ORD 1859

WESTERN SHORE

Painted by W. S. Stephenson for Grace Kruse Dement

Western Shore, built in North Bend in 1874, the fastest clipper ship of her time, from Oregon to Liverpool in 97 days. R. W. Simpson drew the sail plan, A. M, Simpson designed the hull, and John Kruse built her. See the portrait of Kruse in the page of North Bend pictures.

A CENTURY OF

COOS and CURRY

HISTORY OF SOUTHWEST OREGON

By

EMIL R. PETERSON

AND

ALFRED POWERS

ASSISTED BY MANY HANDS

COOS-CURRY PIONEER AND HISTORICAL ASSOCIATION

COQUILLE

1977

Lithographed and bound in the United States of America by
The CAXTON PRINTERS, Ltd.
Caldwell, Idaho 83605
130549

SPONSORS

THE FOLLOWING pioneer families and friends have, by their financial contributions, made possible the assembling of the material for this book:

BAILEY, MRS. KATE LEHNHERR	*Gold Beach*
BANKS, MR. AND MRS. ROBERT	*North Bend*
BERG, MR. AND MRS. J. ARTHUR	*Coquille*
BLANC, MR. AND MRS. L. A.	*Coos Bay*
CARL, MR. AND MRS. J. D.	*Arago*
CHANDLER, MR. AND MRS. BEN R.	*Coos Bay*
CHASE, MRS. INEZ R.	*Coquille*
COMPTON, MR. AND MRS. LAFE	*Bar View*
CLINTON, JESSE D., ESTATE	*Myrtle Point*
DEMENT, RUSSELL C., FAMILY	*Myrtle Point*
DEMENT, WALLACE B.	*Myrtle Point*
DIX, DR. GEORGE E.	*Coos Bay*
FIRST NATIONAL BANK AND AFFILIATES	*Portland*
GARRETT, MRS. ROSE CHANDLER	*Myrtle Point*
GILES, DANIEL, HEIRS OF	*Myrtle Point*
GOULD, MR. AND MRS. A. N.	*Coquille*
HARRY, ALVA E., FAMILY	*Sitkum*
HANSEN, H. H.	*Langlois*
HORSFALL, DR. AND MRS. WILLIAM	*Coos Bay*
KERN, HENRY G.	*North Bend*
KEISER, MRS. RUSSELL	*North Bend*
KNAPP, LOUIS L.	*Langlois*
KRONENBERG, J. L., ESTATE	*Bandon*
LAIRD, MRS. BELLE	*Sitkum*
LAIRD, P. W. AND FLORA M., FAMILY	*Myrtle Point*
LORENZ, MR. AND MRS. FRED N.	*Coquille*
LYONS, JAMES A.	*North Bend*
MAST, WEBB AND HARDEE	*Lee Valley*
MARSDEN, MR. AND MRS. ROBERT JR.	*Coos Bay*
MC DANIEL, MR. AND MRS. EDGAR	*North Bend*
MCCLOSKEY, MR. AND MRS. J. H.	*Norway*
MOORE, MR. AND MRS. RALPH T.	*Coos Bay*
MULLEN, MR. AND MRS. JOHN G.	*North Bend*

Sponsors—*Continued*

Myrtle Point Veneer Company	*Norway*
Norton, Mr. and Mrs. J. E.	*Coquille*
Nosler, Mr. and Mrs. S. M.	*Coquille*
Oerding, Mr. and Mrs. George E.	*Coquille*
Peterson Brothers	*Arago*
Peterson, Peter and Hilda, Family	*North Bend*
Purdy, Mrs. Martha Mulkey	*Coquille*
Reed, S. S. and Annie	*Myrtle Point*
Rogers, Mr. and Mrs. Anson O.	*Coos River*
Richmond, Mrs. Georgia	*Coquille*
Rosa, Mr. and Mrs. Archie H.	*Bandon*
Russell, Mr. and Mrs. Elmer F.	*North Bend*
Security Bank	*Myrtle Point*
Schindler, Mr. and Mrs. O. C.	*Bandon*
Schroeder, Mr. and Mrs. Henry A.	*Myrtle Point*
Sweet, Mr. and Mrs. W. J.	*Bandon*
Stauff, Mrs. Clara	*Coquille*
Tower, Morton, Family	*Empire*
Tower, Isaac R.	*Coos Bay*
Ulett, Mr. and Mrs. George A.	*Coquille*
Vaughan, Mr. and Mrs. Wm.	*North Bend*
Williams, Mr. and Mrs. Ralph F.	*Coos Bay*
Weyerhaeuser Timber Company	*North Bend*
Wilson, Jeff D., Family	*Powers*
Yoakam, Jasper A., Family	*Coos Bay*

CONTENTS

Contents—*Continued*

Illustrations

In the text by letterpress, imaginative drawings from old prints; line engravings from camera pictures; a charcoal portrait of Minnie Myrtle Miller by Bernard Hinshaw; a woodcut by H. Macarthey in 1896. Reproduced by offset, thirty-one pages of photographs from the Pioneer Museum at Coquille and from private collections. End-papers are from an old unsigned watercolor painting for many years in the Tichenor family; though the view is dated 1859, it is similar in details of the town to a woodcut in *Harper's Magazine* in 1855.

I

COME THE WHITES

1

Old Mariners Passing By

Back 460 years — legend says in 1492 — an old Chinaman survived the wreck of his junk on the Oregon shore to turn pirate, with a cutthroat band of redskins:

> From broad Columbia down to Coos
> [They fiercely swooped in great canoes]
> To Orford, Coos and far Coquille
> They hewed a way with gleaming steel.

BOLD AND RUGGED CAPE FERRELO, on the coast a short distance from the California line, was named for Bartolome Ferrelo, who was Cabrillo's pilot in 1542 and 1543, only fifty years after Columbus' voyage. Cabrillo died but his dying instructions to Ferrelo were for him to continue north.

> Right royally did Ferrelo carry out his dying chief's instructions. On January 19th [1543] he resumed the exploration northward, and speeding before a fierce gale he reached latitude forty-two degrees and thirty minutes north, on March 1st, and sighted Cape Blanco in southern Oregon. The severe storms continued until, after frightful sufferings and with his provisions reduced to a few seabiscuits, he made for home.

Ferrelo may have seen the cape named for him but historians think he probably didn't.

Cape Sebastian in Curry County perpetuates the name given by Sebastian Vizcaino in 1603 to some high white bluff which historians think was not this one. Vizcaino, from whom Aguilar and Flores had become separated, did not go as far north as they did. On a January day in the Spaniards' latitude of forty-two degress, which must be discounted as too high, they saw the headland which they called Cape Blanco de San Sebastian. Not only had they been in a terrible gale but all except six of the crew were down with scurvy. When the weather cleared, there was the point before their eyes.

In 1774, Juan Perez, who had gone far north, passed along Coos and Curry on his way back, without seeing anything of the country. He was disappointed that on August 15 and 16 the fog prevented him from searching for Aguilar's river and Cape Blanco.

The next year, also in August, Bruno Heceta, likewise on his way south, saw and noted ten small islands in latitude forty-three degrees, and saw three more in latitude forty-three degrees and thirty-six minutes. Bancroft thinks the ten islands were just below Cape Blanco. The expedition's second small ship came along the coast of Coos and Curry in September, 1775, about a month after Heceta. The men were sick with scurvy; only the officers were able to work. They scanned the coast closely where Aguilar's river was supposed to be, but could observe no trace of it. Like Heceta, however, they found a cape with ten small islands — Cape Blanco.

The next visitor was an Englishman, Captain James Cook. He came across from the Sandwich Islands and hit the coast near Yaquina Bay in blustery March weather, 1778. He was sailing in two ships, the *Resolution* and the *Discovery*. He also looked for Aguilar's river. He didn't find it or the Umpqua. But he did find Cape Gregory. His latitude calculations were much more accurate than had been those of the old Spaniards. He put Cape Gregory at forty-three degrees and thirty minutes. The true latitude is forty-three degrees, eighteen minutes, and ten seconds.

Fourteen years later another Englishman sailed along in front of the two counties. This was Captain George Vancouver, Tuesday, April 24, 1792:

> As the breeze that had been so favorable to our pursuits since the preceeding Sunday died away, and as a tide or current set us fast in shore, we were under the necessity of coming to an anchor . . . In this situation the northernmost extremity of the land, is formed by a low land projecting from the high rocky coast a considerable way into the sea, and terminating in a wedgelike low perpendicular cliff . . . This I distinguished by the name of Cape Orford, in honor of my much respected friend the noble Earl (George) of that title: off it lies several rocky islets.

Soon after we anchored a canoe was seen paddling towards the ship, and without any sort of invitation, came immediately alongside. During the afternoon two others visited the *Discovery*, and some repaired to the *Chatham*, from different parts of the coast in sight: by which it appeared that the inhabitants who are settled along the shores of this country, may, probably, have their residence in the small nooks that are protected from the violence of the westwardly swell by some of the larger rocky islets, so abundantly scattered along the coast. . .

We ramained in this situation till near midnight . . . . Cape Orford, which is situated in latitude forty-two degrees and fifty-two minutes, at the extremity of a low projecting tract of land, forms a very conspicuous point, and bears the same appearance whether approached from the north or the south. It is covered with wood as low down as the surf will permit it to grow.

Having now a fine gale with serene and pleasant weather, we ranged along the coast at the distance of about a league, in hopes of determining the existence or non-existence of the extensive river or straits asserted to have been discovered by Martin D'Aguilar. About three in the afternoon we passed within a league of the cape above-mentioned: and at about half that distance from some breakers that lie to the westward of it. This cape, though not so projecting a point as Cape Orford, is nevertheless a conspicuous one, particularly when seen from the north, being formed by a round hill on high perpendicular cliffs, some of which are white, a considerable height from the level of the sea. Above these cliffs it is tolerably well wooded, and is connected to the main land, by land considerably lower. In this respect it seemed exactly to answer Captain Cook's description of Cape Gregory.

Vancouver was a great hand to name things. Farther north his designations of geography were numerous. But his new name for Cape Blanco didn't stick. The noble earl of Orford, however, didn't lose out entirely in the region. His name became one of the two words in the name of a town. And an excellent choice it was, not in honoring this peer but because it sounds so good — Port Orford.

Aguilar's River, 1603

Of the streams of Curry and Coos throwing their volumes out rapidly into the Pacific tides, which was Aguilar's river? This was seen but not entered by Martin

Aguilar and Antonio Flores on a winter day three and a half centuries ago. They approached its mouth in their small frigate, the *Tres Reyes,* but the force of the current would not let them sail in.

The *Tres Reyes* and the *San Diego* were the two vessels under Sebastian Vizcaino. The ships parted in a southwest gale on January 7, 1603. Aguilar in the *Tres Reyes,* thinking Vizcaino had gone on ahead in the *San Diego,* sailed up the Curry County coast close enough to be favored with a good view of it, so that in his log is the first description of it. But that description was not sufficiently detailed and accurate so that other navigators could afterwards find his river or so that historians could definitely tell which one of the modern rivers it was.

During the storm the *Tres Reyes* ran before the wind to a shelter behind a great Mendocino cliff. Then, says the ship's log:

> When the wind became less violent they continued their voyage close along shore, and on the 19th of January [1603], the pilot, Antonio Flores, found they were in latitude forty-three degrees, where they found a cape or point, which they named Cape Blanco. From that point the coast began to turn northwest; and near it was discovered a rapid and abundant river, with ash trees, willows, and brambles, and other trees of Castile on its banks, which they endeavored to enter, but could not from the force of the current.

From here the *Tres Reyes* turned back to Mexico. They had already sailed farther north than their instructions called for, and they had much sickness aboard. Aguilar thought, however, that the river was the famous Strait of Anian — that long-sought channel supposed to go clear through the continent.

The short paragraph about the stream in the old Spaniard's log book caused the *Rio d'Aguilar* — the river of Aguilar — to be placed for a long time on ancient maps. The De l'Isle map of 1752 shows Cape Blanco sticking out like a cow's teat, and just beyond it is *Ent Aguilar* — entrance to Aguilar's river. Above it is *Ent. Fuca.* Both go into the *Mer De L'Ouest,* which is Puget Sound brought away south to cover much of Coos and

Curry. In Jeffery's map of 1768 the river is shown just south of *C. Blanquial.* A bay is marked *Ent. Aguilar,* which is also called River of the West (French), and going back from the same bay another river just north is called River of the West (Russian), both streams heading in the Mountains of Bright Stones. In Carver's map of 1778 the stream is marked as a wide one and called both Aguilar and River of the West. The Strait of Anian runs in from the north, from the Western Sea or Puget Sound. Cape Blanco is shown several miles south of the entrance.

The historians, Bancroft in particular, went on the theory that Aguilar's river was north of the cape, Blanco or whatever cape it was. The language of the log as quoted indicates this position but doesn't say so; the words "near it" are used following the statement about the turn of the land above the cape. But to admit the possibility of its having been south of the headland, wouldn't help much. In the case of Cape Blanco it would be Elk River, and the one north Sixes or Flores Creek, neither of which would qualify as an "abundant river." Also from Cape Blanco the coast does not turn northwest, the cape itself being the westernmost point. And the Spanish navigators overestimated their latitudes. All this greatly muddled the historians in their speculations as to what stream it was.

How would Cape Arago and Coos Bay qualify?

Bancroft doesn't discuss this possibility. Here also the latitude would be against it, but if that could somehow be accounted for would the geography and the trees tally at all with Aguilar's description?

One old navigator rather favored this idea of it. This was Captain George Vancouver. In speaking of Cape Gregory, now Cape Arago, he said: "This induced me to consider the above point as the Cape Gregory of Captain Cook, with the probability of its being also the Cape Blanco of Aguilar, if land hereabouts the latter ever saw." The day before, on April 24, 1792, he had seen the real Cape Blanco. There was some speculation on board his ship whether this was the one Aguilar and Flores had found and named; the position and its dark color "did not seem to entitle it to the appellation of Cape Blanco."

Or is it just possible that it was Flores Lake they saw? Is there any evidence that it might have been connected with the sea by a sizable outlet three and a half centuries ago? Anyway the lake and the creek perpetuate the name of the pilot, and if Lakeport had turned out the way the promoters expected and become a substantial town, then that beautiful body of water, with ships many times the size of the *Tres Reyes* coming into it, would have kept much more importantly alive the memory of Antonio Flores.

Captain Robert Gray, 1788

Captain Robert Gray almost landed at Port Orford but in the upshot went on without doing so.

Captain Gray, the Columbia River's celebrated discoverer, spent two August days in 1788 rather close in to shore, cruising in front of Curry and Coos counties. At the time he was captain of the *Lady Washington,* which had started out from Boston as a consort of and a kind of tender to the *Columbia,* but the ships got separated and were not together on the whole trip up the coast.

Captain Gray was thirty-three years old in that August of over a century and a half ago.

The *Lady Washington* was a sloop of ninety tons, with a crew of twelve. The second mate, Robert Haswell, has left a narrative describing the voyage in front of Curry and Coos counties.

Some time on Tuesday, August 5, 1788, the sloop passed the mouth of the Winchuck River. They apparently went along the southern edge of Curry County in the night.

Wednesday, August 6, 1788. On the 6 favourable breezes and pleasant in the morning about 8 o'clock we were abrest a cove where tolerable good shelter from a Northwardly wind may be had it is formed by a small bay to the Northward and a little

Island to the Southward here wood and water may be procured but what sort of anchorage remains unknown

[Bancroft asks if this was not Rogue River or Mack's Arch. Which was it, or was it either? You who may have gone this way by sea or many times along U. S. 101, do you find the description applying at all to the familiar rock or the mouth of the familiar river?] The people were very anxious to come onboard they Paddled after us an amazing distance with great alacrity waving something I suppose skins but we had at this time a good wind and pleas[an]t weather and it was judged best to seek a harbour while they continued we ran along shore with a Cloud of sail passing within a Quarter of a Mile of a Bould sanday shore in 5 or 6 f[atho]m water above the beach appeared a delightful Countrey thickly inhabited and Cloathed with woods and verdure with maney Charming streems of water gushing from the vallies most of the inhabitants as we passed there scatered houses fled into the woods while others ran along shore with great swiftness keeping abrest of us maney miles. Cape Mendocino bore North distant about 5 Leagues [Not Cape Mendocino but Cape Blanco].

Thursday 7th. we now ran for a place that looked like an inlett this place was in a large deep bay to the southward and Eastward of Cape Mendocino [Cape Blanco] having ran in within about a mile of a small Island we hove the Jolley Boat out and sent her to sound the Channel between the Island the Main and explore the Harbour if aney she soon made a signal that there was plenty of water within the Island

we then followed her but soon discovered what we supposed to be an inlett to be no other than two hills separated by a deep valley we wore ship within ½ a Mile of the Land and found no bottom with a long scope of line we now took the boat in and stood our on the other side the Island which could be compared to nothing elce but a hive with the bees sworming the birds were so numerous they were of maney speces but most of them Pelicons [Bancroft asks if this wasn't Port Orford. Could it have been any other place five leagues or so from Cape Blanco? You who know the vicinity so much better than Bancroft, do you find that the description fits and can you identify the bird-infested island?] at 4PM foggy at 6 Cape Mendocino [Cape Blanco] bore NNE distant about 6 or 7 Leagues a long and very dangerous reef of rock ran out westward of this promontory we stood of a proper distance to give this Ledge a proper berth, and then stood to the Northward for the Land obs[erve]d in Latitude 43 20 No.

There is a very deep bay to the Northward of the Cape in which probably there may be some deep Sound and rivers but in the night we were imperceptably drifted by a current from the Eastward far from the Shore [Bancroft says, "This agrees if not for preceding difficulties with Cape Arago and Coos Bay." Do you find that it fits, including the outthrusting current?] this prevented us from exploreing this part of the Coast [And kept Coos Bay from having a famous discoverer before the Columbia River had him]. a knoledge of this situation might be asential for if there should bee a harbour here no doubt there would be great numbers of sea otter skins its situation is by no means too far to Southward for these animals to exist in abundance, . . .

On a fur-hunting expedition in April, 1792, Captain Gray again sailed along the shores of Coos and Curry counties, reaching within two leagues of Cape Blanco before he turned back north to a very great destiny. This time he was captain of the *Columbia.* A month and a day later he crossed over the tumultuous Columbia River bar, to make his name immortal.

2

Exploring Trappers

"The Great California Trail" was the way a missionary in 1837 spoke of the horse and foot tracks south from Fort Vancouver through the Willamette, Umpqua, and Rogue River valleys. There was no such route west of the Coast Range through present Coos and Curry. This region was pathless except for Indian trails, the crooked, trodden paths of animals, and the ocean beach.

The first whites to have dominion over Coos and Curry, the first ones to travel there, were Hudson's Bay men. With an occasional exception, like Jedediah Smith's party, the fur brigade from Fort Vancouver represented the total of white intrusion for 20 years or so after 1826.

And even these didn't travel it overmuch, for Coos and Curry didn't seem to be the best beaver country. The Hudson's Bay Company had a fort on the Umpqua. The references to trading in the country south of there are not as frequent as one might expect to find in four volumes of the correspondence of Dr. John McLoughlin.

The principal leaders of the beaver-hunting and beaver-buying troops were Thomas McKay, Dr. McLoughlin's stepson; Michel Laframboise; and especially Alexander Roderick McLeod.

McLeod, after a trip to the Umpqua in the summer of 1826, reported to McLoughlin that "the country was destitute of Beaver." The Indians, however, told him "as they had previously informed us that there was a large River two days march South of the Umpqua—which abounded in Beaver." Two days march? Was this Coos River and Coos Bay? McLeod didn't have time that summer to go and see, but it was to appear later not to be exactly abounding in Beaver.

Some months later, in January 1827, McLeod got

down as far as Rogue River and visited the entrance. It came to be sometimes called McLeod's River in honor of this discovery by him. The following summer Thomas McKay led a hunting party there. In speaking of it McLoughlin called it the River Tootonie, meaning Tu-tut-ne, one of the names the river had at that time.

When Jedediah Smith's party was killed, McLeod went down among the Umpquas with 60 men to make them restore Smith's stolen furs and horses. He was about to start out anyhow on an expedition to that area and on south through Coos and Curry. Said Dr. McLoughlin:

> "Mr. McLeod then proceeded . . . to California and returned the following year without having had any quarrel with the Indians, except at Rogue's River, which owes its name to the conduct of the Natives who were very impudent and troublesome, and went so far as to take the people's kettles from the fire and help themselves to the contents; and when the men proposed to drive them out of camp and then punish them for their impudence, Mr. McLeod . . . would not allow them . . . saying to his men, "Take pity on the Indians and give them food." From Mr. McLeod's humanity and forebearance those Indians took a footing, and have been troublesome to the Whites ever since. However as the H. B. Co's people were in large parties and knew their character they never had rupture with them."

He explained that now and then "when an opportunity occurred they would fire their arrows at Hudson's Bay people and into camp."

In replying to criticism regarding the big profits secured from the southern territory, he quoted his American critic, Captain Josiah Spaulding:

> He writes, "their trapping party this last year, consisted of 70 men, under Laframboise . . . they brought in, an average quantity of 260 Beaver to each man." . . . how false and exaggerated? Lafambroise had about 30 men, who averaged about 40 Skins, of which two, were caught North of 42 degrees, because there were none in the route the trappers travelled from this [Vancouver] to there.

That is how poor a beaver country McLoughlin claims he found Coos and Curry. In 1835 Laframboise had been ordered to hunt the country along the coast between the

"Umpqua and Clamet River. Laframboise found no furs where he had been directed to go. Yet in September 1836 he was ordered with 25 men to hunt the country "South of Umpqua." When he got back to Fort Vancouver towards the end of October, McLoughlin could observe, "His returns are better than last year."

McLoughlin's relatively few references to Coos and Curry in his correspondence becomes understandable on the basis of the area's fur scarcity. McLoughlin always wrote Beaver with a capital B. The abundant presence of that animal is what made him enthusiastic for a country, and Coos and Curry afforded catches that were too disappointing. Yet McKay, Laframboise, and McLeod, with their parties and brigades, saw much of the country in its wilderness days. It is too bad that they left us such a scant record of what they saw and experienced.

Campsites of Jedediah Smith *By Alice B. Maloney*

[The noted trapper Jedediah Smith was the first white man with a sizable company to make the land trip between California and Oregon along the sea coast instead of through the Umpqua and Willamette valleys. The year was 1828. The party, which had 300 horses, numbered eighteen men, who trapped as they went. By the time they had reached the ill-fated Umpqua River they had taken several thousand dollars worth of furs.

At the Umpqua fourteen of the men were killed by the Indians. Jedediah Smith thought at first sixteen. He and Richard Leyland escaped together and made their way eventually to Fort Vancouver. Later two other survivors showed up there.

This record of Jedediah Smith's trip through Curry and Coos counties from June 23 to July 10, 1828, is by Alice B. Maloney, a Coos County woman who has become well known as a historical writer. Her husband was at one time publisher of the *Coos Bay Times*.]

From their rocky lookouts the Indians of this remote coast had seen ships of many nations come and go. But this band of white men with their strange animals brought a menace and aroused a savage enmity that was soon to make itself felt. Jedediah Smith, not unmindful of increased dangers, led his brigade northward to their first resting place in Oregon territory.

Oregon Camp No. 1, North Bank of Winchuck River.

June 23d North West 8 Miles At 3 Miles I arrived on the shore and from thence I traveled along the shore and sometimes immediately on the beach for 5 miles and encamped after crossing a creek 20 yards wide. The hills came within ½ mile or a mile of the sea, and were generally bare of timber. The Low land along the shore and in the valleys covered with high breaks and has some Miry springs. Many indians visited camp in the evening bringing berries small fish and Roots for trade. In the course of the day one Mule gave out and another ran back on the trail.

This is Smith's entry for the day. Jedediah capitalized words he wished to emphasize and it will be noted that "Mule" is important—"indian"is not. Both Smith and Rogers mentioned the "breaks." This name is still in general use along the lower coast for the tall sword ferns which grow so lushly in that well-watered country.

Oregon Camp Site No. 2, South Side of Chetco River.

June 24 West North West 3 miles and encamped at the mouth of a river 50 yards wide rapid at the mouth but as it was high tide I could not cross. The hills about the same distance from the coast as the day before and the low land thick covered with brakes scotch caps and grass. When starting in the morning I sent two men back for the Mules that had been left the day before. They came in the evening without the mules and I immediately sent two men back but they soon returned as the indians at a village close at hand did not appear friendly.

Near my camp was a village of 10 or 12 Lodges but the indians had all ran off. Among the indians of this country I have seen a small kind of Tobacco which is pretty generally cultivated. These indians Catch Elk in Pits dug in places much frequented. They are 10 or 12 feet deep and much larger at the bottom than top. They are completely covered over and some of my hunters with their horses fell into one and got out with considerable difficulty.

Indian tobacco still grows on sandy stretches along the coast and traces of elk pits used by these tribes may be found in remote, heavily-wooded areas.

Oregon Camp No. 3, Thomas Creek.

Oregon Camp Site No. 4, South Side of Pistol River.

June 26th N N West 8 miles. On leaving camp I struck out from the Ocean following a ridge on a circuitous route until It came into the Ocean again at the mouth of a creek 20 yards wide where I encamped.

Rogers' comment on the day's travel clears up the question of how the brigade was able to travel on the ridge: "We followed and Ind. Trail from the time we started in the morning until we enc." Some axe and shovel work must have been necessary.

Oregon Camp Site No. 5, South Side of Rogue River.

June 27th North 7 Miles. With the exception of two or three steep points which I was obliged to pass over I was able during the day to travel along the beach. I encamped on the south side of a bay and close to its entrance which was 150 yards wide. The Bay itself was 3 Miles long and 1 Mile wide. At low water I found it quite fresh, from which circumstance I infered that it received a considerable river. After encamping I made rafts that I might be ready to cross the bay early on the following morning. On each side of the Bay were several indian villages but the indians had all run off. On a creek which I crossed 3 miles back was some beaver sign and also some in the bay.

The brigade had now reached the Rogue River and were encamped in the flats south of the entrance, approximately on the later site of Fort Gunnybags, the crude fortification thrown up during the Indian war of 1855-56. There was a large number of Indian lodges on both sides of the river. Upon the approach of the strangers all inhabitants fled, the women not even stopping to carry off their large baskets. The whites tore down one lodge to get puncheons to make rafts, as timber was scarce along the beach. The Indians raised smoke signals on the north side of the bay.

Oregon Camp Site No. 6, Probably at Euchre Creek.

June 28th N N West 6 Miles. Early in the morning as it was low water I commenced crossing. And when I had finished I had lost 12 or 15 drowned in the middle of the water. I know not the reason for their drowning unless it might perhaps be ascribed to driving them so much in a body. In three days I had lost by various accidents 23 horses & mules.

The exact site of this camp remains uncertain. Smith was weary and made but a brief entry for this day's travel.

Oregon Camp No. 7, Mussel Creek.

Oregon Camp Site No. 8, Brush Creek.

This section of the trail is readily identified. Humbug Mountain rises 1750 feet directly from the ocean, with no passable beach even at low tide. The Indians had already found their way around this obstacle by climbing to the sources of Brush Creek and following it down around the eastern slopes, turning west toward its debouchment directly into the ocean on the north side of the rocky eminence. The old Indian trail still in use in 1855 crossed Brush Creek seventeen times in four miles, occasionally using logs for bridges.

Oregon Camp Site No. 9, South Side of Sixes River.

July 1st 1828 North 9 Miles. At 5 Miles from camp crossed a creek the outlet of a small Lake on which was some beaver sign. At this place the hills receded from the shore leaving a bluff from 30 to 100 feet in heighth. Immediately on this bank is a narrow skirt of prairae and further back low Pine & brush. The soil is thin and loose. Encamped on a river 60 yards wide on which was some beaver sign. I found the tide too high to cross. For three past days but one deer had been killed but as we had dried meat we did not suffer from hunger. We saw appearances of Elk have been abundant in the vicinity when the grass was tender. For many days we had hardly got sight of an indian and but one had visited camp since my horses were killed. In the course of the days travel one of my horses was crowded from the cliff and killed.

The small lake mentioned by Smith is Garrison Lake just north of the town of Port Orford. One Indian came to camp. The camp was on the north shoulder of Cape Blanco, oldest identified spot on the Oregon coastline, dating from the early Spanish explorers. The river which flowed past the camp was Sixes River. The trail from the south crosses the cape far out on the promontory through a gap that may be plainly seen.

Oregon Camp Site No. 10, Bluff South of Bandon.

July 2nd 12 Miles North principally along the shore at 6 Miles from camp passing a small Lake. During the days travel the hills were generally 3 or 4 Miles from the shore the intermediate space being interspersed with grassy prairae brush sand hills & low Pines.

Both journals agree on the mileage traveled this day which would bring the brigade to a small stream just south of the present town of Bandon on the land included in the first donation claim on the southern Oregon coast, filed upon by Thompson Lowe in 1853. The old Indian trail was still in use in the early 70's and I was able to locate portions of it in 1934 with the assistance of the late George Williams whose first job upon his arrival at the mouth of the Coquille River in 1873 was the brushing out of the path to make a sled road to the ferry.

Smith's small lake was Flores Lake. Rogers thought the broken hills along the route due to earthquakes. A check-up of men and their articles was made by Rogers indicating that wages for most of them amounted to $1 per day but that Martin McCoy, for reasons not stated, drew $2.

Oregon Camp Site No. 11, Whiskey Run.

July 3d 5 Miles N N West. At 2 Miles from camp I came to a river 200 yards wide which although the tide was low was deep and apparently a considerable River. On first arriving in sight I discovered some indians moving as fast as possible up the river in a canoe. I ran my horse to get above them in order to stop them. When I got opposite to them & they discovered they could not make their escape they put ashore and drawing their canoe up the bank they fell to work with all their might to split it in pieces.

This was the Coquille River.

After traveling along the ocean shore, camp was made that night at Whiskey Run, a small creek emptying into the ocean, later to become the scene of a gold rush.

This is the last entry made by Jedediah Smith in his journal. Fatigue and the exigencies of travel made writing difficult for the overworked captain, and for further information we rely upon the journal of Harrison Rogers.

Oregon Camp Site No. 12, Cape Arago.

Friday, July 4, 1828. We made a start early, starting N.N.W. 9 m and enc. The traveling pretty bad, and as we were obliged to cross the low hills as they came in close to the beach and the beach being so bad that we could not get along, thickety and timbered and some bad ravines to cross. We enc. on a long point where there was but little grass for the horses. Good deal of elk signs, and several hunters out killed nothing, the weather still good.

Rogers' spelling is not so good as Smith's. He always records the weather. Traveling would still be "pretty bad" over the route chosen for this day's progress and the bad ravines, known as the Seven Devils, have given their name to the road traversing that stretch between the Coquille River and Coos Bay. The present highway takes a course far inland at this point. Smith seems to have deviated from the old Indian trail, later to be blazed and used by miners and settlers and called to this day, the Randolph Trail. He hugged the shoreline for reasons not given in Rogers' journal and found the going very difficult.

Oregon Camp Site No. 13, Shore Acres.

Saturday, July 5, 1828. We traveled 1½ miles today N. and finding good grass enc. as our horses was pretty rited (?) Two inds. who speak Chinook came to our camp; they tell us we are ten days travel from Catapos on the Well-hamet which is pleasing news to us. Plenty of elk sign and several hunters out but killed nothing.

One and one half miles travel would place the brigade on the land of L. J. Simpson where his country home, Shore Acres, stood on a high cliff directly over the ocean.

Oregon Camp Site No. 14, Sunset Bay.

Sunday, July 6th N 2 miles and enc., the traveling very bad mirey and brushey several horses snagged very bad passing over fallen hemlock; after encamping two elk killed.

The distance marks this site as Sunset Bay which offers shelter, water, wood and some grazing. It is difficult to place the last item, as burned-over woodland soon springs back to forest along this well-watered coast but the obvious advantages mentioned make this place a resort today. It is not unlikely that these inducements influenced Smith to remain over two nights at this resting place. The carcass of the elk killed figures in the Indian tradition of the visit of the party to this tribe.

Oregon Site No. 15, near Charleston.

Tuesday, July 8, 1828 We made and early start, directing our course N. along the beach and low hills, the traveling very bad on accounts of ravenes, fallen timber and brush. We made 2 miles and struck the river and enc. The river at its mouth is about 1 mi. wide, the inds. very numerous they call themselves the Kakoosh. They commenced trading shell and scale fish, raspberrys, strawberrys and two other kinds of berries that I am unacquainted with, also some fur skins. In the evening we found they had been shooting arrows into 8 of our horses and mules; 3 mules and one horse died shortly after they were shot. The Inds. all left camp but the 2 that acts as interpreters; they tell us that one Ind. got mad on account of a trade he made and killed the mules and horses. The weather still good. One horse left today that was mamed.

Rogers appears to have slightly underestimated the distance covered. This location has remained an Indian village site and from descendants of the chief [of those days] I secured the traditional story of Smith's visit as it had been passed on by father and son. The story was related to me in 1931, three years before the publication of Smith's journal and before any knowledge of Rogers' journal had reached the surviving members of the tribe.

Oregon Camp Site No. 16, East Shore of Coos Bay below Empire.

Wednesday, July 9th We made and early start again this morning and crossed the first fork of the river which is 400 yards and got all our things safe across about 9 o c a m then packed up and along the river N. and traveled about 2 miles and enc. We crossed in Ind. canoes. A great many Inds. live along this river bank; there houses built after the fashion of a shed. A great many Inds. in camp with fish and berries for sale; the men bought them. We talked with the chiefs about those Inds shooting our horses but could not get but little satisfaction as they say they were not accessary to it and we, finding them so numerous and the traveling being bad, we thought it advisable to let it pass at present without notice. We bought a number of beaver, land and sea otter skins from them in the course of the day.

This camp was at the Indian village of Melowitz, a place about which many tales are told in the Coos tribe. I talked with one Indian woman who remembered being taken there as a child.

Oregon Camp Site No. 17, Ocean Beach, North Spit.

Thursday, July 10, 1828 We commenced crossing the river early as we had engaged canoes last night; we drove in our horses and they swam across; they had to swim about 600 yards. Our goods was all crossed about 9 a. m. and 2 horses that was wounded and one was much, remained that Capt. Smith and 5 men stay to cross; the 2 horses dyed of there wounds and Capt. Smith swim the mule alongside one of the canoes. He was somewhat of the opinion the Inds had a mind to attact him from there behavior and he crossed over where the swells was running pretty high, and here being good grass we enc. for the day, the Inds. pretty shy.

The river we crossed today unites with the one we crossed yesterday and makes an extensive bay that runs back into the hills. It runs N. and S. or rather heads N.E. and enters the ocean S.W. at the entrance into the ocean it is about 1½ miles wide.

Rogers' description of lower Coos Bay is accurate but the channel reverses its direction at the N. E. point he recorded and thus the peninsula upon which they traveled north is formed. The brigade crossed the bay at some undetermined point but one near enough to the ocean for the ground swell to make itself felt.

Jedediah Smith, the celebrated trapper leader, through Curry and Coos June 23 to July 10, 1828.

Prudential Insurance Company of America

3

Coos and Curry Indians

THE INHABITANTS which the first whites found, had owned the land for unmeasured centuries.

Said Coquille Thompson in reply to a question of how long the Indians had been in possession, "Well, the Indian people I think were the first people there, and they owned that as a home, that was their little world right there, I believe, from time immemorial."

Lucy Smith, who had a Rogue River father and an Euchre Creek mother, made this response, "I guess ever since there was — ever since God put them on earth here."

The same opinion was held by John P. Harrington, ethnologist, " Indian ownership of the coast reaches back doubtless for a hundred generations, and a map in 500 A. D. probably would have shown the same ownership as that made by Lewis and Clark 1300 years later."

If your ancestors had lived on Sixes River since perhaps the birth of the Lord and then you were dispossessed in the 1850's, wouldn't you have felt perpetually nostalgic and inconsolably desolate as did the wrinkled old squaw, Mamie Strong's great-grandmother?

Mamie Strong was asked, "When was it that you heard your great-grandmother discussing where she had lived?"

She answered, "Oh, I have heard her talk about their old home country so many times . . . She would sit and talk to herself about it. She was getting old and that was all she had on her mind."

THE TRIBES

The Coos — The Coos tribe occupied the Coos Bay region and the Coos River drainage basin. The ocean, of course, was in front. Their northern boundary was Ten

Mile Lake. On the east they joined the Yoncalla Calapooyas; on the south the Coquilles.

Of the latter boundary, George Wasson, who had listened to his Indian grandmother tell tribal folklore, said in reply to his questioners that the divide was the irregular watershed between Coos Bay and the Coquille River. (On the coast the boundary started at Whiskey Run, went north of Randolph and above the head of South Slough.)

Question: Did the Coquilles occupy and claim to the summit of this watershed?

Answer: There was nothing definite about it. If the Coos Indians went over and went to catching beaver out of Beaver Slough, there might be war; but if the Coos Indians went over the top of the summit and killed an elk or something, there was no trouble about it at all. The valuable part of it was the fishing and the trapping. There was a definite understanding between them in regard to the fishing and trapping on the lower grounds, but there was nothing definite on top of the flat ridges.

Wasson said that beyond the site of the present town of Coquille the Coos Indians would catch eels in the North Fork where the falls were but never used the Middle Fork. At the head of Camas Valley they gathered camas and myrtle nuts.

Lewis and Clark in 1805 estimated the Coos population at 1500. The name *Coos* or *Kusa* is said to have had the Indian meaning of "lake," "lagoon," or "inland bay." They didn't flatten their heads. Their closest neighbors doing it were the Alseas at Yachats.

The Coquilles – Their ocean front was rather narrow, from Whiskey Run to Flores Creek, but their territory fanned out to the eastward, going as far as Camas Valley.

In 1890, anthropologist Owen Dorsey learned "from Coquille Thompson, the chief, and an old man called Solomon" the names of 32 Coquille villages. One was on the north side, one on the south side of the river near its mouth. One was on the present site of Coquille, and one below town. Others included "people at big rocks." "people at the big dam," "good grass people," "village on the dark side of a canyon." There was one designated as the village "where there are many of the insects called dul-dul," which in summer and autumn nights flew with a humming noise.

The Rogues or "Rascal" Indians: the Tututni — These embraced a large territory from Flores Creek to Sebastian Cape along the coast, and up the Rogue River to nearly the mouth of the Illinois. There were about a dozen bands.

One band called the Quah-to-mahs included the Flores Creeks and the Sixes Indians. Numbering 133 in 1850, they had villages at the mouth of those streams. George Wasson said, "New River is the outlet to Flores Creek. It flows north along inside of the sea wall, and every fall when the heavy rain comes that river breaks open and then the salmon come in, and it is a natural place to catch salmon. The Too-too-to-neys [The Rogues] came there and occupied that definitely. If any other Indians came in there, there was war, but if they picked huckleberries north of that there was no trouble. So the boundary [between the Flores Creek band of the Rogues and the Coquilles] is some place between Bandon and New River."

The smallest of all the coast bands in 1850 was the Port Orfords, with a population of only 27, nine men, nine women, and nine children. Their village was on Rhinehart or Hubbard Creek. But the little bunch duly had a five-syllabled chief—Chat-al-hak-e-ah.

The Euchre Creeks, with 102 persons in 1850, had the territory from Sisters Rocks south to some point between the mouths of the Euchre Creek and the Rogue. How the Rogue bands intermarried is indicated by the testimony of Lucy Smith at a hearing.

Question: Who was your father?

Answer: Jim Tom, born mouth of Rogue River—Gold Beach, they call it.

Question: Who was your mother?

Answer: She was a Euchre Creek.

Along Rogue River the Yah-shutes or Joshuas had

villages on the north and south sides near the mouth, and one three miles upstream. Their territory went north to that of the Euchre Creeks and south nearly to Cape Sebastian. Seven villages on Hunter's Creek belonged to this band.

Upriver from the Joshuas were the Tu-tu-tunne whose 120 people in 1850 occupied both banks to a short distance above Lobster Creek. Next were the Miko-no-tunne, with a population of 145, who claimed about 12 miles of the river, with an undetermined area of hunting grounds back from the stream. The Shasta Costas were in the Agness vicinity, numbering 145.

The Pistol Rivers owned the drainage area of that stream and the coast from Cape Sebastian to Mack's Arch. An adjoining band went on south to Whale's Head, occupying only about an eight-mile width of country. The records are rather vague to to the occupancy of the next strip down to Cape Ferrelo.

The Chetcos — These people, related to the California Indians to the south, spoke a dialect somewhat varying from the Rogues proper. Said John Van Pelt, "Well, there is just a very little difference between the Chetco and Rogue River [languages]. Some words are a little different." Lucy Smith, when asked about the similarity of speech, said, "The Chetcos was just about half way twisted."

The Chetcos occupied the Chetco River, living mainly along its lower 14 miles. They probably occupied the Winchuck River also. Their southern boundary was just about the Oregon-California line; their northern Cape Ferrelo. They had 9 villages, including Baldwin Fairchild's on the north side of the river at its mouth, and one on the south side.

"What was the southern boundary of the Chetco land?" Harry Van Pelt was asked.

He said, "Out to those islands. They went out and got seagull eggs and mussels."

"What was the western boundary?"

"Along the Pacific Coast, taking in some of the islands.

They even used to go out on Southwest Seal Rock and get sea lions for their food."

In regard to Chetco food, Mrs. Mamie Strong said, "They lived on acorns—they made their own meal out of it. They hunted and fished and had things from the ocean, sea food. They had sea weeds and dried them, and a lot of things that I could name that they lived on. They had what they called Indian carrots, and they had Indian potatoes."

How the Coos Indians Lived *By Gwenedde Maple*

[Gwenedde (Mrs. James) Maple was born and grew up in Empire, center of the dwindling Indian population during the past 90 years. She still lives in the old Tower home that has a big letter T in the glass of the front door; it was built in 1870 by Dr. W. C. Tower, well known in early Coos history. Mrs. Maple's close neighbor is Daisy Wasson Codding, whose mother was a full-blood Coos Indian.]

The four small Coos tribes lived in the present western portion of Coos County—the Me-lu-kitz on the north side of Coos Bay; the Nah-see-mi on the south bank of the Coquille River, perhaps more properly Coquilles but speaking the same language as the Coos; the Mil-luk on Coos Bay from Coos Head to Tar Heel Point; the Hon-us from the southern end of present Empire to the downtown district of present North Bend.

Thus we find two tribes living very close together on the shores of Coos Bay and being very congenial and neighborly with one another. There Mil-luk and Hon-us Indians fished, hunted and lived within the boundaries of what is now known as Lakeside and Tenmile Creek on the north, to Whiskey Run on the south. For why should they travel any further? In this small area they could obtain all they needed or desired. If ever God created a Paradise here on earth for the red man, it certainly was this locality. Truly for the Indian it was a Paradise lost and for the white man a Paradise gained.

The weather was moderate the year around; the mountains, hills and valleys were literally alive with deer, elk, bear, panther, wildcats, California lions, and lynx, and there were even some wolves and coyotes. There were rabbits, mink, beaver, otter, and squirrels in great abundance. In the fall and winter the air was almost darkened with ducks and geese, to say nothing of the quail, grouse and partridge to be found at other times. The streams and bay contained all kinds of fish, as well as clams, crabs, mussels and other shell fish. Many kinds of berries in season covered the divides of various valleys [salmonberries, blackberries, thimbleberries, huckleberries, blueberries, salalberries.]

The swamps provided wild onions and many kinds of greens. The woods gave them fern roots and medical herbs. Even the sea gave them eatable sea weeds; and, most important of all to those Indians, the sand hills provided them with the ha-wooded plant and camas. Can you wonder why they did not travel far?

These Coos Indians were square built of medium height, wearing their straight black hair and only cutting it when in mourning. Often they used small bones or shells for ornaments in their noses or ears. Some of them, more especially the women, tattooed themselves, favoring the chin and forearm for this type of decoration. They had no uniformity in dress, each individual dressing as he wished, mostly depending on what the weather was like and what the person was doing at that particular time. Sometimes they were nude, or practically so. The women, however, always wore at least a small apron both in front and back, made either of grasses or skins. At other times they bedecked themselves in rich attire of skins and furs worth thousands of dollars. They even had rain resistant coats for the long wet season. Those were made from a grass and cattail rushes and so woven that the water ran down and off the garment instead of soaking in.

The Mil-luk and Hon-us dwellings were of two types — the semi-dug-out sand hut and the pole-and-grass shelter. The former was more the permanent home; the latter, a temporary shelter. But even the grass and reed houses kept dry throughout our long wet season because of the kind of grasses and reeds used and the way it was woven.

Lottie, daughter of Chief Jackson, last of the Coos full-bloods

SAND DUNES

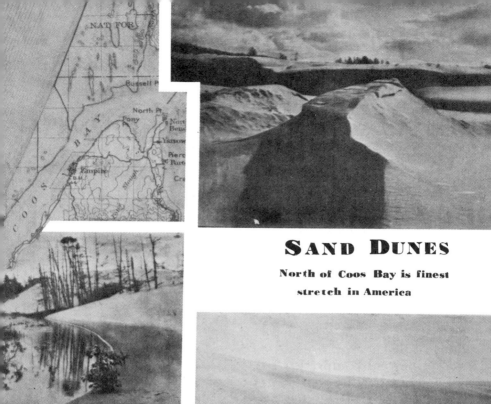

North of Coos Bay is finest stretch in America

News Press, Coos Bay

Staddon Studios, Coos Bay

They always seemed to know just which grass, bark, root or bough to use for each different purpose they intended to put it. The women usually gathered all these kinds of things—it was their particular work. They would make many, many trips into the woods at different seasons of the year and under different climatic conditions in order to gather just the right root, grass, bark or bough in just the right condition and period of growth. Then by careful and proper handling or treatment they finally attained the desired product.

The Coos woman could not have kept house without her basket. She made them in all sizes and shapes. She used them for liquids or solids; for cooking, for storing for winter use, for preserved or dried foods, for carrying everything from firewood to berries. The baskets were woven so as to be strong and durable; some of them were water-tight and flexible. Often they were decorated with Indian symbols, but some were plain. The large burden basket was loosely woven, light in weight but strong beyond comprehension. It was large at the top, tapering to a point at the bottom and had a woven band about two inches wide attached to either side at the top. This band was placed around the forehead and the basket rested upon the back between the shoulders of the carrier. Very, very heavy loads were often carried in this way. The favored basket of the Mil-luk and Hon-us women were made from fir boughs, spruce roots and sea grasses with nothing else in them. Less favored baskets contained in addition fern roots, willow boughs and cedar bark. The spruce roots were carefully dug, usually with the bare hands, in order to get them as long as possible and unbroken. After they were gathered they were buried in hot sand until the outside cracked and dried, so it could be peeled off. Then the roots were split to the desired size, either with the teeth or thumb nail. The willow or fir boughs were either soaked and dried into desired shapes or made so thin they would take any desired shape in the weaving. The sea grasses were bleached white, then either left white or dyed different colors for decorative purposes.

The Indian women also wove mats of all sizes and kinds, exceptionally close-woven and soft. They were used for drying things upon, for covering things like we might use a cloth, or as plates to hold hot foods until cool enough to handle and eat.

Their fish traps were made with willow or fir boughs and spruce roots—in the shape of a large funnel and had the small end laced together. These were taken to the small streams or creeks; barriers were built of sticks and branches across the creek; the trap was placed at an opening with the small end up stream. When the fish got into the small end, there wasn't enough room for it to turn, so it was trapped. The Indians would then unlace the trap, take out the fish and replace the trap for the next catch. These traps were used mostly for catching eel, a favored morsel.

The Mil-luk tribe made four trips a year in order to obtain certain roots. These trips were from a few days to several weeks duration. The whole band went together. One trip was up the north fork of Coos River for catching eel, though they caught trout and many other kinds of fish also. It was from these eel fishing trips of the Mil-luk tribe that Millicoma Creek got its name. They would stay up the river several days camping and enjoying themselves, but also working to catch all the fish and ell they could for winter use.

Another trip was made when the salmon came in. Their favorite salmon fishing grounds were at Ten Mile Creek. So when the salmon run was on they all got into their canoes, went across the bay, then walked up the sand spit to Ten Mile Creek. While the men speared the salmon, the women gathered the ha-wooded roots. The spears were made of elk horn sharpened to a fine point and fastened into long sticks for the handles. The Indians were quite expert at this way of fishing, and the big ones did not usually get away.

They would also go out to Cape Arago and camp while they caught and prepared for winter the shell fish that they used. This Cape Arago trip was the biggest event of the year for the Mil-luks. They all went—men, women and children. And they all worked, each one having certain work to do and doing whatever he was most capable of doing. First they dug a great big pit in the sand, then fitted rocks into the bottom until they had a solid, almost smooth rock floor. Upon this they built great fires from the driftwood and kept their fires burning all day and night until the rocks were red hot. Then the fire was all scraped off the rocks and great bundles of wet sea weed thrown on top of them. Upon this sea weed the fish were placed in their shells which previously had been thoroughly washed of sand. Then on top of the shell fish came another thick layer of sea weed, then sand, skins and anything else they had on hand that would hold the steam in and keep it from evaporating. Water was added around the edges at intervals to make more steam. After this steaming was completed, the clams and oysters were taken from the pit, taken out of their shells, strung on thin sticks and hung over a fire of dead seasoned alder wood to smoke and dry. Thus preserved or dehydrated they would keep all winter. After they were smoked and dried they were stored in the big burden baskets and hung up in the living quarters.

Their fourth trip was to what we call Merchant's Beach and Whiskey Run. It was here that the camas grew. The camas bulbs were dug while they were green, then steamed in a pit the same as the clams and oysters. After steaming, they were spread out on the large drying mats and dried in the sunshine. Thus dried they would keep all winter. Eating before drying and after steaming they were soft and of a transparent dark yellow color. They looked something like citron and tasted very much like an overly sweet sweet-potato. The dried ones were used by grinding them between stones, adding water to make a paste or dough, shaping into flat cakes and baking them on hot stones. This was a most nourishing food as well as a very palatable one.

The ha-wooded root was treated and used in the same way as the camas. But it had a different taste. It grew on and was gathered from the sand hills just across the bay. These roots were about two inches thick and grew several feet long. After they were steamed, they had to be stripped of a tough thread that ran through them. But this thread was the only part of the root that was not eatable.

They also dried the huckleberry, blackberries and blueberries. They were very fond of the salalberry fresh, but never dried it. They liked to pick the salalberries on long stems, dip them into hot melted elk tallow and eat them off the stems. The red elderberry juice was a much relished beverage. They also drank several kinds of tea—bush tea, vine tea, yerba buena, swamp tea, fir tea.

From this we can see that these Indians had a great variety in their diet and through their own efforts by preserving it, had it not only in season, but all the year around. An admirable belief of theirs was that because the Good and Great Spirit had provided them with something, none of it must go to waste.

4

The Land

Latest studies of geologists do not support the popular belief that the Coquille once flowed into Coos Bay. They find evidence that in remote ages, just as now, it went down directly to the sea.

HOW IN REMOTE GEOLOGICAL AGES Coos and Curry uprose out of the ocean is told in *The Two Islands,* by Dr. Thomas Condon, noted pioneer fossil-hunter of Oregon:

> At Cape Blanco, near the lighthouse, one may see an old sea beach elevated 210 feet above tideland, in which shells, for the most part like those now living in the neighboring bays [including the large blue clam] . . . A similar raised beach may be seen near the mouth of the Coquille River on the hill above the town of Bandon. Here the number and variety of shells found were still greater, but at less elevation . . . in an elevated beach 100 feet above present waters, and so entirely undisturbed as to leave no doubt as to their having been deposited there by the ocean.

SOME COOS BAY TOPOGRAPHY *By J. S. Diller*

[Diller was a noted geologist with the United States Geological Survey. These descriptions were published in 1901 in the Coos Bay Folio of the *Geologic Atlas* of the United States. His account here is very much shortened.]

Location and Area—The Coos Bay quadrangle, between parallels 43 degrees and thirty minutes north latitude and meridian 124 degrees west longitude and the Pacific Ocean, at the western base of the Coast Range, embraces 640 square miles.

General Features—The streams have cut into the plain so extensively that from the valleys the country seems hilly. The hilltops, though flat, are rarely broad, and the slopes toward the valleys are steep.

Drainage—The northern half of the quadrangle is drained by the Coos River and the southern half by the Coquille. Both streams have cut deep canyons in the Coast Range. Crooked courses constitute one of the most striking features of the principal and subordinate streams. The North Fork of the Coquille, rising only a few miles from the South Fork of the Coos and scarcely more than 25 miles from the ocean, flows south for over 25 miles to near Myrtle Point, where it joins the South Fork of the Coquille and turns seaward, having yet over 30 miles to travel to its mouth.

The Coos River Valley is remarkable for its fertile plains, which rise in places 15 feet above low-tide level. Above [the tide limit] the stream is shallow and flows in a rocky or pebbly bed in a narrow valley, presenting a strong contrast with its lower course. The river enters Coos Bay, which differs from the river especially in the greater extent of its tidal flats and in having tidal branches or sloughs. The bay itself may be considered in two parts. Of these the southwestern has the greater expanse of tidal flats and several sloughs; the other arm has but a small margin of tidal flats and one slough. This difference is due chiefly to the mode of development, the one arm of the bay being very much older than the other.

The Coquille River is ascended by the tide nearly to Myrtle Point, a distance of about 34 miles, although only 15 miles in a direct line from the ocean. In the Coos River the tide ascends about 30 miles and reaches a point 17 miles in a direct line from the beach. This difference is due to the greater crookedness of the Coquille.

Relief—As the streams are irregular in their courses, so the hills, which are carved out by them, are irregular in outline. The rainfall is heavy and the rocks are generally so soft that erosion would proceed rapidly but for the protective influence of the dense vegetation, which breaks the dash of the rain.

The highest point is between the forks of Coos River, 1700 feet. The next highest is on Sugarloaf Ridge. The most prominent upland, and the only one commonly called a mountain, is Blue Mountain, which for nearly three miles has an elevation of 1500 feet. Bill Peak [is] over 1500 feet within eight miles of the coast. The tops of the highest hills and the crests of the highest ridges are generally somewhat flat, although rather narrow, and the slopes are usually steep. The arrangement of the hills is digitate.

Some years ago the Harrison Brothers discovered the tusk of a mastodon in the river bank along the North Fork of the Coquille about one and a half miles east of Myrtle Point. The bone, although not waterworn, was found close to the stream about five feet above low water, resting on a terrace of sandstones and shales and covered by a thin layer of alluvium.

This is a region, too, of elevated beaches. They are well displayed about the mouth of Coos Bay and the hill of Seven Devils. The first terrace, about 60 feet above the present sea level, is well displayed between Yoakam Point and Cape Arago. Above 800 feet elevation the beaches are less distinct, although they may be detected about the summits of the highest peaks near the sea. On the southwest side of Bill Peak, at an altitude of about 1500 feet, a terrace is cut in the fissured sandstone. That this is an ancient beach is shown by the presence of occasional pebbles and cobblestones upon its surface. Terraces may be seen also at points along the road from South Slough to Bandon.

The black auriferous sand, which has attracted so much attention, is found locally not only along the present beach but also along the elevated beaches.

The Sand Dunes *By William S. Cooper, Professor of Botany,* University of Minnesota

Back in the early twenties I began a study of the sand dunes of our Pacific Coast. I had seen plenty of big and fine dunes, but I found that the great masses that begin at Coos Bay and extend north to Sea Lion Point surpass all others—in extent, in height, in bulk, and in beauty. Fifty-three miles coastwise, in some places three miles wide; depth of sand up to two hundred feet at least.

At one point the great ridges, because they mount a sloping terrace, appear to be five hundred feet high. As for beauty, there are few things in nature that can match a dune in grace of curve and contour and in play of light and shadow. In Oregon the great forest adds variety to the dune landscape, and in the background are sea and surf. Low clouds move overhead, and their shadows follow them across the smooth surface of the sand. Is it any wonder that through the past quarter-century I have gone back to the Oregon dunes whenever opportunity offered, to continue my studies there?

The dune landscape on the coast of Oregon is compounded of three elements. First, of course, is the sand, the stuff of which the dunes are built. Its immediate source is the sea; it is cast upon the beach by the waves. If we trace it back to the solid rock from which it came, we would find that part is derived from the coastal cliffs and may not have traveled very far. Another part, however, is brought to the sea by rivers, and some of this has made a long journey.

The second element in creation of the dune landscape is wind. On the coast of Oregon the winds of summer and winter differ greatly. In summer, pretty regularly every afternoon, they blow from the north-northwest, often attaining a velocity of forty miles per hour. In winter, direction is inconsistent, but the important ones for the dunes are the frequent heavy gales from the southwest. The winds of summer, constant in direction, are responsible for a very definite dune pattern — a system of low ridges spaced at regular intervals, lying transverse to wind direction. Each ridge has a gentle slope to windward, while to leeward the angle is as steep as the sand will lie. Sand is constantly removed from the windward slope and dumped over the crest; the ridge itself is thus in constant motion. The transverse-ridge pattern develops on low-lying areas next to the shore.

On the landward side of the transverse-ridge system, where the sand is very deep and fully exposed to the alternating winds of summer and winter, another pattern arises. Here we find parallel ridges of enormous size—as much as a hundred and fifty feet high and a mile or more long—lying roughly at right angles to the shore. In summer they shift southward slightly, in winter northward. These are the most spectacular features of the dune region, and their inner ends, rising high above the tree tops, are plainly visible from the coast highway, particularly between Saunders Lake and the Umpqua River.

Wind acting on the sand brings activity, mobility; plants, the third element in the dune landscape, make for stabilization. First to be considered are the beach grasses, which hold a part of the sand almost as soon as it is lifted from the beach. These grasses like to be buried, and grow up with the precipitated sand, binding it into a coherent mass. A ridge thus forms parallel to the shore, which is called a "foredune."

Interestingly enough, the most efficient of the beach grasses is not native. It was introduced in the Coos Bay region about 1910, and from there it has spread naturally along the shore, producing in many places a foredune where previously there was none.

Farther inland, wherever the winds are weak, plants take hold and gradually gain the upper hand, first herbs, mosses, and creeping shrubs like kinnikinnick, then tall shrubs—blueberry, huckleberry, salal, manzanita—and finally trees. In many places dunes, once in active motion, bear dense forests of pine, spruce, and Douglas fir. Many of the trees are several feet in thickness, and on one stabilized dune I found a Douglas fir five centuries old.

Sooner or later this condition of stability is bound to be disturbed. Blowouts develop at points of weakness. The forest floor is undermined and the trees go down. Burial takes place too, and the various kinds of trees differ in their ability to cope with this danger. The pines die if only their bases are buried. Douglas fir is fairly resistant. But spruce and Port Orford cedar seem to thrive on burial. They put out roots from their trunks into the surrounding sand, and as for their projecting tops, it is business as usual—continued growth and extra heavy crop of cones.

Stabilization and destruction go on simultaneously, giving infinite variety to the dune landscape. Areas of open blowing, sand with a covering of gray mosses, sand firmly bound by a mat of kinnikinnick, thickets of shrubs, some of them scattered young trees, forerunners of the forest.

What about the dune mass as a whole—is it advancing inland at the present time? The answer is definitely yes, and this holds not only for the dunes of Coos Bay, but for all those of our Pacific Coast. The rate, however, is very slow. Measurements made at a number of places, covering several years, show that the inner margin of the active sand is moving inland at an average rate of about five feet per year. At most points the active dunes are invading earlier ones stabilized centuries ago, burying the forests that grow on them. In some places the present wave of advance has overpassed all older dunes and is trespassing on territory never before invaded.

II

SETTLEMENT

5

Early Colonies

SETTLEMENT OF PORT ORFORD, 1851

IN ALL THE LAND of Coos and Curry, Port Orford was the first to be settled by the whites. On June 9, 1851, nine men were landed a few miles south of Cape Blanco, brought down from Portland by Captain William Tichenor on the little steam schooner *Sea Gull.*

The nine men were headed by Captain J. M. Kirkpatrick, who later wrote:

> . . . On the morning of the ninth of June, 1851, we were landed on the beach just below Battle Rock. There were a few Indians in sight who appeared to be friendly but I could see that they did not like to have us there. . . .
>
> We lost no time in making our camp on what was to be called *Battle Rock* . . .

The cannon was set up, commanding the narrow passageway, the only approach to their camp on the rock. All other sides were sheer cliffs of rock, dropping off into deep water a hundred feet or more below. Some writers have referred to the gun as a four-pounder, others as a five-pounder. Kirpatrick, the leader, wrote:

> We put in a two-pound sack of powder and on top of that about half an old cotton shirt and as much bar lead cut into pieces from one to two inches long as I could hold in my two hands, then a couple of old newspapers on top. We then primed the gun with some fine rifle powder and trained it so as to rake the narrow ridge in front of the muzzle and the gun was ready for business . . .
>
> I stood by the gun holding a piece of tarred rope with one end in the fire ready, as soon as the Indians crowded on the narrow ridge in front of the cannon . . .
>
> When . . . a red shirted fellow in the lead was not more than eight feet from the muzzle of the gun, I applied the fiery end of the rope to the priming . . . At least twelve or thirteen men were killed outright, and such a tumbling of scared Indians

I never saw before or since . . . We counted seventeen dead Indians on the rock and this was the bloody baptism that gave the name of Battle Rock to our old camp at Port Orford on the tenth day of June, 1851.

After the fight was all over, probably an hour, an Indian chief came up the beach within hailing distance, laid down his bow, quivver of arrows and knife and then stepped forward and made signs that he wanted to come to our camp. I went down to the beach, met him and brought him up to the camp . . . He made signs to us that he wanted to carry away the dead Indians. I made him understand that he could bring another Indian to help him. He called out for one more to come up to the camp. They would take the dead ones on their back, pack them down from where they lay, across the narrow sandy beach and up a steep trail toward the north and over the ridge and out of sight. They did this eight times and where they laid the dead was

Coos Bay Times

Battle Rock, scene of the celebrated skirmish with the Indians on June 10, 1851.

over 300 yards from our camp. Some of the Indians were quite large, several of them weighing over 200 pounds. As a feat of strength and endurance it was simply wonderful. They carried away all the dead except the fellow who wore the red shirt. I tried to get the big chief to carry him off but he shook his head and stooped down and tore his shirt in two and then gave him a kick with his foot and turned and walked away. We had to drag the fellow afterwards and bury him in the sand. We all remarked that he was very white for an Indian, he had yellow hair and a freckled face . . . He turned out to be a white man who had been among the Indians for many years, they having saved him from a wreck of a Russian ship lost on the Oregon coast many years ago. . .

In our talk with the big chief we made him understand that in fourteen days more the steamer would return and take us away. And for fourteen days we were not molested . . . But on the morning of the fifteenth they were there in force . . . Now we had lied to them, the steamer had not arrived as we had promised . . . We could not make them understand why the steamer did not come.

The big chief was now their leader. He had his warriors all drawn up around him about 250 yards from us. He made a speech to them so loud that we could hear every word he said above the roar of the surf. . . When he got within about 100 yards from us, I raised my rifle to my shoulder and said, "Fire!" Had a hundred thunderbolts dropped among his warriors they could not have stopped them as suddenly as the killing of their big chief. They gathered around his body and with a groan that was terrible, picked him up and carried him away to the north out of sight.

Another great tall fellow, wearing a red shirt came up to the beach and began calling the Indians around him . . . We could see by his frantic gestures and talk that he was urging the Indians to rush on us and wipe us out . . . We were ready for him and when he came close to where the other chief was killed, we fired and he dropped dead. This ended all efforts on the part of their chiefs to induce the Indians to rush on us . . .

Now was our chance. We left everything we had in camp . . . And with nothing but our guns and an ax and all the small ropes we had, with two or three sea biscuits apiece, we bid farewell to our old camp on Battle Rock, and started on our fearful retreat through an unknown country.

Kirkpatrick and his eight men went north, evading supposedly hostile Indians, aided by some friendly ones, till they reached Umpqua City.

The *Sea Gull,* after leaving the nine men at Port

Orford, had been laid up in San Francisco for some repairs. When Tichenor did return, he believed that his men had all been killed. He proceeded on to Portland and shortly after reaching there, he received the report from Kirkpatrick that all the men were alive.

Tichenor did not abandon the plan to make a settlement at Port Orford. He gathered new recruits. Men of means became associated with him. In the autumn of the same year he landed again at Port Orford, this time with 65 men, besides six who were financially associated with him. Others, too, arrived on the same ship, the *Columbia*. Some of them have been referred to as "agents." Still others came perhaps out of mere curiosity or for the adventure.

Tichenor, obtaining a Donation Claim, lost little time in plotting a town. Port Orford city lots were soon offered to the public.

Federal agents came to establish peace and make a treaty with the Indians. Troops were sent to protect the white settlers; blockhouses and log cabins were built.

In May, 1852, Tichenor brought Mrs. Tichenor and three children, Jake, Anna, age fifteen, and Ellen, not quite four. The latter was to become the "Belle of Curry County," an active young woman who rode horseback up and down the beaches, was always sympathetic with the Indians, taught school, finally married a well-to-do attorney of San Francisco, and become the mother of eleven children.

During the Indian wars in the early fifties, the women and children crowded into the little log fort.

To keep little four-year-old Ellen Tichenor occupied and contented, she was put to piecing a quilt. Nearly a hundred years later, one of Ellen's nine daughters said, "We still have pieces of that quilt."

With the discovery of gold on the beaches and in the creek and river beds, Port Orford became the scene of great activity. Hotels, stores and saloons lined the streets and for a few years did a flourishing business.

On March 25, 1855, a post office was established.

Six voting precincts were established in 1856 — Flores

Creek, Ellensburg, Big Bend, Whalesburg. Chetco, and Port Orford.

Troops had been brought in the latter part of 1851 and during the four or five years that followed. A military post had been established and named Fort Orford. Dr. Rodney Glisan, chief medical officer with the troops, in 1856, observed:

> Adjoining the military reservation of this fort is a small village called Port Orford, which was located or laid out in 1851, during the mania upon the coast of townsites. Having the best port between San Francisco and the Columbia River, it was thought to be an admirable site for a large city, but like many similar attempts, it has proven a failure. For notwithstanding the additional advantage of gold having since been discovered along the sand beaches for many miles above and below the town, and the touching here of a regular steamer every fortnight, it still numbers only about forty houses, and one third of these are tenantless. It has a good summer harbor, as the wind during this season is from the northwest; but in the autumn, winter and early spring it is generally very dangerous for vessels to attempt to "lie to" in the harbor, or even to enter it, as the prevailing winds are then from the south, southwest or southeast.

And in spite of its gold and open harbor, its timber and salmon fisheries, its prospects of coal and copper, the town failed to prosper. Someone wrote:

> In the year 1859 Port Orford was no longer the live place with its many people and places of amusement. Every year since 1856 saw it decline and soon it was deserted, with only three families remaining: Mr. Burnapp and family; Mrs. Knapp, known throughout the country as Grandma Knapp, and one of the dearest, kindest old ladies that ever was, and her son Louie; and Captain Tichenor and family.
>
> Weird, silent, ghost-like stood the hotels, the saloons and stores; homes for the birds, storehouses for the woodrats, sport for the north wind that played hide-and-seek through the broken windows and open doorways; broken fences, deserted farmyards, roofless dwellings—all were melancholy evidence of former life.

But the faithful ones stayed on and life came again to Port Orford, in spite of Bancroft's references to it in the following brief comment: "Port Orford is a little hamlet on the wrong side of the mountain with no reason on earth for being there."

There must have been activity in the town in 1858, or why would M. Riley and W. S. Winsor be given a contract to build a jail for $800?

When Dr. Henry Hermann landed with his Baltimore colony near the end of May, 1859, his people were accommodated in the Peter Ruffner hotel. Charles Hilburn was on hand with a team of oxen to transport the Baltimorians and their goods to the Coquille River. Louis Knapp stayed on and became one of the foremost citizens of Curry County. Among other things, he built and operated a hotel that became famous across the country, continuing to serve the public three-fourths of a century.

There was Andrew Nasburg who afterwards became postmaster of Port Orford, and still later became Marshfield's first postmaster. Allen D. Wolcott stayed on as a merchant and postmaster, until he also moved to Marshfield some years later. George Dart, who had married Anna Tichenor, continued to be a faithful citizen.

Port Orford was at least holding its own during the sixties, until disaster struck all that region in the autumn of 1868. It was the demon Forest Fire. From Ellensburg on October 26, 1868, George McSardder wrote to Miss Ellen Tichenor, away at school at the time:

> At Burnapp's the Unican family were stopping, having saved their lives by covering themselves with wet blankets. They lost everything but a few chickens and a few head of cattle.
>
> The fire seems to have come from across the Sixes to the Elk River, burning the Somer place and the Unican's—I think on the 8th and sweeping onward through the woods to Port Orford.
>
> For several days previous the smoke was so dense that candles were necessary early in the afternoon. Finally the fire came on them from every direction and no men in town.
>
> Some Chinamen just came in time to save their goods which they took from Burnap's down to the beach. But Burnap and his son saved their place. Mr. Burnap's loss being some two or three hundred lots of clothing, which they took and threw over the cliff on the beach and which then burnt . . .

Here are 1936 glimpses back at the town in the 70's:

The Winsor Hotel, now being used by the Bennett store. This

building was built by W. S. Winsor in 1874 . . . The Centennial building is the second oldest, now occupied by the Pugh Drug Store, built in 1876 by Louie Knapp. The other is the Bates home now occupied by the John Marsh Store, built in 1879.

The little schooner *Alaska,* the only schooner ever built in Port Orford, was launched by Captain Tichenor in 1869 . . .

Cultural life in the Port Orford region during the years of "growing pains" is indicated in a newspaper clipping furnished by Mrs. Hedgpeth of Walnut Creek, California:

The Lyceum

The Lyceum furnished splendid entertainments, and you might say the population of Port Orford was one great big family. The Lyceum was organized in Port Orford in 1879 by Bates, J. B. Tichenor, Will Blacklock, Sabin, Winsor, Tissie, Annie and Jessie Blacklock. Two of the musicians had received their musical education under the leading tutors of Germany. Once each month the members of the Lyceum would put on a public entertainment, and up and down the coast, men, women and children would come to witness it.

Walling, in his history of Southwestern Oregon, gives the following account of Port Orford in 1884:

Port Orford is the most important point for lumber, the supply being furnished by two of the three sawmills in Curry County; namely, the Elk Creek mill of Joseph Nay; the Hubbard Creek mill, located a mile south of town.

The latter's capacity is 17,000 feet per day. Its beginning was a small concern built in 1874 by J. E. Gould and Company. In 1876 the mill was enlarged by the Port Orford Cedar Company, N. C. Lorentzen, manager; and a wharf was built, 500 feet long, reaching to a rock that extends 160 feet further. The total cost of mill, wharf, timber and dam was $62,000. Some ten or fifteen million feet of first class timber yet remains on Hubbard Creek.

The Gold Beach *Gazette* of November 28, 1890, tells what Port Orford was like at that time. It said the people were hopeful, even confident, that they were to have a railroad from the interior within a short time and that work on the breakwater would soon be commenced by the government.

The *Gazette* went on to say: "Port Orford harbor is

now one of the best on the Pacific Coast for about nine months of the year, and that with the proposed improvement, or even a part of it, it will be one of the finest deep water harbors in the world. The largest ship that floats can lay and load at Port Orford, as it is, at all times except during a southerly gale, and at such times, all the bar harbors on the coast are shut off with heavy seas." So believed the *Gazette's* editor in 1890. The time would come, said he, when the vast commerce of the entire state would center at Port Orford, adding that there was nothing visionary in his remarks.

And so the people of Port Orford lived in hopes of greater developments and better days. The greatest development of its rich dairy lands was to come in the first half of the twentieth century. Streams were being bridged, highways were to be built, timber would flow out in the future, and so the people lived and hoped and struggled on.

"The Coose Bay Company"

It seems to have required a wreck of considerable consequence to attract real attention to Coos Bay. Soon after Captain Tichenor's settling of Port Orford, federal troops were sent in to protect the whites from the natives. The U. S. transport, *Captain Lincoln,* left the Golden Gate late in December, 1851, with 35 or 40 dragoons to be landed at Port Orford. Stormy weather prevented a landing and drove the ship northward. It was leaking badly. On the night of January 1, 1852, the *Captain Lincoln* ran ashore about two miles north of the Coos Bay bar. In the morning, the captain and his men, along with the troops, found their ship high and dry on the sandy beach. They did not know their location. They went ashore and set up a camp, naming it "Camp Castaway." This was the first settlement of whites in what is now Coos County — if we can call it a "settlement."

Goods, supplies, equipment, all were taken ashore and the men prepared for an extended sojourn. They traded with the Indians for ducks, geese, venison and fish, giving in return, articles of clothing, trinkets, hard-tack, rice and other items relished by the natives. News spread to the Umpqua. Men came down to offer help. Among them were S. S. Mann and Patrick Flanagan. Both these men were later to become leading citizens in the early development of Coos County, continuing for nearly half a century.

Four months had passed before Camp Castaway ceased to exist. Men and supplies were transferred over the sand spit to Coos Bay, across that body of water, then down the coast to Port Orford over what later may have become the famous Randolph Trail, approximately what is now known as the Seven Devils road.

It was this event—the wrecking of the *Captain Lincoln* that apparently caused news of the Coos Bay country to be spread to the outside world.

Walling says:

> Coos Bay seems never to have achieved mention . . . until 1852, when a report concerning it was circulated in the Umpqua Valley . . . King, a venturesome individual, got up a company to search for it. The explorers set out from Winchester and went by way of Scottsburg to the seacoast and then southward to the bay. They were P. B. Marple, Fitzhue, Flourney, Peyton, King and two other whites, with two Indians as guides or interpreters . . . In the following May, 1853, we hear of Marple lecturing publicly in Jacksonville on the beauties and advantages of the Coos Bay country, as it was already called and endeavoring to organize a stock company to go there under his lead and take possession of the country.

At this point, let us listen to Esther M. Lockhart, a member of the Coos Bay Company:

> Full of this dream, Mr. Marple . . . discoursed . . . on the great future of this wonderful "Coos Bay Country." Marple was an extremely visionary man, full of grand Utopian dreams. He really believed all he said about his new "discovery."
>
> He was a fluent speaker and had little difficulty in drawing interested crowds of listeners around him as he talked on the streets of Jacksonville . . . Everybody appeared to be interested in it. Mr. Marple undoubtedly drew a very alluring picture of this vast, unexplored region. He offered to guide a party of

strong, active young men to this favored locality, for a price, naturally . . .

Marple had no difficulty in organizing a party of 40 hardy young men, my husband among them. He could easily have secured twice as many members, if he would have taken them. The avowed purpose of this company was to colonize and develop the Coos Bay country. Each member paid to Marple the sum of $250 for being the Moses to lead them to this new Promised Land.

My two babies and I waited patiently in our fairly comfortable quarters at Canonville until we heard from my husband as to whether or not this new location had come up to his expectations. Finally a letter came, saying that everything was thoroughly satisfactory. The country was marvelous, the future was assured.

He also wrote that only 19 men of the original party of 40 had gone on to Coos Bay. Soon after reaching the headwaters of the Coquille River, 21 of the men had expressed dissatisfaction at not finding gold, or even a trace of it. One small vein of coal had been found. With the consent of Mr. Marple, these discontented men left the party and returned to their valley homes.

After their departure the remaining 19 held a meeting, electing William H. Harris as their leader, thus displacing Mr. Marple, who was quite willing to relinquish his position. The name, *Coose Bay Commercial Company* was adopted for the new organization.

Freeman had written that he would be coming for us soon. Accordingly, the latter part of September, my husband arrived to take us down to this wonderful new land. He said that this would be our home for all future time.

There was something mysterious, exciting and thrilling in going into an absolutely new country where white women had never before ventured. The thought fired my imagination. I hoped it would prove to be all that my husband believed it was, but I still had my doubts.

The route my husband chose to return to Coos Bay was entirely different from that which the members of the Marple expedition had taken. They had gone through Camas Valley, and after much devious wandering they had reached the headwaters of the Coquille River, had gone down that beautiful stream in Indian canoes and after a stay of some days at the big Indian village at the mouth of the river, they had laboriously walked over the steep, rugged hills known as Seven Devils to reach their destination . . .

It was a long and wearisome journey even for strong young men like themselves. This route would have been too strenuous for women and little children. It would have been a dangerous one for them all

Mr. Lockhart had learned of another entrance into the Coos Bay country. It meant an extra hundred miles or so, but far less hazardous. Instead of turning west by way of Camas Valley and the middle fork of the Coquille, the chosen route led northward to Winchester, then in a westerly direction to Scottsburg. Now, we'll let Mrs. Lockhart continue:

We rode on mules over the mountains, on trails that were steep, rough and narrow. My husband carried one of our children on his lap and I held my eight-months' old baby in the same way. It was often difficult for me to keep my seat on the mule. I thought many times that we were falling off. In those days all women rode on side saddles, on one side of their mount only. This was really a most ridiculous fashion. It proved scant protection for the rider and was hard for both her and the animal. For a women to ride astride, as they all do nowdays, would have been considered a most unwomanly and immodest thing to do.

At Scottsburg we embarked on the little river steamer *Washington* . . . Coming down the river on the *Washington,* we passed the Curtis Noble family, also bound for Coos Bay. They were obliged to travel somewhat slowly, as they had a scow, towed by a big Indian canoe, with a considerable load. They were bringing with them some cows, horses, pigs, and chickens. This was the first livestock ever brought into Coos Bay, with the exception of horses and mules, which had come with the first white men. We had probably been at Empire City about two weeks when the Nobles finally arrived.

When we arrived at Winchester Bay, at the mouth of the Umpqua, we again mounted our mules for the 20 mile ride along the ocean beach to the settlement at Empire City.

It was about four o'clock in the afternoon of October 18, 1853, when we reached our journey's end. We went at once to the "hotel" a little log cabin, kept by the genial Frank Ross. Here we feasted literally, on fresh salmon, crabs, clams and roasted wild ducks and geese, all of which were delicious. Although we had to experiment with the shell-fish, we liked it from the first. This was fortunate for us, as it had to be a generous part of our future food supply.

The men who had come earlier in the summer met on the east shore or lower Coos Bay, where they formed themselves into an organization which they named the "Coos Bay Company," the purpose of which was for each to take up a land claim, to prove up on it, to secure a patent and then to turn the land over to the Coos Bay Company.

The persons entering into this agreement consisted of the following

William H. Harris	Joseph H. McVay
Rollin S. Belknap	Charles Pearce
Solomon Bowermaster	S. H. Temple
A. P. DeCuis	J. A. Burnett
John H. Foster	W. H. Jackson
A. P. Gaskell	Presley G. Wilhite
F. G. Lockhart	Matthias M. Leam
P. B. Marple	Henry A. Stark
James A. McVay	Benjamin Rohvin
Joseph Lane	C. K. Haskell

Others came later and bought shares in the company.

The Baltimore Colony

Perhaps no other group coming into Coos County formed quite so well an organized band as those often referred to as the *Baltimore Colony*. Descendants of those people, down to the fifth generation, still form a substantial portion of the leading citizens of Coos County.

Their leader was Dr. Henry Hermann, born in 1812 in Germany, where he grew up, was educated and graduated in medicine from the University of Marburg. It is reported that he became involved in the political difficulties of the 1830's, when he emigrated to America, locating in Baltimore, Maryland. In 20-odd years he built up a large medical practice.

By 1858, Dr. Hermann found that hard work and lack of outdoor freedom was undermining his health. He and a few chosen friends had ideas about starting life anew in the far-off western country on the Pacific Coast.

He was joined by a Mr. Bender, Harry Pagels, Mr. Osterhans, James Burke, H. Finkelda and Mr. Coleman. Crossing the Isthmus of Panama, they proceeded northward into Oregon and on into Washington as far as Puget

Sound, not finding any place that entirely suited all their requirements.

Once more they headed south, and in the little settlement of Roseburg, Dr. Hermann fell in with John Yoakam, an early Coos County settler, who had come to Roseburg with a pack load of hides, skins, and furs. Yoakam gave such a glowing report of the Coos County country that Dr. Hermann was induced to see the place for himself. He went with Yoakam, by way of Camas Valley and the Middle Fork, and remained on the Coquille over winter, observing the climate, the land and the general situation. He is reported to have said, "I have found it; I have found the place for which I have searched the entire Pacific Coast."

In the spring of 1859 he returned to Baltimore, where he published a glowing account of this wonderful Pacific Coast region in Southern Oregon.

He gathered around him a party of men with their families, and some who had no families. Many trades and professions were represented, including a shoemaker, a tinsmith, miner, music teacher, cabinetmaker, piano maker, farmers, laborers, ship carpenter, locksmith, carpenter, and himself a medical doctor. And there were two cigar makers, not inappropriately coming to a region where the Indians had been growing the smoking weed since time without record.

Ready to leave Baltimore in April of 1859, Dr. Hermann's party included his own wife and family: Binger, T. Manuel, Washington P., Cass M., Tushelda, and Franklin P.; Henry Schroeder and wife with their family: J. Henry, Augustus H., J. Frederick, Louisa A., William, Charles E.; William Volkmar with wife and son Carl; August Bender with wife and son Edward; David Stauff with wife and child; Mrs. Edward Pagels and children, Caroline, Mary and Edward. Mr. Pagels had come with the first party; Mr. Wilde and family, William Leake, Mr. Julius Gustave Pohl. Later, at San Francisco, they were joined by George Stauff and family, and Mr. Victimier.

The steamer *Northern Light* took the party to Aspinwall on the shores of the Gulf of Mexico, where they were transferred across the Isthmus of Panama, to the Pacific coast, and the steamer *Uncle Sam* took the party on to San Francisco.

There, after taking on some additional supplies, they shipped on the *Columbia,* landing at Port Orford in the latter part of May. While most of the party rested up here at the Peter Roffner house, Dr. Hermann immediately started out on a saddle horse to arrange for a pack train to take their goods over the hill to the South Fork, as well as to arrange for boats on the Coquille River. With the exception of a few men to accompany the pack train over the mountain, other members of the party were to go up the coast to the present site of Bandon and then by boat on up the river. The more bulky goods and equipment were also to go this way.

At Port Orford they first met Louie Knapp and Charles Hilburn (whose wife's sister was later to marry Joaquin Miller). Hilburn did freighting with an ox team and wagon. He was engaged to take the party up the coast to the Coquille River. Their heavier and more bulky goods, camp equipment, and some of the members least able to make the trip afoot, were loaded on the wagon. The first night they camped on the Sixes.

Bennett says:

> This was the first night they had ever spent out in the woods. The comfortable family home, the ship's warm cabin, the hospitable hotel, had now belonged to the past. They had got beyond the bounds of civilization. Those that had been brought up in the refinement of city life were obliged to lie on the ground with a log or piece of rock for a pillow, with a blanket wrapped around them. The twang of orchestral violin, or the ponderous tones of the church organ were now supplanted by the screams of wildcats, or the sullen growl of the bear. Instead of the dainty leg of mutton with caper sauce, those dainty Baltimorians had to be content with the hind leg of a half raw grizzly . . .

It was the end of the third day out from Port Orford, June 1, 1859, that they first saw the beautiful Coquille. Well, not quite the end of the day, for Dr. Hermann was there with two boats to take them and the luggage up the river to the home of D. J. and Y. M. Lowe, opposite Parkersburg. Entertainment in the Lowe home was heaven compared with what they had endured through the two previous nights.

Proceeding on up the river, shortly before reaching the present site of Coquille, a gloom of sadness was cast over the entire party by the drowning of ten-year-old William Schroeder. Binger Hermann, then 16 years old, almost met the same fate when he plunged in to try to save the younger boy. While some remained in an attempt to recover the body, the main party proceeded on the next morning. The body was found 17 days later.

The boat trip on the Coquille came to an end at the home of J. Alva Harry, a short distance up the river from the present site of Myrtle Point.

While locating sites for new homes, the community was again cast into gloom when Mr. Wilde, after selecting a location on Catching Creek, accidentally discharged his gun, killing himself immediately. He left a widow and two small children.

Bennett says:

> The doctor and his colonists took up lands, and commenced clearing them at once and all went to work with a right good will. There was no post office nor even a store nearer than Empire City on the one side, and Port Orford on the other. (About 50 miles either way,) There was no school in the whole country at this time except at Empire, until young Binger Hermann was induced to open one, and he did, as literature was possibly more in accordance with his tastes than cutting his way through logs, ditching, plowing, carting and all the other rough requirements of agricultural pursuits.
>
> Early in the fall more colonists arrived, including Mr. and Mrs. John Kronenberg and their daughter Emma; Mr. Carpenter, Mr. Kohler, J. Grubbe, also Bierbrance and Crady, Mr. Getty and their children, Charley and Fannie Wilmot, also Robert McCleary and Henry Grube . . .

Before leaving Baltimore, the party had made arrangements to send some of their heavier and more bulky goods by ship around the Horn to San Francisco, whence it was reshipped to Empire. Next it had to be taken in small boats to the head of navigation on Isthmus Slough, and transferred over land to Coaledo, at the head of

Beaver Slough. The shipment included, among other things, a grand square piano, a 54-inch Page portable saw mill, an upright 8-horse-power steam boiler and engine, and a pair of 24-inch mill burs for making flour.

Dodge says they were transferred across the divide from Isthmus Inlet to Beaver Slough "by a lot of squaws under the supervision of A. H. Hines." It seems more likely, since this travelway had already been used for six years as the main route connecting the Coquille with the Coos Bay country, that it must have been widened sufficiently at least to admit the use of a sled or a "lizard", and that horses or oxen were used as draft animals to transfer heavy loads.

At the head of Beaver Slough, the cargo once more had to be transferred to boats for passage down that precarious waterway to the Coquille, then up the river 25 miles to the J. Alva Harry place, a few miles south of the present site of Myrtle Point. A short time before reaching that destination, however, one of the boats swamped, soaking its cargo, including the piano, Dr. Hermann's valuable library and instruments, some of the mill machinery and other things. Most of the cargo was saved, though much damaged.

All this freighting with the many transfers was not only hard on the goods and on the nerves of the owners, but also on the cash reserves of the colonists. It is reported that the total cost of the freight bills, including transfers, ran up to more than $60 per measured ton. Some of the families found themselves broke and facing conditions that were not encouraging to say the least. This was especially true of those who lacked strong hearts and stronger backs. Little wonder then that, after a few months, some left to join relatives or friends in California, including the bereaved widow and the two young children of Mr. Wilde.

The stayers brought culture, music, books, good citizenship. Members of the party built up good farms, some of which are still in the families of the original owners of 90 years ago. Others became teachers, lawyers, merchants, mechanics. Some entered politics, becoming state legislators. Binger Hermann became a congressman for 16 years and U. S. Land Commissioner in Washington, D. C.

Several of the names in the Baltimore Colony will be found in other parts of this book.

6

Three More Colonies

From No'th Karliny

In the spring of 1872, William P. Mast, with his family and about 66 other persons, besides the little children, set their faces westward from North Carolina, to Oregon.

The David Wagner and John Hayes families had come west from North Carolina two years before, settling in the neighborhood of what is now Powers.

After a year in Douglas County the Mast party moved on into Coos.

The Coos Bay Wagon Road had been opened during the summer. So, in the autumn of 1873, the North Carolina emigrants pulled up stakes and loaded their wagons and pack animals. Some of them rode saddle horses. Others walked and led cows. Although the wagon road was open and passable for teams and wagons all the way to Sumner, some of the new settlers were obliged to seek claims some distance off the main road. Reuben H. Mast said that their place was four miles off and that it had to be reached over a rough mountain trail —

> . . . over which we had to transport on the backs of our horses, hitherto unused to such work, all our trunks, boxes, cook stoves, chickens in crates, and last but not least, a blacksmith shop, as father could not live on a farm without one. We still remember what a novelty it was to see a small horse loaded with a big trunk on each side and one on top, the whole being lashed by what seemed an intricate network of ropes.

Those early settlers in the communities of Sitkum, Dora, McKinley, Fairview and Lee, and others along the Coos Bay Wagon Road, came into a wilderness with timber everywhere. Away from the main road, there were only trails, and not many of them.

Reuben Mast said:

There was not any means of crossing streams; hence, the settlers would select a place where they could fall a tree across a stream, level off the curvature of the log, erect hand rails. With such a bridge, saddle and pack horses were led and transportation was established and maintained until the settlers built makeshift roads to the Coos Bay Wagon Road at Burton Prairie [Fair View] and later to Norway.

They were soon settled snugly in a board shanty, 12 by 14 feet, which was surrounded by tall fir timber on the north and east and on the south by a stretch of ten acres of black logs which had been cut down in the early summer and burned over in the fall. All through the long winter, they toiled in those black logs, cutting, rolling, burning and grubbing, day in and day out and often till ten o'clock at night, so that when the June roses blushed and nodded in the sun, ten acres were raising as fine a crop of grain and grass as ever grew.

In addition to the W. P. Mast party from North Carolina, others came about the same time and still additional families followed as the years went by. Many worked and did their full share in the slow transformation of a wilderness. Stories of those families will be told in other parts of this book.

The Tenmile Country

In the extreme northwest corner of Coos County is the Tenmile Country forming the watershed that drains almost entirely into two lakes — North Lake and Tenmile Lake. In recent years the western portion of this area has come to be referred to as the Lakeside Country, the eastern portion as the Templeton Community.

The entire district contains 60-odd square miles.

The two lakes are very irregular, having several prongs, somewhat in the form of fingers of badly-mangled hands. They are divided from each other by rather a high ridge which slopes downward from the Millicoma Divide, to about three miles inland from the ocean. At this point it is cut, allowing North Lake to flow into Tenmile Lake through a shallow creek about 2000 feet in length. The combined waters of the two lakes find their way to the ocean through the Tenmile Creek, about four miles in length from the lake to the ocean. This short stream is the gateway for tens of thousands of salmon entering the lakes on their way to the inflowing creeks each season.

The fertile agricultural lands of the region are located along the banks of the creeks that feed the two lakes. The ridges dividing these rather narrow valleys, once covered with a heavy growth of fir timber, had been burned off before the coming of the white settlers. This may have occurred during the big forest fire in 1868, though some seem to be of the opinion that it was burned even earlier. But nature has replanted the forests, largely to alder at first, then to Douglas fir. During this process of natural reforestation, there were thousands of acres of range for elk and deer and later for cattle and sheep.

This portion of Coos County did not begin to be settled as early as were the lands bordering on Coos Bay and the Coquille River, not being similarly reached by water transportation.

There seems to be no definite record as to who were the first pioneers to settle in the Tenmile region.

The first county road established in Coos County was along the ocean beach from Coos Bay to the Tenmile Creek.

During the first 20 years following the settlement at Empire City and around Coos Bay, the greater part of the land travel into Coos County was by this route, down the Umpqua by way of Scottsburg. It seems logical to conclude that the first settlers around the Tenmile lakes came around by the same route, thence up the creek, a distance of only three or four miles, to the lakes.

Boats and equipment could easily have been hauled in on wagons. Water transportation then afforded them means for reaching the fertile lands along the creek bottoms reaching out from the various branches of the two lakes.

Alder, willows and maple crowded the creek banks. Red cedar, killed but not destroyed by the early fires, was still sound and provided splendid building material — boards, puncheons, shakes, posts, rails. Large old growth Douglas fir trees that had escaped the early fires also made first class building timbers.

The Tenmile pioneer found nearby all his necessary food supplies within the bounds of his own homestead and in the nearby surrounding woods, creeks, and the lakes.

Meat, fish and fruits, Mother Nature bountifully furnished the Tenmile pioneer. The streams and lakes teemed with trout; large schools of salmon came up each autumn through Tenmile Creek from the ocean. Deer and elk were plentiful at each pioneer's doorstep. Pheasants, ducks and geese gave meat variety. An occasional fat bear added his supply of lard.

While the pioneer waited for his fruit trees to come into bearing, he was in the midst of an abundance of the native wild berries so common in Coos and Curry counties.

Such was the Tenmile country when the settlers began to locate homes there in the seventies. Among the earliest of these were Nels Monson, Ben Roberts, Steve Johnson, W. N. Adams and his son, B. F. Adams, Jake Nelson, Pete Robertson, William (Wm. F.) Bowron, Charles Carlson, Sr. and his two sons, Charles and Alex, Thompson, Charles Siestreem, Angus McDonald, Gus Carlson, Ole Benson, Eric Erickson, C. W. Sanford, Hibbard, John D. Quick, James B. Servis, as well as others.

During the eighties and nineties others moved in, including the families of John Steinlechner, William McCulloch, John Benson, Harry Wilkins, Ed Wells, Oliver Landrith, Pete Menegat, D. O. Kinyon, Richard Handle.

Around the turn of the century and later, newcomers were arriving, some to buy out earlier settlers, others to find vacant lands yet to be homesteaded.

Those who came in the early seventies first brought only such supplies and equipment as a family might need to camp for a few weeks. They had to make extra trips to bring in tools — axes, saws, a few steel wedges and a sledge, a cant-hook, the pioneers' necessary frow or froe for splitting shakes and boards.

Just when or how the first cows, horses, pigs, chickens, sheep were brought into the Tenmile Country, no one seems to know. No doubt some of them came up the beach route to the lakes and were then ferried on rafts to the desired locations. But over the ridges to the south, Haynes Slough penetrated inland towards the Tenmile Country, leaving a gap of only some seven or eight miles. Settlers on upper Haynes already had grubbed out a summer road and there were trails three or four miles beyond the head of navigation. Ridges dividing the two communities were quite free of brush and timber, and the hardy pioneer soon opened up trails sufficient to enable him to lead in a cow or two, and a couple of pack horses. In this way some of the early chickens and pigs were moved in, as well as furniture, tools, supplies. Trails were widened so that a "frog" could be used to haul some of the heavier articles, such as stoves.

A "frog," be it known, is a kind of sled used by the pioneer. It is somewhat in the form of a letter A, made from the forks of a tree.

As trails were widened, sleds replaced the "frog." Next he built what he called the go-devil. It consisted of a platform mounted on two wheels under the rear end, while under the front end was a "bob-sled," attached by means of a king-bolt.

As years went on and roads were built, wagons were used, replacing the pack-horse, the "frog," the sled, the go-devil, until even the old wagon had to give way to the truck, the pick-up, and the sedan.

In time, roads were opened up over the ridges between the Tenmile Country to the head of navigation on Haynes Slough, called Smith's Landing. But even this could not be reached by boats except when the tide was well up. Three miles farther down the stream, boats could float even at extreme low tide. A road was extended to that point and the place came to be known as Peterson's Landing.

Travel in and out of the Tenmile Country was for years divided between the beach route and the road over the hills to Haynes Inlet. Another road was opened from the head of navigation on North Inlet to the lake at the place now known as Shutter's Landing. Nearly all of the farmers around the North Tenmile Lake used the beach route, for they had two or three additional ridges with only trails beyond the end of the road. Even to this day, some of the North Lake farmers have no outlet except by means of boats down the lake to connect with the roads.

At the lower or west end of the lakes, where Lakeside later became located, a common meeting place was begun early in the history of that section of Coos County. Here it was that boats on the lakes met wagons that hauled freight over the ocean beach route to and from Coos Bay. This common meeting place began to take on life; and, like Topsy, it just "growed." Boat landings, warehouses, cabins, shelters for the horses, over-night stopping places with an occasional meal for the weary traveler, and families began to settle. In 1892 a post office was established and was known as *Lake*.

The dairy farmers established a cooperative creamery in the spring of 1893 and the place became known as *The Creamery*, as distinguished from *Lake*, the post office, which shifted about from place to place in keeping with the residence of the postmaster.

Farm produce in the Tenmile Country, besides dairy products, including potatoes, apples, beef, pork, some mutton and lamb, wool and hides. Beef cattle often were driven overland to Peterson's Landing on Haynes Inlet, where they were slaughtered and shipped by boat to the bay markets. Sometimes buyers brought out bands of cattle, loading them onto barges, to be taken to different points of Coos Bay. One of the earliest of such buyers was E. George Flanagan, eldest son of Patrick Flanagan. He had been associated with H. P. Whitney in the meat business, with a slaughter house on the bay front midway between Old North Bend and Marshfield. Their place was known as Centerville. Other buyers who came later included Henry Holmes, who operated a meat market in Marshfield, and Bill Gamble with a market in North Bend.

"Outside buyers" came in from Douglas County, driving out bands of cattle of all ages from yearlings up to old cows. These bands ranged from 50 or 60 up to as many as 150 head.

In the summer of 1898, an inland mail route was established from Marshfield on Coos Bay to Gardiner on the lower Umpqua River. Three round trips a week were made. A row boat was used from Marshfield to Peterson's Landing on Haynes Inlet, where the carrier changed to a saddle horse, with the mail bag tied on behind. Soon the mail increased till he needed a pack animal besides his riding horse. His route took him east of the lakes, over some seven or eight ridges in all, and across as many little valleys, to a point on Scofield Slough within the present limits of Reedsport. The carrier had to stable his horses again and once more resort to a row boat to carry him and his mail pouches to Gardner. The next day he reversed his journey in the same manner.

Three post offices were established on this route. The first was at Peterson's Landing on Haynes Inlet, named *May,* for the youngest daughter of the postmaster, Peter Peterson. The second was located on the Wm. and C. P. Coleman dairy farm, who had bought out the former owner, Ole Benson. Miss Albina Coleman became the first postmaster, followed by Edward A. Taylor, Benjamin Roberts, Miss Greta Walker, who married and resigned 1916. Mary A. Monson was appointed. But Mary declined the honor, so Greta was required to maintain the office for another six months till Uncle Sam's man could get around to check up and relieve her on February 28, 1917. The post office was known as *Templeton,* named for a bachelor settler of early days. The third office, *Sampson,* was in Douglas County.

At the lower end of the lakes, the old creamery operated with more or less success for 12 or 14 years. In 1906 it was sold to L J. Simpson and C. M. Byler, who bought up considerable land in the vicinity of the creamery. The old *Lake* post office had been discontinued in 1903. In 1908 a new office was established; Simpson and Byler had plotted the land, and *Lakeside* was born.

For some years Lakeside flourished. Hotels were built, summer homes sprang up around the lakes, docks with boats-for-hire lined the waterfront of the new town. Within 16 years it had taken on metropolitan airs and became Coos County's eighth incorporated city. For a few years it boomed. The Southern Pacific railroad had come in 1916, giving Lakeside an attractive depot. Logging camps in the surrounding country provided employment for many workers, till the best timber supplies had dwindled.

But the Oregon Coast highway, opening in the thirties, left Lakeside nearly a mile to the side. The Templeton country at the other end of the lake had been opened up by a fairly good all-year road to the Coos Bay markets and trading centers. Shipping through Lakeside and down the beach route had long since ceased. Came the depression in the thirties and Lakeside became almost a ghost city. It was disincorporated in 1942.

The "Currier Village," with its "thirty-six steam-heated cottages" added considerable life and new hopes during the otherwise dull years of the thirties. A dock was built on the lake front, with a modern restaurant and night club. Boats and launches were for hire. Tourists from distant points spent days and even weeks in the "Village." Week-end visitors from parts of Coos County came for fishing, boating and camping.

Now a sawmill and a planermill in the town, with several other sawmills on the lake shores tributary to the town, add to the activities and the prosperity of the community. Bathing beaches have been added to the lake front. Speed, outboard and sailing boats and hydroplanes — these at times make fleets of buzzing, humming, speeding scenes up and down the lakes. Fishing in season adds to the list of attractions. The town has an airport.

Eckley — "Little Switzerland"

Can you spot Eckley on the map?

If we could follow a crow that had roosted at Powers and was going to Port Orford for his breakfast, straight over the mountains, about midway between the two places we could look down and see the Eckley country, a sort of Switzerland planted in Southwestern Oregon. It drains off into the Sixes River, which flows into the ocean a few miles north of Port Orford.

The pioneers who first entered the Eckley country didn't follow the crow. Not quite, for the going was too rough. They must pick their way through devious passes, over ridges, across canyons. The Indians, however, had trails even before the coming of the whites. Along an Indian trail in the early 50's, east from Port Orford, men made the rich strike which resulted in the name of Johnson Creek. On their way they must have passed through the country that we now know as Eckley.

We next learn of it through Joseph A. Haines, who bought the claim then occupied by Wash Waters:

> We arrived August 15, 1860 . . . It was a lonesome place. The furniture consisted of three or four three-legged stools, a slab table, a few pots and pans, a Dutch oven, blankets, a brush broom, and a lot of pack saddles . . . [Years later, Mrs. Haines told a neighbor that she refused to move into the cabin until the place was cleared of the pack saddles.]
>
> The next day was devoted to house cleaning. My furniture had been sent to Port Orford and in September I got it home . . . Our nearest neighbor, John Leggett, lived four miles away, and the next nearest was twelve miles. Our first visitors were Mr. and Mrs. Leggett. We were very glad to see them . . . and in a short time we returned the visit.

Just when the next families moved into the Eckley country isn't clear. But among those who came were the families of Alfred ("Tim") Greene, some time before 1860; Thomas Jefferson (Jeff) Gibbs in 1870; the Bigelow family; the George H. Guerin family, in 1876.

For the large families of these settlers there appears to have been little in the way of schools in the community. Joseph A. Haines reports that he hired Ellen Tichenor for three terms of three months each at a salary of $25 per month and board. Later they had a man teacher from San Francisco on the same terms.

Another report is of a small school house sometimes referred to as the "chicken house." On one side there was a lean-to that covered a hen roost.

One may know about Eckley from a few of those who were born there, or came when they were barely old enough to remember their first coming. From them it is possible to learn about the gold mines and the pack trains; the wild game, the farm products, the social life; some of the other families and the schools; the mail services and the post offices — yes *offices,* not just one post office. Four different names appear in the official records in the National Archives in Washington, D. C.

Mrs. J. N. Gearhart and Hulda (Greene) Svensen form the main source of information for this story of the Eckley country.

These natural prairies were bountiful with grass and wild clover and today provide forage for large herds of cattle. When the settlers first came, deer and elk roamed at will and fish were abundant in the streams. Bear were not uncommon, and their fat helped to supply shortening for pastries and for frying. The tallow from the deer and elk was used for making candles, while the meat was ever at hand to cook fresh or to eat dried.

To this land of plenty came settlers to make their homes. The Guerins, Haines, Gibbs, Bigelows, and Greenes owned and lived on their land in the Eckley country 50 years or more, till they sold out to the lumbering interests in 1912. The homes of the Haines family, the Guerins and the Greens were stopping places for travelers. Anyone from the outside bringing news was more than welcome, for mail and news were scarce. Some of the first settlers had been there 20 years before they had any regular mail service.

South of the Eckley country was a mining district where much gold was taken out during the early days. The miners in coming and going, often stayed at the homes of the settlers, and many happy hours were spent sitting around the fireplaces discussing the news or spinning yarns of adventure.

The Greens, with the Bigelows, came with their teams and wagons over the old Coos Bay Wagon Road to Dora, then down to Myrtle Point, up the South Fork to the Bill Warner place. While the party waited there, Edwin

C. Greene came down with all his 14 saddle and pack animals to bring them in.

In a recent report, Mrs. Gearhart wrote:

> Within a few weeks each family had a house . . . Boards twelve to fourteen feet long were easily split from Port Orford cedar. Floors made from this white wood were the pride of the women. Very thin strips were split for slats in the beds on which to place mattresses of straw and wool. And good beds they were, too.
>
> [Later an] organ was hauled up Salmon Creek on a narrow sled, with handles behind to help keep it upright, while it was pulled by one horse. Ropes were tied to the top of the organ and an extra man went on the upper side of the trail to keep the organ from rolling over.

"Uncle Tim" Greene was one of the first miners; he with five other men drilled and blasted a tunnel deep into the Salmon Mountain, one of the more famous gold mining spots in that region. Many years later, "Tim" Greene's grand-nephew, Amasa W. Greene, and two other men reopened the tunnel to a depth of 670 feet and still did not reach the end.

Besides mining, "Tim" Greene kept cattle on the Roland and Salt Lick Prairies and finally settled on what came to be known as Deer Park, the cattle ranch now owned by Albert Powers. He would not permit the killing of deer or other wild game on his place. He was one of the first mail carriers to pack the mail in on his back over the mountain trails from Port Orford. He carried no gun, nor even a knife for protection. In 1886 he was buried on the hill back of his house in Deer Park.

Since the coming of the whites, there have been, we might say, three epochs in the history of the Eckley Country.

With the discovery of gold in the Johnson Creek area in the early fifties, miners rushed in, many of them with nothing but what they could pack on their backs. A few had horses.

Flour, potatoes, bacon, tobacco, an occasional change of overalls, shirts and flannel underwear, and tools — these must be packed in. Horses and mules were needed.

So other men came with pack animals. Gradually these

teams, or pack trains, as they were called, increased with the growing demand until some of the individual owners had as many as 20, or even up to 30 pack animals. In some cases a man with his sons might operate the train; or the owner hired extra men to help.

From the 1850's to the nineties, practically all the supplies for the mines and the Johnson Creek and Salmon Mountain district were packed in from Port Orford by way of Eckley. So men brought their families and settled in this "Little Switzerland" in the mountains from which springs the Sixes Rivers.

Travel increased when people began coming in from the Coquille side, up the South Fork, over the divide, adding another spoke in the wheel of which Eckley was the hub. When mail service was established, a carrier started from Myrtle Point at the same time that another one started from Port Orford. Each one would reach Eckley in the evening, stay over night, returning to his starting place the following day. Thus Eckley became a stopping place between Myrtle Point and Port Orford, as well as from the latter place to the mines. A road was built in from the Coquille side in 1895, enabling the residents to go and come in style — in buggies.

Came the second period, or epoch, when the mines began to peter out. Gone were the days of the old pack trains. Men turned to other fields. The settlers who had provided the pack animals, and who had supplied the miners with butter, cheese, eggs, bacon, vegetables, fruits and other necessities, must now look to other means of supporting their families, educating their children. There were large families: 10 Guerin children; 12 Gibbs; 15 Haines.

And so the pack trains gave way to the raising of beef cattle. Some beef was locally butchered to supply the few remaining miners and for home use. Most of the cattle, however, were driven out.

The second epoch ended when the pioneer settlers sold out their holdings in 1912 to the timber interests for lumbering purposes. Much of the timber has been logged off, though a great deal of it still remains. The cleared portions, together with the natural open prairies, provide thousands of acres of forage for range cattle.

Ellis Dement, son of Russell and grandson of Sam Dement, now owns most of the range land in the Eckley country west of the divide, in Curry County. His two sons, Sam and Russell, have leased the land and bought the livestock from their father. They have sufficient range to run 400 head of cattle.

The east portion of the Eckley country, on the Coos County side of the divide, commonly known as the Deer Park area, now belongs to Albert Powers, who carries on a cattle business similar to that of the Dements.

Previous reference has been made to the post offices of the Eckley country and their different names. When the mail service first came to this community, the post office was not named *Eckley,* but *New Castle,* with Charlotte N. Guerin as the first postmaster. She was the widow of William Guerin and had come with her son, George H. Guerin, and his family in 1876.

No explanation is available for the change of the name of *New Castle* in 1885 to *Tell Tale*. The records in the National Archives merely register the fact that it was so changed. But the name *Tell Tale* must have met with immediate dissatisfaction and protest by residents and patrons, for only 39 days later it was changed again, this time to *Eckley*. The office was kept under this name until it was discontinued in 1916. But to this day the community is still known as the Eckley country.

The name New Castle, perhaps, was given to the place on account of coal outcroppings in that vicinity.

The creeping in of the name *Tell Tale* appears to be wrapped in secrecy, and nobody seems to be able or willing to reveal the secret.

7

Some Pioneer Families

JOHN ALVA HARRY, *By Mr. and Mrs. E. A. Krewson*

THE LISTING of John Alva Harry, as one of Coos County's earliest pioneers, can be traced by his diary which he kept up to date through his entire life.

Excerpts from Diary

Oct. 4, 1854 — This morning Alfred Culver, Liness Bushnell and myself started to the Coquille river to look for land claims. Stopped over night at Mr. Day's in Camas Valley. The weather toward noon was cloudy in southwest. At sundown commenced raining gently.

Oct. 6 — Camped at sun down a half mile from Sugar Loaf mountain. Weather fair.

Oct. 7 — Crossed Sugar Loaf mountain and camped at the edge of Kitchen Prairie.

Oct. 8 — This morning we saddled our horses and rode to Hoffman's for breakfast. Turned the horses loose and took a look at my claim.

Oct. 9 — Built a cabin on my claim up the river from [the present Myrtle Point].

Nov. 1 — After looking for the cattle in the fog until noon, got them up and commenced plowing. Alfred built a chicken house.

June 4, 1856 — We attended the first election in the Coquille valley. Miars and his squaw stopped with me. Dulley and Hill went home.

Sept. 6, 1856 — Today we formed Coquille infantry guard. Runners brought in report that Rogue River Indians were on the war path. Mrs. Hoffman and other women and children hid in the nettle patch while the men stood on guard.

Sept. 7 — Commenced work on Fort Kitchen.

Sept. 21 – This morning Hill, Hoffman, Colwell, the two Coopers and myself started up the river. We found Hoffman's house burning. We returned to the fort.

Sept. 28 – The Indians brought in some of the stolen goods. Today 10 of the boys came from Rowlands to Fort Kitchen. We elected Jackson captain.

Sept. 30 – Today the Coos Bay boys went home. The Coquille boys prepared to leave.

John Alva Harry and Chloe Amelia Cook were married in 1857. He was 23, his wife only 17. They moved at once to his land claim on the Coquille River, near Myrtle Point. They made this trip on horseback and, months afterwards, small bits of her dress could be seen where they caught on the wild rose thorns along the narrow trail over Sugar Loaf Mountain.

Here they lived for a number of years, trapping beaver and hunting between Myrtle Point and Coquille, making long, arduous trips twice yearly to Empire for supplies. Mr. Harry became the first assessor of Coos County, when the court house was located at Empire. He was a surveyor and woodsman, leading the expedition that discovered Brewster Valley. He later settled at what became then and still is known as the Half Way House, on the old Coos Bay Wagon Road.

Mr. Harry died in 1874. To him and Mrs. Harry were born five children – Even Neva Harry, who married Phebea Turner; Grant Harry, who married Hannah Krewson; Eva Harry, who married Thomas O. Krewson; Colfax Harry, who married Nellie Norton and Belle Harry, who married J. D. Laird. They are all deceased with the exception of Mrs. Belle Laird, who is now 83 years old and is the assistant postmistress at Sitkum.

To the five children of John Alva Harry and his wife have been born a great number of children and grandchildren who, all together, would make a sizeable city.

Sol J. McCloskey, *By Minnie McCloskey Lester*

Sol J. McCloskey was living in Kansas when he became

afflicted with "Oregon Fever" and sent for literature on the Coos Bay section. The descriptions were alluring. A farm of 160 acres could be homesteaded. Because of the fertile soil, and "Oregon mist," vegetables, fruits, and grains could be grown abundantly; the Bay and streams were teeming with fish; the forests were full of game.

He and some of his neighbors made preparations to move to this "paradise." Some sold their farms; while others rented so they might return if disappointed. Early in May, 1876, he, with his wife, one son and five daughters, started for Coos Bay. Two younger sons, Bertie and Roy, were born after the family was settled in Coos County.

In Brewster Valley they met the Laird family. The party rested for several days before journeying on down the East Fork of the Coquille River. As winter was settling in, they decided not to go on to Coos Bay until spring. That winter, Mr. McCloskey homesteaded a plot of land, and he and his small son cut and hewed logs for a house. When all was in readiness, the neighbors came in for a house-raising.

These pioneers worked very hard, cutting down the big trees and clearing their small farms. Neighbors gathered for a day of "logrolling" so the logs not used as building material could be burned. At the same time, the women of the group held quilting bees indoors. Since there was very little money, these early settlers helped one another by exchanging work. They had grand times together.

McCloskey soon petitioned for a post office and named it Gravel Ford. He was appointed the first postmaster and served until he moved elsewhere. The office was located in his home. He was also justice of the peace and brought in the first threshing machine and went down the river as far as Norway threshing.

McCloskey petitioned the County Court for a bridge to be built across the North Fork at Gravel Ford. This was granted, and J. B. Fox took the contract. Mrs. McCloskey boarded the crew.

The roads at that time were deep in mud much of the

year, so when the wheat was harvested, it was loaded into a large skiff and taken to the grist mill at the Forks, where it was ground into flour.

The first school the children attended was in a small log cabin. For windows, a log was left out on each side. Beneath this they had fastened a split log to the wall with wooden pegs. This was used as a desk. Legs were placed on the other half to make it serve as a bench for all sizes of children.

For the Fourth of July, 1880, McCloskey planned a celebration at Gravel Ford. He cleared off a place in his grove and constructed seats and a platform. A flag to float over the entrance could not be found, so Mrs. McCloskey and her daughters, following Betsy Ross's example, made one from white muslin and blue and turkey-red calico. To this celebration came many from Myrtle Point. Among them were several families prominent in Coos County pioneer history—the Hermanns, Benders, Borders, Dixons, Lehnerrs, and others.

Later, the McCloskeys moved from Gravel Ford to a farm a half mile below Norway. McCloskey soon bought the community store at Norway from Edward Nelson and was appointed postmaster, a position he held until his death in 1908. He was county commissioner when the Middle Fork road was being built, and he had much to do with its construction.

THE DENNIS COLLINS FAMILY *By Ann Truman Connel*

The idea of homesteading in Oregon appealed strongly to Dennis. It would be a fine thing for an Irishman, he thought, coming from that isle where tenant farming is the rule. Honora viewed the plan with misgivings – there were Indians, sh'd heard, in Oregon!

So in 1869, Dennis, Honora, and the four children joined several other Irish families who were taking up land in Curry County, next to the California border.

The trip from San Francisco to Ellensburg, at the

mouth of the Rogue River, where Gold Beach now is located, was made on a small schooner.

The place on Hunter's Creek, three miles from Gold Beach where Dennis had filed, could not be reached by wagon — there was no road. Horses were hired to take them in with such of their goods as they could manage. Honora and the smaller children remained with the goods, while Dennis and Jimmy took the horses back for a second pack load. Even the cook stove had to be taken apart and packed in on horseback over the trail.

The first home was a log cabin, one room with a loft, in which they lived for several years while clearing the land for garden and fields, planting apple, pear and plum trees for the family orchard, and buying cattle and the first of their sheep. Sheep and the yearly wool crop were to be the main income of the years ahead.

The rude cabin, fashioned from trees felled on the place, was close to the ocean, just over the top of a rolling ridge. It was crowded too, with the six of them in it, but the boys had the loft; and for the little girls there was a trundle bed, and there was cozy comfort in the place. Near the stove on a bench were the water buckets, shelves of dishes and tin pans; the table and chairs for dining were in the opposite corner. The spool bed, with its coverlet quilt in Wild Geese pattern — flying triangular wedges of green and daffodil yellow on white — was the most imposing article of furniture, unless it was the big dresser. The spinning wheel soon was one of the busiest. After the first year, it was not long before all were wearing some article spun and knitted from their own wool.

In 1872 the 13th and last child of the family was born in the log cabin, a romping girl, Catherine, or Katie Collins, or mother. Eight earlier children had died, one by one, such was the infant mortality of the times, in the cities.

There was school in Ellensburg in the winter, and for several winters Honora lived in the town with the children so they could attend. For this, the cookstove was taken apart again and taken to a cabin in town, rented for the winter. It was left there for the next and succeeding winters, until this plan was given up because the children were large enough to ride in to school on horseback.

Life was busy and full of meaning in the log cabin; nearly everything used was produced by themselves, except the flour, sugar, (brown, and like the flour, bought by the barrel) molasses, salt, and some bolts of muslin, which were ordered from San Francisco. Oregon cities were so remote from this little hamlet that when anyone spoke of "The City," all knew they meant San Francisco. Goods came in on the little Hume boats. Sometimes there were oranges when the boat came in, peaches from California, or those southern fruits, bananas. But mainly they lived on their own "praties," as Honora called potatoes, their cabbage and kraut, root vegetables which also carried through the winter, their orchard fruits and wild berries. Strawberries, blackberries and huckleberries grew on the hills, and luscious salmonberries grew thick and high along the creeks; gathered by the pailful, red and yellow, and eaten fresh with cream, the salmonberries were one of Katie's dearest memories of childhood. There were salmon from the river for the taking, or four-foot salmon could be bought for not more than a quarter. Rock oysters and mussels from the ocean were used, and these made the only kind of soup considered palatable; such as we use now, of vegetables, to Honora would have seemed only fit for pigs. Some foods were preserved, but mostly they were dried or salted. Mutton was the mainstay of domestic meats, for they raised their own; beef was the rarity. Venison and bearmeat were commonly used. Hogs were allowed to run wild in the woods to fatten on acorns, and were shot when wanted for meat. The fat of these animals was softer, more flavorsome. Dennis smoked hams and bacon, sometimes a salmon. Bees were kept by several families for honey, but best was the wild honey from an occasional bee-tree in the hills.

There were pillows and ticks to be made, ticks of straw to be kept fresh and sweet, and finally replaced by feather ones, when enough feathers had been saved, from hens and wild fowl. There was sewing to be done for the growing children, letting down tucks as they grew, or taking them up to fit garments to the next in line. Honora herself had one little vanity about her dress — she always wore calicoes in shades of lavender, "lay-lac," she called it, in her Irish brogue — to set off her golden hair. Large white aprons, tucked and trimmed with her crocheted lace, went with the dresses. Black silk was for dress wear and for church, which was held about once a year whenever a priest could make the long trip down from Roseburg.

When Dennis and Honore had first camped to build their home, he told her on his second trip down with household goods that he'd learned they had a neighbor very near to them; the house was hidden by trees, but he pointed out the smoke from its chimney. It was a cheering thought to her, and she visioned the comfort of another woman dropping in to borrow odds and ends, and to trade recipes. We can but imagine the shock it was to her, when within the week she met her neighbor and found that she was an Indian! She learned in time to know and respect and be fond of her neighbor, who was kind and good, and cleanliness itself.

Married to a man of German descent, the Indian woman and her children spoke English with his broken accent. He had a long white beard of which his wife was very proud, and she kept his denim clothing bleached almost white to match it. No floors of the community were sanded so white as hers. Her sons taught young Jerry many a bit of woods-lore, and they often went hunting together.

Nearest neighbors up the Creek were the Colvins, among whom the girls found chums, as well as in the Doyle, Riley and Cunniff families. Nearest in point of likeness to themselves, Dennis and Honora, were the McVey families. There were two, Jim and his wife, Mary Ann; John and his wife, Martha, sister to Mary Ann.

There was the one doctor of the community, Dr. M. O. von der Green, whose wife was midwife for the community and instructed many mothers in home nursing.

There was Mrs. Edson, the tragedy of whose early life is marked for posterity by the Geisel monument; her husband and son were killed by Indians in the far-away earliest days of white settlement. There was the Bailey family — Ellen Bailey the beloved teacher of their school; the large Caughell family, the name pronounced as if spelled Call; the Strahans, Judge Riley and family, Judge Huntley and family, the judge, father of Harry Huntley of North Bend. There was Charles Winsor, Hume's business manager, who married Kate Anthony of Crescent City, and they later moved to North Bend. There were Mr. and Mrs. Peter Glynn, who had also lived through famine years in Ireland; she used to call him: "Come in to your tea and eggs, Peter Glynn," as though rejoicing that now there was plenty. There was the Doyle family, of whom one is Mrs. E. C. Mather of Coquille. There were also the Gauntletts, the Cunniffs, the Careys, and many others. Asa Carey — "Acie-boy" to his friends — is a tradition still in Gold Beach, as the man who actually rode a wild bear.

Sturdivant Homestead *By Mrs. Dan B. Keating*

The Civil War was over and conditions in the South were deplorable. In the Holland Dutch Sturdivant family in Virginia, there were 13 children, of whom five brothers had taken part in the war, three with the South and two with the North.

One of the brothers, John M., married to Emily Patterson of Mississippi, learned of land grants being thrown open to homesteaders out in Oregon.

The year was 1873, when wood-burning steam engines were hauling emigrant trains over the railroads to the far west — into California, not yet into Oregon, emigrant groups could charter a car, or several cars, or even whole trains. Into these the emigrants would load all their belongings — household goods, personal effects, cooking utensils, tools, even livestock in some cases. Housekeeping might be set up in the car, where the occupants would cook, eat, and sleep as they went.

It was with such a party that John and Emily Sturdivant, together with their young son, Daily Leander, left Missouri. They reached Empire City on May 2, 1873.

A homestead was found on the East fork of the Coquille River, just a wilderness of tall trees and underbrush, with elk trails through it.

A little spot was cleared and a log house was soon put up. A doorway in one end had a quilt hung over it to serve as a door. Gunny sacks were hung over the small square windows.

John made all the furniture for the log house. The chair backs and legs were of maple and the bottoms were rawhide woven across for the seats. The table and beds were split from logs.

He started clearing the land to plant the seeds they brought with them. One day he went to the lower end of the place to slash brush. He took his gun, a muzzle loader, with him. Emily was alone with the baby at the cabin, when she heard a scream which to her sounded like a woman in distress. She thought someone was lost, and she answered. It screamed again; she answered again. It was closer, coming down the mountain just across the river. It was moving too fast for a person, she thought, as it screamed again on her side of the river. Realizing too late it was a panther she had been answering, she dashed into the cabin and put the baby on the bed. She grabbed everything movable and piled it in the doorway. Then snatching the iron pot from the fire, where she always kept it full of boiling water, she stood by the window with the gunnysack pulled back a few inches, peering out. She was planning to throw the hot water on the intruder if it tried to come through the door. That was her only protection. They had no dogs then. The panther didn't come.

This was her first experience with a wild beast but as months passed and she learned the habits of different animals and the night noises near the house, she feared them less. Something always seemed to be prowling around the house at night. Sometimes it would climb up the logs of the house, then slide down real fast. They never knew what animal was cutting such capers. There were a great many hoot owls in the trees. Their loud hooting at night made the woods seem alive and terrifying.

John found a bee tree. He chopped it down and carried home the honey, placing it on a high log beside the house. That night they didn't get much sleep, as bears came prowling most of the night. A couple of them got into a fight. John went out and shot at them in the dark. They jumped off the log into the brush. The next morning the honey was all gone.

A generous spot was cleared and made ready for planting the garden seeds. The planting was done by the moon. Some in the light and others in the dark of the moon. The soil was very fertile and the plants flourished. It looked like a bumper crop when things began to happen. The deer and elk did a lot of damage, eating and trampling.The coons were very fond of the corn. Fencing in the garden had to be resorted to. Split rails and logs were used. The deer would leap over an ordinary fence with ease, so it was very high.

The first trip out for supplies was made on foot. A group of settlers walked over the trail through Brewster Valley and over the mountain to Roseburg. In the Lookingglass Valley, near Roseburg, they found a grist mill. The flour sold for 75 cents for a 50-pound sack. Each of the men carried a sack home on his back. It took several days for this trip. Finally pack trains were used. Men would ride the horses, load them with supplies, and walk and lead the animals home.

The water supply was from a creek, several hundred feet from the house. Emily would take the baby on her hip and with the bucket in her other hand, would run all the way to the creek, fill the bucket and run all the way back. The brush was so thick on each side of the trail, the baby's legs would often get scratched and its cries would cause Emily to run the faster. She was afraid the crying would bring the wild animals. One day she was about to dip her bucket into the creek when she heard a noise in a chittem tree close by. Glancing up, she saw a cub bear sliding down. She threw the bucket and ran. It also ran, just as scared as she was.

Each pioneer home had a doctor book or medical book. In case of sickness they watched for symptoms, read the book, then diagnosed the case, proceeded with the treatment, and usually effected a cure. Nature had to play a big part in those days. Emily suffered from a bad tooth for days. When she could no longer stand it, she heated the sharp end of a file in the fire till red hot to sterilize it; then when it was cool, she pried the tooth out.

To Myrtle Point, trading center, was just ten miles, but it was an all-day trip. In winter the mud was knee deep to a horse.

The first horse John bought was named Charlie. He would carry the produce from the farm to Myrtle Point. Two kerosene cases would be used, strung across the saddle, balanced on each side. These would be filled with eggs, blackberries, dressed chickens, or farm produce — anything to trade for things that were needed. One day Charlie was in a playful mood and when John tried to catch him, he kicked up his heels, tossed his head and galloped away. As he bounded along he stepped into a hole, fell and broke his neck. John cut Charlie's head off and used it to bait a bear trap. The next day he had a big black bear in the trap. They ate the bear meat.

When a large bird was killed, such as an owl or an eagle, Emily would cut off the wings and set a heavy weight on them to press them flat. When they were dry, they made excellent dusters or could be used to sweep with.

The trapping of fur bearing animals proved profitable. Beaver, mink, marten, skunk, weasel, otter, racoon, and fox, provided plenty of prime pelts.

By donation labor the settlers of the East Fork made a road to connect with the Coos Bay Wagon Road at Dora. Some of the settlers living in our valley were the Weeklys, Brights, McCloskeys, Culbertsons, Hansons, Jacksons, Smiths, Bennets, Swans, Minards, Krantzes, and Taylors.

The name selected for the community was Gravel Ford. The river had to be forded to get to Myrtle Point, as there were no bridges then. At this particular spot was the only gravel bottom in the river for a convenient crossing, so the ford was made there, and hence the name. It was near the forks of the river where the North Fork flowed into the East Fork of the Coquille River.

There were 12 children in the family of John and Emily Sturdivant, each trying to help in his or her small way, even when little tots. They were Daily Leander, Mary J. (Mollie), Nancy Jane, Ella R., Robert, James Alexander (Alex), William Tell, Thomas M., Frances May, Laurabelle, Ira, and George Alfred.

The parents, John and Emily, lived their last years in town, he till he was 88 and she till she was 78.

Elkhorn and the Gould Family

A remarkable family were the Goulds — father and mother, nine children, Aunt 'Elo and Uncle Byron McClay. Into the virgin forest they went — 30 miles of pack trail, the nearest settlement being 15 miles away, and many more miles to the nearest town.

George Gould had grown up in a saddle and in the seat of a wagon. He knew how to pack a horse or a mule. So, in 1882 at their California home near San Jose, the Goulds loaded up and started for Oregon.

Mrs. Gould's sister, Oelo McClay was a member of the Gould household through all their trials, fondly referred to as *Aunt 'Elo.*

Bert, in late years known as A. N. Gould, said recently of the family's coming to the remote place which is still remembered by our older residents as Elkhorn — Home of the Goulds:

> I can still recall that eventful day, back in 1886. I was already at the place, anxiously waiting for the arrival of the folks. Then I saw them coming over the ridge. Father was leading a horse with the twins, George and Georgia. There were two kerosene cases, one on each side of the pack saddle, with a three-year-old child in each, eagerly taking in their first view of the new home. Mother came next with little Lucy, just nine months old. And Grandpa and Aunt 'Elo brought up the rear.

George Gould was a man of action as well as of ideas.

It wasn't long till they had several pack horses loaded with jerked venison and elk meat, as well as buckskin made from the hides of the deer. Furs from coon, mink, beaver, marten, bear and other animals were added; also buckskin gloves and sometimes other wearing apparel; and elk horns and teeth, and bear galls, and honey.

The Gould home was in Coos County, but up to this time their outlet was by way of the 30-mile trail to the Umpqua River in Douglas County. They learned from two hunters who had come in by way of Coos River that there was a settlement about 15 miles distant, at the head of navigation on North Coos River, and that a small steamer made daily trips from there to Marshfield, "a little town on Coos Bay." And so Marshfield became their trading center. The round trip could be made from Elkhorn and return in three days. A day was required to pack out to The Forks (later known as Allegany), where they stayed over night; the second day for the trip on the steamer, a few hours in town, then the return on the boat and another night at The Forks; and the third day to reach home.

Produce from the Elkhorn ranch that couldn't be disposed of at Marshfield was shipped to San Francisco. Some furs, buckskin, and buckskin gloves were shipped to Chicago.

George Gould was a good mixer. He soon took on new friends in Marshfield. One of them was Charles H. Merchant, the pioneer saw mill operator and businessman.

The old Pershbaker mill at Marshfield had been abandoned by Dean and Co. Mr. Gould made a deal with Merchant, whereby he exchanged smoked elk meat and venison, honey and perhaps other products from Elkhorn, for discarded parts of the mill — pulleys and shafts, belting, and other things. These were shipped up the river to Allegany and packed over the trail to Elkhorn. An overshot water wheel was built and set up; a sash saw was installed, a planer and turning lathe were added; and soon they were turning out lumber of every type needed for a complete modern home. Furniture was made for the entire house. There was power to spare, so a washing machine was built to use it.

A school house was built, where Aunt 'Elo taught the nine Gould children through six months of each year.

It wasn't many years till Bert was old enough to ride out and camp at the hunting grounds with his father. Clarence, two years younger than Bert, went along. Bert and the father killed, dressed and hung up the elk and deer to cool; they loaded it on the pack horses and Clarence led the animals home, where the women folks took over, cutting the meat into strips; then salting it over night, and hanging it on racks to be dried and smoked and made ready for market or for home use. The following morning Clarence would go back with the horses to the camp, where Bert and the father would have another load of meat ready.

After the hunting season, came the trapping. Bear hides were not worth a great deal in the market, but the bear must be trapped to protect the sheep, hogs and calves. The bear galls brought a dollar apiece. And bear lard was even more desirable than hog lard. And the meat, too, was relished by many persons. Mink, beaver, otter, marten and other animals added to the marketable produce. Elk horns and elk teeth were marketable in limited quantities.

The river that flowed in front of Elkhorn, nearly dry in the summer, became a turbulent stream at times in the winter. Their trail to Allegany was on the opposite side of the river from their house. This sometimes cut off their travel to the outside. George Gould said he would bridge the stream. More experienced men said it couldn't be done. The first big freshet would wash the bridge away. Came summer and the river was only a trickle. George Gould and the boys went to work. They got out long, straight red cedar timbers and hewed them to the required dimensions. With two yokes of oxen, the timbers were hauled into place; trusses were built on the abutments; the mill furnished planks for the decking; the 72-foot bridge spanned the river, carrying both man and beast for many a year.

In time the children "went out" to school. When Grace, the oldest of the children, learned to play the organ, and had come home for summer, she longed for a musical instrument. Her father, being a lover of music himself, fell in with the idea. Lack of space and time forbids telling the story of the Gould organ here, except to say that they sent to Chicago, had an organ shipped to Marshfield, then by the little river steamer to The Forks, hauled it five miles on a sled, packed it between two horses, tandem fashion, ten miles further, over narrow, crooked, steep, brushy trails that twisted and turned and dipped over ridges and across canyons. It took four persons and three horses — Mr. Gould, Bert, Frances, and Aunt 'Elo. One horse was needed to pack the camp equipment and two horses for the organ. They were four days on the trail, from their home to The Forks, and return with the musical instrument, arriving at home October 5, 1891. (The story of this adventure appeared in the *Youths' Companion* sometime in the 1890's.)

With the completion of the bridge and the new eleven-room house and the opening up of better trails, the remarkable family built 14 miles of telephone line. When the daughters had developed into five charming young women, Elkhorn became more accessible and more attractive than ever.

Aunt 'Elo afterwards wrote:

> People came from far and near, some from Marshfield, Allegany, Loon Lake. Some come horseback, some walked. All stayed over night and some longer. We had plenty of music, for by this time we had an organ, which some of the girls had learned to play. And there was a banjo, a guitar, and of course a violin. We always had plenty of eats.

On another occasion, on January 1, 1892, the Gould family proved that they had plenty to eat. They formed on the front porch and marched in to the tune of *Midnight Serenade,* played on the organ by Grace. The menu consisted of cold roast venison ham, cold roast mutton ham, baked pheasant, fried trout, chicken pie; vegetables of various kinds; hazelnuts, huckleberries, currants, prunes and apples; fruit cake, marble cake, jelly cake.

The Gould family built up and developed a forerunner of the popular mountain resort. Visitors came from San Francisco and other far-off places, some remaining weeks at a time, returning year after year, with George Gould as their trail and hunting guide. Of the five Gould sisters, four became trained nurses. The fifth continued to teach school until she married. Bert became a surveyor and a business man; Clarence took to steamboating and saw mill work; George went to Arizona and entered the cattle business; Leonard, the youngest son, was drowned in the river.

George A. Gould, of so much creative energy, wrote a quantity of verse, including a poem given in the literature chapter and the following lines from one called "Bonny Elkhorn:"

We are leaving dear Old Elkhorn.
The folks get tired and lonesome here alone.
  And we may return no more
To the smoothly beaten dooryard
That was worn by little feet,
  As they played and sang around the kitchen door.

Oh, the brush will take Old Elkhorn,
  And the fences all fall down,
Where we tossed about the fragrant new-mown hay;
  And the trails are choked with timber,
Where we drove the cattle in
  From the pastures in the valley far away.

The Isham Cox Family *By Nellie B. Maben*

My fathers's parents, Isham and Mary Ann Cox, left Missouri in 1845, crossing the plains by ox-team, and settling near Salem, Oregon. In 1865 they moved to Curry County, riding horseback and moving all necessary goods by packhorse.

They stayed the first winter with a Mr. Turner who lived on the hill above Langlois and had been in Curry County about 12 years. It was an especially hard winter, with one storm after another, so that by spring they were so disheartened that they went back to Polk County.

Later, in 1868, my father, Glen Cox, who was 12 years old at the time and the youngest of the family, accompanied an older brother, Doc (Frank K.) Cox and his wife and two small children back to Curry County. It was during the big fire that swept the coast in that year. Part of the way they traveled in the wake of the fire, and logs and snags were still smoking. Glen was holding his little niece in front of him on a horse when a limb fell from a burning snag and struck the horse on the head, knocking it to its knees.

For weeks the sun was hidden behind a pall of smoke. Port Orford was burned out, but soon after, the wind changed and burned back over the same territory.

There was great loss of wild life but after the first rains the grass came up and was soon waist-high. Despite the elk and deer that died in the fire, there were herds of both to be seen everywhere. For several years it was a hunter's paradise.

A year or two later, in 1870, the parents, Isham and

Collection of Alfred Powers

The Gould and Cox families were among the numerous Coos County families who crossed the plains in covered wagons.

Mary Ann Cox, moved to Curry County to join their sons. They bought a place at Denmark, near their son Frank.

Isham and Mary Ann Cox had nine children.

Doctors were few and far between in those days. Mrs. Cox thought nothing of traveling for miles on horseback to nurse the sick or help bring a baby into the world, and considered it just being neighborly.

The following is quoted from a letter by Mrs. Maben in 1950:

> My father, Glen Cox; his older brothers, Jim and Isham; a nephew, Ralph Cox, and a man named Joe Clink, spent the winter of 1895 working Jim Cox's mining claim in the Eckley country.
>
> My mother went along to cook for the men. She took me and my two older brothers. I was too young to remember; but I remember in later years of hearing them tell about the winter we spent at the mine—how the wood rats came into the cabin for the first few nights after we came in; how we had fresh deer meat all winter long; and that the Haynes family were our only neighbors and several miles away at that.
>
> When we went home in the spring, they figured that the men had cleared less than a dollar a day, but they all enjoyed every minute of it and we were all in the best of health the whole time.

QUICK FAMILY MEMOIRS *By Flora E. Dunne*

My parents, Mr. and Mrs. Jonathan Quick came to Coos County in September, 1874 with five children.

When at last we arrived at Coquille City, as it was called then, we camped on the ground where the Schroeders Funeral Chapel now stands.

Father met Mr. Steve Seward who kindly went with him, looking for a location. He found what he wanted on Lampa Creek, about 13 miles down the beautiful Coquille River. The banks were lined with all kinds of trees and brush. The distance has been shortened to 11 miles by the road. There were no roads or steamboats then. Father got a scow, put all his belongings on it and started early in the morning to get the benefit of the tide.

It took all day to get to the landing where they made camp that night near the river. Next morning began the long tiresome task of moving our belongings up the creek to the place which was our home. Father hired a pack horse for part of the stuff. There were logs across the trail and when they came to the logs the pack was taken off.

That afternoon we all started for our new home. All around were logs and brush. Father soon had fires going in the old logs and stumps. I want to say right here that for 15 years or more the fires were kept burning. It was a daily job to clink them up, that was the main way to get rid of the logs and stumps. There was a large red fir log which had been down many years; it was five feet or more through. About 150 feet along this log toward the top, a spruce tree had grown over the fir log. The spruce was five feet through and when the fir log was removed we children could walk through under the spruce.

This old tree gave me many sleepless nights when there was much wind. After a time it became dead. And then I was more afraid. When it did fall it was a calm day in the summer. The top just crumpled down from dry rot, doing no damage.

That first winter during a terrible rain and wind storm, I was awakened by a horrible snarling and screaming by panthers right by the house. Father got the Winchester, rushed to the door, and began firing. This frightened the animals away, but one ran up a tree making great claw marks in the bark. Often when there was much wind we could hear the boom of the trees falling, and how they would sway and bend.

The spring after we came to the homestead, Mr. Steward and Father got a move started for a school. Mr. Steward had several children. He lived across the Coquille River from Lampa Creek. Miss Mattie Henderson was our first teacher. She was sister of Aunt Ellen Robinson now of Coquille. There are four pupils now living who went to the first school. They are Mrs. Annie Clemens Creary now of California; Mrs. Clara Wheeler now of Sweet Home, Oregon; Mrs. Ida Levine now of Eureka,

California; Mrs. Flora Dunne of Monroe, Oregon. More people came to this location, and soon ministers came and Sunday schools were organized.

I must return to when we got to the place to be our home. Mr. Steward got the neighbors to come with tools and make a place to live. They cut down a large cedar tree which they cut up in workable length. Some made shakes for the roof, and others made boards for siding and puncheons for the floor. Yes, it was rough but it kept the rain and wind out.

They made a large fire place in which we could burn large chunks. So we had plenty of wood and water. Such nice soft water. We did not have to use water softener as we did where we had lived. There was a small stream running through the place. Father named it, Pleasant Run, and we always called it that. At the foot of the hill by this creek were two large myrtle trees, beautifully green all the year around. The larger one was hollow at the bottom, and made a nice place for the children to play. This tree had great spreading branches making a good shelter from sun and rain. Under this tree we did our washing for several years.

Father got a large whiskey barrel and sawed it in two making two good tubs, and for a time we used coal oil cans to heat water in. Later we got a 10 gallon kettle.

It took a lot of hard work to make a home out of this land. We used to laugh and say, we couldn't see the sky, except by looking up.

As there were no roads during our days on the Coquille, the young men had boats to take their girl friends for a ride. When the wind was right, the sailing was splendid. The girls, too, could row and sail a boat. This afforded one of the finest forms of our outdoor amusements.

8

Indian Troubles

Chetco Jenny was Agent Ben Wright's squaw wife. She joined with Enos to kill him. Together they made a repast of part of his roasted heart — a fine courage hormone when it was a brave man's.

ALTHOUGH MOST OF THE ROGUE RIVER INDIANS objected to the coming of the white man and his rude disturbance of their leisurely existence, it is worthy of note that the greatest animosities developed where the usurping palefaces coveted the ancestral homes of the natives who had lived upon them for generations, some of the sites being of importance to them as stream crossings, canoe landings, or comfortable dwelling sites.

During 1851 difficulties with the Indians of the Rogue River area were constantly increasing. General Hitchcock at San Francisco ordered Lieutenant-Colonel Silas Casey, with a force of 90 regulars, to Port Orford. A detail of the force was sent out to punish the Coquille Indians. Stoneman in command and later governor of California, reported, "A large number of them were killed and the moral effect of the operation was very great."

Fort Orford was built and garrisoned till the removal of the Indians in 1856, when the post was abandoned. It was in the area dominated by the treacherous Rogues, a people contemptuously referred to by the friendly Coos Bay Indians as "California siwashes," a term of reproach which included all the Indians of the Curry County coast and the Coquille River area. None of these were permitted to pass northward of a certain point south of Coos Bay, marked by a bleached pole set in a pile of rocks.

President Fillmore made Anson P. Dart superintendent of Indian affairs in Oregon. In October of 1851 Dart reported treaties with four bands of Indians between the

Coquille River and the Oregon-California line. The treaties covered an area of approximately two and a half million acres, "represented as being good farming land." And at what a bargain. "Price $28,500 payable in ten annual payments, no part of which is to be paid in money. . . . The total cost, including the treaty expense, was less than one and a half cents an acre."

By 1852 prospectors had spread widely throughout Southwestern Oregon and Indian troubles multiplied. There arose some friction that resulted in the burning of an Indian village. Joel Palmer succeeded Dart.

Palmer's report in 1854 is a synopsis of the conditions he found in Curry County:

About three miles north of our boundary line a stream empties into the ocean, known by the Indian name as *Chetco*. Here are many indications of having once resided a numerous people. In the fall of 1853 one Miller and several associates located land claims in this vicinity. They first built their houses about a quarter of a mile from the river to which the Indians made no objections. Subsequently, knowing that the newly discovered mines would attract an influx of people, the whites projected a town speculation, formed an association and selected a site at the mouth of the Chetco River. The face of the country is such that the crossing must be at the mouth of the river by ferry. Here were two Indian villages on opposite sides of the stream, of 20 lodges each.

This ferry was of considerable importance. The new townsite included one of the villages, and when preparations were made to erect a house within its limits, the Indians strongly protested; but at last acquiescing, the cabin was built and occupied by Miller. Hitherto the Indians had enjoyed the benefit of the ferry; but now Miller informed them that they must no longer ferry white people. The Indians, however, sometimes did so, and were threatened with the destruction of their lodges if they did not desist.

The misunderstanding became so acute, that several men who had been fighting Indians on Smith River, in California, were called in by Miller and quartered in his house for nearly two weeks. Becoming unwilling to remain longer, they were about to return to their homes. Miller objected to their leaving until they had accomplished something for his relief, as on their departure he would be subject to the same annoyance as before. The next morning at daylight, the party consisting of eight or nine well armed men, attacked the village, and as the Indians came from their lodges, 12 were shot dead. The women and children were allowed to escape. Three Indians remained in the lodges and returned the fire with bows and arrows. Being unable to get a sight of those Indians, they ordered two squaws, pets in the family of Miller, to set fire to the lodges. Two Indians were consumed in the conflagration. The third while raising his head through the flames and smoke for breath was shot dead. What added to the atrocity of the deed is, that shortly before the massacre the Indians were induced to sell the whites their guns, under the pretext that friendly relations were firmly established. In the next two days all the lodges in the village were burned, except two, belonging to the friends of an Indian who acted with Miller and his party. This horrid tragedy was enacted about February 15, 1854 . . . In all, 23 Indians and several squaws were killed.

The other settlers condemned his atrocity and told Miller he would have to face the consequences alone. Miller was subsequently arrested and placed in the custody of the military at Fort Orford; but upon examination before a justice of the peace, was set at large, "on the ground of justification, and want of evidence to commit."

In Special Agent Smith's report dated February 5, 1854, he said:

"A most horrid massacre, or rather an out-and-out barbarous mass murder, was perpetrated upon a portion of the Nah-so-mah band residing at the mouth of the Coquille River on the morning of January 28 by a party of 40 miners. The reason assigned by the miners, by their own statements, seem trivial. However, on the afternoon preceding the murders, the miners requested the chief to come in for a talk. This he refused to do. Thereupon the whites at and near the ferry-house assembled and deliberated upon the necessity of an immediate attack upon the Indians. A courier was sent to the upper mines [Randolph], some seven miles to the north, for assistance. Twenty men responded, arriving at the ferry-house in the evening preceding the morning massacre.

At dawn on the following day, led by one Abbott, the ferry party and the 20 miners, about 40 in all, formed three detachments, marched upon the Indian ranches and "consumated a most inhuman slaughter," which the attackers termed a *fight*. The Indians were aroused from sleep to meet their deaths with but a feeble show of resistance; shot down as they were attempting to escape from their houses. Fifteen men and one squaw were killed, two squaws badly wounded. On the part of the white men, not even the slightest wound was received. The houses of the Indians, with but one exception, were fired and entirely destroyed. Thus was committed a massacre too inhuman to be readily believed.

In the spring of 1855 the Upper Rogues grew restless. In March, 1855, Captain Abbott had a skirmish with the Chetcos at Pistol River. In the same month troops attacked a village ten miles up the Rogue. A few days later they victoriously fought the bands of Chief John and Limpy at the mouth of the Illinois.

On April first, a company of citizens again attacked the village near the mouth of the Coquille River, killing ten men, wounded eleven and took forty squaws and children prisoners. About the same time a party of volunteers ambushed a party of Indians in canoes when passing through a swift narrow channel of Rogue River, near Lobster Creek. Only one man and two squaws escaped.

On April 29 a party of 60 regulars were attacked near Chetco River while escorting an army pack train. Three soldiers were killed or wounded, the Indians losing six killed and several wounded. Active in these campaigns were the *Gold Beach Guards,* the *Coquille Guards,* and the *Port Orford Minute Men.*

Said Joel Palmer on March 8, 1856:

A party of volunteers encamped for sometime at the Big Bend of Rogue River, above Agness, returned, and a part of them encamped near the To-to-tin village, three miles above the coast; the remaining portion having passed on to the mining village at the mouth of the river. On the morning of February 22, at daylight, the camp near the Indian village was attacked by a party of Indians supposed to number about 300, and all but two [of the whites], it was supposed, were put to death, one man making his way to Port Orford, the other to the village at the mouth of Rogue River. With one exception, all the dwellings from the mouth of Rogue River to Port Orford have been burned and the inmates supposed to be murdered. Five persons, however, had made their appearance, who at first were supposed to have been killed. Benjamin Wright, the Special Agent of the district, is supposed to be among the killed . . .

The extraordinary success of the hostile bands and the ease with which the Indians had invariably gained a victory, inspired a belief that they were abundantly able to maintain their position, and rid themselves of the white population. In every instance where a conflict had ensued between volunteers and hostile Indians in Southern Oregon, the latter had gained what they regarded a victory . . .

The avowed determination of the people to exterminate the Indian race, regardless as to whether they are innocent or guilty, and the general disregard for the rights of those acting as friends and aiding in the subjugation of our real and avowed enemies, has had a powerful influence in inducing these tribes to join the warlike bands.

It is astonishing to know the rapidity with which intelligence is carried from one extreme of the country to the other, and the commission of outrages (of which there have been many) by our people against an Indian is heralded forth by the hostile parties, augmented and used as evidence for the necessity for all to unite in war against us.

It was at the beginning of this last general outbreak of the combined Rogue River and coastal Indians, that the Geisel tragedy took place at midnight on February 22, 1856. Many others were killed on that fateful night, and practically every home of the white settlers of Curry County was burned. A state park, known as Geisel Monument, has been erected which embraces the site of the Geisel home.

These once large tribes, however, had become greatly decimated by early epidemics of smallpox and measles, coupled with the almost constant friction and wearing down of the tribal manhood in their conflict with the encroaching whites. Their numbers had been so reduced that by 1855 these belligerent Southern Oregon tribes were no longer capable of successfuly engaging in a war against the available military forces and the greatly augmented, well armed, civilian population who opposed them.

Their most capable leader, Chief John, was defeated in the Big Bend battle near the junction of the Illinois and Rogue rivers, on May 27 and 28, 1856. When the defiant scattered element were all brought in, those pitiable, hopelessly defeated remnants of a once large native population realized they could no longer combat the overwhelming strength of the forces arrayed against them.

They surrendered and were transported to the Grand Ronde and Siletz reservations.

Wrote Joel Palmer on July 3, 1856:

> The passage from Port Orford was agreed upon at ten dollars per head, (usual steerage fare twenty dollars) not counting infants, which fare was to include rations and the transportation of baggage. They were put on board in a hurry, and their number could not accurately be taken, but were estimated at six hundred; a subsequent enumeration gives seven hundred and ten souls . . .

Every feature of the treaty that had been entered into between Joel Palmer on the one side and the Indian chiefs and headmen on the other, were carried out by the military forces against the natives, while the higher officials in Washington, D. C., shamefully neglected all the promises that had been made by the well-meaning agents.

The treaty never was ratified by the Senate. It lay gathering dust in pigeon holes of the National Archives, until dug up generations later by representatives of the Indians who were seeking by peaceful and legal means to obtain a semblance of justice.

In 1862, Agent B. R. Riddle reported in part as follows:

> Ever since I have been in charge of this agency constant complaint has been made to me . . . that the government has acted in bad faith with them (the Indians). They say they made a treaty with the government, abandoned their country, and in consequence with the stipulations of the treaty they removed to this reservation where they have continued to live and in doing so have fulfilled their part of the agreement, but not so the government. On the contrary, it never has ratified the treaty and has done nothing but pay them in promises . . . They have waited patiently for the Great Father to fulfill his promises. It does seem to me that the government is very tardy in the matter of ratifying these treaties.

At last the Indians were permitted to sue the government of the United States. They first had to show that they were the *original owners* of the land. There still remained the matter of how much compensation they were entitled to. They claimed interest from the time they were deprived of their property in 1855 to the time of final settlement. This was denied. The 97-year-old claim still drags on.

9

Rise of Towns

Port Orford

The main events in the history of this oldest community in Southwestern Oregon have been given in the chapter on Early Colonies.

Three things perhaps need to be added:

1. In 1918 George M. Cornwall, publisher of *The Timberman,* during a visit to the town stated his belief that Curry County timber should be shipped from local ports. Long-distance trucking was not visualized at that time. So the *Port Orford Tribune* started a campaign for the creation of a port district. Its organization was accomplished the following year. Lumber shipments, however, did not materialize as expected, and when unusually high seas washed away the wharf, the commissioners sold the property and dissolved the organization.

2. Nellie's Cove as described by an unknown writer. The original copy was received from a granddaughter of Captain William Tichenor and has the appearance of having been written many years ago:

> Nellie's Cove is on the west side of Port Orford heads. It is not hard to descend the old trail leading to it, for many people traverse this trail to fish from the rocks below. There are a great many kinds of fish caught and more fishing is done here than in any of the other coves.
>
> In the center of Nellie's Cove is a large round-shaped rock with bushes growing on it, giving it an odd appearance. On the little beach various kinds of mosses and stones are found. It is a good place for outdoor lunches. Narrow headlands extend out for some distance on either side and high cliffs at the back help to protect it, making the cove an excellent refuge for vessels during a north wind. The cove received its name from Nellie Tichenor, a daughter of Captain Tichenor.

At present the cove is used by the U. S. Coast Guard

as a place for the Coast Guard boats. It is reached by a long stairway leading down from the living quarters at the top of the "Heads."

3. One of Oregon's most beautiful cemeteries is located at Port Orford. Visitors there get a peculiarly poetic reminder of the long-ago days. It is the place where the Tichenors and other pioneers lie buried. It is on the flat open summit of a considerable hill. The tops of the trees rise above it all around to fence it in with foliage. Beneath the greenery through the boles of the trees is a view of the sea far below, in perpetual activity, in perpetual life, in contrast to the stillness of the sepulchred summit and the solemn wording on the stones.

Gold Beach

1826—Mouth of the Rogue visited by Hudson's Bay trappers.
1828—Jedediah Smith's party camped there.
1836—Hudson's Bay Company schooner *Cadboro* entered the Rogue.
1852—Schooner *Flagstaff* reported to have landed for water.
1853—Gold seekers swarmed along the beaches. Trouble began with the Indians, continuing to 1856.
1857—First Ferry across Rogue River at Gold Beach.
A. F. Myers started commercial fishing.
1863—Plat of Ellensburg filed; post office established.
1870—Captain James Coughell salted salmon in hold of schooner *Newton Booth;* sailed to San Francisco with his cargo.
1876—Riley & Stewart sold fishery, sawmill and store to Hume.
1877—R. D. Hume built salmon cannery.
1879—Hume began experimenting with salmon hatchery.
1881—Rogue River Grange No. 190 established at Ellensburg.
1882—Newspaper *Curry County Post* established by Walter Sutton
1884—Sutton changed the name of his paper to *Gold Beach Gazette.*
1888—County School Superintendent F. A. Stewart conducted first teachers' institute in Curry County.
1890—The big flood changed the entrance to Rogue River. First wagon road into Gold Beach from the north and south.
1892—*Gold Beach Gazette* sold to Hume, who moved it across the river and published it as the *Wedderburn Gazette.*
1893—Hume's cannery burned. Hume moved across the river and started Wedderburn.

1895—Wedderburn post office established.
1927—Highway 101 graded and rocked.
1932—Rogue River bridge completed.
1945—Gold Beach incorporated.
1951—County hospital opened in Gold Beach.

Just when the first gold was discovered does not seem to be definitely known. However, by 1853 the ocean beaches were swarming with gold seekers. About this time also, serious troubles began to break out between the natives and whites, resulting in the Rogue River Indian Wars of 1855 and 1856.

Other than Port Orford, the mouth of Rogue River became the central point of activity in Curry County. Groups of log cabins and shake shanties sprang up both north and south of the river, each hamlet taking its individual name, including Ellensburg, Whalesburg, Elizabethtown, Sebastopol, and Gold Beach. These names gradually faded away and remained only in the memory of older pioneers—all except Ellensburg and Gold Beach.

When in 1863 a post office was established, the name was recorded in Washington as Ellensberg. The spelling was changed in Washington in 1877 to *Ellensburgh*. Historians all seem to follow the usual form *Ellensburg*.

One report says:

> The town of Ellensburg continued to grow and expand along the river front. The first and only record of a plat of Ellensburg was filed in May 1863 . . . The returns from beach mining began to shrink and salmon fishing became the principal industry. This industry advanced from the primitive salting method to canning.

Following the fishery established in 1857 by A. F. Myers, Stewart & Riley entered the field, with a fishery, sawmill and a general merchandise store. Riley and Stewart sold out to R. D. Hume in 1876.

The report quoted above goes on to say:

> The schooner *Newton Booth* entered in 1870. The first steamer to enter was the *Alec Duncan*. The steamer *Mary D. Hume* was built at Ellensburg, the yard being located at Mill Rock. Other vessels plying to Ellensburg during this period were the *Thistle,* the *Pelican,* and the tug *Katie Cook*.

Although the post office and the townsite were both known as Ellensburg, the place continued to be referred to as Gold Beach. Even as early as 1856, Dr. Rodney Glisan, in his *Journal of Army Life,* speaks of the little *Gold Beach.* When Walter Sutton established his newspaper, the *Curry County Post,* in 1882, he began "drumming" for the change of name to Gold Beach, which was officially accomplished on May 28, 1890.

The principal activities in the Gold Beach region at first centered around gold mining. As this became less profitable, more attention was turned to commercial fishing, which grew to be the largest source of income, perhaps for 50 or 60 years, from the middle seventies through the turn of the century. Then it began to taper off, ending in 1935 when the river was closed to commercial fishing.

For some time previous to 1935, there had been considerable controversy and rivalry between the commercial fishermen and the sportsmen. This rivalry was not confined to the Gold Beach and Wedderburn area; it extended into the upper Rogue River in Josephine and Jackson counties. Zane Grey's *Rogue River Feud* was based upon this rivalry. Since 1935, the Chinook, the Silversides and the Steelheads have attracted sportsmen from far and wide, to Rogue River, giving rise to numerous auto courts and motels in and around Wedderburn and Gold Beach.

For half a century and more, Gold Beach remained very much isolated due to lack of transportation. The flood of 1890 left the entrance to the river even more hazardous than it had been earlier. It wasn't till 1890 that Gold Beach had a wagon road connecting with Crescent City on the south and Coos County on the north. But such a road! From sea-level up to high mountain tops: through the winter months there was deep mud in the valleys and snow on the mountains. Teams with wagons had difficulty in passing when they met on mountain grades. It is reported that two parties with teams met near Humbug Mountain. It became necessary, not only to unhitch one of the teams, but to unload the wagon, to take off its wheels, uncouple the reach-pole, and stack the parts to one side so that the other team and wagon could pass. The first wagon then had to be re-assembled, reloaded and re-hitched. All this required real team work.

It was not till 1927 that Highway 101 provided an all-year outlet for Gold Beach and Wedderburn, when the road was graded and rocked.

Today in many respects Gold Beach and Wedderburn are one. Historically, however, they have always been separated by the Rogue —that is, ever since there was a Wedderburn, which came into being when Hume moved his cannery across the river and gave it his Scotch name, and obtaining a post office in 1895. Gold Beach didn't get its name much earlier, for it continued as Ellensburg until the name was changed in 1890. The ferry across the river changed locations at different times, from near the mouth, to Bagnell several miles up the river. The fine Rogue River bridge was opened in 1932.

Gold Beach, the commercial center, is an incorporated city. Wedderburn can hardly be classed as more than a hamlet. Wedderburn, however, has several modern motels and auto courts and cottages, each prepared to serve the tourist, camper, fisherman, and hunter with boats and gear and guide service. The Gold Beach Rotary Club holds its weekly luncheon meetings in the Del Rogue Club in Wedderburn, indicating the close co-operative spirit between the *City* on the south side of the river and the *Hamlet* on the north side. The former R. D. Hume holdings, which passed to the Macleay Estate after the death of Mr. Hume, and to the Lloyd Corporation in 1935, still maintains its local head-quarters at Wedderburn, in the old Hume building. S. O. Newhouse is the local representative for the Lloyds. The West Coast Telephone Company in its December 1950 directory lists 311 connections for Gold Beach and 51 for Wedderburn.

Wedderburn has the same daily mail service that Gold Beach has, coming by truck from north and south. The two offices have the same service up the river to Agness—

daily except Sundays in summer, three times a week in winter. It is at Wedderburn that you contact the Rogue Boat Service to "climb the riffles of the Rogue."

Approaching Gold Beach from the north, over the big fine bridge, one of the first buildings to attract attention is the myrtle wood shop operated by Mr. and Mrs. Orin Hess. The business was first started by Mrs. Hess' father, Charles Wakeman, back in the early days when myrtle wood was little known. Mr. Wakeman came to know myrtle as few persons then knew it—the wood, the grain, the color, the figures that could be brought out and developed. He began turning out pieces as a hobby. It developed into a business.

Highway 101 passes through Gold Beach its entire length from north to south, as a wide paved thoroughfare.

EMPIRE

1853—First settlers, "Coose Bay Company." December 22 Territorial Legislature passed bill creating Coos County and designating Empire City as county-seat.

1854—April 3, first meeting of county court in split-board court house.

1855—H. H. Luse began erection of sawmill and ship yard.

1856—(Date uncertain) Luse mill shipped first lumber from Coos County.

1858—Empire City post office established; J. J. Jackson first postmaster.

Several hotels, several stores, saloons to make Empire City the most important point in Coos County for about 15 years.

1868—H. H. Luse sawmill turning out 15,000 to 20,000 feet of lumber per day.

1883—Luse sold out to Southern Oregon Improvement Company, which erected a large sawmill with a capacity of 100,000 feet per day; said to be the largest on the coast, perhaps the largest in the world. Business was good. Besides having the county seat, with its court sessions and other transactions to bring people from all parts of the county, bar-bound ships necessitated hotel accommodations for many persons waiting for the ships to sail. A salmon cannery was built about this time.

1886—Lumber market poor. Big sawmill operated spasmodically; work was unsteady and uncertain. New management for a while had the effect of improving conditions.

1893—The big mill closed indefinitely. Hopes continued for its reopening.

1894—*City* was dropped from the name and *Empire City* became *Empire.*

1896—Voters of Coos County designated Coquille as the county seat.

1897—Before losing the county seat to Coquille the population was estimated at about 700. Then Empire became practically a ghost town. The 1900 census showed the population to be 187. It still continued to go down, only 147 being quoted in 1910.

In the late 1920's, L. J. Simpson and Robertson and a number of associates organized a plan for a NEW EMPIRE. They arranged to take over the big sawmill, which they converted into a mill with modern machinery. Many other improvements were planned for the town, some of which were put into effect. The population increased from 182 in 1920 to 493 in 1930.

Many of the old substantial residents retained their homes in Empire. In 1928 the city was re-incorporated; an entirely new charter was adopted, fitted to modern ideas. Reynold Olsen became its first mayor.

1928—Empire had been re-incorporated. The city entered the thirties with a bright prospect for the years ahead. But the unsettled conditions interfered with its progress under the new plan. The big mill failed to get on a sound operating basis. Its machinery was removed and the mill closed.

After 1930 the pulp mill and sawmill south of the town continued to operate and the population of Empire increased even during the unsettled times of the 1930's, adding 172, to show a population of 665 in 1940.

About 1942 the big mill was taken over by a new organization known as the Cape Arago Lumber Company, business became good and the city boomed; more than 232 per cent was added to its population in 10 years, reaching 2,212 according to the 1950 census.

Empire today is a modern little city; many up-to-date business houses, paved streets. An observer might say it lacks only a newspaper, a good hotel and a theatre. It has a lot of new blood; its people are becoming organized; this oldest of all Coos County cities is rising out of its old lethargy and gives promise of a come-back to reclaim its place among the leading centers of Coos County.

A Young Ben Franklin in Empire in the 1890*'s*

By Margaret S. Turkel

Dad had several ways of earning money. He milked the family cows and four other cows and so earned $20 a month. Many sailing vessels came to Empire to load lumber. He sold milk to them for ten cents a quart, delivering to the cooks.

He had a standing order for crabs for the Tim Hayes saloon. Every Saturday he gathered and cooked ten dozen for the magnificent sum of one dollar. Boys salvaged whiskey bottles. Many flasks were found to sell for two for five cents. The boys were met at the back door, and were never inside the saloon.

He retrieved a particular dime on a very cold day in January 1884. Several men were having a game of poker out on a platform over the lake. Dad saw a dime fall on the ice and watched it melt its way down. After the men left he dug out the dime. He believes he had to dig down twelve inches—but he got the dime.

MARSHFIELD, NOW COOS BAY

1853—J. C. Tolman, a member of the Coose Bay Company, settled at what appeared to him to be a good place for a town. He built a cabin and named the place *Marshfield* after his old home in Massachusetts. He induced Crosby and Williams to erect a store and open a trading post.

1854—A. J. Davis acquired an interest in the land, leaving Wilkins Warwick in charge of the property. Tolman returned to Jacksonville. Entry was made in Warwick's name under the Donation act, but 18 days previous to Warwick's entry an act had been passed by Congress whereby no Donation claim could be granted for a townsite or settled upon for the purpose of business or trade, but must be for agricultural purposes. This resulted in a question about the title, causing considerable litigation for a number of years.

1867—John Pershbaker became interested, built a sawmill, established a store, putting his brother Charles in charge. From that time onward Marshfield has been the leading community on the coast of Southern Oregon.

John Pershbaker's property was assessed at $60,000, topping the list of taxpayers in Coos County in 1869—for mill and improvements, $20.000; for store and merchandise, $20,000; for tug *Escort*, $20,000.

1871—Marshfield post office established, Andrew Nasburg first postmaster.

1874—Marshfield became first incorporated city in Coos or Curry. Board of trustees were A. Lobree, Thomas Hirst, W. Richert, C. D. Golden, J. J. Caufield.

1878—Marshfield Academy established, offering instruction in high school subjects, first in Coos County.

1884—Marshfield population reported at 800.

1893—Marshfield became terminal of railway connection with the Coquille Valley.

1899—Marshfield adopted a new charter. E. A. Anderson, mayor.

1900—Marshfild's official U. S. census count is 1,391.
1910—2,980.
1920—4,034.
1930—5,287.
1940—5,259.
1950—6,223.
1944—Marshfield changed its name to Coos Bay.

From 1854 to 1867 Marshfield was little more than a boat landing, a store in a log house and a trading post. With the coming of John Pershbaker in 1867 with his sawmill, shipyard and store, the place soon became the center of activity for all of the coast region of Southern Oregon. Marshfield forged ahead. It built up and grew. It was the first community in Coos or Curry to become an incorporated city. It was the center of all shipping between Coos County and San Francisco. The two leading coal mines, Libby and Beaver Hill, had their bunkers at Marshfield. All freight and passenger steamers and gas boats of the Coos Bay area operated to and from Marshfield. In 1893 the place became the terminus of the railroad connecting the Coos Bay region with the Coquille Valley, reaching south to Powers on the upper South Fork in 1915.

Marshfield took the lead in banking, when young Ralph F. Williams became the first cashier of the Flanagan and Bennett Bank in 1889.

Marshfield had the first high school of the region, an outgrowth of the old Marshfield Academy. The town had the first and at present the only daily newspaper in the two counties, and the first radio station. It is the only center at present with two banks. It has the largest aggregation of mercantile, professional and industrial firms and individuals. It has been and is now the undisputed leader as a metropolitan center. The largest and most modern hotel, the Tioga, is located here. The dairy industry of the entire north end of Coos County centers here. The Greyhound Bus line has its own depot.

Yet it has at least forfeited a quantity of good will by the aggressive nature of its leadership. It started the 20-year fight to deprive Empire of the county seat. The upshot was that the courthouse went to Coquille; then it undertook to have the county divided. Its leaders tried to divert Highway 101 around the east side of Coos Bay into Marshfield.

Perhaps Marshfield's greatest political blunder in all its history came in 1944. Some of its most progressive leaders had believed that a united municipality made up of Marshfield, North Bend and perhaps Empire, to form a single city, would be a great forward step for all the bay area. Arrangements were made for an election in North Bend and Marshfield. The proposition carried in Marshfield but the vote in North Bend was almost unanimously against consolidation.

Many of the conservative and substantial citizens of Marshfield were content to proceed as usual, following a sound course, continuing to be friendly neighbors. The more aggressive leaders, however, undertook to change the name of *Marshfield* to *Coos Bay,* and succeeded in doing so.

The people of the whole area to whom the name of *Coos Bay* had been a heritage for nearly a century had no voice in the matter.

The change caused considerable dissatisfaction within the city as well as outside. It was expensive to individuals, to business concerns, to public utilities and to all who had to change their printed forms, stationery, schedules. Much confusion followed.

Now when *Coos Bay* is mentioned, an explanation is

needed to tell whether the speaker refers to the real *Coos Bay* or to the town. A Portland man wrote to a friend in the Bay area, saying that he would be at the North Bend Hotel on a certain date. The local man asked him for further information, "Do you know that the North Bend Hotel is at the Air Port, that the Coos Bay Hotel is in North Bend, and that the Marshfield Hotel is in Coos Bay? Now, at which hotel shall I meet you?"

Has *Marshfield* been forgotten? The high school is still the *Marshfield High School.* The public library books still have the imprint, *Marshfield Public Library.* In the Coos Bay section of the telephone directory we find the following: *Marshfield Bargain House, Marshfield Electric Company, Marshfield Florist, Marshfield Fuel and Supply, Marshfield Hotel.*

Marshfield Advertisers' Business Directory in the Coast Mail Special 1903.

ATTORNEYS
J. M. Upton
W. U. Douglas
C. F. McKnight
E. L. C. Farrin
Hall & Hall
John S. Coke

BANK
Flanagan & Bennett

BARBER SHOP
Edwards & Kelly
D. A. Curry

BAKERY
Jos. Egle

BLACKSMITHS
G. T. Coleman
W. Duebner
Fred Haglestein

BOAT BUILDERS
John Blomquist
Holland Brothers

BREWERY
Robert Marsden

CIGAR FACTORY
Marshfield Cigar Co.

CIGAR STORES
A. P. Owen
Bonebrake Bros.

CANDY & NOTIONS
C. A. Jensen

CARPENTER & CONTRACTOR
A. J. Savage

CLOTHING SALESMAN
W. E. Dungan

CLOAKMAKERS' AGENT
Mrs. M. R. Smith

DRY GOODS & CLOTHING
Wm. Nasburg
Chas. George
Magnes & Matson

Dry Goods

Mrs. F. A. Payne

Drug Stores

H. Sengstacken
H. Lockhart

Dentists

Dr. A. B. Prentis
Dr. W. A. Toye
Dr. R. H. Walters

Electric Light Works

F. M. Friedburg

Fruit Store

Mrs. E. J. Hansen

Groceries

A. B. Campbell
Wickman & Wickman
F. A. Sacchi
C. W. Wolcott
Gow Why

General Merchandise

Dean Lumber Co.
H. Lockhart

Hardware & Implements

E. O'Connell
J. H. Millner

Harness Shop

Wm. Haskell
E. A. Anderson

Hotels

H. W. Short
John Snyder

Ice Plants

Coos Bay Ice &
Cold Storage Co.

Ice Cream Parlors

Carl H. Winner

Iron Works & Machine Shop

Fred Nelson

Insurance Agent

W. J. Butler

Livery Stables

John Bear
E. A. Anderson

Meat Markets

Henry Holm
Noble Bros.
E. G. Flanagan

Mens Clothing & Notions

H. Finell

Musical Instruments

Chas. Grissen Music Co.
E. M. Furman

Mattress Makers

Coos Bay Mattress Factory

Manufacturers' Agent

F. S. Dow

Painters & Paperhangers

J. R. Rochon
P. M. German

Photographer

J. W. Riggs

Physicians

Dr. Hayden
Dr. Murphy

Racket Store

E. Marsh

Real Estate

I. S. Kaufman

Restaurants

Geo. N. Farrin
J. W. Tibbitts
J. M. Mulkey

Saloons

C. A. Moore
Robert Marsden
A. Heckela
T. F. Crawford
John Herren
Marsden & Quick
Emerson & Ferrey

Shoes & Notions

Peter Clausen

Steam Laundry

Amstein & Hibbard

Stone & Marble Works

A. R. Tenbrook
F. M. Stewart

Tailors

Noris Jensen
L. W. Planz

Transportation Lines

S. C. Rogers
C. E. Edwards
W. C. Harris
Eli Bangs

Variety Store & News Stand

F. P. Norton

Marshfield, the most important town along 400 miles of the Pacific shore line, has a trim, neat appearance it didn't have in the old days. Yet how it was in the nineties is wistfully remembered by many oldtimers, as in the following sketch:

Do you remember the kerosene street lamps set up on posts before the coming of electricity? Of course, you recall the first electric power plant out on Central Avenue on the bank of Mill Slough.

And do you remember the whistling of the passenger steamers at all hours of the day—the *Comet,* the *Blanco,* the *Yarrow,* each making two round trips a day between Marshfield and Empire? When you heard three long blasts you knew you still had 30 minutes to shop around. Two blasts warned you that the boats would be leaving in 15 minutes; one blast meant just 5 minutes.

And the milk cargoes from Allegany and along Coos River? Individual customers came to the dock with empty cans to replace the full ones. There was no other milk delivery in town except where a family kept a cow.

Perhaps you remember when you could buy a salmon — a big chinook—for 35 cents, or a silverside for 15 cents, or four wild ducks for 50 cents.

And what became of the two-bit meal? Do you remember Tibett's Chop House where you could get everything from soup to pie for 25 cents? But they also had a 50-cent dinner—reserved for the drummers. It would never do for one of them to be seen eating at a two-bit table.

North Bend

1853—First settlement—Lockhart family; Wilcox. (*Old* North Bend).
1854—Wilcox trades his claim to Glen Aiken for horse, saddle, bridle.
1855—Aiken sells his claim to A. M. Simpson for $300.
1856—Simpson prepares to build sawmill and shipyard. Work delayed by wreck of schooner *Quadratus* on Coos Bay bar; mill machinery salvaged.
1857—*Brig Blanco* (284 tons) first ship built on Coos Bay.
1858—First shipment of lumber from North Bend.
1872—Post Office established; C. H. Merchant and Robert W. Simpson, postmasters.
1874—Post Office discontinued.
1900—Post Office re-established; L. J. Simpson, postmaster.
1903—North Bend (New Town) incorporated.
1910-1950—Population for each ten-year period beginning with 1910: 2,078, 3,268, 4,012, 4,262, 6,099.
1951—Weyerhaeuser sawmill starts sawing lumber.

When A. M. Simpson took possession about 1855, he immediately began construction of a sawmill and a shipyard; also a store, a cookhouse and a bunkelation for the unmarried men, and several small dwellings for the employes with families.

During the next forty-odd years, the mill whistle continued to sound the time to get up in the morning, the time for dinner and when to quit work at the end of each day.

About 1862 a one-room school was opened, in the north end of what is now Simpson Heights.

The post office, established in 1872, was discontinued two years later. The residents then got their mail at the company store, brought daily by steamers operating between Marshfield and Empire.

Just south of North Bend, a city named Yarrow was platted in 1890. The tract of some fifty odd acres had been bought from the government in 1863 at $1.25 per acre. A year later it was sold for $500 to Charles Merchant, who sold it eleven months later for $400 to Charles E. Eckhoff.

Eckhoff built a house, raised a large family, did some farming, rafted logs from logging camps to sawmills; he fished for salmon each autumn, salting, packing and shipping them to San Francisco, assisted by some of his daughters. One of the girls, Margaret, now Mrs. John Messerle in her 86th year, residing at Catching Inlet, remembers that she was the boat-puller for her father; some of her sisters helped dress the salmon.

In 1889, the land was bought for $16,000 by Thomas W. Symons, who platted the property as the townsite of Yarrow. The Eckhoff family had built a dwelling in the north end of the property years earlier. Some time during the nineties, Charles Hendrickson built a dwelling near the old Eckhoff home.

Following the initial flush, the town of Yarrow seemed to bog down.

In 1902, Symons sold the townsite to L. J. Simpson for $25,000—all except two lots—probably on which ten years earlier Charles Hendrickson had built his home which still stands at 1524 Sheridan Avenue. One of the Erickson daughters who grew up there, is now Mrs. Victor West residing on Simpson Heights.

Immediately after buying the townsite of Yarrow in 1902, Simpson proceeded to replat it, giving it the name of North Bend. Few changes were made from the original map of Yarrow, except some of the street names. Grant Circle and Lincoln Square were retained as originally planned.

A post office had been re-established in the Simpson store, taking the old name of North Bend. Later the office was moved to the new town, The Simpson mill property came to be known as *Old North Bend,* or just *Old Town.*

In 1903, North Bend took its place among the incorporated cities of Coos County, with Simpson as mayor. He retained that office for many years, until he established his legal residence in his new home near Cape

Arago, naming his place *Shore Acres,* the present State Park of that name.

North Bend News

Douglas fir poles, 100 feet long, arrow-straight, before being set up as lofty lamp posts for the North Bend ball park. Such timbers uplifting as masts of sailing ships were admired in many a foreign harbor.

Simpson, a vigorous and active young man of 25 years, brought with him a period of new activity on Coos Bay. Marshfield which had been the outstanding industrial and commercial center of the entire Coos-Curry area since about 1867, now had its first real competitor for top place on the coast of Southwestern Oregon.

Beginning about 1903, new sawmills were built; the old Porter Mill property was bought by Simpson and rehabilitated. Other factories were added, including a woolen mill, a sash and door factory, a milk condensary, an iron foundry, and a plywood mill. Streets were graded and planked. The first store was opened by George Witte in the old Eckhoff building at the corner of Sherman and California. Witte had come down from Portland on the steamer *Breakwater* with a stock of groceries, second-hand furniture, and a stock of clothing for working men.

About the same time, A. J. Davis moved in from Marshfield and opened a dry goods store for women. A little later they erected their own building and gave their store the name of *The White House,* operated after Davis' death in 1923 by Mrs. Davis, up to the time of her death in 1950, then it was taken over by her niece, Miss Pearl Johnson. This is the only North Bend store that has endured and continued to grow from the very beginning, in the hands of one family.

One of the earliest churches in North Bend was that of the Presbyterians on North Union. It was in the basement of this church that the first public school was opened in new North Bend, when the one-room school in Old North Bend became inadequate.

The Central School built on McPherson Avenue in 1904, continued to be used until 1949. The brick high school building in the Bangor district, erected in 1909, was given the name of the Kinney High School, later changed to North Bend High School.

Steamboats and gasoline launches afforded practically the only means of transportation to and from the town. A winding trail connecting with Empire and Marshfield had been widened to permit use of buggies.

Gasoline launches began carrying passengers between

North Bend and Marshfield a few years after the city was incorporated, replacing the earlier steamboats. First on the run with a regular schedule was the launch *North Bend,* to which was later added a second launch, named *Marshfield,* and then the larger and speedier *Bonita.* Fare between the two towns was fifteen cents each way, twenty-five cents for the round trip.

About 1913, Vern C. Gorst and his partner, Charles King, with a six-passenger Cadillac, started a bus line by way of the old wagon road to Ponny Slough and over the hills to Ferndale and Marshfield.

Gorst & King started with a fare of twenty-five cents each way. Some said they would go broke within a few weeks. People wouldn't pay double fare. Just the same the Cadillac ran continuously from early morning till late at night. The two proprietors were their own chauffers. But they soon had to add other cars and new drivers. A year or two later was opened the waterfront road, hardly to be classed as a highway. Mud holes, broken planks and other distressing features were common. Slowly, improvements came year after year, till in 1949, the modern four-lane paved highway connected the two cities. The Gorst & King busses still operated between the places, the only line with a regular schedule on this run.

Water for the mills and other industries, as well as for domestic uses, was a problem even before New North Bend came into being. The town of 6,000 is traversed its full length by U. S. 101, four lanes, a distance of two miles through residence, commercial and industrial districts.

Bandon-by-the-Sea

1853—First settlers, attracted by gold and other inducements.
1877—Bandon Post Office established; John Lewis, postmaster.
1891—Bandon incorporated.

The earliest known white men in the lower Coquille River region were Hudson's Bay Company trappers in 1826. In 1851, Captain Tichenor's men, escaping from the Indians at Battle Rock, crossed the river a mile or two above the present site of Bandon. In 1852, men from the schooner *Captain Lincoln,* wrecked on the beach just north of the Coos Bay bar, crossed the lower river on their way to Port Orford. Among them was Henry H. Baldwin, who was so impressed by the location which later was to become Bandon, that he returned and made his permanent home in the area.

Baldwin reportedly had been a close friend of George Bennett in Ireland; he induced the latter to come and locate here. Both these men, having come from Bandon, Ireland, were instrumental in transplanting that Irish name to the new settlement. (Let it be said in a low hush-hush whisper that Bennett also brought and transplanted the Irish furze, known and hated today as gorse.)

In 1853, gold seekers were swarming the beaches both north and south of the Coquille River. George Bennett reported:

> The first donation claim taken south of the Coquille River was taken in the year of 1853, by Thos. Lowe, commonly known as Tommy Lowe . . . and the second by Chris Long . . . After these and towards the end of the same year, the site of the town of Bandon was taken up, not for the gold that glittered in the front of it, . . . but because of a convenient place for a ferry, and from its admirable position for commercial purposes.

Bennett said that the property passed through several hands, including A. H. Thrift, Louis Turner, Chris Long, Edward Fahy, John Lewis, Neil, Averhill and Alberson, and George Dyer.

In 1874 a voting place was established south of the river and was named Bandon Precinct. According to the *County Archives,* quoting the *Roseburg Review* of Feburary 14, 1889:

> Although the precinct has been named Bandon since 1874, the congregation of houses and other buildings that constitute the town was called *Averhill* until 1889.

The Bandon post office was established in 1877, with John Lewis as first postmaster. In 1891 Bandon was incorporated as a city. The 1900 census showed a population of 645.

Bennett said:

The first sawmill in Bandon was erected in 1883 by Major R. H. Rosa, about two miles inland in a country abounding in the best spruce, fir and white cedar, etc., for which a ready market and at the highest quotations is always obtainable.

O. W. Briggs, writing in 1936 for the W. P. A. project, reported:

Bandon has no railroad. As late as 1886, there was no wagon road between Bandon and the Coos Bay side of the country. Judge D. J. Lowe traveled the 28 miles to Empire, the county seat, horseback, over the Randolph trail, kicking elk out of the path in many places, he often related to friends in court.

All traffic between Bandon and the settlements on the upper river was by steamers, row boats, and later by gasoline launches, with scows for livestock and heavy freight shipments.

After the government constructed two jetties at the harbor entrance in the late 1890's the district had regular freight transportation from San Francisco and Portland.

The city came into prominence between 1905 and 1910, when the river was lined with five sawmills and one or two shipyards.

The city for two or three years was the most prosperous in Coos County. Then the Randolph mill burned down; the Parkersburg mill also was burned; the Johnson mill suspended operations, leaving the industrial situation uncertain and discouraging. Bandon at this peak had a population of over 1800.

It was about 1900 when the Moore lumbering activities got under way on the lower Coquille, resulting today in one of the major lumbering organizations in Coos County.

In 1893 a three-set woolen mill was built in Bandon by T. W. Clark and H. Z. Burkhart. A year later, Burkhart sold out to Clark According to the *Marshfield Sun,* issue of January, 1901, the mill was employing from 45 to 55 people. In 1903 the mill was closed and the machinery moved to the new city of North Bend, under the energetic and aggressive leadership of L. J. Simpson.

But Bandon also had a progressive and enterprising leader in the person of R. E. L. Bedellion, who mustered a following of supporters, and Bandon again had a woolen mill.

By 1906 population was increasing rapidly, the town was out of debt, and industrial production was booming.

In 1908 the first direct steamer line between Bandon and Portland was established.

By 1911 Bandon had two banks, and three good hotels, one of which, *The Gallier,* had 9,126 registrations in 1912.

By 1913 Bandon began to draw many tourists. Picturesque scenery, an outstanding panoramic view of the harbor, river, beach, bar and ocean, and hunting and fishing attracted vacationists and sportsmen.

On June 11, 1914, a severe fire swept Bandon's business district, with damage estimated at $200,000. At that time Bandon had three weekly newspapers, the *Bandon Recorder,* the *Western World,* and the *Surf.* Census reports indicate that Bandon was then at its peak and that it has had periods of ups and downs throughout its entire history,

1890– 219
1900– 645
1910–1,803
1920–1,440
1930–1,516
1940–1,004
1950–1,212

The two heavy drops in population followed the two destructive fires, the one in 1914, the other in 1936.

By 1936 Bandon was a substantial community of about 1500 people, with about 450 homes and 40 or 50 commercial establishments. Approximately 350 persons were employed by Bandon mills and manufacturing plants, and about 200 by small industries, stores, and other establishments. Dairy and stockraising in the surrounding territory added to the stability of the community. Bandon was headquarters for the fleet of fishing boats during the fishing season. Salmon fishing was still an item of importance in the Coquille River. The city also was the center of the promising cranberry industry.

Then suddenly disaster struck Bandon once again on September 26, 1936; a forest fire swept in and practically wiped the city out. The following morning only 16 buildings remained standing out of nearly 500 of the day before. The large lumber mill was spared; also a few small industries.

The immediate problem was to care for the hundreds who had suddenly lost their homes and everything. Commercial activity was set up in the old business district.

At the request of Governor Charles H. Martin, the Oregon State Planning Board gave immediate assistance in developing a replanning program. Within 10 days after the fire there was a joint meeting of the Bandon City Council, the State City Planning Board, and other community leaders. They worked out a *Plan for a New Bandon.*

Just before the fire the assessed valuation of the city was $786,319, reduced in a single day by a large portion—perhaps down to one-third or about $262,000. There was a debt of $280,000 against the city. Bandon was apparently bankrupt.

The debt clearly had to be reduced, scaled down, compromised. It was also realized that the city had been a sprawling, shapeless, planless conglomeration of structures, very much the same as other American cities that had "just growed." Following the fire, Bandon was no less sprawling than it had been, but, in addition, it was a blackened mess of wreckage spread out over an area of more than 900 acres. Less than half of that area was sufficient to provide ample room for housing its people.

The river front, by the new plan, was to be reserved for mills, manufacturing plants, shipping. The city proper was to be protected from possible future forest fires by a wide *green belt* on the east and south sides.

The plan provided for pooling all the property within the city. A great portion of it was already owned by the town, having been taken over for unpaid taxes. Other portions were owned by the county. Individuals who pooled their property were to be given certificates in accordance with the value of their respective properties. After completion of the plan, the certificates were to be redeemable for property within the NEW BANDON.

By reducing the city to 450 acres, the reduced area would require fewer streets, shorter sewer lines, better lighting and power service, shorter distances from homes to schools, safer playgrounds for the children—many advantages that the shapeless, planless city could never hope to have.

But during the process of refinancing, overcoming the numerous obstacles, ironing out the countless difficulties, time was passing on. Many persons who had lost their homes and collected their insurance money, were anxious to become re-established. Some were doubtful about the new plan, fearing that they were being deprived of their properties with no assurance that they would receive just remuneration.

Some whose taxes had been unpaid, their homes destroyed by the fire, collected their insurance money, let the vacant lot revert to the city or to the county, and moved out to build new homes alongside the highway. Businessmen were anxious to get re-established before losing their old customers. They began setting up temporary quarters.

Gradually the old order was taking root. Slowly the city was beginning to grow anew regardless of plans or shape or form. And so the PLAN FOR A NEW BANDON died while in the process of being born. The town once more was on its way to grow and spread and sprawl.

The basic beauty of Bandon, by no means entirely effaceable by man, has been expressed in a poem by L. D. Felsheim, publisher of the *Western World*:

Where breakers roar,
Where white gulls soar,
Where ships pass out to sea;
Where driftwood logs
Mid seafoam bogs
Splash on so merrily;

Where mist and rain
Off bounding main
Sweep hills of rolling green,
And shifting sands
Spread fairy lands
Upon a glittering screen.

1861—Platted as Meyersville
1872—Gets post office named Ott
1876—Name changed to Myrtle Point
1887—Incorporated as city of Myrtle Point

The Christian Lehnherrs had come from Lookingglass Valley, Douglas county, in 1857, and had settled on the South Fork of the Coquille. A man named Henry Meyers had come with the Baltimore Colony and had settled in the vicinity. In 1861 he purchased a donation claim from John Dully, a beautiful section on the bank of the river. He platted a town and called it Meyersville. Several houses were built, and a large store building.

In the following winter, heavy rains all along the coast resulted in destructive floods.

Mrs. Fannie Lehnherr Dixon wrote:

> Our garden on the bank of the river was completely covered with loam and debris. . . . Many members of the Baltimore colony had built small cabins. . . . The high water covered their places and they had to flee to higher ground. Many became discouraged and left their places to return to Maryland. The town Henry Meyers had plotted was deserted. Meyers decided to sell his holdings and return home . . . Father became the owner of 160 acres of land and also possessor of the large building erected for a store. . . . Meyers' furniture, dishes and many things that were great luxuries to our pioneer family, were moved to our Roland Prairie home.

Four years after the big flood had driven the residents from Meyersville, the Lehnherr family moved from their farm home at Roland Prairie on the South Fork, into the deserted town. Said Mrs. Dixon, "The cabins built by the Baltimore immigrants were in fairly good condition and made the place look less desolate, although none were occupied."

Clay suitable for brick-making was located in the community which accounts for a number of clay buildings at Myrtle Point in later years. Of the early history, Mrs. Dixon wrote:

> Two men, both brick masons, were delegated to make and

burn a kiln of brick . . . A fireplace was built in the south end of the building . . . For many years that fireplace was the scene of many gatherings, and sometimes very heated arguments by opposing politicians. Already our home was used by all the settlers who passed along to *Coos Bay* or Roseburg.

The beauty and utility of myrtle wood was being discovered even in those early days. Mrs. Dixon reports that William Cribbins arrived in 1867, with a turning lathe and proceeded to make chairs and bedsteads from the hard myrtle wood:

Settlers came from the eastern states, occupying empty houses of the once deserted Meyersville . . . They came by way of San Francisco to Coos Bay, up Isthmus Slough, down Beaver Slough, then up the Coquille River, a three-day journey and 67 miles.

The enterprising Lehnherr soon added a grist mill and began supplying flour made from the wheat being grown in the community. Hogs roamed in the flats, growing fat on the myrtle nuts that covered the ground under the trees in the fall of the year. According to Mrs. Dixon, her father made bacon, for which he found a market at the sawmills on Coos Bay. After being taken by boat down the river, then up Beaver Slough, hauled on a sled across the isthmus, it was taken by boat to Empire. Mrs. Dixon recalls one of those trips on which she accompanied her father.

I can remember vividly being taken out of a warm bed in the middle of the night, wrapped in a blanket, and placed in a boat to finish the journey to the market. The bacon was exchanged for household necessities: brown sugar that came in barrels, syrup in five-gallon cans, rice in Chinese mats, green coffee also in mats; tea, salt and a few other commodities. Always a bolt of blue and white gingham, unbleached muslin, and Kentucky jeans for the men; and two pairs of shoes for each member of the family; one pair with copper toes, shoes that must last till another hog-killing. But if they gave out, Mr. Schroeder could renew the soles and put on a patch or two.

Such was some of the early life in what is now Myrtle Point. It was still Meyersville. There was no post office.

All mail was brought by sailing vessels from San Francisco to Coos Bay and was held at Empire until one of the settlers from the Coquille side made a trip to the Bay. The mail was placed in gunny sacks, and at every home the sacks were emptied on the floor and the owner selected his individual mail.

A school had been started up the river but it was too far away for children at Meyersville. According to Mrs. Dixon, an upstairs room was fitted up in the big building and "a young man, Alex Stauff, taught the first school . . . Julia Ann Grant taught the school in 1869."

It was not till August 27, 1872, that a post office was established. It was named Ott, with Christian Lehnherr as postmaster. Four years later the name was changed to Myrtle Point, due, no doubt, to the beautiful myrtles in the community. No record seems to be available to explain why it was first called Ott.

In 1887, Myrtle Point was incorporated as a city. The first available census report, 1900 gives a population of 530. Each succeeding ten-year period shows a steady growth, except during the 1930's. 836 in 1910, 934 in 1920, 1362 in 1930, 1296 in 1940, 2033 in 1950.

In the 1890's, when the 20-year fight to take the county seat from Empire was drawing to a close, Myrtle Point announced its candidacy in the *Myrtle Point Enterprise* of February 8, 1896:

> As the time for the final decision draws nearer, there is a great deal being said in regard to the re-location of Coos County's seat of government . . . Now that the other towns are becoming somewhat active in presenting their claims for this much prized plum, it behooves the citizens of Myrtle Point to begin to wake up, rub their optics and prepare for the coming conflict.

It did get the perquisite of the County Fair Grounds.

Myrtle Point is a natural hub in one of the richest dairy areas of Coos County. Highways lead in from each of the three forks of the Coquille and from the lower river, on both sides of the stream. State Highway 42, from Bandon by way of the county seat of Coquille, passes through Myrtle Point and on to Roseburg. Myrtle Point is also the gateway to the city of Powers and the upper Rogue River areas.

1870—On July 1, post office established; Titus B. Willard, Postmaster.
1885—Incorporated.
1896—Became the county-seat.
1950—Population 3,523.

The site had been owned by Evan Cunningham, who had a wharf on the river known as Cunningham's Landing. In 1870, Titus B. Willard acquired the property and had a post office established with himself as postmaster.

Though the name was Coquille from the first, it was pronounced Ko-kwell. Sometime later, perhaps around the turn of the century, someone began calling it Ko-keel. This pronunciation is now commonly accepted, though many pioneers stick to the original Ko-kwell.

By 1876 a move was started by some Marshfielders to have the county-seat changed from Empire City. People in the Coquille Valley felt that if a change was to be made, a geographical center should be selected. For 20 years the fight went on. By a majority vote, in 1896, Coquille became the county-seat. It was incorporated as a city in 1885.

Til M. Vowel had opened a store in 1871, said to have been the first on the Coquille River. Vowel sold to Alkeny Nosler, who later sold to John T. Moulton, a name long to be connected with the mercantile business of Coquille. A newspaper, sawmill, and other enterprises came.

Orvil Dodge said in 1898:

> Coquille is incorporated, population about 1800; has fine merchandise stores, one hardware store, three drug stores, two grocery stores, one drygoods and clothing store, two hotels, three blacksmith shops, two livery stables, two millinery stores, two saloons, two weekly papers, five churches, public school, one academy, one sawmill, one broomhandle and shingle mill, railroad station and Wells, Fargo & Co's. express office, telegraph and telephone offices, a public hall, four attorneys, abstract office, three physicians, silk manufacturing station, court house now building, jail, photograph gallery.

Census figures indicate Coquille's growth as follows: In 1890–449; 1900–728 (not half as many actually as Dodge estimated two years earlier); 1910–1398; 1920–1642; 1930–2732; 1940–3327; 1950–3323.

The *Coos Bay Times* in August of 1922 ran an article by Walter Sinclair *the pioneer* lawyer of Coos County, with a practice begun in 1884:

Do You Remember the first store opened in Coquille? Till Vowell built on the lot where the Lorenz store now stands, which was purchased by John T. Moulton.

Do You Remember the second mercantile establishment opened by Emmerson & Hayes and the third by C. Andrews, with whom W. P. Wright was associated for some time?

Do You Remember the first hotel opened, I think, by M. W. Miller, where the Baxter hotel now stands, and the second opened by Mrs. Robinson on the south side of front street and the extra fine meals we got for 25 cents?

Do You Remember the first express team, operated by J. P. Messer, consisting of a pair of red oxen, Duke and Dime?

The same *Times* issue remarked of George T. Moulton, who held a unique position as a Coquille pioneer:

He was born down the river where his father, John T. Moulton, settled when he took up a homestead in 1866. The father put in the machinery for the Lane blacksand mines. In 1871, the family moved to what is now Coquille and occupied the house which was built by T. B. Willard. Mr. Willard was the only other person in the city at that time. George Moulton was then five years old.

The first school Mr. Moulton attended was a log cabin across the river which burned down and later he attended one which stood where the Farmers & Merchants bank now stands. His first teacher was W. H. Nosler. Mr. Moulton worked for his father in the store.

Eastside

1868 or 1869–First settlement – date uncertain.
1891–Post office established as East Marshfield.
1893–Post office discontinued; reopened in 1897.
1908–Name changed to Eastside.
1915–Eastside incorporated; Richard Whitty, first mayor.

Beach scenes 1915
Fourth of July 1900
Tupper Rock

Collection of Alfred Powers

BANDON

Coos-Curry Pioneer Museum

Myrtle Point

1861–Platted as Meyersville
1872–Gets post office named Ott
1876–Name changed to Myrtle Point
1887–Incorporated as city of Myrtle Point

Milk man about 1908. Christian Lehnherr grist mill 1876. First train, September 15, 1893.

Coos-Curry Pioneer Musem

PIONEER STORE

Binger Hermann's, then Wise Brothers', then Wise & Bender's Store at Myrtle Point. Above: The store and post office in 1877. Third man from right end is Sol Wise, at the end is Ed Bender. Below: Interior of the store in 1892. In the foreground, far left leaning on counter, Ernest Hermann; with arm on pile of goods, Sol Wise; far right at end of counter, Oliver Miller; far back, closest to lamp, Ed Bender. Customers not identified.

Coos-Curry Historical Muse

Loaned by Mrs. M. P. Hughes

Loaned by Mrs. Albert Powers

POWERS

1873–The North Carolina settlement.
1890–Post office established by name of Rural.
1915–Post office named Powers.
About that time the town platted
1945–City of Powers incorporated.

Albert H. Powers. Powers 1915. Building railroad 1920. David Wagner house 1873.

Coos Curry Pioneer Museum

EMPIRE CITY

Oldest Coos Settlement

1855

EMPIRE CITY, COOS BAY.

Harper's Magazine

MARSHFIELD
Coos Bay

Above: Lockart Building, corner of Center and Front Streets, Marshfield, about 1900, housing the Coos Bay Drug Store and W. G. Webster "Gent's Furnishings, Clothing . . . Goods Cheap for Cash." Below: Marshfield in the 90's.

Coos Curry Pioneer Museum

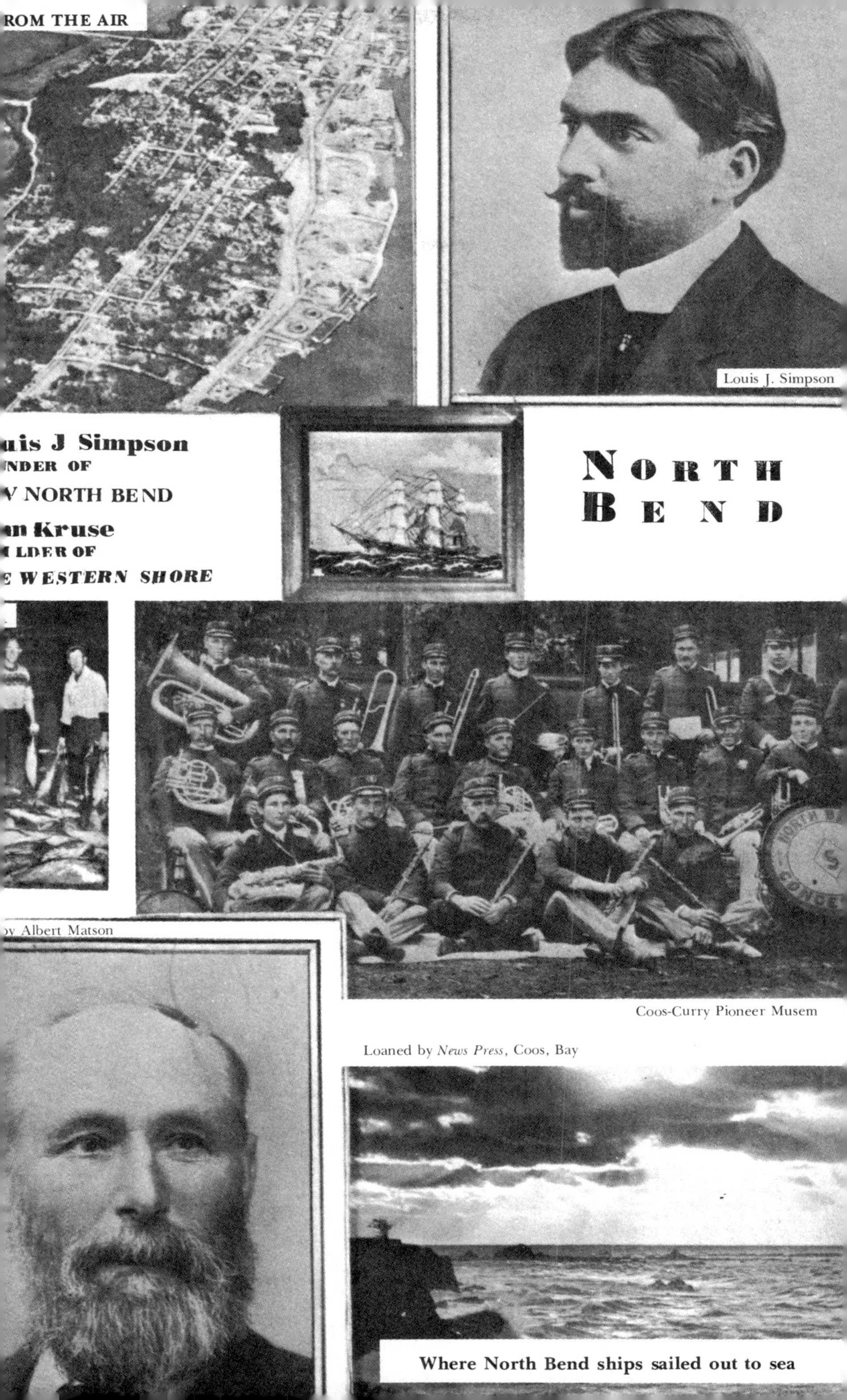

Louis J. Simpson

by Albert Matson

Coos-Curry Pioneer Musem

Loaned by *News Press*, Coos, Bay

Where North Bend ships sailed out to sea

1900

Coos-Curry Pioneer Museum

COQUILLE CITY

1896

Postmasters under the two names of East Marshfield and Eastside, in order of their appointment: C. J. Bishop, John H. Rease, Wm. La Palme, Lucy H. La Palme, Martin B. Pederson, Genevieve F. Bock, Marguerite Neiman, Loretta Cornell, James Zimmerman, Kate F. Prey, Leona Creson.

From its earliest history, the area now embraced by the city of Eastside and its surroundings had been so closely associated with Marshfield that it hardly had a history of its own. It lay just across the Bay from Marshfield and roughly included all of the peninsula between the tide lands of lower Coos River on the north and Isthmus Inlet on the south.

The different parts of the area were variously known as Timmerman's Point, Bay City, and Aaronsville. Before the establishment of a post office named East Marshfield in 1891, the whole area was commonly referred to as Bay City, the name still applied to the area surrounding the big sawmill at the extreme south end.

The Pioneer families included Timmerman, Kern, Dunbar, Jennings, Peterson, Jordan, and *Milk-Man Jones* who kept several cows and delivered milk in Marshfield as well as to his Bay City neighbors.

In 1885, the sawmill of E. B. Dean and Company was discontinued in Marshfield and rebuilt on the east bank of Isthmus Inlet at the south end of Bay City, where a mill under different ownerships has operated ever since.

During its early history, the mill was often referred to as the Lobree mill, A. Lobree being one of the principal owners. He had a son Aaron — hence Aaronsville. Some of the old records indicate that the steamer *Comet* was built at Aaronsville in 1883.

Bay City's transportation was first entirely by water. Each family had a boat or two of its own, equipped with oars and sails. Steamboats operating on Isthmus Inlet also landed at waterfront points.

Later, the Coos Bay Wagon Road was extended from Sumner to Bay City, terminating on Timmerman's Point. A long board walk was extended across the tideflats to the Coos Bay channel opposite Marshfield. At first this was a narrow walk—some say only a foot wide. It may have been. Anyway, later it was widened to accommodate vehicles—horse-drawn and automobiles. A dock made boat landings possible. Later, a ferry service enabled traffic to continue into Marshfield.

A warehouse was built at the end of this Eastside extension as a distributing point for gasoline, used principally for launches. It was the first gasoline distributing plant on Coos Bay and was operated by Jack Flanagan for the Standard Oil Company. The gasoline came in iron drums, each holding approximately 100 gallons, by steamer from San Francisco.

Just south of this warehouse and landing, perhaps a hundred feet distant, was a building on piles driven into the tide-flats. It was commonly known as the Powder House, being used to store powder by the Pioneer Hardware Company of Marshfield. J. Albert Matson recalls that the building was erected many years earlier by Captain Wm. Campbell for use as a grist mill, operated by wind power.

The ferry at this point long continued in use until the highway bridge was constructed across Isthmus Inlet from Bunker Hill to the Bay City side, serving all the Coos River, Allegany and most of the Catching Inlet areas.

Eastside's population according to the U. S. census, was as follows: 1920—453; 1930—556; 1940—638; 1950—890.

At this time Eastside has stores, auto service stations, paved streets and all modern conveniences such as electricity and telephones, as well as its own water system. However, as its early homes were laid out by meets-and-bounds, and as almost every family kept one or more cows, running unrestricted except for a fence around each home, the cows had an important part in laying out the trails, which later developed into roadways and afterwards became improved as streets. As a result, the street system of Eastside, like many other American cities of pioneer origin, follows a cowtrail pattern. But this feature has a decided advantage in modern day life—automobile speeding is practically impossible, helping to make Eastside an attractive residential district.

RIVERTON

When Dodge wrote about Riverton a little more than half a century ago, he referred to it as a *town*. At that time, in 1898, coal mines were employing many men; steamers were carrying the output to San Francisco; river boats were busy up and down the stream.

Around the turn of the century, there was at least one hotel, a store or two. At one time there were said to be seven saloons. The population was reported at somewhat over 300.

Today, Riverton has one store and a rural post office. There is no hotel and none is needed.

Perhaps the only feature that has increased is the school population, which indicates a census of approximately 650 or 700. But the school district is not limited to the village. It is made up perhaps mostly of farm and other rural families.

But look back fifty or sixty years, as told by Dodge:

> The town of Riverton is situated on the left bank of the Coquille River nine miles above Parkersburg and nine miles below Coquille City. The town was laid out by E. Weston, civil engineer, in the fall of 1889. The townsite was originally a part of the fine ranch homestead owned by Nathaniel Thruch. . . . The site contains 20 acres.
>
> The first settler in the town was O. A. Kelly, then employed as teacher in that district. His first residence was a small box house, a part of which soon after became the post office, with Mr. Kelly ·as the first postmaster, . . . in 1890.
>
> In 1896, the population amounted to over 300 inhabitants, with over forty buildings in the town, not including the school house, church, hall, store, meat market or barns. . . . In Riverton is a fine sawmill built in 1890 by Price Bros. & Co.
>
> The chief enterprise of Riverton is the coal business; next comes the merchants and the hotels. At present there is but one general merchandise store in the town and it is managed by E. B. Price, who is also postmaster. There is only one hotel now

running in the town, the Riverton Hotel, O. A. Kelly proprietor. As soon as the mines all resume operation, as they will soon, other business enterprises will again start up as the demand requires.

The coal mines did start up again and operated until about 1940, when the last one, the Alpine, closed.

About 1907, Wesley A. Bean, a school teacher, took over the general merchandise store and the post office. Associated with him was his brother-in-law, Clifford Martin. The partnership continued for about forty years, when Bean disposed of his interest to Martin, who then became the sole owner. Since then, the store has changed hands several times

LAKESIDE

Lakeside received its name on April 18, 1908, when a post office was established and Nels S. Olsen became its first postmaster. L. J. Simpson and C. M. Byler had bought the property, laid out a town and named it. In 1892 a creamery was located there. Milk, cream and other farm produce came from the farms by row boats. From here the outlet was by teams and wagons across the sandflats to the ocean, then 10 miles southward along the ocean beach to Jarvis Landing on Coos Bay to connect with steamers operating between Empire and Marshfield.

In the early nineties a post office was established and named *Lake*.

Lake was somewhat like the hopping flea, for it moved about from place to place with each change of postmasters. But the creamery remained stationery. There was a store, a one-room school, a hotel, and a place to play baseball. The community was commonly referred to as The Creamery. The country surrounding the lakes was called the Tenmile country. In 1903 in a special issue of *The Coast Mail*, a weekly newspaper of Marshfield, a contributor with a free-flowing pen told about the Tenmile country:

There is one reverend or minister of the gospel here, but no lawyers, courts, jails, criminals, gamblers, saloons, dance halls or evil influences of any kind to debase character and corrupt the morals of man, woman or beast. . . . This important part of the country was almost unknown until 1874, when S. F. Johnson and Nels Thompson explored it and located permanently the following spring.

In 1924 Lakeside was incorporated as a city.

Through the thirties business dwindled, fire had destroyed some of the principal buildings; the Southern Pacific Company removed its depot, leaving only a flag-stop. Little by little the population dwindled, making a sick city. Its remaining residents in 1942 voted to disincorporate.

In the past decade, however, Lakeside has taken on new life and a new look.

LANGLOIS

The name Langlois in Curry County dates back to the time when half a day was required to drive to Bandon or Port Orford, a trip now made in twenty minutes.

William V. Langlois had come from the Willamette Valley some time in the fifties. After operating a store for a while in Port Orford, the family moved north some fifteen miles, settled on a homestead and a donation claim approximately midway between Port Orford and Bandon. Eight children were in the family. Frank M. Langlois was one of six sons.

About 1880, Frank entered into a partnership with A. H. Thrift in the establishment of a store on the Langlois farm a mile or so west of the present site of Langlois. A year later, they moved the store to a location on the main road, where a post office was established April 4, 1881, with Frank M. Langlois as the postmaster and Langlois took the family name, which it carries to this day.

Merchandise for the store came from San Francisco by boat, usually to Bandon. From there it had to be freighted by wagon or pack horses. Freight rates were high. It is reported that the famous Curry County horseman and bear rider, Ace Carey, was one of the earliest freighters for the Langlois store.

The Langlois store carried the customary merchandise for farmers, gold miners, loggers, mill workers, and hunters.

Frank Langlois platted his land as a town site, giving it the name which the post office already carried. In the half century that followed the establishment of the Langlois store, the business changed hands several times. In 1898, it was bought by Ed Rackliff, who in turn later sold out to Ed. Thrift, son of A. H. Thrift. In 1920, William J. Sweet took over the store and post office, turning the business over five years later to his brother, Alfred J. Sweet.

With the opening of the Coast Highway, U. S. 101, Langlois ceased to be an isolated hamlet in the wilderness. Truck lines make daily deliveries to the stores, enabling the local merchants to compete in many respects with the larger places.

Perhaps no other single item has given Langlois the wide range publicity as that of the Langlois Cheese Makers, owned and operated by H. H. Hansen, which ships its products far and wide by parcel post.

City of Powers

1873—The North Carolina settlement.

1890—Post office established by name of Rural. James D. Hayes, postmaster.

1915—Post office named Powers. Gustavus A. Brown, postmaster. About that time the town platted.

1945—City of Powers incorporated.

The town's history will be given by means of four interviews with oldtimers by students of the Powers High School in 1931. These then very young historians would be in their thirties now.

Bernice Briggs interviewed Mrs. Dement and succeeded in getting hold of some interesting information:

Daniel Wagner was the first white settler in the Powers area.

He built a house where Albert Powers' house now stands, and then he sent for his family and friends.

The people who were here at that time were called the North Carolina settlers, namely, the Wagners, Bakers, Hayes, Binghams, Arnolds, Gants and Woodbys.

Mr. Albert H. Powers purchased the town site from Mr. Wagner. The people thought about naming it Wagner but as there was a post office already by that name in the state, it was decided to call it Powers.

The south section of town was then a marsh, making it necessary to drain it before houses could be built. The first hotel was built where Morgan's Garage now stands. The first store was on the north side of Powers, close to Ligget's Service Station.

Chinese were mining here when Wagner came; hence China Flat derived its name from the Chinese.

The early settlers had to make their own shoes, clothes and flour, a grist mill being at Mill Creek, where they made their flour. They did not have fruit jars then and saved all the bottles they could get hold of and covered them with cloth, dipping them in sealing wax. It took four and one-half days to drive their cattle to Roseburg, shipping from there to Portland. They could file three kinds of claims: preemption, donation, and homestead.

Gladys Tanner interviewed Mr. and Mrs. Max Dement. The things in her paper that dealt with the same people and events as that of Bernice Briggs, have been left out except the controversial matter of the South Side marsh:

After David Wagner located some likely homesteads, he went to get his family, and in 1873, they all left North Carolina with a group of other settlers. They started a colony called the North Carolina Settlement.

There were Chinese mining here when the settlers came. Those miners bought their supplies from the ranchers. After they had made a purchase, they would go shuffling off to their mines. They were panning out "real pay dirt."

Most of the Indians had left the country before the Chinese came. The few Indians who were left were very peaceful and quiet. The settlers were more afraid of the Chinese than they were of the Indians. Finally they decided they could get along very well without the Chinese who were very superstitious, so it was an easy task for the settlers to scare them out. The settlers could not get along nearly so well with the Chinamen gone as they did while they were here. There seems to be a difference of opinion as to when this happened, some say 1884 and others say in 1887.

As it was a two days' trip to Coquille, the settlers had to do without a doctor. One day a child fell and cut her leg quite badly. Her father sewed the cut up with silk thread. She still has the crossed scar.

The country was full of bears and other wild animals, and one night when Mrs. Wagner heard her pigs squealing as if they were badly frightened, she ran to the pig pen. An old pig ran by, stirring up so much dust she could scarcely see the old bear, which also ran by with a young pig in his mouth.

The first business buildings built were on the North side. Ross's store was the first store built in Powers.

After the railroad was finished in the fall of 1914, the South Side began to grow. There seems to be a difference of opinion as to the nature of this side before any buildings were built there. Some say it was marshy in the winter time and had to be drained before the town could begin, others say the site might have had a little water on it in the winter, but it never had to be drained.

After 1914, the Coos Bay Lumber Company began hauling their logs over the railroad.

In 1916, the bank began and the "big" school building was completed. The post office was moved from Tom Hayes' to Powers. All of the old Main Street was burned in 1923. Then it was moved one block east and has since grown to its present appearance. So Powers has grown from the "North Caroline Settlement" to a small town.

Mildred Nylander interviewed T. S. Zimmerman:

Powers in the early days was just a cow pasture. In 1915, "Pinky" Mathews built the first house in the town section across from where the depot now stands. Meanwhile he and his wife lived in a tent. Later the depot, company warehouse, pool hall, and hotel were built.

Mr. A. H. Powers, general manager of the Smith-Powers Logging Company, carried out the scheme of a town to give the working man a chance to own his own home. This idea was different from most of the companies that built houses and rented them to the workers.

The first school was located by Hayes' ranch. It was a small poorly equipped building, which is now used for a barn.

In 1915, mail came up on logging trains. Mr. Zimmerman, the timekeeper of the company, acted as postmaster. The post office was established in the latter part of 1915, with Gus A. Brown as first postmaster. Prior to the time of the connection line from Portland and Marshfield, mail came in by the Coos Bay Wagon Road from Roseburg.

The first passenger train arrived in Powers on May 1, 1915, with about four or five hundred people from the Bay.

Many of the old settlers have passed away, others moved out of town, while some of them still live in Powers. George Stewart, "Pinky" Mathews, T. S. Zimmerman, Charlie Fesler, George Laingor, Fred and Albert Powers, John and Thomas Hayes, Frank Morris, and Ed Ladell are some of the early pioneers.

Millard Hubbard, the male historian, picked out an oldtimer and used a page to introduce him. This page is omitted so that the interview starts with what the old man said:

When we came here the only inhabitants were old man Bingham, Wiggins, and Wagner. We made a trip back to Myrtle Creek, 20 miles south of Roseburg to Eveline's Mill for flour. We got our start of cattle by driving 40 head in for three of these farmers. We got these cattle from Berry "Happy" Wyland's grandfather.

Our main supply of meat came from the elk. I think there were more elk at this time than there are cattle now. We rendered tallow for candles and dried meat for winter. My mother cooked on a dutch oven or open fireplace and hung her kettles on a lubber pole.

That year I heard my first coyote yell and killed my first game which was a grouse I killed with a rock.

I also earned my first dime. Old man Bingham offered me a dime if I 'd follow him around all day and whistle. At two o'clock he gave me a dime to quit whistling.

At the end, Millard Hubbard satisfied the reader's long suspense by adding this:

As he sat there thinking of his past life, that I could tell by the far away look in his eyes, I thought it would be an appropriate time to butt in and ask his name. I had heard it several different ways, so I kindly asked him.

He replied:

Many folks have mistaken my name because of the pronunciation. They call me "Old Bill Netherly" but my name really isn't pronounced that way. My name is W. B. Neathery.

Brookings

Brookings had its name recorded as a post office on June 4, 1913, when John N. Thornton became its postmaster, followed in 1917 by George D. Wood. The town apparently received its name from the Brookings Lumber Company, which began operations there about that time. The company built a large sawmill, extended a railroad into the redwood section of northern California, shipped its lumber by steamers that anchored close to shore. Loading was done by means of a cable stretched from shore to ship

With the depression of the lumber market, after World War I, the mill was closed and never reopened.

Brookings seemed destined to become one of the ghost towns of the coast. But a few faithful people hopefully held on, as the Brookings locality has always been a beautiful and specially pleasant spot, with a climate that seems to say: "Come, abide with me!"

One who responded to that call was Tony Olsen. Before coming to work in the Brookings saw mill, he had been interested in flowers; he had grown bulbs as a hobby. At his bachelor home just south of the Chetco River, near Harbor, Tony planted some flowers along with his vegetables. The bulbs responded to the soil and the climate and to his loving care. They grew and flowered; the bulbs multiplied. Tony couldn't throw them away; he gave them to neighbors and friends and planted others.

Tony Olsen tells a story about one of the results of his early bulb-growing experiences. A woman living in the neighborhood said to her neighbors, "He can't eat the bulbs, he can't feed them to stock, he can't sell them. What better evidence do you want to prove that he is crazy."

But Tony persisted. He found some distant markets and managed to sell a few of his bulbs. Whether he was the first bulb-grower in the community, is not certain. At least he was one of the pioneers. He had learned the business from the ground up, with all its ramifications. Today, Tony Olsen, though not one of the biggest, is one of the most substantial bulb-growers of the vicinity.

By the middle 1940's, the bulb business was zooming skyward. Many people went "bust;" but bulbs and cut flowers, under careful and studied management, helped to bring prosperity to Brookings.

On July 10, 1951, residents of Brookings decided for city incorporation by a vote of 153 to 85. Brookings postmasters beginning when the office was established on June 4, 1913, to and including 1951, are as follows: John H. Thornton, four years; George D. Wood, twenty years; Goldie V. Smith, fourteen years.

Brookings has a twin — Harbor over in the Chetco's south bank. It has 13 business telephones to Brookings' 73. The newspaper, published by Dewey Aker, is called the *Brookings-Harbor Pilot*.

Curry County Post Offices

Mail service of a sort reached into the most remote sections of Curry County. Many of the post offices have been discontinued.

Name	Established	Discontinued	Postmaster
Bennett	1883	1884	John R. Miller
Bagnell	1894	1895	Ary Bennett
Blain	1891	1891	Eliza Woodruff
Chetco*	1863	1910	Augustus F. Miller, 1863; Henry Simons, 1869; Robert Moore, 1870; Thomas Van Pelt, 1871; Jeanette Cooley, 1873; Miller Cooley, 1875; Henry M. Cooley, 1886; Frederick G. Blake, 1888; Frederick H. Blake, 1889; Ida Cooley, 1905; James A. Cooley, 1906
Corbin	1901	1910	Richard D. Jones, 1901; Charles R. Wilson, 1901; Samuel R. Dartt, 1902; Dietrich Quellen, 1905
Cumtux	1895	1895	Henry P. Moore
Ellensburg**			
Eckley***			
Elkridge	1902	1903	James R. Hall
Esoms	1899	1899	Geo. W. Billings
Gray	1884	1887	Loftin Gray
Fern	1888	1888	John Sedgwich

Name	Established	Discontinued	Postmaster
Hare	1898	1913	Joseph Hare, 1898; Frank H. Strain, 1908; George Heebler, 1911
Illahe	1895	1943	Elijah H. Price, 1895; James James R. Hall, 1898; Ellen Fry, 1902; E. R. Russell, 1905; Eliza H. Price, 1908; Lewis Hostetler, 1914; Rose Meservey, 1914; Bessie Billings, 1915; George W. Meservey, 1918
Lakeport	1910	1915	Emil Berg, 1910; Richard Walker, 1911; Helen M. Walker, 1913
Moore	1902	1902	Charles M. Neil
Newcastle****	1879	1916	Joseph Haines, 1897; George Martin, 1908; Charles W. Haines, 1908; Hugh C. Hamilton, 1911; Charles H. Bramley, 1915
Pistol River	1927	1930	Richard E. Guthridge
Quosaton	1895	1895	George W. Meservey
Ragic	1898	1900	John H. McElhaney, 1898; Elvin R. Miller, 1900
Sandstone	1890	1891	Annie J. Blacklock
Seaforth	1890	1892	Robert McKenzie
Triangle	1914	1916	Elinor Lehnherr
Winchuck	1917	1918	Beulah McKeiser

* Chetco business transferred to Harbor post office nearby.
** Name changed to Gold Beach in 1890.
*** First established as Newcastle.
**** Changed to Tell Tale and then to Eckley in 1883.

The nature of early-day mail carrying in southern Curry County has been described by H. T. Stewart:

Charles Dewey was mail carrier. He made a round trip once a week between Port Orford and Crescent City. The trail followed ridges over the highest mountains and crossed all streams without bridges. There were ferries at Rogue and Chetco rivers, but otherwise it was ford or swim the many swift streams that came tumbling into the Pacific along the route. Horses that were trained to swim carried their riders and the mail with surprising safety. The mail pouch was held aloft and kept dry during winter storms when streams were high and swimming necessary, but after one such experience the carriers rode the rest of the day soaked from the waist down.

10

Ghost Towns

Randolph

Gold was discovered at the mouth of Whiskey Run in the winter of 1852-1853. Before long a camp had sprung up along the beach. Sober citizens soon began calling the place Randolph. The camp grew rapidly. Each day saw the arrival of new miners. Before spring, storekeepers were weighing out flour, sugar, and coffee. Miners, up from the sluices on the beach, warmed chilled bones in improvised saloons, the steam from their sodden garments mingling with the reek of whiskey, wood smoke and kerosene. Along the beach, honeycombed by the workings of the miners, at the mouth of the creek that is still called Whiskey Run, against a somber background of densely-wooded hills, sprawled the town, a jumble of board and log houses with shake roofs, stone and mud chimneys, oiled-paper windows, and puncheon floors. Pack mules floundered deep in the mud of the streets . . .

Randolph-the-First (there were others) was short lived. A terriffic storm that lashed the coast in the spring of 1854 obliterated most of the gold-bearing black sands, burying sluice-boxes and shafts under dunes of prosaic gray grit. While miners loafed, waiting for the sea to sweep the worthless sand away, a prospector, later known as "Coarse-Gold Johnson," made another find on a southern tributary of the Coquille. The stampede to the new diggings half emptied Randolph over night.

Randolph just faded away. But it left a name known as the Randolph Trail, leading out of Empire, through the heavy coastal timber and shrubbery, crossing sloughs and gullies, following ridges, always in a southerly direction through a country now commonly referred to as the Seven Devils, ending at the gold diggings on the beaches north of Coquille River.

But the name of Randolph was not forgotten. On the 18th day of August, 1859, it was recorded in the annals of the National Archives in Washington, D. C., as a post office, with George Wasson as the postmaster, followed by John Hamblock on April 20, 1863.

It must be concluded from these records that Randolph was still a swaddling youth, not yet settled down. George Wasson was associated with Stacy and Fundy in the sawmill at the present Fahy farm home near Bullards Ferry: Hamblock, who became postmaster in 1863, was located where the Bullards Ferry now crosses the river. The old-time post offices moved about from place to place according to the residence of the postmaster. So Randolph moved from Whiskey Run to Fahy Farm and then Bullards Ferry: (Randolph-the-second and Randolph-the-third.)

Adam Pershbaker had established a store on the north bank of the Coquille some two or three miles up stream from the Bullards Ferry. On December 7, 1871, he became the Randolph postmaster. Here, then, was the final resting place where the wandering Randolph settled down. In Randolph-the-Fourth business flourished for more than 20 years. People moved in and settled around the store. It became a central location for commercial fishermen. The whistles of the river steamers were heard several times each day as passengers and freight came and went. A school was established.

In the early 1890's the business in the Pershbaker store began to fall off. Three miles down the river, on the south bank, a new place was springing up — ship yards, sawmills, and a fish cannery. With barges and a river steamer, Pershbaker loaded up all his possessions and moved to the new location, where he set up his store, established a post office, naming it Prosper, with himself as the first postmaster.

Thus, when Pershbaker left, he took with him practically everything except the name of Randolph, which still clings to the place to this day. The post office was discontinued on August 22, 1893, just two weeks after Pershbaker had received his appointment in the new office at Prosper.

Even the channel on the Randolph side of the island in the river has gradually filled and has ceased to be the main waterway for river traffic, open only to small boats. The name of Randolph, established in the very beginning of Coos County history, may soon celebrate its one-hundredth anniversary. But as a municipality it must be put down merely as a ghost-town.

Coal Mine Ghosts

Among our ghost-towns of today, there were several given premature birth by the very promising prosperity offered by the vast beds of coal.

Following successes of early coal mines, ever alert exploiters flocked in, anxious to get in on the ground floor. They succeeded in interesting men of means who were anxious to risk their capital in new enterprises. The result was a considerable portion of the ghost towns of today.

One-time promising communities, which today are mere memories, include Libby, Beaver Hill, Caledonia, Henryville, Utter City.

Libby

Libby, originally known as New Port, was the scene of the Flanagan and Mann coal mines, with store, school and homes for the miners and their families. It took the name of Libby when a post office was established on June 6, 1890, with Enoch Gore as postmaster. After Flanagan and Mann sold out about 1885, the mines continued with more or less success for nearly half a century. But as a center, Libby petered out and was finally absorbed as a residential section or suburb of the city of Coos Bay.

Beaver Hill

Beaver Hill, the most noteworthy of all our present-day ghost towns, being the only one to attain the status of an incorporated city, is so completely wiped out that no trace of it remains today to indicate where it once thrived.

Beaver Hill was in the center of one of Coos County's richest and most extensive coal fields, was located roughly in the headwaters of Beaver Slough.

Oddly enough, as an incorporated city, it never had a post office. No other incorporated city in this area lived through three decades without having an established post office. Some older residents insist that Beaver Hill did have a post office. But they fail to submit any substantiating evidence. It is not listed in the records of all Coos and Curry post offices, beginning with Port Orford in 1855 to about 1930. Inquiry by letter to the National Archives, Washington, D. C., confirms the evidence that Beaver Hill did not have a post office.

In its heyday, Beaver Hill was a lively coal mining town, changing its status to a city on January 11, 1896. The poll book showed 85 registered voters, all voting for incorporation except one. Hugh Cross was elected mayor; J. L. Parker, recorder; and Daniel Richards marshal.

James H. Flanagan said that Beaver Hill was reached by —

> A spur track, mostly on piling, built to the mine from the main line of the Coos Bay, Roseburg and Eastern Railway & Navigation Co., a distance of a mile and a half. Extensive improvements were installed — a large store, miners' dwellings, a bunkhouse, a cookhouse, bunkers, separation plane, hoisting machinery.

Mail was brought in on the company's train to the store and distributed.

About 1920, with the coal market waning, the mine was permanently closed; the people moved out. When a vote was called in 1926 to disincorporate the city, only 16 voters could be mustered. All except one voted to disincorporate. Today no trace remains of the city of Beaver Hill. The story of the Beaver Hill coal mine appears in another chapter.

Caledonia

On Isthmus Inlet there were several centers that once gave promise of becoming thriving towns.

First, Caledonia. Though opened up as a coal mine, it never made a great deal of progress. Several families settled there and the houses remained until well within the memory of present-day residents. A few new houses now occupy the place.

Henryville

Eight miles beyond Coos Bay, on the east bank of Isthmus Inlet, was Henryville, a pretentious undertaking, launched with good intentions, based on the prospects of coal outcroppings. Somebody's money went into the ground — hundreds of dollars — tunnels, trestles, bunkers, docks, houses for the men and their families — money sunk. Henryville even had a post office, established January 28, 1875, with Steven D. Megeath as postmaster. A year, two months and ten days later, the post office was discontinued. The tunnels, the trestles, the bunkers, the buildings remained. A keeper, Matt Bowron, was in charge for many years, remaining there with his family up to about 1913, when the place was abandoned.

Henryville may still be seen in the form of rotted and tumble-down pilings, the remains of the old bunker, trestles and docks, on the east side of Isthmus Inlet, eight miles from Central Avenue in Coos Bay on Highway 101, on the way to Coquille.

Utter City

A mile beyond Henryville, nine miles from Central Avenue in Coos Bay, lies the ghost of one-time very promising Utter City. It was located at the head of deep water navigation on Isthmus Inlet, deep enough for ocean-going vessels. From Utter City a railroad extended over the divide five miles to Carbondale, the mine that was to supply coal for shipment to San Francisco.

At Utter City, besides the coal bunkers, docks, residences, and warehouses, was a hotel, large and pretentious for its time and place. A post office had been established in the neighborhood with the name of Isthmus, December 11, 1871, with Gilbert Hall as postmaster. On February 11, 1875, the name of the office was changed to Utter City, with Gilbert Hall continuing as postmaster, until he was succeeded by Zachery T. Siglin, June 26, 1876. The office was discontinued on June 22, 1880.

Utter City was the scene of much activity for several years during the latter part of the 1870's. As an industrial undertaking, like many of the hastily-engineered coal mine ventures, it proved a flop. More is told of Utter City in the chapter on coal mines.

Incidentally, the Utter City hotel, after being closed, was loaded on two large barges and floated down the bay to Empire to replace Mrs. Jackson's Pioneer Hotel, which had been destroyed by fire sometime in the 1880's.

Coos City

Coos City was not a coal mining town. It was the original terminus of the old Coos Bay Wagon Road from Roseburg, a stopping place, hotel, stables for horses, landing for the boats that met the traffic and mail for Marshfield, North Bend and Empire. A post office was established on June 25, 1873, with Henry A. Costan as postmaster. Other postmasters that followed were Fred Jarvis, Ferdinand Hirschfeld, James M. Arrington, Douglas J. McLaughlin. The office was discontinued on March 18, 1884. In the meantime, a ferry had been established across the inlet and the road continued to Marshfield. Sumner, too, being located at the head of navigation on Catching Inlet, took part of the traffic from the Coos Bay Wagon Road. From Sumner another branch of the road led to Bay City (the present Eastside), with a board walk and a boat landing for crossing the bay to Marshfield. Much of the traffic being diverted from Coos City, that place lost much of its early importance and ceased to bid for a place as a city.

However, with the present development of the Al Pierce saw mill, Coos City seems destined once more to be revived.

Glasgow

There were some semi-sucker-bait towns. They might have had some future possibilities — the *natural location for a trans-continental railroad terminal* located on the bay — where "Rail Meets Sail." Usually two or three good size buildings were constructed — a warehouse, a store, a hotel, perhaps a bank. Pictures of these with a map of the town were sent to agents in various parts of the country. And the suckers bought lots.

Such a town was Glasgow. It was platted in the early nineties. A few buildings were erected and a dock at the edge of the channel of Coos Bay, connected by a long planked approach. Some lots were sold. But people tired of waiting for the railroad. The town failed to grow. Lots reverted to the county for unpaid taxes.

For nearly 30 years Glasgow slept on. Sometime in the early 1920's "Happy" Hoffmeister moved in with a flock of goats. The Oregon Coast Highway was under construction, with Glasgow as its terminus on the north side of Coos Bay. About 1925 Coos County established a ferry service across the bay, connecting Glasgow with North Bend. The *Roosevelt,* a side-wheel steam ferry, capable of carrying about a dozen cars, made a trip about once an hour during daylight in the summer months. Roads were too muddy for winter travel.

People began to buy lots from the county. The usual price was about $25 per lot, lots that had originally sold for $200 or more. Mrs. M. G. Coleman set up a lunch counter, together with candies and soft drinks, thus starting the first business revival. The North Bayside Grange built its large hall in Glasgow in 1928. In that same year the Oregon Highway Commission took over the county-owned *Roosevelt* and added the *Oregon* in 1929. J. C. McCulloch and family, as well as other families, were establishing their permanent homes. And so the ghost-town of Glasgow came back to life. It is one of the thriving little residential hamlets today.

In 1915 two hikers along the Curry County coast, crossed the Flores Creek bridge and took a side road to the west. In about three miles they ascended a low, sandy hill and looked over what was once and briefly the metropolis of a big county — the ghost town of Lakeport.

Its sandy street was hummocky and bunched with grass, the walks were lined with bushes, its suburbs were overgrown with tangled herbage, the brown and weathered buildings leaned drunkenly, the single telephone wire sagged between the poles.

Down a cross street from Main Street was a three-story building, still upright on its foundations — the Lakeport Hotel.

The travelers proceeded there to be received by Jim Murphy, old and rheumatic, who said they could stay and stay for free. Just go up and take any room they pleased. The pair who had been sleeping out under the heavens on their blankets, picked the deluxest room there was. It had a heavy carpet, a thickly-mattressed bed, and eider down quilts, very fine in all its appointments but rather dusty. The two unpaying guests went down to the end of the hall where there was a stack of linen some feet high, just as it had been put there after being laundered six years before. They dug down deep into the pile and took four sheets and four pillow cases — for one bed, not for two. They put two sheets over them and two under, and dressed each pillow with two cases. They were thus protected well enough from all the chamber's dusty luxury.

They soon learned that Jim Murphy was the only remaining resident of Lakeport. The day before there had been three. Two had quarreled and one had killed the other.

The two hikers were tyro journalists. They walked to Langlois and wired the *Journal* and *Oregonian*, asking if these papers wanted them to cover the Lakeport murder. The papers wired back that they did.

So the hikers cooked their food on the hotel's big stove

and occupied their fine quarters while the sheriff and his deputies from Gold Beach organized a posse to find the vanished murderer in the wilderness surrounding Flores Lake and Lakeport. Each morning they walked to Langlois to give the telephone girl there the story for the *Journal;* each evening they sent the one for the *Oregonian.* They headed their dispatches "WITH THE POSSE AT LAKEPORT."

They stayed in Lakeport three days and then felt they had to get on with their hike, though it meant leaving the murderer still unfound and all their readers in suspense. They carried away with them a history of the town, received on the ground without much in the way of confirming record except the faded hotel register. At the beginning in 1908 the pages were filled with signatures of persons from various towns of the Pacific Northwest. Then abruptly they became very thin. In August of 1909 there was an entire week when no one registered. After this the clerk began to invent guests and soberly to put them down in the book, very prominent ones like Jack Dempsey and William Howard Taft. Finally, under date of Thursday, November 6, 1909, he made this entry, "Not a dam sole." It was the hotel's and the town's obituary.

The idea which gave birth to Lakeport on Flores Lake did indeed sound good. Between the lake and the ocean was a narrow ridge of sand. The lake itself was 25 square miles and very deep. Dig a canal and, lo, there would be the finest fresh water harbor all up and down the coast. Room aplenty for ships from the seven seas.

No wonder that twenty blocks were laid out, that a sawmill was put up with a capacity of 60,000 feet a day, that on the payrolls in the town in 1908-1909 were 200 men. Many residences sprang up. Business buildings lined both sides of Main Street. There was a newspaper and there was the three-story hotel with its excellent accommodations. Agents were stationed in various Oregon and Washington towns and cities to sell lots. In Lakeport's heyday there was a population of 400.

After the town had reached such robust proportions

an appalling fact was discovered. When permission was finally secured from the Federal government to construct the canal across the narrow strip of sand between the ocean and Flores Lake, it was found that the lake was higher than the ocean. The canal would simply drain the lake dry.

That discovery ended Lakeport.

Until a few years ago there were a few moldering relics. In a recent clearing of the area none is left. In 1949 one of the hikers revisited the place. He couldn't make out where the hotel had stood, where even the town had been. A nearby resident had to show him.

Not till some weeks later did the hiker pair learn that the remorseful murderer had drowned himself in deep Flores Lake.

11

Pioneer Merchants

THREE CURRY STORES *By H. T. Stewart*

EARLY-DAY GENERAL MERCHANDISING STORES in central and southern Curry County were conducted in the face of many handicaps.

Three of the pioneer stores were those of Riley & Stewart at Ellensburg; Raleigh Scott at Mountain Ranch (now Delmar Colgrove's place); and Seth Blake of Chetco.

The earliest and largest of these stores was that of Riley & Stewart, at Ellensburg, now Gold Beach. It dates back to the late 60's. Merchandise in the early days of this store, particularly in winter months, was at times brought in by pack-train from Crescent City, California, a distance of 65 or 70 miles. Later as the firm expanded its activities by engaging in the fishing and sawmill business, a small schooner, the *Alaska,* was bought and thereafter made regular trips between Ellensburg and San Francisco. Within a few years the *Alaska* was wrecked at the entrance to the Rogue River. In 1876 this business was sold to R. D. Hume.

The store kept by Raleigh Scott was near what is now the highest point in the Coast Highway 101, about 25 miles south of Rogue River. Some of his merchandise came by way of Crescent City, and some was landed at Mack's Arch — a sheltered cove called by most old-timers, Arch Rock. There was no settlement near this store and its trade came from ranchers living for miles round about.

Seth Blake, a southern Curry pioneer, for many years kept a general merchandise store at the location of the old Chetco post office about two miles south of Chetco River. Here, because of the earlier opening of wagon roads and proximity to the harbor of Crescent City, the transportation problem was not so acute. After Mr. Blake's death, his son, Fred Blake, continued the store for a number of years.

These merchants were all prominent in the early political history and development of their sections of Curry County. Among many other activities, Riley, Stewart and Scott, all represented Curry County in the Oregon legislature, while Blake took a leading part in local affairs. Their general merchandise stores were all that the word *general* implied. Patent medicine and food products vied with hardware as best sellers. Star chewing tobacco ran smoking tobacco a close race in popularity. Prices were low where the cost of transportation was not excessive. Wages also were low, as indicated by notes of men working for a dollar a day. All trading was done with San Francisco. Credit was quite general, but the loss from bad accounts was exceptionally low.

In the Rogue River section, beach mining was of considerable importance. The firm of Riley & Stewart handled much of this gold for the miners. The usual procedure was to retort the amalgum and send the gold to the U. S. mint at San Francisco, where it was coined and returned largely in $20 pieces. This beach mining section lay almost entirely along the coast from Cape Blanco south to Pistol River.

THE WOLCOTTS, *Port Orford, Randolph, Riverton, Marshfield*

In few cases in Coos and Curry have father and son continued in the merchandise business continuously for more than 70 years — from the late sixties to 1944.

Allen D.Wolcott, ex-school teacher, came to Marshfield in the late sixties. John Pershbaker and associates had started a saw mill and store in 1867. When Mr. Wolcott arrived some time later, he became the bookkeepr for that firm.

In the early seventies Wolcott is found at Port Orford.

In the official records his name appears as postmaster there from 1872 to 1882. In the Curry County assessment roll of 1875 he is listed among the 20 largest taxpayers. In the *Port Orford Post,* Curry County's first newspaper, in the issue of September 30, 1880, was the following display advertisement:

A. D. WOLCOTT, Dealer in GENERAL MERCHANDISE

Dry Goods, Groceries, Hardware, Drugs.

In the meantime, in 1877, he married Miss Annie Lowe, said to have been the first white girl born in the Coquille Valley, the daughter of Judge and Mrs. David Lowe, prominent pioneers. Three sons were born to the Wolcotts: Herbert E., Chester W., and Dwight O.

After disposing of his business at Port Orford in the eighties, Mr. Wolcott moved with his family to Randolph, where he took charge of the Pershbaker Store, which had been established apparently in the sixties by Charles M. Pershbaker; and was taken over upon his death by his brother, Adam Pershbaker.

As Adam Pershbaker had various interests and activities, he placed Wolcott in charge of his store at Randolph, to which busy little center came fishermen, farmers from up the river, and gold miners from the black sands in the Whiskey Run and Seven Devils region. However, with the dwindling of the gold mining operations and with the greater activities down the river on the opposite bank at the new place known as Prosper, Adam Pershbaker decided to concentrate his business there, along with his sawmill and ship yard.

With a large river barge, he loaded his entire movable Randolph holdings — "lock, stock and barrel" — store building, stock of merchandise, fixtures, furniture, and even the warehouse cat. All were put onto the barge at high tide and moved three miles down and across the river to Prosper.

Wolcott remained with him for a while, then went to Riverton, where for a time he operated a small sawmill and a general store.

In the latter part of the nineties, Wolcott moved to

Marshfield, where he was in charge of the Wells Fargo office and kept books for Henry Sengstacken. Around the turn of the century, he assisted for a while in the latter days of the old E. B. Dean & Company store.

About this time he decided to retire. But when he saw an opportunity in the passing of the old Nasburg & Hirst business, he felt the urge once more to get into harness. Andrew Nasburg had long since passed on. Thomas Hirst who had conducted the business for many years, was now in his sunset days. He had tried to bring up and train his adopted son, Milton, to take over the reins. But Milton didn't seem to "take to" the business.

So Wolcott moved in. He put on a clean-up sale. He sold out the drygoods by auction. On October 4, 1902, he bought out the remainder of the Thomas Hirst merchandise business, and set up a grocery business for his son, Chester W. Wolcott. The father remained until Chester could assume full responsibility as owner.

From here on, the business was that of Chester W. Wolcott. He continued in the Nasburg & Hirst building on North Front Street, for fourteen years.

With the coming of the railroad, passing through the entire length of Front Street, much of the business of the town was shifting in a southern and westerly direction. In keeping with the trend, Chester W. Wolcott moved his business to Market and Broadway, later to Second and Commercial, and finally he rented space in the Union Market, which at that time was owned and operated by Cliff Ruscher. In that last place he continued until 1944, when he sold out and retired from the grocery business, which had occupied his time for 42 years. His father had started in Marshfield in the later sixties or early seventies. Together, father and son — Allen D. and Chester W. Wolcott — cover a period of more than seventy years in the history of Coos and Curry counties — a period of many changes in the grocery business as well as in many other lines of activity.

Pioneer Hardware Store, *Marshfield*

The Coast Mail, in 1903 carried the following story:

One of the largest and most attractive stores in Coos Bay district is the hardware store conducted by Eugene O'Connell. Here can be found a complete line of general hardware consisting of paints, oils, varnishes, fishing tackle, sporting goods, glass ware, crockery, stoves, doors, windows, guns, rifles, revolvers and ammunition. The proprietor is one of the most conservative buyers and consequently can sell goods at a price which will astonish the most economic housewife.

Mr. O'Connell is an old resident of Marshfield and one of the most influential citizens.

The earlier history of this store is a matter of memory. Present-day residents whose recollections reach back to the early 1880's say that Mr. O'Connell was the first owner. As a young man he had worked for H. P. Whitney, who conducted a meat market and grocery store in Marshfield and one in Empire. Whitney had a slaughter house on the bay front, midway between Marshfield and North Bend. He bought cattle in all parts of Coos County, driving and scowing them to his central location, which was commonly known as Centerville.

It may have been sometime in the early 1880's that O'Connell, with the financial backing of Mr. Whitney, entered the hardware business on Front Street in Marshfield. Some reports say that the store had been started by a man named Saunders. Others say that he merely worked as a clerk for O'Connell.

In 1904 the business was incorporated, with the following persons as stockholders and coworkers: Eugene O'Connell, Frank Hague, E. K. Jones. The store was sold in 1908, 1919, 1936, 1946.

The Pioneer Hardware Store has been in its present location on South Broadway since 1932.

Henry Sengstacken, *Marshfield*

Sengstacken was not merely the name of an individual in Coos County for half a century. Sengstacken was an institution — a large-scale merchant; head Wells Fargo in Marshfield for many years; he was agent for a number of steamship lines plying in and out of Coos Bay; he conducted a real estate office; he established and maintained the Title Guarantee and Abstract Company; he represented insurance companies; he built and operated a salmon canneries and a match factory.

Perhaps no other resident of Coos County dealt in real estate to the extent that Henry Sengstacken did. At the time of his death in 1922, it was reported that he owned thousands of acres of land besides many town lots in different parts of the county.

Much of his land contained both standing and down fire-killed Port Orford cedar used for match wood and railroad ties. An unemployed man would call on Sengstacken; if willing to make ties and match wood, Sengstacken would stake him — supply him with tools, working clothes, grub, and even materials for building a shack if needed. And if he peeled cascara bark he could sell that also to Sengstacken, as well as furs of coons, mink, otter and other animals.

It has been said that a person could buy or sell anything through Sengstacken. A story is told that two men were discussing the matter. One of the men said he could stump him. A bet was made between the two men. They went to Mr. Sengstacken. The one who was to stump him, said, "Mr. Sengstacken, I would like to buy a church pulpit."

"All right," said Mr. Sengstacken. "I have just what you want. When the church was closed in Empire after the county seat was changed to Coquille, I bought the property. I'll give you a bargain on the pulpit."

Henry Sengstacken was born in Germany, June 12, 1851; came to San Francisco in 1865; worked for his uncle, Claus Spreckels, the future sugar king; graduated from Heald's Business College. He came to Coos Bay in 1874; he established the Utter City Commercial Company at Utter City; next moved to Empire, where he operated a general merchandise store, including drugs. While continuing that store, he set up another one in

Marshfield in 1879, where he made his home and from where he carried on his business for more than forty years.

In 1884, Henry Sengstacken married Lillian Lockhart. Two children were born: Alton, who died some years ago; Genevieve, who lives in Marshfield, a librarian in the town where she was born. Mrs. Sengstacken died in 1892. Some years later, Mr. Sengstacken married Agnes Ruth Lockhart. One daughter was born, Doris, now Mrs. L. H. Brinkman, residing in California.

PIONEER COQUILLE MERCHANTS *By Lans Leneve*

In the year of 1892 a disastrous fire swept Coquille's entire business section. The fire started in the Olive Hotel and burned to the ground every business establishment.

My grandfather, the late Dr. S. L. Leneve and my father, the late John W. Leneve, lost all their business holdings in that raging conflagration. In view of this latter fact I trust that I may be forgiven for selecting my father as an early merchant of Coquille — for such he was.

However, in passing, I should like to quote from memory the names of other merchants of that early period. At that time, Henry Lorenz, now deceased, was engaged in the general merchandising business, as was the late George and Annie Robinson. Dud Johnson, long since deceased, conducted a meat market but known in those days as strictly "a butcher shop." The Long Brothers dealt in harness. There was a Japanese merchant by the name of Joe Kanamatz. Incidentally he was the only Oriental ever to conduct a business enterprise at Coquille.

R. S. Knowlton, as well as my grandad, owned and operated a drug store — the only difference being the fact that Grandad practised medicine along with the drug business. Prior to the fire my Dad was associated with his father as a pharmacist, filling the prescriptions that Dr. S. L. prescribed for his patients.

J. A. Lamb dealt in hardware. Doc Dean published

the weekly *Herald.* J. P. Tupper was proprietor of the hotel. There were the Murray and Little Livery Stables; Fred Slagle, the tailor; I. B. Fox, dealer in second hand goods; the Tuttle Hotel; Mrs. Moon's Millinery Store.

It was the day of the saloon and four of them did a flourishing business — The Baxter Bros., the Lone Star Saloon, a Mr. Gilkey being the owner; Beckett's saloon and a bar in the Tupper Hotel. There was the confectionery store conducted by Mr. and Mrs. W. C. Rose which also housed the local telephone exchange, and the two jewelry stores owned by the late B. R. Wilson, and W. H. Schroeder.

I am drawing strictly upon my early memory regarding the above and trust that I may be pardoned for omitting other business enterprises. And, oh, yes, I almost forgot to mention George "Josh" Leach's little establishment of confections and soft drinks and "Mother" Wickman's Hotel and Hark Dunham's Pool Hall.

Now let us visit my Dad's general merchandise store — a store typical of that early period. The stock consisted of a complete line of groceries, dry goods, shoes and clothing, and of various other articles too numerous to mention. Anything that was not upon the shelves was cheerfully ordered for any customer.

In those days the traveling salesman's role was a tough one. He would come by rail from San Francisco or Portland to Roseburg and from there to Coquille by stage (horse stage), taking the greater part of two days for the trip between Roseburg and Coquille. It was a long time between calls and Pop (my Dad), used to buy an entire car load of flour at a single order. Coffee was purchased in bulk — whole grain coffee — and would arrive in barrelled 100-pound shipments. Pop specialized on Hill's Bros. Coffee. Customer's orders were scooped from the huge barrel, deposited in a big hand grinder and ground before being delivered. It sold for 25 cents per pound. A 100-pound sack of flour seldom sold for over a dollar per sack. Fresh eggs varied in price from 10 to 25 cents a dozen and butter from 25 to 35 cents per pound. A fine blue serge man's suit could be purchased for $15. Rubber hip boots brought from $3 to $4 per pair. Kid's Buster Brown high top shoes sold for $2.50 a pair. For $4 or $5 the swankiest men and ladies dress shoes could be purchased. Work shoes could be had for the price of $2 to $4, and men's hats were sold at prices ranging from $1 up to $3.50.

Syrup and molasses were drawn from huge barrels by the merchant. It was not syrup that poured like water from a container as does present day syrup; but rich, thick syrup that often tried one's patience, it poured so slowly.

A large barrel of crackers was kept close enough to the old pot-bellied stove to always insure their crispness and flavor and most cookies and candies were sold by bulk.

There was a huge vault that contained a fairly large sized safe that was located at the back of Pop's store. It was the only one of its kind in Coquille and as there were no banks in those days Pop was called upon quite frequently to put the pokes of various customers within the walls of the vault. The creamery that operated one mile up the river from the town used to accumulate fairly large sums; these funds were entrusted to Pop each month and placed in the vault. It was mostly gold coins in those days. At times there was as high as four and five thousand dollars of gold reposing in that old vault.

There was something about an old country town store that can never be duplicated in this modern age — an air of downright friendliness and real, old Western hospitality. What is known to the trade today as a "gyper" was seldom encountered. Then too there was that certain intriguing odor — the scent of bulk spices, such as cinnamon, the aroma of fresh ground coffee forever lingering there.

It was a fascinating spot in which to shop and within which to visit. It had an atmosphere all its own and one that will never again be found in any business establishment. It went its way along with the old horse and buggy, the old river boats, the plank streets and the cherished landmarks that have passed us by.

Nicholas Lorenz *Coquille*

Nicholas Lorenz and his wife (Caroline Bohn), both German born, had six children – Henry N.; Francis George; Charles Fred; Emma Pauline; Edward W.; and Edna C.

In 1887, he came to Coquille, leased the ground floor of the Odd Fellow's Building, and put in a large stock of general merchandise. He later built a large storebuilding on Front Street, where the business was carried on for several years. During this period, the elder Lorenz retired and Henry, who had worked in the store since it was established, took control. When the new Odd Fellow's Building was constructed on First Street, Henry moved his store there. In 1941 he retired. His son, Fred E. with his wife Ruth D. Lorenz, succeeded to the business.

The Lorenz Department Store, one of Coos County's finest, under a continuous ownership and management of father to son to grandson, since September, 1887, is the oldest concern in Coos County – fitting monument to the industry and integrity of this well-known Coquille family.

The Breuer Store *Myrtle Point*

Sale of the pioneer Breuer Store was the occasion for the *Myrtle Point Herald* on July 5, 1951, to review the establishment's history and to mention the two others which with it made the oldest three:

Announcement is made this week that Paul Breuer has sold his interests in the Breuer store, among Myrtle Point's oldest business firms, to his son-in-law and daughter, Mr. and Mrs. Ben Daniels.

The Breuer store was established long prior to the turn of the century and is numbered among three of Myrtle Point's oldest business establishments. Mr. Samuel Breuer, Paul's father, was the original owner. Mr. Breuer died in 1941, and was one of the men responsible for the incorporation of the City of Myrtle Point. Paul was 12 years old when he started helping his father manufacture new boots and shoes by hand, made to measure, and has had an active part in the business since that time. Recalling his early experiences helped his father at the store, Paul said,

"Dad used to take orders for shoes and boots here in the shop and at night would manufacture them at his home out on the ranch."

Mr. Breuer racalled the fact that his father's store was among three of the oldest in Myrtle Point, sons of the original owners taking over following the retirement of their fathers. These three stores are The Breuer Store, Huling, Lundy & Sons Hardware, and the Perkins Drug Store. Mr. Bill Lundy, son of R. W. Lundy, is the present owner. The Perkins Drug Store was established March 10, 1888, by Nicholas Perkins. His son, Flentge Perkins, is the present owner.

The *Herald* reporter asked Mr. Breuer what he planned for the future. He answered: "Who, me? – Oh, hell, I'm going to loaf, run the ranch, help around the store and have a good time – I'll keep busy."

HAZER HARDWARE COMPANY, *North Bend*

Perhaps no business motto in Coos or Curry County is better known than *Hazer Haz It,* which carries the memory back to the days when North Bend had no paved streets; when milk was transported from the boat landing in ten-gallon cans and dished out into containers provided by the individual customers.

It was near Christmas time in 1909 when Roscoe Hazer and his wife, together with Roscoe's father, George Hazer, stepped ashore from the steamer *Breakwater.* Roscoe's mother remained in Spokane, Washington, to keep the younger children, Freda and Bernard, in school.

Roscoe was only nineteen years old at the time. He not only had a wife but he also had had considerable experience as a clerk in a hardware store. Josh Jones was operating a hardware business with limited stock on Union Avenue. Jones wanted to sell out. Roscoe induced his father to buy.

There was little activity at the time. His father went to work in one of the saw mills, while Roscoe managed the store, assisted by his wife.

Hazer & Son soon established themselves permanently in the growing city of North Bend. In 1918 they incorporated as the Hazer Hardware Company, with George Hazer as president, and Roscoe Hazer as vice-president. As the business increased, Mrs. Hazer became active in the office of the company. After the death of George Hazer in 1932, the company continued with little change in policy or methods.

After continuing on Union Avenue for a while, the store was moved to Virginia Avenue, handy to the boat landing through which came nearly all of the farm trade. In 1919 the store was moved to its present location on Sherman Avenue. Today it carries a very complete stock of general hardware merchandise. The management constantly strives to maintain its long-established and well known motto — *Hazer Haz It.*

J. Albert Matson, *Marshfield*

J. Albert Matson was truly one of the *pioneer merchants* of Marshfield.

At the age of 18, in 1893, he began his career as a merchant by going to work for Sam Magness as a clerk. Seven years later, in 1900, he became a partner and the firm became known as Magness & Matson. After another fourteen years, in 1914, he bought out Magness and the establishment became Matson's Quality Store.

Mr. Matson tells of some of the merchandising methods of those days. After a merchant's credit standing was established, he could get any amount of goods on time. Invoices were payable in six months from date of billing. If paid at the end of that time, a discount of six percent was allowed. If payment was made at time of the billing, 12 percent discount was allowed. If the bill ran for a full year, no discount was granted.

All goods came from wholesale houses in San Francisco. It appears that the dealers there were well off financially. Locally, Coos County warrants could be bought at a high discount. Some of the local merchants made a practice of buying up the warrants at a discount, then sending them to the wholesale merchants in San Francisco, receiving the face value of the warrants as credit on their merchandise, thus making a profit on warrants as well as on the goods.

Much of the retail selling locally was done on a credit basis. It was common practice to have purchases charged. Journals of some of the Marshfield stores in the eighties reveal that regular customers in the town — professional and business men — had numerous small items charged to their accounts, even as little as a five-cent purchase. Two or three times a year they would pay up the account that sometimes ran up to several hundred dollars.

J. Albert Matson had many out-of-town customers — farmers, loggers, coal miners, fishermen. Many of them came to town in their boats. In some cases, however, a man working in a mine, a mill, a shipyard, might find himself at the end of the week, wanting to go to his home perhaps out on a farm, without a boat. It was too late to go on the regular steamer. For such contingencies Mr. Matson kept several skiffs, at one time as many as five, to lend to his belated customers, with oars and oarlocks.

Kerosene lanterns also were needed. Matson's Quality Store stocked two dozen lanterns for such occasions, keeping them filled, cleaned and ready for use at all times. Mr. Matson said that he had no losses from such easy lending practices. Even people from North Bend sometimes found it necessary to walk home after dark and came in to borrow a lantern.

Sometimes a man would be in town with his family, possibly several children. They would have to wait for the turn of the tide to avoid having to "buck" it up the river or down the bay. In such cases, it was not uncommon to spread some blankets and bed the children down on the floor of the store, waiting till near midnight before starting for home.

During World War I, lumber markets were "shot to pieces." It was at this time that the C. A. Smith Lumber Company failed. Matson, along with others, suffered heavy financial losses. He went out of the merchandise business.

Following the debacle of that period, J. Albert Matson has made a remarkable come-back. In December of 1918, he entered into a contract as salesman for the New York Life Insurance Company. During the thirty-odd years that have followed, he has consistently been among the ten leading salesmen of the state. For the whole period that he has represented the company, he tops the list of all the agents in Oregon, having sold life insurance to the amount of nearly seven million dollars.

On January 13, 1902, J. Albert Matson married Virginia Alice Kruse, daughter of John Kruse, the well known ship builder for the Simpson Lumber Company. The Matsons had two children, Julius and Virginia.

At the age of twenty-five, Albert became a member of the city council of Marshfield, was mayor 1940-1944. He served for some time as president of the Coos-Curry Pioneer and Historical Association.

Gow Why, *Marshfield*

Little definite information is available about the early life of this Chinese pioneer merchant in Marshfield, though he was well known throughout the bay area for thirty years or more. He was known merely as Gow Why. It is reported that during his early days on Coos Bay, perhaps in the early 1890's, he worked with the construction crew in the building of the railroad from Marshfield to Beaver Hill. He may have been camp cook for the crew.

However, Gow Why's early days on the bay are best remembered by residents of those days as a peddler of vegetables, carried in two large baskets slung over his shoulder. His garden was located somewhere south of Marshfield, towards Millington, then known as Flag Staff. It isn't definitely known whether he brought his produce to town in a row boat or carried it all the way in the baskets.

His business increased until it became too much for him to make house-to-house deliveries with his baskets. So he opened a store at the southeast corner of Broadway and Commercial, in the building that had been occupied by the old Western Hotel. Eventually he bought the building, and the lot, 60 by 90 feet. He added a line of groceries and other goods until his establishment became a general merchandise store.

Apparently Gow Why had attended school somewhere at some time, for he could read and write English, as indicated by his account books. His counting device (an abacus) is still recalled by his old customers. It consisted of a number of counting beads or buttons, strung on several parallel wires in a wooden frame, perhaps approximately 10 by 15 inches, the wires being strung lengthwise. When he had a bill of goods to figure up, he would take the counting machine instrument, count audibly in Chinese as he rapidly shifted the counters back and forth, then write the results with a pen on paper.

The business of this pioneer Chinese merchant increased and developed until his store had become one of the busiest places in town. There seemed to be little system or order, but Gow Why knew just where to find what he wanted when he wanted it.

About 1900 Gow Why went to San Francisco, returning in a short time with an attractive young wife. In the following years, eight children were born. This Chinese family, now entering into the fourth generation since coming to this area, have become thoroughly Americanized.

Gow Why himself, about 1930, turned his local properties over to Mrs. Gow Why and returned to China. If living now he would be past 90 years of age, but his family has not heard from him for several years.

12

Early Doctors

THE FIRST TWO — *Port Orford*

DR. ANSON DART came to Port Orford in 1851 on the steamer *Sea Gull,* accompanied by two missionaries. Larsell in *The Doctor in Oregon* says, "Dr. Dart appears to have been the first medical man in the county. It is possible that he gave some medical attention to the Indians who were wounded in the fighting at Battle Rock, but this is conjecture only."

Dr. Rodney Glisan, though not a general practitioner in Coos and Curry counties, is definitely entitled to more than a passing mention among the medical men of this region. In 1855-1856 he spent fourteen months as chief medical officer with the U. S. military forces at Port Orford, sent there to clean up the mess which the whites had stirred up with the Rogue River Indians. He wrote in 1855:

> There is not a more healthy place on the globe than Port Orford — the only diseases here are some species of intemperance. Indeed, were it not for an occasional accident, there would be no need of a physician at the post.

He gives us a very good picture of gold mining along the beaches, with the skin games perpetrated on the dupes who were easy prey to get-rich schemers.

With the rank of major, Dr. Glisan spent weeks with the men in the field, or rather on the trail, in open camps and in the rough, tough brush of the canyons and mountainsides.

On one occasion he was "hatched" down with sick and wounded men under deck in the "dreadfully small" schooner *Gold Beach* on their perilous journey over the treacherous Rogue River Bar, up the coast at night, to Port Orford.

In 1856 Dr. Glisan moved out with the troops. He established himself in Portland to become one of the outstanding medical men of Oregon.

DR. ANDREW B. OVERBECK, *Empire*

Dr. Overbeck, apparently, was the first medical practitioner in Coos County, though there seems to be little or no record of his medical practice in this area.

Esther M. Lockhart said in telling of their arrival at Empire in 1853, "With us were Dr. A. B. Overbeck, his wife and two little children."

Just how long Dr. Overbeck remained in Empire, is not known. However, it appears that sometime during the fifties he had returned to Jacksonville.

DR. COFFIN, *Empire*

Dr. Coffin . . . N. H. – V. W. – V. M. . . . which was it? There appears to be little information but considerable confusion about this man.

According to the County Archives, N. H. Coffin was named as one of the county commissioners of Coos County by legislative act in 1853. However, when the commissioners met to become organized his name appears as V. W. Coffin.

Ulett says that Dr. V. W. Coffin and Dr. J. H. Foster went to the gold mines with Captain Harris and that they named the boom town Randolph in honor of the noted Virginian, Randolph of Roanoke. He adds that Coffin later lived and died in Empire.

Larsell merely says that Dr. V. M. Coffin came with the gold rush and later he settled at Empire City where he practiced until his death.

DR. J. H. FOSTER, *Randolph and Empire*

Dr. J. H. Foster is described by Ulett, who says that

he went over to the Randolph gold mines with Captain Harris.

According to the County Archives, J. H. Foster became Coos County's first sheriff when the county was created by the legislature in December, 1853.

Larsell says: "With the gold seekers had come Doctors V. N. Coffin and J. H. Foster . . . Foster went to the mines with Captain William Harris and had a part in the founding of Randolph."

His relatives say his name was J. Franklin Foster.

DR. THOMAS MACKAY *Empire*

In *The Doctor in Oregon* by Olaf Larsell is the following reference to Dr. Thomas Mackay:

> He studied medicine at the University of Virginia and at Philadelphia, receiving a medical degree in 1864; did medical service in a Confederate hospital during the Civil War, coming west to California after the end of the war. In 1875 he was placed in charge of the U. S. Marine Hospital then located at Coos Bay, Oregon, where he remained until 1892.

Ulett says, "At the time of the severe diphtheria epidemic of 1880, these two Coquille doctors, Leneve and Angle, worked together with Dr. Mackay and Dr. Cook of Empire City.

DR. FRANCIS O. VON DER GREEN *Gold Beach*

Dr. Francis O. von der Green, German born and German educated, was the first to make the medical profession his life work in Curry County. Coming to America, he practiced for a number of years in Baltimore, and then migrated to California. He practiced for a while in the San Francisco Bay area, where he met and married Katherine Noon, a school teacher. Sometime after their first child, Mary Lou, was born, they moved to Oregon City and later to Curry County.

He and his little family squatted at Ellensburg, where the Rogue River flows into the Pacific. To the north there was a trail, long used by elk and Indians and pioneer whites. Scattered along the way were a few settlers. Some were miners; some were homesteaders. Occasionally along the trail he would meet men with packtrains of mules. At Port Orford there was an ambitious sprouting city that grew and shrank as the years went by. All these settlers and travelers and miners and packers were potential patients for the new doctor.

Southward from Ellensburg, all the way to Crescent City, the conditions and distances were about the same as to the northward. And up Rogue River as far as Indian canoes could be paddled or white men's boats could be pulled; and then on beyond where horses or mules might be led; and still further on where men must go afoot — some took their wives, or married Indian women. Children were born; sometimes there were accidents; occasionally people did get sick, even in this country of which Dr. Glisan had written, "There is not a more healthy spot on the globe."

There would be times when Dr. von der Green would be called; and if it was humanely possible, he went. For many years, in all this country, 125 miles along the Oregon coast and inland as far as high mountains and rushing torrents would permit men to penetrate — in all this country, Dr. Green was the only accredited M. D. He served the wild area as long as God gave him strength to stand on his feet.

Sometimes he would be out and away from his family for weeks. There was plenty of practice, but many times money would be scarce. People would gladly pay if he would take produce they might have. But there was a problem: How could the good doctor accept cows and sheep and chickens with no place and no way to keep them? Dr. von der Green was a man of action as well as of ideas. His German background, his training, his education, his experience, his rugged individualism — all combined with his pioneer spirit to make a man who would not be stymied by little problems.

Some eight or ten miles north of Gold Beach — it was beginning to be known as Gold Beach now — there was a homestead by the side of the trail. Cedar Grove, it was called. It could be bought at a price within the doctor's reach. He obtained it. Here he brought his family, which by this time included three girls. Here they had a place for sheep, a cow or two, some hogs and chickens. And the family could have a garden, a berry patch, and fruit from the trees that had been planted by the former owner. His daughter (now Mrs. T. H. Chapman, a retired school teacher, in her 80th year, in North Bend) spent several years in that home at Cedar Grove by the side of the trail overlooking the restless Pacific. She recalls that the flock of sheep grew to be as many as 400 at one time. She and her sisters did their part in herding the flock. Sometimes, when the girls were at school, a man was hired to tend the sheep.

The wool was packed on horses to Gold Beach, for shipment on sailing vessels to San Francisco. In return they received flour, sugar, coffee, salt, shoes, bolts of cloth to be made into clothing, and other necessary items. "And candy," Florence added as she related bits of their family life. "We children always looked forward to getting our candy when our ship came in."

When flour might get low in their bin and they might not be sure where the next loaf of bread would come from, the girls often divided their time between sheep herding and gazing southward over the ocean for the appearance of sails that would bring their ship with a new supply of flour. When they saw the schooner enter the river, someone would saddle a horse and pack animal.

From this mountain home overlooking the ocean, Dr. Green made his long trips to the sick, usually by saddle horse. Sometimes he had to go afoot; sometimes by boat. His daughter recalls that once he had a call to go to Mule Creek, some fifty miles up Rogue River from Gold Beach, accompanied by two men. After going as far as possible by boat, they changed to saddle horses, and rode on to Illahe, to Foster Creek, to Big Bend, to Billings Creek, to Solitude. When they reached the Devil's Backbone, they found the trail impassable for horses. They had to proceed afoot. The doctor gave out. He could go no further. The two men, backwoodsmen, accustomed to the mountains, took turns in carrying the doctor, reaching the sick bed in time.

On another occasion, when the doctor was on a similar mission, afoot with two other men, he slipped, fell, and found that he couldn't get up. He was carried to Gold Beach. The date was April 26, 1884. Dr. Green had reached the end of his trail. He died that night.

Dr. Charles W. Tower, *Empire and Marshfield*

Dr. Charles W. Tower began the practice of medicine at Empire City in 1870. He carried on continuously for nearly a half a century.

When landing at Empire in 1868, he had to be carried from the ship. Only twenty-six years old, he was a mere skeleton, over six feet tall and weighing but 120 pounds. A broken-down veteran of the Civil War, it was said that he had come west to die. He did — 52 years later.

Charles W. Tower was born in New Hampshire in 1842, was educated at Harvard, with medical training at the College of Physicians and Surgeons in New York and at the Harvard Medical school.

He came out of the Union army with health so impaired that his case seemed hopeless. His sister, Mrs. S. S. Mann, had come west and settled at Newport (Libby) coal mines, where her husband was a member of the firm of Flanagan & Mann, coal mine operators. In the four or five years that followed, he came to be a very busy and active man. After completing his training at Willamette Medical School in Salem, he opened his office and began practicing at Empire City in 1870. Records show that young Dr. Tower didn't sit in his office, waiting for patients. He evidently had been investing in real estate, for on September 12, 1870, the county court of Coos County ordered the issuance of a warrant to Dr. C. W. Tower in the amount of $400 for two lots on which to build a court house.

A bi-weekly newspaper, *The Rustic,* had been established in 1871. In its issue of March 16, 1872, is this ad:

C. W. TOWER

CITY DRUG STORE

Physician's prescriptions and Family Receipts Carefully Compounded From Choice Fresh Drugs. Everything Pertaining to a First-Class Drug Store.

He had erected a building for his office and drug store, with an apartment for living quarters in the rear. He became associated with L. M. Hanscom in the publication of *The Record*, issued every Thursday.

About this time, Dr. Tower was married to Minnie Burrell, daughter of Dr. and Mrs. Burrell of San Francisco. He had erected a new dwelling in Empire for their future home. Incidentally, those two houses built by him during the seventies are still in use as dwellings.

In 1874, the Towers moved to the growing new town of Marshfield, where they built a new home and reared a family of three sons and one daughter. Two of their sons Edward and Jay, died after reaching manhood. The third, Isaac R., is the well known owner of the Tower Motor Company in Coos Bay.

Dr. Tower was not the typical rugged picturesque type of western pioneer, but a gentleman of New England culture, education, and refinement. This writer recalls how he used to come, along with J. W. Bennett, Dr. O. E. Smith and others, to the Peterson home on Haynes Inlet, to hunt ducks, sleep in the deep feather beds and to enjoy Mrs. Peterson's cooking. And the rich aroma of the cigars smoked by Dr. Tower is still associated with the memory of those days; and the doctor's well-trimmed goatee, and his neat appearance and pleasing manner.

DOCTOR WALTON HAYDON, *Marshfield*

"Dr. Haydon was probably the most versatile man who ever made his home on Coos Bay." — O. W. Briggs in the *Coos Bay Harbor*.

"Dr. Haydon's Marshfield headquarters was a gathering place for intellectuals, for scientists and for prominent visitors who sought particular information of the Southwestern Oregon country."— *The Oregon Journal.*

"Dr. Haydon is a scientist as well as a skilled surgeon and physician." — Fred Lockley.

Walton Haydon was born in England in 1854. His father was a barrister and provided a tutor for his son until the boy reached the age of ten, when he went into a private school and then a public school of some 400 pupils. In the University young Haydon studied medicine, and upon graduation he was stationed at St. Thomas Hospital for a few years.

In 1892 Dr. Haydon opened an office in Portland, where he continued his practice for two years, moving then to Tillamook for a year, and next to Bandon for three years. In 1903 he came to Marshfield and set up his office, which, in the following thirty years, came to be known far and wide.

In January of 1932, just a little less than a year before his death, Dr. Haydon accepted an invitation to visit Fred Lockley in the latter's home in Portland. Lockley wrote the following interview:

> Dr. Walton Haydon is one of Marshfield's best known citizens. Twenty years or more ago I dropped in for a visit at Marshfield with Dr. Haydon. His kitchen was as neat as that of a New England housewife and he cooked with the skill of a chemist and a French chef combined.
>
> A few days ago Dr. Haydon returned my call. As we sat in front of the fireplace in my home I recalled the wonderful steak he had served me a score of years ago.
>
> "Yes, I remember your visit to me very well indeed," said Dr. Haydon. "Jack Guyton introduced us, you will remember. How did I learn to cook? While studying for my medical degree in London I made up my mind to see some of the out of the way parts of the world, particularly in the Far North, so I took a course in preparing foods for invalids. Later, when an interne, I put in a year studying diets and cooking. At the same time I took lessons for a year or more in carpentry and metal work, knowing that in the Far North such knowledge would come in handy . . .
>
> "After I had received my degree, I wanted to see some of Europe, so I put in a wander year in Russia and elsewhere in

Europe. I then made a trip as surgeon aboard the *Hope* on a voyage to the Arctic. We had a crew of about 80 men. We were gone a year. I collected specimens as well as taking care of the health of the crew. I made a second voyage to the Arctic, being gone about the same length of time as on the first trip.

"I was next employed by the Hndson's Bay Company, being stationed at Moose Factory. I put in six years there, traveling pretty well all over the country by dog team, in snowshoes or by canoe. While there I made a collection of butterflies and plants for Darwin, who was anxious to study the variations in animal and plant life due to climatic conditions.

"I also did a lot of photographing. In those days I prepared my own wet plates and made many of my own chemicals. In 1922 a fire swept the lower part of Front Street in Marshfield and destroyed all my collections, including the photographic plates. A few years later my brother ran across in a second hand store in London a book of photographic views that I had printed and sent to a friend in England and that had been sold after his death. My brother bought the book and sent it to me, and you can imagine how much pleasure I had in looking over the photography I had made nearly fifty years ago.

"In 1903 I went to Marshfield and have practiced my profession there ever since. I used to contribute articles to *Land and Water,* an English magazine, as well as to the scientific journals. . . . "

Following Dr. Haydon's death on December 15, 1932, O. W. Briggs wrote in the *Coos Bay Harbor*:

At Bandon, Dr. Haydon heard about black sand mining and making some experiments he decided there was nothing to be obtained more than wages from that pursuit. He was often criticised as a knocker because he would not recommend black sand mining for companies whose officers believed they were right. He steadfastly refused to believe there was wealth or even profit in that line, and the loss of many hundreds of thousands of dollars put into dredging activities and alleged perfecting utilities, proved his position had been right.

Dr. Haydon's office and living quarters in Marshfield were for many years headquarters for particular friends, visitors who came from all parts of the globe with letters of introduction, scientists, geologists, foresters and naturalists.

In these quarters he had gathered from many parts of the world curiosities, arms, books, oddities, and in fact so many things of special interest that the place was an archive of priceless information. All this was burned in the Front Street fire [in 1922].

An unsigned, undated newspaper clipping further describes his quarters as an intellectual and gastronomic center:

> His place was famous. With the burning of the doctor's apartments there is wiped out a place which was famous on the coast. Dr. Haydon's family resides at Empire but he had his office in Marshfield and in connection had living quarters. The doctor had lived on the second story of the building for sixteen or eighteen years and had always entertained extensively. Many prominent men of the coast country have been guests of the doctor at his apartments and the place was pronounced by many as displaying the most wonderful collection of curios in this part of the country. . . .
>
> Back of his office was his famous den with its collection of relics and behind it a kitchen from which the doctor had served to his friends for many years the spreads which made him famous as a fine cook.

Still another clipping tells of his collection of plants given to the Academy of Science in San Francisco:

> The collection comprises the plants which he found native of this immediate locality, all within a radius of fifteen miles of Coos Bay. The specimens number about 500 and have all been prepared and named. Some of the specimens in doubt were sent to New York to be properly named scientifically.

Dr. William Horsfall, *Marsnfield*

Dr. William Horsfall has established a record which appears to be equaled by few if any professional men—60 years of continuous medical practice in one locality. It was in 1892 that he opened his office on Front Street in Marshfield. Today, approaching 60 years later, he is still answering to the call of the sick and the lame, at his home office on Johnson Street, less than a mile from his first location on Front Street.

Many of the older families of the Coos Bay area still speak of him as "our doctor." Now, in his 85th year, you might run on to him on the street, when he comes to town, almost any day, bareheaded, without overcoat, slightly bent, but with a firm step. If you call at his home office on Johnson Street, where he now holds forth, you might be directed to have a seat to await your turn following others who came ahead of you.

William Horsfall, born in England in 1866, came to the United States at the age of four, with his parents, the Reverend and Mrs. Dean William Horsfall. In 1886 they landed in Marshfield, where the father had been assigned to the Episcopal pastorate. Young William, then aged twenty, was robust, active, energetic, fond of hiking and swimming, hunting and fishing, boating and camping, boxing and wrestling. He had been educated in the Bishop Military Academy in San Francisco, and Stanford University. Later his education was continued at the Cooper Medical College, and still later by a course in the Mayo Clinic.

During his early years in Coos County, he taught school in different rural districts through the summer months, and attended the Cooper Medical College in California during the winters. In 1892 he received his medical degree, when he opened his office and began his long years of continuous practice.

In his professional work, Dr. Horsfall would go at any and all times, night or day, sometimes afoot with a lantern, sometimes on a bicycle, perhaps in a rowboat across a stream and then on horseback, through forests and over hills. When roads permitted, he drove a horse and buggy. Later came the gas boat and the auto. But for many years there were places still where boat and auto could not go, and the doctor had to continue by the old means of travel.

On April 7, 1896, Dr. Horsfall was married to Miss Lydia Yoakam, a teacher in the Marshfield school. The ceremony was performed by the doctor's father. Two sons and a daughter were born: William (deceased) ; George, colonel in U. S. Medical Corps; Marian, a school teacher in California.

Many interesting experiences occurred during Dr. Horsfall's practice. One was an urgent call from South Slough. It was while he was still a single man, though he had become engaged to Miss Yoakam. He invited her to accompany him, for it meant a pleasant buggy ride over the old wagon road through Empire.

At the farm home, the doctor found that a major operation was necessary. There was no hospital within several hundred miles. What was to be done had to be performed there in that little farm home. An operating table must be improvised; water must be heated; and an anaesthethic had to be administered. Miss Yoakam was a music teacher, not a nurse. But this was an emergency, so she was pressed into service. She followed the doctor's instructions while he completed a successful operation.

Another time he had a call to make a night trip across the bay to the present site of Eastside, then known as East Marshfield. A baby was due to be born. The father had come with a rowboat. The two men started out. The boat, having been exposed to sunshine and drying winds, had developed open cracks on the sides. With the weight of the two men, the boat settled deep enough to permit water to enter through the cracks. While the father rowed, the doctor bailed with a little tin can. But the water gained faster than he could bail. The boat settled till the water was coming in over the top, and the shore was still a hundred yards to the east.

The father clung to the boat with one hand and paddled ashore with the other. The doctor, being an expert swimmer, held his medical kit above his head in one hand and swam with the other. They reached the shore and the maternity bedside. One more baby was added to Dr. Horsfall's growing list. It was only after he reached home that he thought of changing his own wet pants.

In addition to his medical practice and his numerous outdoor activities, Dr. Horsfall has fulfilled many duties that come to an active citizen. He has been coroner of Coos County; medical officer in charge of Naval Radio Station, Medical Reserve Corps, Coos Bay; elected "First Citizen" of Coos Bay, 1939; president, Coos County Medical Association, 1922 and 1940.

13

Coos Plants

THE PLANTS THAT GREW WILD naturally had an enormous influence for the early settlers. They and not the scientists as elsewhere were the first to observe the immense vegetation. The long-ago botanists into Oregon Territory did not get down into Coos and Curry. Captain Vancouver's botanist, Archibald Menzies, didn't come ashore. David Douglas shot down the great cones from trees in the Umpqua country. He did not enter the Coos region at all, only heard about it from his Hudson's Bay companions.

The following list of wild flowers, shrubs, and trees, growing a hundred years ago as profusely and as varied as they do today, is a direct result of wild flower shows held annually in North Bend during the 1920's.

Wild flower exhibits were sent in from all over — Myrtle Point, Arago, Cooston, Sumner, Allegany, Daniels Creek, Coos River, Charleston, Empire, Hauser, Lakeside, Templeton, Shoreacres, Glasgow, Kentuck Inlet, and other places. They were sent by individuals, by schools, by clubs. Some came by mail, some by gas or rowboat.

Dr. Helen M. Gilkey, professor of botany and curator of the herbarium at Oregon State College, was brought in each year to identify, classify, and list all exhibits. On each occasion she devoted several days to the task, including field trips to collect specimens in their natural habitats. She was accompanied on some of the trips by Mr. and Mrs. C.A. Smith, Anna Truman, Jack Greves and others. The specimens were classified and compiled into this list by Dr. Gilkey. She fully supplied the scientific as well as the common names, but as here printed the former have been omitted. The interspersed comments are not by Dr. Gilkey.

Buck bean, Beale Lake. Gentian family.

Buttercup. Hauser. Buttercup family. A different species at Shoreacres.

California wild lilac, Chittam family.
Cascara. Cascara family.

Cat-tail. Cat-tail family.

Cinnamon bush. Mountain balsam. Chittam family.

Columbine. Daniel's Creek. Buttercup family.

Coolwort. Currant family.

Coos Bay Myrtle. (*Umbellularia californica*), Laurel family.

Corn salad. Valerian family.

Creeping buttercup. Low meadows along the coast. (*Ranunculus repens*).

Cow-parsnip. Parsley family

Cream cup. Sunset Bay. Poppy family.

Creeping violet. Violet family.

Crimson Clover. An escape from fields. Pea family.

Curly dock. Dock family.
Cut grass. Beale Lake. Sedge family.

Dandelion. North Bend. Dandelion family.

Deer fern. Fern family.

Dogwood. Bridge. Dogwood family.

Douglas fir. Pine family.

Elkhorn moss or ground pine. South Slough. Club moss family.

Fairy Bells. Lily family.

False broom rape. Beale Lake. Broom rape family.

False dandelion. Dandelion family.

False Solomon's seal. (*Smilacina racemosa*). Daniel's Creek, Lily family.

False Solomon's seal. (*Smilacina sessilifolia*). Lily family.

Feather grass. Grass family.

Field larkspur. Buttercup family.

Fool's Onion. Lily family.

Fox-glove. Snapdragon family.

Goat's beard. Rose family.

Gold-back fern. Fern family.

Groundsell. Dandelion family.

Hedge nettle. Mint family.

Hellebore. Lily family.

Horsetail; Scouring rush. Horse-tail family.

Indian pipe. Heath family.

Inflated clover. Pea family.

Inside-out flower. Barberry family.

Kinnikinnic. Heath family.

Mrs. James Maple of Empire says: "The swamps provided the Coos Indians with wild onions and many eatable greens. The woods provided fern roots and many medicinal herbs.

The sea gave them eatable seaweeds. The sand hills provided them with the *ha-wooded* plant and camas. The *ha-wooded* roots, after they were steamed, had to be stripped of a thread that ran through them, but this was the only part that was not eatable."

Labrador tea. Heath family.

Large dog-fennel. Dandelion family.

Large-flowered Phacelia. Waterleaf family.

Larkspur. Daniel's Creek. Poisonous to stock. Buttercup family.

Lavender iris. Iris family.

Lavender violet. Sunset Bay. Violet family.

Lawson's cypress; Port Orford cedar. Cypress family.

Lily-of-the-valley. North Bend park. Lily family.

Lodge pole pine. (*Pinus contorta*). Beale Lake. Pine family.

Low Oregon grape. Barberry family.

Madrona. North Bend. Heath family.

Maiden-hair fern. Fern family.

Mallow. Cotton family.

Manzanita. Beale Lake. Heath family.

Marguerite. Dandelion family.

Marsh star-flower. Primrose family.

Milk-thistle. Dandelion family.

Miner's lettuce. Portulaca family.

Mitre cap. Currant family.

Mock orange or syringa. Saxifrage family.

Monkey flower. Beale Lake. Monkey-flower family.

Mountain Oregon grape. (*Berberis nervosa*). Barberry family.

Mouse eared chick-weed. Hauser. Pink family.

Narrow leaf plantain. Plantain family.

Ninebark. Rose family.

Oregon grape. (*Berberis aquifolium*). Barberry family.

Oregon tea or Yerbabuena. Mint family.

Pacific Christmas fern. Fern family.

Pimpernel; Poor man's weather glass. Primrose family.

Pine lily or bear grass. Lily family.

Pink bird foot; Trefoil; or Pink lotus. Pea family.

Pipsissewa or Princess pine. Heath family.

Pitcher plant. Pitcher-plant family.

Plume fern. (*Woodwardia fimbriata*). Fern family.

Poison camas. Lily family.

Pond lily. Beale Lake. Water-lily family.

Psoralea. Pea family.

Purple Clover. Sunset Bay. Pea family.

Purple cluster lily. Lily family.

Purple iris. (*Iris tenax*). Iris family.

Of the myrtle trees the misinformation still persists that they grow only in Coos and Curry and the Holy Land. They grow, though less gloriously in Northern California and their scientific name as listed above is *Umbellularia californica;* and they don't grow in the Holy Land at all. The claim can remain undisputed that it is the most beautiful finished wood in the world. One of J. H. Oerding's sons, early and prominent manufacturers at Coquille, tells how he was once summoned home to find Jack London sitting on his doorstep, his knees bunched up and his elbows upon them, in an attitude of meditation. He became alert enough in finding out about Myrtle wood which he wanted for his famous Valley of the Moon place. It is reported that a Bandon business man had a mantlepiece which he valued at a thousand dollars. This was loosely fastened so that in case of fire it could be saved. A fire did come and so suddenly that the expensive piece of timber was lost. The Oerdings once furnished covers for a collector's edition of an Oregon book; it was bound in myrtle wood with a red Morocca back. Myrtle wood novelties are now widely sold. In fine manufacturing, selection of wood can be made according to colors and grain but it is impossible exactly to duplicate a piece; the marbled figures are as individual as human fingerprints. There are three varieties—black, yellow, and white. One of the finest myrtlewood parks is on the Chetco River near Brookings.

Purple violet. Haynes Inlet. Peterson's Landing. Violet family.

Pussy'e ear. Lily family.

Quinine bush or Silk-tassel bush. Hauser. Silk-tassel family.

Radish. Turnip family.

Rattlesnake plantain. Orchid family.

Red Cedar. Cypress family.

Salal. (*Gaultheria shallon*). Heath family. The Coos Indians liked the fresh berries dipped into hot elk tallow.

Salmonberry. (*Rubus spectabilis*). Rose family.

Salt-horn. Pigweed family.

Sand lotus. Pea family.

Scorpion grass. Forget-me-not family.

Scotch broom. (*Cytisus scoparius*). Pea family.

Showy owl's clover. Hauser. Monkey-flower family.

Silver-leaf. Rose family.

Silver-stemmed lupine. Pea family.

Sitka spruce. Pine family.

Skunk cabbage. Hauser. Arum family.

Slender vetch. Hauser. Pea family.

Small hop clover. Pea family.

Red Clover. Hauser. Pea family.

Red elder. Honeysuckle family.

Red huckleberry. Heath family.

Red sorrel. Dock family.

Rhododendron. Heath family.

Seaside daisy. Daisy family.

Seaside tansy. North Slough. Dandelion family.

Sea-thrift. Leadwort family.

Sedge. *Cyperacease.*

Sheep sorrell; Wood sorrel. (*Oxalis oregana*). Oxalis family.

Small lupine. Hauser. Pea family.

Small speedwell. Snap-dragon family.

Snow plant. Sand Hills. Heath family.

Speedwell. Snapdragon family.

Spring beauty. Glasgow. Mustard family.

Take a look at one of our commonest trees, one often thought to be unworthy of our attention—the red alder. Take a look at any tract denuded by logging; in a few short years the area has been made green with alders. Soon other trees spring up in the protecting shade. These are nursed and sheltered by the benevolent alder. The other trees in time overshadow it; crowd it out; and when its usefulness has been accomplished it returns its fertile elements to Mother Earth. Picknickers find the cool freshness of the alder on a warm day beside a little brook; its leafy branches are sought as nesting-places by the robins; cows after grazing chew their cuds in its shade. The pioneer seeking a garden spot didn't go to groves of firs, hemlocks, or cedars. He sought out a grove of alders. He didn't know why. He only knew that his vegetables and his berries and his young fruit trees did better where the alder had grown. In the old days near the present site of Hauser, when barefoot boys went fishing, where did they get their worms for bait? Not under fir trees, or spruce, or hemlock, or cedar. They found them in the alder groves, and where you find worms you are quite likely to find some good plant soil. And the pioneer homesteader found that the trees made very good fuel for his fireplace and cook stove. In the fireplace it gave off an enjoyable aroma in addition to its snug warmth.

Star flower. Haynes Inlet. Primrose family.

Stinking currant. Currant family.

Twin-flower. Honeysuckle family.

Twisted stalk. Daniel's Creek. Lily family. Reddish berry.

Wake robin. (*Trillium ovatum*). Lily family.

Waterleaf. Daniel's Creek. Water-leaf family.

Stone crop. Stonecrop family.

Sundew. Hauser. An insect-eating plant. *Droceraceae.*

Tarweed. Hauser. Borage family.

Thimbleberry. Glasgow. Rose family.

Tiger lily. Beale Lake. Lily family.

Twin-berry Honeysuckle family.

Valerian. Daniel's Creek. Valerian family.

Vari-leaved Cilia. Phlox family.

Vegetable wool or Cotton grass. Rush family.

Vine maple. (*Acer circinatum*). It has caused a lot of profanity by woodsmen who are tripped by its recumbent diabolic branches. Maple family.

Water lily. Water-lily family.

Wax myrtle. Haynes Inlet; Cooston. Sweet gale family.

Western dogwood. *Cornaceae.*

Western hemlock. Beale Lake. Pine family.

Western winter-green. Sand Hills. Heath family.

White cedar. Cypress family.

One June day a party visiting Cape Blanco Lighthouse, went out along the edge of the gusty promontory which juts out so far towards the sunset. They were struck by the varied bloom all around at their feet. They picked as many kinds as they could find in an area no bigger than a city block. Their off-hand harvest resulted in sixteen varieties, some of surprising delicacy to thrive in that strong blowing.

White cluster lily. Two species. Lily family.

White lupine. Pea family.

White violet. Beale Lake. Violet family.

Wild blackberry. (*Rubus vitifolius*). Rose family.

Wild cucumber or Old-Man-in-the-Ground. Cucumber family.

Wild currant. Hauser. Currant family.

Wild geranium; Crane's bill. Geranium family.

Wild Ginger. Haynes Inlet. Peterson's Landing. Dutchman's pipe family.

Wild Lily-of-the-Valley. Lily family.

Wild morning glory. Morning-glory family.

Wild radish. Turnip or mustard family.

Wild strawberry. Shoreacres. Rose family.

Wood fern. Fern family.

Wood rose. Rose family.

Yarrow. Dandelion family.

Yellow cluster lily. Lily family.

Yellow elder. North Bend. Honeysuckle family.

Yellow false broom rape. Sand Hills. Parasite on salal. Broom-rape family.

Wild daisy. Empire. An escape from gardens. Dandelion family.

White Forget-me-not. Forget-me-not family.

Wild geranium. Common. Geranium family.

Wild turnip; Wild mustard. Turnip or mustard family.

Wild wall-flower. Turnip or mustard family.

Wine-bush. Dandelion family.

Wood Oxalis. Shoreacres. Oxalis family.

Yellow iris. Iris family.

Yellow Owl's clover. Snap-dragon family.

Yellow violet. Shoreacres. Violet family.

Yellow wood violet. Shoreacres. Violet family.

Youth-on-Age. Currant violet.

GORSE, *By D. D. Hill,* Oregon State College

Gorse or Irish furze, *Zlex europeaus,* is a leguminous shrub which closely resembles Scotch broom. During the blooming season, normally from January until June, gorse is covered with a profusion of showy orange-yellow blossoms.

It grows especially well on sand dunes, gravel bars, fence rows, on logged-off and burned over forest lands, along roadways, in pastures and in other areas where it is not disturbed by tillage or where it is not shaded by other plants. Once established, i' excludes all other vegetation. The mature plant in covered by sharp spines which seriously discourage its use by animals. The plant contains a moderate amount of oil. Under normal conditions of development the oily plant grows from the center outward, leaving a mass of dead, dry matter in the center. When the plant is fired, this center burns to form a chimney or draft which rises in increasing intensity of the fire.

Gorse is most serious in Curry, Coos and western Lane counties. Estimates indicate heavy gorse infestation of not less than 25,000 acres.

In the area of heaviest infestation, namely, in the vicinity of Bandon in Coos County, on the Elk River in Curry County, and on Heceta Head in western Lane County, gorse was introduced as an ornamental shrub. Early records indicate that gorse was introduced to the Bandon area late in the nineteenth century. The following letter was introduced as part of a record at a public hearing on gorse control held at Bandon in August, 1944.

Bandon, Oregon, August 15, 1944

TO WHOM IT MAY CONCERN:

I can recall back to May, 1894, when I saw two rows of gorse approximately twelve feet long and two feet high at the place known as Lord Bennett's, an early resident of Bandon. He stated to me at that time that he had brought the seed from Ireland. I cannot recall any other gorse in this area. Since then the gorse got out of control and spread in the area of Bandon until by 1936 it was scattered all through the area around Bandon and was a great aid to the fire that destroyed Bandon. Since 1936 it has spread more rapidly than it ever had before.

MICHAEL BREUER

The distribution of gorse is largely by seed, which is quite similar to that of Hairy vetch. On warm dry days the seed pods will pop open and will often spread the seed for a distance of several feet. The principal distribution, however, is by means of animals, cars, trucks, and logging equipment. Gorse growing along streams is distributed by water. It has also been scattered in gravel used for road construction when it is taken from streams along which gorse is growing.

The initial spread of gorse is slow. The seed is very hard and apparently will lie in the ground for many years before natural germination occurs. . . . Observations indicate that gorse seed as much as 25 years old may germinate and grow. The hard seed of gorse is rather resistant to fire. Observation following a complete stand of gorse from six to eight feet high show heavy seed germination within sixty days. Samples from the different areas indicate as much as from four to nine million seeds per acre in the surface inch of soil. Fire may destroy many of the plant crowns but seems to encourage plant reestablishment by hastening seed germination. Gorse seedlings appear in fields many years after the original stands have been destroyed. Any system of control, therefore, must recognize that the seedlings must be kept destroyed for an extended period.

[The writer devotes considerable discussion to control methods, including control by tillage, the use of goats and other farm or range animals, by chemicals, and by reforestation.]

The people of Bandon in 1950, recalling the terrible fire of 1936, and mindful of the fact that the despised gorse was one of the principal fuels that made an inferno of that fire, rose up in anguish and ire to declare war upon that enemy. The local paper, *The Western World,* proclaimed:

ALL OUT DRIVE ON GORSE SCHEDULED FOR SUNDAY

"Gorse Riddance is Good Riddance" will be the battle cry this Sunday, when every Bandon family is urged to join in a community-wide attack on the area's worst menace – gorse.

Large stands of the fire-spreading gorse will be exhibited to show citizens the methods being used by the city to control the plant with a program financed by a special tax levy by the people in the spring.

The principal phase of the Gorse-Killing Day program will be that of old-fashioned cutting and slashing, plus treatment on scattered gorse patches throughout the city.

14

Wild Life

It is estimated that not less than one thousand elk were killed in one year in Coos County alone, for the skins only. FRANCES FULLER VICTOR, 1891

On his Coos ranch in 1871 John Neal ate "elk flesh fried in bear oil." JOSEPH GASTON, 1912

Coquille is also said to be derived from a kind of lamprey eel so palatable that the white man as well as the natives preferred it to salmon.
GEORGE BENNETT

THERE IS A BEAVER SLOUGH sure enough, but beaver were not plentiful to any such extent as they were in other parts of Oregon in the fur-hunting days. Few tall hats worn by fine gentlemen in London, came from the Coos, the Coquille, or the Rogue. Trapping expeditions into the country south of the Umpqua were usually disappointing to Dr. McLoughlin of the Hudson's Bay Company. This considerably accounted for Coos and Curry's being such an untouched paradise for the settlers to come to.

Dr. John McLoughlin of the Hudson's Bay Company didn't think much of Coos and Curry. They were poor beaver country.

His trapping expeditions came back with disappointing catches. Apparently they never found Beaver Slough.

THE HIDE HUNTERS, *By Lans Leneve*

When the first settlers blazed trails into the fastness of

the big timbered hills, and scouted the lowlands and flats, they were amazed at the great number of elk and deer that they encountered. There were bear in abundance, bobcats, marten, fisher, rac-coon, mink, civet cats, skunk, otter, and muskrats by the thousands. Even the big timber wolf, now practically extinct in Oregon, were here in great numbers. Probably not another spot within the entire Pacific Northwest boasted more game birds and animals per square acre than did Coos and Curry.

Had some one ventured to remark in those days that some time in the future there would be legislation for the protection of those animals, he would have been laughed at. Surely these countless thousands could never be decreased to any great extent, what with their mating and breeding season after season and with all the natural cover furnished them. Laboring under this impression and with the object of easy money in sight, many men sighted up their muskets and took out upon the trail.

The wholesale slaughter inflicted upon the deer and elk herds was tremendous. Appalling is a better word for it. They were slain, their carcasses left to rot in the

"Often whole herds of elk would be slain and only a ham be removed from a single animal."

woods, only their hides being taken. In the case of the elk their two ivory teeth were taken along with their hides, both bringing fair prices on the market. Often whole herds of elk would be slain and only a ham be removed from a single animal, to be used for food, the rest being left for the predators.

My Dad told of five hunters making their way by trail and taking along pack animals over into the Eden Valley country during the early pioneer days. They returned a couple of weeks later with 300 deer hides and not even a mess of venison.

Down on the old Snead Place on Bear Creek, on the lower Coquille River, three hunters killed 85 elk within a period of three days and took only the hides and teeth.

A Curry County resident shot down 24 elk — killing every single elk in that particular herd. In this case the animals were not even skinned and only one ham was removed from a carcass.

Elk and deer hides were towed down the Coquille River after being loaded upon large scows — hundreds of hides at each trip and shipped from Bandon to the various markets and dealers.

The worst violators of today — men frowned upon by law abiding sportsmen and citizens — cannot hold a candle to those hide hunters of early days, the only difference being that the violator of today knows better and is perfectly aware that he is robbing the law-abiding sportsmen in general. At least the old time hide hunter did not realize that he was robbing future generations and those of his own blood of a great heritage.

Many old timers were real conservationists at heart. They killed only what was needed to supply their families with food, meat was never wasted, and they never went in for hide hunting.

Bear Hunters, Bear Dogs and Bears

Said the 1915 *Oregon Almanac*:

Some authorities claim that over one-fourth of all the deer, bear and cougar of the Pacific Coast states are in Curry County . . . that 20,000 deer and thousands of bear and cougar roam the county, the inner recesses being the home of unnumbered wild game.

At that time, on the Rogue in the Agness-Illahe region, was a group of celebrated bear hunters — Jake Fry, Frank Fry, Will Lake, Walter Fry, Delmar Colgrove, and Elmer Miller.

The greatest of these was Jake Fry, who had been hunting Curry County bears for 50 years, since he was 11 years old. During the period he had owned 100 bear dogs, keeping four on hand steadily for half a century. Eight years was the ordinary life of the bloodhounds and beagles he used; in eight years, often before, he went to the Valhalla of brave bear dogs. Jake Fry remembered the heroic services of dogs that had been dead 40 years. During retrospective evenings the ghosts of the hundred that he had owned came back to him, eager for the hunt, nimble of foot, musical of voice.

Jake Fry killed as many as ten bears in a day. He thought a low average would be 25 a year. That would be 1250. He believed he had killed more than that.

Frank Fry had killed an estimated 25 a year for 33 years; Walter Fry, Miller, Lake, and Colgrove, though not equaling the records of the two Frys who had accounted for 2,000 bears between them, yet in every case had an impressive total that would have brought renown to a city man.

According to the natural history of the hunters, the bears in summer traveled along the river. In the fall they ate huckleberries and acorns and such miscellany of food as they could find. In the spring the main items of their menu were clover, skunk cabbage, and grass.

Big Cats

Panthers, cougars, puma, mountain lions, or in the Chinook Jargon *hyas puss-puss,* whatever name he might be called by, America's big cat with the debatable human scream has in days gone by thickly inhabited Coos and Curry.

In one year 135 cougars were killed in Coos County. In 1919 the state game protection fund paid bounties on 18 cougars in Curry County and two in Coos County.

Perhaps the two best known panther hunters in the period between 1910 and 1920 were Hathaway Jones of Marial who estimated that in 29 years of hunting he had killed over a hundred, and Jack Warner of Powers who in five years killed 24 panthers along with 78 bobcats. When Warner had Grit and Foxie, his pair of famous cougar dogs, he would guarantee from one to four big cats to anyone who would go out with him.

Panther tales are an exciting part of American folk literature. Yet Coos and Curry, notwithstanding all the actual animals they have had, are decidedly short on the kind of stories of them that would make a boy listen with shivering absorption. "Two Panthers and the Two Jones Boys," with a setting on Rogue River, was published in *St. Nicholas Magazine*, New York, in the 1920's, but it was fiction.

Wild Hogs in Curry County

Is there a *native* wild hog in Curry County as distinguished from the *domestic* hogs which have strayed from the farms and gone wild?

Matt Coy, a former long-time resident of that section, with years of experience in hunting the wild hogs, says definitely that there is a *native* wild hog with characteristics different from those of the domestic hog.

J. S. Spoerl, a resident of long standing in Curry County, with many years of handling wild hogs, says, "I have encountered many hogs that were as wild as deer, but never have I seen one that was not a stray or a descendent of a stray from some rancher's farm band of hogs." Other old time residents of Curry County seem to be in accord with Mr. Spoerl's opinion.

However, Matt Coy offers evidence to substantiate his claim that there is a real native wild hog:

Mr. Coy hunted wild hogs for twenty years or more and killed many of the animals of both types. The *native* type, he said, is always of the same color, a battleship blue. The domestic type may be of any color. Another characteristic of the *native* wild hog, is a protective cartelage as much as a half inch in thickness, under the skin, running from the shoulder to the hips. The native hog also has a different tail — 18 to 20 inches long, always white and always ending with a tassel eight inches to a foot in diameter. These animals were known in early days as *flag-tails.*

The native animal also had habits that were different from those of the wild farm hogs. The *native* always built his nest on a hillside, using a bunch of sour grass, covering it with any small brush. He alweys slept with his head down hill. When disturbed, the animal shot out and down into the ravine, making a very difficult mark to shoot at.

The ordinary wild hog, according to Mr. Coy, does not take such precautions. It makes its nest of any material at hand, under a log or overturned tree or stump. His home was a temporary one, to be used only as long as there was a supply of feed nearby. The occupant then moved on to other pastures.

Turning now to Mr. Spoerl's testimony in support of his theory, that all the wild hogs of Curry County originated from farm bands:

I have had many years of experience in running hogs on the ranges of Curry County and during that time have encountered many hogs that were as wild as any deer, but never have I seen one of them that was not a stray from some rancher's or homesteader's band of hogs. If there is such native wild hog in this part of the country, I have never seen one of them.

Curry County had large stands of tan oak timber and usually from October first to June first the acorns from this timber furnish much of the feed for range hogs, deer, bear and other wild game. The hogs get very fat on such a diet and often stay out in the timber and brush for months at a time, sometimes bedding in hollow trees, under logs or in other protected places, living very much as wild animals do. Under such circumstances some of these hogs become quite wild and hard to handle. . . . Sometimes it is possible to drive such hogs right home, but more often they have to be shot in the timber, or where you find them, and taken out on pack animals.

Often it happens that a few of the animals will be captured and the rest escape. Hogs of this kind that have been run by dogs a number of times usually get much rough treatment, which causes them to become wilder and wilder, with the result that they are increasingly difficult to find in the timber. The offspring of such hogs seem to be endowed with the instinct of the wild animal more than that of the domestic and as these hogs mature they become quite fierce and aggressive; when cornered, they usually charge man or beast. It is not unusual to have dogs killed in this manner. In fact, I know of an instance when a wild boar killed five dogs after being bayed up in a hollow tree.

Tusks of the wild hogs of Curry County are reported as being semi-flat and curved upward to the points, where they are bevel-edged. They have strong roots and measure six to eight inches in length, and sometimes up to as much as ten inches.

Some Wild Bird Watching *By Lans Leneve*

[Lans Leneve's grandfather, Dr. S. L. Leneve, was a pioneer medical man in Coos County. As a small boy, Lans trudged through the woods with his father, John Leneve. As they camped and hunted and fished, Lans came to know each feathered creature. He says, "Ornithology has held a fascination for me since I was a very small lad. I started out very early in life making studies of each particular species."

Tom Tit

The Tom-Tit, not much larger than your thumb, is easily identified. He is brown in coloring and always on the go. He searches for bugs and insects beneath the eaves of your home or in your wood-pile. He is not regarded as a songster and is believed by many to be voiceless.

Yet to me, after many years, I was granted the privilege of hearing his voice raised in song. I was deer hunting and stopped to rest. I leaned my back against the trunk of a friendly tree with my rifle resting across my knees. Suddenly, from a nearby thicket, a little Tom-Tit came winging toward me and alighted upon my gun barrel. I remained perfectly still. He lifted his head and burst into song — a sweet trilling song that would have done credit to a canary. It was so wild, so carefree, that I burst out laughing and broke the spell and Tom-Tit took off for the shelter of a nearby bush.

Sparrows

Of the 60 American species, several are found in our coastal section.

Perhaps the best known and friendliest is the Rusty Song Sparrow, being a more frequent visitor to our yards than any other bird.

The rugged little English Sparrow is a professional "bum." He may be encountered upon the streets of almost any town or village — with his cocky appearance as he hops about the city curbs in search of food, and gazes unafraid at the passerby. He has made such a nuisance of himself in many districts that he is warred upon, but he manages to hold his own wherever he happens to dwell. Occasionally he will take up his abode around a country home. We fed a pair of them here at Remote, but they are usually found upon city streets — independent little urchins of the gutters but lovable none the less.

Camp-Robber

Upon the Camp Jay or Camp Robber we long ago bestowed the name of "gray ghost of the forest" owing to its noiseless flight.

The Camp Robber is a natural born thief. While homesteading at one time, we had to move all loose articles inside our cabin. They would even steal our soap when given the opportunity.

My wife used to step from the cabin and call them and they would come floating from the trees and alight upon her shoulders, cling to the sides of her dress and bum for a handout.

The Camp-Robber frequents the higher elevations and is seldom glimpsed in the lowlands.

Owls

We have several species of Owls — the little Barn Owl, an occasional White Owl, or Alaska Owl, the little Screech Owl, Long-eared and Short-eared Owl, Spotted Owl, and the Great Horned Owl.

The Long-eared Owl is forever taking over a crow's nest and fights are frequent between them and the crow.

At one time, during a freezing spell of weather, I came upon a Great Horned Owl sitting atop a stump with each huge wing placed protectingly about a couple of its offspring. I silently withdrew from the scene.

Western Evening Grosbeak

These birds make their appearance at the time the maples are budding. They usually stay for a period of a week or two and then resume their flight.

When I was a small lad a flock of these birds came each spring to my Dad's place at Coquille. For over thirty years they never failed to make an appearance each season.

Ducks and Geese

In the good old days when the railroad ran the full length of Front Street at Coquille and the vast bottom lands on both the south side and the north side of the Coquille River were covered by willows and tall swamp grass, the Coquille Valley boasted of one of the greatest hunting spots in the northwest, especially for duck shooting. My Dad, the late John W. Leneve, bagged mallards along the banks of the small swamp on Elliott Street in the heart of Coquille. In addition, deer ambled about within the city limits; the blue grouse hooted from the lofty branches of the big firs that bordered the town; the late A. J. Sherwood shot quail in his front yard.

During the fall months, the wild geese winged southward and at that time their line of flight was almost directly over the Coquille Valley. For days thousands upon thousands of the big birds moved in their long V-shaped formations over the present site of the county seat — by day and by night they winged ever southward. Often, during extremely foggy weather, they would become confused. Attracted by the lights shining from residences of the little city, they would circle low overhead, their voices making sleep impossible.

Starting as though by prearranged signal, during all the winter months there was a migrant of ducks from the Fish Trap country. This migration usually started around 4:15 p. m. and seldom varied over five or ten minutes in time. These birds were known to the old time duck hunters as "The High Flyers," owing to the fact that most of them flew high out of range as they winged for the mud flats of Coos Bay. The return of the birds from the Bay section was of no such orderly nature and never one of great concentration. We believe that thousands of them returned sometime during the night; the remainder sometime during the daylight hours whenever it suited their whim. Yet each evening they again took off from the Fish Trap country on schedule.

That daily migration continued until darkness blotted out the sight of the birds in flight. It was like a giant army passing in review — ducks of all species being represented by the tens of thousands — teal, widgeons, sprigs (pin-tails), bluebills, red heads, canvasbacks and, the king of all waterfowl, the mallard. One might then have witnessed ducks in greater numbers during just one such evening than may now be seen upon the marshlands of Coquille Valley over a ten-year period of seasonal hunting.

Such ducks as the butterball, ruddy, wood-duck and black whistlers took no great part in the general daily migration, but remained behind in great numbers. In addition to this, the willow-covered marshlands were fairly teeming with mallards and teal at all times of the day and night, and especially were the flights extremely heavy during the late evening. They swept in by the tens of thousands to roost.

There was no such a thing as a bag limit or a time limit placed upon migratory waterfowl in those days. A hunter was allowed to shoot throughout the night if he so desired — spotting the incoming birds against the moon.

The Merganser

This bird, generally known as the "Fish Duck," frequents our coastal streams in great numbers. It lives almost exclusively upon small fish. While it is thought to be very destructive to our game fish, it has been proven in many cases that its diet consists mostly of the slower moving fish considered as trash fish.

Years ago while gunning for Wood Ducks along one of our coastal streams I came upon an old Merganser with at least twenty young. The young ones were unable as yet to use their wings in flight. I came bursting out of the brush at the stream's edge and plunged into the midst of the flock. The little fellows set up a commotion and started beating their wings upon the water in order to propel them beyond my reach. The old bird, utterly fearless, flew straight at my face and sought to beat me with her flailing wings while allowing her little flock to escape. It was a case of downright loyalty and devotion on the part of the mother bird that I have never forgotten.

The Long Billed Curlew

This bird is fast becoming extinct throughout America and it has been many years since one has been seen along our coastline. At one time they were fairly numerous. As a kid, I remember my Dad bagging two of the big birds upon the sandy beach in the vicinity of Charleston, Coos County. The birds were lined up and killed by one bullet from his rifle.

The Curlew stands upon long stilted legs and has a very long curved bill. Its call is an eerie whistle and once heard is never forgotten.

The Water Ousel

The little "Dipper" or Water Ousel, frequenter of mountain streams, is the only bird known to actually submerge and walk along the bottom while it feeds. Naturalists have spent days hoping to be rewarded by the notes of its rare song, which I have been fortunate in hearing on several occasions. Once heard it is never forgotten, for it carries in its lilting sweetness all the rich splendor of the mountains, of laughing, splashing streams, of forest retreats and the pungent spice of Mother Nature, all rolled into a melody that tugs at the heart strings. It contains a quality that stops you dead in your tracks with straining ear until the song is finished and causes you to feel that The Great Red Gods of the Forest have indeed smiled upon you to give you the privilege of listening to what has been termed by many as a mythical song, on account of its rarity. It is too bad that such a song cannot be recorded.

WILSON JACK SNIPE *By Ben Hur Lampman*

The little game bird, the Wilson Jack Snipe, is now protected, like the Curlew, by Federal law, with a continuous closed season. It is of the Snipe family and used to be much sought by hunters. Its flight is very erratic, causing it to present a very difficult target to the gunner.

Ben Hur Lampman, sportsman, writer and poet of Portland, penned a piece which he called "Joe Bennett's Snipe Hunting," here quoted in part:

> Maybe you don't remember J. W. Bennett, we called him "Joe" — used to be a banker in Marshfield.
>
> When I think of him I recollect the times he used to hunt jacksnipe on North Slough above Marshfield. The jacksnipe is a tricky little fellow, and J. W. Bennett always said that he'd rather hunt jacksnipe than anything else. Up they fly from the swamp grass, long and coarse, and away they corkscrew, zigging and zagging, and saying "scaipe! scaipe!" You've get to be quick, you've got to be sure, or you won't get one. When Joe missed he used to laugh, for, the kind of sportsman he was, he didn't mind missing. As a matter of fact, he was simply glad to be out there on the slough, with the salt wind coming over the dunes. And he liked a gray day best.
>
> Jacksnipe have been protected for a good many years, and rightly, for the time came when they got to be scarce. But those were the times of the righthand drive, before the railroad came to the bay, and when a man looks back on them he wonders if ever again there will be times half so happy as those were. I suppose J. W. Bennett shot his share of jacksnipe, but the snipe that he bagged couldn't have hastened the closed season for them. There were market hunters then who shot jacksnipe for $2.50 a dozen, and they made good wages at it. The birds were in great demand, small as they are — just two morsels of breast — for they are fine eating. And in the times I recollect there were a great many jacksnipe. North Slough was a favorite place for them, in the salt grass and the pools that jacksnipe love. And

when I close my eyes to remember better, I can see J. W. Bennett trudging slowly through the swaying swamp grass, with his shotgun at ready, and the look of a boy in his eyes.

"The trick of it," he used to say, "is to shoot while they are flying straightaway, for a jacksnipe can be depended upon to fly straight for maybe thirty or forty feet before the bird begins corkscrewing. But when your snipe starts to corkscrew, heaven help you! Here, Sheila! Here, Mike!"

They were his two Irish setters, and he loved them as he loved his friends, and small blame to him, for though the breed is headstrong it makes a good dog when it does – none better. Those two setters had coats so lustrous that even on a dull day, out in the marsh with Joe Bennett, they shone as though they were on fire. Good dogs, both of them. Beautiful dogs. Of course, you didn't need a dog, not really, to hunt jacksnipe when birds are plentiful. You merely walk through the grass, sniffing the smell of the marshes – and its better than flowers – and once in a while a jacksnipe jumps up at your feet and goes boring away. You've got to be quick. But if you don't happen to score, why you've still the rest of the day, and the sea wind, and the dogs, and the feeling of being out there on North Slough. That's the way J. W. Bennett always looked at it.

I've got a lot of memories of J. W. Bennett and every last one of them is as wholesome as a drink of spring water. I think all his friends that are left would say the some thing. His father founded Bandon. Did I mention it? I meant to.

SWANS *By Emil R. Peterson*

Though swans are migratory, several families of them seem to have adopted the Coos Bay region as a permanent place of residence. Perhaps half a dozen pairs have been here a number of years.

One pair of Swans have nested on Haynes Inlet near Lone Rock each season during the past eight or ten years. In 1949 they raised a family of five signets, making a fine-looking family of seven as they proudly paraded in battleship-formation, with Papa Swan in the lead.

In 1948, Mr. and Mrs. Swan had succeeded in raising one lonely signet. When it had practically reached full growth, one day a two-legged animal stopped his car, got out with his gun and shot the beautiful bird, blinding it but did not immediately kill it. Apparently it swam off and died. The animal with the gun got into his car and drove off, supposedly getting a great thrill out of his act of *prowess*.

One of the most pathetic tragedies in the experience of a local Swan family was told by the *Coos Bay Times* in the spring of 1947:

> For several years the pair of beautiful wild swans that settled on Pony Slough about 1940 has been trying to raise a family.
>
> Each year the graceful birds became tamer, and were quicker to accept food put out by North Bend people grateful for the sereneness they lent Pony Slough.
>
> It seems that something always happened each nesting season. Several vandals broke up the nest and smashed the eggs. This year the proud pair was incubating several eggs.
>
> But the brood will never be raised by the parents. Nor will they probably ever start another family. Yesterday the mother was shot and critically wounded. . . .

Mrs. Andrew Varga of North Bend took the wounded bird in charge. The story was continued a few days later by the *Coos Bay Times*:

> The mother swan shot and critically wounded on Pony Slough Sunday died last night.
>
> A veterinarian attempted to save the beautiful bird by amputating the left wing nearly severed by the .22 caliber slug. He gave the swan gas and performed the operation yesterday afternoon. . . . Too much water had leaked into the swan's lungs through the torn wing and this killed the bird, the veterinarian believes. He explained that swans breathe partly through their wings.
>
> Meanwhile, Mrs. Andrew Varga has put the six bluish-green eggs into an incubator, rigged up from an electric heating pad.
>
> Extremely tame, the dead swan was one of a pair that had been living on Pony Slough for several years. They depended much upon Bangor residents for bits of bread and other food. Originally quite wild, the heavy, graceful birds became so tame they ate from the hand of anyone who offered food. . . .
>
> The father swan is heart-broken. He swims half-heartedly today on Pony Slough with wings tucked in and head hung low.

Mrs. Varga succeeded in hatching the eggs and fed the signets for a few days. But apparently she did not know the ways and needs of a family of baby swans, for one by one the little fellows weakened and died.

Just what became of the Widower-Swan is not definitely known. However, there is a *single* Swan that has made his home on Haynes Inlet during the past several years. It is possible that he may be the one who lost his family in that Pony Slough tragedy in 1947.

Early Day Fishing, *By Lans Leneve*

When I first accompanied my parents upon a fishing trip on the Coquille River, it was not unusual for three or four in one family to catch 500 "shiners" (now known as young silverside salmon) and trout, within a single day's fishing. During spring and fall, it mattered not where one might cast a hook within the tide waters of the Coquille, he was assured of good angling. Excellent fishing could be had off the many sand bars and wharves, in fact from almost any spot where one might be able to cast a hook along the entire length of the river, and the same held true of all forks and tributaries of that stream.

On the lower Coquille during the various runs of salmon, thousands of the big fish could be seen sporting about the surface of the water, leaping and rolling – the water fairly boiling as a result of their capers. The big seines that were drawn by horses driven along the flats between Bullard's Ferry and the mouth of the river, yielded tons upon tons of fish each day.

Down at the mouth of Sixes River, in Curry County, the farmers would drive to the mouth of the stream, where the salmon during their runs fairly choked the mouth of the narrow channel. Armed with spears and pitch forks, they would soon load their wagons with the big fish. The salmon taken in this manner were salted or smoked and the surplus used for fertilizing orchards.

Coos River in those days boasted some of the finest fishing to be found anywhere in the United States. Bait casting, trolling and fly casting – any one of the three methods – assured the taking of both large salmon and cut-throat trout by even the rankest novice.

Every stream of any size and the various lakes of both Coos and Curry counties fairly teemed with trout. It was nothing unusual for an angler to catch a hundred or more game fish within a single day. When legislation was finally enacted to protect our game fish, they were still so abundant that the first limit imposed upon the angler was 75 a day. After several years had passed the limit was cut to 50, later to 25, then to 15, and finally, as at the present, to 10 trout.

Yet in spite of the strictest conservation methods employed by game and fish agencies, there will never again be one tenth of the game fish that at one time were to be found by the millions within the borders of Coos and Curry counties. Those days are but a memory.

A Wild Fish Story — But True, *By Emil R. Peterson*

In the late summer of 1898, when I was 16, father came home after all the rest of us had gone to bed. We heard his excited voice as he burst into the house, "The slough is alive with fish!"

We were soon all out of bed.

"Get some buckets!" father said. We did — and followed him down to the slough. Our boat landing float was made of several big logs, eight or ten of them. The fish had got in between the logs — hundreds of them. We scooped them up in our hands. In a little while we had the buckets full. We brought more buckets, then the wash tubs, then boxes and barrels.

The fish were something like herring, but at least twice as large. We found out later that they were pilchards. The next morning we began cleaning fish and preparing them for salting. Neighbors came and we gave them all they could carry. The fish kept on coming, and we continued to catch them. We salted them down, filling barrels and wooden tubs.

The fish still kept coming and we kept fishing — just for fun. We couldn't possibly use any more. Sometimes at night when a big run was on, we would hang a lantern over the water. The fish would dart up to the light and we could catch them in a dip net, from one to half a dozen at a dip.

It sounds unbelievable, but we could sometimes hear the fish coming at night when they were nearly a mile down the slough. They would come in large schools, droves, multitudes. I guess there must have been millions. Apparently something would startle them and they would go to jumping. They roared like rapids or falls in a river.

The fish remained in the bay several weeks. It may have been months. I'm not sure how long. Then they began to die off. They must have starved to death. Anyway, when they died, they formed floating islands — acres of islands. It was a time for the sea gulls. They came by the thousands. I never saw so many sea gulls before nor since. Sailors on ships that came in said that all the sea gulls from San Francisco to Seattle were in Coos Bay attending the fish festival. It was fortunate for the residents that the sea gulls did come.

I remember it was in 1898, the year of the Spanish-American War, because a neighborhood boy, Walter Westman, said that when Admiral Dewey sank the Spanish fleet in Manila Bay, there was so much shooting that the pilchards became so frightened that they scooted across the ocean and came to Coos Bay for protection. But they ran into their Waterloo.

Other runs of pilchards came in some of the following years, sometimes large runs, but never did they begin to approach that run of 1898.

Striped Bass Come to Coos Bay

The following account is condensed from *The Coming of the Pond Fishes* by Ben Hur Lampman:

> In the salmon season of 1914 a flabergasted Marshfield commercial fisherman, tending his gilnet, took from its meshes two strange and beautiful fish, such as never before had been taken from the waters of Coos Bay or elsewhere along the Oregon coast. *Roccus Lineatus,* the striped bass, acclimated in San Francisco Bay since 1879, was on the march northward. . . .
>
> The most celebrated saltwater game fish of the Atlantic coast

was not enthusiastically welcomed. An insatiable predator, he was certain to play havoc with the native salmon and trout.

Indeed, Albert Jutstrom, who netted the first bass, had but to glance at the stranger to know that its food was the living flesh of other fishes. From the stomach of a 14-pound Coos Bay bass, eleven cutthroat trout, averaging eleven inches in length, have been taken. It was obviously an ill day for our salmon and trout when this glorious glutton was freed in the Pacific coast waters. The statement has been positively made by members of the Coquille River salmon fishery that the fine salmon runs of

Coos Bay Times

In 1914, "a flabbergasted Marshfield fisherman took from his net two strange and beautiful fish such as never before had been taken from the waters of Coos Bay."

that stream presently will be exterminated in the capacious maw of the striped bass.

The appearance of the striped bass in Coos Bay in 1914 was followed by a consistent increase in frequency, so that in 1928, a catch which heretofore had been incidental to other fisheries assumed importance in its own right. The year 1931 saw the inclusion of striped bass in the Oregon commericial code, with regulations prescribing areas in Coos Bay where the taking of bass was permitted by angling only. It was in 1931 that the striped bass catch was included in the official records of the Fish Commission of Oregon.

The commercial catch for 1931, with bass reported only from Coos Bay, was 18,153 pounds. In 1945, that catch (incomplete) totaled 231,005 pounds from Coos Bay, 725 pounds from the Coquille and 18,582 pounds from the Umpqua.

Oregon anglers have taken striped bass from Coos Bay weighing up to 60 pounds, though the average is far less.

15

Rogue River

IF YOU KNOW ROGUE RIVER WELL, you may find fault with some of the names and explanations given here. However, the names are local and most of them do not have any official confirmation. The Old Rogue goes on a rampage once in a while and leaves the riffles, the rocks, the banks and the channel changed . . . sometimes very much changed. Different people give different names to riffles and other landmarks.

Here is a log of the Rogue from the ocean up to Agness:

(N denotes north side of river; S, south side; C. in river). Beginning at mouth of river, heading up stream:

1 South spit.

2 N Doyle Rock — named for pioneer rancher.

3 N Hume or Hunt Rock — north abutment of bridge.

4 S Mill Rock — named for Riley & Stewart sawmill. The Hume salmon cannery was just west or down the river from the rock. The Hume fish hatchery was on Indian Creek about a mile up the river on the south side. Riley and Stewart sold their salt-packing fish plant to Hume, who later moved his cannery and store across the river and named the place *Wedderburn*. Hume tore down the old Riley and Stewart sawmill, floated some of the hewn timbers across the river and used them in his Wedderburn buildings — warehouse, cannery, store. H. T. Stewart recently wrote, "I presume those timbers are still supporting that warehouse."

5 Lower and Upper Alder Riffles, about a mile above bridge, named for former strip of alder trees, later mostly washed away. This strip of river was famous as a *drift* for commercial fishing in early days.

6 Woodruff Riffle — named for Lyman Woodruff, father of Calvin, Cornie and Chancie Woodruff.

7 S Elephant Rock.

8 C Johns' Hole — named for Jacob Johns, a set-net fisherman; half a mile up from Elephant Rock.

9 C Cannery Riffle — named for Seaborg cannery, a competitor

of the Macleay Estate interests, 1915-1919. The site has been washed away, leaving the riffle.

10 N Flemming Slough.

11 Ferry Riffle. At lower end of Ferry Hole.

12 Ferry Hole – site of the old Bagnell Ferry, in operation in 1876 when the Wakeman family moved in. About 1915 to 1927, a free ferry was operated there by Curry County.

13 N Squaw Creek – an Indian woman was drowned in this creek.

14 N Canfield Riffle named for Canfield family.

15 S Jim Hunt Creek – Hunt family were early settlers.

16 C Wakeman Riffle – Wakeman family. Theodore F. Wakeman said, "It was here that my grandparents got their first glimpse of the Rogue River after coming from Camas Valley by pack horses.

Wakeman farmstead was completely eradicated by flood in spring of 1890 . . . "

17 N Emery Riffle – Emery family, early settlers.

18 Libby Riffle – just below Libby Creek. Sometimes called Bill Ash Riffle after a fisherman who camped there.

19 N Libby Creek – named for Dave Libby, Indian war veteran; also scene of an Indian battle in 1856.

20 N Libby Hill – good deer hunting ground.

21 N Tom Smith Ranch. Hardy Stewart recently wrote concerning Tom Smith:

"He was my uncle by marriage. When he first came to that section he was foreman of the Riley and Stewart seining crew. Later he bought the place where there were some of the best fishing eddies on the river. He sold his fish to Hume at 20 cents each and paid Hume two cents each to boat them to the cannery. Several times he tried to organize the fishermen, but so many of them owed Hume store bills, he was unsuccessful. His wife, my aunt, was a good cook and set an excellent table. For many years people stopped there for meals or to spend the night and no thought or mention was made of pay. I boarded there for $8 per month when I taught school at what was then known as *Round Grove.* I taught three months for the sum of $100."

22 N Kimble Riffle at the foot of Kimble Hill — one of the best steelhead riffles on the river; and Kimble Hill, a splendid hunting region.

23 N Jim Davis Riffle — named for Jim Davis family, part Indian.

24 C Coffee Riffle — a bad hole close to north shore, sometimes called the *Devil's Coffee Pot.*

25 N Lobster Creek and Lobster Rock — lobsters or crawfish said to be plentiful in this stream. Scene of Indian ambush during the Indian war of 1856.

26 C Lobster Creek Riffle.

27 C Shallow Riffle.

28 C Jennings Riffle.

29 N Panther Creek.

30 C William Miller Riffle — an early settler.

31 C Hawkins Riffle — named for Angie (Billings) Hawkins, who still lives on the south shore with her son, who is a well known river guide and navigator.

32 S Quoseton Creek — Indian name.

33 C Silver Creek Riffle.

34 N Silver Creek.

35 C Annie Lowery Riffle — named for Annie Lowery, who operated *Lowery's on the Rogue.*

36 C Bacon Flat Riffle.

37 C Big Fish Riffle.

38 C Lowery Canyon — named for Jim Lowery, early settler.

39 S Skookum House Butte — site of Indian stockade and battle with Indians in the war of 1865.

40 C Bradford Riffle — name of an Indian.

41 S Bradford Creek. Indian Bradford lived there with two wives.

42 C Coal Riffle — scow load of coal lost there.

43 Slide Creek Riffle.

44 Sherman Riffle — boat landing of Sherman, a homesteader.

45 S Wake-Up-Riley Creek. Hardy T. Stewart tells how this creek got its name:
"My grandfather (Michael Riley) grubstaked a miner. The miner came at midnight, rapped on the window of Riley's cabin and exclaimed excitedly. 'Wake up, Riley! We're rich!' He thought he had made a rich gold strike. It turned out to be *fool's gold,* or mica. And so the name."
46 C Rachel's Delight Riffle.
47 C Aurberry Riffle – named for a homesteader.
48 N Tommy East Creek.
49 N Tommy East Riffle – veteran of Indian war.
50 Nail Keg Riffle – canoe upset, losing a keg of nails.
51 Nail Keg Creek.
52 Little Canyon – difficult to navigate when water is high.
53 Ran's Creek – named for Ran Tichenor, early settler.
54 New Riffle – built up in recent years.
55 C Bear Riffle.
56 Sundown Creek – men with Indian wives reached there at sunset and camped over night. Thus, the name.
57 C Bean Riffle – boat upset with load of beans.
58 C Boiler Riffle – Steamer *Rogue River* wrecked there in 1902. Its steam boiler marked the place for years.
59 N Stonehouse Creek.
60 C Painted Rock Riffle.
61 N Painted Rock Creek.

62 N Painted Rock – an overhanging rock used by Indians on sheltered side to paint signs with colored clay, giving directions to travelers; a kind of guide post.
63 C Copper Canyon – copper prospect worked there.
64 C Petter's Riffle.
65 Twin Sisters Riffle.
66 C Twin Sisters Rock.
67 Crooked Riffle.
68 Allen Pool – steelhead water.
69 C Smith Riffle.
70 N Agness Boat Landing.
71 S Illinois River Junction.

A few years after the turn of the century — it may have been in 1906 or 1907 — Henry Moore secured a contract to carry the U. S. mail by motor boat from Gold Beach to Agness. A year or two later he was succeeded by Frank Lowery, who knew the river well, for he had grown up on it.

Frank's father, Jim Lowery, had come in 1868 with his Indian wife, from Sailor's Diggings in the upper Rogue River country in Josephine County. They settled on the north side of the river about midway between Wedderburn and Agness, where their son, Frank, grew to manhood. Few persons, perhaps, were so well prepared by nature and by experience to navigate that treacherous stream. And so, through twenty years or more, Frank Lowery provided a boat service on the Rogue.

In 1930 Lowery sold his business to Carter and Miller, who continued the service for about twelve years, selling to Bob Elliott in 1942.

Four years later, in 1946, Elliott transferred his interest to Keneth Meservey and De Forest Sorber. A few months later, Meservey sold his interest to Lex Fromm, resulting in the partnership of Fromm and Sorber, who now make six round trips per week in summer and three in winter, in keeping with their mail contract, besides carrying passengers and freight. Special trips are made when called for, sometimes as many as five trips a day in the height of the hunting and fishing seasons.

A boat, equipped with a high-powered outboard motor and a tunnel-enclosed 16-inch propeller, sometimes glides in as little as six inches of water in climbing the riffles. The man at the controls must know the river. Also he must know his boat and just what it will do when he "gives 'er the gun."

Settlers

Climbing the riffles of the Rogue didn't develop in a day. A whole century and more has been given to its growth. Even before the Indians were driven from their homes in the war of 1855 and 1856, men paddled and poled and pulled their canoes and boats from the ocean up stream some thirty miles to where the Illinois flows into the Rogue. From there they went by trail into the mountains. Gold was the chief attraction. Fish and game were had for the taking. Patches of fertile land induced the growing of potatoes and a variety of vegetables and such fruits as apples, plums, pears, peaches, grapes, and different kinds of berries. Wild blackberries and huckleberries were plentiful in season. Open prairies provided range and pasture for horses, cattle and sheep. Hogs grew fat on acorns and myrtle nuts.

And so men began to settle along the rivers and up the smaller streams. Some of them brought their families. Others married Indian women. Children grew up, boys became men. Fishing and hunting had become a part of their very lives. They learned to know the trails leading to the best hunting grounds. Fishing eddies and riffles were as open as books to them. Shooting the rapids of the Rogue was as natural to them as sleep at the end of a weary day.

Guides

Fame of Curry County as a paradise for hunting and fishing became known far and wide. Sportsmen, coming in, needed guides. Who could be better prepared for such service than the boys and men who had grown to be a part of the country itself? At first they did it for pure enjoyment. Demand for their services increased and guiding became a profession.

Among the early guides in Curry County, Bill Coy appears to be the choice of several oldtimers to top the list. One of his lifelong friends said of him:

> Will Coy was one of the finest and best guides in Curry County. Pages of interesting material could be written about him. . . . His home was at Eucher Creek, in which section he was born and lived until moving to Reedsport in 1950, shortly prior to his death. His hunting and guide experience was largely in the central part of Curry County from the coast to Josephine County line. He was noted for his rugged endurance and prodigious

strength, the latter being illustrated on one occasion when he put an iron on his shoulder that weighed over 700 pounds and walked away with it.

A Dr. Cooper of San Francisco, for many years made annual trips to Curry County and always hired Coy as guide for his party. The Doctor was an expert rifle shot and Coy credited much of his own skill to the training he received on those hunting expeditions. It always took one horse, he said, to carry the ammunition, and daily shooting practice was routine.

The same informant said of two other guides:

Delmar Colgrove, Sr., living on the mountaintop between the Rogue and Chetco rivers, earned an important place among the guides and hunters of Curry County. He owns a valuable stock ranch of several thousand acres in a section where bear and panther have been plentiful. Self preservation as a stockman and the thrill of the chase made a serious and active hunter of him.

Colgrove hunted with a pack of dogs, chaining them together in pairs, excepting the start dog, so they would stay with him until he turned them loose on a hot trail. If a panther was jumped it usually treed quickly, but a bear generally required the united efforts of all the dogs. One of his favorite start dogs was known to have picked up a cold track two days old. The number of bear and panther killed by this combination of man and dogs would run into many hundreds.

As a game shot, Colgrove is near the top in a country noted for the markmanship of its native hunters. His ability to keep within hearing distance of the cry of his dogs when in full chase, and his long experience as a big game hunter, were so outstanding that Jack London, after one hunt with him, said that he would return and write a novel with a Curry County background and with Colgrove as the central figure. London died before he could fulfill his promise.

Tom Carey, now a resident of San Jose, California, is another outstanding hunter and marksman of past days in Central Curry. Tom was born and grew to manhood in the midst of a splendid game section about twelve miles south of Port Orford. His experiences as a youngster were exciting and dangerous. On one occasion his dogs treed a panther when his only weapon was a 38 pocket revolver. After many shots he knocked the panther out of the tree. When it hit the ground it sprang and caught a small tree near where Carey was standing, and tore great scratches in it when it raked down with its hind legs, evidently thinking it had caught its tormentor.

When getting a new rifle, the first thing Carey did was to knock off the sight and mount a peep. He used only this peep and a bead and shot with both eyes open. As a quick game shot he was without a peer.

Up in the Agness country were several other guides, among them Walter and Martin Fry, the Blondell brothers, and Charles Pettinger. Their hunting grounds included Fishhook Camp; Burnt Ridge, or High Ridge; Brandy Camp; Sugar Loaf; Squirrel Camp; Hole-In-The-Ground, a deep little valley almost surrounded by ridges, appearing like a deep hole when viewed from higher ridges; Bear Camp — good bear hunting; Bob's Garden, where Indian Bob once had a home; Sour Grass Camp; Silver Creek Prairies; Bald Mountain Camp; Bark Cabin Camp. Charley Pettinger also had for his hunting grounds such places as Iron Mountain Camp, Mount Brinn or Bald Knob Camp; Hunter's Camp, at head of Lobster's Creek; Cedar Springs Camp.

Charles Billings, living in the Mule Creek country, guided in the areas which embraced Big Meadows, Cold Springs, Eden Valley, Buck Camp, Panther Camp, Hanging-Rock, and Nine-Mile Camp at head of West Fork.

Guides down in the Chetco country included Fred Gardiner, Bill Tolman, and Delmar Colgrove. Their stamping grounds were such places as Hazel Camp, Long Ridge, High Prairie, Barclay Butte, Windy Valley, Bosley Butte Camp, Stack Yards, and Denet's Rock.

Five Sections of the River

For an over-all glimpse of the Rogue from its source near Crater Lake to the sea, the stream might roughly be divided into five sections.

First, the rough and turbulent waters come bubbling out of the west side of the Cascades not far from Crater Lake.

Next, slowing down somewhat into placid stretches, it flows into the broad and populated area commonly referred to as the Rogue River Valley.

The third begins a few miles below Grants Pass and ends at Agness. Only the lower ten miles of this section, from Big Bend to Agness, may be traveled by road. From below Grants Pass to Big Bend is a wild part which few persons travel by boat and none by road, for no road follows this portion of the stream. Of this section, Zane Grey, in his *Rogue River Feud,* says:

> The river twisted and chafed and fought its way through Hell Gate, and rushing over Alameda Rocks and the ledges of Argo mines, it entered the canyon wilderness of the Coast Range.

If you itch with a longing to shoot this stretch of the Rogue in a boat, the only thing that I know for you to do it safely is to make a date with the *River Sharks,* men who grew up on and with fighting-mad rivers. They know every rock and rapid and riffle from Grants Pass to the sea. There are several outfits prepared to serve you. They have boats that are sturdy and staunch but light enough to be portaged over two or three of the worst rapids. Outboard motors are used in stretches where the river runs gently. One seasoned guide mans each boat. Two passengers with their tackle, guns and luggage, and the guide, make up a full cargo of 800 to 900 pounds.

There are several stopping places along the river where guest houses are prepared to offer the traveler good meals and comfortable overnight accommodation, such as the little community of Marial.

It is reported that the earliest boating ever done on the upper "white water" of the Rogue was by John Aubury, when he freighted supplies from Josephine County to the gold miners at Marial, about 1906. Glen Woolridge writes: "I started running the Rouge from Grants Pass to the sea in 1915. . . . Have made five motorboat trips up from Gold Beach to Grants Pass." Woolridge had a story of his experiences in *Field & Stream,* for August, 1948, in which he said:

> For many years my burning desire was to make a journey up the river, from the sea to Grants Pass. Wise old river rats said it never could be done. . . . When I was a small boy I spent most of my time wading, swimming and fishing, and learning to handle a boat on the smooth stretches before I ventured into the rushing currents. . . .
>
> During the past twenty years I have made hundreds of down-river trips from Grants Pass to the sea, and for quite a while had been studying the possibilities of coming up the Rogue from the sea to Grants Pass. . . .

Together with Chuck Foster and Bob Prichett, two of the ablest boatmen of the Rogue River, I made a number of preliminary runs. . . . On the morning of the start of the big run — Wednesday, May 14, 1947 — we put off from the old Ferry Landing at Gold Beach. . . . After the motor became thoroughly warmed up, I gave her the gun and she streaked on her way. We shot up through the head of tide-water and took Canfield Riffle, through Copper Canyon, and on to Marial we sailed like a dream. . . .

The beach in the Grants Pass city park was the end of our journey at 6:45 p. m. on the third day — 14½ hours actual running time. A grand experience!

Names of other *White-water* Rogue River guides include Everett Spaulding, Pres Pyle, Prince Helfrich, Veltee Pruit, Howard Montgomery.

The fourth section of the Rogue is the navigable portion from its junction with the Illinois down to where it meets tidewater. The fifth section is the tidewater or lower river.

Prior to 1907 or 1908, a trip to Agness from Gold Beach or Wedderburn offered a choice of two routes — one by water, the other by land. The Rogue with its riffles was there just about the same as today. But the modes of navigation were different. A boat was rowed and poled and in some places pulled by means of a rope, the "puller" wading over riffles or sometimes walking on gravel or sand bars by the side of the river. In some places where the river was not too swift and if the wind was favorable, a sail might be brought into service. One did well to make the trip of about 30 miles in a day.

If no boat was available or if walking was preferred, the path was a narrow, uneven one along the north bank. The road has been gradually extended until it reaches Lobster Creek, about 15 or 16 miles up from Wedderburn. From the end of the road, the hiker took to the trail, climbing ridges, crossing gullies and streams. What might be encountered on this trip has been described by Zane Gray in telling of this trip in *Rogue River Feud*:

The trail climbed to the mountain side above the river. The rain fell steadily. The Rogue roared below. It looked like a dark brown swirling torrent. Uprooted trees, their foliage green against the water, told the tale of the mountain storm. Long before Kev reached it, he espied the hamlet of Agness, recognized by the white suspension bridge which spanned the river.

Besides a trail in from Roseburg and later from West Fork, the only other entrance to the Mule Creek area was by way of the upstream trail along the north side of the river. This, no doubt, had been used by the Indians through untold generations. Today you can drive in from Powers. Marial is one of the regular stopping places for the river rapid-shooters on their way from Grants Pass to the sea. A mile down the river from Marial the road ends and the trail begins.

About midway between Marial and Big Bend is a more or less mysterious or mythical place called Solitude, chosen by Zane Grey as the home of the fictional heroine in *Rogue River Feud*.

Big Bend is at the foot of the hill where the road from Powers first reaches the Rogue River. From there to Illahe is about two miles and another eight miles to Agness.

The name of Big Bend is famous in Indian War history of 1855-1856. Here is perhaps the largest single tract of fertile river bottom land for many miles in either direction. H. G. Plumer has been developing the place as a beef cattle ranch. He and his neighbor across the river have a private airfield. Several fine lodges are located along the river between Big Bend and Agness, some private and others public, on both sides of the stream.

At Agness the Illinois River joins the Rogue. A suspension bridge, just wide enough for an auto, crosses the

Rogue at Agness, and a road leads up the Illinois to Oak Flats, a distance of four miles. Except for this short branch, the road ends at Agness. And here also ends the river boat run from Wedderburn and Gold Beach.

From this central junction where rivers, boats and autos meet, numerous trails lead out in various directions to homesteads, mining camps, hunting grounds, camp sites, and forest lookouts. Also the old Indian trail from Port Orford, wending and winding through the forests and across gullies and canyons, over ridges and mountains, leads the traveler to the Illahe-Agness-Big Bend country.

Agness post office was established in 1897, with Amaziah Aubery as its first postmaster and with the office named after his daughter. Besides the post office, Agness has a school, a hotel, a store and a U. S. Forest station.

Stop anywhere along the Rogue within a hundred miles from the ocean and ask any oldtimer about Illahe and he'll answer, "Oh, yes, that's where George Meservey lives, eight miles up the river from Agness."

Or ask about George Meservey and the answer will be that he lives at Illahe. Meservey and Illahe are practically with Elijah H. Price as postmaster.

George's father, Captain Elisha H. Meservey, a Mexican War veteran and U. S. marshall, had an active part as a volunteer in the Rogue River Indian War during 1855-1856. After the war was over, he married an Indian woman. Perhaps no living person today knows Curry County better than does George Meservey. In the neighborhood of 90 years of age, his memory is excellent. He recalls the old hide-hunters who slaughtered elk and deer for the skins. He remembers his father's first-hand stories of the Indian War.

George served as postmaster at Illahe for 22 years, from 1918 till 1940, when he was succeeded by Rose L. Meservey. Though the office was discontinued in 1943 the name lives on. Address a letter today to *George Meservey, Curry County, Oregon,* and it will be delivered to him at Illahe. The office was first established in 1895, with Elijah H. Price as postmaster.

III

CULTURE

16

Education Since 1854

By Maude Liddell Barry

At Empire, in the autumn of 1854, Mrs. F. G. Lockhart taught the first Coos County school. She had five pupils—Russell Dement, Jasper Yoakam, Joe Yoakam, William Noble, and Lyman Noble. F. G. Lockhart became the county school superintendent, serving till 1857.

In September of 1857, C. Alderson was sent by Bishop Edmund S. Janes to Empire City to establish Methodism in Coos County. He visited around the different settlements and in 1858 taught reading and orthography to the children up Coos River. Later he went to Coquille where he held Sunday services at the Yoakam cabin, teaching the children of that locality during the week.

In 1860 Binger Hermann, then 18 years old, opened a school for the neighboring children of the south fork of the Coquille River. This was called district 2 and the village was later called Broadbent. It was the Coquille Valley school, standing on property owned by J. J. Jackson and later by R. C. Dement.

At "Old Town" or North Bend a school building was completed in 1862. The first teacher was Mr. McNutt, the second, Mrs. John Butler, wife of Captain John Butler, whose son, John, later became city recorder at Marshfield.

Meanwhile, Empire had been an attractive spot for new settlers. The school population was so increased that more room was needed as well as more teachers. George Stauff, a contractor and builder, was employed in 1866 to build a real school house.

It is interesting to note here that in 1868 Mrs. Minnie Myrtle Miller, wife of Joaquin Miller the poet, was one of the teachers at Empire.

At Marshfield, John Howlet, had built several tug

boats on the bay and had also built a bunk house for his men. When they moved to other quarters, John Howlet donated this building to the town for a school house. It was located on what was later called North First street. In 1867 Miss Mary C. Norris, who later became Mrs. J. L. Barker, held the first school and the district was called No. 9. It was formed from a part of the Empire district. Later Mrs. E. A. Anderson and Mrs. G. Webster and others taught until 1873.

In 1867, school was also begun near where Coquille was later established. This school house was built of logs on Cunningham Creek and was taught by Chester Rowell. Later, Rowell became one of the leading physicians of San Francisco.

During these thirteen years there were many settlers so isolated that it was impossible to send their children to any of the early schools. So they either taught them at home or employed a private tutor. Many of the early schools had very few, if any, books from which to learn. They were taught their A, B, C's from the Bible. The school day was long but the term was short, due to the weather, and the trails, and roads over which they had to travel.

In 1873 Brewster Valley built a log school house for the children and employed Miss Annie Robbins as the teacher for a term of six months.

A year later, 1874, D. M. Lowe, who with his family lived on the lower Coquille River not far from where Bandon is now located, decided to make a trip to Empire, thirty-one miles away. His purpose was to establish a school district near his home. He had six children of his own and there were several families not far away, but the nearest school district, at that time, was at Empire. It took him a week to make the trip but he obtained the necessary papers, properly signed, and District No. 11 was established. It was located at a place called Myrtle Grove, across the river from where Parkersburg now stands. Their first teacher was Miss Lucy Norris.

In 1875 a school house was erected at Dora and one at

Gravel Ford. A short time later the Shiloh school was built near the I. T. Weekly place.

To the Haines Inlet school, started in 1874 and later called District 26, came children from territories which later had their own districts.

Leslie's Weekly drawing made in 1878 of a schoolgirl of that time.

In Coos, great-grandma was trim and neat like this, and very winsome.

Let us summarize the first ten school districts:

District	Year	Teacher	Co. Superintendent	
Empire—6	1854	Mrs. F.G.Lockhart	F.G.Lockhart	1854-1857
Coos River—36	1858	C. Anderson	G. H. Hodgkins	1857-1859
Broadbent—2	1860	BingerHerman	ECCunningham	1859-1860
North Bend—13	1862	Mr. McNutt	C. Herman	1860-1863
Forks of Coos R.	1862	Isaiah Hacker	Wm. T. Perry	1863-1865
Marshfield—9	1867	Mary C. Norris	Anson Rodgers	1865-1868
Cunningham	1867	Chester Rowell	Anson Rodgers	1865-1868
Parkersburg—11	1871	MissLucyNorris	J.H.Schroeder	1868-1872
Brewster Valley	1873	Miss Annie Robbins	I. Hacker	1872-1874
HaynesInlet—26	1874	FannieMcKnight	J.H.Schroeder	1874-1876

In 1855 the school tax levy was one mill, in 1873 it was three mills and by 1897 it had been increased to five mills. (Now in 1951 the levy is 37.2 mills.) In 1897 there were 72 school districts, 4,025 children over 4 and under 20 years of age. (In 1951, 33 districts, 11,243 children.)

Return now to the first ten courageous school districts and see just how far their influence has spread since those very early days. Suppose we begin at the southern part of the county.

In 1872 the Wagner family, Henry Wygant, Hayes and T. C. Land settled in what is now the town of Powers. They came west from North Carolina and chose this location because it reminded them so much of their old home. They called their little settlement "North Carolina."

In 1912 A. H. Powers, vice-president and general manager of the Smith-Powers Logging Company, bought the Wagner ranch of 166 acres. It was platted for a town and Block 8 was deeded for a school. The town was named Powers in honor of A. H. Powers. A very nice school was built (District 31).

North from Powers, we come to Broadbent, District 2. In 1903 the one-room school was moved to the present location and in 1916 a second room was added.

Next we come to Myrtle Point, District 41.

In 1881 W. L. Dixon became a teacher in the village school. In February 1887 the town was incorporated. In 1888 Border and Bender laid out and platted an addition of nine blocks to the town, east and adjoining the land of

Collection of Alfred Powers

oaned by Emil R. Peterson

PORT ORFORD

llen Tichenor, to Port Orford in 1852, first white child in Southwest Oregon.

Port Orford 1888. Battle Rock.

Walter Sutton started the *Port Orford Tribune* in 1892.

Loaned by H. T. Stewart

The Sutton Family,

Taken September 25th, 1889:

Walter,	Aged 39	Years.
Louesa Annie,	" 30	"
Luly Alpha,	" 12	"
Walter Frank,	" 10	"
John Adam,	" 8	"
Bertha Francis	" 5	"
James Henry,	" 3	"
Mary Gertrude	" 10	Months.

Skookum, the Mule, aged 22 Years.

Collection of Alfred Powers

GOLD BEAC

Above: Main Street, looking south, in the old muddy days. Below: Wedd
across the river before the bridge. Bottom: Smallest Catholic church in A

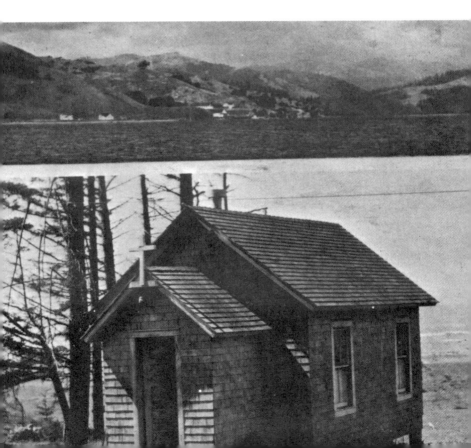

Chris Lehnherr. They donated block 5 to the school district, and a school house was built — District 31. This school was also used as a church. However, with the growing population the quarters became too small and in 1891 a brick building was erected at a cost of $15,000.

You will remember that J. M. Lowe walked to Empire in 1874 to create District No. 11, the first public school in the Bandon area, at Myrtle Grove across the river from where Parkersburg was later established. It was taught in 1874 at the Asa Hinch homestead, known as the Fourteen-Mile House on the Randolph Trail on what is now known as Cut Creek. In 1876 the school site was moved north to a building on land donated by Edward Fahy.

In 1880 a schoolhouse was built near Bullards Ferry. Robert Bullard taught this school for four years. In 1884 a large school was built on the hill near Rocky Point and Bullard taught here two years, marrying Malinda A. Hamblock, of the old pioneer family and one of his former pupils. He left the teaching profession and established a store on his property and the Bullards Ferry.

As you see, there were many little school districts in this area. Bandon itself did not show much improvement until after 1880 when an appropriation of $10,000 was received for improving the mouth of Coquille River. By 1886 it was decided that there was a great need for a school house in the town. This was District No. 54.

Up the Coquille River we come to the former coal mining town of Riverton, at one time a busy, romantic, fascinating village. The present school house that replaced the primitive one was built in 1909.

Now on to Coquille. In the Cunningham Creek district as previously stated, the first school was built in 1867 and the teacher was a young man by the name of Rowell, who later became a celebrated physician in San Francisco. The next teacher was Miss Lockhart, who later became Mrs. Henry Sengstacken. Later, Mrs. Hathaway, Miss Ann Hatcher (Mrs. A. L. Nosler), and John Overholtzer also taught at this school.

The Cunningham school soon became too small. It

also seemed too far away from the town. So a larger school was built, a box-house on the site where the First National Bank was built in later years. Soon this school house in turn became too small so the building was sold to John Messer who enlarged it for a livery stable.

The next school house was a frame building but before very long, it too became too small. So the Presbyterian Church took over the building and another new school was constructed in 1881, with 82 pupils for a term of three months. The teacher's salary was $30 a month. In 1882 there were 100 pupils. Two years later a second teacher was added and the following year the school term was increased to six months. By 1890 the enrollment had increased to 170 students and the teacher's salary was increased to $60 a month for men teachers and $40 a month for women.

In 1890 the Bunch family with other teachers and friends decided to build an academy on the north side of the Coquille Valley. The members of the faculty were W. H. Bunch, Principal; May Bunch, Mr. and Mrs. R. W. Airey, and Mr. and Mrs. Frank Bunch. The curriculum consisted of high school studies and a normal school course which drew teachers from great distances.

As the town of Coquille built up the followers of the Adventist Church felt that the town influences were not conducive to the healthy growth of the academy and it was decided to move this school to Gravel Ford. Some years later it was bought by J. L. Lutrell, a retired Christian minister.

In 1895 it was decided to build a new high school. This was later replaced by the Washington grade school, and a new high school was built in 1921, followed by a junior high school in 1926. The Washington school was replaced in 1939 and in 1949 the first section of the Lincoln elementary school was erected.

During all this time the rural districts realized that the children of their communities could receive a much better education and have many more advantages if they consolidated with the city schools. So it was decided to transport the pupils by bus and to do away with the little one-room schools of pioneer days.

On Coal Bank Slough the Newport and Eastport mines were opened in 1856 and the little town of Libby was a busy place. A schoolhouse was built. Its large bell was the pride of the community. However, like the other coal mining towns, Libby too became abandoned and the once prized school bell was installed in a new school house built at Englewood in 1913. Englewood school consolidated with District 9 in 1916.

In 1874 Donald McKay and others platted a town across from Marshfield and many buildings were erected, including a school. In early days there was a ferry connecting the two towns. Now we have a bridge and highway. Following this highway up Coos River, we come to a very large schoolhouse at the forks of North and South Coos River. This large building resulted when several rural schools decided to consolidate. In 1951 Coos River school together with Eastside consolidated with Coos Bay District 9 C.

Before the highway was built, however, the pupils were transported to and from school by boats. One afternoon the writer stood on the bank in front of the school house overlooking the river. It was time for school to close for the day and out of the building came the boys and girls. Two by two they walked down the many, many steps to the bank of the river where each pupil stepped aboard the boat that was going in his direction. The loading took but a few minutes and as the whistles blew the boats glided out into the channel. Now there is a highway up the river and its forks, and buses take the place of the boats.

Bunker Hill schoolhouse was replaced by a very fine building in 1909 when there were two teachers. Since that time it has been enlarged and now it too has consolidated with Coos Bay District 9 C. The Millington and Delmar schools also joined District 9 C.

District 9's first school has been described. From time to time a few additions were made to this building as the public school enrollment continued to grow. Marshfield was incorporated in 1874. When John Howlet gave the District his old bunkhouse for a school building,

George Stauff donated the seats for the children. Mr. Hacker was hired to teach. He had twenty-one students but many others began coming from nearby settlements until the enrollment became so large that not only was it necessary to employ more teachers but also to build additions to the building. Mrs. Hacker, Mrs. S. B. Rotnor, Mr. Siler, I. H. Atkinson, Mrs. O. Ralsten were some of these early teachers.

On January 7, 1878, J. T. McCormac and Mrs. S. B. Rotnor opened up a private school in the academy building located on the block bounded on the north by Highland Avenue, on the east by Third Street, on the south by Market and on the west by Fourth Street. It was erected by subscriptions of the Marshfield citizens for the purpose of a Presbyterian Church and an Academy. However, they became financially involved and the building was bought by E. B. Dean and Company in order to protect their interests, as they had donated part of the land and furnished the lumber. The 1879 monthly tuition was $5 for the primary department, $7.50 for the junior department, and $10 for the senior department.

The following text books were used at that time:

Orthography	Watson
Reading	Watson
Penmanship	Spencerian
Grammar	Clark
Composition and Rhetoric	Hart
U. S. History	Barnes
Political Science	Hopkins
Geography	Monteith's Series
Natural Philosophy	Quackenbos
Botany	Gray
Chemistry	Youman and Atfield
Philosophy	Steele
Bookkeeping	Bryant and Stratton
Arithmetic	Thompson's Series
Higher Arithmetic	Robinson
Algebra	Brooks and Loomis
Geometry	Loomis
Trigonometry and Surveying	Loomis
Latin	Harkness

This academy and the large school building at Bandon that was built in 1886 were considered the most westerly places of learning of their character at that time in the United States, and were certainly a great credit to this part of the country. The enrollment increased, as students came from many parts of Oregon. In June of 1881 the enrollment was 175 students and there were four teachers. The following September, D. L. Rood and his wife took over the school. Through their efforts a settlement was brought about with the E. B. Dean Company and the district bought the portion of the property which the latter owned. In 1883 J. N. Knowles and wife donated the northern part of the block to the district. Now the entire block belonged to School District 9.

From this time on the school was conducted under the management of different people: J. D. Hawes, Allen Arrington, W. D. Reedy, J. M. Peebles, and Mrs. Huden. However, it was not until 1892 when Professor F. A. Golden took charge that the school was established as a graded school. Three years later it was decided that the size of the town and the increased enrollment warranted a new building. The old Academy was moved to the west side of Third Street between Commercial and Market streets and a new building was erected on the old site. Eight rooms were completed in February of 1896, when the attendance had grown to 471 students, with eight teachers.

In 1909 came a high school building, in 1923 the Harding School used as a grade and junior high school, in 1942 a senior high school and gymnasium.

Many districts have consolidated with District 9 C — Coos Bay (formerly Marshfield), Coos River, Bunker Hill, Millington, Delmar, Sumner, Allegany, and Eastside.

As in other districts in the county, there were several private schools. One was conducted by Mrs. Sarah Horsfall, mother of Dr. William Horsfall — on Pine Street, later in the second story of the Manse on Market Avenue.

During the summer months a teacher was sent to Marshfield by the Seventh Day Adventist Church to teach, primarily, sewing to any who wished to enroll. Later a church was established on Seventh Street and Commercial Avenue and in 1930 one room was added for a school to accommodate children of the first six grades. In 1950 they had two school rooms, and taught the first ten grades.

Another religious private school was built in 1920 by the people of the St. Monica's Catholic Parish — at the corner of Sixth and Bennett Avenue. The first enrollment was 73 pupils and was taught by the Sisters. The school was later moved to its present location on Sixth Street next to the Catholic Church. It was enlarged and modernized and fully certified by the State Board of Education in 1941 and is now under the management of the Holy Names Sisters of Marylhurst, Oregon.

At North Bend the first school at "Old Town" in 1862 became too small to house the pupils and it was necessary to teach some of the children in a church on North Union.

In 1904 was built a very fine schoolhouse, called the Central School and located on McPherson and Vermont Streets, since torn down. In 1905, on the west side of the town in the area called "Bangor," a building was used to accommodate the growing school population in that section.

In 1908 a beautiful high school was built next to this west side school and in 1949 another class room building was built just north of the high school.

The Roosevelt school was built in 1924 on Sherman Avenue; the Hillcrest School in 1948 on South Meade Street. The growing population, on the west side of the town near the airport, called for a school in that area, known as the Sunset School.

We now return to Empire, the scene of the first school in Coos County. Some of the students that attended the Empire school in the early days are people that many of us remember: John and James Flanagan, Chas. Stauff, James Watson, Mrs. Brando, Flo Farley; and some of the early teachers were Mr. Rood, Mr. Dalrymple, Mr. Porter, Mrs. Short, Mrs. Lehman and Mrs. Vandenburg.

The school at Empire soon grew from the one-room shack to a four-room school house. The several rooms of today are at the original location.

Farther towards the ocean at Charleston, at first a small one-room building was erected for a school on the Seven Devils Road. This later was moved nearer the town to a more central location. At present there is a very fine building with four classrooms, a gymnasium, and cafeteria.

17

The Churches

By Ralph T. Moore

RELIGION AND SECULAR EDUCATION, during the first 25 years of Southwestern Oregon development—1851 to 1876 — was very largely at mother's knee or in neighborhood gatherings under leadership of civic-minded volunteers. The austere difficulties of obtaining a bare living and the extreme hindrances to ready transportation combined to confine family activities to the near environment of the home. But the devotion of pioneer mothers and fathers to the spiritual welfare of their children was not in the slightest diminished by travail and hardship. The foundation for the substantial and influential organized church developments that accompanied later economic progress was well laid in pioneer homes.

Every record of early church organizations among the major denominations contain statements indicating the prior existence and militant vitality of home worship. The high courage and resolute determination that characterized the men and women of substance who comprised the constructive leadership in every early community found source and substance in adherence to God's word. Where the printed word was either inadequate or entirely missing, as it often was, devoted Christians supplied from memory or inspiration. Organized church work had but to gather together these consecrated elements into formal parishes and the present church began.

In spite of the firm foundation of resolute faith upon which early church work was established, there remained many grim obstacles to overcome. The gold rush to the sand coastal area in the early 1850's followed by rapid expansion in the lumber industry that accompanied establishment of water transport to California ports, brought many lawless and godless transients. Ridicule and disinterest proved even more formidable handicaps than the earlier natural hazards. Church maintenance imposed heart-breaking burdens upon the faithful. But truth and reason eventually prevailed. Organized religious works soon acquired the place of influence it now occupies.

The common failing of every historical endeavor of this nature is that important and interesting detail, deserving of prominent mention, must be sacrificed for the welfare of the whole. The innumerable labors and ministrations of simple, God-fearing folk that have woven the very fabric of the present Christian churches and that constitute a priceless heritage, must go largely unrecorded except in the archives of heaven. The heart-aches, the desolate watches of the night, the heroic self-sacrifices, the saintly ministrations of that early day, must be passed over with mere casual mention.

It must suffice to say that the joint endeavor of church people in this area, irrespective of the denomination within which their work has been carried on, has had dominating influence on public policy both locally and over the state as a whole. Coos County in 1951 ranks high in organized church effectiveness. It's coordinated Protestant effort, in particular, now serves as a model for such endeavor in the Pacific Northwest.

Scores of interesting anecdotes characterize the history of many of the older church organizations in the area. One relates how the Coos Bay Methodist church structure once fell into the bay after a Christmas program practice. Another tells how a Baptist church building became an apartment house and still serves in that capacity. There is the story of Bandon's indomitable Presbyterians holding services in a condemned school building until resources could be mustered for a new structure to replace the burned church. There are stories of meetings in groves, in homes, in business and farm buildings, in public schools and even in open fields as the people resolutely held fast to the worship of their God in the face of early hardship and poverty.

CATHOLIC

The first organized Catholic mission into Coos Bay country seems to have been the tour of Father James Croke.

In August 1853 he reached Empire, a little settlement then being built as Oregon's future chief seaport. Father Croke said that it's population was about 20 people at that time.

Father Croke explored both Coos Bay and Coos River to the head of tidewater. He noted the farm lands along the river, the fine white cedar timber, the extensive coal fields, and the extraordinary land-locked harbor with it's easy entrance. These observations caused him to predict a great future for the community and to arrange for a Catholic mission at Empire where a donation of four city lots for the site was obtained.

The Croke letters make no further mention of the Coos Bay country.

Father Croke was transferred to San Francisco in early 1859 after having started the development of Catholicism in Southwestern Oregon on an organized basis. There is small doubt but what early communicants of that faith had set up their own devotional procedures in many instances. These were later developed into Catholic churches when it became possible for trained missionaries to reach the scene.

The Catholic faith has grown steadily in importance and influence as the area's industries developed. Lack of quick transportation induced the building of small chapels to serve the most remote districts. Among these were chapels at Bandon, Langlois, and Cape Blanco.

Catholic churches have been built in North Bend, Coos Bay, and Coquille. The other major communities are served by missions in the general plan of efficient ministry now being used. Chapels at Reedsport, Myrtle

Point, Powers, Gold Beach and Brookings are evidence of the recent expansion of the Catholic ministry.

The Mercy Hospital at North Bend, later converted into Mercy Home for the Aged, has been operated by the church since 1906. For many years it was the only first-class hospital in the entire area. But after requisition of the McAuley Hospital in Coos Bay in 1939 the church was enabled to serve the community with more modern equipment, the Mercy Hospital became the Mercy Home and is, as such, filling a very compelling community need in the care of the aged.

The Saint Monica parochial school in Coos Bay, adjacent to the church structure bearing the same name, was instituted in 1920. It has operated steadily since then in the education of Catholic children. It's continued growth has now confronted the church with the necessity for substantial expenditures for plant expansion. Foresight has fortunately provided sufficient added space for this development.

Thus has the tiny mission established by Father Croke grown into a great church organization that capably serves the entire area of Southwestern Oregon.

Presbyterian

There is record of Presbyterian work in Coos County in 1873. Congregations were established at Empire and Marshfield during that year. As in the case of other major denominations, it is virtually certain that the formal organization of congregations served to coordinate earlier neighborhood communions and that the advent of Presbyterianism dated a decade sooner.

Active Presbyterian work started at Bandon with the arrival there of the Reverend Eneas McLean in 1890. This stalwart trail-blazer had served several years as missionary for Presbyterian Board of Foreign Missions in Chile.

Reverend McLean was sent to Medford. Hearing of the need for ministry in the rapidly growing communities of Southwest Oregon, he decided to leave Medford and head for Bandon at the mouth of the Coquille River. He organized the church at Bandon shortly after his arrival and also undertook to minister to Presbyterians in the vicinity of Myrtle Point. A church in the latter city was soon established and Reverend McLean served both fields during the balance of his stay in the county. Church structures were built in each city. That at Bandon was destroyed by fire in 1910, rebuilt in 1915, again destroyed by fire during the 1936 conflagration, and again rebuilt in 1937. It stands today as a monument to the indomitable spirit and faith of the Presbyterian congregation it serves.

The Myrtle Point edifice has had a more fortunate career and stands today much the same as in the original plan. It has become a landmark in this interesting little city and no small part of the community life has for many years revolved about it.

The growth of the Marshfield, later Coos Bay, church was steady but unspectacular. The records of this institution are studded with the names of those prominent in the industrial and economic progress of that community. The original church structure built in 1892 was increased in size from time to time by additions made necessary by the gradual expansion of the church functions. In 1949 the congregation began work on a new church structure badly needed to house the present congregation. The old church property was disposed of and the proceeds used in erecting the new. The new location, fronting Elrod Street above Fourth, is more centrally situated for the residential district.

The North Bend church, until the projected completion of the Coos Bay structure the most modern of the Presbyterian churches in the county, has had steady growth since it's organization. It prospered particularly under the ministry of the Reverend Levi Snyder to whom must go major credit for it's substantial position in the community. Like the Coos Bay church, it's history has not been spectacular. But the commonplace has not detracted from it's effectiveness nor from it's moral power.

A church was undertaken in the City of Coquille in

the late 90s. It prospered for a time, was later suspended then revived, and again suspended about 1925 for good. Improved transportation and lack of enough contributing communicants made the suspension advisable. Those of the Presbyterian faith were absorbed by other denominations or attended services at Myrtle Point, Bandon or Coos Bay.

An interesting activity of the Bandon Presbyterian Church in 1913 was the sponsorship of the church at Langlois. Dedication of this church took place in the summer of that year under the direction of the Reverend A. Haberly, a long-term resident of Bandon and a retired Presbyterian minister. The Langlois church later became a community church under other sponsorship. But it has functioned actively since 1913 and continues its work today.

Lutheran

The early arrival of many lumber and shipping workers of Scandinavian ancestry made inevitable the organization of a Swedish Lutheran Church.

Consequently the first of such organizations took place on September 8, 1884, when the Swedish Lutheran Church of Coos Bay came into being. The congregation at that time was composed of 44 communicants, a sizeable start for those days. A church building was completed during the ensuing winter and spring in time to be dedicated in May of 1885.

The church added a substantial utility building as the congregation grew in size. It's plant stands on the original site of Coos Bay's downtown section and is one of the best equipped Protestant organizations.

Other Lutheran congregations were organized throughout Coos County as communicants of that faith increased in number. These include a Norwegian Lutheran Church in the city of Coos Bay. There are six churches of this denomination to date and all are active in their respective fields.

It is a matter of course that the early establishment of the Lutheran faith made it a major factor in community life. While little of the spectacular seems to have marked it's history, it nevertheless has been the spiritual haven for scores of influential citizens and has witnessed the baptisms, weddings, and funeral services of a considerable portion of the population. The most significant thing about it's work is perhaps the fact of it's almost immediate establishment after the coming of it's communicants to the new country around Coos Bay. This gives evidence of the deep-rooted spiritual motives of the Scandinavian people.

Salvation Army

This remarkable service organization operates from its headquarters in Coos Bay. Community cooperation resulted in the housing of this denomination in the present quarters at Third and Market streets which serve as a center for the county.

Formal operations commenced in the early 1900s and have contributed so largely to the care and sustenance of unfortunates that the Salvation Army has virtually become a recognized branch of local government. Work of the denomination extends throughout southwestern Oregon and its services are readily available to every community.

It is sustained by public voluntary contributions and by the personal gifts of its members.

A fortunate choice of executives to head its local operations has contributed both to its success and to its accumulated prestige.

Baptist

The first Baptist Church in this area was organized in Marshfield during 1879. A report of its organization included a statement that the city had numerous saloons and that the populace was sodden with drink at that time. Prospects for launching a church venture were said to be very discouraging but the congregation proceeded with the organization despite the forbidding outlook.

The steady growth of the Baptist movement since that time vindicated the early judgment. A fine modern structure now houses a large and influential congregation. It replaces an earlier frame structure built in 1884, on the present site of the Salvation Army building.

Churches in Coquille, Reedsport, and Bandon were later built and are now flourishing. That at Bandon was destroyed in the 1936 fire but was immediately rebuilt and with substantial improvements. It houses a large and active congregation influential in community life.

A new Baptist Church in North Bend, and of the Southern Baptist faith, completes the present list of Baptist Churches in the area.

The development of the Baptist movement is plainly highlighted by the unusual ministry of the Reverend G. L. Hall, a former Baptist missionary now living in McMinnville, Oregon. Noting the difficulties of transportation at the time of his coming to Coos Bay in 1912 and observing that people lived chiefly along the several rivers and inlets, he conceived the idea of ministering by boat. A trim cabin-cruiser, *Lifeline,* was built by subscription in the Columbia Boat-shop of Eastside and placed in Reverend Hall's service.

The boat became nationally known as it literally brought the church to the people. The congregation was gathered as the boat cruised along its scheduled route. Thereupon its skipper, the Reverend Hall, would tie up at the final landing, doff his overalls, and proceed with the service, in the boat's roomy cabin. The congregation was returned to its several homes after the services. No regular appointments were established because of tide conditions and the need for freedom to serve upon call. The boat was used for weddings, funerals, and evangelistic services. It often encountered trouble by grounding on mudflats during fogs which frequently hamper navigation in fall and winter months.

When water transport was superseded by highway the

Lifeline work was closed and the boat sold in order to equip the Reverend Hall with a land cruiser. He continued preaching to the pastorless and in churchless places for the balance of his active life. Perhaps he was materially aided in his work on Coos Bay by the natural curiosity of hard-bitten loggers and ranchers to see the man who could operate a gasoline engine of those days and remain in good ministerial standing. The *Lifeline* engine usually cooperated. The need for use of the usual lurid expletives was thus obviated.

METHODIST EPISCOPAL, *By Dr. W.W. Youngson, Portland*

The first church was organized by Reverend Alderson who came to Coos County from Corvallis. The church was established in September, 1857, over the Foley Drug Store in Empire. From there Reverend Alderson made periodic trips to the settlers as far away as Camas Valley and Port Orford. Presumably this early Empire church was instrumental in the establishment of Methodism throughout the area.

In his memoirs the late Reverend Thos. F. Royal, doughty veteran of the saddle-bag era, tells of riding the Coos County circuit. Since he arrived in Jacksonville in 1853, it is probable that he was one of the first such circuit-riders in Coos County. His experiences with mud, snow, and winter floods and storms, give a glimpse into the almost incredible hardships endured in that early day.

The advent of Methodism in Coos and Curry Counties probably antedates that of the other major Protestant denominations by a considerable period. The institution of the Empire church in 1857 indicates this. It is also probable that the division of Methodism into the several branches handicapped the growth of that faith until their union in 1939.

With active congregations in virtually every major community in Southwestern Oregon, Methodism now ranks among the first in Protestant ministry. Its growth from 1940 to date has taken place not so much in the institution of new fields as in the strengthening of existing congregations. Well established congregations in North Bend, Coos Bay, Coquille, and Myrtle Point make it difficult to select the outstanding field, if there be any such. But the Coquille church is perhaps the most interesting in early history. Its initial organization was at the hands of the Methodist Episcopal Church—South, which entered Oregon in 1858.

The first M. E. South church building was erected in Roseburg during 1866. This church probably sponsored the strong Coquille M.E. South church which built a house of worship in that city during 1888. The memoirs of the Reverend H. S. Shangle tell of the active pastorates at Coquille, Myrtle Point, and Bandon which he found when he arrived in Roseburg in 1890. This means establishment of the Coos County churches in the late 70s or early 80s.

The Coquille church was the strongest of the Protestant denominations in this area at that time and for many years later. It is still one of the strongest and a spearhead for Methodism in Southwestern Oregon.

Episcopal

The first organization under the Episcopal faith seems to have taken place in Empire during a visit to Coos County by Bishop Benjamin Wistar Morris in 1872. But prior to this time there is tradition of Episcopal Church services being held in Cave Rock on the beach at Bandon. Such services were held during summer months to the accompaniment of a roaring surf whipped up by the summer tradewinds. They were important social functions to the early settlers of Episcopal faith.

Episcopal churches were subsequently organized in Bandon, Marshfield, and Coquille. Churches were built in Bandon during 1893, in Marshfield during the late 80s, and in Coquille during 1898. The latter city records use of a church structure of sorts as early as 1877 and the later joint use of the M.E. South structure built in 1888. This sharing continued until erection of the present Coquille structure several years later.

The highlight of Episcopal development in this area is the long and effective ministry of the Reverend Wm. Horsfall, vicar of the Bandon church and outstanding as an early pioneer. Through Dean Horsfall's efforts the Episcopal faith was sustained during its most trying period. It has rewarded his efforts by becoming one of the strongest and most influential of the Protestant denominations of today.

The Horsfall family went on to make very substantial contributions to the community welfare in other fields than religion. Probably best known to the general public is the work of a son, Doctor Wm. Horsfall, physician and surgeon, whose long and spectacularly successful career has contributed so heroically to Coos County development.

All three Episcopal churches in this area are very active. The Coos Bay parish has erected a fine new modern structure on ground that permits substantial expansion and enhances the imposing dignity of the new structure. This action was taken after condemnation of the old structure because of foundation failure, it being built on an old fill of an arm of Coos Bay.

The Bandon Church was rebuilt after the 1936 fire and is an excellent example of good chapel structure. The addition of a social hall, the gift of the late Mrs. W. J. Sweet, has greatly helped with the parish work by enabling an expansion of the social and church school programs. This well organized church plant has become an important factor in Bandon community life.

The Episcopal ministry has been particularly effective in civic affairs and continues to contribute substantially to such efforts. The early establishment of this faith in pioneer community life gives it a well-earned prestige.

Church of the Brethren
(German Baptist Brethren or Dunkards)

In the year 1872 a group of settlers of this faith left Ontario, Iowa, for Oregon. They were 21 in number and were of one family name, the Barklow brothers and their respective families.

They traveled by train to San Francisco then to Red Bluff, California. Here they bought teams and wagons and came on to Grants Pass, overland.

Being dissatisfied and discouraged by the appearance of the country, they were about to return to Iowa when they encountered Binger Hermann from the Coquille Valley. He told them of the mild climate, fertile bottom lands, and the excellent opportunity to secure good homesteads. Three of the Barklow brothers, David, John, and Samuel, left their families at Grants Pass and rode over to the Coquille Valley on horseback via the so-called Elk Trail over the Coast Range. The brothers, having been favorably impressed with the valley, bought land for themselves near Myrtle Point, then returned for their families.

They arrived at their respective homesteads in mid-August of 1872 and were able to get land cleared and living quarters erected for man and livestock before the winter set in.

David Barklow immediately established the first Church of Brethren a week after the arrival. The services were held in a grove near the mouth of North Fork below Myrtle Point. However, formal organization was not effected until next year, 1873, when Coquille Valley Church of this faith was duly instituted, with David Barklow as its first elder, an office he held until his death.

Services were held in groves, homes, school houses and barns until 1878 when a church building was erected on a site donated by William Rackleff near his home just south of the mouth of the North Fork. This building was used for 20 years or until 1898 when it was torn down and the material used in erecting the building in the City of Myrtle Point which housed the church until 1949. It was sold in order to secure a more suitable church site for a new building.

The services of the early church were supervised by a free ministry, with assignments for specific periods being distributed among several elders ordained for the purpose. In 1924, and thereafter, the pastor system was installed with a regular ordained minister in charge. The most rapid growth was attained during the period from 1902 to 1906 under a strong evangelistic program. This growth compelled major addition to the church plant in 1904 when the building was modernized extensively. It also led to establishment of a church in Bandon in 1912.

Many well-known and influential early Coos County settlers found sanctuary in this church and it remains one of the strong Protestant institutions of the county.

FIRST CHURCH OF CHRIST, SCIENTIST *By Leonard Love*

In the year 1908 a small band of earnest students of Christian Science met for the advancement of their spiritual growth and organized a Christian Science Society. The first services were conducted in a home, then in the old Masonic Building on Front Street, also in other downtown locations, and later in the Knights of Pythias hall. In 1917 the members took steps to organize a church which was incorporated under the laws of the state.

In 1932, on the corner of Seventh and Central, a church building was dedicated, entirely free from debt.

"In his memoirs Reverend Thomas F. Royal, doughty veteran of the saddle-bag era, tells of riding the Coos County circuit."

18

Coos and Curry Newspapers

By J. E. Norton

PAPERS OF THE PERIOD covering the 1870's and through the 1890's were usually edited by men whose main object was a medium for the expression of ideas and opinions, and they had opinions and expressed them freely. In many cases the effect this might have on the financial success of the enterprise made little difference to the editor.

Politics was the issue upon which many papers and their editors starved, bled and died. The investment was not large—a few hundred dollars would buy the needed material for a start and if the owner was also a practical printer, and many of them were, he was owner, editor, reporter, and printer, usually aided by some local youth who wanted to learn the trade.

Coos and Curry county papers, having to depend on ocean transportation for their supplies, were at the mercy of the elements in winter. Bars were rough and, in many cases, only small sailing vessels making the port. Paper supplies sometimes became exhausted and the printer cut the size down to two pages and used all his colored poster paper and, failing in that, the town merchants' flat manila wrapping paper was resorted to.

The early-day country newspaper carried considerable foreign advertising—that is, out-of-state tobacco and patent medicine ads. This fact made the proprietor, to a considerable extent, independent of local pressure. If he was the crusader type, an interesting writer, with the right command of English, his subscription list usually held up, since a part of the population wanted to see what he said about the other part, and the others were equally interested from a personal standpoint. So, if his local advertisers boycotted him, his foreign ads would buy his supplies and his subscribers would provide living needs, though subscriptions were often paid in potatoes, chickens, wood, or what have you.

The wages of printers, like nearly all workers, was low at this time. In the late 1880's and early 1890's the big city dailies installed the Linotypes, throwing many typesetters out of work. Many of these joined the ranks of the "tramp" printer, following the railroad tracks, working a day here and a day there on country weeklies. Eventually they adjusted themselves to that manner of life and many of them followed a regular route, starting north in the spring and south in the fall. They kept a schedule of sorts and would not work more than two or three days in a place, as they said they were "behind schedule." Weekly papers along the railroad always tried to have some work they could do, as they had to be fed anyway.

Coos and Curry saw little of this phase, as they were off the regular line of travel. The writer recalls only two or three coming in here; one in particular, an old-timer named Hazlett, who usually wintered in San Francisco and subbed on the *Chronicle*. Another, who followed a different plan, was William Miller. His method was to make a deal to handle the job department, and he usually stayed several months, helping to put on dances and arousing the interest of the younger element in any form of entertainment that would require advertising — creating a demand for handbills or posters.

While mail service was slow and all methods of transportation difficult and many times dangerous, the early-day papers went far afield for news. A greater percentage of their available space was devoted to state and national affairs than is the case today with the country weekly.

Coos County

Empire

The following from the *Rustic,* published at Empire

City, Thursday, December 5, 1872, will be of interest to the musically-inclined, and no doubt informs us of the date of Coos Bay's first band:

> The instruments of the Coos Bay Band have arrived and all who attend the Ball at Marshfield for their benefit, may expect a musical treat as the boys will "toot" their own horns on that occasion.

Again from the *Rustic,* Volume 1, Number 2, Saturday, November 18, 1871:

> Watsonville is the name fixed upon for the town now being surveyed off by Mr. Flint at the Noble place on Isthmus Slough. It will some day be a place of considerable importance. Its location is at the terminus of the C. B. Wagon Road and the Slough up to that point is of sufficient depth to float any vessel that can come into the Bay over the bar. The site is owned by the C. B. W. R. Co. [Coos City].

Information on the first publication in Coos County is rather hazy and of doubtful authenticity. Dodge's history says:

> The first newspaper to appear on the Bay was a six by nine sheet called *The Bumblebee* in 1869.

We are unable to corroborate this. Again, in writing of the Coos County election in 1874, Dodge's history says:

> There were at that time no newspapers published in the county but a little sheet originating on the Bay came to the assistance of the Republicans, called the *Bumble Bee.* Also the *Town Bull* for the Democrats. These two little papers were of short duration.

The *Coos Bay News* was in the field in 1873 so Dodge probably meant to say no paper with political affiliations was published in the County.

In the Museum in Coquille is a copy of the *Bumble Bee,* Coos Bay, Tuesday, May 26, 1874, by Bumble Bee Publishing Company — no volume or issue number — four pages, six by nine, and mostly devoted to a campaign against Judge Lowe, the Democratic candidate for re-election as county judge. Another copy, Volume 1, Number 4, July 29, 1874, says,

> "Published every Wednesday morning at Empire City, *Bumble Bee* Publishing Company."

This would indicate that Volume I, Number 1, was dated July 8, 1874, and that the May 26 issue was just an irregular campaign sheet, not a regular newspaper publication. This leaves us in doubt about the 1869 date.

The *Monthly Guide,* first appearing in October, 1870, was a four by six, four-page publication. This seems to have been short-lived and was followed by *The Rustic.* This paper has apparently been overlooked by the writers of early Coos County newspaper history. Our attention is called to this oversight by Mrs. Mary Randleman, custodian of the Coos-Curry Pioneer Museum in Coquille, where several copies of early issues of *The Rustic* have been placed. These copies were in the possession of former Coos County judge, James Watson, no doubt having been preserved by his father, D. L. Watson, an early-day attorney of Empire City and Marshfield. In the collection is Volume 1, Number 2, a three-column, four-page paper, dated November 18, 1871, T. G. Owen, Publisher. Number One is missing but we find other copies issued every two weeks, first on Saturday and later on Thursday, with a few missing, up to and including Number 22, December 5, 1872. In the last two numbers available we find the publisher, T. G. Owen, attempting to arrange for an enlarged paper to be published weekly. We quote from the last available issue of *The Rustic,* December 5, 1872: "We have a prospect of a weekly newspaper being published here in Empire City at an early day if the people of Coos County give it the necessary encouragement."

This is the last we find of *The Rustic.*

About three months later appears the *Coos Bay News* a four-column, four-page weekly. Volume 1, Number 1 has not been located but Volume 1, Number 2, comes to light under date of Thursday, March 27, 1873, with the same T. G. Owen as publisher, J. M. Siglin, editor, and E. C. Phelps, foreman, and continues at weekly intervals until Number 9, May 15, 1873, when T. B. Merry appears as editor.

This leaves little doubt that the *Coos Bay News* was the successor of *The Rustic,* and that the *News* was Coos County's first weekly newspaper. It appeared first as size twelve by eighteen — four-page, four-column paper. It was later enlarged and in 1875 was moved to Marshfield under the management of T. G. Owen, with J. M. Siglin as editor, T. B. Merry dropping out due to ill health. In 1877 Owen sold to G. A. (Gus) Bennett, H. R. Gale and J. M. Siglin, with Siglin as editor. The paper was now a twelve by eighteen, eight-page publication. Some time later the *News* became the property of G. A. Bennett, who changed to a four-page, Wednesday paper, carrying the banner of the Democratic Party.

G. A. (Gus) Bennett, published the *News* for about forty years, until the plant was destroyed by fire in 1922. Bennett had for many years been gathering material for a history of this section, but being ill at home when the fire occurred, this valuable material, much of it irreplacable, was lost. He passed away on December 23, 1926. The impact of his life on the community was such that in conversation with people who have resided in Coos County for a number of years, his name is still frequently heard.

The *Coos Bay News,* Coos County's first weekly newspaper, with its wealth of early Oregon history and folk lore, was reduced to ashes, after forty-nine years of service to the community.

A small sheet, usually about nine by fifteen, called *The Argus,* appeared first in 1873, published first in Empire City, by Marquard. It soon ceased publication, but came to life occasionally over a period of fifteen to twenty years, as a medium of expression for the literary-minded — the last copy recalled by the writer about 1889, edited by Robert Starkey, a picturesque figure and prolific early Coos County writer [He is briefly sketched in the chapter on literature.]

The *Coos County Record* came on the scene about the same time, apparently in 1874, that being the year shown by Ayer's Directory, and as published in Empire City by Watson and Webster — four pages, twenty-three by thirty-two. It seems to have changed hands and location, as in 1875 it is listed as a Republican paper, issued Thursday by C. W. Tower and M. K. Hanscom in Marshfield. It was sold in 1875 to Marquard and moved to Empire City. In 1877 it was listed back in Marshfield under Watson and Webster. This appears to be its last move, as there is no further account of the *Record.*

Another paper, of which there seems to be no record in early histories, was started in Empire — the *Coast Ranger,* a four-page, seven-column paper which was edited by a man named Nat Baker, probably about 1877 or 1878. It apparently did not last long, as we have failed to find anyone who remembers it. There was such a paper, however, as in 1889 the writer helped to distribute the type of the last issue. The story as we got it at that time was that Baker got into trouble which led to shooting and he left in such a hurry that the forms were still on the press, with the roller part way across. He never came back and the type was not distributed but was tied up in takes and placed in type boxes for storage. This type was borrowed by John Dean of the *Coquille City Herald* in 1889, to use in the publication of a special edition, both papers having used long primer. In reading the type we found the article of about one column to be headed: "Coos Bay-Roseburg & Eastern Railroad Now an Assured Fact."

This article could have been run by any Coos Bay or Coquille Valley paper twelve years later without change, as current material.

Marshfield

The *Coast Mail* was started in Marshfield in 1878 by Webster and in 1879, I. Hacker, later Coos County Treasurer, was associated with him. In 1881 Andrew Lockhart was connected with the paper. Then John Church was in charge until 1884. During the last years of his regime an evening daily was published in addition to the weekly. At the time Church retired, or soon after, John A. Gray became editor. Gray was an attorney and much in demand as an orator. His tenure was the longest of anyone connected with the paper at any time, continuing until his death in 1896.

Following Gray, came Thomas H. Barry. In early 1898 — our country being at war with Spain — the demand for news was so keen that Barry arranged for some telegraphic news service and published a small daily — one page, printed on one side. This was sold at one dollar per month and was continued until the close of the war. Then followed a period of change and finally the Coos Bay Publishing Company, with Percy C. Levar as editor — with a daily, every morning except Monday, and a weekly, continuing until the plant was sold to the Coos Bay Times Publishing Company, in 1906.

Levar then started the *Coos Bay Monthly,* a remarkable literary magazine for a single county.

The *Marshfield Sun* was established in 1891 by Jesse A. Luse, a native of Coos County, son of one of its oldest families. The *Sun* was started as a seven-column, four page, Thursday weekly, Independent, later turned Populist.

We now have the early newspaper picture on the Bay into the pattern which existed for many years. The *Coos Bay News,* under G. A. Bennett, Democrat; the *Coast Mail,* with John A. Gray, Republican; and the *Marshfield Sun* with Jesse A. Luse, Populist.

The *Marshfield Sun* had an unusual record. This paper, started in 1891 by Luse, never changed hands but was published by him until his death, July 2, 1944, a period of 53 years. It was hand-set and printed on a Washington hand press during its entire existence, probably another record for its time. At last account, the plant was still locked up in an old building on Front Street in Coos Bay.

The *Advertiser,* owned by Ernest Kramer and edited by his brother, Gus W. Kramer, was next on the Marshfield scene but in 1906 was sold to the organization which formed the Coos Bay Times Publishing Company, and Gus Kramer became the first editor of the *Times.*

The *Coos Bay Times* resulted from the efforts of a number of Coos Bay business men interested in a stronger paper for the Bay area. The Coos Bay Times Publishing Company was organized in 1906. Its board of directors consisted of C. D. Temple, chairman, George W. Kaufman, secretary, G. W. Kramer, Alva Doll, J. M. Blake, attorney, and Andrew McClelland of Pueblo, Colorado. This group took over the *Advertiser* from the Kramers and the *Coast Mail* from P. C. Levar. Gus W. Kramer was employed as editor and manager. The salary of $100 per month loomed large for the limited income of the paper but small to Kramer for the amount of time and effort required to get out a daily paper and he stayed less than a year.

Then came the Maloney brothers — Michael C. as editor and publisher and Dan E. as city editor and later as manager. Then followed a long period — twenty years — under the same ownership and management. The *Times* was changed to an evening paper and, in the face of most difficult competition, continued to make progress. Mike Maloney had worked as an editorial writer on the *New York World* and *Chicago Tribune* and was a forceful writer — so much so in fact that he had to face suits for libel. In looking back over his career in the newspaper field, we are reminded of many early-day editors. When they decided they were right — never mind the consequences. The *Record* — an evening paper — entered the field in 1909 and the struggle for supremacy was fiercely fought.

For a time, in 1914 and 1915, the *Record* passed the *Times* in circulation but later the *Times* forged ahead until its circulation was more than double that of the *Record*. The middle 1920's saw the newspaper fight reach a most regrettable stage. In 1925, during the Gordon management of the *News,* the point of personal combat was reached. Politics and religion, combined with the battle for newspaper supremacy, was causing such an upheaval in the community that a committee of Marshfield merchants decided to try to work out a solution.

The committee consisted of George C. Huggins, George A. Martin and J. O. Fisher. They arranged a meeting attended by over sixty business men. A plan was agreed upon whereby E. J. Murray, newspaper man of Klamath Falls, was induced to come to Marshfield to see what could be done. With this support and the cooperation of the Maloneys, he took over the *Times,* and the *Southwestern Oregon Daily News* returned to weekly publication.

The *Times* had developed from a small beginning to a paper running sometimes as high as sixteen pages, and with the fight settled and the daily field left to it alone, the future looked more encouraging.

The Maloneys went to Santa Anna, California, where for some time they published *The Daily Register* . . . M. C. Maloney met with an accident and died in San Francisco in 1931.

The story of the *Times* would not be complete without mention of Albert E. (Jack) Guyton, for some time city editor under the Maloney ownership. Guyton brought the *Times* many years of experience on midwest newspapers and was an outstanding news man. At the time of his death in 1924 he was Southwestern Oregon correspondent for a number of publications, including the *Portland Telegram, The Timberman, Four-L Bulletin,* and San Francisco and Seattle papers.

The *Times* was purchased in 1930 by Sheldon F. Sackett who was interested in the *Salem Statesman.* C. J. Gillette of the Forest Grove *News-Times* was brought in as editor-manager. In 1935 Gillette took over the *Examiner* in Lakeview and Mr. Sackett took personal charge of the *Times.* During the term of Charles A. Sprague as governor, Sackett returned to the *Statesman* and left Wm. L. Baker as managing editor of the *Times.* Later, when Baker moved to Alaska, Harrison P. (Red) Hornish became managing editor, Sackett spending much of his time with interests elsewhere. During Mr. Sackett's control of the *Times,* the following editors have served for varying lengths of time — Clayton Bernard, Wendell Webb, David Eyre, Francis W. Hilton.

The *Evening Record* was started in Marshfield by A. R. O'Brien, an Alaska publisher, in 1909. The fight between the *Record* and its successor, the Southwestern *Daily News,* and the *Coos Bay Times,* was spirited and at times a bitter one. The *Record* gained the lead in subscriptions in 1914. In 1915 the lead was increased by a cut-rate campaign, but it dropped behind and by 1921 O'Brien decided to quit and sold to the Southwestern Oregon Publishing Company, and Lew A. Cates was installed as editor.

O'Brien went to Ukiah, California, where he published a paper for a number of years and was also chairman of the Golden Gate Bridge Commission at the time of his death.

Under the new owners the name of the *Record* was changed to the *Southwestern Oregon Daily News.* After a few months the paper was placed in charge of Wm. L. Carver as receiver and editor-manager, with Wm. H. Perkins as editor part of that time. Then in 1923 and 1924, C. W. Parker, who had been secretary of the Marshfield Chamber of Commerce, was in charge, with Earl W. Murphy, formerly with the telephone company, as editor the last year. Then came Lionel D. Gordon in 1925, as editor-publisher and two years of bitter strife between the *News* and the *Times.* Then the sale of the *Times* and return of the *News* to the weekly field. In 1929 Gordon gave way to Edwin Rose as editor. C. T. Nunn became editor-manager in 1930. He carried on until 1938 when the paper ceased publication and the plant was converted to a commercial printing establishment, with W. K. and Bessie M. Brownlow in charge. It is now operated by the *News Press,* owned by Lloyd Quick and Sheldon Sackett, with Lloyd Quick as manager.

North Bend was without a newspaper until 1903 when Chester R. Ingle started the *Citizen,* a weekly Republican paper and was later joined by his brother, Roy Ingle. This continued until 1906 when publication ceased.

The *Evening Post,* published by Frank X. Hofer, was in the field for a short time in 1904. This was a daily, inspired by world happenings. The Japanese and Russians being at war, people were anxious for news, but the time for a daily newspaper was not yet and the *Post* folded up.

North Bend

In 1905 came the paper that was to succeed and become representative of the city of North Bend. The *Coos Bay Harbor* was established by C. M. Sain and C. H. Keith, as a Republican paper, issued on Saturday. Two years later they sold to A. Whisnant and Edgar McDaniel. Whisnant soon withdrew and McDaniel, who came to North Bend from South Dakota, had a long and successful experience as editor-publisher of the *Harbor*. In September, 1927, the paper moved into its own new building on Sherman Avenue in North Bend.

The esteem in which Edgar McDaniel was held by his employees and friends was shown by a two-page spread in the issue of September 27, 1927, under the caption "An Appreciation to Edgar McDaniel" followed by this quote:

> In the belief that too seldom is appreciation expressed to the living, we wish to express, as friends and neighbors, our appreciation of your untiring efforts during the past twenty years to make North Bend and Southwestern Oregon a greater city and a greater community.

This was followed by the explanation that this was one of the few pages of printed matter ever appearing in the *Harbor* without the knowledge of the editor. The announcement was flanked on each side and below by the names of seventy business and professional individuals and firms. Failing health finally compelled Mr. McDaniel to seek relief from the responsibilities of the paper and on July 1, 1945, he disposed of it to Mr. and Mrs. J. W. Forrester, Jr. Mr. McDaniel was much interested in photography and could usually be relied on when anything of interest was happening, to be on hand with his camera. It was while taking some pictures at the library in North Bend, May 28, 1949, he died from a heart attack. Present owner is Fred Haas, who changed the name to *North Bend News*.

North Bend had another small but spicy little paper called *The Agitator,* which changed its name in 1915 to the *Sunday Morning Bee*. It was published by Frank B. Cameron, and whether *Agitator* or *Bee,* it kept things stirring in the community. Scandal was its stock in trade and so bitter was the feeling on the part of some people that one attempt was made to blow up the plant. Fortunately, the dynamite failed to explode. Cameron carried on until 1927 when, to the surprise of some people, he died peacefully and the plant was sold.

Westernmost Missions, a Catholic paper devoted to Church work, was started in 1925 and continued publication for a number of years.

Coquille

The *Coquille City Herald,* first paper in the Coquille Valley, made its bow in 1882, with John A. Dean as editor-publisher. Mr. Dean, a young man, came to Coos County from Rolla, Missouri, in 1873, and taught school for a time before starting the *Herald* — a four-page, seven-column weekly. Independent paper — subscription price $2.00 per year. A friendly, cheerful man, not a printer, but a good writer and news gatherer, he made the paper interesting and it had a rather wide circulation for an isolated small town publication. Associated with him was his brother, D. F. Dean, who came from Missouri in 1881 and was later in charge of the mechanical department of the *Herald.* When the Peoples Party became of some importance, the *Herald* went under that banner but later became again independent.

In 1890 J. A. Dean sold his interest to J. S. McEwen, a life-long printer and editor. D. F. Dean retained a half interest. McEwen, whose newspaper career had been an interesting one, became editor. He had been a life-long Democrat; but the Populist Party was becoming very active in Coos County and the *Herald* took up its cause — in fact, so definitely that in 1892 J. S. McEwen was elec-ed as Coos Representative to the Oregon Legislature and, in 1894, D. F. Dean, as county clerk of Coos County.

McEwen for many years carried on a bitter fight in the newspaper business in Coquille. Extremely patriotic, but with radical tendencies, and ever suspicious of big business and political greats, he soon was in the midst of a political fight which involved his advertisers and the

Brookings

Above: Left — Mrs. J. M. Finch, adventuring pioneer of bulbs, collector of rare mountain ones, 1910-1925. Right—Headwaters of the Chetco, a regular gathering place. Below: Early housing for mail and money. Center: Chetco before there was a Brookings. Bottom: Seashore, Brookings.

Collection of Alfred Powers

LAKEPORT

Ghost Town on Flores Lake

Above: As pictured by promoter in *Bonville's Western Monthly,* June 1909, first called Crittenden. Center: Hotel as it was in 1916 when two hikers slept there for free; of paying guests the old register said years before, "Not a dam sole." Below: Main Street in 1916. Now not a vestige of the town remains.

boycott was on. In 1901 he disposed of his interest to D. F. Dean and went to Lake County, California, where for a number of years he published the *Kelseyville Sun*. In his declining years he returned to Coquille where he passed away in his 86th year. When not aroused by conflict, he was a friendly, kindly gentleman, fond of music and children.

The *Herald,* in 1904, became a semi-weekly, Tuesday and Friday. After four years it again became a weekly. D. F. Dean continued at the helm until 1912 when he went to Halsey and started the *Enterprise*. The *Herald* was taken over by P. C. Levar, under lease from Lew A. Cates, who had purchased the plant. In 1914 Cates sold to H. W. Young, who had purchased the *Sentinel.* The *Herald* continued under lease to Levar until his death in 1915, when it was leased to J. C. Savage, former owner of the *Sentinel.* On September 1, 1917, the *Herald* was consolidated with the *Sentinel.* Thus, after a varied career of thirty-six years, Coquille Valley's first newspaper passed into oblivion.

Now came one of those unfortunate happenings for the writers of history. Due to crowded storage space at the *Sentinel* office, the files of the *Herald* were burned and much valuable history of Coos County's early days was lost.

(Before leaving the record of the *Herald,* an incident comes to mind to show what was sometimes undertaken by early newspapers with their inadequate facilities. In 1889, John Dean of the *Herald,* contracted with a transient, M. B. Goodkind, to print five thousand copies of an eight-page, seven-column special booster edition. Goodkind was to furnish copy for write-up of space users. This would entail the printing of 40,000 impressions on the Washington hand press, in addition to running off about 1,000 copies of the *Herald* each week, printed both sides. Shortage of type caused the borrowing of type from Empire, as stated elsewhere. By keeping the hand press going nearly day and night, the job was accomplished.)

The second paper to enter the Coquille field was the

Bulletin, started December 7, 1894, by J. M. Lasswell, as an independent, Friday weekly. The *Herald* being a strong Populist advocate, there seemed to be an opening for another paper. Most of the business men being either Democrats or Republicans, supporters were offering encouragement. Lasswell was inadequately equipped and was soon succeeded by Ben F. Lawrence and J. A. Lamb, with Lawrence as editor. In 1895 they purchased the plant of the *West Oregonian,* which had been published in Myrtle Point, and added its equipment to that of the *Bulletin.* Mr. Lamb soon gave up newspaper work to enter the hardware business with his father, J. J. Lamb, and Lawrence continued as editor-publisher until 1899. E. E. Johnson then took charge for a time. He was followed by J. J. Stanley, who continued until 1902. That year E. C. Holland took over and carried on until 1904 when the *Bulletin* ceased publication.

For a short time the *Herald* was alone in the field. Lawrence who had set type on the *Herald* as a boy, went to the *Oregonian* and later went east and spent some forty-odd years with the *Indianapolis Star* organization. At the time of his retirement a few years ago, he was general manager.

The *Coquille Valley Sentinel* began publication in Coquille in 1905, with Orvil Dodge, Coos and Curry historian, as editor and publisher. It was an independent, Friday weekly, and continued under his regime until 1909 when he sold to J. C. Savage. In 1913, Lew A. Cates, who had purchased the *Herald,* which was under lease to P. C. Levar, bought half interest in the *Sentinel* and became editor and publisher. Mr. Cates remained about a year, when he sold his interest in both papers to H. W. Young, a veteran newspaper man from Woodburn, Oregon, but earlier from Independence, Kansas.

Mr. Young was joined in Coquille by his son, Allen, an all-round printer, and his daughter, Marian, linotype operator. Having purchased all of the *Sentinel,* the Youngs later purchased the site at First and Willard Streets, Coquille, and erected a modern, concrete building, which continues to be the *Sentinel's* home. H. W.

Young died in 1927, at the age of seventy-nine, being at the time the oldest active newspaper man in Oregon. His wife having preceded him in death, the ownership of the paper passed to the son and daughter, H. A. Young becoming editor and the daughter, Mrs. Marian D. Grimes, still linotype operator.

The *Sentinel,* a good country paper, continued under the management of H. A. Young until, due to failing health, he disposed of his interest to the present editor, Ralph P. Stuller. Mrs. Grimes still retains her interest.

The *Coos County Courier,* an independent weekly, edited by W. E. Hassler, appeared on the Coquille scene in 1928. This paper had been published in Powers by Hassler for several months under the name of the *Powers Patriot*—the mechanical work being done by one of the other Coos County papers. In 1932 the political outlook being favorable, the policy was changed from non-partisan to Democratic and the name changed to *Oregon Coos District Courier.* The ownership later passed to Miss Anna Jerzyk, of Rainier, then to R. B. and R. N. Cummings, father and son, followed by B. M. and L. J. Kaster, husband and wife. Under the Kasters the name was again changed to the *Tribune.* In 1938 William McKnight purchased the *Tribune* and entered into a joint ownership of the *Tribune* and *Herald* with the Youngs. Both papers were finally absorbed by the *Sentinel.*

Myrtle Point

The *West Oregonian,* Myrtle Point's earliest newspaper, was first published on December 3, 1889. W. L. Dixon, Myrtle Point merchant was the owner, Dr. Gussenhover was made business manager, and Orvil Dodge, who in 1898, published a history of Coos and Curry counties, was installed as editor.

The population of Myrtle Point was small and no doubt one inducement for the starting of a paper there at that time, was the taking up of timber claims in the vicinity. Groups of men were coming in, each filing on a quarter section of timber. The notice of intention had to be published in the nearest paper of general circulation, and as there was no paper south of Coquille, the notices automatically went to the *West Oregonian*. The paper received ten dollars for ten weeks publication and this, being cash, was quite an item to any paper at that time. The *Herald* had been running nearly two full pages set in small type—minion and agate, probably more than sixty at a time.

Like nearly all small-town weeklies of the time, the *West Oregonian* was printed on a Washington hand press. G. M. Short of Marshfield was employed as foreman and John N. Roberts of Myrtle Point soon became an apprentice typo.

The management proved inefficient and Gussenhover was released by Dixon. The paper was then carried on for a time by Dixon and Short. Then Short took over with Orvil Dodge as editor. The Board of Trade of Myrtle Point soon after purchased the plant and installed Orvil Dodge as editor-publisher. John H. Roberts later purchased it from the Board of Trade and moved it into his own building and sold it to Dodge, who, in turn, sold to W. O. Phillips, a lawyer, who moved it to a new location. Phillips failed to click as a newspaper man and Dodge had to take it back. So after many changes in management and location, the plant was finally sold to Lamb and Lawrence of Coquille and consolidated with the *Bulletin*. Myrtle Point was now without a paper, but not for long.

The *Enterprise* had been published at Riddle by Thorp and Conner. Myrtle Point appealed to them as a more desirable location and, on November 16, 1895, the *Myrtle Point Enterprise* was a going concern, with W. C. Conner in charge. This paper met with better success and soon enlarged from a seven-column, four-page paper to eight columns and in 1898 to five columns with eight pages.

The next year the paper was sold to G. M. Short and J. C. Roberts. In October, 1901, E. C. Roberts took over Short's interest, which he sold in May, 1905 to L. J. Roberts. L. J. Roberts in 1909 sold to L. C. Bargelt, who, had purchased J. C. Roberts' interest and he, in turn, sold to C. M. Shultz. W. R. Smith succeeded Shultz in 1917, and Smith changed the name of the paper to *Southern Coos County American*.

Then in 1923 came J. M. Bledsoe who, in 1925, his health failing, sold to George E. Hamilton, from Washington state. Mr. Hamilton disliked the paper's long name and changed it to *Myrtle Point Herald*, on March 29, 1928. Hamilton continued to publish the *Herald* for seven years, during which time it became the owner of its own home. In February, 1932, he sold to R. L. and J. L. Tucker, who came from Woodland, California. The Tuckers sold to Arthur Jones, who continued in charge until 1947 then the ownership passed to Logan White. White remained for about a year and October 1, 1948, sold to the present owners, E. F. and G. W. Hall. Located on the main street in Myrtle Point, in their own building and well equipped, a successful operation seems assured for the Hall Brothers.

Bandon

The *Recorder*, first newspaper in Bandon, was moved there from Denmark, Curry County, where it was started in 1883 by P. O. Chilstrom and J. M. Upton. In about 1885 it was moved to Bandon and edited and published by Chilstrom. The paper was taken over about 1887 or 1888 by David E. Stitt, who carried on until 1906 when George P. Laird became publisher, with S. W. Scottin as editor. Then came several changes of editors with Irving I. Bath in 1907, Graydon T. Treadgold in 1908, and C. E. Kopf in 1909 to 1916.

During the time from 1912 to 1916, Kopf published a semi-weekly, but in 1916 went back to weekly publication and that year the paper became bankrupt. R. B. Swanson, printer employed by Kopf, was placed in charge as manager for the creditors but finally, June 27, 1916, it suspended publication.

The *Western World* was established in Bandon in 1912 by Butterfield, a practical printer. He then was joined by A. J. Weddle, a blacksmith. Butterfield soon withdrew and his brother, Ollie Butterfield, became associated with Weddle as editor.

In 1913, L. D. Felsheim, W. B. Pressey and James H. Howe purchased the paper. A few months later Pressey sold to Felsheim and Howe and moved to California. The partnership of Felsheim and Howe continued until 1920 when Howe sold to Felsheim. The paper had been established as an independent weekly and by 1916 had outstripped the old *Recorder* in circulation and that paper folded up. The *Western World* went through the disastrous fire in September, 1936; and, though considerably damaged, managed, with some assistance from the *Coos Bay Times,* to continue to get out a paper without a break. Mr. Felsheim was appointed to the office of Coos County judge by Governor Earl Snell and was elected to the office by the voters in 1946 and was a candidate on the Republican ticket to succeed himself in the 1950 election.

In 1946, L. L. Felsheim, son of L. D. Felsheim, came home from the Navy and became editor and in 1949 became editor and publisher.

Bandon had an additional paper, the *Surf,* which was started by M. A. Simpson in 1913 but with the *Recorder* and *Western World* both in the field at that time, the *Surf* found the going tough and gave up in a few months.

This completes the record of Coos County's newspapers and brings us down to the present time with one prosperous paper in each of Coos County's five principal towns: North Bend, Coos Bay, Coquille, Myrtle Point and Bandon. The future looks bright for the publishers.

Curry County

The *Port Orford Post,* Curry County's first newspaper, was launched May 27, 1880, by J. H. Upton and Son — a five-column, four-page, independent weekly.

It had been Upton's plan to publish the paper in Ellensburg (now Gold Beach) as the *Curry County Post.* A boom was on, however, at Port Orford, in expectation of the government's building a harbor of refuge there, so he cast his lot with Port Orford.

The Uptons continued to publish the *Post* until 1882, when it was sold to Walter Sutton.

Sutton began his printing career on the *Oregon Sentinel,* Jacksonville, in 1862. In 1864 he was employed in a job office in Portland. He soon returned to Jacksonville as foreman with the *Sentinel.* After three years he went to Portland as a compositor on the *Oregonian.*

In 1870, while on a vacation trip to Curry County, he was so pleased with the coast country that he remained. He followed various pursuits till he was elected county clerk in 1876, serving six years. Later he was in the state legislature and was county treasurer for six years.

A month after buying the *Port Orford Post* in 1882, Sutton moved the plant to Ellensburg by boat. He enlarged the paper to six columns and changed the name to *Curry County Post.* He enlarged it to seven columns in 1884 and changed the name to *Gold Beach Gazette.*

R. D. Hume, founder of Wedderburn, owner of several miles of river frontage, and operator of a salmon cannery and hatchery, was displeased with the policy of the *Gazette.* He offered to purchase it and Sutton accepted. Hume wanted him to agree not to start another paper, insisting on a $500 bond, not being willing to accept Sutton's word for it. This was perhaps a mistake, as other parties, not liking Hume, raised the money and paid the bond, and Sutton went to Port Orford to start a paper.

Hume moved the *Gold Beach Gazette* across the river and called it the *Wedderburn Gazette.* After publishing it for about two years, he discontinued it as a "white elephant." It was later revived and was issued by E. M. Bogardus until 1901.

Sutton bought a new plant in San Francisco and started the *Port Orford Tribune* on May 10, 1892.

After publishing it for ten years he sold it to Walter Riley, and a year later bought it back. In 1904 he sold it to his half-brother, Frank. A Stewart and the latter's son, Hardy T. Stewart. In a short time Hardy Stewart became owner, editor, and publisher, continuing for sixteen years. In 1920 he sold it to the Tribune Publishing Company, which in turn sold it to Walter Sutton and his son George W. Sutton, now Curry County assessor.

A year later they first leased and then sold it to Thomas W. Fulton. Two more years and the *Curry County Reporter* at Gold Beach bought it and suspended publication. Walter Sutton, its founder, continued to reside in or near Port Orford until the time of his death in 1929. An informal Sutton family portrait is included in the page of Port Orford pictures.

The *Southwest Oregon Recorder* was started at Denmark in September 1883 by J. H. Upton and Son, J. M. Upton, and was published for about two years. P. O. Chilstrom and J. M. Upton then moved it to Bandon as that town's first newspaper, as previously related.

The *Southwestern Oregon Reporter* began publication at Langlois on September 16, 1897.

It was a four-column, eight-page paper, subscription price $1, with J. H. Upton as editor and publisher. The first issue carried less than one and a half columns of advertising. Said an item "Quite a number of local and other advertisements left out of this number will appear in next" — evidence that the main purpose was not financial gain. The last issue of it found is Volume 1, Number 23, June 17, 1898.

The *Chetco-Harbor Herald* was started in the early 90's by John L. Childs at the instigation of a group of Chetco River citizens enthused by prospects of a Federal appropriation for harbor improvement.

Childs was publishing the *News* in Crescent City at the time and also teaching school at Smith River. He was promised $1,500 to start the paper, a sufficient sum in 1911 to induce almost anyone to start a paper any place. Ten individuals signed up for $150 each. Childs moved the hand press and some other equipment from the *News,* ordered a rotary press for the *News,* and started the *Chetco-Harbor Herald.* He later installed Mrs. Margaret Hughes as editor. In a recent conversation Judge Childs was asked, "How many subscribers did you have?"

"No one subscribed," he replied. "They just said, 'Send me the paper.' No one paid."

After about two years of publication only one of the sponsors had paid anything. The company having repossessed the rotary press from the *News,* Childs moved the hand press back to Crescent City and the *Chetco-Harbor Herald* was discontinued.

The *Curry County Recorder* was started in Gold Beach in 1902. August J. Krantz was editor and publisher. It was sold in 1904 to Frank A. Stewart. In that year, as previously stated, Stewart also bought the *Port Orford Tribune,* with which the *Recorder* was merged.

The *Radium* was published in Wedderburn from 1904 to 1909 by R. D. Hume. Its first editor was O. W. Briggs, who later for many years was employed on Coos Bay newspapers. Briggs was followed as editor by Hume himself. Next came H. F. Crippen, then W. E. Thresher.

The *Globe,* another Gold Beach paper, was started in 1900 by an association of its citizens, with Colonel Munsey as managing editor. Ed Marsters later obtained the controlling interest and became the publisher, continuing until it was merged into the *Curry County Reporter.*

The latter was first published on September 15, 1915, by E. M. Bogardus. It was sold in 1917 or 1918 to A. E. (Jack) Guyton of Marshfield and John A. Juza of Coquille.

Juza was in charge and published it till it was sold in 1922 to the Macleay estate. Then W. E. Hassler, later of Coquille, became editor, followed by Robert L. Witherow of Portland. Juza, who for several years before going to Gold Beach had been foreman on the *Coquille Valley Sentinel,* went to Crescent City where he published the *Del Norte County Triplicate.* He is now a realtor in Crescent City.

In 1932, Reuben Young, formerly of Eugene and Redmond, became editor and publisher of the *Reporter,* continuing until 1941 when he sold to S. L. Burton, present editor and publisher, a long-time printer and newspaper man of Oregon.

The *Port Orford News* was started in 1926 by George W. Sorenson, who at the same time acted as secretary of the Port Orford Chamber of Commerce, a wide-awake, progressive influence in the community. He continued with the *News* until his death in 1933 when publication ceased.

The *Port Orford Post,* with the same name as Curry County's first newspaper, was started about 1936, with Frank Fay Eddy as managing editor.

It was later edited by Reeves Taylor until June 1, 1941, when Gilbert Gable became the owner and Francis W. Hilton the editor. Gable, who was promoting a large harbor and industrial development at Port Orford, died about the time of the Japanese attack on Pearl Harbor. Hilton continued to publish the paper until April of 1942, when it was discontinued.

Brookings Harbor Pilot was first published March 7, 1945, by the present editor and publisher, Dewey Akers — the first and only paper ever published in Brookings.

A five-column, ten page tabloid, well supported by advertising, it is a neat, well-printed paper which shows the hand of an experienced printer in its make -up. Mr. Akers, with 38 years experience in the business, was at one time head of the University of Illinois printing department.

The boom town of Pacific City, often referred to as Lakeport which is described in the chapter on ghost towns, brought into being another newspaper in Northern Curry County. The *Floras Lake Banner,* a seven-column, four-page paper, subscription price $1.50, made its bow on March 26, 1910, with Smith and Quarles as editors and publishers.

The project was doomed to fail. People drifted away, buildings yielded to the elements, and nature gradually covered the scene of men's hopes and disappointments with a new growth of brush and salal. The *Banner* ceased publication. Quarles left for other parts. C. N, Smith moved the plant to Langlois and for a time published the *Curry County Leader,* but the field was small and it soon faded from the picture. Smith remained in Langlois for a number of years, operating a store and cannery. He later moved to North Bend.

There may have been another paper in Langlois in the 90's. The *Oregonian,* on February 25, 1896, in writing of new Oregon newspapers, makes reference to the *Langlois Rural,* but it has not been possible to find any actual record of it or anyone who remembers it.

19

Literature

By Ruth McBride Powers

Indian Literature

THE FIRST PERSON to write down any portion of the Indian literature was Agnes Ruth Sengstacken of Marshfield, who in 1909 brought out a little volume entitled *Legend of the Coos.* Otilie Parker Kronenberg, daughter of the renowned Captain Judah Parker, of Parkersburg, wrote a charming story, "The Legend of Face Rock," and also wrote and produced in 1917 a pageant of Indian days from the stories and legends related to her by her nurse, "Indian Mary," at Bandon.

In 1913 and 1914, Dr. J. L. Frachtenberg, working under the anthropological department of Columbia University, wrote a pamphlet *Lower Umpqua Indians* and made a few references to Coos Dialects. He noted the main two, Miluk and Hanis. In 1914 he phonetically wrote down a number of Indian stories in Hanis entitled *Coos Texts.* His informants were Jim Buchanan of Empire who died in 1935 and Frank Drew of Florence, Coos Indians.

In 1933 and 1934 Melville Jacobs of the University of Washington lived at Charleston and made phonographic recordings of many Coos stories as told by Annie Miner Peterson who was born at the Indian village near Cooston about 1860. Her father was a white saw mill worker who soon deserted her mother. She went to Yachats with her mother when the Indians were put on the Siletz Reservation but drifted back to Empire about 1880 where lived her sister, Fanny, the wife of Coos Chief Jackson. She later lived in Portland and met Peterson whom she married and, after a vacation at Charleston, they settled there.

Annie spoke both Miluk, which was the speech of the Indians on the Coquille River, and Hanis, the language of the Indians at Charleston and Empire. The native stories, recorded in two dialects and then translated into English, frankly and exactly, are a contribution to Coos County literature that deserves wider circulation and study. Here is a sample entitled "The Blue Jay Shaaman," which may be found on page 138 of Jacobs:

There was a girl who was always picking myrtle nuts.
Once the girl became ill, she became extremely ill.
"We must get a shaman. I wonder where there is a shaman?"
"They say that Bluejay is a good shaman."
"Very well, then, you go get him."

And so indeed they went for the shaman.
Sure enough he came and labored over the girl.
And so he doctored her and said,
"Ha! It is my own poison-power that they are speaking of."
"Keep watch on him, That blue jay is tricky."
And sure enough, he then flew up, carrying the girl on his back!
He leaped through the smoke hole and disappeared.
"Hahahahaha, she has become my very own wife," said Bluejay.
He stole the girl.

S. S. Mann

Samuel Stillman Mann, born in Massachusetts in 1819, and a graduate of Brown University, arrived in San Francisco in 1849. During the gold excitement on Klamath River in 1850, Mann and others chartered the bark *Katie Heath* and, loading her with supplies, sailed up the coast. They entered the Umpqua River and laid out Umpqua City at its mouth, the first white men to sail in. Mann lived at Scottsburg until 1854 when he purchased an interest in the Newport Coal Mine at Coos Bay from Patrick Flanagan and made a fortune. He became the first judge of Coos County in 1859 and served until 1862. He returned to Randolph, Mass., to marry Miss Ella Tower and on his return to Empire was reelected judge and served until 1870. In 1883 he sold his mining interests and moved to San Francisco where he died in 1888.

Samuel Mann was the author of *The Settlement and*

Early Settlers of Coos Bay subtitled *Personal Sketches, Eccentric Characters and Historical Reminiscences written by a Pioneer Resident of the Bay,* and published anonymously at Marshfield in 1879 by the Coast Mail Book and Job Printing Office. This rare pamphlet, 37 pages with an appendage of quaint business advertisements, was the source of Bancroft's history of the Coos Bay area. The trenchant flavor of Mann's vivid prose is apparent in the following extract:

Paucity of Females

In these early days angel women "uncertain, coy and hard to please," were commentably few and scarce. Bachelors halls were in the majority. The occupants were under the necessity of being their own cooks and housekeepers. The advent of a marriageable young lady produced a lively sensation. All the bachelors rushed in hot haste to secure a chance in the matrimonial prize. The fair one was perplexed to choose among her many offers and could select her own time to restore "the lost rib" to some happy swain. This terrible lack of female loveliness and companionship made men desperate. There were many native maidens camped about who could be purchased from their fond parents for a few pairs of blankets. Rather than live on hopelessly languishing for fairer loves, many embraced the opportunity and provided themselves with companions from the wigwams of the "noble red men" and lived clandestinely without any marriage ceremony. Suddenly black clouds arose, darkening the horizon of their domestic felicity. An order was issued from the Indian Department that all the Indians from Coos Bay should be REMOVED TO THE SILETZ RESERVATION.

This order would ruthlessly include all those dusky companions to whom these men had become attached, turning them adrift again to solitary single life. These Indian maidens, strange as it may seem, had wound themselves deeply into their affections. They looked with horror on such a separation. Lucky thought, Happy discovery! Marriage would make them wives and American citizens beyond the control of Indian agents. The danger was imminent. The emissaries of the Indian Department were gathering Indians for removal. There was a rush of these couples to the Justice of Peace in the county and about thirty couples in this vicinity were joined in the bonds of wedlock. Some of them proved faithful wives and some of their leige lords are among us, respectable, honored, thriving citizens.

George Bennett

George Bennett was born in Bandon, Ireland, in 1827 and was a graduate of Trinity College, Dublin.

In Vols. 28 and 29 of the *Oregon Historical Quarterly*, appears his "History of Bandon and the Coquille River" written shortly before his death on October 15, 1900. He prepared Chapter Ten, "Bandon Beach," in Dodge's *Pioneer History of Coos and Curry Counties.*

Three stanzas of a six-stanza poem written in 1887, are indicative of his literary talents:

O', we love to stroll
Where the billows roll
On a cheerful and cloudless day;
And roam o'er the strands
With their jewelled sands
And to watch the waves at play.

The water it raves
In the sounding caves
In the gloomy and dark defiles . . .
Rushing and dashing
Seething and splashing
Through the echoing somber aisles.

Sitting on a rock
Beyond the shock
Of the incoming angry wave
We think of this life . . .
Its sorrow and strife
And the life that's beyond the grave.

H. H. Baldwin

H. H. Baldwin was born in 1825 in Bandon, Ireland, where he was a schoolmate of George Bennett. He came to Coos Bay in 1852. He was one of the 36 Dragoons wrecked near Coos Bay in the *Captain Lincoln* on January 3, 1852. Following this experience, he went to Randolph to mine, then took a claim on Rowland Prairie, and later settled at Bear Creek.

When Ralph Williams arrived from Ireland and settled on a neighboring claim in 1880, he was asked to stay at the Baldwin cabin while Baldwin went to town. The cabin was a one-room log house with a large fireplace and many shelves filled with papers and notebooks bearing the fruits of Baldwin's literary efforts. Baldwin was a careless housekeeper, never emptying the coffee pot until the grounds accumulated to the top. Sour dough bread and salt mutton were his staple foods.

On the fortieth anniversary of the wreck of the U. S. transport *Captain Lincoln,* Baldwin wrote a 53-line poem here shortened to a dozen lines.

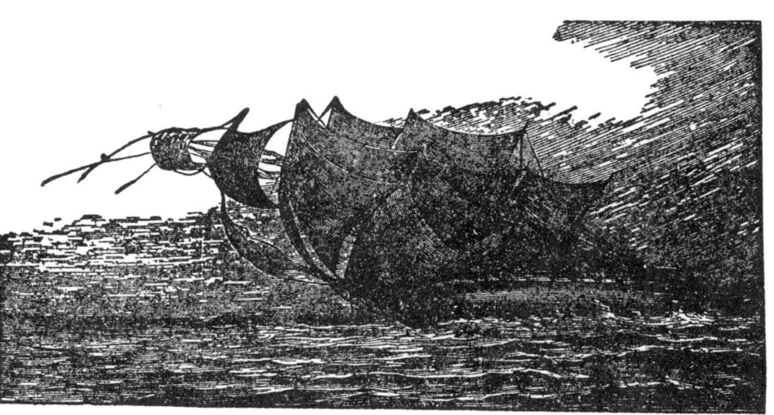

The Wreck

Come listen to my shipwreck tale, a deep and dismal one,
Which happened thirty-five dragoons, close to the wild Cowan.

The morning of the thirty-first, and last of the old year,
It filled all hands with joy, for each knew the port was near.
Alas! how short is human bliss, the wind commenced to blow,
Which forced our poor, short-handed crew, all canvass safely stow.
For three long days and dismal nights the tempest blew its best;
The water broke into our hold, the pumpers saw no rest.

At five a.m., "Great God; she's struck," the morning of the third;
Then fore and aft and either side were roaring breakers heard.
Again she struck with giant force, the mad waves leaped her deck,
Another giant, parly blow, "then *Lincoln* lay a wreck."

H. H. Woodward

Henry H. Woodward arrived on the Umpqua River in the fall of 1850 as a member of the Umpqua Company. He later joined Company C and fought in the Rogue River Indian War. Between 1857 and 1867, Woodward was a resident of Coos County, having filed on a donation land claim on what is known as the Ben Gant Ranch at the entrance of Powers, Oregon. Woodward Creek, in this area, bears his name.

He published two pamphlets of poems entitled *The Pioneer's Offerings* in August and September, 1867, through the newly established Roseburg *Ensign*. The poems were given little praise by the *Oregonian* or Jacksonville papers, but inspired many other pioneers to enliven their solitude with poetic effort.

On a visit to England, Woodward had a second volume published entitled *Select Poems* in May, 1875. In 1870, Woodward had taken up a permanent residence in Roseburg. In 1889 he published his last volume entitled *Lyrics of the Umpqua* which was printed by John B. Alden of New York City.

Woodward died in Roseburg June 11, 1915, and is buried in the Roseburg Cemetery. The following poem, taken from *Select Poems*, gives the style of his writing and are significant as examples of pioneer taste. (Johnson Mountain is, of course, the mountain south of Powers named for "Coarse Gold Johnson" who discovered gold there in 1855.)

To Johnson Mountain

"O Towering steep, the muse shall turn to thee,
High pinnacle overlooking Pacific's proud sea,
Vast mines of wealth in thy bosom do teem
And run at the base Coquel's auriferous stream.
Hardy adventurers full of hope and faith
With buoyant hearts have trod thy craggy path
Thy glittering quartz add brilliancy to the scene,
On thy benches the grassy swards are rich and green.

In winter thy peaks glaze in the mid day sun
And oft is heard the echo of bold hunter's trusty gun

Famous mountain, the Coquel' annals renowned
Wild herds in numbers on thy slopes abound
Once noble Mount, the aborigines trod thy steep
Grim warriors who now are laid in peaceful sleep
Traditions tell of their once swift rudelike chase
After herds of elk, whose trail they'd often trace.

Johnson's! with thy angled crooks and steep ascents
Thou stands a stately type of nature's monuments.
On thee brave hunters many a bear have tracked and slew.
The muse now bids thy golden slope a kind adieu.

George A. Gould

Early editions of newspapers in Coos County carry many poems contributed anonymously by the pioneers. George A. Gould, born in Iowa in 1853. In 1875 he married Harriett McClay, aged 15, and in 1886 we find him established on the Elkhorn Ranch 30 miles from Coos Bay in a teeming wilderness. The family, which consisted of nine children, industriously dried venison and elk meat, sold hides, fur, elk horns and teeth, bear galls, honey and cattle and hundreds of pairs of buckskin gloves. Later Gould acted as guide for hunters who came for summer sport.

Alone By the Campfire by Hearsay

[With four lines omitted]

Sitting alone by the campfire, by the fitful flickering light
Watching the embers falling apart . . . it is lonely here tonight.

One hears a hoot owl now and then, a mountain lion's startling scream,
But through it all a low refrain . . . a steady droning, soothing dream.
The sound is scarcely a sound at all, not like the coyote's quivering bark,
But just a dull monotony one always hears when it is dark.

The fire is slowly burning out, the light is getting dim and gray,
Fit emblem of the human life . . . we all full soon must pass away.

Willis White

The following poem by Willis White of Port Orford details a famous pioneer event that occurred in 1870 at Ellensburg, Curry County. It is copied from a manuscript by Frank Tichenor, who was planning to publish a history of Curry County but had not completed it at the time of his death. White was born in Maine and was 24 years old when he settled on Rogue River in 1871.

Ace Carey and the Bear

You have heard this story though strange tis true as well,
And not one fancy painted like I've heard others tell,
But really a true story a fact I will declare and emphasize with firmness,
Ace Carey rode a bear.

This happened down in Curry a part of this fair state,
Which now seems forging to the front a coming out though late,
Like a blossom on the sweetest rose, but really I declare,
I quite forgot my story – Ace Carey rode a bear.

Ace went and set a bear trap beneath a spreading oak,
Trouble then was brewing for Bruin – this was no joke,
And to a limb suspended he placed a bill of fare,
I think he called it "Marwich Bearmeat," and
Acey caught a bear.

He caught it by a hind leg – well up and thus secure.
He went and called a neighbor to have a witness sure.
The neighbors came and saw him throw a rope that landed fair
Around the neck of Bruin; to this tree he snubbed the bear.

Horatious at the bridge is naught, Thermopylae is tame,
This ursine ride of terror entitles greater fame,
Ace stood there like a Spartan, erect, serenely fair,
Then bowing to his audience he calmly rode the bear.

Bear *with* me just a moment, my story has been told,
There was no tragic end, to this I should mere unfold,
Ace rode this one for pleasure, next time he'll ride a pair,
The hall of fame should claim the name of Ace who rides a bear.

T. C. Land

T. C. Land entered the Coquille Valley on November 1, 1871. In 1872, the "North Carolina Settlement" was established on the South Fork of the Coquille River about the present town site of Powers, and "Squire" Land was its first school teacher. The Wagners, Hayeses and T. C. Land were the original settlers.

Land took up a homestead on the edge of what is now the Siskiyou National Forest. His name is commemorated in "Land Creek." He was a man of gentle habits, never carrying a gun, and was the first teacher in the community (1881-1884) which had the post office designation of "Rural." He was a neighbor of H. H. Woodward and H. H. Baldwin, both pioneers of the South Coquille. Land is the author of the poem:

Our Beautiful Coquille
[28 lines omitted]

Coquille River, grand and graceful,
  Gently gliding to the sea,
Through our valley, rich and fertile,
  As any soil on earth can be.

High above our fertile valley,
  Rise the undulating hills,
Thickly covered with a forest,
  Interspersed with limpid rills.
Gracefully the towering cedar,
  Rears its head to kiss the sky,
Tall majestic stand the fir trees,
  None like these so large and high.

Many of these stately fir trees,
  Rise three hundred feet or more,
While the graceful, fragrant myrtles,
  Seldom rise above four score.
Maple, live oak, yew and elder,
  Flourish well on hill and dale,
Ash and balm, also madrona,
  All are found in Coquille vale.

When relieved of trees and shrubbery,
  Vegetation grows apace,
Fruits, potatoes, grains and grasses,
  Every nook and corner grace.

Rutabagas, peas and carrots,
  Onions, radishes and beans,
Turnip, cabbage and tomatoes,

All will help to load our teams.
O, how lovely is our valley,
How delightful 'tis to dwell
In this mild and healthy climate,
In our beautiful Coquille.

On our hills and lovely valleys,
Elk and deer in concert graze,
Bear and panthers, too, are plenty,
On our rivers, creeks and bays.

Geese and brants, at times, are plenty,
Grouse, and pheasants, ducks and quails,
All along our bays and marshes,
On our mountains, hills and dales,
In our clear and limpid river,
Fish by millions do abound,
Such as salmon, trout and suckers,
Fine as those on Puget Sound.

Many things I still could tell you,
But, at present, will not tell,
All who love a pleasant region,
Come and see our dear Coquille.

Robert Starkey

Robert Starkey was born in New York state in 1830. A veteran of the Mexican War.He married Rosita Diaz in 1856 and came from San Francisco to Coos Bay in 1862. He contributed verse anonymously or under the nom de plume of "Le Garcon" to various county newspapers. In 1884 he was a member of the staff of the *Coquille Herald.* He wrote the article on "Climate of Coos and Curry Counties" in Dodge's history in 1898. He was the author of many eulogies in the *Coos Bay Times,* as well as acrostics. In 1880 he brought out a collection of poems entitled *Sparks of Poetic Fire.* It was printed at the Coos Bay News Printing House, Marshfield. Its subjects are varied, "The Coal Miners Evening Chime," "The Office Seeker," "Lines on the Chinese Question." Starkey spent his last years at the Roseburg Soldiers' Home and died in Marshfield in 1925.

The following lines recount the effects of taking the Coos and Curry Indians to the Siletz Reservation:

Our Indian Civil Service is not good,
That costs a mint of treasure, lakes of blood,
And all for what? To feed some idle knaves
Who cheat the nation and also the braves,
While the much plundered "Lo" in vain contends
Not one to aid him, none his rights defend.
In January Eighteen Sixty Eight
At the Siletz, in this Sunset State
'Twas cold; and yet not colder than the man
That was in charge when that cold snap began.
Psalms he would sing and shout "Let the Lord be thankit,"
Then cheat the "Diggers" out of half a blanket.
And when the Indians loudly did implore,
He'd talk Chinook and in that jargon swore
Were they to "Memeloos" they'd get no more.

If one requested it, he'd get a pass
Then he could go to work or go to grass.
Returning, buy his own from out the store,
The goods that his "Great Father" sent before.
Of mathematics, books were there the pride
'Twas healthy too . . . no Indian ever died.
Dead or alive, the Indians shoes and flannels,
Poured money in his purse from sundry channels.
As school was kept where everything went merry
And quibs writ to the papers for "School Jerry"
This Indian made to cut a mimic caper
"Wanted" . . . of course a Digger wants . . . a paper.
The squaws were taught by rule, retro gradation
Fair graduates all . . . in foul miscegenation
Thus are they ruled . . . no effort to retrench,
Good Sirs, go take a lesson from the French."

G. A. Bennett

G. A. Bennett, born in Ireland in 1856, came to Coos County in 1872 with his father and brother. He hunted elk and trapped for wild game and shot many sea lions for their fur at the mouth of the Coquille River. At times he carried the mail from Port Orford to Gardiner during the winter season. In 1878 he lived in Empire and in 1881 bought out the interest of J. M. Siglin in the *Coos Bay News* and published it until his death on December 25, 1926. When the business section of Marshfield was destroyed on July 23, 1922, the priceless files of the paper together with much historical data gathered by Mr.

Bennett was lost. The following paragraphs are from a sketch entitled, "Elk Hunting:"

One of my hunts that I remember well occurred in the late summer of 1874. My partner, Bill Perkins, and I had picked out a portion of the country below the mouth of the Coquille River, as the place for securing a supply of meat while elk were in their prime.

We spent the night at the cabin of Harry Baldwin, plainsman, U. S. trooper and Indian fighter, on Bear Creek [the poet previously considered]. Next day, after killing a four point and a five point, we dressed them out and were sitting on the ground, taking a rest and smoking before commencing to pack our horses, when we heard the first whistle of the season.

It was a shrill, high pitched, piercing whistle which hung for a while on the shrillest note and then died away gradually. This is the whistle of the young buck, probably a four pointer. Almost immediately at the cessation of the whistle, we heard the breaking of brush and dry sticks on a little spur which jutted out from the hill on which we were sitting and which was beneath us to our left about 150 yards away. A magnificent buck burst into view and hurried to the end of the spur, where he could survey the surrounding hills and the table lands below.

He was in his prime, as fine a specimen of a bull as one could hope to see; rolling fat, probably seven or eight years old and carrying a pair of horns that Bill said were like a rocking chair. He threw his horns back until they seemed to touch his hind quarters and with his nose pointed upwards he sent out his challenge to the youngster that had dared to whistle in the vicinity of the big fellow's herd. He started in with a sound somewhat resembling a steam whistle, low at first but gradually rising until it changed to a sound resembling the whinny of a horse, and then gradually died down to the pitch on which he had started.

Hunters used to refer to young bucks as "whistlers" and to old bucks as "buglers." I have heard a great many bucks whistle but I doubt if I have ever heard any two whistle exactly alike. When the big fellow commenced bugling everything suddenly became as still as death and remained so a few seconds. It was nature's tribute of veneration to the monarch of the hills. The big fellow stood perfectly still for a while listening anxiously and eager for an answer to the challenge, but none was forthcoming. Had it been a few days later in the season there is no doubt but that other buglers would have answered the challenge promptly and the hills would have resounded with the clashing of horns as buck met buck and fought to a finish for the coveted position of boss of the herd.

I heard five bucks answer a challenge on the Seven Mile Ridge near Randolph on the lower Coquille one morning and my friend and I stood among the limbs of a fallen fir tree within 40 yards of the "stamping ground" and saw two big fellows fight with one another until one of them laid down to die. But that is another story.

Frank A. Stewart

Frank A. Stewart was born in Illinois in 1843, crossed the plains to Oregon in 1854. He settled at Ellensburg in 1865. He served as treasurer of Curry County and was a member of the state legislature two terms. His poems appeared in the *Gold Beach Gazette* and the Port Orford *Tribune*.

Frances Holmtsrom

Frances Johnson Holstrom was born in Michigan in 1881. She attended the Cleveland, Ohio, Art School for two years. Her family came to Oregon where the future poet taught school, married and became the mother of four children. Her son, "Buzz" Holstrom, was the first man to navigate the Colorado River alone. She lived on a farm near McKinley from 1919 where she began to write verse. These poems have been published since the early twenties in the *American Mercury, Sunset, Ladies' Home Journal* and *Forum*. She has published three volumes of verse, *Western Windows,* 1938; *Rich Lady,* 1941; *Oregon Mist,* 1951. Mrs. Holmstrom lives with her son Carl in Coquille and records many Coos County scenes in water color. A new form of art using Myrtle wood plaques and oil paint has been developed by her.

The following is an example of her delicate perception and superior literary craftsmanship:

Curry County

Curry County, you who sit
With your back to the world, disdaining it,
With your back to the world and your feet in the sea,
Reading its riddles endlessly —

Curry County, you who wear
Nests of eagles in your hair,

Who bind your forests with golden streams,
Hiding treasure for miners' dreams,
Who wear white bones of the sunken hosts
In a cruel necklace about your coasts:
To whom the sea-gull's cry is a song
Tuned to the breakers your shores along:
You who clasp to your jealous breast
The last frontier of the fading West –

Curry County, do you know
A lover leaves you when I go?
And if it happens I die some day,
A friend, let his name be what it may,
So that he loves both thee and me,
Shall seek some height that is part of thee:
Cooley's point or Battle Rock,
Or some unnamed ledge where the seabirds flock,
Shall take up a pebble and fling it down
Into the caldron whose angers drown
The sound of its falling, and as it drops
The wind shall chant thro the torn tree tops,
Curry, Curry, beside thy shore
Hold thou this memory evermore.

Agnes Ruth Sengstacken

Agnes Ruth Lockhart Sengstacken, fourth daughter of Freeman Goodwin and Esther Lockhart, was born in 1859 in a two-room log cabin on the Coquille River at a place now known as Myrtle Point.

Her childhood and young girlhood was spent in Coos County, mostly in Empire. She attended normal school in San Francisco, later teaching at Knight's Ferry and Buena Vista, in Stanislaus County, and at Ramona, near San Diego, California.

She married Henry Sengstacken and lived in Marshfield. Mrs. Sengstacken was active in all civic, club, church and social life of the community. Always an avid collector, the attic of her home bulged with a splendid Indian collection, including 150 Indian baskets and other specimens of Indian life and culture. In addition, she had an outstanding collection of semi-precious metals and shells.

She wrote numerous poems, articles, non-fiction, including *The Legend of the Coos,* published in 1909 and *Destination West,* published in 1942.

For the last two years of her life, Mrs. Sengstacken lived in Long Beach, California, where she died November 24, 1948.

Destination West details the life story of her mother, Esther M. Lockhart, her trip to Oregon in a covered wagon and her life as pioneer teacher, wife, and mother. Mrs. Lockhart was the first woman president of the Coos and Curry Pioneer Association and the first school teacher in the county.

First Coos "White Squaws"

The people at the settlement had been expecting the arrival of ourselves, the Overbecks and the Tolmans, and soon after some loud shouting by our men, we perceived several large canoes coming across the bay. The stream appeared to be a mile or more in width. The mules, greatly frightened, were finally induced to swim over and before long we were all safely landed on the other side. It was really very beautiful where we landed at the tiny settlement of Empire City. It was still in its wild natural state with splendid dark forests coming down almost to the water's edge.

It was about four o'clock in the afternoon of October 18, 1853, when we reached our journey's end. We went to the "hotel," a little log cabin kept by genial Frank Ross. Here we feasted literally on fresh salmon, crabs, clams and roasted wild duck and geese, all of which was delicious.

That night we slept on a "puncheon floor" in a big room with about forty other persons, both men and women, having only our own feather beds between us and the uneven logs of the floor. But we slept in peace and safety lulled to rest by the surf beating musically on the ocean beach a few miles away.

It is probable that we three were the first white women who had ever set foot in the Coos Bay Country. It is more than likely that there were women and children among the seventy-five emigrants on the brig *Katie Heath* which came into Coos Bay by mistake in 1850 on its way to the Umpqua. We have no record that any of the persons of this pioneer vessel ever went ashore. Apparently we were the first white women that many of the Indians along our route had ever seen. They gazed at our white faces in undisguised admiration. Anxiously and openly they besought our husbands to trade wives with them. They offered all their blankets, their lovely hand woven baskets and matting, their prized wampum, most of which belonged to their women, in addition to their dusky partners. They even put up their precious ponies thinking that would clinch the bargain. But even then the strange pale faces were obdurate. They could not be induced to give up their "white squaws."

Minnie B. Tower

Minnie Burrell Tower was the wife of Dr. C. W. Tower, pioneer physician for the Newport Coal Mine and editor of the first newspaper in Coos County, *The Monthly Guide,* printed briefly in Empire City in 1870. Mrs. Tower was born in San Francisco and was gifted in music and painting. She married Dr. Tower in 1883, and, coming to the Bay, became active in dramatic and musical assemblies in the pioneer community, and a favorite soloist at weddings, funerals, and civic celebrations.

The following song reported in the *Coast Mail* of May 21, 1885, is indicative of the custom of the period:

Arthur's Gone to Sleep

(Written and sung by Mrs. C. W. Tower and Miss M. E. Thompson at the funeral services of little Arthur Ramsdell at this place on the 13th instant.)

There's a pair of little hands
Laid to rest for evermore,
There's two pearly dimpled cheeks
Whose rich blossoming is o'er.
Death has sealed two little eyes,
That will no more smile or weep,
Tiny windows of the soul,
Little Arthur's gone to sleep,
Little Arthur's gone to sleep.

Angels bore him safely home
So for him we may not weep,
Softly to the doorway came,
Little Arthur's gone to sleep,
He has only gone to sleep.

Minnie Myrtle Miller

(Poetess of the Coquille)

In 1857 Aaron Dyer and his son George came to Southwestern Oregon seeking gold. They located a home at the mouth of Elk River, Curry County, and George returned to Iowa to escort his mother and sisters to Oregon.

Theresa Dyer, or Minnie Myrtle as she was known as a poetess, thus came to Curry County in 1859 and later sent poetry to various newspapers. Verses printed in the Eugene paper arrested the attention of Joaquin Miller who was editing the *Democratic Register*. The poet rode to Curry County, causing much comment among the settlers with his saddle which "was a full Mexican pattern covered at the fastenings with silver half-dollars and twenty-five cent pieces."

Binfords & Mort

Minnie Myrtle Miller, wife of famous Joaquin Miller and a gifted poet herself, whose home was at the mouth of Elk River that flows into the ocean a few miles south of Cape Blanco.

Mrs. C. Y. Lowe was a child living in the George Dyer home when Minnie Myrtle brought her children home to her mother, Mrs. Aaron Dyer, pending her divorce from Joaquin. She states that Minnie Myrtle was very pretty and capable and conducted the funeral services of a child of Alexander Thrift when no minister was available.

Minnie Myrtle taught school at Empire City in 1869 just before her divorce in 1870. She died in New York City in 1884. Her daughter Maud was born on Sixes River in 1864 and died in New York in 1901. She left one son, Alloysius McCormick. Minnie Myrtle Miller's sons George and Harold, born in Canyon City both are dead. George attended school in Marshfield and stayed with his aunt, Emma Hilborn.

Said Joaquin Miller of her marriage to him and of her death:

> In the summer of 1861 I was attracted by her writings in the newspapers. I wrote, and had replies. Then, when I came down from the mountains, her letters grew ardent and full of affection. I mounted my horse and rode till I came to the sea, at Port Orford, and first saw "Minnie Myrtle" – tall, dark, and striking in every respect. In her woody little world there by the sea, the bright and merry girl was brimming full of romance, hope, and happiness. I arrived on Thursday. On Sunday next we were married! Oh, to what else but ruin and regret could such romantic folly lead?" [Eleven years after their separation she came to him in New York]. "I have come to you to die," she said. And so Minnie Myrtle died last May, 1884. Much that she wrote was better than any writing of mine. But she lacked care and toil and sustained thought. I bought a little bit of ground in Evergreens Cemetery, and there laid the poor, tired lady to rest, forgiving, and begging God to be forgiven.

The first and last verses of her most famous poem, "Sacrifice Impetro," which appeared in *The New Northwest* edited by Abigail Scott Duniway, are here presented:

> Why did I dream of thee, darling,
> In the sweet wild hours of the night;
> Why did thy spirit come near me
> Moving in mystical light?

Why did you bend above me,
With the old and passionate sigh,
In this world, where there's no one to love me,
Making me long to die?

To the splendid grave they have made him,
Where the tropical drowsiness floats,
Where a bird in the plumage of Eros,
Is tolling his funeral notes
I will come, sometimes with the shadows,
I will hush the wild notes of the bird;
And then in the listening silence
The voice of my heart shall be heard.

Alice Bay Maloney

To Alice Bay McCormac Maloney goes the distinction of being one of Coos County's most distinguished scholars. The daughter of Dr. James Thomas McCormac, principal of the Marshfield Academy from 1877 to 1882, she was born on September 19, 1885, and attended the Marshfield public schools and graduated from St. Helens Hall in Portland. She then attended the University of Oregon and the University of California.

In 1909 she married M. C. Maloney. She was active in the management of the *Coos Bay Times* of which her husband was publisher, and in the civic and women's clubs of Coos County until moving to California in 1928. After the death of her husband in 1931 she devoted her entire time to historical research. She was a member of the historical societies of British Columbia, Oregon, and California; of the Hudson Bay Company's Records Society; and was elected a Fellow of the American Geographical Society.

Fur Brigade to the Bonaventura was first published in five successive issues of the *California Historical Quarterly* in 1943-44 and then issued in 1945 in one volume.

This magazine published six other research papers by her. She also contributed a total of 15 historical articles to the *Oregon Historical Quarterly, Western Horseman, Oregonian, The Covered Wagon,* and the *Beaver*. Substantial portions of her well-known essay on the camp sites of Jedediah Smith are given in Chapter 2.

Grace McCormac French

Grace McCormac French was born in Marshfield in 1881, the daughter of Dr. J. T. McCormac and sister of Alice McCormac Maloney. She was for many years conservation chairman for the Oregon Federation of Women's Clubs and a student of Oregon birds. She is now a resident of Carlton, Oregon.

Coos Bay

I live in an inland valley
But my heart yearns for the sea
I come from a race of sailor men
And they left that love to me.

Fog enfolded all the landscape
On a cool October day
And my thoughts began to center
Round my old home on Coos Bay . . .

And then — I heard a steamer whistle
As it left the lower bay,
Yet I knew 'twas the noon time signal
In a town six miles away,
But to me it seemed to say —
Come back, come back you wanderer,
Come back to old Coos Bay . . .

I know — I'll hear the sea gulls screeching
When my ship sails in the bay
Past the cape where stands the lighthouse
And the cliffs all wet with spray,
Then my happy heart will say —
You're home, you're home, you wanderer,
It's home on dear old Coos Bay.

Ruth McBride Powers

Ruth McBride Powers was born in Michigan in 1903, spent her girlhood in Berkeley, California, and graduated from Stanford University in 1925. She edited a children's page for the Berkely *Daily Gazette* in 1925-26. She married Albert H. Powers and lived in Powers, Oregon, in 1926. They are the parents of Diana, Albert Junior and Quincy Powers. She has contributed poetry to various women's publications and six sonnets in *Oregon Poets, 1935*. She was editor of the Junior Page of the General Federation of Women's Clubs magazine *The Club Woman* from 1936 to 1938. She served on the General Federation of Women's Clubs Board for eleven years and on the state boards of American Association of University Women, Save The Myrtles League, Council of Republican Women, Oregon Trails Association, Daughters of the American Revolution, and Oregon Federation of Women's Clubs. She organized the first twelve Junior Womens clubs in Oregon, as well as the Coos Bay Community Council and the Coos Bay and Coquille Community playgrounds. She has carried on extensive research in Coos County and written many sketches of pioneer life.

William J. Sweet

Dairy Ranch Rhymes and Sweet Family Yarns was written by William Sweet and published hy him in 1942. He was born in 1882, in Nova Scotia, Canada, and came with his parents to Humboldt County when one year old. He studied at the College of the Pacific and College Park near San Jose, California, and came to Oregon in 1902. His interests are in banking and timber as well as maintaining a pure bred dairy farm at Elk River.

Beatrice K. Noon

Irish-born Kate Noon, truly a frontier poet, was married to Francis von der Green, a young doctor from Munich, Germany.

In her girlhood days she learned dressmaking from her aunt but turned to school teaching in wartime 1861. After her marriage she often helped her husband in nursing the sick in sparsely settled Curry County, where they came in 1866.

She loved the mountains and hills of Curry County and, above all, the ocean and beaches. Many rhymes were written about these hills and forests. "Scenes Near the Mouth of the Rogue River" appears on page 112 of

Dodge's *Pioneer History of Coos and Curry Counties*. An ardent advocate of Woman's Suffrage, she often wrote for Abigail Scott Duniway's paper, *The New Northwest*.

Their home was nine miles north of Ellensburg, where her husband had a drug store. She lived in Portland following the death of her husband but died in North Bend in 1911 at the age of 76.

Russell Cook Dement

Russell Cook Dement, whose father, Samuel Dement, was a member of the 1853 Coos Bay Company, wrote his pioneer story for R. L. Tucker of the *Myrtle Point Herald*. It appeared August 6 to November 19, 1931. Dement was a child of four when he came to Empire City. His home was in Myrtle Point but he owned ranches throughout the county. He died in 1936.

Daniel Giles

Daniel Giles, when only 16, worked his way across the plains in 1852. In October, 1853, he arrived in Empire City and proceeded to the Randolph gold fields. His Diary was also published in the *Myrtle Point Herald* in 1933.

O. W. Briggs

O. W. Briggs, journalist, columnist and historian became a resident of Coos Bay in 1906 and worked on the *Coast Mail* and the *Coos Bay Times*. He was special correspondent to the *Oregonian* and *Journal* for 20 years. He carried on research in 1933 in the county records and wrote for the W. P. A. Coos County History.

Mary Lucile McLain

Mary Lucile McLain was born in Marshfield in 1904, the sixth child of Judge and Mrs. Hugh P. McLain. She graduated from Marshfield High School in 1921. She was a student at the University of Oregon, leaving in her junior year to resume full-time work as reporter and feature writer for the *Coos Bay Times.* Her metier was pioneer history and vignettes of early Coos. In 1930 she completed a series of 68 sketches entitled "Romance of the Southwest Empire."

She was married in 1944 to Ross D. Slane of Seattle. In 1951 she returned to the *Times* as news and feature writer.

Robert Harrison

Robert Harrison, born in 1868, in California, came to Marshfield with his parents in 1879. The family settled in Brewster Valley. In the early 1890's, Harrison contributed to Coos County newspapers under the name of "Nimrod." Articles on trapping, hunting, fishing, mining and frontier life have appeared in the *Myrtle Point Herald, Coos Bay Times,* and *Coos Bay Harbor.* He wrote *The Tribe of Swalalahist,* a book of Indian legends and lore.

Olive Barber

Olive Maxson Barber was born in 1889 in a log cabin in Kansas. For two years she was secretary to Emma Page, blind lecturer for the WCTU. She attended Bellingham Normal School and taught school for more than nineteen years. She served as official bird observer for the U. S. Biological Survey and her textbook on birds is used in Coos County schools. Her column on birds in the *Coos Bay Times* in 1930 was expanded to human interest stories and appeared in eighteen Pacific Coast papers. She also presented human interest programs over radio stations KOOS, Coos Bay, and KOL, Seattle.

The following column appeared in the *Coos Bay Times* in August, 1944:

Modern Dance

The teen-agers were having a dance. Asked to look in on the affair, I did so. My first reaction was amazement. Not only do present day teen-agers have joints they never had in my teen-age day but they have more knee and hip gear shifts, all in the speedier brackets. No longer can dancing be called the poetry of motion, or if it is, its free verse, anyway free. If the rugged individualism of the teen agers' dancing is indicative of their activity when they grow up, then indeed democracy is safe, for they will follow no set pattern.

One of the dancers who intrigued me was a maid of 15 summers perhaps. Bespeckled and dressed in a gingham frock right out of Godey's, her hair was done in pigtails. Only the use of a monkey wrench could have accomplished those tight little braids. Finally one of the white bows on one braid escaped and lay on the floor, a poor little butterfly come to rest. I wished I could have rescued it but soon was past all rescue, crushed by the feet of the dancers.

One lad was in overalls and danced with his knees bent at what seemed to me a punishing angle. He ricocheted rather than danced, hurled about by some invisible force outside of his control but he never missed a dance. I wished that he and the maid with the braids would get together, but they never did.

Lans Leneve

W. Lanson Leneve, born in Coos County in 1890, has contributed to the *Coquille Valley Sentinel* and the *Myrtle Point Herald.* Some of his wildlife sketches appear elsewhere in this history.

Dr. Walter Haydon

Dr. Walter Haydon, gathered a collection of butterflies and ants for Charles Darwin, the great naturalist. He contributed articles to *Land and Water,* an English magazine; to scientific journals; and Indian tales to the *Coos Bay Monthly.*

He is considered more fully in the chapter on pioneer doctors.

Orvil Dodge

Orvil Ovando Dodge, author, editor and compiler of the *Coos and Curry County History* (1898), was born 1839 in Pennsylvania, at 16 drove stage in Indiana, at 18 was in Illinois, at 19 married Alice Walrod, at 21 set out for California in a covered wagon in the spring of 1860.

He farmed and then operated a sawmill in California.

Burned out by the Indians, he mined in Jackson County. He served 13 months in the First Oregon Cavalry in the Snake River Indian War. In 1863 he was divorced and given custody of two children. In 1867 he married Louisa A. Schroeder of Myrtle Point and settled in Empire City where he opened a drug store and also made photographs. In 1889 he established a newspaper in Myrtle Point called the *Western Oregonian* and edited it for five years. In 1906 he established the *Coquille Valley Sentinel* but sold out in 1909. A rare pamphlet was published by him in January, 1904, profusely entitled:

THE HEROES OF BATTLE ROCK
OR
THE MINERS' REWARD.

A Short Story of Thrilling Interest.

How a Small Canoe Done Its Work.

Port Orford, Oregon, the Scene of the Great Tragedy.

A Desperate Encounter
Of Nine White Men and Three Hundred Indians.

Miraculous Escape after Untold Hardships.
Historically True.

Savages Subdued and Rich Gold Mines Discovered.

The *Coos and Curry County History* was written under an appointment from the Pioneer Society of Coos and Curry County in 1896. In his preface, Mr. Dodge mentions that he gathered material enough for two volumes but unfortunately only one was ever published. He died in Myrtle Point on August 30, 1914.

Though somewhat scrambled up in its organization, Dodge's work in the fascination of its narrative is unmatched among the early county histories of Oregon. Again and again the present history has drawn upon it. Its vivid characters and events were the stimulus of a boy's adventure novel, a black sand story.

The Coos Bay Monthly

It is something of a cultural phenomenon for a county to have a literary magazine of its own. *The Coos Bay Monthly* evidently started publication at Marshfield in September of 1906; the earliest issue in the Marshfield Public Library is Volume 1, Number 4, December 1906. The latest issue in the library is Volume 3, Number 5, September 1908. The periodical seems therefore to have had a life of three years. It started out fat and big, almost equal to the *Pacific Monthly* of the same period in Portland. The final number on file is thin and sad. A county — even Coos — was not large enough to support permanently such an enterprise of poetry, essays, stories, history, and legends.

The man back of this remarkable effort was Percy C. Levar who had been editor of the *Coast Mail* and later, for two or three years before his death in 1915, was publisher under lease of the *Coquille Herald*.

The Marshfield Public Library has altogether about twenty numbers of the magazine. Some of the contents even now make good reading.

20

Folk Literature

There is a legend that Baptiste Lavelle and two companions were stranded on a Coos Bay island, perhaps Squaw Island, in 1808, two years after Lewis and Clark. They waited to see a passing sail till they despaired. Then they struck off across the continent. In about 18 months they reached Natches on the Mississippi.

Kingdom of Quivira

Sixes River was approximately the northern boundary of the mythical Kingdom of Quivira. For about 200 years the old makers of maps, charts, atlases, and globes soberly located this kingdom along the coast of what is now Curry County and northern California. It appeared very much like something real on Mercator's map in 1569. It continued to be shown on maps in 1570, 1582, 1587, 1592, 1597, 1600, 1630, 1637, 1671, and even as late as 1750.

The king was a long-bearded, hoary-headed fellow by the name of Tatarrax. One imaginative report had Chinese ships in the harbor of the the City of Quivira. This was located on a bay at the mouth of a big river. Far up the river was another important town by the name of Tuchano.

Philip III of Spain discovered among his father's secret papers "a sworn declaration that some foreigners had given him," relating how "they came in sight of a populous and rich city named Quivira . . . All this moved his Majesty to make every effort to find out about such a famous city and discover its situation."

The river that Martin d'Aguilar was reported to have discovered and that could never be located by later navigators, was supposed by some to be "the one leading to a great city . . . and that the city called Quivira is in these parts."

Since most of Curry County was in the Kingdom of Quivira, a much noted and much looked-for land during nearly two centuries, the county could have cashed in on the ancient publicity by taking the name instead of that of an Oregon governor. And Quivira County would have sounded nice too.

Mermaid of the Rogue, *By Arthur Dorn*

[A number of years ago, Arthur Dorn, former San Francisco lawyer, settled high up on the south side of Rogue River across from Agness, reached only by a trail. He has gathered together a whole manuscript volume of folk tales of that remote, fascinating region. Among them is a different version of the classic boulder — about 12 feet through — which Hathaway Jones of Marial pushed down the canyonside. Its momentum took it about the same distance up the other side and back almost to where Jones stood in his astonishment. "It got right near to the place I'd pushed it off from, and stopped, and down she went again." In two years Jones came back. "I heard the queerest rattlin' sound, and here come a little rock about the size of a little marble. That big rock I pushed over two years before must have been a-rollin' all that time till it was wore down." Mr. Dorn not only had an assertedly truer version but had the rock itself, found after the animation was finally gone out of it. It is quite round, and dark gray, and pock-marked rather than expectedly smooth, and somewhat larger than a baseball. He gave permission to the Coos - Curry Pioneer and Historical Association to choose any folk tale in his manuscript collection. The rolling stone one, having already been considerably publicised, was passed up for this one, never before printed.]

The fate which befell a beautiful Indian maiden, known through the centuries by only one Indian family, can now be told. Old Johnnie Fry, who lived along the Illinois River, was the last descendant of that family, the last custodian of the strange historical story. He lies now in the little Indian graveyard overlooking the Valley of the Illinois and the blue western mountains. But the story did not die with him, and it is this wise that it can now be told.

Many years ago there lived on an island of the Klamath River an Indian named Waukill Harry, the favorite of his great-grandmother who was very old. He was charged with killing a Swede with a two-bitted ax; but the jury, because of the work of a young lawyer, found him not guilty.

Not long after the trial the lawyer returned to the Klamath on a fishing trip and stopped to visit Waukill. He was not at home but when the great-grandmother realized the visitor was the man who helped her Waukill, she wanted to give him the house, the island, everything, including a couple of great-granddaughters who were twins, and quite pretty. But the young lawyer had no use for the house, nor the island. The twins, however, were eager to go with him, and though he always denied it, he would have taken them had he dared. He would have dared, too, had he not dearly loved his wife, and wished always to please her.

However, he encouraged the old squaw to talk about the past. Eventually she told him some things about the mermaid in the Rogue River, claiming that he was the only white man who had ever heard them. She said that Johnnie Fry's mother, who was a primitive medicine woman, was one who knew the facts. She would certainly have intrusted the details to Johnnie, and the young lawyer could get them from him.

This did not turn out to be a simple matter. Johnnie Fry, during many years, never repeated nor even mentioned the story. Shortly before he died he said he had never told it to any other human being. Many hunting trips in the far mountains, excursions upon the rivers, gardening together, or sitting by the fireplace while storms raged, gradually developed perfect understanding and trust. Then one evening, while we sat in his boat which was anchored at a certain place in Mermaid Pool, he spoke thus in substance:

A long, long time ago, during ages primordial, the topography of the country around the confluence of the Rogue and Illinois rivers was quite different from what it is now. Erosion has worn away much of its ruggedness. The low mountain under which the Illinois found its way into the Rouge, through a long, dark, rocky passage, has disappeared.

During that remote period, while the Illinois flowed under the mountain, a very fine race of people inhabited the region along the coasts of Southern Oregon and Northern California. Their center of government was near what is now called Mermaid Pool. These prehistoric people were large and white. They all had red hair and sky-blue eyes. The ancestors of what are now called Indians were their slaves. Those slaves were the progenitors of Waukill Harry's great-grandmother, and Johnnie Fry.

That ancient race lived under strict customs, or laws. They were monogamists. Upon reaching the age when he desired to be accepted as a man entitled to have a wife, each youth was required to undergo a test respecting his bravery and physical strength. He had to swim from the Illinois, under the mountain, into and across the Rogue at a time when the rivers were at flood and when the passage was full of backed-up waters to a great depth.

His bride-to-be always stood alone across the treacherous waters, waiting. Great uprooted trees with limbs and roots threshed around. All kinds of drift hurtled out of the passage into a roaring whirlpool caused by the meeting of the two rivers. Everything coming from the Illinois was caught within the circling clutch and dragged to the bottom of the river.

Across this perilous maelstrom the swimmer fought his way or perished. Under the mountain the water passed with appalling speed. Should a swimmer, in the total darkness, be dashed against top, side, or bottom, he would be battered to death instantly. If he failed to come through alive, or was sucked down by the whirlpool, his sweetheart jumped in and went with her man. That was the law.

Among those ancient people there once lived a lovely maiden, the most beautiful girl in all the nation; but at heart she was selfish, and flirtatious. However, the time came, eventually, for her marriage to a fine, handsome youth. The rivers being at flood stage, all was ready for him to make his supreme test of manhood.

The girl was taken to a place across the Rogue from where she had a clear view of the outlet from the Illinois, and of the whirlpool. She was left there alone. Of course those were not the names of the rivers at that time. It was storming; rain was falling in sheets; lightning flashed; thunder crashed overhead and over the mountains. She was wet and very cold. Her thoughts were concerned with her discomfort more than they were with the young man who was braving the terrors of the treacherous underground passage for her sake. She had not long to wait. He was hurled out of the passage, dead. The whirlpool sucked his body down and away.

Now, according to the inexorable, primordial custom, the girl should have jumped into the whirlpool and gone with her sweetheart. Instead, she decided that she did not want to die.

Her thoughts were not of the youth who was gone; they had turned to another. So she went back alone to her home.

It was the first time such a thing had happened. Always before, bethrothed girls had jumped without hesitation, upon the failure of their men to survive their trips through the underground passage, and across the whirlpool. That night the elders gathered in the council chambers, where the girl was brought before them. They asked her why she had not jumped and she answered that she did not want to die.

Some of the elders thought she should be thrown into the whirlpool. Several were not so hard hearted. After all the others had spoken, a very old magician arose and stated that if the rest of the elders were willing, he would dispose of the matter justly. They agreed because they were not at all happy over the prospect of drowning a girl who was so very beautiful.

The old magician gazed intently into the face of the girl as she stood before them, tall, straight, and fearless. Just for a fleeting moment she thought compassion flickered deep within his cold, faded-blue eyes, but his stern mind scorned all emotions. Soon he pronounced judgment:

"Unhappy, selfish maiden, you are beautiful, and to men you are very appealing. I now cause you to become more beautiful and even more appealing. You say you do not want to die; so you shall live a long time. I now change you, from your waist down, into the body of a fish. I shall throw you into the river, where, under the power of my magic, you shall live for ten thousand winters. You shall not know heat, cold, hunger, nor thirst."

Time passed slowly after that lovely girl was metamorphosed and thrown into the river by the old magician. Her people migrated eastward over the mountains, leaving no trace behind, except the girl and the magic. Time did not dim her radiant beauty, nor change her appearance at all.

She sought a place where the river flowed deep against the northern bank. Luxuriant ferns grew there and hidden reefs gave protection. Huge alders shaded the river during the long summer days. Azaleas fragrantly hung great clusters of flowers over it in the spring. For many years, many hundreds of years, she hid herself in shame. Then slowly she began taking interest in the birds and other wild creatures. She loved most of all the robins and meadow larks, because they stayed and poured out their melodies all the year round. A spell still lingers around that place, causing the birds to sing there almost every day, even during the storms of winter.

In 1866, when Johnnie Fry was six years old, he came to the Illinois Valley with his father and with his stepmother, a young squaw for whom a mule had been traded. But before the small boy departed, his left-behind real mother took him aside and told him some words he was to use in the event he should discover the mermaid in that swift river where he was going and where she lived.

His mother instructed Johnnie to confide in no one until he had grown into manhood. Then he would know whom he could trust. She said he had descended from the woman who had been the mermaid's childhood nurse and companion. With these words she taught him, he could make himself known.

Johnnie loved the rivers; so he soon acquired a boat. Always, while rowing, sailing, or poling upon the Rogue he watched for the mermaid, yet he had reached the age of twenty before he discovered her. She was greatly surprised and very happy when Johnnie told her about himself. They were soon able to converse freely, though she would not permit him to come close to her. A few years after he found her, he rode across the mountains to the Klamath, where he told his mother about his experience.

Through the years that Johnnie knew her he saw only the upper part of the mermaid's body, and her head. He said she was so utterly beautiful she seemed like a being from some Paradise. Her eyes were large, and blue as the color in a rainbow; while her eyebrows and lashes were quite dark. Her hair was abundant and wavy, and shone with a golden splendor. Her skin was very white. Her cheeks were colored the prettiest pink, like the delicate tinting of some rare sea shell. Her lips were red and quite inviting. While Johnnie talked to her she had a way of reaching up, fixing her hair, and smiling. Only by seeing her could anyone realize her sweetness when she smiled.

One day in midwinter, when the sun was shining, Johnnie decided to call upon the mermaid. He poled his boat up to the place where he always anchored, but she was not at the spot where she usually greeted him. Suddenly she leaped upon a great boulder, changing from a mermaid, back to the perfection of her youth. But with her release from the magic, ten thousand years of time which had been held in abeyance, was also released.

She changed from youth to old age so fast Johnnie just held his breath. Death and disintegration followed so quickly that, where a moment before she had stood in her glorious beauty, now was only a puff of golden dust shimmering in the rays of the setting wintry sun – drifting down, some upon the earth, some upon the water.

Ancient City of Curry County

In the fall of 1881, near Flores Creek, a storm uprooted a large tree that grew on a mound, one of many mounds thereabout. The big spruce's whole bed, several feet thick, had lifted up like the lid of a box.

It was on "Mr. Cox's place" but it is not stated whether it was Mr. Cox or someone else who passed along and was astonished at the nature of the rock exposed. It was unmistakably cut stone, "bearing quite plainly the marks of the stone-cutter's chisel." Moreover, the blocks seemed to lie "as if the wall had tumbled down."

After this hewn sandstone was thus accidentally brought to view, others of the numerous mounds were prospected. In all of them were similar relics of ancient masonry. The Flores Creek diggers, and the neighbors who had collected by this time to help him, made another discovery as they poked about with their spades. They came upon "what to all appearances had been a mining ditch," coursing along the hill slope and "walled up on the lower side" with the same character of shaped stone contained in the excavated mounds.

The editor of the *Port Orford Post* duly wrote up this archeological find in his paper and told his readers he would "personally inspect these alleged 'ruins' at no distant day," hoping to be able "to give a detailed description of the 'town' and its surroundings." Whether he actually did or not, and what opinions he formed, are not known because the files of the *Post* no longer exist. His original report is preserved by having been reprinted in a Portland magazine, which failed to run any follow-up if there was one at Port Orford as promised.

All further testimony can be counted upon to have perished. There is one way, however, to rediscover the ancient city and give it a thorough investigation. The location of the old Cox place can no doubt be learned in the recorder's office at Gold Beach. Then it oughtn't to be hard to find the mounds. After that it is only necessary for a group of amateur archaeologists to have enough spade energy.

They might well be spurred on by the prospect that this was perhaps one of the towns of the Kingdom of Quivira, built by the enlightened inhabitants ruled over by "horie headed" King Tatarrax.

Tom Billings, now just a little past eighty, grew up at Big Meadows. When he was old enough he went with his father's packtrain to Roseburg. Sometimes, on the way, he stopped at Camas Valley while his father went on to Roseburg. Here he met a girl. Her name was Sarah Alice Noah.

Tom Billings, after seeing a great deal of the world, returned to Big Meadows, settled down, took part in getting a post office established in 1903, and became its first postmaster. The office was given the name of his little daughter — Marial.

It was at his home in Marial in September 1949 that Tom Billings told this story about the hunt for the Pot of Gold.

A few years ago, he said, a man by the name of Oxenrider — a queer name, Mr. Billings remarked — came to the Billings home. He was from the Coos Bay region.

This man Oxenrider said he had married a woman who had lived in Camas Valley when she was a child. Her folks took in travelers sometimes. Two men had come and stayed several days. (This was the Noah home mentioned earlier in this story and the girl was Sarah Alice Noah) . The two men were from the East, but they had been mining gold on the Rogue River and had come out by way of the trail to Camas Valley.

These two men — the names are forgotten — seemed to take a liking to the Noah family. After disposing of their mules and horses, they were preparing to leave for their homes in the East. But before leaving, they told their story to Mr. Noah. Sarah Alice, being a wideawake girl in her early teens, listened with open ears.

The two men had struck it rich on the Rogue a few miles below Mule Creek. Indians were causing uneasiness, and the two men decided to get out. But fearing that they might be waylaid and their gold taken from them, they selected a fairly large madrone tree, dug holes nearby, covered the cache with earth and leaves. In a circle around the tree they placed a ring of rocks. Then in their minds they formulated a map of the country with details to enable them to find the hidden treasure when they should return. Then they pulled out. Over the Devil's Backbone they went, up Mule Creek, followed the winding trail through the forests, over ridges and across streams until they arrived in Camas Valley.

Now that they were ready to leave Camas Valley for their eastern homes, they reconstructed the map that had been carried in their minds; gave the map to Mr. Noah; told him that if they failed to return within a reasonable time, he might go to the place and recover the hidden gold.

It seems that the men did not return. Or if they did, they must have by-passed the Noah home. And, perhaps, Mr. Noah had little or no faith in the promised riches. At any rate, he did not pursue the rainbow. Might some day. But that day did not arrive.

In time they moved to Coos County, where they settled on Coos River. Sarah Alice married John Yoakam. She had fallen heir to the map of the Pot of Gold. Several members of the family are still alive. John Yoakam was killed by a bull. The Yoakam house on Coos River was destroyed by fire and the Pot of Gold map was lost. But Sarah Alice had studied it so often that it was clearly impressed in her memory — every detail.

Across the river from the Yoakam home lived widower Oxenrider. He married the widow, Sarah Alice Yoakam. She told him about the map of the Rogue River treasure. In time she died; Oxenrider sold his farm and moved to Marshfield. The gold and the map were firmly fixed in his mind. He now had time on his hands. A Ford pick-up, camp equipment, including tools, bacon, coffee, flour, potatoes, and other necessities — and he was off. Coquille, Myrtle Point, Powers — these were passed, and Oxenrider, now a Ford-rider, in due time arrived at the home of Tom Billings, where Mule Creek empties into the Rogue River.

Oxenrider knew that he must be in the vicinity of the buried cache. But he needed the help of someone who was intimately acquainted with the lay of the land. He had been told that Tom Billings, nearing his four-score-and-ten period of life, had grown up in that part of Curry County. He would know the country if anybody did. So he told his story to Billings, who concluded that the place must be down the river, perhaps some six or eight miles, with only a trail to reach it. Oxenrider had to leave his Ford and go on afoot, taking only what he could carry on his back. Billings did not feel like going, but directed him to a couple of men who lived in the vicinity of the supposed cache.

Oxenrider went down the trail that leads through the Mule Creek gorge. He returned the next day for some additional supplies from his Ford and again went down the trail. After that, Billings saw no more of him and had not heard of him again. He wondered if I knew anyone in the Coos Bay area by the name of Oxenrider. Yes, I told him, I knew a man by that name.

In the evening of October 28, 1949, I called at the home of Mr. Oxenrider at 886½ South Fifth Street, Coos Bay. He confirmed all that Mr. Billings had told me, adding a good many details.

Down the river somewhere beyond Blossom Bar, perhaps in the Neighborhood of Solitude (Zane Gray's home at one time) Oxenrider met two men — father and son, I believe. They lived in a cabin, did a little mining, some hunting and trapping, fishing a bit in season. They were interested in Oxenrider's story; would gladly cooperate with him in exchange for a share in the find.

One of the men, the older one, had a six-shooter strapped to his belt; the other carried a large knife in his holster. They went up a creek with which they were familiar and where they knew a large madrone tree to be located. After a few hundred yards, they came to a madrone somewhat more than three feet in diameter.

"Is this the tree?" they asked.

Oxenrider sized it up. "No," he said, "it is too big. It was less than a foot in diameter when the gold was buried and it could not have grown so much since that time."

The younger man, who carried the big knife, remembered a madrone tree on another branch of the creek.

Perhaps that was the place. He would lead them there. They found the tree, but it appeared to be too small, less than a foot and a half in diameter. It should have been larger. But Oxenrider pointed out that the top had been broken out, perhaps by a severe storm. Its growth had been checked. Besides, it was located in a little flat where the soil appeared to be rocky and of poor quality, not inducive to rapid growth.

"I believe this is the place," he told the men.

They had carried a shovel with them and the man with the gun in his holster began to dig, searching for the ring of rocks around the tree. But they found the ground so hard that they could not penetrate it with the shovel. It was like trying to dig into solid rock.

They must have other tools. One of the men volunteered to return to the house for a pick and a bar. In less than half an hour he was back, and the picking and prying with the bar began to make some headway. They found what appeared to be parts of the circle of rocks around the tree. But it was incomplete. Some of the rocks were missing. But enough remained to convince them that they had the right circle with the cache in the center.

But the fact that the circle was incomplete, had been broken — what did that mean? Had the cache been discovered? Had it been dug out by someone else years before? The digging was hard. But gold miners were used to hard digging. With the pick, the bar and the shovel they worked on. After they had broken the surface, the digging was not so hard. With every shovelful of dirt they looked for some yellow substance.

All the way around the tree they dug, some ten feet in diameter and about two feet deep. No gold. Perhaps they had not made the circle wide enough. Another two feet they went out. Then four — and six. Still no gold. Darkness was coming on. They must quit.

Oxenrider returned with the men to their cabin. He had brought bacon, coffee, flour and some other things. Together they had supper. Then, as they sat before the open fire, they talked about their venture. If someone had found the treasure ahead of them, it must have been years before. All indications of previous diggings had been obliterated by the growth of shrubs, ferns and small trees. The fact that some of the stones were missing from the circle around the tree seemed to indicate that the place had been disturbed.

Could they have dug deep enough? Perhaps not. They would go back next morning and try again. Once through the top crust and loose rocks, a couple of feet deeper would not be difficult.

In the morning, after a breakfast of bacon, eggs, hot-cakes and coffee, they were back on the job. Down another two feet, then they probed still deeper with the sharp bar. Once they struck something that felt as though it might be a rotten buckskin sack with nuggets in it. A hurried digging revealed it to be a root from a nearby fir tree that had died before, had completely rotted away, leaving the bark in the form of a tunnel. In this a squirrel had built his winter nest of moss, littered with shells of hazelnuts.

Once more the sun was going down behind the high ridges. Darkness was closing down on the gold diggers. The day was done, was gone. And so was their ardor. They had reached the end of the rainbow. But, like other rainbow ends, the pot of gold had flown.

Oxenrider still wonders if they had found the gold — would the six-shooter and the big knife with which the two men were armed — would these have had any part in the sharing of the spoils? He thinks not. These things were merely in keeping with the custom of the time and place.

COOSBERRIES, *By Albert Sidney Roos*

In Tupper's Hotel, on Nineteen Two's
June 1, Coquille, in County Coos,
In Or., the state of wealth and views.

To Mister Samuel Hendershott,
In Mich., the town of Wyandotte,
At corner of 10th and West Pequot.

DEAR SIR: Yours of the 6th I've got;
It differs from the average lot
By simply asking whether or not
  Much berries grow out here in Coos.

Yes, it's a natural berry spot
  For blacks, and rasps, and straws, and dews,
  And crans in bogs along the sloughs;
  Salal and huckle, prickly goose.

  Out here in Coos
  Them we produce
  From tart to sweet, in all the hues.
  We have besides the reds and blues
  A saffron *Rubus,* if you choose
To speak of it in botany-glot –
  The salmon – deceptive as the deuce,
  All ochre fluff, small meat or juice,
  Just good for salmon fish's use.

(Some laugh at it as tommyrot
  That its plump fruit gets ripe, turns loose,
And drops with sure, obliging shot
  To chinooks that wait below in crews
With open jaws – straight stuff, I wot.)

  And myrtle berries for your *Sus,*
Your hogs, that is – why, Hendershott,
  They'll get so fat they'll only snooze.

  You finally ask, "Now don't refuse
  To answer me with absolute truths –
Of poison oak how much you got,
That evil berry for man and tot?
Do patches all the hillsides dot,
  Existing there since the first papoose?
  I'm not among the don'ts but do's,
  A very vulnerable fellow whose
Afflicted eyes can't tell what's what
  As around them swollen flesh accrues."

  Be calm, dear sir, for here's good news –
  That cussed plant, white-berried *Rhus,*
  Ain't hardly found out here in Coos.

Yours truly

ALBERT SIDNEY ROOS,
(No realtor as you might deduce)

21

Libraries

A LIBRARY has its beginning in the mind of some individual.

In 1853 Mrs. F. G. Lockhart came with the Coos Bay Company to Coos County. After several years she had occasion to make a trip to Roseburg.

> While in Roseburg I laid in a stock of useful little articles for the Children's coming Christmas and also purchased a few books for them. We still have in 1942 a few of the books that I bought in that distant time, and they are all in fair condition, considering that my six children read and re-read them, and I fancy that some of my grandchildren also glanced through them.

One of Mrs. Lockhart's six children grew up to become Agnes Ruth Sengstacken, author of *Destination West,* of whom it was said:

> The Marshfield Public Library . . . started in 1906 when the earliest glimmer of interest was sparked by Mrs. Agnes Sengstacken, backed by the members of the Progress Club . . .

Can there be any doubt as to where and when the seed was sown that many years later resulted in the Marshfield Public Library?

One more thought-seed is gleaned from the biographical sketch of Christian Lehnherr, written by his daughter, Fannie Lehnherr Dixon:

> Regular trips with pack teams were made to Roseburg, bringing in flour and other necessities . . . A library of 100 volumes of Harpers Family Library was bought from a lawyer who had brought it around the Horn . . . Mother read the books aloud to the family during the long winter evenings by the light from candles made from elk tallow in tin molds brought in the covered wagons. A taste for good literature was implanted in the minds of the family that continued through the years.

The influence of that old library is still being felt in the third, fourth, and fifth generations.

Bandon

Mrs. Dal M. King has sketched as follows the early beginning at Bandon:

> In 1893 a lending library was started by Mrs. George Williams in the store owned by them and a man named Frank Rupert. This library was in operation only about a year. In 1899, Mike Breuer, a shoemaker by trade, and Mr. John Chase, manager of the Bandon Woolen Mill, decided there should be a place for sailors to go besides the numerous saloons. They rented the lower part of the building owned by David Stitt, publisher of the *Bandon Recorder*. Adam Pershbaker of Parkersburg donated lumber for the shelves. Many books were donated. These men also furnished light and heat. Breuer's young son, Vic, tended the fires.
>
> There was no librarian or custodian. Borrowers were put on their honor. They wrote their names and title of books on a paper which hung on the wall. When books began to disappear, the project was abandoned . . .
>
> The beginning of the present day library was a reading room in the Lorenz building, instigated by Professor Harry Hopkins, J. Ira Sidwell and the Rev. Harry Hartranft . . . The members of the *Hurry Up Bible Class* took turns in being responsible for the reading room. When it became too large a job for them, the public was requested to take over.

In 1914 Miss Amelia Henry became the librarian and continued in that capacity for 28 years, including the trying and critical period following the disastrous fire in 1936.

From the report by Harriet Long, state librarian, after she had visited Bandon following the fire:

> In the 24 years that the Bandon Library had existed, it had collected approximately 5,400 books. The library had for many years one of the highest per capita circulation in the state, reaching a 23,000 figure last year (population 1500) . . .
>
> It was finally decided to use the tent (14 feet square) vacated by the State Police that morning. The tent had a board floor and a conical sheet iron stove in the center. Shelves were made of a few boards and packing boxes. When the floor was swept, two long benches rescued, a table and chair for the librarian,

with the gay colored bindings and the gay colored books, the room was really attractive.

People began to flock in. First patron was an old gentleman who had lived 41 years in Bandon. A woman said, "Oh, we need books so badly. Everyone is getting on his neighbor's or his family's nerves now because we are so congested and uncomfortable." The National Guard brought a cot, mattress, blankets, and wash basin for Miss Henry, who was to live in the library.

In 1942 Mrs. Bessie Young became librarian. In 1949 there were 3,400 volumes.

MARSHFIELD

According to a State Library report, the Marshfield Public Library was established in June 1910. It had 1,554 volumes, there were 452 borrowers registered, and 1,013 books were loaned the first month.

It was first opened in the Henry Sengstacken Building on Front Street. It was later moved into the Coke Building, now known as the American Bank Building.

Headed by Mrs. Sengstacken, a move was made to secure aid from the Carnegie Foundation for a library building. A grant of $12,500 was received and the building was completed in 1914.

A source of revenue that has always been highly appreciated is the Nancy Noble Fund, a bequest of $2,000 left to the library by Nancy Noble in 1918. Memorial donations of books and money have added greatly to the library. In 1949 the Coos Bay Pirates Club made a handsome contribution in memory of Clarence Coe, a president of the organization. The Soroptimist Club made a generous gift of books in 1949.

The following is a list of Librarians in the Marshfield Public Library:

Mary Jameson, 1910-1911.
Emily Blake, acting librarian, January and February, 1912.
Ida Adams, March through July, 1912.
Elizabeth Topping, 1912-1915.
Gladys Diment, 1915-1916.
Ruth Cowan, one month, 1916.

John S. Richardson, 1916-1918.
Laura Snyder, February and March, 1918.
Nelly Latham Snyder, April to December, 1918.
Miss Norsworthy, 1919-1920.
Georgia Donnelly, 1920-1924.
Elizabeth Edwards, 1923.
Sarah Sissler, 1924-1926.
Eva Blood, 1926-1929.
Ruth Montague, 1929-1930.
Helen Stack Bower, 1930-1965
Genevieve Sengstacken, head assistant since 1926.

North Bend

It appears to have been sometime during 1912 that the people of North Bend, led principally by a few enthusiastic women, undertook by various means to raise money for starting a library. In the beginning a dinner was given in the Winsor Building on the corner of Sherman and Virginia. The admission was *A Book and Fifty Cents.* Says a report, "Over a hundred dollars was cleared, and this was the first money they had."

The following article appeared in the *Coos Bay Times* on May 26, 1914:

> Beginning today, North Bend has a public library. Some months ago Mrs. Fredrick Hollister gave the use of a large handsome billard room located in the basement of the beautiful Hollister residence, provided the ladies of North Bend would furnish the room for that purpose. This they have not been slow to do. The room now has shelving for several hundred books.

The library was soon moved to the Myers Building. Captain A. M. Simpson died and left the library his collection of books.

During the first six months the library was open, there were 97 borrowers, 50 of whom were children. The total receipts were $220.47. The library was open ten hours a week. The librarian and her assistant had received $90 each as salary for the six months.

The following librarians have served during the 37 years from 1914 to 1951:

Mrs. L. A. Woodbury
Myrtle Helm (Mrs. Sig Anderson)
Viola Helm (Mrs. Herman Anderson)
Mary Gurnea (Mrs. Sheldon)
Bessie Hinch (Mrs. Basil Durflinger)
Mrs. Howard Imhoff (supervising librarian)
Mrs. Leonard Russell
Illma Langworthy (Mrs. C. S. Lehmanowsky)
Bertha (Mrs. C. A.) Langworthy

The present librarian, Bertha (Mrs. C. A.) Langworthy, has served 27 years, starting in 1924. The annual report in 1950 showed 9,622 volumes owned. The library is financed by a city property tax of 1.47 mills.

Coquille

Coquille's Public Library was established on February 1, 1914. However, the people of Coquille and vicinity had library service several years prior to that time.

The following information has been gathered and reported by Mrs. Dal M. King:

Around 1900 a reading room was maintained in a building on Front Street, kept open by Mr. and Mrs. J. H. Cecil, who lived in the back of the same building. Books and magazines were donated by local people and by the J. G. W. Club.

July 20, 1908, the Coquille Library Association was formed. The board of directors included R. S. Knowlton, R. H. Mast, J. E. Quick, Mrs. L. H. Hazard, and Mrs. Fred Belloni. A reading room was opened in the Moore Building, corner of Second and Taylor Streets.

October 28, 1912, the Coquille Library Association accepted the proposition to take a room in the newly built City Hall. Mrs. T. M. Dimmick was appointed librarian at a salary of $8 a month. The records do not indicate what the hours were.

In 1931 the City of Coquille took over complete control of the library, all property of the association being given to the city, including books, furniture and cash on hand. In 1949 the amount budgeted for the library was $3,150. Donations each year continued to come from the Coquille Woman's Club, the Rotary Club, and the Professional Woman's Club.

Perhaps the most noteworthy advancement in the Coquille Library came in 1942, when the Coquille Community Building was completed, including a room for the library.

According to Mrs. Dal M. King's report, the librarians have been Mrs. T. M. Dimmick, 1908-1921; Mrs. Alice Eveland, 1921- 1927; Mrs. Pearl Ellingsen, 1927-1946; Mrs. Patsy Barkwell, 1946- .

Miss Harriet Long, state librarian, reported after a visit in 1934: "This is one of the libraries it is a joy to visit. Has distinct personality, and an effort to meet the needs of the community."

Myrtle Point

At a 1921 meeting of the Myrtle Point Woman's Club, it was moved that a Library Club be in charge of the Woman's Club, and that the W. C. T. U. be asked to move their books to the club room, then in the Woodmen Hall. The library was kept open on Wednesday of each week, with Mrs. E. C. Barker in charge. Later the Library was open on Saturdays from 3 to 5 p. m.

In 1923, the Woman's Club, with Mrs. Belle Whitaker as president, decided to undertake the establishment and maintenance of a city library.

By this time a new City Hall had been erected. So the book committee met there. The minutes of the December 16 meetings show that $400 worth of books had been ordered through Perkins Drug Store and a dozen magazines from the Schneider Music Store.

The library was kept open then six days each week by volunteer librarians. In 1925 Mrs. E. C. Barker, who had been in charge of the staff of volunteer librarians, was employed as the first paid librarian, receiving $30 a month. By then the number of volumes in the library totaled about 900, in addition to the State traveling library of 150 volumes which were renewed every 3 months. The number of registered borrowers was 557.

From 1926 on, the city library operated on funds received from pledges of the townspeople, Chamber of Commerce, and benefit parties given by the Woman's Club.

Lucy (Mrs. Ed) Barker resigned as librarian in 1935, and Mrs. Belle Whitaker was appointed, serving until

March, 1944, when Mrs. Anita Gill Howe became librarian for six months. The present librarian, Florence (Mrs. Tom) Sumerlin was employed in September, 1944. The Myrtle Point City Library became a member of the American Library Association in April, 1936.

A bequest of $8000 for the construction of a new City Library and two lots upon which it is to be built, was made to the city in 1943 by the will of the late P. W. Laird. The Library will be known as the Flora M. Laird Memorial Library, honoring his deceased wife.

The 1948 report gave the total number of volumes as 5904, and the number of registered borrowers as 1561.

PORT ORFORD

This library has had a career of rather rough sledding through a period of nearly 24 years since it was first established in 1923.

The available historical information is rather limited and broken. The following data is based upon reports from the State Library:

1927—One Port Orford Public Library established November 4.
1940—Another one established December 1.
1927—Mabel Gillings, librarian. No officers listed. The State Library report says, "There are 315 volumes owned by the library."
1928 - 1931—No report.
1932—No librarian listed.

The State Librarian included the following in her report after a visit in 1940:

> Library has had a checkered career, open, shut, even two rival libraries at one time. Letters of inquiry from several people indicate the time was ripe for action. Therefore, I had asked rival groups to meet me in the community house where the collection owned by the Women's Club is housed. There was determination to do something. Women's Club is really ready to turn collection over to a city library. So we went to work and sorted for discard and mending, which I really think will be done. Then Mayor Gable took me around to see a little building formerly used by the bank, which could be moved to city property and

fixed up. Left a new traveling library, and expect something to happen.

In 1940 Fannie G. Eddie is librarian; Douglas Johnson is president, Ruth Corson, secretary. No other report.

In 1942. No report.

In 1945-46 Mrs. R. E. Thomas is librarian. No further report.

The 1950 *Directory of Oregon Libraries* listed 1,128 volumes in the library.

Powers

The Powers Library came into being as a result of an inspiration engendered in the minds of Mrs. Albert H. Powers Jr. and Mrs. James Gamwell. A meeting had been called in 1934 at the home of Mrs. Powers for the purpose of organizing a Junior Women's Club, which decided to make its major project a library for Powers.

Arrangements were made with the school board for housing the library in the school building. Lumber for shelving was donated by the Coos Bay Lumber Company. The Boy Scouts and husbands of the club members helped with the installation of the shelving. A book drive was conducted. The library was officially opened June 15, 1935. For a while, each club member in turn acted as librarian, keeping the library open two hours in the afternoon, three days a week.

In 1936, money was raised to pay a librarian, with a number of young people of the town serving in that capacity for several years. Miss Ruth Crawford was the first paid librarian.

In 1938, when the Junior Women's Club no longer functioned, the library was accepted as a civic responsibility of the Powers Woman's Club. In 1946 the city took over the financing, budgeting $400 and increasing the amount later to $450.

In her 1938 report to the State Library, Mrs. James W. Gamwell, library chairman, wrote: "During the long period of unemployment this winter, the library has certainly been of untold value — and we do hope to keep it going and to improve it as we can."

Brookings

The Brookings Public Library was established on November 1, 1924, with the following board members: Mrs. G. G. Wood, who served as librarian, Miss Florence Hill, Mrs. N. Crowdace, Mrs. A. Smith, Mrs. C. C. Cannon.

In September, 1933, Miss Harriet Long, State Librarian, visited the library and reported:

> The librarian is paid fifty cents a week by the Chetco Woman's Club. Local library sponsored by the Woman's Club, and housed on balcony of principal store. Open only on Saturday afternoon, in charge of a high school girl, who performs function in a routine manner . . . Book collection fair . . . condition fair . . . Advised borrowing 50 volumes from the State Library.

On April 26, 1951, the *Brookings-Harbor Pilot* was able to say:

> Chetco Community Library has been a very busy place since it was reopened a month ago, in the VFW hall, with over 350 volumes being taken out in that time—a good percentage by the children . . . Two large donations of books have been received recently, one from Mrs. Rose Poole and the other from Mrs. Bob Perkins.

For the year ending June 30, 1950, the library had Mrs. Gladys Brainard as librarian, 772 volumes, a registration of 275, and a circulation of 3,954.

Empire Public Library

The library was established very belatedly indeed in this old town in 1923, consisting of about 350 donated volumes, supplemented by the State traveling library.

Seventeen years later, the next recorded information appears, following a visit by the State Librarian in September, 1940:

> Looking up! Have acquired a little building, shabby but their own. Have purchased a few books, discarded all too few, but are beginning to sit up and be noticed.

Mrs. Dorothy Haaga is listed as the librarian in 1940, Mrs. Hal Gray in 1943-44, Miss Nina Lyon in 1946-47, Mrs. G. Eikenberry in 1947-48.

Following is the 1950 report on the library: Librarian, Mrs. Edith Trochim; volumes, 2,432; registration, 427; circulation, 6,436; total receipts, $692.

Publicly Owned Books

Summary statement of the Coos and Curry Public Libraries for the year ending June 30, 1950, condensed from the *Directory of Oregon Libraries*:

Library	Volumes	Borrowers	Circulation	Receipts	Per capita
Bandon	3872	1346	40835	2350	1.94
Brookings	772	275	3954	269	......
Coos Bay	19298	2476	42434	10843	1.80
Coquille	8420	2543	27981	4597	1.08
Empire	2432	427	6436	692	.28
Myrtle Point	6371	928	16899	2008	.94
North Bend	9622	1600	33382	5990	.86
Port Orford	1128	125	384	18	......
Powers	2374	214	5574	450	......

This adds up to 56,289 publicly-owned books in the two counties, to 9,934 persons who borrow and read them.

It is interesting to note that the little city of Bandon — in spite of all its set-backs — has a public library history truly outstanding, including its per capita library expenditure of $1.94, topping the list of all Coos and Curry communities, and exceeded in the entire state by only one other, the cultural city of Ashland, $1.97 — 3 cents higher than Bandon.

22
Music and Drama

> Oh, you hungry Lucile from Coquille,
> You seem to be made out of steel,
> Your eyes they shine brightly,
> You do things uprightly,
> In a way that's a shame to reveal.
> —*Bandon High School Opera,* 1909

Empire Dramatic Society — J. M. Siglin, editor of the *Coos Bay News,* has left an account of the visit of famed Thespian troupe to Bandon's first Fourth of July celebration, 1878:

> On the morning of the 2nd, we in company with the members of the Empire City Dramatic Society, left the bay for Coquille to attend the celebration at Bandon . . . On the evening of the 3rd we arrived at the ferry, the place selected for the celebration, where we found numbers already encamped quite home-like with tents, some in flat boats or scows. We found a hall built for the occasion, 40 by 100 feet. About 10 o'clock of the 4th the assemblage was called to order. Judge Lowe read the Declaration in good style, after which "The Red, White and Blue" was rendered by a quartette, the audience heartily joining in the chorus. After dinner the "Dramatic Society" gave an entertainment as per programme, acquitting themselves very creditably, and to the great delight of the audience which filled the large hall. J. W. Bennett sang "The Hat Me Father Wore" in character, and being but a few years from the "auld counthry," his mimic of an Irishman was a complete success, and was received with a storm of applause. C. C. Dryden sang "Marching Back to Georgia" in character in good style, and brought down the house.

Golden West Quartette — Vince O. Pratt was 22 years old when he walked from Roseburg to Marshfield with his father, Calvin C. Pratt. They arrived on New Year's Day 1890.

He was one of the best vaudeville entertainers on the Bay, an outstanding show man. His banjo playing and singing were in much demand. Members of the Golden West Quartette were Jay Tower, Charlie Lash, Mr. Niles, and Vince Pratt.

Corn-Fed Canaries — J. L. ("Jay") Smith, who came

to Coos in 1913, was the first country agricultural agent.

In 1915 he solicited the support of the Coquille Chamber of Commerce for some form of entertainment for the farmers in connection with the judging of corn. Out of this developed the Coquille Corn Show, a two-day celebration with all the entertainment free, which was continued for 20 years. A feature of this event was a singing group dubbed the "Corn-Fed Canaries" which entertained during the two days, any time, any place.

The "Canaries" held a reunion in August, 1949 at Coquille, with a program broadcast over KWOR. Those present were Jack Lamb, Ken Talley, Spike Leslie, Aaron Wilson Eugene, J. E. Norton, Sam Nosler, Frank G. Leslie (Oakland, California), "Jay" Smith, E. D. Webb (Empire), George Taylor, Brick Leslie (Oswego), F. C. True, Jack Cramer (Portland).

Coos Bay Pirates – Organized in 1924, "they attract attention by their fierce looks and piratical garb." At Gold Beach in July 1941 they joined the Rogue River Rogues and the Grants Pass Cave Men in a feast of raw cougar meat. They attended the Golden Gate Exposition garbed in "true Captain Kidd style." No. 1 Pirate officer is the Chief Skull, No. 2 is the First Mate, the treasurer is the Yeoman. The governing board of seven are the Quarter Deck. In 1941 as they traveled and extolled the beauties of the Coos Bay country "they were seen and of course admired by 3,000,000 or more."

BANDS AND ORCHESTRAS – For the years 1904, 1909, 1913, the bands and orchestras of the various towns, and their leaders, were as follows:

Marshfield: 1904, KIRKMAN'S ORCHESTRA – E. J. Kirkman; MARSHFIELD FIRE DEPARTMENT BAND – W. A. Toye, dentist and assistant chief. 1909, MARSHFIELD ACME BAND – Charles F. Ellerbeck, a railroad fireman; SWASTIKA ORCHESTRA – Frank Bowker, a barber. 1913, COOS BAY CONCERT BAND – R. N. Fenton, another fireman on the Coos Bay, Roseburg & Eastern; ELLERBECK'S ORCHESTRA – the same Ellerbeck as above; KEYZER'S ORCHESTRA – Lew Keyzer, a music teacher, in competition with a very musical 27½ miles of railroad. At this time there was the CHAMINADE MUSICAL CLUB – Mrs. William Horsfall; and the MARSHFIELD DRAMATIC CLUB, meeting at call in Masonic Hall – Rebecca Luse, elocution teacher.

North Bend: 1904, NORTH BEND CONCERT BAND, meeting at the Pavilion – Charles S. Kaiser, brick contractor. 1909, same band, meeting in the City Hall – P. L. Swearingen, barber; ECKHOFF ORCHESTRA – C. A. Painter, a painter; BAY CITY ORCHESTRA – George Langenberg, bookkeeper at the Coos Bay

Brewing Company. 1913, same band, again directed by Kaiser but now meeting in the Meyers Building.

Coquille: 1909, Fire Department Band – George O. Leach; Gage Orchestra – C. A. Gage. The sheriff's office here had even more of a monopoly on musical leadership than the railroad had in Marshfield; Leach was the sheriff's bookkeeper and Gage was his deputy. 1913 – Same band, same orchestra, same leaders.

Myrtle Point: 1904, Myrtle Point Orchestra – Herman A. Tucker, who listed no other occupation for himself; he lived at the Guerin Hotel.

Coos Bay Times

The Coos Bay Regatta, one of the community events which Coos and Curry have had through the years, including Paul Bunyan Celebration, Marshfield; Corn Show and Flower Show, Coquille; Wild Flower Show, North Bend; Agate Carnival, Port Orford; Fat Lamb Show, Gold Beach; Azalea Parade, Brookings; Cranberry Festival, Bandon; Coos County Baseball League about 1900-1904; ship launchings at Old North Bend; pioneer horse races at Arago; log-rolling contests; steamboat races; land-clearing teams; picnic excursions up Coos River or to Charleston, with demonstrations by the Life Saving crew; beach-combing gatherings at wrecks; camp meetings, principally up Coos River; an occasional whale exhibit, always good for a big crowd, no matter how hard to get to.

BANDON: 1904, BANDON CONCERT BAND – W. F. Harris, music teacher; MCCULLOUGH'S ORCHESTRA – C. S. McCullough, a surveyor. 1909, same band but now directed by E. B. Kausrud, a music teacher, who was also leader of the SEASIDE ORCHESTRA. 1913 – Same band and Kausrud still the leader but the two motion theatres now had the orchestra.

Riverton: 1904, SMITH'S ORCHESTRA.

OPERA HOUSES AND THEATRES – 1904, Masonic Opera House, Marshfield; The Pavilion in Old North Bend; Coquille Grand Opera House. 1909, Benson's Opera House, Myrtle Point; Bandon Opera House. 1913, Motion picture theatres – Marshfield: Grand, Orpheum, Royal; North Bend: Joy, Star; Coquille: Royal, Scenic; Myrtle Point: Unique; Bandon: Grand,Orpheum, neither owned but both directed by H. H. Morton, who additionally directed both orchestras. George J. Lhemanski was proprietor of the Coos Bay Vaudeville and Moving Picture Circuit.

The present Mrs. J. N. Gearhart, the seventh child of Edwin J. and Emma Bigelow, says of the pioneer days in the Eckley country:

Many of the oldtimers could fiddle and whenever enough gathered, a square dance was enjoyed. When they came in great enough numbers, they danced all night. Miss Ella Bigelow could play the organ and sing and she was always ready on request to respond for the entertainment of the old miners, who, being isolated for years, enjoyed such a rare treat. And she played and sang for the neighbors whenever they called.

Mollie and Wade Wilson, brother and sister, who lived west of the Eckley Sugar Loaf Mountain, also could sing, and they always added a bright spot and a cheerfulness to the gathering when they came to visit.

23

Coos Officials

IN 1879 A LIST of Coos County officials appeared in a 40-page booklet printed in Marshfield and titled *Settlement and Early Settlers of Coos Bay*. No authorship was revealed except that it was "Written by a Pioneer of Coos Bay." However, the authorship is generally accepted as that of Stillman S. Mann, first probate judge of Coos County, and a partner in the firm of Flanagan & Mann, pioneer coal mine operator. [He is sketched in the literature chapter.] The list covers the period from 1854 to 1878 inclusive.

It was not till 1921 that the county clerk's office started a register of the different officials.

The gap of 40 years from 1880 to 1920 has been covered by two Marshfield High School students, Emogene P. and Orlando F. Furno.

Probate Judge

Charles Pearce Apr.–Oct. 1854
F. B. White ....Oct.–Dec. 1854
R. S. Belknap ....No date
A. N. Foley ....No date

County Judge

S. S. Mann 1859-1862
Gilbert Hall 1862-1866
S. S. Mann 1866-1870
D. J. Lowe 1870-1874
J. H. Nosler...............1874-1882
George M. Dyer 1882-1886
D. L. Watson 1886-1894
J. Henry Schroeder ..1894-1898
L. Harlocker 1898-1906
John F. Hall 1906-1914
James Waston 1914-1920
C. R. Wade 1920-
R. H. Mast 1921-
D. F. Thompson 1935-
Hugh McLain 1939-Died
J. E. Norton (appt.) 1939-1940
Ervin L. Peterson......1941-1943
L. D. Felsheim 1943-1950
James W. Harrison....1951-

Coos and Curry 1852-1952

Four administrators of the Coos and Curry County Pioneer and Historical Association, the publishers of this history. Left to right: J. E. Norton, chairman of the history and finance committees; Inez R. Chase, now in her sixteenth year as secretary-treasurer; Mrs. Ralph Stephens and Mary Randleman, who for many years have had charge of the museum in Coquille.

Bill Dixon
Bill Welch
Clark Miller
E. Bender The Leader
Aurelius Todd
Charles Dietz
Charles Schroeder, Sr.
Carl Vokmar

Mr. Pape
J. Henry Schroeder
Steve Steward
August Schroeder
Henry Schroeder, Sr.

First Brass Band in Myrtle Point
Probably the first in Coos County

Coquille Women's Band About 1894

-Curry Pioneer Museum

Four Grandmas

randma Leneve, Grandma Bender, Grandma Guerin, Grandma Norris

Six Lumberjacks

Isthmus Slough Camp 1889.
Villiam Lawhorn, Jerry Grow, Ed Thompson, Joe Reister, Martin Flick, Jack Boone.

ed by Warren Dick

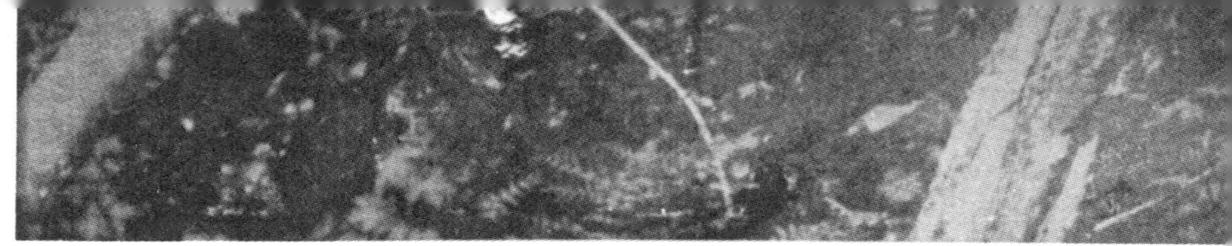

Joaquin Miller in Coos

With Mr. and Mrs. Norris Jensen

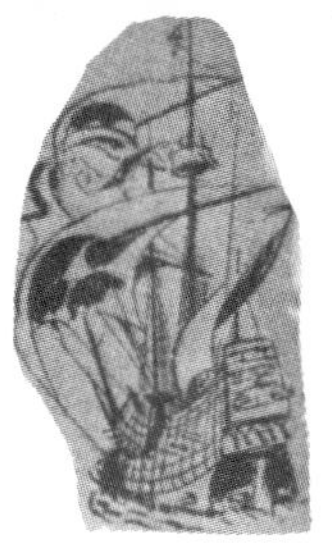

CAPE BLANCO

Left: Lighthouse built in 1870: Below: Ruins of the westernmost church on the mainland of the United States, photographed by Edgar McDaniels about 1945. Left center: Map of the Cape Blanco area. Bottom: James Langlois, assistant keeper and keeper of Cape Blanco Light for more than 40 years.

Gold Beach 1915

BLACK SAND

Mouth of the Rogue

WHISKEY RUN 1855

HARPER'S MAGAZINE

BEACH GOLD DIGGINGS

yrtle Trees

Collection of Alfred Powers

10 INDEPENDENT CHILD'S SPELLER. THE ALPHABET.

O o R

O o R

Ox ox Rat rat

SCHOOLS

Top: From a Coos primer of the 70's. Left: Off Haines Inlet School. Above: The old school Coquille. Below: Lower South Coos River Sch 1889.

Assessor

H. G. Fernald 1854-
John B. Dully 1955-
Wm. Bagly 1856-
E. Cunningham 1857-
C. H. Hodgkins 1858-
W. H. Packwood 1859-
Samuel E. Smith 1860-1861
A. J. Moody 1862-1863
John A. Harry 1864-1865
E. D. Sewell 1866-
F. G. Lockhart 1867-
Wm. T. Perry 1868-1869
G. W. Sleeper 1870-1872
W. F. Hill 1872-1873
Jas O. Shinn 1874-
Raleigh Isaacs 1875-
Alex Stauff 1875-1878
John Lane 1879-
John J. Lamb 1880-1882
L. Harlocker 1882-1886
F. M. Garrison 1886-1888
W. C. Bullard 1888-1892
J. H. James 1892-1894
K. H. Hansen 1894-1898
J. S. Lawrence............1898-1902
T. J. Thrift 1902-1916
J. P. Beyers....................1916-1940
Charles W. Forrest....1941-1951
Hiram R. Clark..........1951-

Sheriff

J. H. Foster ....Apr.-June 1854
C. H. Haskell 1854-Dec. 1856
W. H. Jackson ..1856-Apr. 1857
John A. Chick ..1857-Dec. 1857
J. S. Macnamara 1857-July 1858
J. C McKay ......July-Dec. 1858
J. S. Macnamara 1858-July 1860
Stephen Davis ..1860-July 1861
Jod. Burgess (Act.) Aug. 1861
Wm. S. Dryden 1861-June 1863
I. Hacker 1863-July 1864
A. J. Moody 1864-July 1870
C. A. Hanscom 1870-July 1872
G. W. Sleeper ..1872-Apr. 1873
T. G. Owen 1873-July 1874
Jos. Ferry 1874-April 1785
Jay Tuttle 1875-July 1876
A. G. Aiken 1876-1879
John Lane 1880-1884
W. R. Simpson..1884-July 1885
Isaiah Hacker..............1885-1886
L. Harlocker 1886-1890
Z. T. Siglin 1890-1892
R. H. Wieder 1892-1894
W. W. Gage 1894-1902
Stephen Gallier 1902-1906
W. W. Gage 1906-1920
E. P. Ellingsen 1921-1925 (died)
W. W. Gage 1925-1929 (died)
Henry E. Hess 1929-1935
William Howell 1935-

County Clerk

H. C. Boatman 1854-1855
D. L. Lount ....1855 July-Dec.
F. G. Lockhart 1855-1858
Wm. Romanes 1858-1860
Geo. T. Sullivan Jan.-July 1860
J. S. Macnamara 1860-1862
D. Morse Jr. 1862-1868
W. H. Jackson 1868-1878
Alex Stauff 1878-1884
J. J. Lamb 1884-1892
J. J. Stanley 1892-1894
D. F. Dean 1894-1896
Edward Rackleff 1896-1900
L. H. Hazard 1900-1904
James Watson 1904-1914
Robert R. Watson 1914-1916
L. W. Oddy 1916-1920
Ines P. Bunch............1920-1921
A. B. Collier 1924-
Robert R. Watson 1929-
L. W. Oddy................1933-1950
Georgiana Vaughn 1950-

County Treasurer

N. C. Boatman April 1854 to July 1855 (County clerk at same time.)
A. N. Foley 1855-July 1859
H. B. Cammann July-Sept. 1859
P. Flanagan 1859-July 1860
H. B. Cammann 1860-1862
Geo. Cammann 1862-1864
James T. Jordon 1864-1866
Henry Wykoff 1866-1870
Geo. Cammann 1870-1872
D. Morse Jr. 1872-1876
John Flanagan 1876-1878
D. Morse Jr. 1878-
Frederick Schetter 1880-1884
A. P. Owen 1884-1890
H. G. Ploeger 1890-1892
S. B. Hatch 1892-1894
W. W. Hayes 1894-1900
J. B. Dully..................1900-1910
T. M. Dimmick........1910-1930
Charles Stauff ..1930-1948 died
Clara Stauff 1948-

County School Superintendent

F. G. Lockhart 1854-1857
G. H. Hodgkins 1857-1859
E. Cunningham 1859-1860
C. Hermann 1860-1863
Wm. T. Perry 1863-1865
H. Hermann (Elected 1864 but failed to qualify)
Anson Rogers 1865-1868
J. H. Schroeder 1868-1872
I. Hacker 1872-1874
J. H. Schroeder 1874-1876
John S. Coke..............1876-1878
J. F. Moore 1878-
A. B. Camp 1880-1884
Dr. J. T. McCormac 1884-1886
A. J. Sherwood 1886-1888
W. H. Bunch 1888-1892
A. N. Knight 1892-1894
J. H. Barklow 1894-1898
W. H. Bunch 1898-1912
Raymond E. Baker ..1912-1920
C. E. Mulkey 1920-1925 (died)
Martha Mulkey (Purdy) 1925-

County Surveyor

E. Cunningham
J. Malcolm
J. Aiken
Wm. Hall 1873-1874
S. B. Cathcart 1874-1875
Wm. Hall 1876-1880
E. L. Price 1880-1882
J. F. Hall 1882-1884
John F. Neall 1884-1886
S. B. Cathcart............1886-1904
C. S. McCulloch 1904-1906
S. B. Cathcart 1906-1908
A. N. Gould 1908-1914
C. S. McCulloch........1914-1924
E. H. Kern 1925-
E. L. Vinton 1933-
J. N. Gearhart............1937-

County Coroner

Louis Monroe 1880-1882
(Acting Coroners) 1882-1888
W. J. Butler 1888-1892
D. M. Brower 1892-1894
Geo. W. Canning 1894-1896
Wm. Horsfall 1896-1904
E. Mingus 1904-1908
T. J. Lewis 1908-1910
Dr. R. E. Golden 1910-1912
F. E. Wilson................1912-1928
Dr. Russell C. Keizer..1929-1936
Dr. Ennis Keizer........1936-1942
Wm. O. Campbell 1942-1947
Brewer Mills 1947-

Coos-Curry Representation in Oregon Legislature

When Oregon became a state in 1859, the approximate population of 53,000 and 16 senators meant one for about 3,300 persons. However, if a county exceeded half of that, or a few more than 1650, it could have a senator by itself. For a representative in the house the number was about 800. In 1860 Coos' population was 445, Curry's 393. Neither had enough but they could combine for a joint representative. The first one was S. E. Morton in 1860.

Not until 1870 did Coos have enough for a representative by itself. Curry's population was still not enough. So, not to deprive it entirely of representation, it went on being given a joint representative with Coos, an arrangement which continues today. Coos has a full representative and a joint one, Curry only the joint one. The latter may be a representative of either county but as a matter of courtesy he has with few exceptions been a Curry man.

Neither Coos nor Curry alone has had sufficient population by itself to have a whole senator. At the beginning even the two together lacked the required number, so a third county — the former Umpqua County — was included. With the demise of Umpqua County in 1862, Douglas County was the third area in the partnership. In 1872 Coos and Curry could qualify without Douglas. Yet from 1899 to 1901 Josephine County was a part of the Coos-Curry senatorial family. Since then it has been just the two.

Coos-Curry Territorial Legislators

House	*Council*
1855-56	1855-56
William Tichenor (Coos)	Hugh D. O'Bryant (Douglas & Coos)
1856-57	1856-57
A. E. Rogers (Coos & Curry)	No Coos & Curry listed
1857-58	1857-58
T. J. Kirkpatrick (Coos & Curry)	Hugh D. O'Bryant (Umpqua, Coos & Curry)
1858-59	1858-59
William Tichenor (Coos & Curry)	D. Wells (Umpqua, Coos & Curry)

Joint Coos-Curry Senators

1860—William Tichenor (Also Umpqua)
1862—J. W. Drew (Also Umpqua)
1864—James Watson (Also Douglas)
1866—Watson & G. S. Hinsdale (Also Douglas)
1868—Binger Hermann & C. M. Pershbaker (Also Douglas)
1870—L. F. Mosher & C. M. Pershbaker (Also Douglas)
1872—J. F. Watson & Gaius Webster (Also Douglas)
1874—J. F. Watson & Gaius Webster (Also Douglas)
1876 and 1878—A. G. Brown
1880 and 1882—J. M. Siglin
1885 and 1887—J. M. Siglin
1889 and 1891—W. S. Sinclair (Also Josephine)
1893 and 1895—W. S. Vanderburg (Also Josephine)
1897 and 1899—C. E. Harmon (Also Josephine)
1901 and 1903—T. M. Dimmick
1905 and 1907—J. S. Coke
1909 and 1911—W. C. Chase
1913 - 1919—I. S Smith
1921 - 1931—Charles Hall
1933 and 1935—John D. Goss
1937 and 1939—George H. Chaney
1941 - 1951—William E. Walsh

Coos-Curry Representatives

[The joint legislator for each biennium since 1874 was the one listed first]

1860	1862	1864
S. E. Morton	Archibald Stevens	Isaiah Hacker
1866	1868	1870
F. G. Lockhart	R. J. Pendergast	F. G. Lockhart
1872	1874	1876
M. Riley	H. Blake	E. J. Gould
1878	John P. Dully	R. H. Rosa
M. Riley	1880	1882
J. H. Schroeder	Raleigh Scott	Frank A. Stewart
1885	William Morras	William Morras
Walter Sutton	1887	1889
John H. Roberts	A. H. Crook	A. H. Crook
1891	John H. Roberts	John H. Roberts
A. H. Crook	1893	1895
J. D. Garfield	J. H. Upton	Frank A. Stewart
1897	J. S. McEwen	Thomas Buckman
W. H. Nosler	1899	1901
Thomas Buckman	E. S. Platts	R. D. Hume
1903	George P. Topping	A. H. Black
R. D. Hume	1905	1907
Schiller B. Hermann	Robert Burns	Ed Rackleff
1909	Schiller B. Hermann	W. C. Chase
I. N. Muncy	1911	1913
R. E. L. Bedellion	S. P. Pierce	S. P. Pierce
1915	Ed Rackleff	J. S. Barton
S. P. Pierce	1917	1919
Charles R. Barrow	Frank B. Tichenor	J. R. Stannard
	Arthur K. Peck	T. J. Thrift
1921	1923	1925
S. P. Pierce	S. P. Pierce	S. P. Pierce
T. T. Bennett	T. T. Bennett	Dal M. King
		1931
1927	1929	Louis L. Knapp
S. P. Pierce	Louis L. Knapp	J. E. Norton
Dal M. King	J. E. Norton	1937
1933	1935	Roy E. Carter
W. H. Bennett	Roy E. Carter	J. H. McCloskey
J. H. McCloskey	J. H. McCloskey	1943
1939	1941	Stella A. Cutlip
Roy E. Carter	Roy E. Carter	Ralph T. Moore
J. H. McCloskey	George C. Huggins	
1945	1947	1949
Fred B. Adams	Fred B. Adams	Fred B. Adams
Ralph T. Moore	Ralph T. Moore	Ralph T. Moore
	1951	
	Fred B. Adams	
	Ivan C. Laird	

24

Pioneer Association

> Binger Hermann was out elk hunting with Samuel M. Dement, Coos pioneer of 1853. Hermann, shaking with buck ague, discharged his gun prematurely. Dement asked him what he was shooting at. "At random," said he. "Zooks, Binger, I didn't know that there was any randoms in this country. What kind of animals are they?"

THE OLD *Pioneer Minute Book* begins with a newspaper clipping and reports the first annual meeting of the Coos County Pioneer Association at Coquille City on November 5, 1891, with Orvil Dodge as secretary. The book ends with the fifteenth annual meeting at Bandon on August 30, 1907, with Viola L. Rosa as secretary. This report is in the form of a newspaper clipping pasted into the book, on page 70. The next sheet apparently has been removed, containing pages 71 and 72. No further recordings appear in the book, except that a copy of the constitution and bylaws is pasted in on the fly leaf. It bears no date; but, by deduction, it appears to have been formulated in 1893. It gives the name as the *Coos County Pioneer and Historical Society,* whereas the original name adopted at Coquille during the first meeting is recorded in the following statement: "This organization shall be known as the *Coos County Pioneer Association.*"

From the old pioneer minute book, page 51, on the meeting in Marshfield August 15, 1899:

> Mrs. Jackson, Mrs. Yoakam and Mrs. Lockhart, the first three white ladies who settled in Coos County, were escorted to the platform by Judge D. J. Lowe, being surrounded by many prominent pioneers, among whom were John Hamblock, S. H. Hazard, Judge J. H. Schroeder, W. D. L. F. Smith and many others.

Said S. H. Hazard, orator of the day:

It is right and proper that we assemble and honor the men and women who first settled in Coos County, for they made it what it is today. . . . Particular credit is due to that litle band who first settled at Empire City on the remote and picturesque banks of that beautiful sheet of water – Coos Bay; for they it was who planted the first seeds of civilization, and every pioneer present should feel grateful that the three ladies who accompanied those heroes and shared the dangers of that day are with us on this happy occasion. And though their venerable locks are sprinkled with the frost of age, yet they are able to point back nearly a half century and tell us of the hardships and suffering they endured when they helped to break down the first wild shrubbery that began to yield to the white man's progress.

I saw what the pioneers had done 25 years ago, when I first came, and I wondered at the achievements . . . When they came, they followed elk trails, but I came just as the Coos Bay and Roseburg wagon road was completed. I had stopped on the way at C. H. Howe's. He had a peculiar table, invented by himself, I suppose. By turning an upper platform, the eatables would come around and the large luscious strawberries that were brought in front of me by that ingenious mechanism fairly astonished me, and I wondered at such products.

When I arrived at a tributary of Coos Bay, I took a small boat and found after a long pull the excellent abode of comfort, Mrs. Lockhart's hotel.

Not in the minute book, but in a copy of the *Coquille Valley Sentinel* of September 11, 1908, a lengthy report is given of the 1908 meeting in Coquille.

September 3, 1908, opened a day of joyous expectations, and at an early hour the citizens of Coquille were astir, and as the train and river boats came puffing into town, crowds took up their march to the beautiful groves of myrtles, whose balmy odor added comfort as it mingled with the invigorating zephyrs that breathed through the tree tops.

After this, Mayor M. O. Hawkins delivered a splendid address of welcome to the pioneers and veterans, which was responded to by C. R. Barrows, Esq., for the two societies [G.A.R and the pioneers] in a very interesting manner.

Mr. Hermann's oration was a masterly effort and was pronounced by many as the best ever heard on such an occasion. . . . Officers elected for the ensuing year included Dr. C. W. Tower, president; William H. Schroeder, secretary and treasurer.

It had been previously planned to hold the next annual

meeting in the grove on the old Hermann homestead and make it a celebration of the fiftieth anniversary of the arrival of the famous Baltimore Colony in the Coquille Valley; but when Dr. Tower presented the joint invitations from the Marshfield Chamber of Commerce and the Marshfield City Council, it was unanimously decided to accept them. Instead of converting the fiftieth anniversary of the arrival of the Baltimore Colony, the latter event will be celebrated separately by a picnic at the homestead of Dr. Henry H. Hermann, who led the group into the Coquille Valley. It is thought the four generations will be in attendance at the picnic, making about 200 in all.

The Coquille meeting in 1908 was the seventeenth annual gathering of the old Association. The one scheduled for Marshfield in 1909 would have been the eighteenth. However, if the meeting materialized, no record or report of it has been found.

The meetings of the old Coos County Pioneer Society usually lasted three days. Some of those who came from the more distant parts of the county required five days in all, including the coming and returning. Camping on the way and at the meeting place was common.

The meetings very often were held in conjunction with the G.A.R. There was always at least one brass band, but more often two or three. Four were reported to have taken part in one place.

There was always a picnic dinner, usually furnished by the host community, and a *Speaker of the Day* to present an oration. A favorite speaker for such occasions was Congressman Binger Hermann. He gave the oration at the Fourth of July celebration at Meyersville (Myrtle Point) in 1861. He was speaker 63 years later at a Port Orford celebration.

The *first* and the *last* of the seventeen meetings of the old Coos County Pioneer Society were both held in Coquille, the first in 1891 and the last of which we have any record in 1908. The 1908 report previously referred to in the *Coquille Valley Sentinel* contains the following:

Wm. H. Schroeder, the permanent secretary and treasurer of the Pioneer Association, was instructed to compile a roster of the living pioneers and a memorial of those who have passed to the Great Beyond.

Following is the membership list taken from the old minute book, giving the year of enrollment and the year when the member first came to Coos County.

Pioneer	Came to Coos
Mrs. E. M. Lockhart	1853
Mrs. Yoakam	1853
W. H. Harris	1853
W. M. May	1853
A. G. Aiken	1854
D. J. Lowe	1856
W. D., L., F. Smith	1853
John Kronenberg	1859
J. H. Schroeder	1859
J. F. Schroeder	1859
Mrs. O. T. Bender	1859
Mrs. Menitta Stauff	1859
W. T. Lehnherr	1859
Dora Schroeder	1859
Mary B. Harris	1862
Mary Schroeder	1863
T. C. Stillwell	1864
G. T. Moultin	1864
J. A. Collier	1865
B. F. Collier	1865
Orvil Dodge	1866
Thos. R. Willard	1868
Geo. W. Leneve	1865
C. A. Lowe	1857
G. S. Wells	1850

Pioneer	Came to Coos
Mrs. Capt. J. J. Jackson	1853
Mrs. J. F. Schroeder	
B. F. Ross	1853
James Aiken	1854
C. L. Scales	1856
B. F. Figg	1856
Y. M. Lowe	1857
H. Schroeder	1859
A. H. Schroeder	1859
C. E. Schroeder	1859
George Stauff	1859
Carrie Stauff	1859
Emily Schroeder	1859
G. A. Brown	1861
Elizabeth Lehnherr	1863
E. W. Stillwell	1864
Christina Norris	1865
S. L. Leneve	1864
Jos. Collier	1865
H. J. Collier	1865
W. C. Paxson	1866
Chas. Collier	1865
Elizabeth Leneve	1865
Vail N. Perry	1858

Additions in 1892 to the list:

Pioneer	Came to Coos
R. J. Cussans	1859
Mrs. Ada Egenhoff	1860
Mrs. Mary R. Smith	1858
Adda G. Hacker	1867
Charles Eckhoff	1858
Comrade Linderman	1859
D. W. Haywood	1853
Henry Ploeger	1867
John Flanagan	1850
J. B. Gilbert	1866

Pioneer	Came to Coos
David Morse, Jr.	1860
George Chard	1866
J. J. Jackson	1856
P. A. Peterson	1868
Anson Rogers	1856
Delia M. Rogers born	1870
Lizzie Pendergrass b.	1860
H. Grotget	1868
Henriettta Eckhoff b.	1868
William Kloelin	1868

Pioneer	Came to Coos
Innis E. Ross	1868
Mrs. C. M. Cammann	1859
Miss Georgenia Cammann	1863
Isaiah Hacker	1862
Mrs. Charlotte Eckhoff	1864
Henry Miller	1860
Lottie Eckhoff (b. in Coos)	1867
Mrs. Catherine Mullen	1862
Alexander Stauff	1861
James Magee	1867
Dr. C. W. Tower	1868

Pioneer	Came to Coos
Thomas C. Wyman	1867
Agnes R. Sengstacken	1859
A. W. P. Baker	1868
George W. Jackson	1867
Elizabeth Rogers	1869
Emma A. Hilborn	1856
Patrick Flanagan	1850
E. D. K. Bevins (no date)	
Mrs. Fannie Hazard	1866
Mabel Hacker born	1875
Mrs. Mary Majory	1868

Additions in 1893:

Pioneer	Came to Coos
C. L. Hilborn	1856
W. P. Hermann	1859
Allen Urquhart	1868
Daniel Giles	1853
Fannie Dixon	1860
W. W. Phillips	1855
Mrs. Lina Norris	1865
Mrs. Annie Decker	1861
T. M. Hermann	1859
Mrs. Grover	?

Pioneer	Came to Coos
Daril Pulaski	1857
J. A. Lehnherr	1859
O. J. Grant	1861
W. L. Hayter	1865
Lizzie G. Lehnherr	1863
Elizabeth Hermann	1859
Mrs. W. Volkmar	1859
Mrs. Laura Hansen	1853
Mrs. Carrie Hermann	1859

Additions in 1894:

Pioneer		Came to Coos
Mrs. Ellen Rooke		1858
C. W. P. Mack		1865
W. O. Christen		1867
John A. Lennon		1867
Miss E. Stephens		1867
Miss Josephine Nay		1866
Miss R. E. (Rose) Rooke		1877
W. A. Colver (b. in Coos)		
Carline Eckhoff	"	1873
Mrs. Margret Messerly	"	1867
Minnie Stephens	"	1873
Frank Stephens	"	1876
Thos. Rooke	"	1869
James B. Davis	"	1869
Julie F. Getty		1868
John H. Eckhoff		1870

Pioneer	Came to Coos
J. W. Rooke	1854
Isaac Landrith	1860
Dora A. Cathcart	1860
S. B. Cathcart	
Mrs. Catherine Nay	1866
R. C. Dement	1853
James Rooke Jr. (b. Coos)	1873
Eliza R. Rooke	1871
Mrs. Emma Eckhoff	1873
Miss Ida Eckhoff	1874
Emma Stephens	1874
Henry Grotegut	1868
J. M. Davis	1853
Wilmot Getty	1859
John Nasburg (Port Orford)	1854

Additions in 1895:

Pioneer	Came to Coos	Pioneer	Came to Coos
H. H. Baldwin	1852	L. B. Feller (Fetter)	1862
Mrs. Viola L. Rosa	1859	Mrs. Mary A. Lowe	1857
Mrs. Annie Wolcott	1859	Mrs. Mary J. Thrift	1854
Mrs. C. Figg	1867	Mrs. Emma Craddock	1868
Mrs. Sarah Fay (Fahy)	1859	Mrs. Edward Fay (Fahy)	1854
Mrs. Julia A. Randleman	1866	A. C. Thrift	1853
R. E. Summers	1851		

Additions in 1896:

Pioneer	Came to Coos	Pioneer	Came to Coos
Mrs. C. A. Laird	1857	Grant Harry	1864
W. A. Stillwell	1865	Mrs. A. C. Butler	1868
Mrs. E. Fouts	1866	Mrs. Mary E. Norris	1868
W. P. Bovee (?)	1854	J. B. Fox to Oreg.	1853
A. D. Boon to Oreg.	1846	Mrs. J. Collier to Oreg.	1872
Mrs. S. C. Rogers	no date		

No list in 1897. Page 48 shows evidence of sheet being removed. The 1898 report gives no new names but lists a number of those present. The clipping which reports the 1899 meeting says, "Several new members were admitted and annual dues were paid to the amount of $20.50." But no membership list is given.

New members added in 1900:

Pioneer	Came to Coos	Pioneer	Came to Coos
Levi Snyder	1873	Samuel Hunter	1873
T. P. Hanley	1868	Dora Hanley	1862
Maryette Morse (b. Coos)	1872	Parlee Blackerby (b. Coos)	1869
Nannie Giles	1870	R. H. Rosa	1870
E. A. Lowe	1857	J. J. Lamb	1873
Mary A. Lamb	1873	J. C. Brown	1869

New members in 1901:

Pioneer	Came to Coos	Pioneer	Came to Coos
M. G. Pohl	1859	Shad Hodson	1875
Mrs Alice Hite (b.in Coos)	1872	E. W. Hermann (b.Coos)	1864
Edwin F. Schroeder "	1868	Mrs. A. F. Linegar "	1875
Mrs. Stephen Gallier "	1862	Mrs. J. C. Moomaw	1874
Mrs. L. J. Paxson	1865	J. H. Nosler	1870
Mrs. Henrietta Nosler	?		

New members in 1902:

Pioneer	Came to Coos	Pioneer	Came to Coos
Percy Hanley	?	George F. Ross	1867
Mrs. Sarah Lewis	1864	Henry Sengstacken	?
Herbert Lockhart	?	Mrs. Lou Lockhart	?

New members in 1903:

Pioneer	Came to Coos	Pioneer	Came to Coos
L. A. Roberts	1873	Mrs. T. M. Hermann	
W. H. Rogers	1874	Mabel A. Roberts	
Alice Arrington	1860	Lois Marcy (b. in Coos)	1867
Mrs.WT.Dement (b.Coos)	1870	W. T. Dement "	1869
Edward M. Jenkins	1870	J. A. Martin	1870
Mrs. Edward M. Jenkins (b. in Coos)	1876	M. H. Dement (b. in Coos)	1876
Clay Dement (b. in Coos)	1873	Mrs. Lillie Dement	
Mrs. Clay Dement "	1875	Edward Hoffman	1858
James T. Guerin	1873	Mrs. Edward Hoffman	1873
Mrs. Celia Guerin	1876	Geo. H. Guerin	1876
J. C. Whiting	1872	Inia Rose	1877
Mrs. J. A. Haines	1860	J. A. Haines	1869
Price Robinson	1873	L. L. Haines (b. in Coos)	1863
		Dr. Geo. E. Eldin	?

In 1904 no names were listed. In 1905 there was no meeting. No names are in the newspaper clipping pasted in the book on the 1906 meeting, and no minutes for that year.

New members in 1907:

Pioneer	Came to Coos	Pioneer	Came to Coos
Perkins, T. J.		Quick, Jonathan	1874
Bullard, R. W.	1867	Paull, B. B.	1874
Aasen, S. E.	1873	Hansen, Mrs. L. J.,	1853
Oddy, Wm.	1875	Lamb, J. J.	1873
Levine, Ida Quick	1874	Gallier, Wm.	1873
Strang, Mrs. Viola	1881	Wilson, John D.	1881
Baxter, F. M.	1878	Hunt, J. H.	1875
Patterson, Joel	1856	Jenkins, E.	1872
Schroeder. J. F.	1859	Jenkins, Mrs. E.	1876
Wilson, John D. and wife		Matheny, J. H.	1873
Stanford, H. H.	1883	Brown, Maryle	1859
Neatherby, W. B.	1868	Ellingsen, O. P.	1873
Cawfield, S. F.	1869	Ashlon, Thomas	1873

Pioneer	Came to Coos	Pioneer	Came to Coos
Moomaw, Carrie	1874	Ross, B. F.	1853
Broadbent, C. E.	1874	Swan, G. G.	
Henry, G. C.		Wilson, Bertha	1881
Mollie Bender, Mrs.	1881	Rosa, R. H.	1870
Elden, George D.	1871	Schroeder, Mrs. W. H.	
Schroeder, August H.	1859	(b. Coos)	1874
Schroeder, W.H. (b. Coos)	1866	Butler, C. H.	1868
Schroeder, Mrs. W.H. "	1874	Ploeger, Henry G.	1867
Bullard, Malinda "	1872	Figg, Catherine	1867
Hermann, E. W. "	1864	Fox, J. B.	1870
Hermann, Mrs. S.E. "	1872	Ellingsen, Mrs. C. A.	1873
Gallier, Wm.	1873	Ashlon, Margant	1873
Oddy, Ellen,	1876	Hermann, Mrs. W. P.	1854
Strang, D. P.	1871	Prey, Mrs. L.	1877
Baxter, Mrs. F. M.	1878	Collier, J. A.	1865
Hollen, S. B.	1878	Butler, Mrs. C. H.	1868
Quick, J. E.	1874	Endicott, Margaret	1903
Schroeder, Mary		Schroeder, Dora C.	1859
Stanford, S. M.	1877	Grant, Mrs. Mollie	1877
Epperson, M. A.	1868	Aasen, J. L.	1882
Wilson, M. J.	1870	Dean, D. F.	1881
Cawfield, Mrs. J. J.	1869	Bender, Mrs. O. T.	1859
Dodge, Orvil	1866	Hermann, Mrs. Y. M.	1868
Hoskin, B. H.	1877	Goodrich, Mrs. G. N.	1876
Aiken, A. G.	1854	Perkins, Eliza	

The seventeen annual meetings of the old Coos County Pioneer Society are here listed, as compiled from the *Pioneer Minute Book* and from old newspapers:

Date	Place	President	Secretary
Nov. 5, 1891	Coquille	J. D. Lowe	Orvil Dodge
Oct. 21, 1892	Empire	J. D. Lowe	Orvil Dodge
Sept. 14, 1893	Myrtle Point	Wm. Harris absent	Orvil Dodge absent
August 15, 1894	Marshfield	Patrick Flanagan absent	Alex Stauff absent
August 15, 1895	Bandon	J. Henry Schroeder	Mary C. Harris
August 15, 1896	Coquille	J. Henry Schroeder	Mary Harris
August 16, 1897	Empire	John Flanagan	Mrs. S. B. Cathcart
August 15, 1898	Myrtle Point	J. H. Schroeder	F.G. Dixon (acting)
August 15, 1899	Marshfield	J. D. Lowe	Viola Rosa
August 15, 1900		J. D. Lowe	Viola Rosa
1901		Isaiah Hacker	J. J. Lamb

Date	Place	President	Secretary
August 15, 1902	Marshfield	S. B. Cathcart	Ada Dungan absent
August 14, 1903	Myrtle Point	J. H. Schroeder	E. H. Hermann
August 15, 1904	North Bend	Charles Eckhoff	Ada Dungan
1905 (didn't materialize)			
August 31, 1906	Myrtle Point	J. D. Lowe	Viola Rosa
August 30, 1907	Bandon	R. H. Rosa	Viola Rosa
Sept. 2, 1908	Coquille	J. Fred Schroeder	**D. F.** Dean

During the twenty years following the 1908 Coquille meeting the society was apparently dormant. Meetings began to be held again about 1929, out of which grew the present association.

ACROSS THE PLAINS TO COOS

By J. E. Norton

From ivied halls of learning,
  From humble worker's abode,
They held the same great yearning,
  To travel the Westward Road
Far on and on to the end . . .
  With restless soul
  And a distant goal,
Their weary way they wend,
Strewing it with their substance,
Marking it with many a bier,
  Yet able to smile
  Upon the last mile —
Thank God for the Pioneer.

IV

AGRICULTURE

25

Farmlands and Farming

Coos County

AGRICULTURE HAS HAD AN IMPORTANT PLACE in Coos and Curry counties since Captain Tichenor landed at Port Orford in 1851. Just about every pioneer had at least Bossy Cow and a garden. There can be little doubt that the earliest settlers included seeds in their precious luggage — vegetable seeds, the stored-up dormant future home gardens they visioned.

Garden seeds were saved from year to year. Berry plants came later, as did fruit trees; the former were slipped and shared with neighbors. The native wild crabapple and wild cherry were found to be receptive to scions for grafting.

The virgin fertile bottom lands soon produced more than the family could consume — potatoes and a wide variety of vegetables.

If the pioneer's homestead was on one of the inlets or streams entering into Coos Bay, he might load his boat with garden produce, perhaps a few dozen eggs and several two-pound rolls of butter. Then, sometime between midnight and daylight, when the tide was right, he would start with his load, headed for town — Empire City or North Bend or, if it was later than 1867, to Marshfield. Arriving in town when the smoke was just beginning to curl upward from the various homes, he might find that some other farmer had beat him to the landing. So instead of finding Nasburg & Hirst ready to offer him a good exchange deal, he would find himself in competition in a very limited market. He might try Pershbaker's store, or he might go out and peddle his stuff from house to house.

Within about 30 years most of the desirable land adjacent to navigable streams had been homesteaded. The later comers had to settle farther back in the wilderness. On his remote claim he had game and fish and berries by just going out and getting them. He could produce an abundance of potatoes, milk, butter, cheese, eggs, beef, pork, mutton, chickens. He usually had a barrel of corned beef, another of pork, perhaps a third of salmon or other fish. In the smoke house he could take down a ham, a slab of bacon, a roll of beef, or a smoked salmon.

But a few things had to come from the stores — cloth, yarn, sugar, coffee, flour, baking powder, salt, sometimes tobacco and even snuff. Soap may have been on the store list but more likely it was made at home. Coal oil was needed for the lamps that had begun to replace the home-made tallow candles. For the children shoes and stockings had to be bought and maybe a bottle of Castoria once in a while.

The farmer usually went out to work in the coal mines or lumber camps at least part of each year, leaving his wife and children to take care of the home. European immigrants first sought jobs but soon learned that Uncle Sam was offering free farms. Such a one was Alfred Stora. He came in 1881 from Finland, worked for a while in his uncle Matt Stora's logging camp, and then began to look around for a piece of that free land. He found it on the east fork of the Millicoma River where Glen Creek comes in near the Golden Falls. The place had the making of a good farm, but a bachelor on an isolated homestead finds the long winter evenings rather lonesome.

This was the case with Alfred Stora. He thought of a girl he had known in Finland when both were in their teens. Possibly he sent for her, possibly she just chanced to come to Coos Bay. Anyway, she arrived about 1890. Her name was Hannah Strandell.

Just the other day she laughed as she recalled those days of 60 years ago. She remembered her boat ride up South Coos River to the McKnight place; she remembered how kind Mrs. McKnight was, showing the strange, bashful foreign girl to her room and asking her what her name was. Hannah, not understanding English, just shook her head — "No understand."

In 1893, Hannah Strandell became Mrs. Alfred Stora and went to reside on the Stora homestead near the Golden Falls, 11 miles above Allegany.

Four children were born. Neighbors moved into the community. The Glen Creek school was built.

At first there were no roads, only rough trails that soon were widened into sled roads, and later made passable for wagons.

For a third of a century the Storas lived here. In the early years, Alfred worked in the logging camps while Hannah cared for the home; looked after the children, made garden, milked 10 or 12 cows, made butter which was put up into two-pound rolls and sold at 35 cents a roll, or often put up in tubs or barrels and sold to the logging camps and mills at about 15 cents a pound.

They raised some beef cattle, and sold dressed beef at four cents a pound when they could sell it at all. Once the Storas butchered five small hogs. Leaving home at three o'clock in the morning, Mr. Stora hauled the pork 11 miles to Allegany; put it into a skiff; rowed all the way down the river to the bay, then down Coos Bay to North Bend, where he thought he would find a ready market for the pork. He sold half a hog there at three cents a pound. Then he rowed back up to Marshfield, where he made the rounds and managed to sell one hog to a boarding house on time — and the time is still running.

Then he had to row back up Coos River to Allegany, where he hitched up his team and drove the 11 miles, arriving home 24 hours after he had started out. The Storas then had three and a half hogs to salt down for their own use. In recalling the incident, Mrs. Stora said, "We had pork and pork and more pork."

Later, with the building of a wogon road, Mr. Stora would drive the 11 miles to Allegany in time to catch the *Alert* or some other steamer at 7 a. m. to go to Marshfield; then return in the afternoon and drive the 11 miles home again.

The experience of the Storas is fairly typical of many

families who arrived after the close-in lands had already been occupied by the first wave of pioneer settlers.

The principal cultivated crop grown by the pioneer farmer for the market was potatoes. A limited quantity could be exchanged locally for groceries and other necessities. But the real potato market for Coos Bay was San Francisco.

The best potato land was on the river and creek banks. If water transportation was close at hand, transfer to the most convenient point was fairly simple, but for the farmer with a homestead two, three or more miles from the boat landing, an additional problem was involved.

Most roads were usable for heavy loads only during the dry season. Mud became deep during the winter. The potato crop must be moved ahead of the autumn rains, though the market was not ready to accept them then.

Storage facilities were provided adjacent to the boat landing. A small building contained storage bins to protect the potatoes against possible freezing. The same building usually had a room with a stove and two or three bunks.

Come shipping time — anytime during the winter or even into early spring, the potatoes must be picked over, sprouted, sorted, sacked and loaded on a barge or flatboat capable of carrying 10 to 15 tons to the most convenient shipping point. The barge might have a small cabin at one end, with stove and two or three bunks. Usually two or sometimes three neighbors joined to make up a crew.

A typical boat landing was located at the head of navigation on Haynes Inlet, the natural outlet for homesteads ranging from a mile to four or five miles up the creek. The principal early potato growers along the creek were S. H. Crouch, Alfred McCulloch, H. W. Sanford, C. W. Sanford, and J. P. Davis.

Empire City was the most convenient shipping point, as it could be reached on a single tide under favorable conditions. This meant that by starting from the landing at tip-top-high tide, moving with the ebb, Empire could be reached before meeting the incoming flood tide.

The barge is loaded during daylight, ready to start

at the zero-hour, when the high tide begins to ebb—sometime during the night. The men "turn in" for a bit of sleep. Then up at the scheduled time for a hurried breakfast. The lines are cast off. The channel is narrow and crooked for a mile or two; poles are used against the banks. On reaching deeper and more open water, sculling oars propel the flatboat with its cargo a little faster than the ebbing tide.

If all goes well, the voyagers will reach Empire ahead of the incoming flood tide. Then, too, another well-planned operation might enable the shipper to make contact with an outgoing ship, bound for San Francisco. It might be the steamer *Emily,* the *Arago,* or the *Homer.* The potatoes might be transferred direct from the barge to the ship.

But the shipper is not always so fortunate. His journey might be interrupted by fog or an unfavorable wind, misguiding him from the channel to a mud-flat, holding him with his cargo, making him wait while the ebb tide ran out, and for the coming of the next flood tide to refloat the flatboat. Then it is that the cabin with its stove and bunks serves its purpose.

Twelve or more hours behind schedule in reaching Empire, the farmer-shipper has missed the boat. His potatoes must be carried or hoisted up onto the high dock; then moved by hand trucks to the warehouse to be stored,waiting for the next out-going ship. A rough bar might hold up the next ship for several days, even weeks. On reaching Marshall-Taggert or some other commission merchant in San Francisco, the potatoes have not improved by their wait in storage. Or in any case the market might be in over supply.

Here the farmer-shipper encounters another IF. If he strikes a lucky market, if his shipment is well handled and is sold out readily, he might receive a favorable return for his year's operations. Prior to 1890, his return would be in the form of gold coins, shipped by Wells Fargo Express, for then Coos-Curry had no regular banking facilities.

Potatoes gradually surrendered their leading place in

Coos agriculture with the coming of the creameries in the early nineties. Potatoes did well on new land, but rapidly "wore out" the soil when not rotated with other crops. Potato lands became more profitable when used for dairying purposes.

Along about 1930 and later, with the coming of the highways and the big truck lines, even the local markets were provided with "shipped-in" spuds. Many of the local farmers today do not even grow their own.

In the early days of settlement bull teams were used on Coos County farms as well as in the logging camps.

The U. S. Department of Agriculture gave the following Coos County ownership of land in 1937:

Type of Owner	Acres	Type of Owner	Acres
Corporate	245,330	Municipal	12,887
Private (non farm)	144,256	National Forest	67,434
Private (farms)	261,648	Miscellaneous Federal	21,505
State	44,595	Indian Lands	1,165
Revested Land Grants	178,700	[He who owned it all once has the least of all now.]	
County	64,400		

Of Coos County's commonly estimated 1,041,920 acres, about 290,000 are now included in farm ownership. Agriculture today is summed up in the following report by the Coos County extension agent, George H. Jenkins:

The land in farm ownership should be divided into around 50,000 acres of tillable land and 240,000 acres of grazing land. Most of the grazing area is cutover hill land. To obtain a better picture of the land in Coos County which supports 16,000 dairy cows, 7,000 head of young beef cattle and other miscellaneous livestock and crop enterprises, we could divide it into 1,750 farms each containing 170 acres of which 30 are tillable. The estimated gross income in 1950 was $6,487,500:

Dairy	$3,354,000
Beef and Sheep	1,584,000
Wool	96,000
Poultry and Eggs	360,000
Forage crops	80,000
Potatoes and truck crops	145,000
Small fruits	104,000
Specialty Horticultural products	85,000
Farm woodlot products	550,000
Other products	129,500

For comparison with some of these 1950 production figures, there is an assortment of historical statistics for 1896, 1910, and 1915:

Horses and mules: Not mentioned by Mr. Jenkins because they have so nearly passed out of the picture. In 1896 there were 2,112 of them, assessed at $36,385. *Hogs,* not mentioned either, numbered 4,567 then, eating mast under the myrtle trees and being eaten by the bears and the bears being eaten by the farmer in a kind of circumlocutory meat deal. *Cattle*: 12,145 head were assessedly valued at $107,939 in 1896. *Sheep and goats*: 7,452 with a value of $7,455. The county board said that's what they were worth—$1 a head with $3 added to the total to make it look good—and the state equalization board let it stand, though Benton County's sheep and goats were taxed at $1.52 apiece.

Poultry and eggs: Just chicken feed, to use a pun. Historians don't say much about them; the pioneer farmer biographies are silent oftener than not about the number of hens around the place. There is a reference, however, to the experiences of Joseph Davis Magee in 1897 on his cleared eight acres three miles from the later Lakeside. "He engaged in the poultry business for some time, but the difficulty in procuring grain and other incidental disadvantages hampered his success. He remained upon his homestead claim for about ten years, at the end of which period he abandoned the poultry business and removed to what is now Lakeside."

Fruit calls for a fuller historical annotation. Coos in 1910 ranked 3rd in apples. (Hood River soon shoved it down to 4th place). It ranged from 11th to 17th place in pears, prunes, and five kinds of berries, Negligible were its peaches and nectarines, 527 bushels; cherries, 1,692 bushels; quinces, 106 bushels (but still in 11th place because nobody else was raising them much either); walnuts, 1,115 pounds—and apricots just two bushels.

Thomas Hirst, 1859 Coos pioneer, has told of the harvesting of the first wild abundance: "The pioneer had a plentiful supply of wild fruits in their season, consisting of salmon berries, raspberries, blackberries, huckleberries, and crabapples. Sunday was the day for gathering the fruit. The canoe telephone operated by our women would send word to our neighbors to meet at a certain point or bend in the river. Then with lunch and pails, our ever-ready canoe would glide down the river to the place of meeting. Having filled our pails with fruit and enjoyed a pleasant chat over our lunch, we would return home for milking time."

In Dodge's history A. R. Bottolph described how he started the first fruit nursery in Coos County: "In the fall I went south from Lane County with a wagon and two yoke of oxen loaded with fruit trees, intending to peddle them. While in Camas Valley there came a heavy frost one night that ruined some of my trees. Next morning I buried the roots in the ground. I had been told that the Coquille Valley was open for settlement, and I conceived the idea of starting a nursery in that country. So I started on foot. The second day I arrived at Mr. Lockhart's near the junction of the North Fork. I looked around for a place to start my nursery and finally settled on a place called Fishtrap, bought out a squatter's right of John Dully, and commenced clearing to set out trees."

An alien kind of farming (the first attempt to compete with the Japanese, bulbs being the second) caused quite a flurry from 1893 to 1897. In the former year the Southern Oregon Silk Station was founded at Coquille to investigate the practicability of Coos silk culture. After a series of experiments with 18 different imported breeds, a new variety was obtained by cross-breeding the *O-Gon* (Japanese) and the *March* (Italian).

To go with the eggs of the new variety there was *A Handbook in Silk Culture.* Up to 1897, the book was asked for by 382 persons, both the book and the eggs by 156 more. The promotion was persuasive all right, for 2186 mulberry trees were secured through the Coquille station. At least 100 more were bought directly from nurseries. "These trees," said Orvil Dodge in his history, "are thriving well, and in the course of a few years, when they reach their full growth, will feed an enormous army of silk worms."

At the end of four years, however, the Coos cocoon output was 228 pounds, which were duly reeled into 76 pounds of raw silk — "of the first grade" and valued at $456.

Curry County

The Curry County pioneer was practically self-sustaining — a garden, a berry patch, a few fruit trees, some hogs, two or three cows. The wilds gave him deer, elk, fish, and acorn-fattened bears. He had some sheep; wool was a crop that could be taken by pack horses to central markets for shipment to San Francisco. He could also pack out bacon, hams and lard, cheese, and butter in 50-pound barrels. He sometimes drove out beef cattle to markets.

Rogue River was about all the inland water transportation he had. Some smaller streams provided it to a very limited extent. Chetco River presented a unique example of a waterway. It had three stages, varying according to season — flood, navigable, dry.

In flood stage the Chetco became a raging torrent; the traveler took to the trail along the bank. In navigable stage, except for deep pools at intervals of a mile or so, a boat had to be poled through ripples or towed through the rapids by waders above. In dry stages the river could be "navigated" by means of a team and wagon. A gravel bar served as a driveway for a mile or so. Then by fording across, another gravel bar was reached on the opposite side. Thirteen bars and a dozen crossings brought the traveling homesteader to the "head of navigation," about 18 miles inland from the ocean. From there he proceeded to his cabin by trail.

"Swiss Family Payne" pioneered on the Chetco. Remembering the highland pastures amid the Swiss Alps, they saw grazing opportunities on the mountain prairies in Curry County. Come spring to melt the snow, grass soon covered these prairies 10 or 20 miles up beyond the Payne homestead. They used these meadows as summer pasture for their cows.

When the sunny days came, all necessary equipment was packed on horses; cows were led by ropes, with calves and dogs following; mother and father Payne and their two sons were on their way. It may have taken two or three days.

At journey's end, camp was established. Calves were tied or corralled to keep the cows from straying off. Cream skimmed from the milk in big pans or shallow tubs, was churned into butter, which was packed into 50-pound barrels. Three full barrels just made a good load for a pack horse. At Chetco, the butter was sold to Merchant Blake, who kept a store and post office a short distance south of the present Harbor. Ten cents a pound was a fair price for the butter. Twelve cents a pound was considered a very good price. The butter that was not sold locally to miners and campers was shipped to San Francisco. An occasional ship would anchor near the mouth of the river. Lighters, each manned by seven men, transferred the barrelled butter to the ship.

Prior to the coming of creameries to Curry in the nineties, several farmers carried on dairying by the old method. Cows were tied to spots in corrals or driven into crude barns. Calves were let loose to take their share of the milk, after which they were tied up and the hand-milker took what was left. The milk was strained into pans or shallow tubs. Later the cream was skimmed off and made into butter. Some farmers made cheese rather than butter. After the family was supplied, the surplus was packed in and sold to the nearest local store, somewhere on the 100-mile trail. Or it might be packed to Port Orford or Gold Beach or Chetco for shipment to San Francisco.

Beginning about 1893, perhaps a little later, a few creameries were built. Since then several large dairy farms have been developed. The largest in the county, the Star Ranch, carried up to 150 cows. Several others in Curry kept from 40 to 80 or 90 each. One that has been in the same family perhaps longer than any other in the county, is the Knapp place a short distance north of Port Orford. Settled first in the 1860's by Louis Knapp, it was passed to his son, Louis Jr.

Three of the largest pioneer dairymen who made their own solid pack butter and shipped it to San Francisco, had big herds on expansive pastures by 1911 — Patrick Hughes, 1867, 100 cows on 1,000 acres at the mouth of Sixes River; Robert McKenzie, in the 70's, 60 cows on 1,000 acres at the mouth of Elk River; Alfred J. Marsh, 1882, 50 Jerseys on 480 acres on Elk River.

Robert M. Knox, who resigned in 1850 after 20 years as Curry County's first agricultural agent, reported on progress since he took office in 1930 — in the *Curry County Reporter,* here but briefly high-spotted:

> Marketing of fat lambs was not an established practice in 1930. Surplus sheep were marketed as yearlings to aged wethers. The first shipment of lambs from the Wedderburn ranch to San Francisco topped the market by two cents and beat any truck-ins by 250 miles. At the peak, 15,000 lambs were marketed in one year.
>
> The lily bulb industry brought two million dollars before over production demoralized the market. It has since been stabilized at one-half million.
>
> Car lot distribution of seeds, fertilizers, fencing wire, and feed supplies have saved farmers thousands of dollars. The number of farms have doubled. After the subdivision there still remain 300 good livestock farms in the county. Ten colonies of beetles have been established in major St. Johnswort infested areas. Lumber trucks have back-hauled 300 tons of alfalfa hay from Southern California.

26

Coos Bay Dairymen

By F. B. Rood

Out in the open, the sky is the limit
For man's vision; there's nothing to dim it,
That's where Coos County begins.
There's, oh, such a charm about cows on a farm,
Where nothing can harm and no cause for alarm,
Out where Coos County begins.
—Ethel Rood

IN THE YEAR 1853 Alfred Collver, father of T. M. and Howard Collver, still living on Catching Inlet, purchased a herd of cattle near Roseburg and drove them over the old Roseburg trail. This may not have been the first cattle brought into Coos Bay, but they surely were some of the first and formed a foundation for a large part of the cow population of the Coos Bay Country. Later the early Durhams were crossed with other breeds. At the forks of Coos River on the ranch now owned by Mrs. James Landrith, was developed a cross between the Durham and Holstein. Across the river on the ranch now owned by R. G. Rooke and Sons, the Durham was crossed with the Jersey.

As the number of cows increased the commercial possibilities of dairying were recognized. Butter was first to be manufactured, made on the farm and sold to the mines, logging camps, hotels and local stores. There is a story told of this time about a woman having "leeky" butter and her resourcefulness in selling it. The cows had eaten some wild onions or "leeks," giving the butter an off-flavor. It was customary for storekeepers to taste butter before buying it. So the lady bunched some green onions from her garden, took them to the local grocer, and asked him to taste them and see how sweet they were. The grocer complied, and said he would take all the onions she had. The lady then casually remarked she had some fresh butter, could he use it? The grocer tasted the butter, and his already oniony tongue being unable to detect the strong flavor, he accepted it without question.

Butter was churned every day on the J. M. (Mark) Davis ranch on North Coos River. At the forks of Coos River, Jasper Yoakam — father of Mrs. William Horsfall — also made butter. On the South fork of Coos River, the Bessey Brothers (Everett and Elmer) established a small creamery on the farm now owned by Mr. H. F. Heep. They shipped much of their product to the San Francisco market where it commanded the highest market price.

Anson Rogers manufactured the first cheese in Coos County on his South Coos River farm, and by 1875, was going strong. This farm is still in the Rogers family, the present owner being Anson O. Rogers, a son. By 1887, T. M. Collver was making cheese on Catching Inlet, on the farm on which he resides at the present time. Captain W. C. Harris made cheese at Sumner; the J. C. McCulloch family had a cheese factory on Haynes Inlet, the dairy now owned and operated by Mr. and Mrs. Charles F. McCulloch. Julius Larson operated a cheese plant on the farm now owned by Herman Brelage on Larson Inlet. W. D. L. F. Smith made cheese at the forks of Coos River where the Coos River Farmers' Co-operative cheese factory is now located. C. L. Landrith made cheese on North Coos River. Nathan Smith was another cheese maker on a farm still in the Smith family, now operated by Stian Smith.

Stephen C. Rogers came to South Coos River some years after his brother Anson, and located in the same community. He also shipped cheese to the San Francisco market. His daughter, afterwards Mrs. A. J. Sherwood, made the cheeese in those early days. This fine place, one of the "Riverview Farms," is now owned by a granddaughter, Mrs. Leah Barnes, and a great-grandson, Roger Barnes. S. C. Rogers built up a fine dairy herd, with the Holstein breed predominating. Some of the individuals in this herd were outstanding. The mention of "Babe" and "Hector" still revive old memories in the minds of men who served as milkers under S. C. or his son Frank. At a later date a cheese factory was operated on the farm in the forks of Coos River then owned by Ephraim Enegren. Afterwards this factory was leased by S. Robinson. James West was the cheese maker. There were other cheese factories, but these are typical. The San Francisco buyers of most of the product of these factories were Hills Bros., now extensive coffee importers and processors, and Marshall Taggart & Company, commission merchants. These firms paid for the cheese in gold, which was sent here by express, as there were no banks in Coos County.

As time passed, the dairy farmers came to realize how great an advantage a large centrally-located creamery and cheese factory would be to them. In 1892 was organized the Coos Bay Creamery Association, forerunner of the present Coos Bay Mutual Creamery Company. The building was near the mouth of Coos River on the Dan McIntosh ranch. Many pioneer names were associated in establishing this useful institution: H. E. and E. L. Bessey, S. C. and Anson Rogers, Yoakam, Smith, Ross, Condron, Collver, Harris, Larson, Landrith, Clinkenbeard, Davis, Cutlip, and still others. The Coos Bay Creamery was organized as a Farmers' Co-operative, all the profits being disbursed to the farmer patrons. At first the stockholders received six percent interest on the amount of their stock subscription; subsequently this payment was discontinued. Attorney J. W. Bennett rendered the Coos Bay Company valued assistance on many occasions.

Dan McIntosh was the first creamery manager, followed for 20 years by his son-in-law, H. E. Bessey. George Ross was secretary year after year. J. J. Clinkenbeard was president for some time. Anson Rogers, Stephen Rogers, W. H. Smith, Ivy Condron, and Frank Hodson were among those on the board of directors. Walter Christensen, son-in-law of Dan McIntosh, was cheesemaker for a long period. The Christensen heirs still own the McIntosh ranch. Peter McIntosh (not a relative of the Dan

McIntosh family) served as manager for a short time after H. E. Bessey; Andrew Christenson served for several months before L. A. Blanc, who was the last manager.

From the time of the founding of the Coos Bay Creamery the dairy industry in the Coos Bay country was on a firm basis. Competing institutions entered the field, yet the success and permanence of Coos dairying should be largely attributed to this creamery, untimely ended by fire in 1919. By it the reputation of Coos Bay cheese had been firmly established. The late W. B. Piper, while visiting Los Angeles in 1913, was told by one of the commission merchants there that their best cheese came from the Coos Bay Creamery. Thus the Coos Bay dairy products had outgrown the San Francisco market.

Also in the early 1890's, a farmer's cooperative creamery and cheese factory was constructed at Lake, later named Lakeside. A man named North supervised the building of the plant and he is thought to have been the first manager. G. W. Perkins, W. R. Glass, G. T. Schroeder, and Ralph Schroeder were among those serving at different times as cheese or butter makers. The milk was transported to the creamery in large skiffs about 20 feet long and capable of carrying 20 or 25 ten-gallon cans of milk. There was one such boat on North Lake and one on Ten Mile Lake. Eventually the gasoline launch superseded these skiffs. Later, L. J. Simpson and C. M. Byler bought the Lake Creamery and manufactured butter under the brand of "S & C."

After the railroad came to Coos Bay, creameries in San Francisco and in Portland made a strong bid for cream, especially in the Ten Mile area near Lakeside, and a considerable amount was sent to these cities.

About ten years after the organization of the Coos Bay Creamery, the Coos Bay Ice and Cold Storage Company was formed by Charles E. Nicholson, who had come here from England. A plant was built, with one department known as the Marshfield Creamery. Although cheese was later manufactured, it was originally planned to receive only cream from farm separators. Nicholson was a close friend of Dr. William Horsfall, a stockholder in the company. Carl Arlandson, now a refrigerator mechanic in Coos Bay, was engineer. Came financial difficulties about 1919 and sale to the Coos Bay Mutual Creamery Company, which now has a fine modern plant on the same site.

In 1904 a milk condensary was built in North Bend, and for about 15 years turned out a product known as Sunrise Condensed Milk. Many Coos dairymen will recall the years when J. H. Keating was manager, and later George P. Sheridan. For a time C. F. McCollum was associated with the condensary. The launch *Sunrise* was built to carry milk from Coos River. Walter Harring was captain of this boat for a couple of years, followed by Harvey Russell. Owing to the dairymen's strong feeling of loyalty to the Coos Bay Creamery, it was difficult for the condensary management to obtain as much milk as desired. Eventually it discontinued operations.

Some years later William Werth opened the Bay City Creamery in North Bend, which made butter under the brand of "Bay City Maid" and did well for about 20 years. Many patrons were from north of the bay. Werth sold in 1946 to P. T. Russell, who conducts the Zero Food Lockers there now.

In 1941, the Coos River Farmers' Co-Operative Cheese Factory was built at the forks of Coos River on the pioneer W. L. D. F. Smith farm, operated at present by a grandson, Max Smith.

Bottle milk has become important, more so each year. Indeed, if the bay cities continue their rapid growth one can visualize a time when nearly all the milk produced in the area will be required for the bottle trade. However, like the manufacture of butter and cheese, the sale of fluid milk began in a small way. In pioneer days the family cow supplied the milk for the individual family. Occasionally the cow would provide a surplus, which was sold to a neighbor.

As the ready sales increased another cow would be added — then another, and another. This was especially true in Marshfield, where there was an abundance of pasture the year round on the low marshlands. Thus there grew up many small delivery routes. Also there was another early-day method of supplying milk to Marshfield families. That was the custom of sending it from the dairy farms in small cans, half-gallon or larger, on the Coos River and Inlet boats. Each customer in town had two cans. An empty can was taken to the dock each forenoon and a full can which had been delivered to the dock was taken home. In most instances the owner's name was soldered on the can. Among the farmers who sold milk in this manner were John Hendrickson, Charles Mahaffy Sr., Anson Rogers, S. C. Rogers, W. H. Smith, J. A. Smith, H. L. Russell, James Cully, and T. M. Collver. Later the custom was discouraged by the dairy inspectors as being unsanitary and was finally discontinued.

F. A. Sacchi and H. W. Sanford were among the first to open milk depots in Marshfield, but there were many dairymen who operated milk delivery routes, among them being: A. Gunnell, Dwight Nash, R. F. Greif, Charles McCulloch, Dr. George Dix, George Landrith, and Brunnell Brothers.

In North Bend it was quite different. There were fewer dairy cows than in Marshfield, due perhaps to less available pasturage. Nevertheless the citizens of North Bend had plenty of milk. One of the first to supply it was W. L. Walker of Willanch Inlet. The milk was transported by row boat across the bay to North Bend each morning, and was delivered around town by Walter Westman, and later by Lafe Crouch. At first a ten-gallon can and a wheelbarrow were used. In the winter of 1905 and later C. J. Van Zile had a delivery route. Many still living in North Bend will remember his white horse and spring wagon used in his work. In 1906, Ross and Black were the first to establish a bottle milk route in North Bend. The milk was brought from the George Ross "Cherry Grove Dairy" on Catching Inlet and delivered in town by George Black. About 1907, J. W. Russell and Sons bottled milk on North Coos River and delivered it in North Bend. They owned a gas launch, the *Lozier,* which carried the crates of bottled milk from the farm to town each morning. The ranch that J. W. Russell had under lease at that time and where the milk was produced and bottled, is the farm now known as the "Brookmead Dairy," which has been built under the ownership of Dr. George E. Dix and under the management of G. H. O'Connor, into one of the finest in the state.

The Coos Bay dairyman has ever been on the alert to do as much of his work as possible by machinery; he often used home-made devices until the more improved dairy appliances were invented. On the J. M. Davis ranch in early days, the cream separator was driven by an over-shot water wheel which harnessed the water power of a creek. This creek, years later, was to suggest the name "Brookmead" when Dr. Dix became the owner of the farm. The story is told that at one time the separator on one of the Riverview farms was driven by the tread power of the herd bull. It saved labor and was good exercise for the bull. Other aids came through the years. Barrel churns replaced dash churns; home-made butter-workers helped speed the working of the butter; the hand-operated separators saved time in skimming the cream. As time went on motor-driven churns and separators replaced the hand-operated ones.

The means of transporting milk from the farm to the milk plant was at first by boat. The rivers and inlets were the highways. Each highway had at least one boat, often more.

Improved highways reduced the dairy fleet year by year until on December 11, 1948, Captain Jess Ott of the *Welcome* made the last trip of a milk boat. These milk carriers usually left the head of navigation at 7 a. m., gathering the milk cans at each farm's dock on the way to town, where the boats arrived about 10 a. m. The milk cans were unloaded, the milk weighed and sampled, and the cans washed and returned to their respective boats. The boats left town at 2 p. m. for the return trip, leaving the empty cans at each farm dock.

In 1920, the Oregon Dairyman's League, a statewide co-operative movement, took over the Coos Bay Mutual Creamery, with other Coos County cheese and butter factories. The individual dairyman had to sign a five-year contract to sell to the League all of his milk or cream except what he retailed. There was much starting expense incident to the organization and the overhead expense was heavy.

The result was a price to the dairyman so low as to place him on the edge of financial ruin. After operating only a little over a year, the League liquidated and the factories were returned to the original owners. Much credit for putting the plant back into the hands of the dairyman themselves, as well as bringing the unhappy arrangement to an end, was due Ivy Condron. The whole League experience is one which those who lived through it would prefer to forget. However, there were two compensations which resulted directly from the League. The first was getting J. A. Larson as manager, who saw the company brought back from insolvency to a debt-free status and more, because the fine modern plant now in use was built during the closing years of his management. The second was the trade brand "Melowest" originated by the League, and in liquidation proceedings salvaged for the Coos Bay plant by Mr. Condron and Judge J. T. Brand.

The average butter fat production per cow has been greatly increased during the last two decades, lagely due to the Dairy Herd Improvement Association or "testing association," as it is often called. The first Coos association was formed by J. L. Smith of Coquille when he was the county agent. The following method was practiced:

> Not less than 26 dairy farmers made up an association, one farmer for each working day in a month. A tester was employed who went to each farm each month. He weighed each cow's milk evening and morning, taking a sample from each cow each milking. The samples were tested with a Babcock testing machine on the farm, and from the data obtained a month's production was computed for each cow, the record being entered in a herd book furnished by the government. Thus it was easy for the dairyman to locate the unprofitable cows and send them to the butcher. He also learned the best cows from which to save calves to build up the production of his herd. At first no cow was listed as profitable unless she produced 300 pounds of butter fat a year, later raised by most dairymen to a minimum of 400 pounds.

During the years the plan has been changed somewhat. Coquille is now the center for the Southwestern Oregon Dairy Herd Improvement Association. Field men work out from there in the standard association set-up and in what is known as the Owner-Sampler Association. The dairyman does his own sampling and weighing. A field-man leaves the sample bottles one day and gathers them up the next morning, and takes the samples with the barn sheets and weights to the central laboratory in Coquille for testing and computing.

Much credit is due the county agents, who have been well trained, understanding, and cooperative — J. L. Smith in 1913, followed by C. C. Farr, C. R. Richards, Harvey S. Hale, and in 1930 George Jenkins, who has served continuously down to the present time.

For many years Coos Bay was handicapped by the lack of veterinary service. Veterinarians were on the Coquille side of the county but none in either Marshfield or North Bend, meaning considerable delay and expense in calling one over to this area. The result was when a cow became sick, it received home treatment. Sometimes the animal recovered and often it did not. Sometimes it was as much of a problem for the animal to recover from the effect of the medicine administered as to recover from the ailment for which she was treated. In 1935, Dr. J. H. Bennett located in Marshfield and from that time on skilled veterinary service has been available to the Coos Bay dairyman. In time, others located in Marshfield so that for a number of years there were four college-trained veterinarians on Coos Bay — Doctors Morgan, Hannawalt, and Werth in addition to Dr. Bennett. Coos County is a T. B. accredited area and progress is being made each year toward a Bangs-free area for the county.

Probably no single item has undergone a more radical change than the matter of feeding the dairy cow. The custom formerly prevailed of drying up the cow about Christmas and having her freshen not earlier than March. Often, during this "rest period," the cow was allowed to run in the hills except in extra severe weather. Expense of wintering the herd was reduced to the minimum. If the hills had been slashed, burned and seeded, the cows often came through the winter in fair condition. But at other times they were thin and not in proper condition for freshening. Thus many dairymen concluded it was much better to feed the cow well during her rest period, having her in top condition when she came fresh. Also much more winter milking has been done in recent years.

Helping to bring about the change is the availability of baled hay, especially alfalfa. Another is the feeding of grain. The Coos Bay area does not produce much grain and the idea once was that it did not pay to buy it. Now, however, it is figured that the market justifies a reasonable grain ration. The amounts of outside hay and grain bought and fed to dairy cows, have increased many times in the past 40 years.

The silo began to make its appearance as early as 1900. Early ones were on the Elmer Bessey farm, South Coos River (now owned by H. F. Heep) ; on the George Ross Sr. farm on Catching Inlet (now owned by Bert Smith) ; on the Bay View Dairy farm on Catching Inlet; and on Harry Walker's farm at Cooston. For C. C. Johnson of Cooston (on the farm now owned by Frank Rood Jr.) Charles Kaiser of North Bend constructed a concrete silo which received considerable publicity because of the fine workmanship it represented. It would no doubt still be standing if the barn hadn't burned down; the heat cracked it and it had to be razed. By the time of World War One, silos had become quite general on dairy farms on the inlets and on Coos River — mostly of wood, some hoop-and-stave, and many of the Wisconsin type called the "Coquille" in this county. Silage was sometimes clover and green grains but most commonly corn. The cost of labor was a big item; silo-filling time was when the rains had started to make it a very disagreeable job; often the silage did not keep well and molded. So dairymen became dissatisfied and discontinued their silos. Recently they are being revived, with use of a much better type —metal. Field cutters pulled by tractors reduce the labor required. With improved equipment and the use of molasses, silage is economically made.

The passing years have brought a very marked improvement to the dairy barn. The Humbolt type gave way to the "hip roof" in turn being replaced by the Gothic roofed barn. In early days unplaned, unpainted lumber was good enough; in recent years regular house lumber has been used and the dairy barn is painted as thoroughly as the farm residence. Many sets of Coos Dairy buildings are outstanding not only in their generally neat appearance but in their efficient arrangement. Increasingly stringent sanitary requirements have resulted in the modern milking parlor, a far cry from the pioneer custom of milking in an open corral. The very general use of cement and sheet-metal — both steel and aluminum — in dairy barn construction has been helpful in maintaining high standards of sanitation. An example of modernized dairy buildings is the fine plant built and operated by Herman Brelage and his son, John Brelage, on the pioneer Julius Larson farm on Larson Inlet.

Another milk product has assumed commercial proportions only in recent years — ice cream. At first the small hand-turned freezer was used. Older Coos Bay residents will recall the time when J. W. Tibbits, of the Palace Restaurant on Front Street in Marshfield, made and sold ice cream; or when it was made in the rear of the Charles Stauff Grocery also on Front Street — with the freezer turned by a gas engine. The first actual ice cream factory in the Coos Bay area was built in North Bend in 1923 by Lorenzo D. Cutlip, whose son now owns and operates it with the slogan "Made Its Way by the Way It's Made." Other present plants are Coos Bay Mutual Creamery Company, Mohr's Super Creamed Ice Cream Company, Hosking's Ice Cream Company, and Rich Mix Ice Cream Company.

What the Coos Bay Company did to stabilize dairying from 1892 to the disastrous fire of 1919, the present Coos Bay Mutual Creamery has done in a larger way from 1919 down to the present time.

During World War Two the government commandeered for the armed forces 70 percent of the butter and cheese manufactured. The creamery met the exacting quality requirements without any rejects in shipments of 5,500,000 pounds of cheese and 1,500,000 pounds of butter. The present able and broadly-experienced manager, R. W. Van Auker, took office in 1948. The directors are Clyman Collver, Gus Witt, Charles Mahaffy, Everett Messerle, and Frank Rood Jr.

The Coos Cooperative, previously referred to, has an output of over 500,000 pounds of cheese a year. Present directors are George Landrith, Reuben Hendrickson, William Morgan, Don Gray, and Fred Brunell, president. Graydon Thom is manager.

The Holstein breed predominated 40 years ago. James Landrith owned one of these herds which included a cow that gave a ten-gallon can of milk a day for a time. Other notable Holstein herds were built up by Ivy Condron on the farm now owned by Leonard Rood and John Hendrickson on North Coos River. In more recent years, due largely to market conditions, there has been a swing to the Jersey breed.

Dairying in retrospect since it began in the Coos Bay area, shows impressive improvements — motorized equipment for the younger men who have taken over, electricity in their homes and barns, irrigation systems where needed, better dairy appliances, better-bred cows, and better-seeded fields.

The Holstein breed formerly predominated in Coos County, notable herds being built up by James Landrith, Ivy Condron, and others. In recent years there has been a swing to the Jersey herd.

[Based on information furnished by J. E. McCloskey for plants in addition to those listed above by Mr. Rood]

Coos County

Place—Owner and Date	History
Arago—J. Henry Schroeder, 1893	First in Coquille Valley
Myrtle Point—C. E. Broadbent	He built others at Lundy, Arago, and Broadbent
Arago— John Carl	Broadbent's Arago plant
Gravel Ford —Fred Mosier	Active for several years
West Norway—Fred and John Carl	Located on their farm; operated till farm sold
Norway—J. E. McCloskey, 1913	A cheese department added to old Norway Creamery
Lee Valley—J.E.McCloskey, 1913	Run by him while owning the Norway plant
Coquille—J. E. McCloskey, 1917	No. 3 for him; sold to Swift in 1928
S. of Coquille—Lawrence Rackleff	Ran a few years
Parkersburg—Henry Miller	First on Lower Coquille
Bandon—Co-op	Burned in Bandon fire, 1936

Curry County

Place—Owner and Date	History
Pistol River—J. W. Walker	The plant is still operating
Euchre Creek—Carl Linky	
Sixes River—Zumwalt Brothers	
Sixes River—Swift & Company	A large plant
Denmark—Ed. Britton	
Langlois—H. H. Hansen	Only Blue Cheese factory west of the Rockies, with extensive mail-order business

27

Bulbs and Bulb Growers

Bulb and flower growing on a commercial basis has become a major agricultural project in Curry County, leading all cultivated crops during the 1940's, topped only by dairy and livestock. During the past 10 years it has come through a *boom-inflation, survive-or-bust* cycle, emerging battered but with plenty of life for a future of sustained yield.

Booming and Stabilizing

The following is shortened from a paper by Willis B. Merriam in the May 1946 issue of *Northwest Science Magazine*:

Prior to World War Two, over 25,000,000 lily bulbs were imported from Japan, with Holland and Burmuda also contributing. American production was less than 1,500,000. The [war cut off] both Japanese and Holland sources, and Bermuda's supplies were sharply reduced, providing a high priced market for domestic Easter lily bulbs.

Curry County, with sandy loam soil and a unique combination of climatic factors on the old beach terraces, was found to be ideal for the production of bulbs.

The story starts with Sidney Croft, a migrant farmer from Michigan, who came to Oregon in 1939. Familiar with bulb culture in Michigan, he put in an experimental acreage near Brookings. Croft succeeded in producing good bulbs within two or three years, but without an established market name he was forced to sell bulbs for five cents that three years later were to bring a dollar. Croft died shortly after pioneering the industry, and today, in his memory, the leading bulb from Oregon is known as the Croft.

As a result of these early efforts the renaissance of Curry County came about. In 1944 stories that rivaled the tales of Paul Bunyan were being told in the streets of Brookings. One grower reported the sale of $6,000 worth of Croft bulbs from a crop produced on a corner lot. Land values catapulated. One newcomer bought a single acre in 1942 for $1,000. In 1944 over 50,000 bulblets and 5,000 commercials were sold from another small acreage, valued at $9,000. In 1945 actual transactions involving sales of small acreages of lily land at $2,000 per acre were recorded.

The upshot of the bulb development up to 1945 . . . nearly 1,000 lily growers in Curry County; profits from an acre of ground from $10,000 to unverified yields as high as $20,000; total bulb sales during the fall of 1945 approximated $1,500.000.

But what of the future? Opinions differ. However, the big boom is over. Land is now high priced; two years of meticulous care are required in bulb production. Hence it is expected that few new growers will enter the field after this year [1946]. A new agricultural specialization, however, has been achieved in Curry County . . . one that promises to remain of importance to the region.

The Croft Easter Lily *By Mrs. May T. Stafford*

Louis Houghton was very free with his bulbs. They became very common in the dooryards of Bandon, but no one seemed to think of them commercially. He gave two bulbs — one each of what he considered the best types — to the late Mr. Rasmussen of Bandon. One of these two was the mother lily now known as the Croft. Mr. Rasmussen propagated them carefully. In a couple of years he had a row across the front of his city lot.

For five or six years Houghton grew his lilies in Bandon and at Crooked Creek south of Bandon. Then he moved them to Tillamook. In 1925 he persuaded some business men to go in with him. They incorporated in 1927 and were getting along profitably in competition with Japanese bulbs. In 1930 the depression overtook them and the corporation was liquidated. Houghton took his share of the lily bulbs back to Maryland where they failed to grow. He went back to work for the U. S. Department of Agriculture and is still with them. His advice is, "Don't give up to depressions."

Geneva (Mrs. O. C.) Schindler of Bandon got a look at Mr. Rasmussen's row of beautiful lilies and admired them so much that he gave her two large bulbs when he dug that fall. She planted them in her yard and let them grow. After two or three years she noticed they were not doing too well. She investigated and found the ground was just full of bulbs. She dug them up, divided them, planted back what she wanted, and piled the others on the ground.

Just as she was about to finish the job, Sidney Croft, who lived next door, came along on his way home. He asked her what she was doing. She said she wished him to take those bulbs home with him and plant them for his wife.

He said he had to spend his time raising things to eat; she mustn't put such notions into his wife's head.

Thus they kidded one another, and he started for home. But her mind was made up that he should take those lilies. So she pretended to be mad about it. He turned back, saying, "Give me the darn things."

She says she put them all into his hands, a round double handful. He took them home, made a trench in one of his garden rows, dumped them in, and covered them up. The lilies in his garden bloomed so beautifully and profusely that he became interested. His wife said he never before could get interested in flowers. He conceived the idea of selling lily bulbs to tourists at 50 cents each. He sold a considerable number that way, but in two years he had so many he didn't know what to do with them. He said he couldn't give bulblets away. His wife suggested that he put an advertisement in the local newspaper: "Bermuda Lily Bulbs 5c each."

[A response to that ad in the *Bandon World* came from] Mr. Davids of the Armcrost & Boyston Bulb Company, Los Angeles. He secured some of the stock and sent small quantities to many different greenhouses throughout the United States to see how they would set in different climates. All reported them "tops." Not one could find out where Mr. Davids got them.

All this time Mr. Croft was getting more and more interested. Of the two kinds of lilies he had, he liked the shorter. He segregated them and later named the shorter one "Croft." The other he sold to W. L. Crissey at Brookings who established it on the market as the "Estate." He was by now convinced that his pet lily was worth something He talked lilies to everyone. His wife often heard him say. "Come over and see the Croft lily." He dug up much of his vegetable garden and planted all his ground to lily bulbs. He was just starting to make some money when the Bandon fire came along in 1936 and burned his home.

By that time Mr. Crissey (who had bought Mr. Croft's stock of the longer kind) had been very successful at Brookings, together with his friends.

My neighbor at Harbor, Mrs. LaVerne Olson, had tried raising all kinds of bulbs, was very liberal in interesting others in them, and said the people of the community could begin paying their taxes if we could only get a market for them. I'll never forget the way she persuaded me to turn salesman.

She had talked repeatedly to me, offering half of all I could sell. I finally accepted, but I didn't know anything about bulbs or bulb marketing. Anyway we loaded our car full of bulbs and headed north, peddling door to door to make expenses as we went. We sold $25 worth to the greenhouse operator at Myrtle Point. The balance of our load went to Mr. John Bergen of Marshfield for $93.

Many a thrilling sales trip followed until we gained some real experience. When Mr. Croft moved in across the road at Harbor, he heard of our bulb peddling, for most of our neighbors who had bulbs let me sell them, giving me half,

Well do I remember the first time I ever saw Mr. Croft. He came puffing up our driveway where my car was being prepared for a trip. He had a shoe box and cigar box and several other small boxes in his arms, and a lily bulb in each hand.

He said, "Do you suppose you could sell some of these?"

"I think so," I replied, "if you'll tell me what they are."

He said, "White iris, yellow callas, yellow iris — but these (the ones in his hand) are *Gigantum longiforum Bermudas* lily bulbs. I'll let you have two boxes of them provided you don't tell anyone where you got them."

"Well!! Such things as Mr. Croft's *Gigantum longiforum Bermudas* lilies can't be held down. I sold the two boxes to Paul Peters at Clackamas greenhouses. A traveling salesman saw them and recognized them as the lily introduced to the market by the Los Angeles Mr. Davids who wouldn't tell where he got them.

Mr. Peters of the Clackamas greenhouses got excited. He called us on the long distance telephone. He said, "I bought two boxes of lilies from you. I will buy 10,000 every year. I will come to see you.'"

Not 24 hours later I heard a noise in the kitchen and before I could get there Mr. Peters met me at the living room door, hat in hand. He seemed very anxious. He made that same speech again, "I've come to make the deal."

I said to my husband, "I guess I won't have to peddle any more."

My husband answered, "It sure looks like it."

Mr. Peters told all who asked him where he got the two boxes of lilies. Consequently we got so many orders we were unable to fill them.

Meanwhile Mr. Croft plodded away in his lily patch across the road. He asked Mr. Stafford to help him dig bulbs which he had grown in Harbor just the one year. He liked Mr. Stafford's careful handling, and his interested listening to his lily stories. When it became evident he must give up, he asked Mr. Stafford to take the bulbs on shares, for a half. After being reduced financially by hospital bills. Mr. Croft died in 1941. By that time lilies were going high. That summer before his death in October my sales amounted to $10,850.25.

The work he started goes on. As for the Staffords' part, many blame us for letting the stock out, but we have always felt that the world is a big enough place for us all.

28

Cranberries

THE FATHER OF PACIFIC COAST CRANBERRY CULTURE, Charles Dexter McFarlin, fathered it at the age of 50 in Coos County. Born in 1835 in Massachusetts, he had built a bog in that state 10 years before he built the Pacific Coast's first one in Coos, in 1885. He was married in Marshfield in 1897 and died near his home on North Inlet in 1908.

McFarlin's 1885 bog in Coos was at the place now known as Hauser. Following his death, it passed through several ownerships, becoming badly neglected and run down, until it was bought by Louis Dubuque, who completely rejuvenated it and replanted it. The place at present is owned and operated by Mr. and Mrs. Frank O. Zorn.

In developing a small but well-built bog in 1875 at South Carver, Massachusetts, McFarlin had obtained wild vines from a natural bog on Cape Cod. He later wrote:

> This berry, under cultivation, became the largest variety known. It took my name and is known all over the United States as the McFarlin berry.

Disposing of his Massachusetts bog, Mr. McFarlin came to Oregon about 1878 or 1879. In searching for a suitable location for cranberry culture, he examined several places from Humboldt Bay in California to the Columbia River.

Before leaving Massachusetts, he had arranged with his brother, Thomas Huit McFarlin, to send him some of the McFarlin variety. When the vines came, apparently in 1879, McFarlin, not having selected a location, is reported to have "stuck the plants into a mud bath." Frank Terry, who worked for McFarlin for a number of years, has recently identified the location of that "mud bath" as the Beaver Slough swamp, where traces of the vines may still be found growing right up to the present time.

Finally in 1885 he located the place that he considered ideal for his purpose. He obtained the necessary ground on North Inlet from George W. Beale. With an ox team and some hired men, he turned a bit of extremely rough and stump-infested swamp into the first and one of the finest cranberry bogs ever developed on the Pacific Coast.

In December, 1898, McFarlin wrote:

> I have been cultivating cranberries in Coos County for 13 years . . . I have about five acres from which I gathered 687 bushels in 1898 . . . I have gathered as high as 400 bushels from a single acre. At no time during ten years have I taken less than 565 bushels from my five acres. One year my crop was 940 bushels, and it would have reached 1200 but for a heavy frost. There is money in a well managed cranberry bog.

During the 1890's McFarlin did considerable experimenting in an attempt to develop a variety of berry especially adapted to local conditions.

Referring in this connection to the variety that bears his name, he wrote:

> It is not an early variety, and for that reason is not the best for our climate. I prefer an early variety. I grow the following varieties on my place here: McFarlin, Early Black, Black Veil, True Blue, Cape Cod Belle, Cape Cod Beauty, Black Diamond, Jersey Cherry, Clinkerpin, Berlin Belle, and Saint Claire.
>
> I am experimenting to get a cross between the Early Black and the McFarlin. The Early Black is my earliest variety but it is a small berry. I have hope that I shall succeed in uniting the early qualities of the Early Black with the size of the McFarlin. Seedling vines of the cross are making healthy growth. Though I got a few berries from those vines last year, I am not certain that I shall produce a cross which will be suitable to our climate. I shall know definitely this year [1900].

If McFarlin made any further reports on his experiments, the records apparently have been lost. It seems likely that he did not succeed.

In discussing cross-pollination, Superintendent D. J. Crowley of the Cranberry-Blueberry Laboratory at Long Beach, Washington, defined the difference between this and selective breeding:

Mr. McFarlin must have been a very unusual individual if he was at that date attempting to make crosses between different varieties. There was little breeding work of any kind being done in those days . . . Actually, up to the present time, there is no man-made variety, unless we can classify the Stankavich as such, and most plant breeders who are familiar with cranberries have concluded that this is merely a selection from the Prolific variety. In other words, a vine which had large berries was selected out and propagated by Mr. Stankavich until he had sufficient to plant a few acres. This, as you know, is one of the standard ways of improving many berries, but it is not to be confused with plant breeding.

The conclusion seems to be that McFarlin did not succeed in his attempts at producing an outstanding new variety by cross-breeding. However, the fact remains that improvements (in which quite likely different persons had a part) were made in the McFarlin berry, most likely by selection. Reports indicate that considerable development in this respect was accomplished in the State of Washington. Though the original came from Massachusetts, where McFarlin first planted it and gave it his name, it did not prove to be a favorite variety in that state. But on the Pacific Coast, in both Washington and Oregon, it has taken the lead until it outranks all other varieties combined, three to one.

The Coos County Agricultural Conference in 1936 reported that the State of Washington had 546 acres planted to cranberries and that Oregon had 142 acres, of which 77 acres were in Coos County. The report showed further that of all the cranberries being cultivated in the two states, 75 percent were of the McFarlin variety.

In 1946, a cranberry acreage survey of the county agent's office showed 177 acres producing at that time, with varieties as follows:

Variety	Acres
McFarlin	112
Stankavich	34.75
Howes	14.50
Searles	13.00
Centenial	1.50
Bennett	1.25

New plantings of 76 acres not yet producing:

McFarlin	66.00
Stankavich	7.50
Howes	1.50
Searles	1.00

A conservative estimate in 1951 indicates about 350 acres of producing cranberries in Coos County.

The three or four years leading up to 1946 had been one of those periods of *boom* or *bust* in cranberries just as it had been with bulb-growing in Curry County. At the peak, cranberry growers were reported to have been grossing over $4000 per acre in some cases. Such inflated profits always result in a mad rush of inexperienced and uninformed individuals to "get into the swim." A considerable percentage of the misguided ones found themselves floundering in a whirlpool of distress.

Those who have followed the advice offered by McFarlin many years earlier have succeeded. Others have

Coos Bay Times

Wheelbarrows run on planks are used for taking berries from the meadows because the ground in the bogs is too soft for teams.

found that it was not the easy game which they had pictured it to be. He wrote as early as 1906:

> To plant a berry marsh and go off and leave it for three or four years to mature won't do. The vines want constant care, the same as other farm crops. Keep the weeds out and in three or four years the marsh that is *propertly planted and cared for* will produce 150 bushels of berries per acre per annum for an indefinite time.

By 1951, the surplus stocks have been pretty well cleaned up; the market is pretty well established; better facilities have been developed for handling the crop; harvesting is largely being done mechanically, thus shortening the picking season and reducing the cost.

In recent years considerable interest in cranberry culture has been indicated in the north end of Curry County, an extension of the Bandon cranberry area of Coos County.

Reported the Curry County Agricultural Committee, in 1947:

> Over 1000 acres of good undeveloped cranberry land located between Port Orford and the Coos County line should be developed. In normal times and with conservative prices, this crop should net $1,000 per acre. Three acres should be considered a minimum economic unit. Two hundred growers can produce a million-dollar income in northern Curry, matching a comparative income in southern Curry in floral products.

In 1949, about 225 cranberry *"growers"* were listed in the Coos-Curry area. Perhaps the list should be subdivided as follows: 1, Actual cranberry producers; 2, Experimenters misguided by a rainbow pot of gold; 3, Hobby planters with a few square rods. If reduced to the actual full-time producers, perhaps the number would not exceed one hundred.

The cranberry crop in the Coos-Curry area is marketed mainly through three agencies:

> 1. The National Cranberry Association, with a receiving station at Coquille, including a cold storage plant and a cannery. Its product carries the brand of *Ocean Spray.*

2. The American Cranberry Exchange, with a receiving station at Bandon. Its berries are marketed fresh in celephone bags under the name of *Eatmore Cranberries.* Its surplus that the fresh market does not consume is turned over to the National Cranberry Association plant at Coquille.

3. The Bandon Cranberry Producers Co-Op markets its product in celephane bags.

Of the nation's entire annual cranberry crop of about 915,000 barrels, the Coos-Curry area produces a little less than two percent, or about 17,000 barrels.

29

The Grange

COOS RIVER GRANGE NO. 45 was organized by R. M. Gurney on October 27, 1873, with Cyrus Landrith as master. In 1874 Gurney organized four more granges. In 1875 Henry Schroeder organized Laurel Grange, with L. Leneve as master.

Then there was a lapse of 23 years until Joseph Castro organized Arago No . 288, with Henry Schroeder as master. Two were organized in the eighties in Curry County – Rogue River No. 190 in 1881 by D. S. K. Merriman as master; Flora's Creek in 1882 by F. Green, with J. H. Upton as master.

Since 1873, during 78 years, 38 subordinate granges have been organized in the two counties, besides two Pomona granges and nine Juvenile granges. Of the 14 subordinate ones in 1851, the oldest is Myrtle Grange No. 289, now in its 54th year – organized in 1898 by Joseph S. Castro, with Erick Amerson as master.

Historical coverage is impossible for all these 38 existing during the three-quarters of a century. Two of them, however, have furnished summaries of their activities which are fairly typical.

Myrtle Grange No. 289

The report on the Myrtle Grange is by Mrs. Paul Davis, who has supplied the minutes of the first meeting:

Myrtle Point, Oregon, February 8, 1898.

After a lecture by Bro. J. S. Castro on the benefits of Grange work, he proceeded to organize a Grange in Giles' Hall. After organizing, the Grange proceeded to elect a Master and Secretary. After balloting Bro. Areson was declared elected Master and Bro. E. Jenkins, Secretary. Ordered that the Grange be called Myrtle Grange 289. Ordered that the third Saturday in March being the 19th be arranged as date of first meeting. The Master appointed Bros. Matheny, Giles, and Jenkins as committee on Hall. Grange closed informally.

At the next meeting the following officers were elected:

Overseer, Bro. D. Giles; Lecturer, Bro. Frank Sowash; Steward, Bro. A. McDonald; Asst. Steward, Bro. J. Matheny; Chaplain, Sister M. E. Arenson; Treasurer. Haines; Gatekeeper, Bro. Louis Strong; Pomona, Sister McNair; Flora, Sister Rose Sowash; Ceres, Sister Strong; Lady Asst. Steward, Sister M. E. McDonald. The installing officer was Bro. J. Henry Schroeder.

"It is very interesting," says Mrs. Davis, "to read the minutes, as many of our present members are children or grandchildren of the first members."

The 831st regular meeting of Myrtle Grange 289 was held on December 16, 1950, with John Caudle, master. The number of present members is 133.

There have been 31 masters of Myrtle Grange No. 289, during the 54 years from 1898 to 1951 inclusive, listed here chronologically:

E. Arneson, 1898
B. C. Shull
Lewis Strong
E. Arneson
W. O. Cooper
J. Henry Schroeder
Ed Jenkins
Price Robinson
Henry Strong
Price Robinson
Arthur Brown
C. C. Robinson
J. F. Schroeder
Price Robinson
Mrs. Laura Robinson
J. H. Barklow
Price Robinson
J. F. Schroeder
W. Lee Ray
Rev. C. C. Hulett
Martin Schmidt
Roy Robinson
Frank Southmayd
J. D. Carl
Joe Mast
Roy Robinson
Walter Laird
Donald Schmidt
Rudy Rochek
John Caudle
Ellis Southmayd, 1951

North Bayside Grange

The history of this grange was described in the *Coos Bay Harbor* for September 25, 1947, here condensed:

The North Bayside Grange Hall, which was totally destroyed by fire last Friday night, had for 20 years contributed largely to the building up and the development of the entire north end of Coos County.

It was on September 17, 1927, that a group of citizens met in the Kentuck Inlet school house to hear Arthur Brown explain the procedure for the organization of a grange. Then followed the election of officers, including Henry Gustafson as master, Al Kingston as secretary, and Mrs. George Emmerson as treasurer.

Some of the records are missing, but so far as available, the following is a list of the masters during the grange's 20 years:

Henry Gustafson	John M. Hanson	Calvin Conner
Gus Witt	Hilda Reiher	Russell Anderson
Abe Grossen, Sr.	John Reiher	George Bessey

Since the total destruction of its hall in 1947, North Bayside Grange has erected a new concrete building valued at $40,000, nearly all of the labor being donated by members.

Juvenile Granges

The Juvenile Grange is patterned after the regular organization, with similar officers. Meetings are conducted under the supervision of an older person, a woman called the matron, or a man called a patron.

Juvenile granges in Coos County include North Bayside, McKinley and Bridge, which have their own juvenile grange halls; and Greendell, Sumner, Coquille, Fairview North Fork. In curry County the Sixes Grange has a juvenile organization.

The 38 Granges

Data on all 38 granges have been furnished by Harry A. Caton, national grange secretary, who said:

> Attached you will find a list of the Granges in both Coos and Curry counties, with the date of organization, the Deputy and the first Master . . .
>
> Some of the names were a bit difficult to make out inasmuch as some folks do not write plain, and back in the earlier days of the Grange there were few typewriters in use in the rural areas.

Coos County

Name and No. Grange	Date Organized	Organized by	Name of First Master
Coos River, 45	10-27-1873	R.M.Gurney	Cyrus Landriff
Halls Prairies, 164	5-23-1874	R.M.Gurney	J.Henry Schroeder
Coquille City, 167	6-3-1874	R.M.Gurney	William Morras
Myrtle, 171	8-4-1874	R.M.Gurney	Charles Wilkins
North Coquille, 173	8-24-1874	R.M.Gurney	Thomas Norris
Laurel, 180	2-21-1875	Henry Schroeder	L.Leneve
Arago, 288	2-12 1898	Jos. Casto	Henry Schroeder
Myrtle, 289	2-18-1898	Jos. Casto	Erick Amerson
Coquille, 290	3-5-1898	Jos. Casto	N.Lorenze
Gravel Ford, 304	10-8-1901	Lewis Strong	Taylor Weekly
Remote, 318	5-24-1902	Lewis Strong	Edward Jenkins
Willowdale, 319	6-7-1902	Lewis Strong	J.W.Strong
Coquille, 396	9-3-1909	C.H.Walker	George Peoples
Coos Bay, 397	9-18-1909	C.H.Walker	Charles Mahaffy
Bandon, 398	10-2-1909	C.H.Walker	Frank F.Eddy
Arago, 580	9-8-1919	P.S.Robinson	C.E.Schroeder
McKinley, 582	10-7-1919	P.S.Robinson	Arthur Brown
Lakeside, 589	3-28-1920	F.M.Gill	L.D.Walker
Catching Inlet, 690	8-6-1927	Arthur Brown	Mrs.Robt.Green
North Bayside, 691	8-17-1927	Arthur Brown	Henry Gustafson
Coos River, 701	4-18-1928	Arthur Brown	Wm. Morgan
Bandon, 702	5-15-1928	Arthur Brown	R.H.Christensen
Broadbent, 729	6-21-1919	Arthur Brown	Fred C.True
Bridge, 730	8-28-1929	Arthur Brown	Harold James
Fairview, 739	11-1-1929	Arthur Brown	L. A. Sunneland
Allegany, 762	8-25-1930	Henry Gustafson	True Saling
Greendell, 834	8-27-1935	Henry Gustafson	George Bessey
Gravelford, 859	8-13-1936	HenryGustafson	CMBonniksen
Sumner, 865	9-28-1936	HenryGustafson	Emil Backman
West Most, 884	5-13-1938	HenryGustafson	Jas.A.Heyward

Curry County

Name and No. Grange	Date Organized	Organized by	Name of First Master
Rogue River, 190	5-9-1881	D.S.K.Busick	S.D.Merriman
Flora's Creek, 191	9-16-1882	F. Green	J. H. Upton
Flora, 299	7-27-1901	LewisStrong	C.P.Blumenrother
Chetco, 765	10-6-1930	HenryGustafson	F.B.Hassett
Ophir, 767	10-12-1930	HenryGustafson	FannieL.James
Lower Rogue, 768	10-21-1930	HenryGustafson	Chas.H.Bailey
Arch Rock, 849	3-12-1936	ArthurBrown	Harvey Crook
Sixes, 856	1937	Fred Adams	Ralph Cope

V

INDUSTRIES

30

Gold

"Big Mac" (as smart as big), the black sand feller,
Finds in the black a lot of shinin' yeller;
A shovelful, and soon he ups and hollers,
"It pans an ounce, by cracky — sixteen dollars."

Perks up the inland placer cuss. He thinks
As how each stream plays out, then come the Chinks;
As how the sea'll last. Poor son-of-a-gun,
He's off in Fifty-Three for Whiskey Run.

Black Sand

Whiskey Run 96 years afterwards!

The pair of investigating authors of this volume turned west from the Seven Devils route into a road not only marked private but posted against trespassers. They drove on neverthelsss and in a few minutes of downhill came to the lower canyon of the small creek, on which, a little more than a stone's throw from the beach, was a ranch house. The man there was inclined to resent the intrusion and to make it abortive right now, but he softened up when he learned the purpose was history. The place wasn't his; he worked for an absentee owner who didn't fancy visitors to Whiskey Run.

Leaving the car, the two historians walked on down to where the little stream spilled out upon the sand, which, as sure as anything, had black streaks and black patches here and there.

On the biggest drift log, amidst a criss-crossed jumble of bleached timbers, they ate their sandwiches and drank their coffee, while their eyes took in all the features of that celebrated landscape, where at one time a thousand men toiled for riches and got not a little. A big piece of machinery was nearby in a red-rusted and far-gone condition. They judged it to be the remains of the $60,000 contraption brought to Whiskey Run by some Minnesota men in 1910 to prove itself to be no good in short order.

One of the men tried panning in his coffee cup of the sand he scooped up from a particularly black streak which seemed to have glistening particles in it there in the spring noontime. The bottom of the cup, after the amateur panning, showed color, or he thought it did.

The age-old gold fever took transitory hold of him and his imagination. Couldn't there have been, during the early workings, great banks of black sand out in the ocean a short distance that weren't touched? Possibly big storms had washed them into off-shore shoals and they lay there submerged during 1853-1854. In the long years since couldn't other big storms have washed them back, perhaps off and back repeatedly? In the winter following the first mining activity, enormous tides did sweep away a vast tonnage of the rich beach right out from under the shovels of the thousand diggers. Maybe a man could put up a tent here, and have no boss, and live the life of Riley—just work a little as he felt like it and take out eight or ten dollars a day; and what a small quantity of the tiny, flaky particles would be required to do that.

Then he thought how, even during the dark days of the depression, Whiskey Run and the other black sand localities hadn't furnished much employment. No, this wasn't the way to lick the rigors of living.

Yet how could the inexhaustible ocean be exhausted of those rich deposits? There was an answer to that too. It wasn't the present ocean, not the present one in a manner of speaking which mostly piled up the black sand placers; it was this Pacific's great-great-grandpa geological ages back. And what was deposited by that old ocean was not renewable. If the early Whiskey Runners took it, there would never be anymore to take.

After these sober reflections the historian guessed he wouldn't put up a tent at Whiskey Run to be free and independent.

Some remnants of weathered houses stood on the site

of old Randolph. These could scarcely have been the building of the original town in 1853-1854, but shelters put up for some later workings now also become long ago.

The canyon sides and all the open country were covered with gorse. Through the thicket of this alien scourge, narrowly parting it at the bottom of the ravine, was the little creek of Whiskey Run, little and short but centuries old and in its long existence cutting through the upper ancient beaches. If the McNameara brothers, "Big Mac" and "Little Mac," sometimes come back here in the moonlight, what a sad pair of ghosts they must be. This place which once belonged to them and a thousand other robust, happy men, now belongs to just one crusty fellow who doesn't like trespassers, to him and the gorse.

Tools of the early placer mines – pan, rocker, gold-borer.

Said Elwood Evans in *History of the Pacific Northwest* 1889:

. . . discovery of gold mines near [Port Orford] in the summer of 1853 secured a rush of miners, and brought the locality into prominent notice. The first news [in] a San Francisco newspaper, stated that about 50 miners were making from $70 to $75 per day to the hand near Port Orford . . . on the beach.

Similar deposits were found above and below the mouth of Rogue River, which was properly named Gold Beach. About the same time, two half-breed Indians discovered the placers at the mouth of Whiskey Run . . . After working them a short time, they sold them to the McNamara brothers. . . . The rumor of these rich mines having got abroad, thousands of miners flocked to them and began prospecting along the coast . . . Upon the beach near Whiskey Run, not less than a thousand men were congregated. A town sprang up at once, containing stores, lodging houses, saloons, restaurants, tents and cabins in large numbers, which was named Randolph. The beach mining during this season was very profitable, but as soon as the season of high tides, which accompanied the rainy season, set in, the work had to stop.

The brilliant prospects offered by the beach mines of Coos Bay in 1853, and which attracted so large an immigration, were not fulfilled in 1854. The great sea that had deposited untold wealth upon its shores in the previous season, with its usual capriciousness removed it all the following winter.

Frances Fuller Victor, early woman historian who helped to write the famous Bancroft histories, visited Coos and Curry counties in 1890, and wrote of the beach mining:

The black sand . . . has been mined quite steadily ever since its discovery . . . by some half-breed Indians, at a place a few miles north of the Coquille River. In 1853 they sold their claim to McNamara Brothers for $20,000. Pans of black sand taken from their claim yielded from $8 to $10. Over $100,000 were taken from this claim, which led, as might be expected, to a rush from the valleys to the seashore. But few locations paid like the first one, and, although the sand continues to be worked, no one makes more than fair wages.

An ancient sea-beach, three miles inland, was discovered by Mr. Hinch, who took up a claim there which he sold for $10,000 to John Pershbaker Co., who sold it again for $30,000. Like the first location on the beach, it was better than any afterwards taken.

The beach sands are black in color because they are composed chiefly of magnetic iron, [identified by being attracted to a magnet]. The particles of gold are extremely small [in size from a small pinhead to microscopic specks] and so flaky that often they will float upon water, nor can they be brought to unite with quicksilver . . . It is easy to see that, with the sand so heavy and the gold so light, it must be difficult to capture a fortune from beach mining, the sand of the ancient beaches yielding an average of $3 per ton.

There are more than 100 of these auriferous beaches, extending from Gray's Harbor on the north to Gold Bluff in California. Twenty-seven of them have been worked . . . The production varies. The estimate for 1883 in Curry County was $20,000. On the other hand, one mine in Coos County yielded $18,000 in 12 months.

George Bennett said that "Big Mac" McNameara (the

way Bennet spelled it) was the first black sand discoverer rather than the two half-breeds. On Bandon beach, while still in the army, he idly stirred up some sand with the toe of his boot. He excitedly recognized the shining mixture as gold but kept mighty hush-hush about it till he got his soldier's discharge. Then he and his brother, "Little Mac," went to work. This is how they got the $20,000 to buy out the Whiskey Run half-breeds.

"The Whiskey Run mines proved to be the richest of the entire coast." More than once "Big Mac" and "Little Mac" would take out $1500 in a day, nearly eight troy pounds. "Big Mac" used to tell of some gloriously-remembered shovelfuls containing an ounce apiece. For a long time they went on getting four ounces a day from their claim. In two seasons a 120-foot area yielded them $80,000.

No wonder men flocked to Whiskey Run. It was better than an ordinary placer miner had ever dreamed of before—this idea of the sea washing up gold with its interminable tides. The first miners didn't know as much as is known now about the principal deposits being made ages before on higher beaches. The cuts of descending creek channels revealed them to later, keener eyes. The miners of 18 to 20 years afterwards were mostly the ones to learn about them and work them.

Subsequent mining, with the exhaustion of these anciently laid deposits, got so it wouldn't pay. Yet the fascination of black sand gold would never completely subside. Through the years it led to sporadic activity and to a sizable quantity of scientific literature.

As early as 1854, W. P. Blake contributed a short piece, "Gold and Platinum of Cape Blanco," to the *American Journal of Science.*

Mining and Science carried an article in 1894, "The Black-Sand Gold Question," by A. B. Paul, and one in 1907, "The Black-Sand Problem," by T. Powell. In 1904 the University of Oregon published a bulletin *Beach Gold and Its Sources,* by C. W. Washburne.

In 1906, D. T. Day and R. H. Richardson wrote a 150-page bulletin, *Investigations of Black Sands from Placer*

Mines; and in 1918 R. R. Horner was author of a technical paper, *Notes on the Black Sand Deposits of Southern Oregon and Northern California*—both published by the U. S. Bureau of Mines.

The U. S. Geological Survey in 1914 published *Mineral Resources of Southwestern Oregon* by J. S. Diller, and in 1934 *Beach Placers of the Oregon Coast* by J. T. *Pardee.*

The Oregon Department of Geology and Mineral Industries published *Oregon Metal Mines Handbook* by the staff in 1940, containing ten pages on beach mines; and *Origin of the Black Sands of the Coast of Southwestern Oregon* in 1943 by W. H. Twenhofel of the University of Wisconsin.

In Coos and Curry in the summer of 1917, R. R. Horner was mainly looking into platinum. What he saw, and what he said about the history of the old mines, is here summarized rather than quoted:

> At the Chickamin Mine, on the M. J. Mathews property at the head of Brown Slough, he found a black sand bed 10 feet thick, about 60 feet above sea level, formerly worked by a tunnel 30 feet long. On top of the black sand were 25 to 50 feet of fine sand, clay and soil covered with vegetation, timber, and fallen logs. [The owner of the Chickamin Mine in 1940 was W. H. Wann of Coquille.]
>
> The 20-acre Eagle Mine, about 6½ miles north of Bandon, was discovered in the middle 60's, was worked till 1873, and was the greatest yielder. The workable bed was 6 to 8 feet thick, 200 to 250 feet wide, and several hundred feet long. Tunnels were driven with the outcrop above water level, with drifts following definite pay shoots. Finally pumps were installed to enable workings below water level. This was too expensive and one mine closed down. Horner thought that anyhow by then it had been mostly worked out. In 1914 a Seattle man obtained a lease on the tailings, impounded to the extent of several thousand tons in an old lagoon through which Cut Creek flows. The attempt to re-treat the accumulations failed in a few days.
>
> The Pioneer Mine of 19½ acres was located in 1866 by A. H. Hinch and John Dame. Simon Lane bought it and worked it till the middle 70's. Then it was closed. Some years later it was sold to Captain Smith & Son of San Francisco. It had remained idle but at the time of Horner's visit in 1917 C. W. Smith "was on the ground for the purpose of interesting men in the property."

The Rose Mine, about 7 miles north of Bandon at a 150-foot elevation, was located and worked for a number of years, reportedly with considerable success, by Abraham Rose. Some years before 1917 a Detroit, Michigan, company had bought it. They installed a gasoline centrifugal pump to operate a hose and nozzle; this renewed operation lasted four months.

The Fletcher-Myers Property, joining the Rose claim on the north, was at an elevation of 140 feet above present sea level. In the late 60's a tunnel 95 feet long "was driven on a bed of soft, loosely consolidated black sands more than seven feet thick." The outcrops were on the main branch of Twomile Creek and on a small tributary. Horner found the old tunnel "caved;" a logging camp had later been there and left; brush, timber, and fallen logs covered the surface.

The Geiger Mine, on the south bank of Fairy Creek, was opened in the early days by John Geiger, who worked two acres of ground and is said to have taken out a good deal of gold and platinum. As activity progressed toward the hillsides three things happened — 1, the cover became heavier; 2, the gold and platinum content lessened; 3, the pay sands were gradually getting below water level. The mine closed, but there were later attempts to work it. Horner in 1917 found "the wrecks of numerous gold-saving devices."

The Madden or Cape Blanco Mine, about 7 miles north of Port Orford, was discovered by Cyrus Madden in July of 1871. Madden still owned it when Horner visited there in 1917, the latter saying, "It has never been a large producer, but has maintained a small output for nearly 40 years." Work was found by Horner to be then intermittent, though previously carried on six or seven months in the year. A hydraulic giant was on the ground and he saw that several acres had been worked to a depth of 20 to 25 feet.

The Zumwalt or Butler Mine, 9 miles north of Port Orford, on a Flores Creek tributary, "was worked extensively some years ago, but at the time of the writer's visit it was idle, the ditches, flumes, and other equipment being in a state of ruin. The remains of a hydraulic elevator, spiral iron water pipe, and giant were to be seen. Altogether three acres of ground has been mined."

The Peck Mine was about 10 miles northeast of Port Orford on a tributary of Crystal Creek, which in turn is a tributary of Sixes River. Said Horner, who found it idle and littered with ruined machinery. "This alluvial deposit is especially interesting, as it shows a second ancient beach line . . . nearly 800 feet above sea level. The mine representes only a small remnant, preserved on the top of a rounded hill . . . , of what was perhaps an extensive deposit."

In the early 1930's, the depression stimulated an

amount of renewed activity. South of Cape Blanco, in the very early Port Orford area, J. C. Rowan, E. C. Britton and others mined the beach between high and low tides, using rockers and other movable equipment. Men were busy on stretches at Gold Beach. The Pioneer or Lane Mine was being operated with sluice boxes; a drag-line scraper removed the 15 or 20 feet of overburden. And here another effort was being made to re-treat the enormous heaps of tailings in the lagoons; in July of 1931 a machine was installed to test the deposits; "the result was not learned." The Pioneer just didn't seem to let hopes permanently die.

There was also life again at Whiskey Run. Hal Stutsman and others were at work with a scraper, elevator, trommel, and riffle boxes. The most spectacular effort, however, at this celebrated old place was in 1910. Said Horner:

> Smith R. Bassett, representing Minneapolis parties, designed and built a dredge, mounted on hollow cylindrical wheels about 6 feet in diameter and about 5 feet wide . . . probably the most unique mechanical curiosity of all the devices for recovering the gold from the black sands. On the steel frame of the dredge was mounted an endless-chain bucket digging device operated by steam engine. The machine was propelled by its own power and was designed to work the beach deposits lying between high and low tides. It proved a complete failure, as it was unstable and nearly capsized on the first trial run. With great difficulty it was finally dragged back to a place above high tide, where it now rests. This venture is said to have cost between $60,000 and $75,000.

How much money, how much labor, how much ingenuity have been spent in 96 years on the black sands, which perhaps all in all add up as better takers than givers.

JOHNSON CREEK DIGGINGS, by *Bob Harrison*

[Condensed and to some extent adapted from an article by Mr. Harrison in the *Coquille Valley Sentinel* of October 29, 1942]

It was the evening of a midsummer day in the early 1850's. Two bearded men sat in front of a logging bunkhouse in the Port Orford region. One, a short, sandy-haired squaw man, was known as "Sandy" Summers. The other, a tall ox teamster in the logging camp, had earned the name of "Bovine" Johnson.

Johnson and Summers, after crossing the plains together, had drifted into the Port Orford country to prospect for gold. Their finances being very limited, one would work for wages to keep the other fellow going. As Summers knew the mining game best, and had an

Indian woman for his wife, he naturally had better access to the country.

On this summer evening Sandy took out of his wallet some nuggets to show Bovine, saying, "Now listen, Bo, ole Big Injun Jo give me these. Said he found 'em at the forks of a creek over on yon side of Bald Knob. I jest now got back from thar. We've got to play foxy so the Injuns won't git mad at me fer tellin whar it was. Tonight, as soon as the moon comes up, I'll go with you as far as Bald Knob. The rest of the way you go in by yoreself jest like you done the findin.When you git camp started, then I can be the packer. Everything's fixed up fer the trip; all you've got to do is to git yoreself ready."

Bovine went to Cal Cavanaugh, the Irish logging boss. On account of feelin bad, he was askin for a few days off. Reluctantly Cavanaugh said yes, but to make it short.

By early dawn they reached the end of the horse trail and ate breakfast. Then Johnson took off along a much dimmer Indian trail towards the supposed new Eldorado. Summers returned to the settlement to make himself conspicuous in order to ward off any suspicion that he had betrayed the Indians.

Johnson, following his partner's directions, picked his way very carefully. About mid-afternoon he found what he felt was the place and made his camp—on a bar at the forks of a small mountain creek. Sitting on a boulder besides the stream, he thoroughly surveyed the surrounding landscape and said to himself, "If the gold is here, this sure will be Paradise. After fixing up camp and eating something, he took up his shovel and pan and started digging among the boulders. To his great surprise, the first pan of sand yielded almost an ounce of gold.

Standing there alone in the wilds, Johnson raised his hand high above his head and shouted, "Eureka!"

For several days he made locations and took out as much of the precious metal as he could. Then he found that his supplies had dwindled to the vanishing point. In early morning he left. By dark he was at the Summers place with the good news. They arranged to return the very next day. They got off early, Johnson meanwhile having managed to keep out of sight of the men at the mill and logging camp.

But Cal Cavanaugh, the logging boss, had missed Johnson, whose rather extended vacation had worked a hardship on him. He was having a difficult time trying to get another bull driver and was beginning to inquire around trying to locate Johnson and get him back on the job.

Some of the men had often heard Johnson and Summers talk about prospecting, and had made them the butts of jokes about it. Now Johnson was gone and Summers was acting rather strange. They decided to look about and see what was really going on. One evening in the bunkhouse surmises were passing back and forth, particularly since Summers was now also gone. An old Indian fighter, Ira Bray, ventured a guess on the matter:

"I'll tell you, boys, jest what I've got figured out on old Bovine and Sandy. Them coyotes have been lookin fer diggins fer a long time—and, by gum, I bet a cookie they've struck it. Old Bovine would never quit his whackin bulls less he'd hit it derned rich. If I'm alive in the mornin, I'm a-goin to pick up their trail and see jest what they're up to."

"And, Ira, I'm agoin right along with you," broke in Joe Sweat.

Daylight the following morning found the larger part of the camp crew, headed by Bray, wending their way over the old Indian trail which they had rightly guessed was the route taken by Johnson and Summers. About mid-afternoon they located their men.

Rounding a sharp bend in the trail, Bray and his loggers had a full view of a bar at the forks of a wildwood stream. They had a full view of Bovine Johnson, out in front along the bedrock with his pick and pan, gathering a golden harvest. A loud shout burst from a dozen husky mouths. Johnson, amiable and not resentful, straightened up to wave his right hand in a welcoming salute.

By nightfall the place took on the look of a rip-roarin mining camp. In the evening when the crowd was all gathered about a big log fire, Ira Bray rose and called the meeting to order:

"In callin this august body together, I first want this here beautiful stream named fer the man takin the first nugget from its bedrock—meanin it shall be forever known as Johnson Creek. And since he has shown such nice nuggets, I wish him to be known as Course Gold Johnson and the name Bovine be dropped forever."

Meantime back in the logging camp everything was topsy-turvy. No crew, no bull driver. The old schooner *Sea Gull* was still lying at the dock awaiting its lumber cargo. Cavanaugh had personally gone into the barn to curry the oxen and got kicked. Whereupon he grabbed the remainder of his crew and took off after the long overdue first contingent. He told the old Chinese cook to keep the bean pot and the rice kettle agoin; he'd be back with the gang in a jiffy.

To which the aged slant-eye replied, "No foolee old Wong. Maybe so big bossyman no come back quick. Maybe so big bear catchee him too."

Dawn the following morning found Cavanaugh and his loyal half dozen crewmen out along the old Indian trail. They passed the great Bald Knob and broke over into the headwaters of Johnson Creek. Towards the end of the day the logging boss and his faithfuls arrived in sight of the mining camp. The little caravan halted for a moment and then with a loud whoop they advanced, and were soon at ease on the mossy carpet beneath the great maples.

After a great powwow of welcome, the newcomers were made comfy for the night. As they all sat around the evening campfire, Cavanaugh stood up to address his logging apostates:

"Well, b'ys, I can't blame yez fer what yez did, an' what's more, I'm agoin to stay right here meself and git rich wid the rest of yez."

Back in the logging camp, as the days went on, Sam Wong was in a deep stew. Some of the managers of the enterprise had arrived from San Francisco. From him they were trying to find out what had happened to cause he shut-down. All they could get was, "Me no sabee. Allee men go. Tellee Sam cokee heap lice, heap beans. They no come and getee."

Johnson Creek soon developed into a very busy and bustling mining camp. All hands prepared for the coming winter by building cabins, making sluice boxes, digging trails, and doing other necessary work. Owing to the isolated location and difficulty of access, news of the Johnson Creek discovery did not reach the outside world for almost two years. During this time what few extra men had drifted into the region, were well established on the very best of the claims. With the general rush, mining went on in about all the tributaries of Johnson Creek and a lively camp sprang up on Flanagan Bar along the Coquille River — below the mouth of Johnson Creek where a company of Chinese were doing a stroke of business until moved out by the whites.

Some of the names of early-day miners have been perpetuated in the names of gulches, bars, and creeks, and other geographical features.

> Flanagan Bar at the mouth of Johnson Creek and across the Coquille from it Kelley's Bar. Then in succession up Johnson Creek — Flander's Bar, Jefferson Falls, Collier's Camp, Ragsdale Flat, Hayes Creek, Dean's Point, Green's Rock, Stauff Gulch. We also find Brays Ridge, Barklow Mountain, Sweats Saddle, Land Creek, McLeon Flat, Phols Waterloo or the place where he died "mit cramps."

Johnson Creek was famous for its nuggets. Salmon Creek, Rusty Gulch, Butcher Gulch, Dixie, and some other strikes followed the discovery on Johnson Creek. About all the streams which flowed down from Salmon Mountain and Iron Mountain, were known to be good placer gold producers. Some very good pocket deposits have been taken from the upland in that region, but as a rule hard rock mining never flourished in the district.

The black sands and Johnson Creek just about cover the really important gold operations. A 1940 record of the non-beach mines in Coos County gives nine for the Powers and Johnson Creek areas—the Juniper Group on Sucker Creek, the Nicoli Group south of Powers where the winter might bring 12 feet of snow, the Anchor & Daisy on the north side of Poverty Gulch, the Divilbiss Mine of which it was said, "No one has been able to make it pay," the Old Gold Lode Claim in later years at least quite suitably a Poverty Gulch enterprise, the Roberts Group of five quartz claims occupying 100 acres

on the south side of Iron Mountain, the historic Salmon Mountain Mine which was operated for 13 years in the 1880's and 1890's as a hydraulic placer, the four Rock Creek placer claims of 1600 acres, and the Schiller placers consisting of 17 claims on famous Johnson Creek three miles above its mouth. That was the size of it right after a long depression, when men are more likely to take to hills than at other times.

The 1940 situation was different in Curry County where there were still dozens of gold mines. The following table has been made to cover them, with a geographic rather than an alphabetical listing:

Mine	Kind	Location	Date	Production and development
Gold Bar Mine	Placer	Illhae	1856	$156 in one month, 1911

The man who did so well in 1911 ($156 a month not being chicken feed in those days) had some awful bad luck in 1912. He stored 7½ tons of sand averaging $270 a ton which high water washed away. In 1913 a Sweet Gold Machine was used but the clay in the gravel clogged it up and it wouldn't work. Oh, hum, the life of a miner!

Night Hawk Prospect	Pyrite kidneys	4 miles SE of Agness		
Stephens & Stear	Quartz	4 miles SE of Agness		Last worked in 1915
Empire Prospect	Quartz stringers	In Chetco China Diggings area	1915	
Lucky Girl, Big Joe, Perseverence, Patience		China Diggings area	1935	A 1935 pocket produced $12,000
Gold Basin Placers		China Diggings area	1875 or 1876	Tunneled on bedrock for 30 feet
Golden Eagle	Quartz stringers	18 miles W of Selma	1936	Worked continuously in a small way
Hilltop Group (*No.* 1, *No.* 2, *No.* 3)	Greenstone	12 miles W of Kerby	1934; *No.* 2, a grubstake claim 1937	2 samples—$2.10 and $3.85 a ton
Bacon Mine (Later *Peck Mine*)	Rotten Rock	Chetco area		2,760 foot ditch
Robert E. Mine		Chetco area		Produced $100,000 but owned by U. S. government in 1940
Stone Foot Claim		17½ miles W of Selma	1936	Location work; snow gets 12 feet deep
Webfoot Group		18 miles by forest road and trail from Selma	1936	No production
Young Mine		In Chetco area		R. D. Young reportedly found a thousand-dollar pocket in 1937.

Mine	Kind	Location	Date	Production and Development
Yellow Jacket Claim		In Chetco area		2 shallow open cuts
Collins Mine	Beach Placer	4 miles N of Wedderburn	1914-1915	"Good Wages"
Red Flat Placer		8 miles SE of Gold Beach		Some loose rocks assayed 70 cents a ton
Smedberg Beach Placers (formerly *Rock Claim, Idaho*)		A beach mile S of of Gold Beach		Experimental plant
Wedderburn Trading Company	Placers	N and S of *Gold..* Beach and up the Rogue		"Holdings may be leased"
Grizzly Bear, Big Four	Placers	Lobster Creek area		"Bedrock has never been reached"
Bonanza Placer Mine		8 miles NW of Illahe	1874	$150,000
Otter Point and Hubbard Knob	Beach placers	3 and 4 miles N of Rogue mouth	Several years before 1934	First notice of Chinamen in the black sands. They mined it in 2 big pits
Star Mine	Placer	Lobster Creek	New mining started in 1915; place known as Old Diggings	4,800 foot ditch, dam, other improvements
Kalamazoo Ocean Beach Mine	Beach placer	Mouth of Euchre Creek		J. S. Diller in his 1914 report said this was then Curry's most productive mine
Parker Mine	Placer	Lobster Creek		"Rich pockets occasionally found
Rainbow, Golden Dream, Golden Lamb	Greenstone	4½ miles by trail from Marial	Earlier Bert Owen Lode; Alexander Brothers filed exemption in 1937	Cabins, blacksmith shop, Ellis mill

Mine	Kind	Location	Date	Production and Development
Battle Bar	Placer	On Rogue above mouth of Ditch Crek		Property idle a long time
Blossom Bar	Placer	3 miles below Marial		Owner plans to bring water from Blossom Creek
Dinawadja Group	Free gold	On Mule Creek (Diller in 1914 called it "John Mule Creek")		
Golden Cargo Group	Quartz stringers	Mule Creek area		Tunnel; some shallow cuts
Lucky Strike, Golden Cabin, Golden Economy	Altered porphyry	4 miles from Marial on Mule Creek		4 tunnels
Golden Fraction Prospect	Altered porphyry	Slope of Rooster Peak	Old Bert Owen Ledge	50-foot tunnel
Golden Oak Prospect	Quartz stringers	6 miles NW of Marial		3 tunnels
Golden Rattler Group	Altered porphyry	West Fork of Mule Creek	1932	Cabin; prospecting tools
Good Luck Prospect	Quartz stringers	West Fork of Mule Creek		A number of open cuts
Home Lode Claim	Quartz	3 miles from Marial	Once worked by W. W. Cardwell	A tunnel
Keystone Property		2 miles SW of Marial	Old George W. Billings property; sold 1930 or 1931	An old and new tunnel
Lancaster Claim	Altered porphyry	West Fork of Mule Creek	1929	A tunnel
Lone Wolf Group	Porphyry	Rooster Rock, Marial area		Open cuts; a tunnel
Mammoth Group (*Rogue River Mine*)	Quartz	2½ miles from Marial	"An old property;" 1940 owner had it since 1915	A tunnel; 10-foot water wheel. Owner had 43 assays made

Mine	Kind	Location	Date	Production and Development
Margarette Claim	Altered porphyry	West Fork of Mule Creek	1938	Opencut tunnel
Marigold Mine (formerly *Lucky Boy, Tiny H*)	Pockets	On Tiny H Creek in Marial area	Sold in 1920, 1930, 1937	"No work in the last 25 years"
Mule Mountain		On Mule Mountain less than a mile from Marial	Part of it on Old Bur Oak Placer; George W. Billings sold it in 1930 or 1931	Shaft and 300-foot tunnel
Paradise Mine		Saddle Mountain	"Prior history unknown"	3 tunnels
Paul Junior Placer		Marial is on part of it		

One of the owners mined it in 1938 with a Fordson tractor dragline with a one-third yard bucket, getting about 1500 yards that averaged 24 cents a yard. "There remains approximately 7 acres of gravel . . . about 12 feet in depth."

Mine	Kind	Location	Date	Production and Development
Red Dog Placer		On Mule Creek		Gravel 10 or 12 feet thick
Winkle Bar Placer		Mule Creek area	Worked before 1914	

Diller in 1914 found the Winkle Bar Developing Company getting ready to do things. They apparently didn't, for a famous writer came along and got it. Records of the U. S. Forest Service showed that Zane Gray, Inc. patented 32.53 acres of placer ground on Winkle Bar. In 1940 it was being used as a homesite.

Mine	Kind	Location	Date	Production and Development
Yellow Moon Claim	Quartz stringers	Hanging Rock in Marial area	1939	No equipment
Bear Cat Group	Quartz	Up Sixes River		Two open cuts
Big Sunshine Placer (formerly *Big Johnson Placer*)		Elk River; 16 miles SE of Port Orford		Gravel ran 75 cents a yard
Cape Blanco Mine	Beach placer	Running 2½ miles along the ocean south of the cape	Dates back to 1853	1938 operator used a truck to haul black sand to his sluicing plant

Mine	Kind	Location	Date	Production and Development
Cliffside Lode	Quartz vein	Mouth of Bald Mountain Creek	1938	Outcropping on very steep cliff
Corbin Property Placer		On Sixes above mouth of Dry Creek	Worked in old days by N. C. Divelbiss	He said its left bank produced $5,000 an acre
Elkhorn Group	Placer	On Elk River	"An old property"	Largest nugget found $5
Fall Creek Group	Placer	Elk River, mouth of Cedar Creek		Handwork, $250 a season
Guerin Claim	Placer	Butcher Gulch	Guerin Brothers were ground sluicing in 1914	Apparently abandoned in 1940
Harison Claims (*St. Patricks, Golden Fleece, Mountain Daisy*)	Salty rock and greenstone	Rusty Butte		Fine gold in veins
Hydro Sixes Mining Company	Placer	Above junction of the Sixes		Ditches and flumes; unsuccessful
Inman Mine	Placer	Below and above the Sixes forks	Inman Mines Company orgazined in 1920	

The Inman Mines Company which had 30 mining claims and owned 2½ miles of the Sixes below and above its forks, went into receivership in 1929. The mines were idle for three years. At a sheriff's sale in 1933 the property was bought by the Oregon Engineering Campany.

Mine	Kind	Location	Date	Production and Development
Madden Mine (Once known as *Blanco & Blacksand Mine*)	Beach placer	7 miles N of Port Orford	1871	500 feet of sluice boxes; 2-mile ditch. Operated by Cyrus Madden for more than 40 years
Little Otter Placer		Up Sixes River	"Located and relocated for years"	"No work done"
McCormick Mining and Mineral Company	Placer	40 acres owned but where not given		Claimed to have spent $5207 in 1935

Mine	Kind	Location	Date	Production and Development
Meek's Mine	Beach placer	Near Port Orford		Concentrates claimed to run $8,000 a ton
Myrtle Group	Placer	10 miles SE of Port Orford on Sixes River		Handwork—$300 a season
Oregon Engineering Company (buyer of the Inman's 30 claims)	Placer	On Sixes River		Policy of leasing. Bars small, each requiring a special set-up
Siskiyou Gold Mining Company	Placer	On Sixes River	Portion of old Inman Mine	Small suction dredge in 1936
Sixes Beach Placer		Near mouth of Sixes		A hydraulic elevator to get drainage for sluicing
Big Nugget, Big Foot, Nut Wood	Placer	Mouth of Rusty Creek, in Sixes area	1915	Output was admittedly but $14.60
Sunrise Gold Mining Company	Placer	Hells Hole in Sixes area		Lease on 8 placer claims
Wagner Claims	Placer	Below mouth of Butcher Creek		Streams damned; 2 lines of sluice boxes suspended on numerous logs
P. L. Wall Claim	Placer	Sixes area	1915	20-foot open cut
Wallace & Hadley Claims (originally Thompson Flat)	Placer	South Fork of Sixes	Relocated 1915	160 feet of pipe
Rainbow, Robert Harrison, Nugget Patch	Placer	South Fork of Sixes	Bought from earlier owner in 1912	800 feet of flumes; 600 feet of pipe

31

Coal

A SMALL COAL SHIPMENT was made from Empire on the schooner *Chansey*, perhaps in 1854; but it was lost in crossing out over the Coos Bay bar.

A. G. (Glen) Aiken said in 1913:

> I came out with my two brothers in 1854. We spent the winter getting out coal from Jim's mine on Boatman's gulch. We got out 200 tons and Flanagan & Rogers shipped it to San Francisco for us.

Other shipments that followed, met with less success as explained by Orvil Dodge, "There was a small cargo of dirty coal sent from North Bend that injured the reputation of the Coos Bay product."

Dodge goes on to say:

> In the autumn of 1855, Capt. Park Butler, in charge of the *S. R. Jackson*, took a cargo from the Eastport mines. Although the coal was bright and good as any mined at the present day, it was rejected at San Francisco. Freight was $10 a ton, and Simonds was obliged to sell the corgo at seven dollars and fifty cents a ton. The actual cost of the coal put down at San Francisco was $14 a ton.

Much of the early history of the mining in Coos County may be summed up by quoting from County Archives:

> Scattered like pockmarks over the twenty mile peninsula between the shores of Coos Bay and the Coquille River are sites of coal mining towns that, in the days that King Coal reigned, bustled for a few weeks, a few months, a few years. A dozen endured for more than a year. Most of them died aborning. Their histories lie buried in the files of old newspapers, in old manuscripts, old books, and in the memories of old men and women who lived in earlier days.

Perhaps those early failures are best explained by James H. (Jim) Flanagan:

> Based upon many coal prospects and outcroppings, promoters would organize companies, sell stock, or induce men to "jump into the venture," without adequate investigation. Merely upon the theory that vast amounts of good coal lay buried just beneath the surface, waiting to be mined and taken to market, reckless expenditures would be made for surface developments – buildings, bunkers, trestles, ships, tools, shops, and equipment of various kinds. Then followed the opening of the mine – only to find in too many cases and too late that the vein was broken, or the coal was of an inferior grade, or mining conditions were so unfavorable that successful operations could not be carried on.

But there were also bright spots. At least four mines in Coos County were worked successfully for many years on a fairly large scale.

At present only one small Coos coal mine is operating. The South Slough project by Leonard H. Gibbs under lease from the owners. The coal is trucked to the Krome road and delivered to individual customers for domestic use. The output is approximately 4,000 tons a year.

Before going on with a somewhat detailed record of the early important mines, perhaps some attention should be given to some of the big failures and to some of the general features of Coos Bay coal mining.

Perhaps the first failure of any consequence in Coos County was the Davis venture in 1855. According to Dodge, A. J. Davis together with Joe and Gabe Cooper discovered some coal at the present site of the McKenna fill on Isthmus Slough. Dodge says they obtained capital from persons in San Francisco but that the enterprise lasted only about three months.

Next came the Hardy Mine at the mouth of Kentuck Slough in 1870. Dodge says, "Hardy proceeded to erect costly works and spent upwards of $100,000 endeavoring to make a paying property." Remains of the old tunnel and the old trestle may still be seen as reminders of "Moneysunk" in early coal mining ventures.

Perhaps the most colossal coal mining venture in Coos County to hang on for many years with never a penny of profit was the Henryville Mine on Isthmus Inlet, where old piling stumps still remind us of the one-time "Blaze of Glory" of the 1870's.

> The one elaborate mine opening of the Coos Bay district was the Henryville mine in 1874 . . . a $5,000,000 corporation of San Francisco capitalists . . . Buildings and wharves were erected and the town began with a grand start. Tunnels were sunk several hundred feet and everything looked propitious, when the vein was lost and never was relocated. It was hardly more than two years after the town started that the mine closed down and the town was abandoned. The company kept a watchman there for 40 years watching the buildings and wharves rot away.

Matt Bowron, a well known Coos citizen, was the watchman at Henryville.

About the same time the Utter City operation was started, a few miles upstream from Henryville on Isthmus Inlet, with a narrow-gauge railroad leading about five miles further south to their mining undertaking, which was known as Carbondale.

> The Utters and a man named Ojeda met reverses at every turn. Their mine output dwindled and the quality of coal deteriorated. Cost of transportation was high and the demand lessened. They turned desperately to their railroad to recuperate their fortunes, futilely attempting to develop it into a common carrier, principally of logs, to Isthmus Inlet. This venture failing, the Utter brothers became bankrupt. There was an almost overnight exodus from Carbondale and Utter City.

The Beaver Hill Mine would no doubt be placed in the list of coal mining failures by some observers. Its coal is reported to be as good in quality as any in the entire district. During the 30 years when the Beaver Hill Mines operated, they are said to have produced as much coal as the combined output of all the other mines of the Coos Bay area.

However, the original investment appears to have

been handled by inexperienced management and became unbalanced. Next a disastrous gas explosion resulted in a fire, necessitating the flooding of the mine and causing it to be abandoned. Then, finally, large investments were made on a scale of production up to 500 tons a day, actually maintained for 20 days during March 1905 and one day reaching 600 tons. A fairly successful and profitable operation appears to have been carried on up to about 1910, when output began to be curtailed because fuel oil was beginning to take the place of coal in the bigger markets. In 1923 the Beaver Hill Mine was closed and the entire undertaking was abandoned.

In at least two respects coal mining was a leading factor in the pioneer development of agriculaure and farm life in Coos County.

1. The mines provided a market for farm products—butter, cheese, eggs, beef, pork, potatoes, apples and vegetables. This, in some cases, could be transported all the way from the farm to the mine-market by boat.

2. Many of the leading Coos farm homes were started by part-time coal miners. Mining was somewhat seasonal, with a brisk fall and winter market and a lagging market in spring and summer.

Miners thus relieved during the summer, took advantage of the opportunity to go out and locate homesteads. A little garden, a cow or two, a few chickens, a team and perhaps a pack animal—with these the family was settled for the winter while "Dad" went back to the mine.

One such farmer-miner, who became a leading Coos citizen, was Thomas Hirst:

> I arrived in Coos County in January, 1859. John Canyon and I worked at the coal mines (Eastport) during the winter and improved our places in summer. Our wives lived together during our absence, that being convenient, as our farms joined.

Among the early miner-farmers in the north end of Coos County were such well-known men as Ben Roberts, W. F. (Billy) Bowron, Nels Monson, McCullough and his several sons; William Weir, Alex (Sandy) Simpson, James Yates, and John Steinlechner.

During the coal heyday, covering about 60 years, the San Francisco market was the main outlet for the numerous mines in Coos County. As much as 100,000 tons a year were consumed in that market. Indeed, Coos Bay at one time was a household word in San Francisco and Oakland. It was a common sight to see signs advertising Coos Bay Coal throughout the two cities.

But the market was seasonal. In the fall and winter the demand would become brisk; it was not unusual to see carts lined up blocks long in San Francisco and Oakland, waiting for loads when a vessel would arrive with a cargo of coal. In the summer months the market would taper off. Storage problems prevented stockpiling in summer for winter use. There was always slacking while in storage for any length of time and there was danger of spontaneous combustion.

Another disadvantage was the loss due to the many handlings it had to undergo in water shipments—mine to cars, to bunkers at the mine, to other cars for hauling to bunkers at the bay, dumped again into bunkers, from where it was once more dumped into the hold of the ship. At the end of a 400-mile ocean trip, it once more had to be taken out of the hold of the vessel, placed in bunkers or storage piles, and loaded into carts for its final destination. Each of these handlings caused more or less breakage, resulting in piles of screenings, thus reducing the volume of marketable lump coal. These screenings were marketed at a lower price to small manufacturing plants. But even this market vanished with the coming of oil and gas.

The history of the Newport-Libby Coal Mine, as given by James H. Flanagan, is here condensed:

The Newport-Libby Coal Mine

The Newport coal mine was opened by Rogers & Flanagan in 1855. Patrick Flanagan bought out Rogers and became associated with his brother James. The firm was then Flanagan & Flanagan. Patrick took and kept active management of the mine for 30 years. Soon Stillman S. Mann was taken in, and the new firm became Flanagan & Mann.

The mine was developed slowly and conservatively, made largely to develop itself out of earnings.

At first the coal was conveyed by car on a wooden track to tidewater where it was loaded on scows, which were floated down Coal Bank Slough to navigable water for ocean-going vessels, to San Francisco. Later the road was extended a mile further down the slough, mostly on piling, where ocean-going vessels could come alongside and load by means of chutes. This location was about a half mile above what is now Englewood, then Eastport.

Coal Bank Slough at that time was navigable, at high tide, for vessels drawing 13 feet. The steamer *Arcata* used to come up to this point to load. After being cut in two and lengthened 40 feet, increasing her carrying capacity to 600 tons, she used to back up the slough, a distance of a mile and a half from the bay. The slough was too narrow for her to turn around.

In the meantime a bunker holding 700 tons was built at the mine; also a bunkhouse for the single men, a store and other buildings. The miners, in many instances, put up their own homes, and took pride in keeping them painted or whitewashed, which was also true of the company, giving the village a neat and attractive appearance.

The Newport mine was operated almost entirely above water level. It drained itself and the coal came out by gravity.

About the year 1878 the coal road was extended a mile and a half to the bay, to the mouth of Isthmus Slough, where loading chutes were installed.

In 1883 Captain George Holt, of the steamer *Arcata,* conceived the idea of buying the Newport Mine. Before this, James Flanagan had died, and Patrick succeeded to his interests. Captain Holt was a New Englander, a man of force, a persuasive talker, but sowewhat visionary. He organized the Newport Coal Company, consisting of himself, a Mr. Hawley and a Mr. Peters, of San Francisco. The new company first bought out Mr. Mann, paying him $75,000 cash, then about a year later Mr. Flanagan, paying him $100,000, of which $15,000 was represented by stock in the company.

The mine up to this point was successful, shipping from 30,000 to 40,000 tons of coal a year. Holt had visions of a larger turnover. He built a 1000-ton bunker at the end of the road to take the place of the loading chutes. He bought a new ship, the first steel vessel launched on the Pacific Coast, the *Arago*. He subsidized the Eastport and Southport mines, paying them each a thousand dollars a month to close.

Holt insisted on Mr. Flanagan's remaining as superintendent, although Flanagan did not approve of some of the former's acts, especially the subsidizing of the two mines.

About a year and a half after Holt had taken over, large quantities of foreign coal was dumped in San Francisco and Oakland, brought as ballast by ships seeking return cargoes of wheat. Coal became a drug in the market. The price went down lower than ever before. In addition, the miners having seen how prodigally money had been spent, struck for higher wages. The mine remained closed for many weeks.

The company had borrowed $40,000 from a multi-millionaire money lender in San Francisco, named Nicholas Luning, giving him as security a mortgage on the whole concern, including the ships. When the obligation came due, the mortgage was foreclosed.

Luning organized the Coos Bay Coal and Navigation Company. He added another vessel to the fleet, a wooden ship named the *Ajax* which in a heavy fog in 1901 went to the bottom with a load of coal. However, Luning's proverbial luck stayed with him in this venture. The following year after he acquired the property the reverse happened in the San Francisco-Oakland coal markets. There had been a crop failure in California that year and few ships arrived with coal ballast. As a result there was a coal famine and the price went sky-high. The new company took full advantage of the situation. Coal was rushed into the market to the limit of mine capacity. This demand lasted over a year, and in that year (according to the book-keeper, Richard Walter) the mine cleared $300,000. But the coal and shipping business was out of Luning's line. After operating the property for a few years he sold to Goodall & Perkens.

The latter took the corporate name of Coos Bay Coal and

Navigation Company. Shortly after they acquired the property, Patrick Flanagan resigned as superintendent, in 1888, and moved his family to Empire City where he retired from active business.

Richard Walter succeeded Flanagan for a short time, and upon his retirement, William Campbell took charge, to be followed shortly by his son-in-law, Patrick Hennessey, who continued as superintendent until the mine closed.

In 1889-90 the Libby Post Office was established. The name had to be changed because there was already a "Newport" post office in Oregon. The new name was most appropriate, being that of an Indian squaw who had settled at Newport before the advent of the whites, a daughter of the chief of the Coos Bay tribe of Indians. The site of her wigwam was a knoll where Mr. Flanagan later built a 14-room home. Libby's wigwam was torn down and a new house built for her a short distance from the site of her old home, where she lived for many years.

Goodall & Perkens operated the mine until it was found that coal mining was approaching its end as a major operation. The property remained idle for a few years until purchased by the Reynolds Development Company in 1911. Shortly afterwards George Doll leased and reopened the mine, employing a few men for a number of years and operating in a comparatively small way. His market was mainly local.

The Southport Mine

The Southport Mine, opened in 1877 by B. B. Jones, was and is owned by the Black Diamond Coal Company, controlled by D. O. Mills and A. Hayward, both multi-millionaires. P. B. Cornwall of San Francisco was the agent as well as one of the owners, and the moving spirit in the enterprise. Jones was a practical mining man. He acquired 2600 acres of land and made a thorough investigation of the field before opening the mine.

At this place the coal seam, called the four-foot vein, is smaller than the Newport Vein. The operation was above water level. A large bunker was built at the mine. The coal was transferred in cars, by gravity, to the shipping point, a distance of 2000 feet, on Isthmus

Slough. The empty cars were hauled by horses. A small village sprang up in connection with the mine. After operating for seven years, the Southport Mine was subsidized by the Newport Mine, as previously mentioned, to stay closed.

After some 36 years the Southport Mine was reopened under lease, by James H. Flanagan in association with A. H. Edlefsen of Portland. During this partnership, considerable coal was shipped by rail to the Portland market. In addition, the Southern Pacific was in the market for coal for its cabooses and its stations, both locally and on the main line. Also the Smith-Powers Company burned this coal on their pile-drivers and steam shovels. These outlets together with the local domestic market made an aggregate of 10,000 tons a year. Flanagan reacquired the lease in 1932 and operated the mine until 1943, when he sold his lease to Paul Murphy of Portland.

Beaver Hill Mine

The following account is based on information secured from James H. Flanagan:

> The Beaver Hill Mine, originally owned by John Norman, was first opened by R. A. Graham, a man without mining experience. A spur track from the main line of the Coos Bay, Roseburg and Eastern, was constructed a mile and a half to the mine; extensive surface improvements were installed; and a large bunker was built on the Coos Bay waterfront just south of Marshfield for water shipments.
>
> Graham is said to have spent half a million dollars of Spreckles Company money in this venture, which resulted in failure.
>
> Graham, understandably, was ousted. William S. Chandler, an experienced man, was put in charge. The Graham underground development was abandoned and another slope was opened, using the same surface improvements. Sometime after the mine was producing a considerable output, occurred the gas explosion previously referred to.
>
> After the Southern Pacific acquired the mine and the railroad from the Spreckles interests, another attempt was made to exploit the field, under the management of T. C. Russel, a

mining engineer from Montana. Another slope was sunk to a distance of 3,000 feet, the most elaborate undertaking on the entire property. The plan was to do all the "dead work" before removing coal in quantity.

When everything was ready, the San Francisco coal market went stale and the Southern Pacific Company had converted their main line locomotives to oil burners. The mine was in shape to produce a thousand or so tons of coal a day, but there was no market for such a quantity. Much of the coal which had been "blocked out" was eventually lost.

Russell resigned and was succeeded by A. L. Wheareat, a civil engineer but not a mining man. After a few years, George W. Evans, a mining engineer from Seattle, was engaged as a consulting engineer. He introduced new mining methods, but the market was limited to what coal the Southern Pacific Company consumed on its local locomotives and in its various stations and cabooses on the main line, plus the restricted local market. This did not add up to a sufficient output to make the mine a paying business.

So in 1923, the Beaver Hill mine was closed. The machinery and rails were removed from underground as well as from the surface tracks and the village soon vanished. Today no trace of it remains.

The Crescent or Maxwell Coal Mine

The Crescent Mine, opened in the late 1890's, was situated on the east side of Isthmus Slough not far below the Henryville opening. The property was originally owned by James Wall and a mine was opened by his two sons, John and James, on the croppings.

They afterwards sold to a company called the Crescent Coal Company. The Wall brothers had built a bunker on the water frontage. The new company built an additional bunker of larger capacity. These two landmarks are still in evidence. One or two shipments of coal were made to San Francisco and it supplied local trade. Water trouble developed in the slope, and keeping the mine clear caused heavy pumping expense. After operating two or three years the mine closed. The property afterwards fell into the hands of a Mr. Maxwell, and the name was changed to the Maxwell Mine. Maxwell, who had an associate with considerable money, was reputed to be a mining man, but his knowledge did not apply to local conditions. He sank a shaft about 1000 feet down, east of what was known at the Watson place at Coos City. He struck coal all right, but it was too deep. The expense had exhausted his resources and his associates were unwilling to sink good money into what appeared to be a doubtful venture. The dilapidated bunker still offers evidence of an additional "moneysunk" dream of earlier days.

Riverton Coal Basin

The more recent Riverton district has produced coal since the 1890's. The Alpine Mine was operated from 1930 to 1941 by W. T. Alpine, with a total production of about 100,000 tons. The mine in 1938 averaged about 20 tons a day.

(During the 1930's, Frank Kenworthy, a Curry County dairyman, trucked in hay from the Roseburg area. In order to have a load each way he took on coal at the Alpine Mine, hauling it to Roseburg and selling it to a fuel dealer.)

The first Riverton operation was the Timon Mine, opened in 1895. The Liberty Mine was opened in 1897 near the edge of the river, its slope going down 1300 feet on a 20-degree dip. It produced from 50 to 75 tons a day until 1902.

The Gage Mine was active from 1912 to 1915 and had a possible production of 25,000 or 30,000 tons. Others in Riverton district were the McGee Mine and the Bandon Block Mine.

Cliff Martin, a Riverton resident since early childhood, recalls the strip-mining of coal on the Coquille:

> On or about 1895 Wert Kight of Riverton was mining coal on his place by digging the clay off the coal with a grub-hoe and shovel and using a wheelbarrow to wheel the dirt away. There was about six or seven feet of dirt over the coal, which lay almost flat. Some of that coal could be lighted with a match.
>
> After the coal was dug up, it was sacked in barley sacks and hauled to Riverton, where it was delivered to homes at from two to three dollars per ton.
>
> Later, Mr. Kight used a team of horses and a small scraper to remove the clay from the coal. In the years that followed,

coal was discovered in other sections and was mined on a larger scale by driving tunnels into the hill. Mules were used to haul the coal from the mines to bunkers at the river, where it was loaded on ships for San Francisco.

Mr. Martin remembers the Bandon Block Coal Company. He says, "A bunch of Bandon men formed the company." He adds that Negroes were employed in the mine and that 35 to 40 men were required to carry on the work. There were seven saloons in the town during the early coal-mining days. The coal was shipped by steamboat to San Francisco.

Coos Coal in Many Places

Seventy-four separate *Coals, Coal Prospects,* and *Coal Mines,* in Coos County are listed in *Bulletin No.* 27, of the State Department of Geology and Mineral Industries. The term *Mine* is applied to properties which have had some commercial production; *Prospect* to those which have no production, although some development work may have been done; and *Coal* or *Coals* to undeveloped outcrops.

Upper Coal Group

North Bend Basin coals

1. Wilcox mine

Newport Basin coals

2. Libby mines
3. Englewood mines and project
4. Reservoir mine
5. Flanagan mine

Beaver Slough Basin coals (west side)

6. Southport mine and project
7. Thomas mine
8. Maxwell mine
9. Henryville mine
10. Delmar mines
11. Overland mine
12. Martin mine

13. Beaver Hill mine
14. Klondike mine
15. Fahy-Muir mine

Iverton Basin coals (south end of Beaver Slough basin)

16. Riverton mine and project
17. Smith-Kay mine
18. Panther mine
19. Lyons mine
20. Sell mine
21. Eureka mine
22. Scorby-McGinty mine
23. Fat Elk Creek coals
24. Cedar Point coal
25. McClain mine
26. Bituminous Coal Company

South Slough Basin

27. Yoakam Point coal
28. Big Creek mine and prospect
29. South Slough project
30. Olands mine
31. Vey prospect

Coquille Basin coals

32. Empire mines
33. Marsters prospects
34. Lyons mine
35. Albee mine

Undifferentiated Coal Group

East Side coals (Steva and Hardy beds)

36. Hanson coal
37. Black Diamond tunnel
38. Lone Rock prospects
39. Glasgow mine
40. Gilbertson mine
41. Carlson coals
42. Willanch Slough coals
43. Ward prospect
44. Worth prospect
45. Smith mine
46. Lillian mine

Catching Slough coals to Coaledo

47. Gunnell coals
48. Messerle coal
49. Huntley coals
50. West prospect
51. Smith-Powers mine
52. Coaledo mines

Sumner Basin coals

53. Standley coals
54. Noble Creek prospects
55. Newcastle mines
56. Sumner coals
57. Ferberish prospect

Lower Coal Group

Sevenmile Creek coals

58. Hall Creek mine
59. Lampa Creek mine
60. Donaldson prospect
61. Woomer coal
62. Sevenmile Creek coals
63. Seven Devils coals

Undifferentiated

64. Archer & Sengstacken coals
65. Bunker Hill mine
66. Belfast mine
67. Caledonia mine
68. Davis Slough coals
69. Thirty-Six Coal mine
70. Brown Slough coals
71. Stainbeck coal

Other Coals

72. Bandon coals
73. Lakeside coals
74. Remote coals

Curry County Coal

The upper Rogue coal on Shasta Costa Creek has been found to be in four to six foot beds, with a remarkably low water content but with a large content of ash and fixed carbon.

The thickness of the coal in the Eckley district may be 50 feet. An outcrop is at the eastern part of Sugar Loaf Mountain. A number of other outcrops occur on the small tributary streams.

Outcrops of small beds have been reported along the southern Curry Coast—on the north fork of the Chetco and in the bluff above the mouth of Thomas Creek.

32

Ships, Builders, Captains

By Victor West, Jr.

WOODEN SHIPBUILDING STARTED soon after white men came into the area. It turned out to be one of the major industries of Coos County. At Port Orford, William Tichenor built one of the first vessels, the small two-masted schooner *Alaska.* The same year, James C. Fitzgerald, Daniel Giles, and Thomas Hall built a small schooner on the Coquille River, making one trip from there to Port Orford; she never had a name.

The first vessel built on Coos Bay was the brig *Blanco* built at Captain A. M. Simpson's sawmill at North Bend. His shipyard continued till 1902, turning out 58 vessels, including the first five-masted schooner built in the United States.

The various builders of ships down through the years are given in the following list:

VESSELS AND THEIR BUILDERS

Abbreviations used for the rig of the vessels are:

Bg–Brig
Bkn–Barkentine
Drg–Dredge
Gas–Gas screw
*Gap–Gas stern wheel
Ols–Oil screw
Sch–Schooner
Shp–Ship
Slp–Sloop
Sts–Steam screw
Stp– Steam side-wheel
*Stp–Steam stern-wheel

The figures under *Size* are for the lengths in feet except when marked (T) for tonnage.

Name of Vessel	Rig and Size		Place Built	Year Built and Builder
A. M. Simpson 1	Sts.	193	North Bend	1911—Kruse & Banks
Active	Gas	42	Prosper	1913—Herman Bros.
Addenda	4m Bkn	176	North Bend	1895—E. Heuckendorff
Adel 2	Gas	35	Marshfield	1905—W. Holland
Admiral	4m Sch	173	North Bend	1899—K. V. Kruse
Advance	2m Bg	210(T)	North Bend	1862—W. Robison
Advance	3m Sch	139	Parkersburg	1902—S. Danielson
Akutan	Sts	101	North Bend	1913—Kruse & Banks
Advent 3	3m Sch	151	North Bend	1901—K. V. Kruse
Alaska	2m Sch	48	Port Orford	1857—Wm. Tichenor
Albatross	Gas	36	Empire City	1912—Fred Shelin
Alert	Sts		Marshfield	1881
Alert	*Stp	69	Bandon	1890—Hans Reed
Alice H.	Gas	44	Marshfield	1909—W.Holland
Alma 4	Sts	41	Marshfield	1899—Rogers Bros.
Alpha 5	Sts	65	Empire City	1868—H. H.Luse
Alpha	3m Sch	143	North Bend	1903—H. Heuckendorff
Alton	2m. Sch	83	Marshfield	1886—H. Sengstaken
Alumna	4m Sch	189	North Bend	1901—K. V. Kruse
Amelia	3m Bkn	153	Marshfield	1870—R. Murray
Anastasia Casman 6	2m Sch	51(T)	Empire City	1880—H. H. Luse
Annie Hanify 7	Sts	235	North Bend	1920—Kruse & Banks
Annie E. Smale	4m Sch	200	Marshfield	1903—K. V. Kruse
Annie Stown	2m Sch	119(T)	Marshfield	1870—McDonald
Antelope	Sts	60	Marshfield	1886—Hans Reed
Arago 8	2m Bg	103	North Bend	1860—McDonald

Arago—Second brig built on the Pacific Coast – cost $13,000. After 1880 she was used as a codfisher for 24 years, and was withdrawn from service in 1905.

Name of Vessel	Rig and Size		Place Built	Year Built and Builder
Arago 9	4m Bkn	176	North Bend	1891—John Kruse
Argus	4m Sch	162	Marshfield	1902—E. Heuckendorff
Arrow	Gas	45	North Bend	1908—Geo. D. Smith
Arrow No. 3	Ols	61	North Bend	1925—Kruse & Banks
Arctic	Sts	145	Bay City	1901—Hans Reed
Astoria	Sts	104	North Bend	1884—John Kruse
Aurelia	Sts	162	Prosper	1902—G. Ross
Baladan	Sts	275	North Bend	1918—Kruse & Banks
Balliett	Sts	275	Marshfield	1918—C. B. Shipbuilding
Bandon 10	Sts	172	North Bend	1907—Kruse & Banks

Name of Vessel	Rig and Size		Place Built	Year Built and Builder
Banshee	Gas	38	Pleasant Point	1907—Wm. Ross
Barnacle	Gas	37	North Bend	1914—Fred Harris
Bear	Gas	31	Marshfield	1913—Max Timmerman
Beaver	Gas	35	Marshfield	1907—W. Holland
Big Chief	Gas	30	Marshfield	1913—Max Timmerman
Billy Moore	Ols	48	Prosper	1925—Herman Bros.
Beda	Sts	152	North Bend	1883—John Kruse
Bertha	Sts	37	Empire City	1879—R. C. Cordes

Blanco—In 1864 her hull washed ashore near the mouth of the Siletz River, found there with masts gone, deck broken in, and the hull split from deck to keel, with no sign of her crew. Indians living nearby had in their possession 2 kegs of nails, 5 sheets of zinc, 1 oil coat, 7 pairs of garters, 2 pairs of boots, 1 calico dress, and rope and sailcloth. It was never known just how much the Indians knew of the wreck or what they knew about what happened to the crew.

Name of Vessel	Rig and Size		Place Built	Year Built and Builder
Blanco 11	2m Bg	284(T)	North Bend	1859—E. G. Simpson
Blanco	Sts	61	Marshfield	1893
Bonita	Sts		Porter	1887—Wm. Ross
Bonita	Gas	45	Marshfield	1907—Max Timmerman
Bowdoin	Sts	192	Prosper	1907—E. Heuckendorff
Bowhead	2m Sch	90	North Bend	1891
Brant	.01s	100	North Bend	1926—Kruse & Banks
Brunswick	Sts	161	North Bend	1898—A. Sperry
Buffalo	Gas	34	Prosper	1905—Nels Nelson
Buffalo Bill	Gas	35	Marshfield	1905—W. Holland
Bunkalation 12	3m Sch		North Bend	1868 — John Kruse
Burnside	Sts	266	Marshfield	1919—C. B. Shipbuilding
C. A. Smith 13	Sts	275	North Bend	1917—Kruse & Banks
C. C. Funk	3m. Bkn	163	Marshfield	1882—Hans Reed
C. M. Brewer	Ols	54	Prosper	1930—Herman Bros.
Casco 14	Sts	160	Marshfield	1906—Kruse & Banks
Ceres	Sts	51	Marshfield	1877—O. Reed
Charm	Ols	75	Prosper	1913—Herman Bros.
Charles H. Merchant	3m Sch	120	Marshfield	1877—Hans Reed
Churchill	4m Sch	178	North Bend	1900—Vic Anderson
City of Coos Bay 15	Gas	40	Marshfield	1907—Max Timmerman
Coast 16	Gas	45	Empire City	1908—Pet Olson
Coaster	Gas	50	Marshfield	1910—Max Timmerman
Cononino	Sts	275	North Bend	1918—Kruse &Banks
Columbia	Sts	102	North Bend	1891—John Kruse
Comet	Sts	82	Aaronsville	1883—A. Campbell

Name of Vessel	Rig and Size		Place Built	Year Built and Builder
Comet	Gas	34	East Side	1903—Max Timmerman
Coos	Stp	58	Empire City	1874—W. H. Luse

Coos—A sidewheeler which ran for several years from Empire to all the points on Coos Bay and Coos River. Captains W. H. Luse, H. H. Luse, Lanfare, Floyd and Ernest commanded her at different times until late in 1884 when H. W. Dunham rebuilt her at Marshfield. Captains A. M. Campbell, H. W. Robert and J. F. Dunham were in control of her until 1890 when A. F. Hurd took charge, and 10 years later removed her to the Siuslaw where she became the *Margaret.*

Name of Vessel	Rig and Size		Place Built	Year Built and Builder
Coos	Drg	100	Marshfield	1920
Coos Bay 17	Sts	180	Marshfield	1884—Hans Reed
Coos Bay	Sts	275	Marshfield	1918—C. B. Shipbuilding
Coos Bay 18	01s	46	North Bend	1929—Kruse & Banks
Coos King	01s	48	Marshfield	1923—C. T. Holland
Coos River	Sts	44	Marshfield	1890—R. C. Cordes
Coos River	Gas	37	Marshfield	1916—Frank Lowe
Copper Queen 19	Gas	53	Coquille	1899—A. Ellingston
Coquille	Sts	76	Coquille	1908—Frank Lowe
Coquelle	2m Sch	92	Parkersburg	1883—S. Danielson
Coquille River **20**	**Sts**	**146**	Prosper	1896—W. Muller
Cordelia	Stp	68	Coquille	1873—W. Rackleff
Cruiser	Sts	70	North Bend	1886—John Kruse
Cumtux	Sts		Marshfield	1890
Curlew 21	Gas	40	Marshfield	1903—J. Bloomquist
Cyclone	2m Sch	31	Sixes River	1891
Daisy 22	Sts	174	Bandon	1911—J. H. Price
Dakota	3m Sch	143	Marshfield	1881—Hans Reed
Dare	3m Sch	130	North Bend	1882—John Kruse
Davenport	Sts	200	North Bend	1912—Kruse & Banks
David Evans	4m Sch	200	Marshfield	1901—E. Heuckendorff
Dawn	2m Sch	41	Bandon	1891
Diesel	01s	45	Randolph	1923—Herman Bros.
Dispatch	*Stp	92	Bandon	1890—Hans Reed
Dispatch 23	*Stp	111	Parkersburg	1903—Chas. Tweed
Dispatch	Gas	34	Marshfield	1906—Max Timberman
Dixie	Gas	35	Marshfield	1903—Holland Bros.
Dixie	Gas	43	Marshfield	1907—Max Timberman
Donna II	Gas	31	Prosper	1945—Levi L. Bunch
Dora	*Stp	70	Randolph	1910—Herman Bros.
E.[illegible] F Rippley	Sts	115	Marshfield	1907—Kruse & Banks
Eagle	Gas	46	Marshfield	1903—C. T. Holland
Eastport	Sts		Marshfield	1872—Hans Reed

Name of Vessel	Rig and Size		Place Built	Year Built and Builder
Echo	4m Bkn	183	North Bend	1896—E. Heuckendorff
Echo	*Stp	66	Coquille	1901—A. Ellingston
Elmore	Gas	35	Empire City	1905—Peter Olson
Emily	Sts	37	Myrtle Point	1897—Wall Bros.
Empire	Gas	50	Empire City	1911—R. H. Olson
Enegren Ferry	Ols	56	North Bend	1930—Kruse & Banks
Enterprise	2m	100	North Bend	1863—J. Howllett
Enterprise	Gas	53	Coquille	1908—E. Ellingston
Encore 24	4m Bkn	181	North Bend	1897—E. Heuckendorff

Encore—In July of 1917 she was captured and burned by the German raider *Wolf* in oriental waters. The crew was taken aboard the raider and kept there for sometime. Some of them were later cast away on the Danish coast to be rescued by the Danish authorities. The remainder were taken to Germany to spend the rest of the war in a prison camp.

Name of Vessel	Rig and Size		Place Built	Year Built and Builder
Escort 25	Sts	88	Marshfield	1869—J. Howllett
Escort	Gas	60	Prosper	1911—Nel Nelson
Escort No. 2	Sts	92	Marshfield	1882
Exchange	Gas	33	North Bend	1905—Vic. Wittick
Express 26	Sts	62	Pleasant Point	1890—H. Sengstacken
Express	Gas	43	Marshfield	1907—W. Holland
F. S. Loop	Sts	139	Marshfield	1907—W. Holland
Fairhaven	Sts	185	North Bend	1908—Kruse & Banks
Fanny Jane	2m Sch	120(T)	Marshfield	1869—J. Sutherland
Favorite	Sts	72	Coquille	1900—A. Ellingston
Favorite	Ols	50	Marshfield	1922—Frank Lowe
Fawn	Sts	38	Marshfield	1892—A. J. Campbell
Fay No. 4	*Gap	136	North Bend	1912—Kruse & Banks
Fifield 27	Sts	160	North Bend	1912—Kruse & Banks
Fish	Gas	39	Empire City	1903—John Swing
Florence E. Walton 28	Sts	75(T)	North Bend	1860—Donaldson
Florence Olson 29	Sts	213	North Bend	1917—Kruse & Banks
Forest Home 30	4m Sch	173	Marshfield	1900—E. Heuckendorff
Fort Laramie	6m Sch	266	North Bend	1918—Kruse & Banks
Fort Leavenworth	Sts	266	North Bend	1918—Kruse & Banks
Fort Logan	Sts	266	North Bend	1918—Kruse & Banks
Freak	Gas	42	Marshfield	1912—Frank Lowe
Fred Baxter	Sts	213	North Bend	1917—Kruse & Banks
Frithiof	2m Sch	242(T)	Marshfield	1874—Holden
Gardiner City 31	4m Sch	169	North Bend	1889—John Kruse
Gasgo	Gas	36	Marshfield	1900—Holland Bros.
Gem	2m Sch	106	Parkersburg	1885—S. Danielson
Gen'l. Siglin	2m Sch	80	Marshfield	1894

Name of Vessel	Rig and Size		Place Built	Year Built and Builder
Geo. C. Perkins	3m Bkn	142	Marshfield	1880—Hans Reed
Gleanor	Sts	97	Bandon	1908—J. H. Price
Glen	2m Sch	106	Marshfield	1883—Hans Reed
Gotoma	2m Sch	119	North Bend	1872—John Kruse
Hannah Louise	2m Sch	83(T)	North Bend	1863—Howlett
Harold	Gas	35	Parkersburg	1903—C. W. Aston
Hercules	Ols	42	Marshfield	1909—Max Timberman
Hercules II	Gas	44	Marshfield	1920—Frank Lowe
Homer	Sts	146	Bandon	1891—Hans Reed
Hope	Gas	49	Marshfield	1915—Wm. Bjorquist
Hope	Gas	41	Prosper	1925—Herman Bros.
Horace X. Baxter 32	Sts	214	North Bend	1917—Kruse & Banks
Hugh Hogan 33	3m. Sch	160	Marshfield	1904—K. V. Kruse

Hugh Hogan—In 1918 she was sold to San Francisco owners with Mexican connections but was detained in port on suspicion of being really intended to become a German raider. She was wrecked off the southern Oregon coast in 1922.

Hulda	Ols	70	Prosper	1911—Nels Nelson
Hunter	Sts	95	North Bend	1883—John Kruse
Imperial	Ols	59	Prosper	1924—Herman Bros.
Isabella	2m Sch	107	North Bend	1864—J. Howllett
Ivanhoe	2m Sch	86	Marshfield	1869—J. Walworth
J. J. Loggie	Sts	145	Bandon	1908—J. H. Price
J. Warren	Sts	35	Coquille	1901—A. Ellingston
James Sennett	4m Sch	194	Marshfield	1901—E. Heuckendorff
James A. Garfield 34	3m Sch	140	North Bend	1881—John Kruse
Jennie Stella	3m Sch	132	Marshfield	1876—Hans Reed
Jennie Wand	3m Sch	124	Marshfield	1883—Hans Reed
Johanna Smith 35	Sts	275	North Bend	1917—Kruse & Banks
Joan Kernam	Ols	57	Marshfield	1924—C. T. Holland
John G. North	3m Sch	143	Marshfield	1881—Hans Reed
Joseph L. Eviston 36	3m Bkn	190	Marshfield	1900—E. Heuckendorff
Juno	Sts	56	Coos River	1876—A. Campbell
Juno	Sts	60	Marshfield	1906—W. Holland
Juno 3	Ols	53	North Bend	1923—Kruse & Banks
Juventa	2m Sch	191 (T)	North Bend	1865—Howllett
K. V. Kruse 37	5m Sch	242	North Bend	1920—Kruse & Banks
Katie O'Neil 38	Stp	89	Coos River	1890
Kate Piper	2m Sch	71 (T)	Empire City	1868—H. H. Luse
Katie Cook	Sts	57	Parkersburg	1876—Capt. Parker
Kickapoo	Sts	275	North Bend	1919—Kruse & Banks
Klihyan	Sts	89	Bandon	1908—J. H. Price
Klikitat	3m Bkn	163	North Bend	1881—John Kruse
Koos	Gas	39	Marshfield	1907—W. Holand

Name of Vessel	Rig and Size		Place Built	Year Built and Builder
Koos No. 2	Ols	49	Marshfield	1924—Frank Lowe
Koos No. 3	*Ols.*		North Bend	1915—Buehner Lumber Co.
Koos No. 4	Ols		Empire City	1948—John Swing
Laura May	3m Sch	121	Marshfield	1875—Hans Reed
Leader	Gas	33	Marshfield	1905—W. Holland
Liberty	*Stp	90	Bandon	1903—Herman Bros.
Liberty	Sts	66	Bandon	1889—S. Danielson
Life-Line	Gas	36	Marshfield	1912—W. Cavinaw
ing	1m Slp	35	Jordans Cove	1893
Little Annie 39	*Stp	69	Myrtle Point	1887—W. Rackleff
Lizzie Prien	2m Sch	94	Parkersburg	1884—S. Danielson
Louis	5m Sch	193	North Bend	1888—John Kruse

Louis—The first 5-masted schooner built in the United States. She had a steamer hull and was rigged with five masts for the voyage to San Francisco to have the engines installed, but she sailed "so good" no engines were put in her. She was also the first of her rig to sail around the world. She was lost on June 18, 1907, on South Farallon Islands in the fog.

Name of Vessel	Rig and Size		Place Built	Year Built and Builder
Louisa Morrison	2m Sch	95 (T)	Marshfield	1869—Howllett
Mae	Gas	42	Marshfield	1909—Max Timmerman
Maggie Ross	Sts	115	Pleasant Point	1888—J.Ross
Mandalay	Sts	142	North Bend	1900—G. Ross
Manila	4m Sch	183	North Bend	1899—E. Heuckendorff
Maple	Gas	61	Randolph	1911—C. Herman
Marconi 40	4 m Sch	176	North Bend	1902—Peter Loggie
Marshfield 41	Sts	148	Marshfield	1901—E. Heuckendorff
Marshfield	Sts	275	Marshfield	1918—C. B. Shipbuilding
Marshfield	Gas	41	East Side	1908—Arthur Mattson

Marshfield—The Anza Trading Company was using her to run full cargoes of liquor into San Francisco during prohibition, but she was shortly thereafter seized and sold by a United States marshal. She was reduced to a barge for a while but was later beached at Martinez, California, where parts of her can still be seen.

Name of Vessel	Rig and Size		Place Built	Year Built and Builder
Mary	Sts		Coquille River	1871—W. Rackleff
Mary Ann	Gas	36	Marshfield	1917—Frank Lowe
Mary D. Hume	Sts	98	Ellensburg	1881
Mascot	2m Sch	70	Prosper	1892—Hans Reed
Mawmell	Gas	31	North Bend	1908—J. H. Cullon
May	Gas	46	Randolph	1910—A. L. Herman
Mayflower 42	Gas	37	May	1902—Peterson
Mayflower	Gas	37	Marshfield	1915—Frank Lowe

Name of Vessel	Rig and	Size	Place Built	Year Built and Builde
Mecca	Gas	60	Marshfield	1924—Frank Low
Melacthon	3m Bkn	133	North Bend	1867—J. Murra
Mendicino	2m Sch	84	North Bend	1861—Robinso
Messenger 43	*Stp	90	Marshfield	1873—Capt. M. Lan
Messenger	Gas	35	Marshfield	1907—G. Elliot
Milton	Sts	44	Porter	1890
Millicoma 44	*Gap	55	Marshfield	1909—Frank Low
Minnie Mitchell	Ols	34	Marrshfield	1905—W. Hollanc
Mirene	Ols	61	North Bend	1912—Kruse & Bank
Mizpah	2m Sch	70	Prosper	1898—S. Danielsor
Moon	Gas	47	Prosper	1923—Herman Bros
Myrl	Sts	38	Myrtle Point	1894—Wall Bros
Myrtle	Sts	72	Prosper	1908—Nel Nelsor
Myrtle	Sts		Marshfield	1879—Hall & Lightne
Myrtle 45	*Stp	67	Myrtle Point	1909—C. S. Kim
Myrtle	*Stp	60	Prosper	1922—Herman Bros
Myrtle W	Gas	53	Randolph	1912—Wheele
Mud Hen	*Stp	32	Coquille River	1878—Capt. Dunhan

Mud Hen—Traveling between Coos Bay and the Coquille Valley was quite an excursion in the 1870's and 1880's. A person would have to take a steamer from towns on Coos Bay to Kings Landing at the head of Isthmus Slough and a railroad ride over the Isthmus to Beaver Slough. Captain Dunham and nephew Robert ran the steamer *Mud Hen*. She wasn't a handsome craft but served her purpose well. Her route governed her size — 23 feet long and 6 feet beam, a few inches narrower than the stream. The shrubbery on both sides of the stream formed a complete arch the greater part of the way. Every night the beavers would build numerous dams across the diminutive marine highway, making gum boots standard equipment for the crew so they could wade up the stream and kick a dam out of the way. "What you need are locks instead of dam," suggested a passenger on a trip when the tide had ebbed to leave only a light depth of water in the slough. "Don't mention it," retorted another passenger, a frequent traveler on the vessel, "there are locks of my hair on every tree between here and Coquille."

Name of Vessel	Rig and	Size	Place Built	Year Built and Builder
Multnoma	Ols	45	Marshfield	1928—L. McDonald
Narhel	Gas	45	Brookings	1917—C. S. McRay
Nellie & Cressy	Gas	33	Bandon	1903—L. H. Wolf
No. 2	Drg	70	North Bend	1910
Nonoha	2m Sch		North Bend	1892—John Kruse
Norma	Gas	61	Radolph	1911—Herman Bros.
North Bend	3m Bkn	153	North Bend	1877—John Kruse
North Bend 46	4m Sch	204	North Bend	1918—Kruse & Banks

North Bend—Inbound from Adelaide to Astoria for lumber on February 5, 1928, she stranded on Peacock Spit at the mouth of the Columbia River. She resisted all attempts of the tug *Arrow No. 3* to refloat her. She was finally stripped of everything of value and abandoned to the elements. After several months, reports started to come in that the *North Bend* was moving. At the end of 13 months the schooner had refloated herself in Bakers Bay, traveling through about 12,000 feet of sand. Inspection showed that her hull had suffered no damage while she was on the spit, but because there was no demand for sailing vessels in 1929 she was taken to Youngs Bay near Astoria and tied up for a few years. She was finally converted into a lumber barge, and later brought to Gardiner. On her first trip with lumber from there she sprang a leak off Coos Bay. The pumps were unable to keep her from being waterlogged. So an attempt was made to bring her into Coos Bay. In crossing the bar she struck North Spit, damaging her so badly that when she was refloated and unloaded she was towed back to sea and turned loose, to drift ashore between the Cape Arago Lighthouse and Mussel Reef, where she was finally burned for what scrap iron could be salvaged. She was next to the last schooner built on the Pacific Coast, originally intended as a steamer but, before she was launched, she was converted to a 4-masted schooner.

Name of Vessel	Rig and Size		Place Built	Year Built and Builder
North Bend	Sts	275	North Bend	1918—Kruse & Banks
North Star 47	Gas	36	North Bend	1908—C. A. Johnson
North Star	Gas	35	Marshfield	1905—Max Timmerman
Nora Harkins	2m Sch	121	Parkersburg	1882—S. Danielson
Novelty	Str	71	North Bend	1884—John Kruse
Novelty 48	4m Sch	168	North Bend	1886—John Kruse
Oakland	Ols	103	Marshfield	1905—K. V. Kruse
Omega	4m Bkn	163	North Bend	1894—John Kruse
Onward	3m Sch	134	Parkersburg	1901—S. Danielson
Oregon	3m Sch	139	Prosper	1905—E. Heuckendorff
Oregonian 49	2m Sch	246(T)	North Bend	1872—John Kruse
Occident 50	3m Bkn	297(T)	North Bend	1865—John Dumphy
Oshkosh	Ols	89	North Bend	1909—Kruse & Banks
Owl	Gas	60	North Bend	1911 Kruse & Banks
Osprey 51	Gas	58	Coquille	1908—A. Ellingston
Pacific 52	Gas	58	North Bend	1920—Kruse & Banks
Pannonia	2m Sch	106	Marshfield	1875—Hans Reed
Parkersburg	2m Sch	100	Parkersburg	1883—S. Danielson
Pastime	*Gap	45	Coquille	1900—A. Ellingston
Patsy	Gas	94	North Bend	1911—Kruse & Banks
Peddler	Sts	124	Marshfield	1908—S. Gilroy

Name of Vessel	Rig and Size			Place Built	Year Built and Builder
Polaris	4m	Sch	195	Marshfield	1902—E. Heuckendorff
Port Angeles		Sts	233	North Bend	1916—Kruse & Banks
Port of Bandon		Ols	80	Prosper	1938—Victor Laivo
Portland 53	3m	Bkn	161	North Bend	1876—John Kruse
Powers		*Stp	89	North Bend	1909—Kruse & Banks
Prosper	3m	Sch	128	Prosper	1892—S. Danielson
Queen		Ols	43	Marshfield	1907—W. Holland
Quibinic		Sts	275	North Bend	1918—Kruse & Banks
R. D. Inman		Sts	186	North Bend	1907—Kruse & Banks
Rainbow		*Stp	64	Marshfield	1917—Frank Lowe
Ralph 54		Sts	45	Myrtle Point	1896—Wall Bros.
Ralph J. Long	2m	Sch	87	Bandon	1888—S. Danielson
Rambler		Gas	34	Marshfield	1913—John Matson
Randolph 55		Gas	60	Randolph	1910—Herman Bros.
Ranger		Sts	106	North Bend	1887—John Kruse
Ranger 56		Ols	44	Marshfield	1908—W. Holland
Raymond		Sts	132	Prosper	1906—E. Heuckendorff
Rebecca	2m	Sch	105	Empire City	1875—J. Murray
Relief		Ols	31	Marshfield	1901—Holland Bros.
Relief		*Stp	64	Coquille	1916—A. Ellingston
Repeat	3h	Sch	148	North Bend	1897—E. Heuckendorff
Restless		Sts	45	Parkersburg	1887—Capt. Leneve
Reta		Sts	53	Prosper	1889—A. Ellingston
Robert Emmett.	2m	Sch	34(T)	Empire City	1880—H. H. Luse
Roamer		Ols	60	North Bend	1914—Kruse & Banks
Rogue		Gas	52	Marshfield	1927—A. Windiger
Roosevelt 57		Stp	95	North Bend	1921—Kruse & Banks
Ruby	2m	Sch	41	Parkersburg	1885—S. Danielson
Rural		Gas	34	Marshfield	1911—Kruse Bros.
Rustler 58		Gas	60	North Bend	1911—Kruse & Banks
Ryder Hanify		Sts	235	North Bend	1920—Kruse & Banks
S. Danielson	2m*	Sch	91	Parkersburg	1883—S. Danielson
Samson		Ols	45	Bandon	1910—Wm. McKay
San Ramon 59		Sts	199	North Bend	1913—Kruse & Banks
Santa Ana		Sts	182	Pleasant Point	1900—Hans Reed
Santa Rosa	2m	Sch	61	Marshfield	1879
Satellite		*Stp	72	Empire City	1872—W. Luse
Sea Foam		Gas	49	Prosper	1914—V. Nelson
Shamrock		Gas	35	Marshfield	1908—W. Holland
Signal		Sts	150	North Bend	1887—John Kruse
Silver Wave	2m	Sch	54	Bandon	1889—Hans Reed
Sparrow		Gas	37	North Bend	1903—Victor Wittick
Speedwell		Sts	192	North Bend	1912—Kruse & Banks
Standard		Gas	51	Pleasant Point	1911—Ervin Ross
Stanwood 60		Sts	206	North Bend	1916—Kruse & Banks

Name of Vessel	Rig and Size		Place Built	Year Built and Builder
Star	Ols	40	Prosper	1909—Carl Herman
Staghound	2m Sch	136 (T)	Marshfield	1868—Howlett
Success	*Gap	45	Gold Beach	1903—E. B. Burns
Sunset	Gas	40	Prosper	1909—Carl Herman
Sunshine 61	3m Sch	326 (T)	Marshfield	1875—Holden

Sunshine—In 1875 a mysterious fate overtook those on board. On her first trip on October 8 to San Francisco, after discharging a lumber cargo, she sailed for Coos Bay on November 3, with 15 passengers and a crew of 10. On November 18 her hull was seen floating bottom up close to shore, north of Cape Hancock. A few days later she drifted ashore near Long Beach, Washington, so badly wrecked that no clue could be discovered as to the exact fate of the crew and passengers. In addition to an $18,000 cargo, she had $10,000 in coin aboard.

Name of Vessel	Rig and Size		Place Built	Year Built and Builder
Swan	Gas	32	Prosper	1908—A. Herman
Tam O'Shanter	3m Bkn	170	North Bend	1875—John Kruse
Taurus	4m Sch	161	Marshfield	1902—E. Heuckendorff
Teal	Ols	73	North Bend	1926—Kruse & Banks
Telegraph	*Stp	103	Prosper	1914—Carl Herman

Telegraph vs. *Charm*—In the Coquille River steamboating days many small vessels plied between Bandon and Coquille and up as far as Myrtle Point. These were the farmers' only way of getting their produce to market, getting their mail, going to church in Bandon or Coquille, and for their Sunday excursions and picnics. One day in 1915 the passengers of the gas boat *Charm* and the steamer *Telegraph* were having a quiet ride between Bandon and Coquille when things began to happen. The stories of the rival captains of the boats were a bit contradictory and confusing. The captain of the *Charm* in his detailed account stated that at 2:16 p. m., while he was running from Bandon and was half a mile below Cedar Point, he saw the *Telegraph* coming up behind him. She was showing every inclination and determination to run down the hapless *Charm*. He whistled four times but the *Telegraph* gave no answer except to keep coming on at full speed. Naturally the *Telegraph* rammed the *Charm* and sent her limping to the beach to avoid sinking, with her port bulwarks damaged and her fender ripped away from stem to stern. But the captain of the *Telegraph* had a different report. He stated that it was 2:23 p. m. at a point two miles below Coquille. The *Telegraph* was at a landing when the *Charm* came into sight. Just as the *Telegraph* pulled into the stream, the *Charm* came alongside and attempted to cross the bow of the *Telegraph,* contrary to all the rules of the road.

As she crowded in, the *Telegraph* was pushed against a boom that forced it to skid into the *Charm,* and damaging her somewhat when the *Telegraph* backed off. Take your choice of the stories.

Name of Vessel	Rig and Size		Place Built	Year Built and Builder
Telephone	Gas	36	Marshfield	1903—Frank Lowe
Tiger	Gas	52	Empire City	1919—John Swing
Tillamook 62	Gas	150	North Bend	1913—Kruse & Banks
Tioga	Gas	63	North Bend	1907—Z. A. Kanick
Tramp 63	Gas	56	Empire City	1911—John Swing
Transfer	*Gas	27	Allegany	1907—H. McCallom
Transit	Gap	60	Marshfield	1908—Park & McCallom
Traveler	Sts	160	North Bend	1886—John Kruse
Traveler	Gas	36	Pleasant Point	1908—J. D. Ross
Triumph	Sts	64	Parkersburg	1889—Hans Reed
Tropic Bird	3m Bkn	136	North Bend	1882—John Kruse
Trustee	3m Sch	133	North Bend	1878—John Kruse
Turtle	Gas	44	Marshfield	1912—Max Timmerman
Union	Gas	38	Marshfield	1912—Frank Lowe
Vega	Gas	40	North Bend	1908—Peter Peterson
Venus	Sts	39	Coquille	1901—C. H. James
Victor	Gas	37	Marshfield	1908—Victor Wittick
Viking	2m Sch	108	Marshfield	1882—Hans Reed
Virginia Olson 64	Sts	225	North Bend	1917—Kruse & Banks
Volante	2m Sch	87	North Bend	1891—G. L. Hobbs
Vulcan	Ols	46	North Bend	1926—Kruse & Banks
Wahtaswaso	Gas	55	Marshfield	1911—Matson & Bjorkquist
Washcalore 65	Ols	140	Marshfield	1906—K. V. Kruse
Wasp	Sts		Marshfield	1879—C. Winchester
Washington	Gas	36	Marshfield	1903—P. B. Holland
Web Foot 66	3m Bkn	146	North Bend	1869—John Kruse
Welcome 67	*Stp	56	Coquille	1900—S. H. McAdams
Welcome	Ols	47	Marshfield	1919—Frank Lowe
Wellesey	Sts	186	Prosper	1907—E. Heuckendorff
Wenona	Sts	60	North Bend	1904—E. Heuckendorff
Western Shore	3m Shp	186	North Bend	1874—John Kruse

Western Shore—R. W. Simpson drew the sail plan, A. M. Simpson designed the hull, and John Kruse built her in North Bend in 1874. She was one of three full-rigged ships built on the Pacific Coast. In her heyday she was classed as a clipper ship, making several fast voyages. In 1875 she left San Francisco behind the steamer *Oriflame,* arriving at Astoria two and a half hours ahead, making the trip in a trifle over two days. A year later she established another record; she sailed from Portland to

Liverpool in 101 days. The next year she went from San Francisco in 103 days and returned in 110 days. Another voyage was made from the Columbia River to Liverpool in 97 days. These voyages established for her the record of the three fastest consecutive runs on the route. She was not only a fast sailer but also had a large cargo capacity. Never considered a lucky ship and being a 3-skysailer, may have contributed to her destruction. Enroute from Seattle on July 11, 1878, she struck Duxbury Reef and went to pieces in short order. At the time she was speeding before the wind at 12 knots an hour. When she grounded, her entire bottom went out on the port side, letting the cargo sink into the sea. She had cost $80,000.

Name of Vessel	Rig and Size		Place Built	Year Built and Builder
William Vaughn	Ols	43	Marshfield	1930—L. R. McDonald
Willis R. Hume	4m Bkn	183	North Bend	1874—John Kruse
Wilhelmina	Ols	80	North Bend	1908—Kruse & Banks
Wilmington	Sts	199	North Bend	1913—Kruse & Banks
Winchester	2m Sch	98	Prosper	1893—Hans Reed
Wolverine	Gas	50	Marshfield	1908—Max Timmerman
Yarrow 68	Sts	63	Porter	1890—Capt. Pendergrass
Zebra	Gas	54	Empire City	1921—John Swing
Zenith	2m Sch	54	Bandon	1900—E. P. Anderson

1—Renamed *Martha Buehner*
2—Burned at Gardiner on 2-10-1920.
3—Lost on Coos Bay on 2-18-1913.
4—Renamed *Jauniata.*
5—Renamed *Gov. Tilden* then *Walter Hacket.*
6—Renamed *Felix.*
7—Renamed *Salina Cruze* (Panama).
8— Converted to 2m Sch.
9—Renamed *Aurrera* (Peru).
10—Foundered off Southern Oregon coast. Renamed *Atrevedo* (Mex.)
11—Hull came ashore near Siletz River, Oregon in 1864.
12—Burned at Cape Blanco Lighthouse in 1870.
13—Lost on North Jetty of Coos Bay on 12-16-1923.
14—Lost off Piedress Blancas in 1913.
15—Renamed *Sunrise.*
16—Renamed *Enterprise* then *Arrow No. 5.*
17—Lost at Ventura, Calif. on 12-18-1914.
18—Renamed *Happy.*
19—Lost off Cape Blanco.
20—Renamed *Winchester.*
21—Ran down by tug *Columbia* at North Bend on 2-6-1912.
22—Renamed *Thos. H. Elliott* then *Redwood.*
23—Renamed *John Widdi.*
24— Burned as a Sch. by a German raider in Oriental waters on 7-14-1917.
25—Boiler exploded at Empire City on 12-22-1886.
26—Burned at Marshfield on 9-7-1891.
27—Lost on Coquille River bar on 2-29-1916.
28—Lost between Coos Bay and Rogue River.
29—Renamed *Willapa.* Lost 8 mi. south of Port Orford on 12-3-1941.
30—Renamed *Holmwood* (British).
31—Converted to 3m Bkn. Converted back to 4m Sch. and renamed *Kitsap.*
32—Renamed *Port Orford.*
33. Renamed *Ozmo.* Foundered off Port Orford on 5-17-1922.
34—Renamed *G. Garibaldi* (Peru).
35—Used as gambling barge off southern California in the 1920's.
36—Renamed *Fookien* (Philippines).
37—Sold to a Canadian Company in 1939 as a barge. Wrecked in British Columbia in 1940.
38—Renamed *Barclay Golden.*
39—Wrecked on Coquille River near Bandon on 2-3-1890.
40—Lost on Coos Bay bar on 3-23-1909.
41—Renamed *Bertue M. Hanlon.*
42—Burned in lower Coos Bay on 12-30-1912.
43—Burned at Marshfield on 5-3-1876.
44—Converted to gas.
45—Scrapped in 1922.

46—Lost on Coos Bay bar as a barge in 1940.
47—Capsized in lower Coos Bay on 1-20-1912.
48—Lost north of Coos Bay on 10-23-1907.
49—Lost on Coquille bar on 1-16-1877.
50—Lost on Coos Bay bar on 5-3-1870.
51—Lost on Coos Bay bar on 11-1-1912.
52—Renamed *Barbara C.*
53—Lost in San Pedro barbor on 6-19-1906.
54—Wrecked on Umpqua bar in 1923.
55—Capsized on Coquille River bar on 4-24-1915.
56—Renamed *John A.*
57—Dismanteled and laid up after the Coos Bay bridge was completed.
58—Burned 4 mi. south of Fox Rock on 8-24-1919.
59—Renamed *Katherine Donevan.*
60—Sold to a Philippine Company in 1946.
61—Lost on return trip from San Francisco to Cos Bay in 1875.
62—Renamed *Norco.*
63—Renamed *Pilot.*
64—Renamed *Yolande* (French)—Virginia Olson—Sierra.
65—Lost on Hunter Point on 5-25-1911.
66—Converted to 3m Sch.
67—Stranded near Myrtle Point on 1-11-1907.
68—Renamed *Flyer* and converted to Ols.

A large number of small boats were built on Coos Bay and Coquille rivers which were under 5 tons and ran as common carriers. These are a few that had names:

Steamers *Mink, Butcher Boy, Sierra, Nimrod.* Gasboats *Custon, Rose Bud, Central, Elk, North Bend* (renamed *Ivy Leif*), *Sumner, Trojan* (renamed *Hilda*), *Nira, Milly S., Swan, Monsoon, Pen-nel-o-py.*

During World War One, Coos Bay Shipbuilding Company in Marshfield and Kruse and Banks in North Bend launched 10 hulls each for the U. S. Shipping Board but only four were completed as steamers from the Marshfield shipyard and eight from Kruse & Banks.

During World War Two, Kruse & Banks built six Y.M. S. minesweepers and four A. T. R. tugs for the U. S. Navy, the last vessels of any size built on Coos Bay

Hillstrum Shipbuilding Company of North Bend built the tug *Klama* for the U. S. army engineers, several B. S. P's, L. T. tugs, and patrol boats for the U. S. army during World War Two,

Ship Captains

Captains on the small boats running on the Coquille River and Coos Bay, became as well known to the residents as the boats they commanded. A few captains who retired from the sea thinking they could stay from the water, found themselves back running small boats and happy doing it.

Young lads from the farms and towns with a longing for the sea, would start as deckhands or just by being a nuisance around the wharfs until someone asked for help. Before long they too would be engineers or captains.

On the smaller boats the captain was engineer and deckhand and sometimes the whole crew. When a vessel was owned by one person, he was usually captain; when owned by a group or company, the captain was hired and would change quite often from one boat to another. So it is impossible to get the names of all who were captains and all the boats they commanded, but this is an attempt to list the ones that were commonly known:

Captains Abbott, Lyman D. — gas boats *Transit, Bear* and *Bonita;* Anderson, Edward–tug *Triumph;* Anderson, John–gas boat *Randolph;* Anderson, R.–tug *Multnomah;* Anthony, James –steamers *Favorite* and *Welcome;* Assen, Edwin–steamer *Despatch;* Ashton, C. W.–gas boats *Moon* and *Cham;* Ashton, Rosa –gas boat *Star.*

Captains Bailey, S. S.–Steamer *Messenger;* Bash, John–tug *Klihyan* and coastwise steamers; Baumgartner, Clarence–gas boat *Maple;* Bertrand, J. M.–tug *Triumph;* Bester, J. A.–Steamer *Relief;* Bjorkholm, B. J.–gas boat *Roamer;* Bjorkquist, Wm.–gas boats *Hope, Wahtawaso* and *Marshfield;* Boye, F. L.–gas boats *Buffalo Bill* and *Bonita;* Boye, W. H. — gas boat *Tiger;* Bruce, Wm.–Steamers *Alpha, Escort* and *Comet;* Bumgartner, C. R. — gas boat *Moon;* Burns, E. B. — gas boat *Success;* Burrows, Chas.— Steamer *Relief;* Butler, C. H. — Steamers *Fearless* and *Liberty* and coastwise steamers; Butler, J. R.— gas boat *Tiger;* Butler, Parker — Steamer *Escort.*

Captains Cameron, Frank–gas boat *Rustler;* Campbell, A. J. M. — steamers *Mink* and *Coos;* Campbell, C. C. — steamers *Juno, Fawn, Comet* and *Mink;* Campbell, J. C. — steamers *Comet* and *Mink* and coastwise vessels; Carr, W. P. — gas boat *Telephone;* Carlson, Carl T. — gas boat *Maple;* Cassaday, H. N. –gas boat *Rogue;* Cassaday, W. M. — gas boat *Rustler;* Caughell, James — steamers *Mary D. Hume* and *Katie Cook* and coastwise steamers; Cavanaw, Milton, tugs *William Vaughn, Koos No. 3,* and other tugs; Christensen, Ludwig — steamers *E. P. Ripley, Powers* and *Klihyan* and gas boats *Wilhemina* and *C. M. Brewer;* Cherry, E. M –gas boat *Coast;* Clough. Wm. — steamers *Argo* and *Escort* on Coos Bay and coastwise and Puget Sound steamers; Colner, C. J. — gas boat *Minnie Mitchell;* Condon, J — gas boat *Shamrock;* Copeland, J. E. — tug *Triumph;* Cormbley Wardlow — steamer *Myrtle;* Cordes, R. C. — steamers *Bertha,* and *Coos River*; Cornwall, Neil — steamers *Juno, Eva, Hunter, Bismark, Gleaner, Antelope, Ceres* and *Dispatch;* Crone, Wm. W.— gas boat *Coaster;* Crough, Wallace — gas boat *Vega;* Crumley Wm. W. — steamers *Dora* and both *Myrtles;* Cutlan, L. — gas boat *C. M. Brewer.*

Captains Daley, D.—gas boat *Tiger;* Dann, G.—gas boat *Bonita* DeLong, N.—gas boat *Waikiki;* Donaldson, A.—tugs *Barclay Golden* and *Oregon;* Drane, F. E.—gas boats *Active, Diesel, May Sunset,* and *Samson;* Dunham, H. J.—steamers *Coos, Antelope Myrtle, Little Annie, Telegraph* and gas boat *Charm;* Dunham J. H. W.—steamers *Comet, Coos, Myrtle, Ceres, Mud Hen Montesano, Yarrow, Favorite* and *Telegraph;* Dunham, Robert steamers *Little Annie, Dispatch, Ceres, Antelope, Mud Hen,* and coastwise vessels; Dunham, Roy W.—tug *Hercules* and other tugs.

Edwards, Chas.—steamers *Antelope, Alert, Blanco, Juno, Little Annie, Liberty* and *Powers;* Edwards, C. O.—steamers *Coos River* and *Favorite;* Edwards, G. M. — steamer *Favorite;* Edwards, Herman—steamers *Alert, Liberty, Rainbow* and ferry *Roosevelt* Egdendorff, Wm.—tugs *Coos King, Alice H., Rustler* and *William Vaughn;* Ellingston, D.—gas boat *Moon;* Ellsworth, John C.— steamer *Satellite;* Elrod, W. F.—steamers *Cumtux, Express, Milton,* and *Katie Cook;* Erickson, John — steamers *Montesano Liberty, Juno* and tug *Astoria;* Ernest, Jacob—steamers *Messenger, Coos, Satellite, Yarrow, Butcher Boy, Blanco, Myrtle* and *Rita;* Exon, John W.—steamers *Myrtle* and *Telegraph.*

Captains Faster, H. G.—gas boat *Imperial;* Fulton, Herman— gas boat *Beaver;* Floyd, J. A.—steamer *Coos;* Floyd, Thomas— steamers *Satelite, Coos, Alpha* and tug *Katie Cook;* Frederick A. W.—tug *Vulcan;* Frederick, Robert—steamers *Dispatch, Alert* and *Restless;* Freelund, C. — tug *William Vaughn* and other tugs

Captains Galloway, Ned—gas boat *North Star;* Gibson, R. E.— gas boat *Owl;* Goodele, Thomas—gas boat *Curlew;* Goodman Cy—steamer *Relief;* Godfrey—gas boat *Banshee;* Graham, Carr— tug *Escort No.* 2; Graham, Dan—tug *Escort No.* 2; Graham, E D.—gas boat *Beaver;* Graham, Geo. C.—steamer *Juno;* Graham John—steamer *Juno* and ferries *Roosevelt* and *Oregon;* Graves S. F.—steamers *Little Annie* and *Satellite* and schooner *Rebecca,* Gray, C.—gas boat *Mecca;* Gray, E.—gas boat *Hope;* Guchee Martin—tug *Port of Bandon* and other coastwise tugs; Gunstab E. B.—tug *Cruiser;* Gunnell, Julius—gas boat *Union;* Gunnell Andrew—gas boat *Union.*

Captains Haggblom, J. E.—tug *Hunter;* Hall, A. J.—steamers

Little Annie, Cumtux, Alert, Coos and coastwise vessels; Hall, Chester—gas boat *Sunset;* Hall, J. T.—steamers *Coos, Myrtle, Restless, Yarrow, Little Annie, Cumux, Alert* and tugs *Escort, Fearless,* and *Sol Thomas Jr.;* Hammerberg, Wm.—steamer *Cordelia;* Hancock, Richard—gas boat *Maple;* Hancock, Wayne—gas boat *Beaver;* Harris, Clarence—gas boat *Sumner;* Harris, F. D.—gas boat *Owl;* Harrison, J. A.—gas boat *Eagle;* Harvey, L. P.—tug *Oregon* and bar pilot for oil companies; Haynes, J. W.—gas boat *Randolph;* Helborn, Oliver—steamer *Satellite;* Henderson, L. F. B.—steamer *Kate O'Neil;* Herman, A.—gas boat *Norma;* Herman, J. C.—gas boats *Imperial* and *Norma;* Hill, James—tugs *Fearless* and *Sol Thomas Jr.;* Holden, Dale—gas boats *C. M. Brewer, Pilot* and *Tiger;* Holden, David — gas boats *Transit, Pilot* and *Atomic;* Holland, C. T.—gas boat *Eagle;* Holland, Thomas—steamer *Myrtle;* Holm, A.—gas boat *Union;* Hufford, E. D.—steamers *Dora* and *Telegraph* and gas boat *Charm;* Hufford, Sherman—gas boat *Maple;* Hultin, Roy—gas boat *Beaver;* Hurd, A. F.—steamers *Coos, Mink* and coastwise vessels.

Captains Jacobsen, H.—gas boat *Randolph;* James, H. E.—steamers *Welcome* and *Echo;* Jensen, John—gas boat *Oshkosh;* Johanson, Nelson—steamer *Satellite* and *Coquille* and coastwise vessels; Johnson, A. P.—gas boat *Roamer;* Johnson, Charles—steamer *Yarrow* and coastwise vessels; Johnson, Erick — tugs *Fearless, Escort No.* 2 and coastwise tugs; Johnson, Gustaf—gas boat *Osprey;* Johnson, John—steamer *Liberty* and tugs *Triumph* and *Klihyan;* Johnson, Theo.—steamer *Satellite;* Jones, Robert—steamers *Butcher Boy, Milton, Alert, Bismarck, Yarrow* and tug Hunter; Kay, Wm.—gas boat *Wolverine;* Kernan, F. J.—gas boat *Joan Kernan;* Kiel, H. C.—gas boat *Union;* Kime, C. I.—steamer *Myrtle;* Knapp, Arthur—steamer *Rainbow;* Knutson, Louis—tugs *Koos No.* 2, *Koos No.* 4 and other tugs; Knutson, Harold—tugs *William Vaughn, Koos No.* 4 and other tugs.

Captains Laivo, Viktor—tug *Port of Bandon;* Lane, Nat Sr.—steamer *Messenger;* Lane, Nat Jr.—steamers *Messenger* and *Satellite;* Lanfare, Robert—steamers *Coos, Alpha, Satellite* and coastwise vessels; Lapp, John—gas boat *Turtle;* Lawson, Robert J.—tugs *Fearless, Astoria* and several of Simpson vessels; Leach, Henry—gas boat *Tiger;* Lee, Alva—steamers *Dispatch, Bismarck, Coquille, Telegraph* and ferries *Transit* and *Roosevelt;* Leneve, Geo.—steamers *Antelope, Myrtle, Little Annie, Alert, Favorite, Fawn* and gas boat *Charm;* Leneve, J.—steamer *Myrl;* Lenlton, Raymond—gas boat *Standard;* Lichtwerk, Chas.—steamers *Bertha, Express* and *Yarrow;* Lightner, J. K.—steamers *Yarrow, Myrtle, Milton* and *Antelope;* Lockwood, J. H. B.—steamers *Comet* and *Antelope;* Loughlad, G. B.—steamer *Reta;* Luse, H. H.—steamers

Alpha; Luse, Wm. H. – steamers *Alpha, Satellite* and *Coos;* Lyster, Richard – gas boat *Buffalo Bill;* Lyster, L.–gas boat *Buffalo Bill.*

Captains Magee, James – tugs *Escort, Fearless, Columbia, Hunter* and coastwise vessels; Magee, W. A.–tug *Astoria* and coastwise vessels; Mall, J. T.–steamer *Montesano;* Malstrom, Elmer E.–gas boat *Maple;* Marie, J. P.–steamer *Myrtle;* Masters, Andrew–gas boats *Mary Ann* and *Telephone;* Masters, Chas.–gas boat *Rose Bud;* Masters, Chas.–gas boat *Rose Bud;* Masters, John A.–gas boat *Mary Ann;* Masters, Leonard–gas boat *Curlew;* Mathews, H. A.–tug *Columbia* and gas boat *Hulda;* McAllett, J. W.–tug *Columbia;* McClintock, W.–tug *Cruiser;* McCormick, Wm.–gas boat *Dixie;* McCloskey, F. W.–gas boat *Pastime;* McCloskey, J. W.–gas boat *Big Chief,* steamers *Welcome, Echo* and *Telegraph;* McCloskey, T.M.–steamers *Myrl* and *Reta;* McCue, Chs. steamer *Dora* and gas boat *Star;* McCue, Elmer–steamers *Maple* and *Relief;* McGrath, Frank–tug *Oregon;* McLeod, Don–gas boat *Beaver;* McNelly, Ralph W.–tug *Oregon;* Medahis, Julius –gas boat *Rogue River;* Miller, Alonso B.–tugs *Rustler* and *Coos King;* Miller, J. C. steamers *Echo, Enterprise, Coquille* and *Favorite;* Moomaw, John – steamers *Favorite, Liberty* and *Coquille;* Moon, C. A.–gas boat *Roamer;* Moore, F. R.–gas boat *Mecca;* Moran, M.– tug *Cruiser;* Morgan, M.– tug *Cruiser;* Morgan, Wm.–gas boat *Marshfield;* Morris, E.–gas boat *Tiger;* Morris, F.–gas boats *Active* and *Billy Moore;* Morris, Harold– gas boat *Billy Moore;* Myers, J. L.–steamer *Coquille;* Myres, John E.–steamers *Dora, Echo, Myrtle, Relief, Welcome* and gas boat *Charm.*

Captains Nabb, J.–gas boat *North Star;* Neil, L. E.–gas boat *Eagle;* Nelson, Julius–gas boat *Messenger;* Nelson, Chas.–gas boats *Beaver* and *Atomic;* Nelson, Fred L.–gas boats *Beaver* and *Atomic;* Nelson, Nels P.–steamer *Myrtle;* Nelson, H. C.–steamer *Pedler;* Noa, Wm.–gas boat *Alice H.*

Captains O'Kelly, J. A.–gas boats *North Bend* and *Marshfield;* Olson, R. H.–gas boat *Empire;* Olson, Peter–gas boats *Rustler* and *Roamer;* Olsson, B. W.–coastwise vessels and bar pilot; Ott, H.–gas boats *Coos River, Hope, Mecca, Mary Ann* and *Welcome;* Ott, J. J.–gas boat *Mecca, Coos River, Millicoma* and *Welcome.*

Captains Painter, C. A.–steamer *Flyer;* Panter, Albert, steamers *Dora* and *Telegraph;* Panter, Allen R.–steamers *Dora, Myrtle, Telegraph* and gas boat *Charm;* Panter, F. W.–steamer *Dispatch;* Panter, S. O.–steamers *Coquille, Dora, Myrtle, Telegraph* and gas boat *Charm;* Panter, W. R.–steamers *Dispatch, Liberty, Echo, Myrtle, Dora* and *Telegraph;* Panter, T. W. – steamers *Dora,*

Telegraph, Myrtle and gas boat *Charm;* Parker, Judah—tugs *Katie Cook, Triumph* and coastwise vessels; Pendergrass, M. P.—steamers *Comet, Liberty* and *Flyer;* Pepper, G.—gas boat *May;* Perkins, D. L.—steamers *Coquille* and *Relief;* Peter, Louis B.—gas boat *Owl;* Peterson, Emil R. gas boat *North Bend;* Philips, Percy—gas boats *Banshee* and *Zebra;* Philpot, Wm. H.—gas boat *Hope;* Provorse, John—gas boat *Rambler;* Peterson, Peter — gas boats *Mayflower* and *Vega.*

Captains Rackleff, Wm. E.—steamers *Mary, Cordelia, Little Annie, Myrtle* and coastwise vessels; Randaman, M.—gas boat *Norma;* Reed, J. C.—tugs *Cruiser, Traveler* and other tugs; Reed, Ol—steamers *Ceres, Antelope* and *Dispatch;* Reed, Ed—steamers *Ceres;* Roberts, C. M.—gas boats *Bonita* and *Valcum;* Roberts, Daniel—steamers *Coos, Satellite, Juno, Yarrow, Coquille,* and *Coquille;* Roberts, M.—steamers *Comet, Blanco* and *Montesano;* Rodgers, S. C.—steamers *Butcher Boy, Alma, Coos River* and *Express;* Russell, Chas.—steamer *Reta* and gas boat *Diesel;* Russell, Walter—gas boats *Hope, Welcome, Vega* and steamer *Reta;* Rydquist, Moris—gas boat *Atomic.*

Captains Safley, W. H.—gas boat *Bear;* Safler, D. G.—gas boat *Roamer;* Sadine, A. R.—gas boats *Vega, Ivy Leaf* and *Telephone;* Savage, N.—gas boat *Mecca;* Sckoltens, Ben—steamer *Juno;* Silen, Ben—gas boat *Telephone;* Skible, Max—steamers *Cruiser* and *Powers;* Skog, Ed. L.—gas boats *C. M. Brewer* and coastwise vessels and bar pilot; Smith, A.—gas boat *Gasgo;* Smith, E. G.—steamer *Rainbow* and gas boat *Vulcan;* Smith, Norman—tugs *Alice H.* and *William Vaughn;* Smith, Ralph—tug *Alice H.;* Smith, Thos. F.—steamer *Rainbow;* Snyder, J. H.—steamers *Little Annie* and *Myrtle;* Snyder, Percy—tug *Klihyan;* Snyder, Levi—steamers *Little Annie, Triumph, Liberty, Ceres, Katie Cook, Myrtle, Favorite,* gas boat *Roamer* and coastwise vessels; Spooner, Chas. — gas boat *Mary Ann;* Sprague, Ed — tugs *William Vaughn, Queen* and other tugs; Sproull, A. M.—tug *Cruiser;* Stancup, B.—gas boat *Banshee;* Stevens, Victor—gas boat *Active;* Stout, Earl—gas boat *Hulda;* Stanbuck, Andrew—gas boats *Mary Ann* and *Union;* Swing, John—gas boat *Ranger* and other gas boats.

Captains Tanner, J. W.—gas boat *Minnie Mitchell;* Thompson, Ed — steamer *Katie O'Neil;* Toller, W. R.— gas boat *Maple;* Toozer, Ted—gas boat *Tiger.*

Captains Vancamp, B.—gas boat *Turtle;* Vancamp, W. M.—steamer *Rainbow;* Vellenga, Chas.—tug *Cruiser.*

Captains Wade, Henry—steamers *Restless, Dispatch, Juno,* and *Argo;* Walker, Harry — gas boat *Banshee;* Wallace, David — steamers *Coos, Alpha* and coastwise vessels; Ward, Paris—gas boat *Maple;* Wathrop, O.—gas boat *Multnomah;* Webb, F. A.—gas boat—*Union;* Wenterdale, G.—steamer *Juno;* Wirth, Louis—gas boat *Hercules;* Wirth, M. M.—gas boat *Multnomah;* White, Thos.—steamers *Coos, Yarrow,* both *Dispatches, Favorite, John Widdi* and ferries *Roosevelt* and *Oregon;* Wheeler, W. S.—tug *Traveler;* Willard, A.—tug *William Vaughn;* Willard, E. E.—tug *William Vaughn;* Willard, O. R.—steamers *Welcome, Favorite, Liberty,* and gas boat *Charm;* Willborn, Oliver—steamer *Alpha;* Wilson, Chas.—steamers *Relief* and *Dora;* Woodard, C. H.—gas boats *Diesel* and *Express* and steamer *Favorite;* Wittick, Victor—gas boats *Sparrow* and *Victor;* Wittick, Geo.—gas boat *Vega.*

Captains Yeager, H. H.—steamer *Antelope;* and Yonkers, Joe gas boat *North Star.*

33

Forests, Timber, Lumbering

VERY LITTLE SAWED TIMBER was used in the first few pioneer years in Coos and Curry. In the early 1850's some building lumber came in by ship from San Francisco or from the Columbia River.

The first Coos lumber was whip-sawed, the "mill" being operated by two men, one at each end of a saw. Onto a platform built over a pit, the log was rolled. One man above and the other below sawed up and down till a board was ripped off.

When Daniel Giles, aged 17, came by way of Scottsburg and the ocean beach to a point on the west side of Coos Bay near the end of October of 1853, he looked across the bay to Empire City to see "a small new house on high ground. It was made of white cedar and showed very plain."

Giles swam his fine white saddle horse across to Empire City and then headed for Randolph to join the black sand miners. Securing a claim, he needed lumber for sluice boxes. At the "sawmill" he found so many orders ahead of his that he would have to wait at least two weeks. But he was offered a job at $4 a day. So he went to work at one end of a whip-saw:

> I soon got onto the thing. Being young and stout, I stayed with it for a while and when I wanted to quit and go to mining, they insisted on me taking a third interest in the business. We sawed all winter . . . made near $20 a day each.

Giles' lumbering partners were James Fitzgerald and a man named Hall. Orvil Dodge, in reporting it, commented, "This was no doubt the first lumber enterprise started in Coos County."

The first real sawmill was started in 1854 at Port Orford. An unpublished manuscript, apparently by Frank B. Tichenor, says:

The first sawmill arrived at Port Orford on the steamer Sandiego in 1854. The proprietors were Neefus and Tichenor. The mill was later moved to just south of the road turning in to the Knapp ranch. Eighteen days after the Sandiego unloaded the machinery, the mill was in operation.

The mill employed 25 men and had a capacity of 5000 board feet per day; the lumber was loaded on vessels by lighters and brought $125 per thousand board feet in San Francisco. William S. Winsor, the mechanical manager, was among those to prepare this first shipment to the market. He gave it the name of Port Orford cedar.

Walling in 1884 reported that lumber was shipped by three mills in Curry County, two of them located near Port Orford, "namely the Elk Creek mill of Joseph Nay, and the Hubbard Creek mill located a mile south of town. The latter's capacity is 17,000 feet per day."

The Stacy-Fundy-Wasson mill appears to have been the first power-operated sawmill in Coos County, at a date not definitely established. The story of this mill was told by George B. Wasson substantially as follows:

The first sawmill in Coos County was built by Stacy, Fundy and Wasson a short distance north of the Coquille River near the present site of the Bullards Ferry. The date was thought to have been 1853. (It may have been a year later). It had an upright saw known as a Muley sash saw; powered by an under-shot flutter water wheel. Logs were hauled to the mill by George Wasson with his six-ox team, said to have been the first team of its kind in Coos County.

Edward Fahy bought the mill from the original owners and operated it for many years. He rebuilt it two or three different times, putting in an overshot wheel, remains of which yet stand in the original site, where the son, Charles Fahy still resides.

It was in the 1850's also that the building of sawmills was begun on Coos Bay. Perhaps it was in 1854, but more likely in 1855 when actual construction was started at Empire by H. H. Luse and at North Bend by A. M. Simpson. A son of H. H. Luse, W. A. (Bill) Luse, was in charge of his father's mill. His widow, still residing on Coos River, recalls that a race was on between the Luse mill at Empire and the Simpson mill at North

Bend to see which would be first to make a shipment out of Coos County. Simpson might have won had the machinery not been delayed by the wrecking of the schooner *Quadratus* just after it had passed over the Coos Bay bar. Simpson reportedly made his first shipment to San Francisco in 1858; Luse in 1857.

The first shipment out of the Coquille River was in 1861 according to Edward Fahy, as quoted by Dodge:

> John Hamblock, W. D. L. F. Smith and I took a contract to saw white cedar for exportation and before finishing said contract the two former partners withdrew and I shipped the cargo on my own account, on the Florence E. Walton . . . This was the first cargo of lumber shipped from the Coquille River.

An early—perhaps the first—*steam* sawmill on the Coquille was brought by the Dr. Henry Hermann Colony from Baltimore in 1859. Dodge says:

> Among the goods was a 54-inch portable sawmill belonging to Henry Schroeder, Sr., and an eight horse-power boiler and engine and a pair of 24-inch mill burrs belonging to Wm. Volkmar . . . The mill was put up on the South Fork and was operated for several years, Wm. Volkmar filling the position of engineer and Henry J. Schroeder that of sawyer and miller.

A mill of considerable capacity was constructed on the north bank of the Coquille about a mile east of Parkersburg. According to George Bennett, its first board was sawed on the seventh day of May, 1868 by J. Henry Schroeder. The first cargo was bought and shipped by Captain William Tichenor in the schooner *Alaska* to San Francisco. The mill was located on the farm of Judge J. D. Lowe, whose son, Frank Lowe, still resides in Marshfield. Frank, a small boy growing up while the mill was still in operation, recalls those days very vividly. The mill, he says, had an undershot wheel. Later this was replaced by a very large overshot wheel. Frank's recollections tell him that it was about 40 feet in diameter.

A. M. Simpson

Perhaps no other individual on the Pacific Coast was

better known in his time in the lumbering industry than was Captain A. M. Simpson.

From the start Simpson saw that ships were necessary to reach the markets of the world. Up to this time saw mill operators had mainly depended on the San Francisco market, about which Rodney Glisan, in his *Journal of Army Life,* wrote at Port Orford in 1855:

> Sawmilling is another example of our speculation. From 1847 to 1852 there was great demand for lumber, especially in San Francisco . . . Its supply had in the meantime increased about twenty-fold, as a large number of persons had been induced by enormous prices of $200 to $600 per thousand feet, to erect sawmills; it is now a drug on the market.

But Simpson was not dismayed. In the years that followed, with his ever-growing fleet of vessels, he reached the world markets.

Charles H. Merchant, becoming general superintendent at North Bend in 1860, continued for 13 years, until he went to Marshfield in 1873 to join E. B. Dean & Company.

Another of Simpson's key men was John Kruse, who at North Bend about 1867 joined Simpson as master shipbuilder, a title which he still retained when in 1875 he succeeded Merchant as general superintendent. Some 25 ships are credited to John Kruse during his 30 years at North Bend. At his death in 1896 his son, John W. Kruse, became superintendent.

In 1899 general management of the Simpson properties was taken over by Simpson's eldest son, Louis J. Simpson, then 24 years of age and bringing with him a life of vigor and plenty of ambition. The Porter mill, built in the 1880's about midway between North Bend and Marshfield, had been idle for some years. Young Simpson acquired the properties and put the mill into operation at a capacity of 80,000 per ten-hour day. Later it was sold to the Buehner Lumber Company, who rebuilt the plant and still further increased its capacity.

Oakland Company

About a mile south of the Porter mill, the Oakland Box and Stave Manufacturing Company built a mill, commonly referred to as the Stave Mill, with a rated capacity of 25,000 to 30,000 feet of lumber, 10,000 box shooks, and 15,000 keg and barrel staves per day.

Pershbaker Mill

The Pershbaker Mill at Marshfield was inaugurated by John Pershbaker and associates in 1867.

He immediately began to build ships and opened a store, with his brother Charles in charge. After five or six years of more or less success, the property was taken over by E. B. Dean & Company. It was abandoned at Marshfield in 1885 to be replaced by a new mill at Bay City on the east bank of Isthmus Inlet, present site of the McKenna mill. Store and offices remained in Marshfield on the waterfront. Old residents still have a clear recollection of the store and its manager, Charles H. Merchant.

Under Merchant's management the new mill prospered until he withdrew in 1891. Five years later, in the beginning of 1896, the company was facing financial difficulties. One partner had died; hard times of the 1890's were presenting their problems. Affairs were placed in a receivership with Charles H. Merchant as receiver for many years.

C. A. Smith Lumber Company

Charles A. Smith dreamed of a great industrial organization based upon timber tributary to Coos Bay.

In 1907 the C. A. Smith Lumber and Manufacturing Company, having acquired the old E. B. Dean & Company mill on the east side of Isthmus Inlet, began operating it to make lumber for a big new mill on the west side of the inlet, opposite the old mill. The new one, planned to be as modern and up-to-date as experience and ingenuity could make it, began turning out lumber in 1908 at a rated capacity of approximately 300,000 board feet a day.

As the area had no rail connection with outside markets, Smith acquired California property on a branch of San Francisco Bay, about 40 miles northeast from San Francisco. Bay Point was the name given to the place. It was set up as the distributing center for the Marshfield mill with lumber yards, planing mill, box factory, and other facilities for finishing and distribution.

Rail connections afforded contact with all inland markets; ocean ships could load at Bay Point and sail to any or all parts of the world; barges would carry cargoes to various retail yards on San Francisco bay and its tributaries; trucks would haul lumber to the inland markets of California.

For transporting the lumber from the Marshfield mill to Bay Point, ships were designed and built with a view to easy and quick loading and unloading, to carry a cargo of about two million board feet, with a draft shallow enough to enter and leave Coos Bay unhampered by having to wait for tides. The round trip, including loading and unloading was made in six days or less.

The company owned large tracts of timber tributary to Coos Bay. For getting this to the mill, a subsidiary company was organized, known as the Smith-Powers Logging Company, with C. A. Smith president and A. H. Powers vice president and general manager.

The first five-year output of logs of the Smith-Powers Company has been reported as follows:

1907	25,000,000
1908	65,000,000
1909	85,000,000
1910	100,000,000
1911 (estimated)	150,000,000

The logging company operated seven camps, all in Coos County; used 43 steam donkey engines in handling the logs. In several cases, the logs were transported on railroads to the nearest streams, where they were rafted and towed to the mill booms.

Douglas fir made up the bulk of the company's Coos Bay holdings, but it also contained considerable stands of Port Orford cedar, some western red cedar, western hemlock and some large stands of Sitka spruce. Of the latter there seemed to be a surplus; more in proportion to the other types than the market would consume readily. A limited amount, especially the choicest logs, made excellent plywood for airplane construction and for other building purposes. It also made first class pulp stock.

Pulp making requires large quantities of water, a factor that was not readily available at the Smith mills at Marshfield. Two brothers from Finland, Hjalpe and Rolf Nerdrum, reported to Mr. Smith that they had a process by which he could make pulp by using salt water from the bay. A setup, represented an investment of several million dollars started operations and several shipments of pulp were made. Unforseen difficulties arose, due principally to the variation of the salt in the tide water. It varied according to season, being saltier in summer than in winter. It varied also between high tide and low tide. It was additionally affected by heavy rainfall and by dry spells. Those "bugs" might have been ironed out in time, but they were complicated by other difficulties. World War One came on; financial problems were encountered. Pulp making was wiped off as a bad investment.

The *American Lumberman,* in 1911 reported all was going well with the Smith Lumber and Manufacturing Company and its affiliates, but during the next ten years or so markets were cut off by World War One. Shipments were interrupted. Large investments had been financed by bond issues bearing interest as high as eight percent. Taxes were increasing; fixed operating and maintenance costs piled up.

With the general slump in the lumber markets, inventories of lumber and logs accumulated. Trees already cut in the camps had to be moved to water, where the booms were filled to their capacity. Yards were overstocked with millions of feet of lumber. In a desperate attempt to meet accumulating obligations, the company dumped its finished products on the market at prices below cost, causing further gluts and continued depression in the business.

The company's holdings were placed in the hands of receivers. A new company was formed, the Pacific States Lumber Company. New bonds were issued in the early 1920's. A. H. Paulson, treasurer, called 1924 "the worst in the history of the company." Net operating loss that year was reported to have been over $800,000. Following the debacle of the 1920's, a new company was formed to take over the holdings of the old organizations. C. A. Smith had died in 1925.

The Coos Bay Lumber Company became successors to the holdings and operations of the old C. A. Smith Company and the Pacific States Lumber Company. The story is too long and too complicated to be included here. However, it is too important in the annals of the great industry of lumbering in this area to be omitted. This new company has prospered. According to the 1950-1951 tax roll it headed the list of all taxpayers in Coos and Curry counties. Operations are centered around the headquarters at Coos Bay, with large timber holdings in different sections of Coos and Curry counties. It has four distinct plants:

1. The original large mill of the C. A. Smith Lumber and Manufacturing Company, modernized; capacity, approximately 325,000 board feet per 8-hour shift.

2. On the same grounds, a hardboard manufacturing plant to utilize the slabwood waste, put into operation in 1951 with a capacity of 150 tons per day.

3. The Millington saw mill, about two miles east of the big mill, reached by rail, water and truck; capacity, 100,000 board feet a day

4. The Coquille plant (former Smith Wood Products) manufactures lumber, plywood, battery separators, venetian blinds, doors. Capacity – lumber, 50,000 board feet; plywood, 250,000 square feet; battery separators, 2,000,000 pieces; venetian blinds, 10,000; doors, 1000.

Coos Bay Logging Company

The following story is based largely on a report in a special 1942 number of the *Coos Bay Times.* Revisions and changes have been made to bring it up to date, by contact with the persons concerned, including Bill Vaughan himself:

Whenever any group of loggers or logging operators meet anywhere in the Northwest, sooner or later the name of William "Bill" Vaughan, head of the Coos Bay Logging Company, is bound to be mentioned.

A Coos Bay resident since March, 1900, he came here fresh from business college as a bookkeeper for the Simpson Lumber Company in North Bend.

Vaughan's history is a half century of the history of Coos County logging. From the time he became associated with Jack McDonald, he has adapted logging equipment to meet natural progress of the business and the many handicaps to taking big logs from among natural resisting barriers.

One of Vaughan's best-remembered and most noteworthy feats was the logging of Blue Ridge by way of Daniels Creek. The Simpson Lumber Company had built a railroad up Daniels Creek to the base of the mountains just after the turn of the century. McDonald & Vaughn extended this road up the steep mountainsides along the ridge, hauling logs to a sturdy lowering machine. This was a huge donkey with a special brake. Here the loaded cars were lowered a full mile at the end of a thick cable down a grade of 30 to 38 per cent. Another locomotive took over at the base, hauling the logs to the river.

The spool donkey and the white horse, came in 1905, when McDonald & Vaughan started work on the north fork of the Coquille. The spool donkey hauled the logs to the loading platform, and the white horse took the line back into the woods for another log. (The horse has been dead many years, but the donkey is preserved as an exhibit at the pioneer museum of the Coos-Curry Pioneer and Historical Association in Coquille. In 1950 the donkey was overhauled, put into operating condition, delivered at the museum and presented to the Association by Mr. Vaughan.)

In 1907 McDonald & Vaughan moved over to Daniels Creek and logged that area until 1916. During that time they rode herd on a hard-fighting band of loggers known as the *Blue Ridge Tigers.* These doughty lads had their own baseball team — complete with fancy uniforms — and were a tough outfit to lick in any kind of competition. The loggers came to Marshfield twice a year with their pay in twenty-dollar gold pieces and proceeded to make their presence known in no uncertain fashion.

In 1915, the firm opened a camp at Lakeside that continued to operate until 1922. They had another camp at Beaver Hill from 1916 to 1918. They operated the one at Tarheel south of Empire from 1918 till 1922.

About 1920, Jack McDonald died, when the business was taken over by the newly formed Coos Bay Logging Company, headed by William Vaughan and associated with L. J. Simpson and Charles S. Winsor. This company took over the old Simpson mill at North Bend — the same mill where Vaughan began as bookkeeper twenty years earlier.

In 1944 a new organization was formed to take over the operation by lease from the owners, Vaughan and Ben R. Chandler, who had become associated with him. This operating company is still doing business under the name of Coos Bay Logging Company.

Moore Mill at Bandon

The Moore Mill operations in Coos County had their beginning in a logging venture on Lampa Creek by L. J. Cody about the year 1900. Mr. Cody had been in partnership with Geo. W. Moore in a pine logging enterprise in Michigan.

In the late 1890's Cody bought and began logging the extensive Coach tract on Lampa Creek, building a railroad to transport the logs to the Coquille River. At first, Cody sold his logs to different small mills. In 1906, his former partner, George W. Moore, joined him in building a mill at Bandon. Three years later the mill was totally destroyed by fire. The company was then reorganized into the Geo. W. Moore Lumber Company. The present plant was built and placed in operation in 1910. Cody retired in 1912; his interest was purchased by Moore.

When the Lampa Creek operations were completed in 1916, logging headquarters were moved to the Klondike Mine site southwest of Beaver Hill. A new railroad was built from riverbank to the woods, and logging was commenced on the Boutin tract — predominantly of spruce, enabling the company to be a chief supplier of air plane spruce during World War One.

To get through the severe 1930's, the company secured the very able help of W. J. Sweet, a local financier, and of D. H. Miller Sr., a lumber operator of wide experience. In 1942 a majority interest was obtained in the Cape Arago Lumber Company at Empire, a connection which provided participation in offshore lumber markets. In 1945 the majority interest was sold to Mr. Sweet and Mr. Miller, with Ralph T. Moore retaining his personal holding. Mr. Miller shortly purchased the Sweet interest. The company at present is one of the largest fir operations.

Smith Wood Products

The Smith Wood Products, Inc., came to Coos in 1928 when they bought out the Oerding Manufacturing Company at Coquille and established a modern factory on a 17-acre tract at the edge of the city.

Ralph L. Smith and George A. Ulett, respectively president and general manager, had been making separators at Kansas City. They had obtained some small shipments of Port Orford cedar and found this tree to be superior to any that they had tried.

At Coquille the company developed one of the largest plants in the world for making battery separators, venetian blinds, boxes, and other products. In 1945 its holdings were sold to the Coos Bay Lumber Company.

Said James L. Hall, well-known San Francisco wholesale lumber dealer:

> George A. Ulett believed and successfully demonstrated that good plywood could be made from the second-growth hard Douglas fir timbers of this area. Since then many plywood plants have been erected in Coos and Curry counties.
>
> Mr. Ulett also had a large part in showing world markets the unique and unsurpassed qualities of the Coos and Curry Port Orford cedar, proving the value of that wonderful wood for such uses as battery separators, venetian blinds, boat planking, outdoor seating of stadiums, bleachers, grandstands, and parks.

Perhaps the most progressive stride in the Coos-Curry lumber industry has been the entry into this field of the Weyerhaeuser Lumber Company.

With a dozen tree farms and eight operating centers in Oregon and Washington, North Bend was added in 1951. The big plant at North Bend is being supplied with logs from the 205,000-acre Millicoma Tree Farm, described as follows:

> Legend has it that many years ago, before the white man lived on Coos Bay, an Indian chief named Millicoma lived with his tribe at about the present-day site of Allegany. Hence the name for this tree farm . . .

Before trees could be harvested . . . truck roads had to be pushed deep into the forests through fourteen miles of sheer rock cliffs and steep hillsides. A headquarters camp and log dump were built at Allegany, on the Millicoma River, where the logs are rafted and towed twenty miles to the mill at North Bend.

> The birth of the North Bend plant marks another milestone in the company's program of gearing the production capacity of its plants to the growth cycle of its related tree farms and obtaining maximum utilization of the timber crop.

The 1950 report indicates that the supply of logs during the next 30 years will come largely from old-growth timber, with a gradually increased amount taken from new growth. Beginning with about 1980, the yield from old-growth will diminish rapidly and the yield from new growth will be proportionately increased.

An important trend is to avoid the use of public highways for heavy loads of logs and lumber. Weyerhaeuser is fortunate in having its large tree farm so situated that its logs are hauled on its own privately hardsurfaced highways to the Millicoma River, where they are rafted and towed to the mill at North Bend. From the mill, all lumber and other products are shipped by water or by rail.

The splash-dam has long been considered a necessary evil in getting logs from remote areas down non-navigable streams to deep water, where they could be rafted and towed to the mills. This is destructive to fish propagation and damages farm lands. The Weyerhaeuser Company is prohibiting all splash-dam practice within its jurisdiction.

Coos Bay Pulp Corporation at Empire

The Scott Paper Company acquired the Coos Bay Pulp Corporation's mill at Empire in June of 1940.

The Empire mill is devoted entirely to the manufacture of unbleached sulphite pulp. Approximately 70 tons are turned out daily, for use in the manufacture of high quality tissue and towels at the company's large mill in Pennsylvania.

The fine stands of timber in the area provide the spruce, white fir, and hemlock which go into the manufacture of the pulp. The logs come in from the operations of a multitude of independent loggers, some as far distant as 100 miles, as well as from some fine stands of timber owned by the company. As the only pulp mill on the southwest coast of Oregon, it has become the natural user of the pulpwood species not normally used by the sawmills.

It employs directly 165 persons, and supports several hundred others engaged in the logging, transporting and other supporting activities. As a part of the pulp mill property, a sawmill is operated by the Coos Head Timber Company, which turns out approximately 140,000 feet of lumber daily, and a like amount of timber for use in the manufacture of pulp. This provides employment for another 100 persons. The pulp mill has operated steadily for the past 12 years.

Shipments of lumber and other forest products out of Coos and Curry during 1950 are estimated as follows:

Southern Pacific rail shipments, approximately	345,000,000 BF
Ship cargoes by Independent Stevedores Company	485,201,480 BF
Moore-Oregon Lumber Company reports	50,000,000 BF
Total	880,201,480 BF

Estimate of shipments by truck and trailer are not available, but it is known that millions of board feet in peeler logs and green veneer are trucked out, especially from Curry County.

Pulp shipments in 1950 totaled 23,290 tons. Battery separators and miscellaneous items such as broom handles, venetian blind stock and stitched crate material, made up several thousand car loads.

A forest product practically overlooked accounts for many car loads — evergreens — consisting of huckleberry, salal, cedar boughs, ferns, and such medicinal products as cascara bark, Oregon grape-root, and digitalis or foxglove.

A careful estimate of all forest items produced in Coos and Curry during 1950, places the figure at approximately one billion board feet.

34

Fish and Fishing

SAID WALLING, "A. F. Myers established a fishery at Ellensburg in 1857 for the purpose of taking, salting and barreling salmon." According to Dodge, John Flanagan in 1860 did the first commercial fishing on the Coquille River. Just when commercial fishing began on Coos Bay seems not to be definitely known; early fishermen included Harry Graves, George Wolff, and Charles Eckhoff.

At the mouth of Rogue River, R. D. Hume began canning salmon in 1876, buying out Riley & Stewart who had started a fishery in the 1860's or early 1870's. The first Coquille River salmon cannery was started in 1883. The new processing of the big fish began on Coos Bay some time in the 1880's — the first was on lower Coos River, the second at Empire, the third in the late 1890's in Marshfield.

The crab as a commercial fish had a very humble beginning. Charles Stauff, when a boy in Empire in the 1880's, gathered and cooked ten dozen every Saturday for the Tim Hayes Saloon, as told by his daughter in the chapter on towns.

In the early days there were the big Empire clams but none in the upper bay. Until later years shad was used as crab bait. Albecore are recent. Striped bass first appeared in Coos Bay in 1914, as told in the wild life chapter.

In the 1930's pilchard fishing had a flare up and several receiving and reduction plants were built at North Bend. But the industry died as rapidly as it had mushroomed up. Shark fishing also had its spree for a few years around 1940.

Other fish contributed to the food supply locally since the first coming of the whites, including smelt, herring, flounders, perch, tom cod, and others.

Said R. D. Hume, for 30 years salmon fishing king on Rogue River:

> Salmon were more plentiful before civilization had begun its work, and when dams, traps and other obstructions and hydraulic mines were unknown; when the sources of the rivers were unsettled and undefied by the sewerage of the cities, the forests of the headquarters still untouched by man, and the country yet in its natural state.

(One gathers from this that everything would have been just swell if men hadn't mined or lumbered or settled; if the great river continued to flow through a primitive land with hordes of salmon coming in and with just R. D. Hume there to can them. The people who ate them lived somewhere else anyway.)

In the early 1850's, when the whites came first to the Rogue, the settlers reported difficulty in getting their horses to ford the stream because it "was alive with the finny tribe."

Sometime in the late 1860's Captain Caughill sailed the schooner *Newton Booth* into the Rogue to find a great surplus of salmon — many more than the established fishery could handle. Salt was available but Captain Caughill was unable to obtain barrels. He salted the salmon in the hold of his ship and sailed to San Francisco. Reports don't say whether his venture was a success or not, but at least he had ballast in his ship for the run south.

Also in the late 1860's, Riley & Stewart established a fishery at the present site of the Rogue River bridge. Seines were used for catching the salmon; at times the fish were so numerous that the net had to be lifted to let some escape before the haul could be landed.

R. D. Hume, after buying this fishery in 1876, built his first cannery a short distance down the river. Three or four years later, realizing the necessity of replenishing the supply of fish, he built a small hatchery on Indian Creek, about a mile up the river from his cannery. After

FISHING

ɔquille River Fishermen's Co-
e Cannery. Started in 1908
rated for six seasons. Sold in
the Coquille Cannery Com-
ɔonsored by R. L. Macleay and
Kerr of Portland, who ran it
ıes were prohibited on the
River. Center: Chinook sal-
m a drawing by Quincy Scott.
Seiners in the Coquille River
ber 7, 1898, when the salmon
ll remained heavy from the
early days which caused an
to exclaim, "Begorra, sir,
ly ought to catch them."

Loaned by Binfords & Mort

Coos-Curry Pioneer M

Above: Original rolling stock of the line, from a daguerreotype taken in 1870. Gilbert Hall, thought to have been the builder, is in dark clothes. The center man was named Lockhart. The names of the Indian mule driver and the girl passenger, are unknown.
Below: About 1874 it was bought by Bill Utter, who powered it with a little steam engine for pulling coal cars from Coaledo to Utter City. In 1880 J. F. Dunham took it over to haul logs from the top of the hill to Isthmus Slough, but he also carried freight and passengers. By 1890 it was acquired by R. A. Graham; he used part of the old road bed for the railroad to Coquille and Myrtle Point. See the Transportation Chapter.

ISTHMUS RAIL

Loaned by Mrs. James G. Maple, Empire

Above: Beaver Hill coal bunkers

Right: Newport coal train

Below: Beaver Hill, from a photograph by Ernest A. Stauft, Arago

Loaned by Mrs. Jessie J. Ott, Allegany

Pioneer Museum

Loaned by Emil Peterson

Loaned by J. E.

LOGGING

Top: Two logging teams, about 1900. Above: Largest ox team in Coos County, owned by G. Pike. Time of the picture 1907. The camp was on Fat Elk Creek across the valley fro Coquille. From left to right — G. E. Pike, Mike Boone, Ash Doyle. Below: Bull tea activity at Coaledo in 1886.

Coos Curry Pioneer Museu

GGING

Coos River
probably Wm.
, in 1889.

Sheriff W.W.
hoeing
His two
not identified.

Mr. Florence Ott, Allegany

CRANBERRIES

Above: C. D. McFarlin, pioneer grower of Coos County planting its first b[illegible] in 1885. Wild vines were obtained by him from a natural bog in Massachuse[illegible] in 1875, becoming under cultivation the largest variety known. "This berry he said, "took my name, and is known all over the United States as the McFarl[illegible] Berry." Below: Cranberry pickers, mostly Indians, at Fraser's Marsh, 1910.

Loaned by Emil R. Pete

ILDING

uilding the
David Evans at
in 1901. Below:
g crew at Coos
and ship not

Coos-Curry Pioneer Museum

Loaned by Mrs. Alva

Above: Three schooners at Dean & Company Mill at Bay City on Isthmus Inlet about 1900. The first schooner is the *Western Home*. Photo by Ernest Stauff. Below: Stages on the Beach Route. Asa B. Carey and pack train crossing Sixes River. Center: Rogue River Bridge. Coos Bay Bridge. Bottom: Second locomotive in Coos County, in the 80's. Rephotographed from the orginal owned by Mrs. Strickland, Bunker Hill. Parcel Post at Illahe.

Coos-Curry Pioneer Museum

Loaned by Emil

Collection of Alfr

visiting some California hatcheries he engaged Kirby Pratt to take charge of his. Later he established other hatcheries far up the river. He remained the Rogue River salmon king until his death in 1908.

During the time of his operations he had to face considerable competition, but he kept the situation pretty well under control by buying up about 15,000 acres of the river frontage, thus practically eliminating others from getting a location. In 1893 his cannery burned down. After the fire he tore down the old Stewart & Riley plant, towing the timbers across the river to be used in his new plant. There on the north bank he established and named the place Wedderburn.

Hume had other interests than fish. His holdings extended several miles from the ocean up both sides of the river; on this land he established a dairy farm and a sheep ranch and had some beef cattle. He was strong for saddle horses and had his own race track.

After his death, his two nephews for a year or two carried on the enterprise, fish and all the rest, and then sold to the Macleay estate.

Under the new owners the business was continued for many years with some degree of success. But during the stringent period of the 1930's, and especially with the closing of Rogue River to commercial fishing in 1935, the Macleay Estate had its properties foreclosed. It was sold to the Lloyd Corporation of California, which now has 31,000 acres in Curry County. The local representative is S. O. Newhouse, residing at Wedderburn.

The old Hume records reveal some interesting facts about the Rogue River salmon industry:

> From 1880 to 1900 Hume packed an average of 16,000 cases or nearly three quarters of a million cans annually. The fish were mostly sold under four brand names *Crown, Globe, Royal,* and *Oregon.* The first was the choicest and was largely for the English trade.

Following was the Hume pack for 16 years:

Year	No. of cases	Year	No. of cases
1877	7,804	1885	9,310
1878	8,539	1886	12,147
1879	8,571	1887	17,216
1880	7,772	1888	21,062
1881	12,320	1889	20,296
1882	19,186	1890	19,104
1883	16,156	1891	19,960
1884	12,376	1892	11,084

Besides canning, Hume salted salmon during some seasons. His largest pack by the old method was 534 barrels in 1888. A barrel held 200 pounds.

In the shipping records of the Hume fisheries appear the following vessels: steamer *Mary D. Hume* (built at Ellensburg in 1881), schooner *Stranger, Lizzie Prien* (type not stated), tug *Pelican,* schooners *Merriam* and *Thistle, Del Norte* (type not given). James Caughill (who salted fish in his ship's hold), if not the actual master of these Hume vessels, was for the most part pilot who brought them safely into and out of the treacherous Rogue entrance.

For the 13 years beginning with 1923 and through 1933, Rogue River commercially produced 6,290,349 pounds of chinook salmon and 124,540 pounds of silversides. The latter figure is so incomplete that it might be misleading. The silverside catch was almost entirely during the month of September.

Other Curry County streams have supplied considerable quantities of commercial fish. On the Chetco River salting was the common means of curing salmon in the early days. Vessels did not enter the Chetco; the barrels of salted fish were taken out over the bar in lighters. John Van Pelt and his sons were among those who thus freighted fish and other produce out to ships.

Salmon of the Coquille

"Begorra, Sir, Somebody Ought To Catch Them"

By John Flanagan

In the year 1860 I was mining on the Randolph beach. I took one of my men named "Old Jim" and went down to the Coquille to get some goods from John Hamblock who had a little store there.

When we got to the river the salmon were jumping by the thousands. "Old Jim," who was a native of the Emerald Isle, said, "Begorra, sir, it's a pity to see all those fish going to waste. Somebody ought to catch them."

I said, "Jim, what do you know about fish?"

"Well, sir," he said, "I should know something about them, for I have fished on the banks of Newfoundland for 22 years."

There were some Italian fishermen at Port Orford at this time. I heard they had not been successful and wished to sell their seine, which was 600 yards long. I went down to Port Orford, bought the seine, and packed it up on a cayuse. The next thing was to build a boat and make vats, for which Ed Fahy supplied the lumber.

Now I had the boat, seine and vats, but where were the barrels to come from? There were none on the river and I knew of no cooper at that time to make them. So I came to the bay with two of my men by way of Beaver Slough. I got a scow at Empire and commenced the collection of all the barrels I could get, whiskey barrels and others. I got them from Cammann and Luce at Empire, some at Eastport and Newport. I collected 50 in all and had them hauled over to the head of Beaver Slough. I then rafted them down the slough and river to my friend Jim McCune's place, where I put up the fish. I learned that old Mr. Mushnell was a cooper so I employed him to cooper the barrels. I filled them and took a good many to the bay and shipped them to San Francisco.

Coquille Canning and Packing

By John Nielson

The three Gatchells – D. H., Frank N., and E. W. – and several others in 1883 built and operated the first salmon cannery on the Coquille River, near Parkersburg. Two miles farther up the river, J. H. Hume had a cannery in 1886. Mr. Gilstrap built one at Prosper in 1887; it burned in 1894.

At Bandon, C. Timmons ran a salmon cannery from 1896 to 1908. When it closed down, the machinery was purchased by the fishermen's cannery.

The Prosper Canning Company operated a salmon cannery at Prosper from 1904 to 1925, when the Oregon legislature passed a law prohibiting seines on the Coquille River. The company was sponsored by Sam Ness, a Columbia River fisherman from Astoria; Niels A. Pederson of Prosper; and R. W. Bullard of Bullards.

In 1908 the Coquille Fishermen's Cooperative Canning Company's plant was built on a small parcel of land on the McCue homestead on the south bank of the Coquille, opposite Randolph Slough. The machinery it bought from C. Timmons was of the old type and was replaced. The cannery had five years of cooperative activity, until 1913. Then it was sold to R. L. Macleay and Thomas Kerr of Portland, who formed the Coquille Canning Company. This company operated up to and including 1925, when seining on the Coquille became illegal.

The heavy runs of salmon on the Coquille River have apparently gone forever. During the season of 1912, one cannery packed 60,000 salmon, another 40,000. The 1913 season was almost as good. But from that time on the salmon runs have seemed to become smaller each year. There have been a number of theories to account for this. During recent years few hatcheries have been maintained by either the state or Federal government. River waters have been polluted. Some streams have been used to splash out logs, washing out the bars used for spawning grounds.

Prior to 1883, salmon were salted and barreled for shipment to San Francisco commission merchants. Getz Brothers and Dodge, Sweeney Company were the principal buyers.

Alfred Machedo was the first person to salt, pack and ship salt salmon from the Coquille River. Jens Jensen, who had a salting station at Parkersburg, was the second one in this business. R. W. Bullards, Fred Helgren, Neils A. Peterson and others did more or less salting and shipping.

During this period there were several cooperage shops that manufactured barrels for packing the fish. The hoops were made from a very pliable wood, notched at each end so it would lock together when hammered down over the staves. Later these wooden hoops were replaced by ones of galvanized iron, which were a considerable improvement.

The following table shows the catches of commercial fish from 1923 to 1950 in Coos Bay, including Charleston, Empire, North Bend, and Marshfield or Coos Bay:

	Troll Caught in Ocean		*Net Caught*			
	Chinook	*Silversides*	*Chinook*	*Silversides*	*Steelhead*	*Striped Bass*
1923			206,799	361,081	85,660	
1924			356,565	513,050	103,323	
1925	88,153	189,447	292,183	577,156	70,794	
1926	86,506	540,792	133,193	200,783	80,168	
1927	123,591	959,914	99,147	297,339	29,016	
1928	219,800	708,941	184,678	462,763	47,957	
1929	382,100	612,646	68,655	50,063	26,910	
1930	176,184	659,060	51,775	69,507	61,293	
1931	58,672	244,557	105,487	85,335	16,264	18,050
1932	18,356	328,345	54,244	93,140	10,800	17,594
1933	165,288	446,898	21,495	49,113	13,244	21,198
1934	56,386	375,111	13,542	60,392	9,525	25,712
1935	155,744	2,096,485	24,281	202,402	19,074	27,598
1936	427,313	367,407	31,506	74,171	24,274	29,254
1937	217,569	574,990	20,773	76,225	4,187	32,779
1938	239,013	495,768	24,947	67,547	13,794	42,481
1939	80,480	433,420	15,280	28,829	10,664	65,131
1940	388,788	762,953	2,826	37,201	9,561	75,299
1941	197,152	541,997	745	11,582	339	66,090
1942	208,202	481,264	4,372	17,202	1,816	50,534
1943	190,624	242,117	2,656	32,585	467	60,219
1944	672,018	424,578	28	6,834	2,427	89,576
1945	577,974	252,873	96	8,278	382	231,218
1946	621,178	369,860	893	4,162	890	176,422
1947	596,142	546,528	Coos Bay closed to commercial salmon			87,414
1948	492,390	274.099				94,448
1949						23,413

LESSER FISH

Shad

Shad fishing has become important only in recent years. Formerly the shad was taken principally for its roe, highly prized as a rare delicacy in some ritzy restaurants of the country and bringing a high price. The rest of the fish was used for crab bait. More recently the shad is gaining popularity when kippered. Some canneries are making a specialty of canned kippered shad and find a ready market for the product.

The shad apparently does not enter Rogue River or other Curry County streams. The Coquille run is negligible. On Coos Bay the run is considerable, almost entirely in Coos River. During the past ten years the average catch has been between 250,000 and 300,000 pounds.

Striped Bass

The striped bass, an alien coming to Coos Bay as late as 1914, as described by Ben Hur Lampman in the wild life chapter, is now so numerous that 1,184,434 pounds were taken from 1931 to 1950. The biggest year was 1945 with 231,000 pounds. The latest year, excepting the first three was the smallest, only 23,413 pounds. Is he leaving after a twenty-year visit?

Albacore

Albacore fishing in the Coos Bay area, including Charleston, Empire and North Bend, has become important. Albacore, commonly known as Tuna, are caught in the ocean with hook and line, brought into port, packed in ice, and shipped to the packing plants.

The season ordinarily continues for three or four months, but sometimes for five months — July to November. The largest catches usually come in August and September.

Reports by the Fish Commission of Oregon show the following Albacore landings at Coos Bay for the years 1939 to 1949 inclusive:

Year	Pounds	Year	Pounds
1939	493,446	1945	4,463
1940	245,926	1946	27,016
1941	84,096	1947	1,761,280
1942	267,018	1948	584,947
1943	234,611	1949	889,833
1944	158,112		

Oysters

Little definite information is available on the Coos Bay oyster industry. Estimates are only approximate, except that the report on oyster seed plantings for the past five years comes through the Oregon Fish Commission from the Pacific Coast Oyster Growers Association. The seeds for plantings come on shells in boxes, each box containing a little over 100 pounds. The following plantings are given for Coos Bay:

Year	Number of Boxes
1947	8,200
1948	3,400
1949	230
1950	4,400
1951	6,750

The acreage is put at from 1,000 to 1,500. Some of the oysters are sold fresh; others are canned in 8-ounce and 10-ounce cans, 24 to the case. If the entire Coos Bay oyster crop were canned, it is estimated that a total of 50,000 cases would be produced annually. The industry was started about 1935.

Crabs

In 1907 a previous act was amended to provide "for the preservation and protection of salt-water crabs within the county Coos . . . to regulate the sale and transportation of fresh crabs . . . to prohibit the canning thereof."

Crab landings were approximately 40,000 dozen in 1947 and 70,000 dozen in 1948 for Coos Bay; 12,000 dozen in 1947 and 14,000 dozen in 1948 for Port Orford.

Clams

The clam commonly used as a food and relished by many residents of and visitors to Coos Bay for many decades, was the one known as the "Eastern" clam. The following account of its introduction to Coos Bay was furnished in 1949 by Master Fish Warden Arne J. Suomela:

The history of "Eastern" clam (*Mya arenaria*) on West Coast is somewhat indefinite as to origin of the species. However, it is certain that the clam was first introduced from the East Coast about 1860 to 1870 by one means or another. . . The clam was first found in San Francisco Bay by Henry Hemphill in 1874 and reported in 1875 by Necomb as a new species. It was later recognized as the true Eastern soft-shell. . . Its introduction ascribed to the Eastern oyster plantings about 1870 and earlier. Oyster plantings were made at Coos Bay, Oregon, and Willapa Harbor, Washington during the 1870's. . . .

Aided further by natural spreading, it has extended its range so that now it is one of our commonest, most valuable clams, extending from Vancouver Island to San Diego, California.

In a U. S. Fish Commission Bulletin, Vol. 15, 1895, Dr. Stearns is quoted:

". . . Capt. Simpson, a public-spirited citizen of San Francisco, of the firm of Simpson Bros., . . . informed me that he had at various times sent up the coast by their captains a quantity of *Mya arenaria* for planting . . . and it had multiplied wonderfully. . . ."

Said Ethel Simpson Worrel, a resident of North Bend since early childhood, in writing to the *Oregonian*:

Captain Robert Simpson was a cousin of my grandfather, William Simpson, and I was personally acquainted with him when I was a child. When he came to Coos Bay there were no clams in the upper bay. On the flats near Empire there were and are large clams, which we call the big Empire clams. Captain Simpson sent east and had some of the small Eastern clams sent out which he planted on the mudflats. One day, some years later, my father, William Robert Simpson, said, "I'm going over to the flats to see if Capt. Bob's clams grew." That was about 1881 or 1882. He found them so plentiful he took some to what is now Marshfield. Next day, at low water, the flats were black with people after the clams. . . .

The "Eastern" clam continued to be very plentiful on the tide flats surrounding Coos Bay and its various inlets until perhaps, sometime in the 1930's, when the supply began to dwindle. At present it is almost extinct. The reason for its disappearance does not appear to be known. There may be several contributing causes. Digging increased with the growing human population; in some sections hogs were allowed to run on the tide flats and became regular daily diggers at low tide; the dredging of the bay has covered up much of the clam breeding areas; it may be possible that the oyster plantings have taken away the clams' food supply as well as occupying many acres of the flats formerly occupied by the clams. Whatever the cause, the older residents sorely miss that "open and free market" which was always available when the tide was low

Said the *Marshfield Sun* in January of 1901:

> We have fruit, salmon, and various other canneries, but the latest innovation is a clam cannery that is in the process of construction at Marshfield, Oregon, by Frank Fly and James Rolandson. They are going into the business on a small scale or in other words will feel their way as they go, and if things justify they can easily increase the capacity of their plant. There are six different varieties of clams on Coos Bay and the supply is considered inexhaustible.

When this item appeared a half century ago one of the authors of this volume was in his first year in the old Central School. Fly and Rolandson were buying clams, paying 20 cents for a five-gallon can. On Saturday the Central School boy dug clams as long as the tide would permit. He dug five canfuls — 25 gallons at four cents a gallon. He earned one big round silver dollar.

Following were the Coos Bay landings of clams for a recent seven-year period:

Year	Pounds	Year	Pounds
1943	51,439	1947	82,554
1944	82,910	1948	34,962
1945	169,754	1949	18,926
1946	144,437		

Propagation and Protection

Hatcheries in 1907

The U. S. Bureau of Fisheries carried on the hatchery on the upper Rogue. This, in the spring of 1906, liberated into the upper Rogue and its tributaries 5,892,104 salmon fry. A year later it liberated 105,300 steelhead fry.

The lower Rogue hatchery at Wedderburn was privately run by R. D. Hume.

The state operated the South Coos River Hatchery and the Coquille River hatchery. The former bred 5,621,-450 chinook fry in 1907, the latter 226,600 silversides.

Feeding a Million Little Salmon

R. D. Hume at his private Indian Creek hatchery on the lower Rogue, in the spring and summer of 1907 had on hand from 1,363,186 to 1,418,035 fry. There is a record of what he fed them, and how much, from March 4 to July 19, 1907, when he turned them loose, most of them by then being nearly four inches long after they had eaten 33,308 pounds of feed as follows:

Kind of feed	Pounds
Blood	10
Horse meat	356
Herring and other fish	550
Salmon melts	1,000
Germea (fry refused)	1,385
Canned beef	144
Raw beef	2,173
Canned salmon	1,489
Raw salmon	1,657
Salmon heads (cooked in retort 3 hours and ground to pulp)	23,544

Hume's Run-in with the Law

In effect the lofty R. D. Hume told the Master Fish Warden, the prosecuting attorneys, and the judges to go jump in the lake. Though a case in the circuit court was decided against him, he went serenely on running his plant at the mouth of the Rogue; committing "a new offense every day he packs salmon without a license."

On September 12, 1907, Master Fish Warden H. G. Van Dusen, in taking up the situation with the attorney, ended a three-paragraph letter with this paragraph:

> . . . you will notice that the fall fishing season opened September 5th, and I understand that . . . on said date, Mr. Hume had been receiving and canning salmon in the usual manner, and I have no doubt but what he intends to do so throughout the entire season without license, unless there is some way we can compel him to procure the same.

Very promptly, but not too helpfully, the attorney-general wrote an opinion the next day, in which he said:

> . . . the only thing to do, the best thing to do, is when the court meets again in Curry County next spring to reindict him and fine him again . . . You could, of course, arrest him in the justice's court and have him bound over to appear at the next term of circuit court, but I hardly think it worth while to do that. However, you can use your own judgment in the matter.

35

Grist Mills

BREAD REQUIRED FLOUR, which in the 50's came by ship from San Francisco to Port Orford, Coos Bay, the Coquille and Rogue Rivers. Inland it had to be packed on horses or by man. George Bennett wrote:

> The first grist mill ever built on the river was put up in the summer of this year [1860]. It was erected on Mr. Schroeder's place, and the machinery including engine, boiler and burrs, were brought all the way from Baltimore by Messrs Schroeder and Volkmer. The mill was completed and the first graham flour manufactured in the fall of the same year.

Fannie Lehnherr Dixon said in her story of the Lehnherr family:

> Settlers were filling the country and flour was still conveyed on horseback from the adjoining county. Father had learned the art of grinding flour from an uncle in Switzerland . . . The splendid creek running through the farm afforded a suitable site for a grist mill. A large overshot water wheel furnished the motive power. A pair of buhrstones came with the Baltimore Colony but were not utilized. Father purchased the buhrs. . . .
>
> Near the barn a level place was made ready for the threshing floor. The ground was packed firmly and the shocks laid in a circle, the cut ends toward the outside, the wheat to the center. Sometimes there were eight or ten horses tramping round and round. Men stood in the center keeping the grain in place. Once or twice all the horses were taken off, when the hay was turned and thoroughly shaken. The horses resumed their tramp, tramp, tramp again around the circle. When all the straws were broken and the heads empty, . . . the work of separating the grain from the chaff begun. A good sized fanning machine was brought into use . . . several days were always required to winnow the grain. It was put into two-bushel sacks and ready to go to the mill. . . .

Farmers brought their grain on horseback, and the sixth bushel belonged to the miller.

Bolting cloth was stretched over a wooden frame, and the

crushed wheat conducted from the buhrs soon emerged as a fine quality of flour. Some of the crushed grain was not fine enough to go through the bolting cloth, and the bran came from the end of the cylinder and was used to feed hogs.

Sacks were needed to store the flour . . . With a few bolts of unbleached muslin and our Wheeler & Wilson sewing machine, Mother soon turned out sacks that would compare with the best.

Mrs.Dixon did not tell us what became of the old mill after her parents moved to Myersville, which became Myrtle Point, where he again took up the making of flour.

A clue to the next appearance of the old Baltimore millstones is found in a poem by T. C. Land, a teacher at Rural, which is now the town of Powers:

We have a little mill hardby,
A little creek which doth supply
Us all with flour, as fine and good
As any needs for wholesome food.

With the help of Steve Reed, Calvin Gant, Tom and John Hayes, "Aunt Minnie" Hermann, Charles F. Geitner and others, it has been possible to piece together bits of information that seems to establish the identity of one of those old Baltimore buhrstones, now resting in the Pioneer Museum in Coquille.

"Aunt Minnie" — Mrs. Ernest Hermann — was born in the Rural community. She says that her father, John Wagner, grew corn, and he and a blacksmith by the name of Isaac Bingham made something to crush the corn. She was very young at the time and she didn't know just what it was. Her father and some others began building the mill in 1875 and had it ready for use in the autumn of 1876. She added, "They made corn meal. Then we had something to eat. We had no sacks. Father made buckets. Anything to hold the meal."

The Rural gristmill was powered by an overshot water wheel, thought to have been about 24 feet in diameter. Just when the mill ceased to be operated is not known, perhaps in the nineties. It was located just south of Powers on Mill Creek.

Perhaps the old original Baltimore mill stones would have been lost forever had it not been for Charles F. Geitner. When he heard the subject discussed over the radio he wrote that he had lived near the site of the old mill, remains of which were still there when he arrived, and he had found and recovered one of the millstones. Later he presented this to the Museum.

The two old stones had served in the Volkmar-Schroeder mill near present Broadbent; next in the Lehnherr mill on their Roland Prairie farm; then in the Rural mill near present Powers. One of the old stones no doubt lies buried deep in the dam of the log pool; its mate is the one in the Pioneer Museum in Coquille.

A number of grist mills followed these earliest three.

Of the very old ones, perhaps no other person of today has a more vivid recollection than has Steve Reed, whose mother was Catherine Lehnherr. He remembers that his grandfather, Christian Lehnherr, after leaving the Rowland Prairie mill, established a steam-powered one at or near the present county fair grounds and when this burned, built another. Mr. Reed's mother, and father Oscar Reed, after remaining for some time in the Rowland Prairie home, moved to the middle Coquille, about a mile above the forks. By that time Steve Reed was old enough to remember distinctly the building of the grist mill at that place by his father. He recently pointed out the exact spot where the trees were cut down and squared into timbers for the structure, and where the dam was built in the river.

His father, being a blacksmith and all-round mechanic, had a way of his own for harnessing the power of the river. Instead of the conventional overshot or undershot wheel, he built a turbine. Cutting a big sound block from the end of a log, he split it into four equal sections, carefully shaped them, and bound them together with a wagon-tire. Orvil Dodge, the later historian, and Albert Fish, an expert with tools, helped to hew and mortise the timbers for the mill itself.

The Oscar Reed Mill was operated for some years. The high water of one winter washed out the dam, possibly during the big flood of 1890. The mill stones were sold to Mike Breuer, an Indian creek homesteader just across the river, who built a mill with an overshot wheel, only to have it too washed out by high water. The buhrstones were rescued and are still in the possession of Breuer's son. Mike Breuer himself, now in his nineties, still cobbles shoes in his shop in Bandon.

The old Hoover Grist Mill above Coquille was owned by Willis Hoover, whose daughter, Mrs. Carl Carlson, writes from Reedsport:

> I was quite a small girl, not more than four or five years old, but I remember the mill quite well. There had been a sawmill in one part of the building. I remember of my father taking me in the mill and showing me the big funnel where the flour came down. The funnel was made of a kind of silky material, very nice and white. My folks lived quite close to the mill. I remember my father coming in with flour on him.
>
> Men used to come with their wagons and horses to bring their wheat and get flour. I do not remember the man's name who was in partnership with my father. The last time I was there the old mill was still standing but the house was gone. . . The place then was known as the Price Robinson place.

The Saunders Grist Mill near Ellensburg (Gold Beach) appears to have been built and operated even ahead of the Volkmar-Schroeder mill on the Coquille. Information about it comes from two widely separated sources. The *Curry County Reporter* of October 13, 1949, reported that Mrs. Eva Z. Hill, of Smith River, California, but formerly of a pioneer family on the Rogue River, stated in an interview that the first grist mill in Curry County was established on Saunders Creek, and was built and operated by John Saunders. Mrs. Hill stated that she saw it in operation when she was a little girl.

Said Hardy T. Stewart:

> Shortly after the Indian war in 1856, a German by the name of John H. Saunders built a grist mill at Jerry's Flat, some two or three miles up the river from its mouth. For several years he ground buckwheat and other grains into flour for the residents of that section. . . . In 1873 the mill was changed

over into a saw mill . . . Mr. Saunders was an educated German born on the Rhine River. His mill was run by water power from a stream that still bears his name.

George Meservey of Illahe says that Mr. Saunders had difficulty in finding suitable stone for the buhrs. He searched the country over, finally finding just what he wanted on Quosaton Creek.

Mrs. J. R. Wiley writes from Broadbent, saying,

> My father says he can even remember before there was a grist mill here and all the neighbors used a common coffee mill and sieve to make their corn meal—loaned it around from one family to another.

Far up on Big Creek, which empties into North Lake, Charles Siestreem built and used his mill, operated by an overshot waterwheel, reported to have been 12 or 14 feet in diameter, possibly more. His son, now residing at Hauser, remembers the old mill. The family moved from the place in 1902, but the mill had been built years before that time. Pete Jordan, a brother of Mrs. Siestreem, then residing in the neighborhood, says that Mr. Siestreem grew and ground wheat, buckwheat and corn; made meal, flour and feed for cattle and hogs. Mr. Jordan says that Fuller Sprague planned, laid out and shaped the material at his home at Jordan's Cove, on west side of Coos Bay, just below the present railroad bridge.

J. Albert Matson remembers that Captain A. J. N. Campbell built a grist mill operated by wind power. The mill was built on piling driven into the mud-flats just across the bay from Marshfield. Albert was too young to know whether the mill was ever a success.

Twenty or more grist mills are found to have operated in Coos and Curry counties. Only a summary can be given here, based upon information gathered from various sources, much of it relying upon memory accounts passed down from parents or even from grandparents.

Though accuracy has been checked as far as possible, some errors have no doubt crept in.

Mill Owner and Location	Power	Buhrs		
Saunders, J. H., Jerry's Flat	Water	Stone	Curry	(1st)
Volkmar-Schroeder, Baltimore Col'y.	Steam	Stone	Coos	(2d)
Lehnherr, Christian, Rowland Prairie,	Water	Stone	Coos	(3d)
Wagner-Hayes-Gant, Rural	Water	Stone	Coos	(4th)
Panter, John, R. Fredrick place	?	?	Coos	
Billings, John, Big Bend	Water	Stone	Curry	
Lehnherr, Myrtle Point	Steam	Steel	Coos	
Rackleff, Capt., Myrtle Point	Steam ?	Steel ?	Coos	
Oscar Reed, Middle Fork	Water turbine	Stone	Coos	
Breuer, Mike, Indian Creek	Water	Stone	Coos*	
Campbell, A. J. N., Marshfield	Wind	Unknown	Coos	
Fish, Albert, Bridge	Water	Stone?	Coos	
Minard, Dora,	Water	Stone?	Coos	
Hoover, Willis, Johnson Mill	Steam	Stone?	Coos	
Foster-Tichenor, Foster Creek,	Hand	coffee-mill type	Curry	
Siestreem, Chas., North Lake,	Water	Steel?	Coos	
Johnson, Steve, Templeton,	Water	Steel	Coos	
Nelson, Jake, Shutter's Landing	Water	Steel?	Coos	
Canfield, Rollie, Agness,	Water	Steel	Curry	
[Remains of this mill have been seen in recent years but some doubt exists as to its having been a grist mill]				
Jennings, L. B., Remote,	Gasoline	....	Coos	
[During World War One the owner made meal and flour for himself and for livestock]				

36

Electricity

ELECTRIC POWER ON COOS BAY *By Henry Spargo*

MARSHFIELD IN 1890 issued a franchise to George W. Loggie, stipulating that an electric plant be constructed immediately. Loggie didn't start immediately, didn't start at all, thus automatically cancelling the contract.

In April 1891 the same franchise was given to Franklin R. Arson with the same results. But in October, 1891, J. W. and A. H. Carlson received the franchise from the city, and they installed a small plant of 35 K.W. capacity at 8th and Central Avenue, the location of the present storeroom.

The General Electric Company, due to non-payment by the Carlsons, took over the plant in 1896, and sent a party by name of Freeburg to manage and operate the system. Freeburg in 1902 purchased the property from the General Electric Company and in 1904 sold it to Codding and McKenzie.

The Coos Bay Light and Power Company was then organized and the boiler capacity of the plant was increased by the installation of a 12 steam pressure Russell Boiler. Again in 1906 capacity was increased by replacing the old unit with 150 K.W. Crocker Wheeler generator and Allis Chalmer engine.

Back in 1900 the Simpson Lumber Company had installed a 25 K.W. machine to furnish their employees with energy. In 1904 they put in an additional 25 K.W. unit to supply the city of North Bend which was being platted

In 1907 Seymour H. Bell, purchasing the property from Codding and McKenzie as well as the equipment of the Simpson Lumber Company, organized the Coos Bay Gas and Electric Company. Bell received a 50-year franchise from the city of North Bend and a 25 year franchise from the city of Marshfield, cancelling all prior franchises. A 93,000 cubic feet per day gas plant and 250 K. W. capacity electric plant were built at North Bend and in 1908 the plants at North Bend and Marshfield were connected by a transmission line.

The Northern Idaho and Montana Power Company, in October 1910 purchased the property from Mr. Bell and immediately turned it over to the Oregon Power Company under an operating lease. In 1912 the latter entered into an agreement for the C. A. Smith Lumber Company to furnish electric energy.

The expansion of the company included the purchase of Coquille property in 1913 from Frank Morse, who in 1901 had secured a franchise from that city to construct and operate an electric plant.

In 1902 a line was built to Myrtle Point and permission was given to serve the city but without a franchise. Coquille and Myrtle Point granted 20-year franchises in 1913.

1917—The electric plants at North Bend and Marshfield were dismantled, having been out of service since 1913, and a 11,000 volt line was built from the C. A. Smith Lumber Company plant in Marshfield to North Bend.

1918—The Mountain States Power Company was formed, which acquired the contract for the purchase of energy from the Smith mill.

1919—The Coquille-Myrtle Point. 6600 volt line was rebuilt.

1922—The Marshfield-to-Coquille line was rebuilt, and a transmission line was built from Myrtle Point to Powers.

1924—A 22,000 volt line was built from Beaver Hill Junction to Bandon to serve the City of Bandon Municipal Distribution System.

1925—A 2300 volt line was built from the power plant in North Bend to the City of Empire.

1932—The Marshfield-to-Coquille transmission line was rebuilt and brought into the power plant. The line was stepped up to 66,000 volts, and all the distribution in Coquille Valley set back to 19,500 volts.

Since 1933 Mountain States Power Company has consistently increased its distribution system.

Coos-Curry Electric Cooperative, Inc.
By Ivan C. Laird

In 1939 a mass meeting was held at Myrtle Point by the rural people of Coos County for the purpose of organizing a cooperative. Thereupon incorporators were appointed and authorized to incorporate the Coos Electric Cooperative, Inc. Its charter was granted by the state in 1939. The first board of directors consisted of the following Coos County farmers:

Ivan C. Laird, president; Julia Merle Leatherman, secretary; Rosabel S. Brown, Helen M. Pancoast, Marion C. Miller, Elmer Wilson, Lora E. Holverstott, D. V. Yeoman, L. B. Jennings, Richard J. Connarn was the first manager.

The Rural Electrification Administration granted the first loan in the fall of 1939, the sum of $119,000 to be used for the construction of 84 miles of distribution lines, transportation, office, and other necessary equipment.

The contract was granted Homer G. Johnson in April of 1940 to build the 84 miles; in November of 1940 the line was energized. This brought 7,200 volts of electricity to every home owner of the communities of Norway, Lee Valley, McKinley, Sitkum, Gravelford, and Bridge.

Extensions were added by many additional allotments all over Coos and Curry counties. The project was extended to Curry County and the acquisition of Port Orford, Brookings and Gold Beach was made by the Cooperative, the name of which was officially changed in 1947 to the Coos-Curry Electric Cooperative, Inc.

Wholesale power was purchased from Mountain States Power Company at Norway for the project on the north and from the California Oregon Power Company for Curry County. A 60,000 volt transmission line from the California border to Gold Beach is practically completed at the present time. A distribution contract for the balance of the system for Curry County will soon be completed, which in the ultimate will make Coos and Curry counties 99 percent electrified.

At present the Coos-Curry Electric Cooperative, Inc., receives, at Norway and Bandon, power from the Bonneville Power Administration's own transmission line constructed through Coos County. In 1952 it will be completed to Gold Beach to connect with its own transmission line, making a two-way service to Coos and Curry counties.

Headquarters are in Coquille. A shortwave radio station has been installed to facilitate the business and service. The Cooperative has 3,000 members and has invested $2,075,000 in its electric system, in loans from the Rural Electric Administration, which is being paid back to the government over a period of years with interest. Large power contracts are being negotiated with many sawmills, plywood plants, and such other large power users as irrigation, machine shops, and refrigeration plants.

First Electric Service at Gold Beach

James C. Leith, who assisted in setting up the first Gold Beach light plant, remembers it as follows:

> The equipment was purchased in April 1924 from the Fairbanks-Morse Company of Portland. It was shipped by the schooner *Point Reyes,* landed at the dock at Gold Beach, and hauled by team and wagon to a location at the Gold Beach Auto Park. Walter Asplund of the Mountain States Power Company came down from Marshfield to install the plant. Its primary purpose was to furnish lights for the kitchen, shower house, and cabins of the auto park, and a few homes and businesses close by. The first lines were strung between spruce trees out to the county road which is now U. S. 101. From there 4x6 cedar timbers were set up and wire was strung to the Black Cat Garage, several hundred yards north of the power plant. The wire and poles were purchased by the few residents receiving the service. Among these were Roderick Macleay. Reverend J. Whitesett of the Community Presbyterian Church, and the *Gold Beach Reporter* for use in running the Linotype machine instead of a gas engine.

37

Assortment of Enterprises

In 1904 a North Bend man announced he was organizing a company to make brick from ocean sand. He expected to employ about 30 men.

Banks

Four banks were listed in R. L. Polk's first *Coos County Directory* for 1904-05 — Marshfield, Flanagan & Bennett established 1889, J. W. Bennett, president (Polk's data-getter missed the First National Bank of Coos Bay, founded at the time of his census, in 1904) ; North Bend, Bank of Oregon, 1904, L. J. Simpson; Myrtle Point, Bank of Myrtle Point (a private bank), 1901, J. R. Benson, proprietor; Coquille, First National Bank of Coquille (a merger with Coquille Valley Bank), 1903, A. J. Sherwood.

Banks had multiplied three-fold by 1911 (in which simple, uninflated days there were actually two Oregon banks with deposits of only $8,000) :

Town	Bank	Deposits
Bandon	Bank of Bandon	$193,512
	First National Bank	75,000
Coquille	Farmers & Merchants Bank	53,655
	First National Bank of Coquille	214,000
Gold Beach	Curry County Bank	51,692
Marshfield	Flanagan & Bennett Bank	548,267
	First National Bank of Coos Bay	433,000
Myrtle Point	Bank of Myrtle Point	55,470
	Flanagan & Bennett Bank of Myrtle Point	84,811
North Bend	Bank of Oregon	161,184
	North Bend National	110,000
Port Orford	Port Orford Bank	21,710

From 1907 to 1910 there had been the First Trust & Savings Bank of Marshfield. By 1915 there was the Brookings State Bank. In 1919 the Security Bank of Myrtle Point was started. By 1931 there were four banks in Marshfield — the American Bank, Bank of Southwestern Oregon, Coos Bay National Bank, First National Bank of Coos Bay. In 1936 the North Bend National became a branch of the First National Bank of Portland; in 1937 the First National Bank of Coquille and the First National Bank of Coos Bay became branches.

Woolen Mills

1

In 1893 T. W. Clark, with H. Z. Burkhart and F. E. Palmer, established Bandon Woolen Mill No. 1, specializing in flannels and all-wool blankets, with some mackinaw yardage. In 1903 the mill closed down, and the machinery was moved to North Bend. Then Bedillion headed a group that put up Bandon Woolen Mill No. 2 in 1905 or 1906.

Twenty-four-year-old Robert E. Lee Bedillion had just served a two-year hitch in the army when he came to Bandon in 1890. He already had an industrialist's manner but he knew nothing about sheep, about wool, about yarn. He became Bandon's first town marshal and was doing fine until he himself was arrested. What then corresponded to the FBI caught up with him. He was sentenced to a year of hard labor for army desertion. Friends got him off in three months.

Back in Bandon, he was a fisherman, a jetty worker,

the proprietor for six years of the Gallier Hotel. Said the historian Joseph Gaston in 1912:

> During the time he operated the hotel he organized a stock company among the leading business men of Bandon, and built a large woolen mill within the town limits. . . .He owns 50 per cent of the stock, and has always been a forceful influence in directing its policies. His success is the more remarkable because he had not even seen a woolen mill before he took charge of his present enterprise. His factory is now [1912] working night and day. . . . It is a three-set mill and has been in operation seven years, its special product being all-wool head lining.

2

For Clark's new woolen mill in North Bend a special building was erected. Clark's son was foreman of the plant. It began operation in 1904. An old directory has preserved the names of some of the workers:

BOOKEEPER	ENGINEER	SPOOLERS
Fred W. Haynes	John Hosking	Mabel Hayes Cora Stubbs May Stubbs
CARDERS	FINISHER	
Dale Mynatt H. Totten O. Totten Walter Tucker Alias Walser Otto Walser	Estella Walker	WEAVERS
	PICKERS	
	Sidney Richardson Joseph Schrimser	Mary Blackerby Mrs. John Hosking Lily Mynatt Lottie Pope Etta Pope Maggie Shinn Rose Stubbs Flora Walser
SPINNERS	WASHERS	
S. Mynatt Fred Jennings Harvey J. Russell Raleigh Tucker	Edward Moore William Perry Henry M. Tucker Robert Walker Jr.	

Yet in a few years it had passed away like a tale that is told.

TANNERIES

Coos and Curry had the trees to produce tannin — tan-bark oak, 30 percent near the base, 11 percent up 30 feet; western hemlock, 17,04 percent; Douglas fir (sawmill bark), 6.34; western spruce (sawmill bark), 5.88. They had, as elsewhere told, the hide hunters. It was a natural place for tanneries, which nevertheless were very few and not of important size.

Thomas Dimmick had a tannery at Marshfield on Coos Bay which was referred to in the late eighties as turning "out a remarkably good quality of leather" and which was still listed as doing business in 1904.

A group of settlers had one in the 90's on the Middle Fork near Bridge.

In 1898 there was "a small tannery at Chetco."

So pioneer leather-making didn't amount to much. It still isn't too late — the four tannin-producing trees continue to be numerous. Besides, there is the chrome which the oldtimers didn't know was lying around in such quantities and, even if so, wouldn't have had the least idea about chrome alum's being a good tanning agent. The tanbark oak (*Quercus densiflora*) exists like the myrtle in only one genus and one species and like the myrtle and the redwoods is restricted in range — in its case from the Umpqua River to Santa Cruz. The early California bark peelers, sending whole schooner loads to San Francisco, made savage inroads into the supply there.

Of the tanbark in Curry County in 1898, F. A. Stewart said:

> Next to the cedar and fir, our most valuable forests are tanbark oak. Upon the bark of this tree many settlers depend for their living, and upon its acorns hundreds of hogs are growing fat. As the supply of tanbark is nearly exhausted to the southward, the outlook for this industry here is flattering.

Logger's Shoes

O. O. Lund, first trained to the awl and last in Norway, began in Marshfield in 1907 to make "Custom Shoes — Lumbermen's Goods a Specialty." J. A. Thomas located in Coquille in 1926 and established the Coquille Shoe Factory. "This being essentially a lumber country," said the *Coquille Valley Sentinel,* "he specializes somewhat in the making of loggers' boots and shoes, and his work is in great demand."

Men of the big woods, so very, very particular as to how they were shod, could take their choice of two famous shoes manufactured in Marshfield — the "Coos Bay Logger" or the "Marshfield Logger." The former was made by the Coos Bay Shoe Factory, managed by Nils Rong, with 10 workmen in 1925. The latter was put out by William Feitelson & Son (A. H. Feitelson), also with 10 workmen in 1925, who produced 40 pairs of loggers' shoes a day.

Ben Sundbaum has been making shoes in North Bend during the past 40-odd years, specializing in Sundbaum's Loggers. Three of his sons have taken up the awl and last with their father.

Timber Cruisers and Surveyors

1

The Southern Pacific was somewhat too confident with its cruise reports for the Oregon & California land grants, with all copies in San Francisco which was to be hit by an earthquake. Said the railroad's land commissioner in 1916, "Prior to 1906 the company had very complete cruises, but all burned in 1906 and now we only have cruises or examinations on about 41 percent of the grant, not a close cruise by any means as to actual stumpage." Coos and Clackamas were the two counties that had the best cruise reports of their own. In the hearings on the grant in 1916 the commissioner of the U. S. land office said it was the government's idea to divide it into mineral, timber, agricultural and grazing tracts.

"Classify each 40 acres before it is sold?" he was asked.

"Yes,"

"Won't that require an army of classifiers for two or three years?"

The commissioner didn't think so; he figured that $100,000 would take care of it.

Timber cruising was a pretty good occupation in those days. He was in demand by the U. S. government, the state government (whose commissioner at that time had been a Southern Pacific cruiser), the county, private timber companies, claim locaters, real estate firms, and the Southern Pacific with 59 percent of its vast holdings to do over.

For Coos County in 1909 were formally listed the following timber cruisers: Marshfield, James Cowan and William Hutchinson; North Bend, Archie Philip and C. J. Vanzile; Coquille, A. E. Crouch; Myrtle Point, Moses Endicott, Dominick Hanes, B. E. McMullen.

In 1916 the cruiser went through 40-acre tracts on the basis of a 2-times-run, or 4-times-run, or 8-times-run, charging from 10 cents to $1 an acre. In the cheap 2-times-run he and a compassman would carry the lines without other surveying crew. At each 660 feet he would estimate the trees on each side the compass line for 25 paces. Before 1916 the cruiser sometimes received only 5 cents an acre.

The real estate firms active in selling timber lands included Neathery & Gregg, Coquille (also coal lands); H. C. Diers, Crosse Real Estate Company, and the Standard Investment Company, North Bend, (the latter "For Bargains in Agricultural, Timber and Coal Lands"); E. E. Oakes, Bandon; and in Marshfield August Frizeen and the Coos Bay Realty Syndicate, Charles J. Burschke, manager, "Pacific Coast range timber cruising a specialty."

2

And through the years it furnished occupation to a lot of men to work out the Coos and Curry Domesday Books — the metes and bounds of all the real property, from city lots to the line between Curry and California. In 1909 H. C. Diers of North Bend advertised that he had maps of every city, town and township in Coos County; "surveys made and reports prepared for investors and others."

The most particular job of all was in determining and redetermining the southern state boundary. The Oregon constitution of 1857 said this was the 42nd parallel, "beginning one marine league at sea." It was established in 1868-1869; it had to be just right; there couldn't be any ifs and ands about it. So ahead of the surveyors were the astronomers. An observatory was set up and a total of 3,000 measurements or thereabouts were made of lunar distances. The corner was computed to be 9 miles 56 chains north of the sextant station and 4 miles 78 chains east. From this corner 12 chains from the shore of the Pacific Ocean the line ran due west.

The beginning mark was a Port Orford cedar post about four inches square. And, by gosh, after all the care and the lookings at the moon, it wasn't in the proper place.

It was'nt right smack on the 42nd parallel. Its actual position was 41 degrees, 55 minutes, and 55¼ seconds north latitude. It was almost five seconds off — nearly 500 feet. The advantage was Oregon's. For 83 years Curry County has gone merrily along enjoying and getting taxes on this sizable bite of California.

Sometime before 1918 a resurvey was made. The revised line still doesn't exactly follow the 42nd parallel; sometimes it is north, sometimes south. The later surveyors detected its wabbly course; but they were not narrow precisionists to raise Ned with a lot of records; they were content to correct the grossest errors and otherwise let the old work stand.

The Port Orford cedar post, which had been there for 49 years, was moved out of the way very slightly and put back in the ground. In its hole they placed a 3½ inch post with a bronze cap. The cedar post was still standing in 1925 but by 1936 it had disappeared. The iron post, now jacketed with concrete, continues to uplift in solemn error 200 feet west of U. S. 101, a half-mile south of Winchuck River. Remember the next time you go south that you are really in California 500 feet before you get there.

Furniture

A great furniture manufacturing center seemed to be the natural destiny of Coos County. Through the years there was sporadic activity, some of it imaginative and aggressive, but the destiny somehow failed to jell.

Myrtlewood novelties have made their way into wide favor. The Oerding Manufacturing Company at Coquille, the Myrtlewood Crofters at Marshfield (E. O. Duncan), and the Myrtlewood Manufacturing Plant at North Bend (E. H. Rose and J. H. Horstman) were among those who pioneered it into public demand.

Ostlind Furniture, Inc., of Marshfield (Benjamin B. Ostlind) started out about 1928 with the announced expectation of an annual business of $500,000 to $600,000 — not sufficiently apprehensive that there might be a big depression right around the corner. The line consisted of three suites each of breakfast room, dining room, and bedroom furniture, with occasional living room pieces. An exclusive feature was myrtlewood veneer lining for the drawers of buffets, cabinets, and tables. Retail outlets were arranged with big stores in Seattle and Oakland and a continuing display was set up in Los Angeles.

E. B. Gehrke, in Marshfield since 1908, earned a wide reputation for his store and office furniture, cedar chests and other white cedar products.

Frederick Mark came to Marshfield in 1873 and put up a furniture factory; "among other things he manufactured coffins for the dead."

Matchsticks and Broom Handles

Harvey W. Scott, noted *Oregonian* editor, wrote from "Empire City, Coos Bay, Aug. 26, 1868:"

> Large quantities of this white cedar wood are sent to San Francisco to be manufactured into lucifer matches. It is said that the match factories of that place are almost wholly supplied with the wood from Coos Bay. So, also, the broom factories of that city use white cedar handles, which are turned out by the ten thousand here.

It took a long time for the whole broom to be made where the handles were so plentiful. Keeran Brothers of Marshfield were manufacturing them in 1913.

Cooperage Plants

The scarcity of barrels in the early salmon salt-packing period has been described. F. A. Stewart said that in 1898 there were two barrel-making plants at Langlois, operated by O. W. Hawkins and O. P. Haagensen.

Henry Kern and his father were early-day coopers on Coos Bay, making barrels for shipping salmon. He still resides in North Bend. In the meantime he has been a Sourdough in Alaska, a soldier in the Spanish-American War, blacksmith, foundry and machineshop owner past 49 years; bank president; mayor of North Bend.

Brick Manufacture

The first brickyard in the two counties was that of Daniel Giles, Whiskey Run pioneer of 1853, who came to Myrtle Point in 1891, "where he engaged in the manufacture of brick and tile, his yard occupying eight acres of land." His son Samuel is said to have been the actual brick maker as well as a mason. The Binger Hermann building was one of the largest structures made of Giles brick, which went into other structures and scores of fireplaces and chimneys in Myrtle Point.

Some years later Giles sold out to a man named Tracy, who moved the plant to Arago, where brick and tile were made for several years.

Taylor Siglin for some years had a brick kiln on his place at the head of Isthmus Inlet, favored by low-cost water transportation. A man named Renfro had another kiln on Isthmus Inlet, located near the mouth. There was one for some time on Catching Inlet near the mouth of Ross Slough. In the early 1900's a man named Dexter made brick on the Jessie Smith farm near the mouth of Daniels Creek. The Citizens Building, now occupied by the North Bend post office, was made in 1909 of brick made from the Dexter yard.

Marshfield in 1913 had the Coos Bay Brick & Clay Manufacturing Company.

Quarries

The most spectacular source of rock was at Hunter's Heads, of which and of other quarries F. A. Stewart said in 1898:

A government engineer, in looking up the proposed harbor

improvement at Port Orford, found, a few miles southeast, an acceptable mountain of granite. The sandstone quarry at Blalock lies on the coast, a few miles to the north. The very finest freestone is found at Mack's Arch, and in a prodigious quarry at Hunter's Heads. . . . where the splashing surfs of winter have uncovered the stone for hundreds of feet, exposing the horizontal layers that remind one of a gigantic stairway. Bold water fronts this mammoth quarry; and its largest stones could be slid on an incline, or swung by derricks aboard vessels. . . . Twenty-five years ago they were shipping from Japan to San Francisco freestone not equal to this.

The jetty was a voracious devourer of rock. The Hauser Construction Company from July 1924 to November 1927 delivered 1,044,000 tons. In 1928 it began delivery of 600,000 tons more. The work meant a payroll of about $20,000 a month for 130 to 140 employees.

The quarry site extends for some 2,500 feet along North Coos River, where three 25-ton electric loading derricks transfer the rocks from the cars to the barges for towing to jetty operations.
The first step of building the jetty was to find a quarry where rock of the desired sandstone formation could be obtained. It was necessary to go inland 28 miles from the place where the rock would be dumped, and 12 miles up North Coos River from Marshfield.

For a single tremendous shot 26 tons of powder were used. The result was a small earthquake — it moved 150,000 tons of rock. Any piece under 100 pounds was no good. The company had to pay $500 an acre for a dumping ground for this small material.

The Hillstrom Quarry on Kentuck Inlet is at present delivering thousands of yards of coarse, medium and fine rock to roads and highways in the Coos Bay area. A single shot of powder recently brought down enough rock to keep their crusher and trucks going for a year.

Borax

The old Borax Mine was on the Lone Ranch owned by the Moore Brothers, lying along the coast 5½ miles north of Brookings. It was found in boulders or chunks as large as 200 pounds, though ranging to 20 pounds and to pellets no bigger than peas. A 1916 state mineral report said of it, noting that a 75-foot tunnel remained from old workings:

> It is claimed that considerable material was mined here many years ago and was shipped to San Francisco, but that "no one could reduce it" and that the property has lain idle since. It is reported that the Pacific Borax Company now controls the deposit.

F. A. Stewart said of it in 1898:

> Borate of lime has been extensively mined on the coast near Chetco, the bed yielding the largest prices ever found.

Borax is ordinarily thought of as a desert product hauled out by 20-mule teams. Its occurrence in the Chetco area is indeed unique, with no other deposit like it along the ocean shore north or south.

Chrome

Said the 1942 special edition of the *Coos Bay Times*:

> First new mineral processor in the Coos-Curry county area as a result of America's need for domestically-produced strategic metals, is Krome Corporation. . . of El Paso, Texas. The company will have its new $500,000 concentration plant in operation near Langlois by mid-1942, producing a concentrate in brickette form, that can be fed directly into the steel furnace for alloying steel.

In another article the newspaper discussed the investigations into black sand as a source of chrome.

In World War One there had been considerable production but practically all of it from inland deposits. In 1918 the Bald Face Mine in the Chetco area shipped 700 tons of 40-42 percent chromic-oxide ore. On the east side of Iron Mountain 150 to 200 tons were mined but none of it was shipped. At Salmon Mountain Mine several hundred tons were taken out and "a part of it packed nine miles to the end of the railroad at Powers;" it is said to have run as high as 50 percent of chromic oxide.

Krome Corporation's activities didn't exactly pan out the way the *Coos Bay Times* reporter was told they would. Production began in April 1943; it was discontinued by government order on December 1, 1943.

During the nine months, however, there were mined and milled 232,973 long tons of the black sand, averaging 5.39 percent of chromic oxide. A secondary plant at Beaver Hill treated 30,000 long tons of concentrates. The Humphreys Gold Corporation was also awarded contracts.

By mid-1948 nobody at all was mining chrome. Better in peace times to get it from Africa. In 1950-1951 there was a renewed government demand, with a receiving depot at Grants Pass.

Fruit Drying

In 1878 "the business men of Coos Bay published some very interesting statistics."

> Though our surplus fruit crop has, in former years, been mainly shipped while fresh, the introduction of evaporators is . . . establishing a lucrative business in the export of the dried product of these factories.

In the early 80's, Rosa & Hammerberg erected a fruit dryer at Myrtle Point, paying 29 cents a bushel for apples. "The roads for miles out of town were lined with wagons loaded with large, luscious fruit for the new market." The enterprise didn't last. It was closed and the building sold. By 1887 it was all gone.

The Peppermint Project

The pioneer Kokwellers were charming persons for the way they were willing to try anything once. Six or seven years before they took a whirl at silk culture they almost took one at peppermint growing. In the upshot they didn't, and maybe that was too bad, for it is easily conceivable it would have turned out well in light of all the circumstances since. Kalamazoo, Michigan, became known as growing three-fourths of the world's supply within a radius of 24 miles. It can still be asked what does Kalamazoo have that the Coquille Valley doesn't?

The Coquille Immigration Board got out a publication in the late eighties wherein it was stated:

> Many are contemplating going into the business of manu-

facturing oil from peppermint which grows here in profusion. As many as three crops can be raised during the year. It is estimated that the yield of an acre a year will produce at least $500 worth of oil, which can be distilled at small expense to the planter.

The $500 worth meant about 200 pounds, for the price long averaged about $2.50 a pound. The usual yield is 80 to 85 pounds. It looked like they were on the right track. Why didn't they go ahead? By now Coquille might have been a secondary Kalamazoo.

The distilling cost was correctly stated to be inexpensive. It was only 25 to 30 cents a pound 40 years later, perhaps less then. One community-owned still could take care of 50 to 75 acres.

Breweries

Mehl Gottlieb came to Coquille in 1874 and there operated the first brewery in Coos County.

A. G. Walling in his *History of Southern Oregon,* 1884, said, "Randolph has a brewery of very fair beer." In another place he elaborated sententiously, "Joseph Walster: lives at Randolph; is a brewer; was born in Germany. Mr. Waltser has acquired a good reputation as a brewer." In listing Coquille's 1884 establishments, he added at the end, "There is also a brewery."

Twenty years later, in 1904, there were three in the county instead of two, all in new places: Marshfield — Robert Marsden's and Robert Peters' (both also saloonkeepers; Marsden's actual brewer was Herman Roswinkle) ; Bandon Brewery run by George C. Gehrig.

In 1909 the Bandon concern was the same, but at Marshfield was the Coos Bay Eagle Brewery and North Bend had entered the picture with the Coos Bay Brewing Company owned and run by Charles Thom.

Sealion Bounty Killers

For a quarter of a century, off and on, there was a terrible slaughter industry. Men made their living by turning into abattoirs the foamy reefs. The mistaken and awful program was aimed at the thousands of sealions which added a charm of motion to the green waves and presented an atmosphere of contagious contentment when they stretched their sleek masses upon the rocks to warm. In 1900 the Oregon legislature authorized a $2.50 bounty on each sealion scalp. Later this was raised to $5 and even to $10. Still later, in 1926, it was reduced to 50 cents, and then the wholesale and profitable work of extinction practically ceased.

Complaints of them as salmon destroyers, caused the bounty. Said even the State's master fish warden in 1907, "It is a common thing for the net fishermen to find in their nets, after every drift, from one to ten salmon that the seals, by eating the choicest part, or belly, have made unfit for commercial use."

And so the sharpshooters went out and made good money. In addition to rifles, dynamite was used. In 1917, on the Rogue River Reefs and at Cape Blanco, "the crews of gasoline boats were killing 300 or 400 sea lions a month." On a June day in 1923 U. S. Game Warden Ray C. Steele visited the Cape Blanco rocks. With him was W. M. Hunter, a state-employed sharpshooter. The latter looked 106 times along his rifle barrel. He was a good marksman and in each case the target sunning itself there on the rocks was as quiet as it would be forevermore in a moment.

In 1916 a Gold Beach resident hired a crew and went out to the rocks a few miles off shore and in two days killed 300.

Said an early Southern Pacific booklet featuring its Coos Bay line, "One unusual form of sport practiced in Curry County is hunting sealions. It has enough danger to add excitement to the sport . . . Uncounted thousands of these uncouth monsters may be seen on the rocks."

There was a more justifiable epidemic of killing before the bounty one or the simple pastime one. Stated a report of the eighties, "Seal and sealion have formed an important business for several years among the coast people, and valuable cargoes of oil and furs have been shipped to market."

Indians used the animals for meat. One time a group of early Empire City pioneers bought some from the Indians who said it was smoked pork — *cosho*. The whites ate it with relish before they learned it was sealion jerky.

Fur Farming

Two reports, the first by the Coquille Chamber of Commerce in 1938:

> During the past few years a new and highly lucrative farm industry has come into existence in the Coquille River Valley in fur farms, which have been established in several localities. Silver fox, German fitch [European polecat], and muskrats are the most popular animals.

The second report much condensed from the *Coos Bay Times*, 1942:

> Little foxes and little mink in Coos County are paying breeders an estimated $40,000 a year. Mrs. C. M. Hartwell of Riverton has won more trophies and top awards on silver fox furs than any other fox ranch in Oregon. The Coquille Unit of the Fox and Mink Association includes the counties of Coos, Curry, Douglas, Josephine, and Jackson. There were about 700 silver foxes on farms in Coos County January 1, 1942, and approximately 1,800 mink.

Tourist Trade

Even in the old period of isolation tourists were not entirely unknown specimens. The hardy ones liked the adventuring of getting there and back; the imaginative ones were all the more attracted to it as to some foreign land. The Bandon correspondent for the *Roseburg News* on September 21, 1893, expressed the hope the railroad would go ahead and get built, because visiting Bandon-by-the-Sea over the Coos Bay Wagon Road was beset by some incommodiousness. A vacationer from Roseburg to Bandon Beach, said he, must spend six days coming and going and, moreover, "be put to the inconvenience of sleeping in or under their wagons, and also providing food for their horses whilst on their journey and pasturing for them when they get there."

Even over the primitive ancestor of U. S. 101 and in wagons or buggies, Cape Blanco was visited by 4042 persons during the 20-year period from 1896 to 1916.

It is noticeable that people living along an ocean gravitate towards any lake that is handy. A smaller body of water is something they can get their teeth into, so to speak. Not surprising, therefore, that Ten Mile Lake became a popular place. Joseph Davis Magee gave it a hotel in 1907. Within four years there were two others — the Lakeside Resort Hotel and the Lakeside Inn.

One tourist asset made little of in the old days and not enough in the new days, is the sand dunes, among the finest in North America.

A plank road of sorts goes out into them but not clear through to the ocean. For almost a hundred years, however, people have been driving wagons through them without benefit of planks. It takes good piloting.

Promoters

1

Not so many big-league "developers" as in some places, but a few. One of the grandest centered around Lakeport in Curry County — a double-header by the Port Orford Orchard Tract Company for a town and for an orchard development near by.

In *Bonville's Western Monthly* for June 1909 there was a full page advertisement of the new city on Flores Lake. A picture at the top showed the harbor with four vessels in it, the canal with a sailing ship being towed through it, and the town which was then called Crittenden instead of Lakeport. Said the text seductively in part,

> Flora's Lake, the place for you to start anew in a new city, with new ideals, new ambitions, hopes, and prospects. The first comers will reap the first fortunes. . . A shore line on a deep fresh-water lake, 12 miles long, separated from the ocean by a 500-foot strip of land through which a deep water canal is now being cut.

CRITTENDEN: This is the townsite for this property, 800 acres in extent . . . already has sawmill, planing mill, shingle mill, one mile of deep water front . . . town lots as low as $100.
The Best Harbor on the Pacific between San Francisco and Seattle. Flora's Lake. Very deep, about three square miles in area. Large enough for the entire American navy to maneuver. Millions of dollars in undeveloped resources.

The orchard adjunct had a full page advertisement, opposite, presenting a plan for

A man in the course of five years, by making the investment of $10 per month to apply upon the purchase of a five-acre tract, to acquire a growing orchard that will enable him enough income to support his family and be independent for the rest of his life. Apple orchards adjacent to our tracts last year returned a gross profit of $400 per acre. We have employed one of the most expert apple growers in the Northwest, who is planting our orchard, and will have full care of all orchards until they reach maturity.

Everyone who bought five acres of orchard got a town lot in Crittenden thrown in free. A report on how the business turned out has been given in the chapter on ghost towns.

2

S. A. D. Puter who located various homesteads and timber claims in Coos County, was called king of the land-fraud ring. While in jail he wrote a book, *Looters of the Public Domain,* a vivid state's evidence document. Of himself he said, "I don't drink, don't gamble, my family is not expensive." Yet at various times he was declared "a fraudulent exploiter . . . the chief offender . . . a perfect desperado . . . the archconspirator of them all . . . the most unscrupulous scoundrel that ever came from the Pacific Coast . . . the damndest scoundrel that ever went unhung."

He located about 1300 people on the Oregon & California land grant. His contract called for $100 from each to himself. And when the homesteader proved up, Puter was to get a half interest in the claim by returning half his own fee and paying half the land price or $1.25 an acre. With all the 1300, however, he did not complete agreements. "Probably 18 or 20 paid me $100. A couple of hundred paid me probably from $1 to $10, and there were 15 or 20 who gave me $1, which was simply to bind the bargain." Of the whole number he said there were only 14 in Coos County.

But the claim he liked the best of all was in Coos, and he set it aside for himself:

> When I got this abstract I found that a quarter section was vacant. It was one of the finest claims in Coos County for agricultural purposes, right on the flat, the bank of the river . . . although there is quite a little timber on it. I found that there were five applications for the section, but that one quarter section was vacant, and I filed on it. I would go there with my family now [1916] if I had a chance.

3

An old historic municipality was perhaps kept from becoming a ghost town and given a new and vigorous lease on life by promotion of the Empire Development Company, organized in 1927.

4

Orvil Dodge, the historian, who wrote such a fascinating book on Coos and Curry, was secretary of the Salmon Mountain Coarse Gold Mining Company. All the officers were Myrtle Pointers except the two Gallier Brothers of the sheriff's office in Coquille. Dodge wrote the promotion pamphlet for it in 1904; even when selling mining stock he could not quite get away from history and put in it a detailed, dramatic, account of Battle Rock. Placed on the market were 25,000 shares; "if you have a hundred or a thousand to invest you are face to face with an opportunity for rich returns."He secured a quotation from Binger Hermann who said he had "confidence in the extent and richness of the Salmon Mountain Mine."

The mine consisted of 12 placer and four quartz claims. The latter assayed $268.88 a ton for No. 1, $243.50 for No. 2, $600.80 for No. 3, $8.03 for No. 4. "An affidavit of two men set forth the fact that they were fair and true samples of the mine."

38

Land Transportation

Roads

Randolph Trail — In 1852, troopers from the wreck of the *Captain Lincoln* north of the Coos Bay bar, made their way down the coast to Port Orford. In 1853, Perry B. Marple's 40 members of the Coos Bay Company came north approximately along the same route from the mouth of the Coquille. Then there was backtracking over it in the fall of that year from Empire City to the gold beaches of Whiskey Run. The name it took of Randolph Trail appears on some of the official maps even to this day. When a county wagon-way was built years later it was called the Seven Devils Road.

Beach Route — In the fall of 1853 the Coos Bay Company men brought their families by way of the Umpqua to the ocean, thence along the beach and across the sand-spit to Coos Bay. In less than a year, on July 3, 1854, this highway which the ocean made was designated as the first official road:

> Ordered by the Board, That a county road be established from Empire City to a stream known at the Ten Mile Creek. . . And further ordered by the Board that C. G. Abby, Herrick C. Furnald, and M. M. Learn be and are hereby appointed commissioners to locate said road and erect or cause to be erected, suitable monuments, to guide travelers and prevent accidents from quicksands on said road.

This road, long known simply as the Beach Route, continued to be one of the main arteries of travel into and out of Coos Bay until the coming of the Southern Pacific in 1916.

In the nineties the Drain-Coos Bay Stage Line was advertising trips three times a week at $7, including 100 pounds of baggage. Francis Fuller Victor, the woman historian, journeyed that way at that time:

> From Gardiner a beach-wagon conveyed passengers 20 miles to the north side of Coos Bay, where they were met by a steamer and taken across to Empire City. The beach road is wearisome, with the perpetual roll of the broad tire wheels over the unelastic wet sand, and the constant view of a restless waste of water on one hand, with dry, drifting sand between us and the mountains on the other, varied only with patches of marsh and groups of scraggy pines at intervals.

The stages were two-horse and four-horse rigs. Farmers in the Lakeside country opened a driveway from the lakes to connect with the Beach Route. About 1912 or 1913 Vern C. Gorst and associates put auto busses on the route, mostly remodeled Fords, and kept them running till the railroad came.

Over the Isthmus — Whether or not in geological ages back the Coquille flowed into Coos Bay, the pioneers sure wished it did in their time. Negotiating the Isthmus was considered a tough experience by early settlers conditioned to easy boat transportation. The trail across the Isthmus dates back into unrecorded history. The first whites paddled from Empire City to the head of Isthmus Slough, then trekked across the divide to Beaver Slough, and paddled down that sluggish, beaver-dammed waterway to the Coquille.

At the north end Gilbert Hall kept a stopping place for travelers, with a post office named Isthmus, later changed to Utter City. He had rowboats at a dollar a day; Coquille farmers hired them for trips to the county seat at Empire. He built a tramway across the marsh about a half mile to the foot of the hill, then another half mile across a gulch to the summit. At his boat landing freight was loaded on a sled pulled by oxen over the hill to Coaledo. Previous to this development by Hall, loads had gone over the divide on men's backs or on the backs of hired squaws or sometimes by packhorse.

At the south end, Y. M. Lowe likewise kept a guesthouse, with a post office called Freedom. Getting out of Beaver Slough and into the clear Coquille was considered a state of freedom; hence the name.

Coos Bay Wagon Road — Built in 1873, it was given a luscious land grant of 99,819.35 acres, to be sold in tracts no larger than 160 acres and at not more than $2.50 an acre. Not only were these two conditions violated but two others — 1, the road company sold land as far as eight miles off the line when it was only given six miles on either side; 2, it actually secured patents on land which homesteaders had already been occupying and improving for a quarter of a century. The high-handed outfit was finally brought into court. A Myrtle Pointer had another reason for not liking this artery to the outside. "The Coos Bay Wagon Road," said he, "is the greatest curse that ever happened. The people of the valley will ship their produce here and will completely ruin our butter and egg market."

The route was from Roseburg through Looking Glass and Ten Mile in Douglas County, over the Coast Range to Sitkum on the East Fork of the Coquille, ending on Isthmus Slough at Coos City, where were kept stables for the horses, a hotel, and a post office.

Mutual Life Insurance Company of New York

The stages over the Coos Bay Wagon Road had more dash and style than those along the Beach Route. "Comfortable four-horse Concord coaches" were advertised by the stage line.

A ferry was later established at Coos City and a road built down the west side of the slough, then by way of Shingle House Slough, Coal Slough and Eastport to Marshfield.

A branch of the famous road terminated at Sumner, head of navigation on Catching Inlet. Another branch was extended to Bay City, now known as Eastside.

Getting into Coos Bay was a choice of this thoroughfare or the Beach Route. For weeks together winter closed it with mud, snow, and fallen trees, while the Beach Route was always open. But travel over it was in classier rigs as indicated by an advertisement in the *Roseburg Review* for September 21, 1893:

> The Idaho Stage Co. runs daily stages between Roseburg and Myrtle Point, Coquille City, Marshfield, and Empire City. The line is well equipped with four horse stock and large comfortable Concord coaches.

Old Cammann Road — Said Margaret S. Turkel, whose father, Charles Stauff, grew up in Empire:

> It was about 1870 that Marshfield began to rival Empire in importance. The Newport Mine was in operation and Mr. Cammann built a road from Empire to Newport in order to keep the business of the miners . . . This, still called the Cammann Road, went south out of Empire, crossed what is still called First Creek, and went on to the "Letter Box", a landmark in pioneer days. Here the road turned to the left and went down to Newport, and to the right it followed the tops of the ridges to the Randolph and Whiskey Run Mines. Unfortunately for Mr. Cammann, the building of the road exhausted his finances.

Curry County Trails — In the regular sense up to 1878 Curry County didn't have a mile of highway. And whichever was the cause or effect, it "had less than half a dozen wheeled vehicles." But things had changed 20 years later — "of wagons, hacks, buggies, and carts" there were "not less than 200."

Many of the Curry County Trails have history that only Indian tradition can trace. The one from Port Orford to the Illahe country served a big part in the

Indian wars of 1855-1856. The Roseburg-Big Meadows Trail was well-known in the 1870's and 1880's, a 75-mile packtrain route to present Marial. When the Southern Pacific finished its line in the 1880's, West Fork in Cow Creek Canyon became the eastern end of the trail, cutting the distance more than 40 miles. In early days a trail led from Port Orford into the Eckley country and on to the Johnson Creek mines. Later a trail was opened from Myrtle Point to Eckley. A pioneer track used as early as 1859 led out from Langlois over the hills and down Catching Inlet to the Myrtle Point vicinity.

Ferries and Bridges — Pioneer ferries have been referred to here and there in reports of various events. The early capitalists who pocketed the income from the traffic, yielded to government ownership by the county

Packtrains carried goods over early trails such as the 100-mile one along ocean bluffs during the 50's to 90's from Bandon to Crescent City, or through the mountains to Marial, or east from Port Orford over the rough coast ridges to the Johnson Creek Diggings. And the "Swiss Family" Payne packed out barrels of butter from the upper regions of the Chetco.

and the state. The latter in 1927 ran a diesel-powered ferry between Wedderburn and Gold Beach. In 1928 it took over from the county the operation of the steam-powered side-wheeler on the Glasgow-North Bend run and the next year bought the ferryboat *Oregon.*

One by one down through the years the ferries gave up the ghost to progress. Covered bridges followed and themselves became quaint features of the long ago. John B. Fox was the champion builder of these and open ones — the first bridge across the North Fork of the Coquille at Burton Prairie, 1881; at Lee, 1884; across the East Fork of the Coquille at Maynard's Mill, about 1887; covered bridge at Gravel Ford in early 80's; covered one at Fairview, 1894; 18 open bridges built or repaired in Coos County in 1895.

Now the smooth wide pavement of U. S. 101 and State 42 just keep a-going, and the mile-and-a-quarter-a-minute men hardly realize that below them so evanescently just now was a channel that might have held up the pioneer the matter of an hour. Besides many lesser streams, seven navigable waterways in Coos and Curry are crossed by state bridges — Coos Bay, South Slough, Isthmus Slough, Catching Slough, Coquille River, Coos River, Rogue River. The 1,938-foot seven-span concrete arch bridge over the Rogue was completed in January of 1932 at a cost of $646,700. The 5,337-foot Coos Bay Bridge was completed in September of 1936 at a cost of $2,143,390 — and its steel spans, in the harmony of their color scheme with the water 150 feet below, require a fresh paint job about every three years.

Railroads

The Isthmus Transit Rail Road — History of the I T R R is based on information furnished by Clyde C. Lightner, who spent his boyhood and early manhood in that exasperating bottleneck between Coos Bay and the Coquille:

> With the building of Utter City and the opening of the Carbondale Mines, a railroad was projected. Utter sent J. F.

Dunham to San Francisco to obtain a suitable locomotive. This, built to Dunham's specifications, was named the *Isabella.* It was shipped to Coos Bay in the three-masted schooner *Emma Utter* and was towed up Isthmus Slough to Utter City. Dunham assembled the *Isabella* and was its first engineer.

Fare by boat from Marshfield to Utter City was 50 cents; on the ITRR to Coaledo 50 cents; by boat down Beaver Slough to Freedom 50 cents; by river steamer to Coquille City 25 cents—total from Marshfield to Coquille City $1.75.

The Utter Coal Mine failed. The ITRR was operated for a while to haul logs and general freight. Not being well built and without ballast, the railroad deteriorated and became unsafe for heavy traffic.

A man named Springer and a Chinaman named Ming operated a hand car over the ITRR for several years, hauling freight and passengers. It is said the passengers sometimes had to get off and help push the car over the hump.

Later, Dunham took over the ITRR and built a lighter home-made locomotive, using an upright logging steam engine for power. He also built a caboose for passengers.

Contract No. 5844 – This contract of the Oregon & California Railroad Company was with C. A. Smith for the sale of 27,532.70 acres of Coos County land. It was dated September 12, 1900. That railroad didn't come anywhere near Coos and was hesitant about ever coming there. Then why should Coos divvy up those 80 tracts in size from 40 to 15,000 acres in townships 30, 31, and 32?

For the first 15,000 acres, Smith was to pay $5 an acre; for the remaining 12,500 acres he was to pay $4 an acre. The railroad (having meanwhile become the Southern Pacific) had violated three provisions of the granting act, "to wit, that the lands must not be sold to any but actual settlers; that they must not be sold in quantities greater than 160 acres to any one settler; and that they must not be sold at a price greater than $2.50 an acre."

C. A. Smith, originally a Minnesota man himself (his big Coos company is discussed in the chapter on timber) had a very prominent lawyer, John Lind, former Minnesota governor.

Governor Lind also trafficked quite handsomely in

Coos real estate as brought out in the 1915 hearings before the Congressional Committee on the Public Lands:

MR. LIND: Now, in 1905, I bought some timber land in Coos County, in Oregon, in townships—

THE CHAIRMAN (interposing). Some of these railroad lands, Governor?

MR. LIND. No.

THE CHAIRMAN. Railroad-grant lands?

MR. LIND. No. I bought Northern Pacific script and had them located on unoccupied Government lands [in Coos which was far, far away from the toot of any N. P. locomotive], and I think I had about 2,240 or 2,280 acres. They cost me about $10 or $11 an acre. I held them for about five years, until about 1910, and sold them to C. A. Smith for $100,000.

Coos Bay, Roseburg & Eastern Railroad — The project began in 1873 as the Roseburg-Port Orford Line. The Coos Bay, Roseburg & Eastern was started in 1878 by the Umpqua & Coos Bay Railroad Company. Then in 1882 the Coos Bay & Coquille Railroad Company was incorporated. For many years it was a dilly-dallying enterprise.

The far end portion was done in five relays during three years — 1891, Marshfield to Dunham, 5 miles; 1892, to Cedar Point, 5 miles; and to the Coquille River, 5 miles; 1893 to Coquille City; August, 1893, to Myrtle Point. These 27½ miles were all that were ever to be of the original abortive efforts. The Spreckles interest bought the road in 1903; the Southern Pacific in 1906.

Other Coos Railroad Dreams — In the spring of 1909 the home folks on their own organized The Coos Bay & Idaho Railroad Company, to build not just to Roseburg but clear on to Boise. P. Hennessey was president. F. A. Hains was chief engineer and a quick starter; he began surveying the route in June. Marshfield was to give a bonus of $150,000. The Chicago & Northwestern was understood to be kind of back of it. The local group's big expectations and big talk lasted just a year. The project was taken over by The Coos Bay

& Central Oregon Railroad Company, but it also lapsed for lack of funds. Meanwhile a scheme was being promoted by the Coos Bay & Inland Electric Railway for an electric line by way of Roseburg, which, in spite of previous disallusionments, pledged $25,000. Whereupon a Eugene group, not wanting their fair city left off the route to the valuable ocean, got busy and organized The Lane County Asset Company to build a railroad from there to Coos Bay. It lasted from November, 1909 to June, 1910.

Finally the Southern Pacific — The S. P. railroad from Eugene to Coos Bay opened for traffic on July 24, 1916. A girl reporter on the *Eugene Register* wrote a poem, wherein Mr. Eugene jubilantly announced to Miss Coos:

> *I'm comin, honey, and I'm comin hard,*
> *With six grooms to prop me*
> *And a diamond for a callin card.*

Perhaps in waiting till they waited too long the Southern Pacific sometimes thought a little sadly of all the good years they had missed of the kind of good railroad pickin's that were beginning to be irrevocably gone even as they arrived.

Rapid Transit

The ever ingenious J. F. Dunham built a log chute from a place on high ground in the Beaver Hill area. In the spring, when the sap was running in the trees, a barked log went down the chute's mile and a quarter in less than a minute. "You could only see a line of smoke as the log went by."

A similar operation was described by A. G. Walling in 1884:

> Near the town of Randolph is a lumber chute leading from the brow of the bluff . . . and ending at the slough, where the

logs, launched from the steep height, come down like a flash of light, and plunge into the waters.

Livery Stables

There were more livery stables than one might expect in a country of so much water and so many boats. In Marshfield in 1904 were E. A. Anderson; John Bear in the business for 18 years; and L. H. Heisner, "new rigs and fine horses." In North Bend, McCollum & Rennie; in Lake, J. M. Quick; in Coquille, T. J. Little; in Bandon, Hoyt & Garoutte and Jacob Waldvogel & Son. Myrtle Point had as many as Marshfield — L. A. Broden, William Carver, and B. Fenton.

Hotels

Hotels were all the more an accompaniment of travel in isolated sections like those of Coos and Curry, where the traveler and the discriminating drummer had perforce to put up at and sometimes to put up with such inns as he found.

In 1904 the Coos hotels were the Arago (John Morgan) and the Pioneer (Mrs. Jackson) at Empire; the Marshfield (Albert S. Dibble), the Central (John Snyder), and the Blanco (Edward G. Flanagan) at Marshfield; Hotel North Bend and Our House (W.S.Spoor) at North Bend; Hotel Coquille (John P. Tupper) and the Tuttle (Samuel J. Tuttle) at Coquille; the Myrtle Point (John J. Curren) and Hotel Guerin (George H. Guerin & Son) at Myrtle Point; Pacific Hotel and the Tupper House (both owned by Thomas W. and W. Russel Panter) at Bandon; Riverton Hotel (Alexson Martin) at Riverton.

Tupper, at this time one of the biggest of Coos taxpayers, came to Bandon in 1882 as a ship's carpenter. There, before going to Coquille, he built the Ocean House at Tupper Rock and bought the Lewis House. The latter became the Gallier Hotel with 106 rooms under the Gallier Brothers, Stephen and Edmund, afterwards county sheriff and deputy sheriff.

Marshfield until 1867 had "only a humble inn." James

L. Ferry in 1873 started a rooming place which in 1884 became the Blanco. W. B. Curtis, later Marshfield postmaster, was clerk there for 17 years.

Curry's famous hotel was the Knapp at Port Orford, dating from 1867. William H. Seward, Lincoln's secretary of state, stopped there, and Jack London is said to have written a portion of one of his books there.

Benjamin Franklin Ross built the first hotel in Empire in 1853. A *Harper's Magazine* writer in 1855 quoted its sign:

PIONEER HOTEL

Donuts — WOm Meels

MOTOR CARS

About 1905 Dr. Walter Culin of Coquille was owner of the first horseless carriage in Southwest Oregon. It was sort of a buckboard affair which attracted much attention in the county seat — solid tires, no top, a straight stick like a sailboat tiller in place of a steering wheel.

It was about 1908 before Henry Hoeck of North Bend had the first motor vehicle on Coos Bay. It was a *Rambler*. Not long afterwards J. W. Hildebrand had a *Brush* in Marshfield. I. R. (Russ) Tower had the first auto sales agency in Coos and Curry — in Marshfield 1909. In order to get the Ford agency in 1914 he had to contract to take 80 cars the first year. Later he sold Model-T's touring, for $515.70 and raoadsters for $360. (Them was the days) .

Vern C. Gorst introduced to the area motor busses, and ran some varicolored cars along the Beach Route.

39

Communication

Packin' the Mail

Coquille River — The Cokwellers while distant Empire was their post office, until 1871, worked out an R. F. D. Cooperative. Each week, according to Dodge, one of the farmers would go to the county seat by way of Beaver Slough. "A sack was always taken along to get the mail, and a two-bushel seamless sack was the most appropriate for the purpose, as it was always filled to its utmost capacity." As he returned up the river, the sack would be opened at each community point and the mail for the whole neighborhood be extracted, for local subdelivery. "Then the farmer would pull his craft along to the next stopping place" — in turn to "Willards (Coquille City), Fred Schroeder, Hall's Prairie (Arago), W. T. Perry (Norway), "the Forks," Chris Lehnherr (Myrtle Point), John A. Harry, Henry Schroeder, Dr. Hermann." By 1874 there was a weekly mail between Roseburg and Coos Bay.

Gold Beach — Up to 1915 the mail for 113 miles of Rogue River would be put off the S. P. train in Douglas County at a point doubly described in the 1915 *Oregon Almanac* like this:

West Fork—Altitude 1080 feet. (See Dothan). Mail trail station on Southern Pacific Railroad. . .

Dothan—Population 80. Railroad name West Fork, on Cow Creek. Trail leaves here for mail carrier to lower Rogue River points.

The mail was taken on muleback to Illahe post office. Diamond hitches held the parcel post in place. At Illahe the letters, papers, catalogues and packages were transferred to the back of another mule for Agness. Just why the same mule couldn't go on and save a lot of diamond hitching, wasn't explained; the remaining distance was relatively short. At Agness a motorboat became a mail wagon for the lower Rogue River settlers and Gold Beach, to make one of the most picturesque rural routes in the country in 1915. There were mail boxes along the way the same as for a land carrier. These were attached to posts that leaned drunkenly in the gravel at the edge of the water. The carrier's clientele obligingly moved these farther out in the gravel bars as the current got low, and back again when it was high. The boatman became very adept at delivery. He could jump out, stick letters and papers into the box, and jump back in again without stopping the boat. Few dwellings were to be seen but the mail boxes were numerous; no telling from how far inland the isolated inhabitants came to get what the mail boat brought — this boat that was their only connection with the outside world.

Lighthouses

Cape Arago Light — Located 2½ miles north of the cape, off the south entrance to Coos Bay. Built in 1866; rebuilt in 1934. Its white octagonal tower lifts the light only 100 feet above the water — candle power 270,000. Its three four-seconds flashes and its two short and one long eclipses can be seen 16 miles.

Cape Blanco Light — This promontory, though indeed close "to the crimson bars of evening," is not as sometimes believed, the westernmost point on the U. S. mainland. Its longitude is 124 degrees and 33.8 minutes. Cape Flattery 's is 124 degrees and 44.1 minutes or about nine miles closer to Japan and the sunset — and an obscure headland nearby, Cape Alava, juts out still farther than Flattery.

Cape Blanco Light was built in 1870, with its light 245 feet above the water, the highest along the coast except Mendocino. Material for its construction and its $20,000 lens were landed from a boat. From 1875 James

Langlois was a keeper there for 42 years; in all his life he was never so much as in another lighthouse. Two women, a Mrs. Brotherton and a Mrs. Alexander, were assistant keepers before the time their sex was disqualified by law. Cape Blanco's original 45,765 candle power long gave it a first order rating. Now, in the period of real illumination, the candle power is 320,000. It can be seen 22 miles, 1.8 seconds bright, 18.2 seconds in eclipse.

The most striking view of the lighthouse is up the curving beach from the mouth of Elk River — where Joaquin Miller courted Minnie Myrtle. It hadn't been built then or we might have a good poem on it, perhaps two good poems, one by her and one by him.

Previous to Cape Blanco Light, Louis Knapp is said to have kept a lamp burning every night and all night from a seaward window of the Knapp Hotel in Port Orford.

Bandon Light — Officially called the Coquille River Light Station, was established in 1896 and was discontinued in 1939. The light on the South Jetty took its place.

Fire Patrol Stations

In 1909 was organized the Coos County Fire Patrol Association, which now watches over a million and a quarter acres of timbered area during the fire season. Its 15 lookout stations are so situated that a fire is quickly discovered by at least two stations. The double report enables headquarters to determine the location of the fire.

Eccentric First Telegraph *By Alice (Aiken) Schetter*

The name Schetter is closely associated with the coming of telegraphic service into Coos County, and with its operation for 60 years.

Frederick Schetter, with his family, came to Coos Bay in 1869, taking charge of the office and general store of the Eastfort Coal Company on Coal Bank Slough. He had been a telegraphic operator. As all undertakings originated in the minds of some individuals, so did telegraphic service for Coos County begin in the mind of Frederick Schetter.

In the middle seventies, a bonus of about $3000 was raised by Coos County residents to induce the Western Union to build a line in from Roseburg to Empire City. The undertaking was directed by Schetter. The line was considered a marvel. Instead of being supported by poles it was strung from tree to tree through a heavily-timbered country, making it easy to put up and difficult to maintain.

After one of the worst storms experienced in the history of Southwestern Oregon, the snow was said to have been 20 feet deep in some places near the summit of the Coast Range. The line was useless for a period of six weeks. Service was re-established by means of a second line strung above the snow and fastened higher up on the trees.

From Roseburg, the line came through Lookingglass Valley, over the Coast Range to Sitkum, Sumner, Coos City, Empire City. At Coos City a cable was laid across Isthmus Slough, at or near the present bridge by the Al Pierce saw mill. For more than 40 years that old line served Southwestern Oregon as its only telegraph wire.

In 1892 a branch line was established in Marshfield, when Schetter put his 18-year-old son, Otto, in charge. Otto Schetter continued as manager of the Marshfield office up to the time of his death in 1936, after 44 years of continuous service.

A branch line was run to Coquille, where an office was managed by Marshall Way.

James D. Laird, located at Sitkum, midway between Coos Bay and Roseburg, was responsible for the upkeep of the line. His wife, Belle Laird, learned to operate the key and proved to be indispensible in locating line interruptions and in maintaining service. Belle Laird still resides at Sitkum in 1952.

Keeping the wire alive through the winter months was

no small job. Jimmy Laird and his helpers would struggle through snow and mud to repair the line and restore service. The nearest ranchers would provide shelter when night overtook them. Falling trees during every wind storm was one of the greatest sources of trouble for Jimmy Laird. But there were other "bugs" also. It is reported and is perhaps true that at some places farm women found the telegraph wire to be a convenient clothes line. Sometimes the wet blankets or long nighties weighted the line down and made contact with a damp bush or shrub. Thus shorted, the line was dead. Jimmy and Belle had to get busy and locate the "bug."

Many times the wire would carry signals only one way. So, on prearranged hours, the Portland office would send its messages to Otto Schetter and never receive a response or o. k. until the old steamer *Breakwater* would bring the mail. It was always a source of wonder to the Portland operators, how few corrections had to be made when the original messages were compared with the copies made under such trying conditions.

The old wire, strung from tree to tree had an individuality too, so much so that new operators almost went frantic trying to operate it at times. When no one else could handle it, Otto Schetter would take the key and was able to get messages through. He knew every little trick of the old wire.

Many human interest stories center around Mrs. Laird's many years as operator at Sitkum. The team work of Belle Laird, Dr. Wm. Horsfall and Otto Schetter, no doubt saved several lives in the isolated country around Sitkum. The father of a sick child would travel to Sitkum and ask help from Mrs. Laird; she would telegraph Schetter, who in turn would call Dr. Horsfall. The father would give the symptoms and temperature, Mrs. Laird would relay the information to Schetter, who would repeat it to Dr. Horsfall.

Dr. Horsfall would prescribe, which necessarily had to be a home remedy, tell the father to return at a given time and report. Regardless of the hour, Dr. Horsfall and

Otto Schetter would be in the office to hear the father's report and advise further treatment.

When the Southern Pacific reached Coos Bay in 1916, the Marshfield station became a regular Western Union office, and Otto Schetter continued as local manager.

The old wire to Roseburg which followed the Coos Bay Wagon Road, was maintained as an auxillary for a year but was dismantled. The new line following the railroad has three submarine cables between Coos Bay and Eugene — one crossing Coos Bay at North Bend, one crossing the Umpqua River at Reedsport, and one crossing the Siuslaw at Cushman. In 1930 the Morse System was replaced by the new automatic Symplex System.

First Telephones

Early telephone history in Coos and Curry has gone largely unrecorded and is almost completely dependent upon the memories of older residents.

As remembered by Dr. William Horsfall, Frederick Schetter tapped the telegraph wire at Marshfield, plugged in a telephone, and had another plug-in at Empire. A few merchants and professional men installed telephones between their business places and their homes. Among these were Jake (Peanut) Nelson, J. W. Riggs, Dr. Horsfall.

The Home Telephone Company in Marshfield was the first established system, according to J. Albert Matson. Some vaguely seem to recollect an earlier organization, but Mr. Matson is confident this was the first. All agree that W. U. Douglas was its first president and Louis R. Robertson an early manager.

The exchange was set up in the rear of the Norton and Hanson Store on Front Street, with Eliza Ayer as first operator. Other early operators included Lela Border, Mamie Mahoney, Cora Chapman, Alice Rogers, Ella Anderson, Eulalia (Tollie) and Josephine Cordes.

J. E. Norton finds that the first line between Myrtle Point and Marshfield was completed in April of 1893, with an office in the Lyons Store in Coquille and in the Hulling and Lundy Store in Myrtle Point. This was a toll system only. Mr. Norton believes that telephones had previously been installed in the Coquille area around 1900. A farmers' line was established later, but there was no interchange of service. Business concerns were obliged to have two phones to serve their customers.

It was under Louis B. Robertson's management that in the late nineties the Marshfield line was extended northward to Gardiner by way of Old North Bend, Haynes and North inlets. A toll station was located in the Peter Peterson home at Peterson's Landing and one in the Judd Hotel on North Inlet, present site of Hauser.

In the 1920's Charles Hall, among his other large activities, completely reorganized the mixed-up and inadequate telephone systems, forming the West Coast Telephone Company that consolidated all existing lines.

COOS RADIO BROADCASTING *By Roger Spaugh*

Eight years after the first regular broadcasts began from a regular station in the United States, Coos County had its own broadcasting station — a small one set up in 1928 in what is now the Marshfield Hotel Building in Coos Bay, the ancestor of KOOS. The call letters were adopted from the local name, Coos, the change from a C to a K for the first letter being required by international radio regulations. It ceased operations three or four months after its start.The next year the engineer, H. H. Hanseth, resumed operation from his Marshfield home in a spare bedroom. Old timers will perhaps recall that programs of those days were very simple, consisting usually of phonograph records, announcements, and an occasional studio feature with local talent.

The station continued in Hanseth's home until the early thirties when it was moved to the Hall Building and ownership passed from Hanseth to Wallace Brainerd, who later sold the station to Walter Read. Around 1936 the present radio tower atop the Hall Building was constructed — a great advance in broadcasting in those days. Programming still consisted largely of phonograph records, although there were some amateur programs, dance marathons, and similar events of the day. Listeners of those days may recall the broadcasts of the sound from motion pictures from the Egyptian Theater on Sunday afternoons.

The ownership of KOOS passed from Walter Read to Sheldon Sackett on June 1, 1938. At the same time negotiations were completed to bring Mutual network programs to the area. These started June 1, 1938.

Coos County's second radio station started in 1949 when Walter Read in partnership with William E. Walsh, state senator, started KWRO in Coquille. This brought the southern part of Coos County its first dependable day and night radio reception. KWRO has operated as an independent station except for network hookups for football and baseball games.

The third radio voice in the area started in March of 1951 when KFIR, North Bend, began bringing in programs of the Liberty Broadcasting System. Thus Southwestern Oregon radio listeners now have their choice of three programs. The North Bend station is owned by Josephine Bjarnson, Hal Shade, and Roger Spaugh.

40

Inventions and Science

INVENTIONS

1

MECHANICS-CAN-DO-IT Americans have gone on expecting that sometime some inventive fellow will come up with a rig to take from the black sands their last glistening flake. Plenty of ingenious ones have tried their hands; as one failed another came, on and on through five generations; and the belief still exists that it is bound to happen.

In 1940 there was a device down at Ophir Beach at the mouth of Euchre Creek which sure looked like it would do the trick. It was the Parker Electromagnetic Machine, put out by Parker Methods, Inc., Gold Beach. A watertight steel box enclosed a Ford engine and an electric generator-set on iron sled runners and dragged under water by a scraper cable. As it browsed on the river bottom, with the river flowing over it, it picked up the black sand (which goes running to a magnet) .The machine's rate was something over a ton an hour. Submerged right under the current of Euchre Creek, it would move along, attracting to itself a precious load. Now, a Ford engine has to breathe in and out. That was taken care of by two vertical pipes reaching up like a submarine's periscope to furnish an exhaust and intake. The cylindrical magnets were at the four corners of the sled inside the runners. They were energized through cables from the generator. Push buttons on the outside of the box permitted control of the motor. All pretty slick. But why isn't it, why aren't hundreds of it, now working in the beach placers from Whiskey Run to Chetco?

Back in 1914, J. S. Diller, the famous geologist, said soberly in two places in a bulletin published by the United States government:

Mr. J. A. Gardner, of Bandon, Oregon, wrote me on May 29, 1912, that he was using with a good degree of success two of Eccleston's tension concetrators at the mouth of Gold Run, and it appeared that at last a successful method had been found to work these deposits not only on the present beach but also on the elevated beaches. . . . On the Meeks Mine, near Port Orford, Mr. R. G. Eckis has been running an Eccleston tension concentrator 24 hours a day for some time. He is using a giant to wash the sand into a sluice box in the bottom of which he has a screen, thus taking the heavy black sand out in an undercurrent. This product is then run over the concentrator. He reports that he is securing 80 per cent of the gold . . . and he says his concentrates run over $8,000 a ton total value. One machine handles the undercurrent for 150 cubic wards a day.

To get chrome, not gold, was the purpose of the Humphreys Spiral (devised by the Humphreys Gold Corporation), which proved rather successful it is said for producing "primary gravity concentrates from the Chrome beach sands."

2

William Vaughan's famous combination of a spool donkey and a white horse has been mentioned. Fred Powers invented a safety choke hook. And in the timber field there is an invention of another kind that has had an incalcuable value — the invention of a name. The first schooner load of Curry County white cedar went to San Francisco in 1854 as something William S. Winsor inspiredly called it —Port Orford Cedar, destined to be second in world fame only to that of Lebanon.

"High Tide" was a lesser stroke but still a great one in the province of terminology — could a cigar manufactured in a maritime area be more gloriously called? Otto Groke in 1925 was making it at the rate of 25,000 a month at North Bend.

Elijah Smith at Empire City in 1897 was also pretty good at nomenclature. He was just fair with his "Invincible Brand" of canned salmon; he was just about perfect with his "Cape Arago Brand."

3

J. B. Fox, Coos pioneer of 1869, put in Marshfield's first water system, using fir logs for pipe, pierced by 3-inch holes and put together with cast iron couplings. In 1887 he dittoed this system for Coquille, boring the holes through the logs at his home on the North Fork and floating them down the river to Coquille. A second system for Marshfield came in 1895; horsepower was what he used for boring the logs.

John L. Koontz of Marshfield invented the Koontz Hydraulic Press used in the late 1920's by the State Highway Commission — itself but 500 pounds in weight but capable of exerting an 80-ton pressure by hand power.

Stewart Lyons of the pioneer Coos County lumbering family invented the "Koos King," a donkey engine for logging in the roughest of rough country. This powerhorse was manufactured in Marshfield for many years.

A turbine for a grist mill was made by Oscar Reed by using the end of a tough log, cut into four equal and carefully-shaped parts, bound together by wagon tires. This served very well in the grist mill on the Middle Fork in the late 70's, lasting till it was washed out by a flood in 1890.

The Marshfield manufacturer of the Western Picker a $1,075 machine for picking cranberries, has sales representatives in Massachusetts, Wisconsin and Washington, stating "There are now hundreds of Western Picker owners." It harvests the berries at a cost of 50 to 80 cents a barrel against $1.40 and up by hand scooping. It is claimed that a grower with 100 acres or less can do his picking alone with it. "Any normal length vine will be pulled down through the teeth before the sickle will cut. . . . Rubber lugs mounted on the conveyor belt engage the top end of longer vines and pull them into the sickle."

4

Coos and Curry have had three Luther Burbanks — Coos the two men who produced the McFarlin and the

Stankavich cranberries; Curry the man who produced the Croft Easter Lily.

In reversal of the ordinary situation, the agricultural Kokwellers to a greater degree than the more industrial Coos Bayers were economic experimenters, opportunity investigators, new enterprise explorers, flier-takers. This was particularly so in the eighties and nineties, and they must have been a very winsome people in their enthusiasms. Said the Coquille Immigration Board about 65 years ago, "Experiments are being made with reference to the manufacture of sugar, as many of the products of our soil are extremely rich in saccharine properties."

5

R. D. Hume, that celebrated fisherman on the Rogue, was not only a baby specialist for baby salmon, but the U. S. Commissioner of patents on April 21, 1896, gave him a reissue of a patent on a machine for "can-body forming, soldering, and heading," and on December 1 gave him a new patent on a "can heading machine."

Perhaps no more dramatic creation has come out of the minds of Coos Bay men than that (as elsewhere told by Victor West) by the collaboration of three North Bend marine dreamers and doers — one working out a sail plan, one designing the hull, one building with wood and bolts and ropes and canvas. Three men in a small and remote village, in competition with men of great and famous cities, making the fastest sailing ship of its time, making the *Western Shore.*

Science

Coos was the location of a naturalist's exciting, living find. Along in the 1880's the Red Tree Mouse was considered one of the rarest mammals in North America, all but extinct. Only two specimens had ever been collected by naturalists. Then in August of 1890 one was found near Marshfield. It made such a scientific stir as to be described in the Proceedings of the United States National Museum of November of that year. It was then learned that the Red Tree Mouse wasn't so rare after all. He was pretty thick in fact in Coos and Curry:

In 1917 Jewett found them abundant along the lower Rogue River . . . where their bulky nests [some as large as a half-bushel measure] were seen in the spruce trees from 15 to 18 feet above the ground. He secured a couple of the mice alive but they failed to survive a long, hard pack trip.

Institute of Marine Biology

On Coos Head, near the town of Charleston, overlooking both Coos Bay and the Pacific Ocean, the Institute of Marine Biology has held annual summer sessions since 1937. A department of the State System of Higher Education, it offers undergraduate and graduate work in botany, zoology, and paleontology, with special emphasis on marine invertebrates, marine algae, and biology of fishes. Many of the studies and findings relate to economic problems.

Empire Fossil Hunter

William Healy Dall, paleontologist with the U. S. Geological Survey and for a third of a century America's leading conchologist, in 1897 visited his friend J. S. Diller who was investigating coal deposits in the Coos Bay region. As a great shell authority, he found a man after his own heart in one of the oldest settlers of Empire:

It happened that among the inhabitants of Empire was a retired merchant of German extraction and advanced age who, without any scientific training, books, or knowledge of paleontology, except such as he could extract from an old edition of Websters Dictionary, seeking some occupation for his hours of leisure, became interested in the fossil's he found on the beach during his strolls.

He finally formed the habit of patrolling the beach between Empire and South Slough at regular intervals and especially after storms which might dislodge specimens from the bluff. This practice he has continued, according to his own estimate, for about 15 years. During this time he has accumulated, in a disused warehouse, heaps of fossils. Of the common species . . . he had literally gathered bushels. It was possible to select from this accumulation a representative series of the Miocene fossils of the locality such as would have cost the ordinary geologist years of labor to bring together.

I prevailed upon this person, Mr. B. H. Cammann, to part with such a series . . . which rendered possible the preparation of this paper. [A total of 90 species]. Besides the cranium of a fossil sea lion *(Pontolos magnus True)*, Mr. Cammann had accumulated a large number of fragments of celacean bones of large size . . . that may have belonged to a fossil *Megaptera* [humpbacked whale].

The Lost Meteorite

In the year 1859, Dr. John Evans, government geologist for Oregon and Washington, was exploring the region near the coast of Southern Oregon. It was his habit to forward rock specimens to scientists in the East for laboratory analysis. One of these scientists was Dr. Charles T. Jackson of New York. While examining a package of new arrivals, Jackson made a sensational discovery. In the lot was a piece of rock like nothing on earth. It consisted of a metalic network, including a stony material. Chemical analysis showed that the metal was principally iron containing about 9 per cent nickel. This clue confirmed by other evidence, proved that the specimen was part of a meteorite of unusual characteristics.

When the discoverer, Dr. Evans, learned what he had found, he furnished from memory a description of the meteoric mass from which he had taken it. He said that it was "in the mountains about 40 miles from Port Orford and easily accessible by mules." He estimated its weight at fully 22,000 pounds and said that the exposed surface rose about three feet from the ground. When a Boston scientific society prepared a memorial to congress asking that search be made for the treasure, Dr. Evans recalled more details. He wrote: "There cannot be the least difficulty in finding the meteorite. The western face of Bald

Mountain where it is, as its name indicates, bare of timber, a grassy slope without projecting rock in the immediate vicinity of the meteorite. The mountain is a prominent landmark, seen for a long distance on the ocean, as it is higher than any of the surrounding mountains."

But in 1860, before arrangements for the expedition to find and unearth the strange meteorite had been completed, Dr. Evans died. No one else had his exact knowledge of its whereabouts. The missing meteorite has never been found. It is mentioned among the who's who and where's where of meteorites in scientific catalogs with the location given at 42 degrees, 46 minutes N. and longitude 124 degress, 28 minutes W. The Smithsonian Institution offers a reward for its discovery; plenty of scientific bodies would pay a good price for it.

For nearly a century the Port Orford meteorite has remained in its secret hiding place, though many searching parties have raked the region, seemingly, with a fine-toothed comb.

Bob Harrison, the much publicized gold mine prospector and writer of visionary experiences, has reported that he knows the exact location and that he has a mining claim in which the meteorite lies hidden. But to date he has not revealed his secret.

Following a widely-read story in a Portland paper about twelve years ago, a group of Lakeside men formed themselves into a search party, naming themselves *The Society for the Recovery of THE LOST PORT ORFORD METEORITE.*

Head of the group is Myron D. Kilgore, who has made a number of trips into the area. From the National Archives, Washington, D. C., he has secured a copy of the day-to-day journal of the 1859 Evans party, and has obtained an aerial map of the general territory where the enormous heavenly rock is supposed to be. In case he fails to find it during his own lifetime, he expects to leave his data to others so that the search might go on till it is successful.

Coos Meteorologist

Weather figured big with George Bennett, namer of Bandon. It was one of the two main inducements that brought him from Ireland to the mouth of the Coquille River in 1873. In his Bandon Beach verses he put "a cheerful and cloudless sky." In his prose writings on Bandon he described the "fresh and invigorating breeze that comes in there over an ocean expanse of nearly 4,000 miles." He explained why the Japanese current at Bandon was kind of special – it flows in "between Capes Arago and Blanco and between whose arms stretched out from the mainland it is sheltered from all winds save the west." So it was warmer than at the "more exposed portions of the coast." He noted the seasonal growth of native grasses – spring, 7.28 inches; summer, 12.12; fall, 5.27; winter, 4.30.

Aguilar's River, that 300-year mystery to others, was by the evidence of climatology the Coquille. When did Aguilar and Antonio Flores see it? January 19, 1603. What is the Coquille's wettest month? January. What would the foot of rainfall at that time make it? "A rapid and abundant river," just like Antonio Flores said.

Such zeal was utilized by the U. S. Weather Bureau. He became the official observer for Coos County. He served for many years and was always diligent in furnishing the required reports.

VI

BIOGRAPHIES

BIOGRAPHIES

These biographies were selected and the information in large part assembled, as accurately as possible, by the History Committee of the Pioneer and Historical Association, with the assistance of an advisory group. Limitations of space have not allowed the inclusion of many individuals and families who have importantly contributed to the material and cultural growth of Coos and Curry counties. Persons considered with some detail in the main portions of the book, are ordinarily not given again in these biographical pages. All sketches have had to be kept rigidly short.

Aasen, Sivert E., b. Norway 1846; to Coos 1872; bought and operated farm on Halls Creek below Myrtle Point. Married Marie L. Bagge 1873. Children: Mary Magdalene (Fredenburg), Edwin, Lewis, John L., Sigwell A., Magnor E., Olaf H.

Abernethy, Edwin P. S., b. Portland 1875, son of William and Sarah (Gray) Abernethy; to Coos 1891; settled with parents on farm near Dora. Married Ethel Laird, daughter of James D. and Belle Laird. Mrs. Abernethy as Ethel Laird became postmaster at Sitkum January 25, 1917; by January 1952 she will have served continuously 35 years, longest term as postmaster in Coos or Curry. He developed and carried on farming; built a portable sawmill, making planks for the old Coos Bay Wagon Road; later he added a planing mill; built a fine home where he and Mrs. Abernethy still reside, on the old homesite of his parents.

Abernethy, William, b. New York 1831, son of George Abernethy, first provisional governor of Oregon. Father, a Methodist missionary, came to Oregon 1840; located at Salem; William attended Willamette University, James Elliott School in New York, Phillips Academy in Massachusetts, and Yale. To California during gold rush 1849; farmed in Willamette Valley; in business in Portland; in The Dalles; in Boise, Idaho. Married Sarah F. Gray. Children: George Henry, Mary, Priscilla, Annie May (Starr), Caroline A. (Burgess), William G., Edwin P. S., Violet O. G. (Swanton), Daisy S. F. (Hahn), Pearl D. (Miller), Frances May (Hahn), Camilla D., Mizpah I. (Waterman).

Adams, John F., b. Iowa 1880. To Curry about 1900. Farmer; state game warden; U. S. predatory animal hunter; developed and operated livestock farm on Rogue River between Wedderburn and Agness; built mill and sawed lumber on farm for home use. Married Sadie E. Hull 1910. Children: Ellen Burk, George Richard, John F. Jr., Genevieve Hutchew, Jack, Roy, Ruth. Two of the sons, Dick and Jack with their families, have taken over the main part of the farm. The parents, Mr. and Mrs. John F. Adams, continue to make their home by the side of the Rogue, where they keep open house to their friends, especially those who like bear meat, and are interested in fishing and hunting.

Adelsperger, Augustus Edward, b. Illinois 1878. To Coos 1907. Married Mabel Rush 1909. Children: Helen Page, and Bob, both born in Coos County. Mr. Adelsperger came to Coos as timber supervisor for C. A. Smith Timber Company. President Coos County Tax Association; secretary Coos County Fire Patrol Association; president Western White Cedar Company. Died 1937.

Adolphsen, Asmus, b. Denmark, Europe, 1854. To Curry 1886. Homesteaded at Denmark; later operated sawmill at Dairyville; developed homestead into the Wood Lily Dairy Farm. Returned to Denmark, Europe, to marry Anna Festerson. Children: Hans, Henry, Katie, Fred.

Aiken Brothers—John, James and Andrew Glen, early Coos pioneers. Their father, a coal mine operator in Pennsylvania; sons came west 1853 in covered-wagon train, in the first immigration via Natches Pass. South into Willamette Valley and to Coos County. James Aiken, first to arrive, obtained land with coal prospects at head of Coalbank Slough, which later became the nucelous of the Newport and then the Libby coal mines. During winter of 1854-55, the three brothers mined and hauled 200 tons of coal to the bay; arranged with Patrick Flannagan to ship the coal, which is reported to have sold readily in San Francisco at $40 per ton. John Aiken went to San Francisco, where he died later. James and Andrew took up claims at head of Isthmus Slough; conducted logging camps; James also followed surveying and made several early surveys in Southwest Oregon. Both James and Andrew served as volunteers with Capt. William Harris in Indian wars in mid-fifties. Andrew Glen Aiken served several years as sheriff of Coos County and later as postmaster at Coquille. Glen Aiken Creek was named for him. Married Augusta Cunningham 1879. Children: Charles Glen, Alice, Margaret Florence, William. In 1897 the Aiken family moved to Marshfield, where Mrs. Aiken conducted a millinery store many years. Mr. Aiken died 1917.

Albrecht, Carl L., b. Germany 1872; with parents direct to Coos from Germany 1883. From age 18, followed steamboating, surveying, railroad construction, freight contracting by boat and barges; worked at surveying for Simpson Lumber Company. In 1901 married Fannie Warner, daughter of Wm. and Laura Warner, covered-wagon pioneers residing on south fork of the Coquille. One daughter, Vera L. Member of city county of Marshfield for three years, when much of the street paving was begun. Sister Jennie was the late Mrs. Robert Kruger, mother of the present Max Kruger of Coos Bay.

Anderson, Andrew, b. Finland 1866; to Coos 1890; worked in timber and coal mines. Homesteaded near Lakeside 1906, on North Lake; developed dairy farm. Married Mrs. Hannah Stonelake 1904. Her children by first marriage: Stanford, Victor, Emma, Mathew, Esther. Children of marriage to Mr. Anderson: Edna, William, Arthur, Ernest.

Anderson, Edmund A., b. Prince Edward Island 1842. To Oregon by way of Isthmus of Panama and San Francisco 1869. Followed shipbuilding and carpenter work in Simpson yards, North Bend; later in Marshfield shipyard. Began livery stable in Marshfield 1878; brought first buggy to Marshfield; owned up to 18 head of horses; sold wood, coal, grain, hay; did general hauling and livery business. First mayor of Marshfiled; member of several lodges. Before leaving Prince Edward Island, married Caroline Murray. Children: Emma, Herbert, Lillie Luse, Annie Coke, Margaret Wold, Eva Chestnut.

Anderson, John E., b. Finland about 1850; to Coos about 1880; one of the well known logging raftsmen through many years before the coming of power boats. Married Louise Hillstrom. Children: John, Andrew, Hilda, Ernest.

Anderson, Victor, b. Finland 1863; to Coos 1881; several years in logging industry; then learned trade as ship carpenter; employed many years in Kruse and Banks shipyards; bridge building contractor. Owned considerable real estate in North Bend. Married Anna Strong 1884. Children: Emma Matson, Ellen Kruse, Inez Muscus, Malinda, Louis, Fred.

Appleton, John, b. Jackson County 1858; to Coos at early age. Married Sisa C. Robinson 1880, who had come with parents from California. Children: John W., James L., Rosabel, Mary, Lena, Elsie. Family resided on Myrtle Creek, Coos County, running a small farm. He was an early bull-team logging driver. Died 1939. Mrs. Appleton still resides with daughter near the old home.

Archer, Samuel, b. Scotland 1843; began seafaring early in life. Mined gold in California and Alaska; to Coos about 1874. Mined coal at Libby; in 1875 took preemption claim of 179 acres on Isthmus Inlet, which became home of the Archer family. Married Margaret Munroe 1861. Children: William, Neil, Martha, Ellen, Grover. Several generations of the family are among present-day residents of Coos County. Mr. Archer died 1925; Mrs. Archer 1891.

Arnold, Almus McDaniel (Mack), b. Tennessee 1844. Orphaned at age three; reared by relatives. In Civil War, enlisted in First Cavalry; served two years nine months. A lover of horses and cattle, he spent most of his life in cattle business and in the saddle as cowboy in Texas, New Mexico, and Colorado. Married Catherine McDermott Dolan 1881; to Oregon 1884, engaged in cattle business; moved to Washington with herd of cattle; lost them all by cold weather. Returned to Coos with about 100 horses in 1891; briefly on Halls Creek, then to a farm on South Coquille, near present site of Powers. Children: Annie, Eva, Marie, Nellie, Juanita, William, Ranson, Richard, Elizabeth, John. Died at age 84, Mrs. Arnold at nearly 90.

Arnold, Richard, b. Rural, son of "Mack" Arnold; married Lida Morehouse 1928. No children. Owned and operated tavern and eating house in Myrtle Point many years.

Arrington, J. M., b. Portland 1852. Married Alice Haynes, daughter of Mr. and Mrs. Jerry Haynes, 1879. One daughter, Ione. Operated a grocery in Myrtle Point about 30 years. Past master of Masonic lodge, Marshfield.

Asplund, Hans B., b. Finland 1853. First marriage in Finland; two children: Amelia and Carl. Wife died. Hans came to America about 1882. Married Johannah Mattson 1886; brought his two children from Finland. Children by second marriage: Edna Johannah Ausee, John Walter, Esther Charlotte Leyer. Hans Ausplund worked in car shops of S. P. railway for many years. Died 1913; widow 1937.

Asplund, John Walter, b. Marshfield 1891, son of Hans and Johanna (Mattson) Asplund. Educated in local schools and Oregon State College. Married Hazel Christensen 1899, graduate of Oregon State College. Children: John Victor, Charlotte Palmateer. Mrs. Asplund died 1949. Mr. Asplund married Mrs. Jeanette Beckhelm 1950. Following service in World War One, he has been with the Mountain States Power Company, from 1919 to 1948 as division superintendent and since then as manager.

George Bennett, the witty Irishman, as justice of the peace at Bandon in 1878: *A bride and groom present themselves. We read the solemnization of matrimony according to the ritual of the Church of England, and particularly that portion where the woman promises to obey. "Say, Judge, hold on there a minute," exclaims the fair bride. "Obey, obey be damed. I never obeyed anyone since I was born and may I be damned if I am going to begin now."*

Bailey, Charles H. Sr., to Curry 1857; settled near present site of Wedderburn.

Bailey, Charles H., son of Chas. H. Sr., b. on Bailey ranch in Curry 1864; attended local schools; rancher and farmer; Ellensburg postmaster 1886-87; county assessor 1890-92; Alaska *Sourdough* 1897-1903; sheriff of Curry County 1912-17; county judge 1924-36; president Curry County Bank 1920-39. Children: Alice A., Mary Eleanor. Died 1939.

Bailey, Kate Lehnherr, b. near Myrtle Point 1889, daughter of Wm. Tell Lehnherr of pioneer family.

Taught school in Coos and Curry; married Charles H. Bailey 1916. Two daughters: Alice A., Mary Eleanor. Active rancher since death of Judge Bailey 1939. Large producer of sheep; ranch is bordered by the Rogue and the Pacific, where river meets the sea.

Baker, John L., b. Missouri 1850; to Coos 1887; settled at Coquille; livery and feed business. Married Delia Coon 1873, b. Linn County 1855. Children: John, Sarah, Lewis, Allie, Bertha, Preston, Dollie, Lester. Moved to Myrtle Point in the 1890's and engaged in cattle buying.

Baker, Raymond E., b. Kansas 1875. Eduction began in Kansas; continued on through high school in Washington, D. C., while his father was Congressman from Kansas. Married Mary J. Bradbury 1903. Children: Henry, Ellen, Jean (Hornish), William, Raymond, Ned. To Coos 1905, superintendent of Myrtle Point schools; homesteaded on Middle Creek 1909; continued to teach; county school superintendent 1913-18. Pioneered movement from the *Three R's in the Little Red Schoolhouse* introducing athletics, debating, consolidation of one-room rural schools, longer school term, higher standards for teachers, and other features to give rural schools the advantages of city schools.

Baldwin, Henry H., b. Ireland 1825; to sea at age 16; to U. S. 1846; enlisted U. S. Army 1849; to Oregon to help quell Indian uprisings. Member of U. S. transport schooner "Captain Lincoln" wrecked just north of Coos Bay bar 1852. In 1855-56 served as packer, scout and express rider during Indian wars in Curry. Mined in Jackson and Coos counties. After about 20 years of military service, took up 320 acres near Parkersburg; sold out 1895 and retired in Bandon. A man of schoolarly attainments, his poetry and prose often appeared in periodicals of his time. Member of G. A. R. Never married.

Banks, Robert, b. Canada 1870. In 1913 married Margaret Fisher, who died. One daughter: Mary (Mrs. Jack Granger). Married Pearl Stuart 1942. Began as shipbuilding apprentice in Connecticut; later employed in San Francisco yards, where he met and worked with K. V. Kruse. Was attracted to Coos by large sign: "Use Coos Bay Coal." Entered partnership with K. V. Kruse in shipbuilding firm of Kruse & Banks, building scores of all types of wooden ships at their North Bend yards, including many for the U. S. in both world wars. President of firm since 1920. Surveyor for S. F. Board of Underwriters since 1920; member Coos Bay port commission; North Bend city council; active in many civic and community affairs.

Barker, Delroy, b. New York 1847. Served in 7th U. S. Cavalry with General Custer in the Custer Masacree; only man to survive, as he was posted behind to guard the Company's property. Arctic explorer four years with Canadian expedition of Oglesby and Green. Homesteaded on Coquille River 1895. Farmed and operated pack train. First marriage to Christina Myers. Children: John H., Mary E., both of Canada. Second marriage to Mrs. Louisa Hillis. Her children by first marriage: William, Edward, Harry, Roy, Glenn, Thomas.

Barker, Ed C., b. Coquille 1884. Married Mary Lucy Gould 1909. Children: Lucy Aileen Rickard, Grayce Gould Hatcher, Edwin Cecil Barker Jr. Mr. Barker, a graduate watchmaker, has conducted his own jewelry store in Myrtle Point many years. Mrs. Barker, a daughter of Mr. and Mrs. George A. Gould of Elk Horn Ranch, graduated as a trained nurse at Home Hospital, San Jose, 1907.

Barker, John L. b. Missouri 1847, one of 12 children. Started west by covered wagon at age eight. His father died enroute. Mother bought 20 acres in California; she moved family to Roseburg 1860; she died about 1868. John went to work freighting, working with pack trains, driving cattle. He married Mary C. Norris, dauhter of Mary E. (Boone) Norris. Children: Fred W., Verner N., Thomas G., Clyde A., Jessie M., Edwin C., John L., Birdie. M. Bought 160 acres on Coquille River, where he resided 30 years. In 1900 he purchased a home near Fairview, where he farmed and logged; served 27 years as school director and over 20 years as road supervisor.

Barklow, C. H., b. Iowa 1872. Settled with parents near Myrtle Point 1873. Married Etta A. Wagner, b. Illinois 1872. Children: Rachel A., Zelia E. General farming.

Barklow, Daniel, b. Illinois 1865; settled near Myrtle Point 1872. Married Mary J. Pullen, b. in Illinois. Four children. Early day stage driver and prominent Coquille Valley farmer.

Barklow, James H., b. Illinois 1862; settled near Myrtle Point 1872; later moved to Bandon. Married Louisa Randleman. Four children. Principal occupation, teaching school; several terms as county school superintendent.

Barklow, J. D., b. Iowa 1856; settled near Myrtle Point 1872. Married Sarah J. Lewellen, b. Iowa 1858. Five children. Farming.

Barklow, Elder Samuel S., b. Pennsylvania 1841. To Coos 1872. With his brother David he introduced the German Baptist religion in Coos County; served here as a preacher the remainder of his life. Died 1897. (See chapter on churches). His first wife was Mary Studebaker, who died in 1866. Children: J. H. and J. S. Second marriage to Anne Miller 1867. Children: Sarah E. Randleman, Nathan E., John D., Mary Broadbent, Bertha Snell, S. Willie, Alta Annie Abbott.

Barklow, Thomas, b. Illinois 1853; settled near Myrtle Point 1873. Married Anna E. Miller 1871. Children: Charles Henry, Mary Ann, George Wilbur, John Wesley, Eva May, Gracy Myrtle, Nora Belle.

Barrows, Abie, b. Astoria 1869; to Coos 1882. Married Mary Christina Hamblock 1891, b. in Coos County 1875, daughter of Mr. and Mrs. John Hamblock, early pioneers. Followed ship building, farming and sawmill filing work. Died 1945; Mrs. Barrows 1949.

Barrows, Joseph F., b. Kentucky 1822; to Oregon 1847; to California gold rush 1849. Gold miner, merchant, farmer at different places in California and Oregon. First wife was Margaret Stevenson, who died shortly after marriage. Second marriage in 1850 to Dianna T. Lightner. Children: William, Alice, Samuel, Frank, Carrie, Albia, Lee, Cassie, Charles.

Barry, Thomas. In 1892 married Mary Ellen Flannagan, b. San Francisco 1867, daughter of Patrick and Ellen Janes Flanagan. Children: all born at Empire: Jack, Marge (Tofts), Katherine (Beyer). Was first tutor for the Patrick Flanagan children when the family lived at Libby. Later he worked with "The Coast Mail," one of the pioneer newspapers of Coos County. For a short time he was U. S. Collector of Customs, succeeding Major Morton Tower.

Baxter, F. M., b. Iowa. Married Linwoood Watson; to Coos 1879; engaged in logging. Children: Charles E., Mabel, George E., Harry (Hal), Pearl, Cleveland.

Bean, Wesley A., b. Douglas County 1862, son of Stephen and Martha A. Bean. Taught school six years; then formed partnership with J. H. Timmon in a coal mine project at Riverton, the first in that area. Later he worked at carpenter trade and in sawmills. Married Mabel Martin 1897. Children: Bernice and Dorothy D. Opened store in Riverton, later taking in Mrs. Bean's brother, Cliff Martin; the partnership continued for over fotry years, until 1940, when he sold his interest to Mr. Martin and retired, at the same time quitting the postmastership which he had held since 1907.

Bear, John, b. Finland 1841. Sailed many years, reaching Marshfield 1865 from a beached burning ship. Worked at Simpson sawmill in North Bend three years; then establihsed a lumber business of his own; improved, stocked and sold 15 farms in Oregon. Operated livery stable in Marshfield several years. First married Mary Ann Walin; died 1888. Children: Emma, Cynthia Nagle, Edna Walters, Albert, Chester. Married Mrs. Nelson Jenson 1895.

Beatty, John, b. Scotland 1842; to Coos 1870; for a while on Coos Bay, then to Randolph. In 1875 settled on a Coos River farm, where he and his brother resided for several years. Lived continously in Coos County, except five years at placer mining in California.

Belieu, Lorenzo D. b. Douglas County 1857. Married Malinda Josephine Dean, daughter of Provit Dean, 1879. Children: Joseph A., Lorenzo D. Jr., Lou Zetta, Lavina De Etta, Leova M., Leander D., Claude L., Floyd R., Naoma J., Edna E., Edward C. Family residence is at Bridge.

Belloni, Fred, b. Switzerland 1862; to Curry 1897; followed dairying; to Coos 1905, in lumber business. In 1901 married Delle M. Cope, daughter of W. V. Cope. No children of their own but cared for and reared Joseph and Sarah Nye (orphans of Mrs. Cope's sister) ; two nieces; and other children not related. Resided many years in Coquille, where their comfortable and hospitable home is well remembered by scores of persons who had temporary or semi-permenent living quarters with the Bellonis. He died 1949. Mrs. Belloni resides in Bandon with her niece, Mrs. Otto C. Schindler.

Belloni, George, b. Switzerland 1850; to Curry 1896; operated dairy of 200 cows; later bought dairy farm at Riverton. Married Celia Ottoline 1882. Children: Cora, Lena, Nettie — all teachers in Coos County; Henry, Thomas, George, Masie, Agnes, Mamie.

Belloni, Henry P., b. California 1885, son of George Belloni. To Curry 1894. Worked at the Star Ranch, where he did his first butter-making. Did creamery work in Coquille 43 years. Married Belle McLeod 1908. Children: George, Helen, Margaret.

Bender, Edward, b. Baltimore 1841. With parents to Coos 1875; established general store on Dr. Hermann's place, later moving his business to Myrtle Point; postmaster; justice of the peace; notary public; connected with U. S. General Land Office. Married Nellie Hermann 1876. Children: Asa B., Ferdinand, August, Ernest E, Chester L.

Benham, George, R., b. Missouri 1862. To Oregon with parents 1863. Farmed with his father in Coos; later purchased his own farm and engaged in dairying.

Benham, Jefferson Davis, b. Missouri 1864, son of Peter and Nancy Benham. To Coos with parents 1882. His father bought a homesteader's right, but died shortly afterwards; his widow proved up on the land. Young Jeff carried on with his widowed mother; developed their Fairview farm. Planted and developed one of the best orchards in Coos County. Later he bought out his mother. Married Carrie Edda Brownson 1888. Children: Nancy L., Myrtle Irene, Thomas H., Raymond D., Edda Amanda, Elmer Ernest.

Benham, William, to Coos 1863; settled in Fairview district; farmer and blacksmith. Married Susan Miller. Children: John, Samuel, Amanda, James, Nancy, Florence, George R., Martha S., Frances M.

Bennett, G. A. (See newspaper chapter) .

Bennett, Geo. **(See chapter on towns.)**

Bennett, John D., b. Missouri 1848; to Coos 1870; owned and operated a sawmill; carpenter work; bridge building a specialty; farmed near Gravelford. Married Mary Belle Bunch. Children: William, Charles R., Arthur R., Ray R., Eva M., Lois L.

Bennett, Joseph William, b. Ireland 1855, son of George Bennett; to Coos 1873; married Mary Grace Bennett. Children: Elsie, Thomas Tankerville. Established Flanagan and Bennett Bank in Marshfield 1889, first in Coos-Curry area; a leading attorney many years. Mrs. Bennett died 1894; Mr. Bennett 1916.

Bennett, May B., b. Marshfiield 1887, daughter of G. A. and Jennie (Mark) Bennett. Local schools and Stanford University School of Nursing. Sent by Red Cross with group of doctors to Siberia in 1918; later entered U. S. Public Health Service at Port Townsend, Washington; covered many states throughout the nation during the 28 years she was in this service; chief nurse 1924-1948. Retired and resides in the family's former Marshfield home. Member of Coos Head Garden Club, and various nurses organizations.

Bennett, Thomas Tankerville, b. Marshfield July 7, 1886, son of Joseph

W. and Mary Grace Bennett. Educated in Marshfield schools, Bellmont private prepatory school in California; graduated in law from Stanford University 1909; began law practice with firm of Bennett, Bennett and Swanton in Marshfiield 1910. Member of the Oregon State Legislature two terms; president Coos County Bar Association. Died 1929.

Berg, J. Arthur, b. Minnesota 1895. Graduate University of Oregon Law School 1921; admitted to Oregon State Bar same year; law practice in Coquille since then. Married Florence Powers, daughter of A. H. Powers, 1924. Children: Mary Patricia, Martha Suzanne, Joseph Arthur. Served in First World War; mayor of Coquille, 1928-36; chairman rationing board Coos County; Selective Service, Coos and Curry. Member Coos County Bar Association, Oregon State Bar Association, American Legion, Veteran of Foreign Wars.

Berry, John L., b. Scotland; to Curry about 1852. Married Mary Warner. Children: John, Alfred, Horace, William, Olive Shull, Mary Wyland, Alice Strong, Laura Schroeder.

Bessy, Elmer L., b. Massachusetts 1862; to Coos 1887. Married Clara Guptil 1885. Children: Warren, Alden E., Ruth Olive, Frank L. Owned farm on South Coos River. In partnership with his brother, built and operated the Bessey Creamery on home place; bought out his brother's interest 1898. School director and road supervisor.

Bessey, H. E., b. Massachusetts 1860. To Coos 1885; bought and operated farm on South Coos River; with his brother built and operated the Bessey Creamery. Later helped to organize the Coos Bay Mutual Creamery, of which he afterwards became general manager. Married Josephine McIntosh 1894, daughter of Donald and Nancy McIntosh. Children: Catherine, George, Lawrence, Lucy, Fred.

Bettys, Hiram, b. New York 1835.To Coos 1874; farmed in Fairview district. Married Catherine Desmond 1861. Children: William, Albert E., Barbara, Annie, Harry, Walter.

Bettys, William, b. Canada 1862. To Coos with parents 1874; followed farming in Fairview area; drove stage from Sitkum to Coos City. Moved to Coquille about 1917; died 1951.

Beyers, Ephriam H., b. Ohio 1841. To Coos 1883; settled on farm near Sumner. Married Barbara Ellen Weaver. Children: Ophir H., Laura L., Charles W., Alice M., Jesse P., Josephine R., Frank C., Millie I., Nettie V.

Beyers, Jesse P., b. Nevada 1873, son of Ephriam Beyers. Grew up on farm near Sumner; local and Coquille schools; worked for a time as photographer. Assessor 1916-1940. Married Mabel Lawhorn. Children: Llyle, Margaret Zella. Mrs. Beyers died. Later, he married Ruth Nissen, a teacher in the Coquille schools; she died 1950.

Billings, L. L., b. Missouri 1856. To Coos with parents 1872. Married Belle Major 1881. Children: M. E., Hazel, Della, Walter, Clarence M., Alvin, Lester, Lena, Albert, George. Proved up on homestead on south fork of Coquille River 1884. Followed general farming and dairying successfully on different places over a period of years.

Black, Henry, b. Missouri 1838; in Confederate army in Civil War. To Coos 1875. Operated own farm on Catching Inlet till 1907. Married Sarah McGee in Douglas County 1865. Children: John D., William F., Lucy, Mary, George. School director; road supervisor. Son John D. postmaster at Marshfield 1894-1898. William Frank moved away. Lucy married George Ross, son of B. F. Ross, early pioneer of Coos County. Mary early trained nurse of Coos County; married Carl Smedberg; together they operated the Smedberg Hospital in Marshfield till the Wessley (now McAuley) Hospital was established; then moved to Gold Beach, and owned the Smedberg Hospital till the late 1940's. Mrs. Smedberg, now a widow, lives with her brother George Black at Gold Beach.

Blain, Thomas, b. Missouri 1846; became orphaned at early age. Made his home with a family named McGee; came west with them to Douglas County 1867. Married Frances Woodruff 1869; to Coos 1872; settled on North Coos River; developed a fine dairy farm. Children: Laura, Jettie, Lizzie, Mattie. Sold farm 1910 and retired to Marshfield. Died soon after. Mrs. Blain died 1883.

Blanc, Lou, b. Nebraska 1886; married Minnie Coleman 1912; she died 1949. Later married Daisy B. Hayden. Began as signalman and steam engineer in logging camps and sawmills. Operated Coos Bay Mutual Creamery 1918-19. Organized and became principal owner and president of Lou Blanc, Inc. 1919 to date: general automobile sales, service and repairs, in Marshfield, now Coos Bay; director Coast Highway Association; Marshfield city council; active in many local, community, civic and trade affairs; Elk life membership.

Blumenrother, Charles T., b. New York City 1846; resided in both Coos and Curry; in U. S. Army during Civil War; attained rank of lieutenant-colonel. Married Amelia L. K. Meier 1871. Children: Thomas J. G., Charles F. W., Pauline R. W. Farmer; in business in Bandon a number of years.

Boak, Gurley, b. Wisconsin 1861. To Bandon 1889; located on homestead near Bradley Lake. Married Margaret Jane Saunders. Childern: Henry E., Leah Ellen, Hattie F., Carrie Gail. A marine engineer on ocean-going ships, bar tugs and river steamers. Died 1925; Mrs. Boak 1950.

Boak, Henry E., b. Michigan 1883; to Bandon with parents 1890; first employed in the Clark woolen mill; later various kinds of work; clerked in McNair's hardware store 1906; became a stockholder and director 1913. Married Catherine A. McNair 1911. Children: Melvin E.; Rupert G. and Robert A., twins; Ralph A. Member of city council and school board. Died 1949.

Bogardus, E. M., b. New York City 1858; settled on Rogue River 1893; Printing and publishing business 25 years. (See newspaper chapter.) Married A. B. Greene; parents of two children; county treasurer a number of years.

Bogard, Gustave, b. Norway, Europe, 1856; to Coos 1898; settled on Lampa Creek; cleared up, improved and developed one of the fine farms of the Coquilla Valley. Married Christine Lee 1888, b. Norway 1855. Children: Conrad, Lester, Gertrude. Mrs. Bogard died 1926; he 1935.

Boice, Allen H., b. near Langolis 1881. Married Carrie Guerin 1906. Children: Howard Wm., Fred, Edna, Ada May, Courtland A., Hilda, Warren, Alma, Dora, Mary, Allen H., Alden W. Farmed; freighted with six-horse team; later operated truck line; sold out to Central Transfer Company of Bandon. Curry County commissioner and judge. Died 1949.

Boice, Zachari, b. Missouri 1851; settled on Flores Creek 1877; married Eliza Gault 1871. Children: William R., Frank E., Ida, Clarence W., Allen H. Dairying and livestock. Moved to Bandon 1904; worked in Rosa sawmill. Died 1915; Mrs. Boice 1916.

Bonebrake, Charles L., 1864, son of Lorenzo and Lucy A. Granby; father and mother both died shortly after. Then adopted by J. V. and Sarah Bonebrake at Empire City, with giving him the name of Charles Lorenzo Bonebrake. Grew up on Ross Slough; married Janet Munroe 1885. Children: Clara, Zelle L., Malissa L., Lucy I., Charles O., Holt M. Sold his dairy farm and moved to Marshfield 1907. Operated laundry; butcher shop; later the Club Confectionery and Cigar Store. Removed to Olympia, Washington.

Bonebrake, George Alva (Alvie), b. Oakland, Oregon, 1867, son of John W. and Martha A. To Coos with parents 1868; grew up on Ross Slough. Married Mildred A. Tanner 1899. One child, Willa M., died 1945. One of the owners and operators of the Union Meat Market in Marshfield a number of years. Both he and Mrs. Bonebrake are Methodists, Republicans and members of Women of Woodcraft over 50 years.

Bonebrake, Henry S., b. Iowa 1858; settled on Catching Inlet 1866. Later moved to Marshfield and engaged in watchmaking business. Married Ida

M. Newland 1880. Children: Eulalia, Alton E., Verle S.

Bonebrake, Joseph V., b. Indiana 1837; to Coos 1862; worked in Newport (Libby) coal mines. Later moved to farm on Ross Slough. Married Sarah B. Ross. Children: Charles L., Jennie P.

Boone, Alphonso D., b. Missouri 1837, son of Col. A. D. and Nancy L. Boone. Married Nancy L. Barker 1875. Children, all born in Coos County: Jesse A., Lulu L., James L., Mary E., Henry C., Myrtle L. Came to Coos 1869; homesteaded on Catching Inlet; worked on steamboats on the Umpqua and Coos Bay; settled down on homestead near Sumner. Great-grandson of Daniel Boone of Kentucky fame. His sister Chloe married Governor Curry of Oregon; said to have been the first woman school teacher in the Territory of Oregon. Both Mr. and Mrs. Boone died 1915.

Booth, Robert A., b. Minnesota 1880; to Coos 1906. Manager of retail lumber yard of C. A. Smith Lumber Company. Later owned City Lumber and Supply Company at Astoria. Married Katheleen Bennett, daughter of G. A. and Jennie (Mark) Bennett. One daughter, Mary Kathleen. Mrs. Booth, before her marriage, was a teacher in the Marshfield schools for a number of years. She still resides in Astoria, where Mr. Booth died 1931.

Bossen, Edgar, b. Germany 1851; to Curry 1876; acquired 400-acre farm; raised sheep, operated dairy; developed a brick kiln from a rich deposit of clay on his farm; also developed a large apple orchard. Married Mary Bruhn 1872. Children: Alice, Mary, Elena, Jennie, Grace, Henry. Jennie taught school and was county school superintendent in Curry for several years.

Bowman, David, b. Oregon 1870; to Curry 1910; an early cheese maker. Later operated a cheese factory at Parkersburg in partnership with his brother-in-law, Henry Miller. Married Lillian Berry 1903. One daughter, La Verne.

Bowman, J. A., b. Oregon 1864. Bandon and Langlois laborer, blacksmith, plumber, dealer in hardware, implements and plumbing fixtures. Deputy sheriff, Curry County. Married Anna Jordan 1887. Five children.

Bowron, Frank, b. Ohio 1863; to Coos in 1870's; coal mine and logging camp work; saloon in Marshfield; farm on Tenmile Lake near Lakeside; conducted the Lakeside Inn. Married Nellie E. Noble. Children: Cora, Maude, Jack, Ruth.

Bowron, Wm. F., b. Ohio 1855. To Coos 1877; took claim on unsurveyed land in the Tenmile country; helped to build roads and to open up that area; road supervisor; developed dairy and stock farm of about 800 acres. Married Nancy R. McCulloch. Children: Wm. Frank, Alfred Ray.

Boyrie, Arthur M., b. France 1830. To U. S. 1851. Married Maria Kraker 1863. Children: Flora, Edward, Harry, Arthur, Frank Clarence, May, Vesta. To Coquille 1883, where he was one of the early teachers. In later years bookkeeper for Jas. A. Lyons sawmill. Died 1906; Mrs. Boyrie 1921.

Brack, Phillip, b. Germany 1828; to Coos 1852; member First U. S. Dragoons on schooner "Captain Lincoln," wrecked just north of Coos Bay entrance January 1852. With others, made way overland to Port Orford. When mustered out two years later, he settled on Middle Fork of the Coquille. Married Florence Fredenburg. Children: William H., Daniel N., Mahhalia, Suzanah B., Mary E., Emma V., Margaret C.

Braden, Samuel C., b. Douglas County 1866, son of Francis Braden, who with his father operated flour and grist mills. The Braden family, including two-year-old Samuel C., settled at Burton Prairie (Fairview) 1868. The father became first postmaster of Fairview, established in their home 1875. Samuel's father was also one of the first stage drivers between Myrtle and Roseburg. As Samuel grew up he engaged in the transportation business. Married Augusta Prey 1893. Mr. Braden died 1935. Mrs. Braden lives with daughter, Mrs. Harold Watzling, in Myrtle Point; another daughter, Mrs. Ralph Sigsby, lives in Coos Bay.

Brady, Thomas W., b. Minnesota 1858. To Gravelford 1880 to be with his half-brother, Sol J. McCloskey. Married Martha A. Bright 1883. Children: Mary J., Sarah A., Charles M., Electa L., William E., Maxine. Most of life spent on farm near Gravelford; a few years at Grants Pass; last years in Coquille. Died 1944.

Brando, Harriet J., b. Ashland 1866. To Coos 1880, lived with sister, Mrs. David Young. Married Henry E. Nicholls 1889, a marine engineer. Children: Eunice A., H. Allen. Married E. E. Brando 1906. Operated the Brando Apartments. Died 1951.

Brandon, Laura C., b. Iowa 1874. Married Walter G. Brandon 1906; to Coquille 1908. Children: Warren G., Mella J., Marlin J. Mrs. Brandon taught in public schools 43 years, 13 in Kansas and 30 in Coos County. Resided in Coquille since 1908. Retired 1950.

Brelage, Herman, b. Germany 1895; married Angela Lenger 1919. Children: John, Frank; to U. S. 1926; worked in Anaconda copper mills, Montana; to Coos 1933; leased the former Charles Siestreem farm on North Lake near Lakeside; operating it as a dairy. In 1936 bought the Julius Larson farm on Larson Inlet, building it up to one of Coos County's most modern dairies; keeps 75 to 80 cows. President Southwest Oregon Retail Milk Association ten years; member local school board several terms; active in community affairs. In three years' experience Mr. Brelage learned all he wanted to know about cranberry culture.

Breuer, Michael, b. Austria Hungary 1859; began as shoemaker's apprentice at age 13; drafted into Austrian army; deserted at age 21; migrated to U. S. 1881. Married Josephine Andrachofsky 1882. Te Coos 1886 over famous Beaver Slough route; homestead on Indian Creek and Middle Fork Coquille. Helped to build old Myrtle Point-Roseburg road; built and operated water-power grist mill; opened shoe shop in Bandon 1894, developed into general merchandise business; still operates his cobbler shop at age 93. Children: Victor, Ilona, Albert, Joe, Irene, Josephine, Otto. Josephine is keeping house for her father. Mrs. Breuer died 1932.

Breuer, Paul E., son of Samuel Breuer, b. Myrtle Point 1891; early life on farm and in his father's shoe shop and store. Educated in local schools and Behnke-Walker Business College, Portland. Married Eva M. Bennett 1914. Children: Paula M., Eleanor B., Helen M., Melvin B. After the death of his father in 1941, Paul took over the Myrtle Point shoe business. In 1951 he disposed of the establishment to his son-in-law, Ben Daniels, to devote his time to his flock of sheep.

Breuer, Samuel, b. Hungary 1858; To Coos 1887. Shoemaker, cobbler; opened shoe shop in Myrtle Point, later taken over by his son, Paul. Married Maria Elischer 1882. Children: Annie, Gustave, Minnie, John, Emma, Paul, Josephine, Nellie. Died 1941.

Bright, Albert, b. Iowa 1862. With parents by wagon to Roseburg 1871; then by pack horses to Gravelford, slashing trail as they came. Farmer, blacksmith, boat builder, wagon maker. Married Sarah E. Culbertson 1882. Children: John E., Roxie E., Sylvester P., Zeno, Millie E., Alden A., Dorothy.

Bright, J. S., b. Virginia 1820. To Coos 1871, over Brewster trail to Dora, down the East Fork to the North Fork; took up land and established a home. Opened the first wagon shop in the Coquille Valley. Married Augustine Macbeen. Children: Phillip, James, Tom T., L., Albert, Martha, Mary, Minnie, Jesse D.

Broadbent, Charles, b. Pennsylvania 1864. Pioneer cheesemaker. Bought the Sugar Loaf Creamery 1903; later built and operated the Lundy Cheese Factory, the Broadbent Cheese Factory, and another one at Arago. Married Laura Barklow 1904. One daughter, Helen Jo. Post office and town of Broadbent named for his family. Sold his cheese factories and moved to California 1916, engaged in orange and olive orcharding. Died 1930.

Brodie, Ed F., b. California 1878. Married Libbie Soaper 1904. Children: Darrell, Elden. To Coos 1913 to saw shingles at the C. A. Smith Lumber mill at Marshfield. Operated shingle mills at Bandon, Fishtrap, Stout Mill in North Bend. Bought a small farm near Norway 1928, where he and his sons built a shingle mill in 1933, still operating. They also operate a lumber yard in Myrtle Point.

Brown, James G., b. Kentucky 1859; to Coos with parents 1871. Settled near Myrtle Point. Married Mary C. Lehnherr. One son, Grover.

Brown, J. Lee, b. Missouri 1870. Graduated from University of California College of Pharmacy. To Marshfield 1889. Employed as a druggist by Dr. J. T. McCormac. Established Red Cross Pharmacy of Marshfield 1906. Married Elizabeth Greenman 1895. Served two terms on Oregon State Board of Pharmacy. Retired 1947. Resides in Coos Bay. Mrs. Brown died 1951.

Buck, R. E., b. 1844; to Curry 1874; settled near Flores Creek; later to Coquille, where he started the first livery stable. Later moved to Bandon and worked for J. E. Walstrom. Married Lucy E. Grant. Children (adopted): Nettie, Ella.

Buell, James B., b. Virginia 1841; settled on Middle Creek between Dora and Fairview 1870. To Curry 1884-1886; returned to Coos, located on Catching Creek. Married Florence Pearce. Children: Lewis M. P., Julia A., Mary E., James L., Caroline E., Almon P., Laura A., Verner O., Henry P., Rosetta M.

Buffington, Collier H., b. Iowa 1889. Admitted to bar in Idaho 1912; State of Oregon bar 1914. To Gold Beach 1915; same year married Xenia Knoor. Besides an extensive legal practice, he engaged in a number of other activities—dairying, bulb growing, mining, fishing. District attorney of Curry nine years. Active in developing Curry County resources. Died 1951; Mrs. Buffington a few weeks later. Children: Nancy A., Collier H. Jr., Richard I., Anne M., Deborah K., Donald K., Charles K.

Bullard, Robert W., b. Iowa 1857. To Coos 1877; in 1883 married Malinda Hamblock, daughter of John and Jane Hamblock, among the oldest settlers on the Coquille. Operated store, post office, ferry at Bullards; taught school; fished and was interested in fish canning; very active in community affairs. Children: Warren A., Pearl A., John C., Laurence, Christina, Frank.

Bullock, Richard G., b. Kentucky 1831. To Coos 1868. Married Elizabeth Cawfield. Children: James L., Thomas O., John F., Louisa A., Frank R., Rosey B. Farmed on Cunningham Creek. "Bullock" Mountain bears the family name.

Bunch, Frank S., b. Kansas 1865; with parents to Oregon 1872. Taught school in Gravelford Academy, a Seventh Day Adventist institution; later was principal six years. Married Mary Leek 1890. Children: Raymond; Frank L. and William, twins; Edith, Paul Dorsey, Bessie. Bought farm; carried on stock raising and dairying. Removed to Cailfornia.

Bunch, Wm. Hamilton (Ham), well known in Coos County as a sawmill operator, farmer and educator, yet definite data about him is not readily available. Came with parents sometime in the seventies; settled at Fish Trap; with brother and their father, J. C., built first sawmill in Coquille; afterwards sold it to Binger Hermann; it later became the well known Lyons mill. "Ham" Bunch taught school a number of years in Coos and Curry; with others, he established and operated the Coquille Academy and later the Gravelford Academy. Lived several years on his farm near McKinley. Was county school superintendent a number of terms. Later moved to California. Children: Binger, Taylor, Inez, Claude, Irma, Walter, Minnie.

Burmister, Henry E., b. Oregon 1883. Graduate of Northwest Pacific Dental College; practiced dentistry in North Bend from 1905 till time of his death. Mayor of North Bend. Married Maude E. Shelton 1905. One daughter, Kathaline J.

Butler, C. H., b. Main 1841. To Coos 1868; a pioneer steamboat captain on Coos Bay. Married Anna Catherine Perry. Children: Oscar U., Beulah A., Charles H., Cora C., Bertha A., Jay M., Eva M.

Butler, Parker, marine captain, settled in North Bend in 1850's. Captain of the old tugs "Fearless" and "Escort." Took tug to San Francisco; was returning on steamer "Star King" 1872; the ship failed to show up and has never been heard of since.

Byler, Chauncey M., b. Indiana 1866. To Empire City 1890 after his graduation as pharmacist from the University of Cailfornia; pharmacist for Southern Oregon Company. Married Laura Turpen 1895, born in Empire 1872, daughter of William and Alice A. (Stokes) Turpen. Children: Horace, Dorothy A. Huggins, Alice D. Theiring. Later the Bylers moved to North Bend, where he was associated with L. J. Simpson in different projects, particularly in platting and developing Lakeside; he was a member of the Coos Bay Grocery Company in North Bend and continued in the grocery business many years. Died 1949. Mrs. Byler, one of the founders of the North Bend Public Library, died 1939.

Samuel Colt with two others in 1853 entered into a partnership with one Blaisdel, inventor of a gold saving machine for working the black sands. They had several machines made by a San Francisco foundry; one was set up at Port Orford. Said Cox, "We made about $8 a day per man. The test there of the machine showed it possessed no special value. Blaisdel claimed it was a poor mine, but I could see the gold floating away with the sand after passing through the machine."

Caldwell, J. W., b. Missouri 1853. To Coos 1871. Married Christine B. Majory 1878. Children: Grace B., Mary L., Lucy P., George K. Livestock farmer near Myrtle Point.

Capps, Ed., b. Curry County 1894. Attended Heald's Business College, California; World War I veteran, garage and service business in Bandon. Married Maude Lowe 1923. One son, Edgar L. Mrs. Capps died 1944. He married Bernadean G. Wilson. Councilman and mayor of Bandon.

Capps, James Sylvester, b. Tennessee 1864. To Curry 1888; taught school; homesteaded; acquired large acreage; raised sheep and cattle; dairied; store and postmaster at Denmark. Married Mary O. Porterfield 1887. Children: Raymond, Edna, Edgar, John, Eva.

Carey, Asa (See literature chapter).

Carey, David, b. Iowa 1855. To Curry 1872; livestock farmer; also in lumber business. Married Cynthia A. McBride. Children: Frank D. Nellie S., George F., Olive, Lottie W., Ray, Addie, Zella.

Carey, Elwood, b. Iowa 1861. To Curry 1872; settled on what is known as Carey Sheep Ranch. Married Gertrude Annie Crunk 1989. Four children. Stock raising and general farming.

Carey, J. W., to Curry 1869; rail splitter, sawmill worker, sheep herder and shearer, farmer, mail carrier; heavy construction jobs—mills, canneries, bridges. Married Mrs. E. J. Rolls, who died shortly after. Married Martha Doyle.

Carey, Thomas, an early guide. (See chapter on Rogue River).

Carl, August, b. Germany 1835; to U. S. 1859; Civil War veteran. Married Amanda Newcomer; to Norway, Coos County 1881; farmed till 1901, then moved to Newberg. Children: George C., Marcus, Mary E., Millie A., Herman I., Charles E., John D., William N., Ira W. Died 1903; Mrs. Carl 1924.

Carl John D., son of August; born Norway, Coos County, 1881. Married Edna May Schroeder 1909, daughter of A. H. Schroeder. Children: Kenneth E., Melden A., Herbert G.; Wallace J., killed in World War II. John D. Carl has resided continuously in the Arago district; dairy farming and butter and cheese making; a leader in organizing and improving the business; county commissioner; president Coos-Curry Pioneer and Historical Association. Mr. and Mrs. Carl now retired, still reside at Arago.

Carter, Cecil, b. Douglas County 1883, son of Isaac L. To Coos same year. Farming and logging. Married Alta Dodge. Children: Gladys Cummings, Hilda Bergilt, Clarence, Shirley M. Reside in Myrtle Point.

Carter, Edwin O., b. Benton County 1866. Son of Isaac L. To Coos 1883. Married Oliva E. Morris 1896. Adopted two children: Edwin and Harriett. Farmed at Gravelford, later moved to Myrtle Point, present residence. Followed logging many years, long known as one of the best ax men in Coos.

Carter, Isaac L., b. 1836; to Coos 1883; farming and miscellaneous kinds of work. Married Elizabeth Casebeer 1862. Children: Dora, Estella, Mary, Thomas, Clara, Izabella, Elizabeth, Ida, Edwin, Cecil, Florence, Uiresa, Laura Alice.

Carter John W. (Jack), b. Lane Co. 1857. Stage driver a number of years. To Coos and became Marshfield's first elected marshal 1881; continued as marshal and chief of police till he reached retirement age. Died in the 1930's. Married Sadie Murray 1891. Children: Edith, Edward, Jay.

Catching, James, b. Tennessee 1827; to Coos 1871; farmed near Sumner. Married Patsy E. Russell. Children: John W., Mary I., Sarah E., Arthur W.

Catching, John W., b. Oregon 1855; to Coos 1871, son of James. Farmed near Sumner. Married Hattie A. Bollenbaugh. Children: George W., Bertha E., Effie I.

Cathcart, Simon B., b. Indiana 1842. To Oregon 1853. Served in Civil War, Company A, first Oregon Volunteer Cavalry till 1866. To Coos 1871; farmed on North Coos River, raising livestock; appointed mineral surveyor of the district 1873; county surveyor about 20 years. Married Dora Landrith 1879, daughter of Cyrus Landrith.

Cavanaugh, Abraham, b. Canada 1828; to U. S. 1891; settled on farm on Catching Inlet. Married Minerva Buck in Canada. Children: Emma, Herman, Milton, Alfred E., Charles, William, Reuben L., Wilkinson H. Taught school in Canada; farmed in Coos. Died 1903; Mrs. Cavanaugh 1931.

Cavanaugh, Charles, b. Canada; son of Abraham; to Coos with parents 1891; farmed on Catching Inlet, sawmill filer. Married Lavina Shepherd. Children: Herbert C., Albert E., Hubert, Edith, George.

Cavanaugh, Wilkinson H., b. Canada 1881; son of Abraham; to Coos with parents 1891; farmed on Catching Inlet; sawmill work. Married Martha Archer, daughter of Samuel Archer. Children: Ethel M., Herman W., Archer B.

Cavanaugh, William, b. Canada; son of Abraham; to Coos with parents 1891; teacher; dentist. Married Zula Turnbow. Children: Florence, Erna.

Cavanaugh, Reuben, b. Canada 1879; to Marshfield 1891; studied engineering in San Francisco. In 1907 established himself in business as civil engineer; city engineer for East Marshfield (Eastside). Married Edith Miller 1907. Children: Muriel E., Robert Lee.

Chandler, Ben R., son of Wm. S., b. San Francisco 1889; to Coos with parents 1899; married Cecile Wilcox 1913. Children: Ben R. Jr., Jean. Banker: president, First National of Coos Bay; when bank was sold to First National of Portland, he remained as its branch manager. Interested with William Vaughan in logging and sawmill operations; with Charles Fellar in fish packing business; chairman Oregon State Highway Commission. Residence, Coos Bay.

Chandler, William S., b. San Francisco 1858; mining engineer; to Coos 1899, receiver and general manager of the Beaver Hill coal mining properties, including the railroad and steamships. Married Nellie Irving 1882. Children: E. Irving, Wm. G., Helen C., Ben R. Interested in local properties and civic affairs. The Chandler Hotel was named for him.

Chandler, Isaac, b. Missouri 1855; to Coos 1874; settled on south fork of the Coquille. Married Sarah Lamb. Children: Malinda J., Cora L., John H., Dinscilla M., Blanche R., Emma L., Lorance A., Ruba C., Isaac A.

Chandler, Wm., b. Missouri 1853. To Coos 1874; old time minister, farmer, logger; settled in neighborhood of Myrtle Point; made many trips down Coquille, up Beaver Slough, across the Isthmus, then down Isthmus Inlet and Coos Bay to Empire City, bringing supplies. Married Margaret Bird. Children: Ettie Rankin, Sarah Johnston, Corda M. Gilkison, Willis G., Charles W., Rose H. Garret; Arthur A., Calla D. Zumwalt, Rena V. Bilkison, Bernice N. Hillis, Chesta B. Woodcock.

Chard, George, b. England 1854; In Coos engaged in logging, merchandising and other activities. Married Minnie M. Elliott. Children: George H., James O.

Chase, Inez, b. Iowa 1874, daughter of William and Ida Emma (Bell) Rich; to Oregon with parents 1883; attended schools in Grants Pass; to Coos 1888; attended State Normal School at Drain; began teaching 1891 on Flores Creek, Curry County. Married Wm. C. Chase 1895. Children: Pauline Chase (Harvey), a teacher in Coquille schools; Genevieve, consulting psychologist, New York. Mrs. Chase continued teaching until 1900; time out while children were small; began teaching again 1907; taught in Coquille primary grades from 1908 to 1944, when she retired. Mr. Chase taught until after marriage, when he took a law course at Ann Arbor; practiced law in Coquille; represented Coos and Curry in State Senate 1909-1913; died 1924. Mrs. Chase is an active member of Coos-Curry Pioneer and Historical Association; Secretary-Treasurer for many years.

Cheever, E. H., b. New York 1858; to Curry County about 1887; carpenter. Married Elizabeth Russell 1889. One daughter, Ethel. Associated with J. A. Bowman, and later with his son-in-law, Clyde Corrick, in hardware business at Langlois.

Clarno, George W., b. Ohio 1824; to Curry County 1876; farmed on Pistol River. Married Malinda Leach. Children: George W., Melissa, William H., Henry L., Eliza A., Francis W., Sarah, William, Annie, Mary. Mrs. Clarno died. Married Mary E. Engleman. Children: Lucinda, Andrew J., Albert S., Oliver H. P.

Clausen, Alton H., b. Coos County, 1899, son of John P. Calusen. Married Myrtle A. Olsen. Children: Phillip A., Linda K., Joel R. Owns and operates one of Coos County's largest and finest dairy farms near Riverton.

Clausen, John P., b. Denmark, Europe, 1849. To U. S. 1869. Followed the sea for years in early life and sailed as captain on lumber schooners coming to Coquille River. Married Mary Christensen 1881; settled on Coquilla River 1883. Children: Anna M., Martin, Charles, Christina, Mary, George, Louise, Stanley, Alton, Lester. Captain Clausen prospered as a dairyman.

Clausen, Lester K., b. Coos County 1901. Married Bernice Alpine. Two sons: Max and Peter. Owns a large dairy ranch in the Coquille Valley, across from the mouth of Beaver Slough, and has been very successful.

Clayton, Eli M., b. Nebraska 1873. To Oregon 1884. To Coos County 1896. Associated with father and brother in shingle mill—J. Clayton & Sons. Made shingles for court house in Coquille 1898. Later took over interest of father and brother and continued to operate mill at Fourmile below Bandon 1901 or 1902. Moved to Gravelford. Mrs. Clayton died 1931. Children: Myrtle, and Marion, who is assistant postmaster in Coquille.

Clinkenbeard, J. J., b. Portland 1850; to Coos 1875; settled on Daniels Creek; general farming, gardening, livestock, dairying; prominent Coos pioneer. Married Philura Vanderberg. Children: George, Anna D., Jay, Carl S., Ada, Ralph.

Clinton, George T., b. Missouri 1859; to Coos 1873; settled Gravelford; moved to near Norway; married

Teresa J. Kennedy. Children: Ellen P., James I., Sarah M., Thos. I. Followed farming.

Clinton, James A., b. Missouri; to Oregon 1873; settled on North Fork of the Coquille; married Perlina Lamb. Children: Catherine J., Dewitt, Margaret E., W. M., John W., Mary Ann, Nancy J., Joseph E., Robert J., Sarah E., George W., James T., Henry Ison. The family came by boat to Coos Bay; up Catching Inlet; hired teams to haul them to Burton Prairie (Fairview). From there they packed in to their new home on North Fork and it was three years before they could get a wagon to their homestead. It took hardy, determined people to develop Coos County; of such were the Clintons.

Clinton, John W., b. Missouri 1848; to Coos 1873; purchased 40 acres near Norway; engaged in logging and became one of the outstanding operators of his time, progressing from bullteam to steam donkey; also dealt in standing timber and bought and sold logs. Married Eliza Ann Russell 1867. Children: James D., Marion T., Jesse Dewitt, Mary C., Dorlisca E., George H., Albert R., Edward O., Samuel H., Clarence A., John R., and one who died in infancy. The family has had much influence in the development of Coos County.

Clinton, Jesse Dewitt, b. Missouri 1873, son of John W. and Eliza Ann; with parents to Coos same year; parents homesteaded, rented and bought land at different locations in Coquille Valley; finally settled near Norway; farming, logging, while clearing land, developing dairy, and building home. To Coos in diapers; to school in homespuns made by his mother; to dances in long store pants and jean jumper; played fiddle; greased skids and carried water in bullteam logging camps. In 1896 at age 23, married Daisy Bell, daughter of Asa and Susan Myers; moved belongings in a wheelbarrow to logging camp west of Norway, where Jesse worked in woods and Daisy cooked for the men; acquired 20 acres of land, a cow and calf worth $26, a cart and harness worth $40. Kept the land but exchanged cow, cart and harness to two carpenters for building house, didn't say where or how they got lumber. Jesse continued work at logging while clearing and building up farm, adding cows and equipment. Children: Lilas, Lillie, Lawrence, Ardis. School director; road supervisor; active community leader. Bought home and moved to Myrtle Point 1926; capitalist, interested in logging, banking, city investments, insurance agency; on boards of numerous public, semi-public and community activities; mayor of Myrtle Point; Lion, Rotarian, Odd Fellow 55 years; active in Myrtle Point Saddle Club. New bridge across the river at Myrtle Point named the "Jesse Dewitt Clinton Bridge", is his memorial. Jesse and Daisy both died 1949.

Clinton, Robert J., b. Missouri 1855; to Coos 1873; settled on North Fork of the Coquille. Married Mary J. Carter. Children: D. Pearl, Lillian G., Paul P., Dora A.

Clinton, Teodore (Dutch) L., b. Arago 1893, son of James D. and Etta. In 1915 married Mabel Schroeder, daughter and C. A. and Rachel Schroeder. Farmed till 1925; then worked as timber cruiser and log buyer; moved to their modern new home on Johnson Hill near Coquille. Children: Jack, who served with rank of lieutenant and was lost in World War II; Gretchen (Mrs. Jack Laird); two other children died in infancy.

Codding, Daisy, b. Coos 1874, daughter of George R. Wasson and an Indian princess, Adulsa Susan (Hodgkiss) Wasson; grew up on South Slough; learned Indian lore from her blind grandmother; attended the local school; next to the Indian school at Chemewa in Willamette Valley; then to the Indian college at Carlisle, Pennsylvania; and finally two years training in the Chester County Hospital in Pennsylvania. Returned to Coos 1904, one of the first registered trained nurses in the Coos-Curry area; continued her practice more than 40 years, always much in demand. Married Charles H. Codding, a civil engineer, 1908; one daughter, Elizabeth, the present Mrs. Mell Burnette. Mr. Codding died 1917. Mrs. Codding, retired, resides in Empire.

Coke, John Stephen, b. Tennessee

about 1835. Served in Civil War. Married Elizabeth Moore. Children: Frances J., Thomas, Richard S., Paul S., John Storey, Hugh M. To Coos County, where two more children were born: Caroline and James L. County school superintendent; collector of customs at Empire. Family well known in Coos County during the past 80 years.

Coke, Judge John S., b. Tennessee, 1867. Son of John S. and Mary E. (Moore) Coke. To Coos 1872 with parents. Studied law in law offices in Portland and Coos Bay and at the University of Oregon. Practiced law in Marshfield and served as mayor of that city. Served in the State Senate, in 1909 was appointed circuit judge of the Second Judicial District; elected in 1910 and continued in office until 1923, when he resigned and took up the practice of law in Portland, where he still maintains his office. Married, in 1903, Miss Annie Laurie Anderson, daughter of Mr. and Mrs. E. A. Anderson, of Marshfield. Children: Morton, Virginia.

Colbrook, Frederick W., b. England 1818; followed the sea; came as a captain to California; operated a store in the gold diggings area. Several years later, came to Curry County and took up cattle and sheep raising; owned 520 acres in Southern Curry. Married Mary A. Smith 1875. Children: Ella N., Louisa N., Frederick W., William, Annie, George and Mary Smith, a daughter of Mrs. Colbrook by a former marriage. As county surveyor, he surveyed a large part of Curry County. Died 1899.

Coleman, Orange S., b. California 1856. Married Katherine Luper 1881. Parents of five children. General farming in Coquille Valley; poultry, horses, cattle, dairying, fruit growing. Reported to have packed and shipped more apples in 1911 than were shipped by any other individual from Coos County. Seven Day Adventist; director of Gravelford Academy.

Collier, B. F., b. Iowa 1854. To Oregon with parents 1860; to Coos 1865. Parents settled on land now a part of Coquille. Married Judith Morras. Children: Annie (Mrs. E. A. Wimer), W. G. and M. F. died in early childhood. Mr. Collier was a carpenter.

Collier, Joseph, b. Ohio 1817. Married Hannah J. Hathaway. To Coos 1865; bought farm adjoining the original townsite of Coquille. Children: Henry James, Evaline, Joseph Allen, Benjamin F., Latha Jane, Charles E., George, Sarah A., Dora Elizabeth. The family exercised much influence in the community life of Coquille.

Collver, T. M., b. 1869 on Coos River. Married Carrie Moore 1898. Children: Chester A., Vernon W., Gladys L., Gordon M., Enid R., Marshall M. Followed stockraising, dairying and general farming.

Collver, William A., b. Douglas County, 1855, settled on Coos River 1857. Married Neomi Steinon. Children: Josephine R., and Myrtle I. Followed carpenter work.

Collver, Andrew F., b. on Coos River 1863. Married Clara H. Williams. Childrne: Ray C., Floyd M., Ralph A., Lyell F. Homesteaded near Cape Arago. Followed farming and deep sea fishing.

Compton, Lafe, b. in Oregon 1893; orphaned when about five years old; taken in by Lee Bilyeu of Scio, where he spent his boyhood and attended school. Married Flora Stokes 1915. Children: Doris Jane and Marilynn Ethel. Has spent practically his whole life in the hotel business; first employed in Russ House, Albany; later with Albany Hotel; to Marshfield 1916 as clerk in the Chandler, until 1924, when Mr. and Mrs. Compton opened the new Coquille Hotel under lease; continued to operate it 20 years; then purchased the Chandler in Marshfield, taking active management in 1944, continuing to date. They are among the best-known hotel people in Oregon. They live at Barview on lower Coos Bay.

Condron, Ivy, b. Missouri 1867; to Coos 1884; farmer; logger; merchant; dairyman. Among the first to own and operate a gasoline launch on Coos Bay. His trim and neat little launch, loaded with a variety of choice vegetables and fruits from his Coos River farm was a frequent scene still recalled by many of the Bay residents of the early 1900's. Married Elizabeth E. Rook 1889.

Cooley, Miller, b. Kentucky 1822; to Curry 1860; settled near Chetco; stock raising and farming. Married Elizabeth C. Hill. Ten children. Civil War veteran.

Cope, William V., b. Canada 1846. To Curry 1887. Settled on Flores Creek. Married Sarah Emmerson. Children: Ralph E., Leora E., Mary V., Delle M., Helen M., Bessie E., Alexis, William E. Was first of four generations of successful dairy farmers in the same location, his great-grandson, Ralph E. Jr., being the present operator. Moved to Coquille in 1906 and engaged in lumber business and later the butcher business. Died 1909.

Copeland, Wm., b. New Brunswick 1848; to Coos 1874; settled at Coaledo; later moved to Coquille; logged off the timber and sold his land to Sol Spurgeon; now known as Spurgeon Hill. His wife was M. Billing; children: Maggie, Rufus, Bill, Wm. W., Lucy.

Cordes, Romuld C., b. Wisconsin 1852; early life on father's tugboat on Lake Michigan; overland to San Francisco; took side-wheel steamer "John L. Setvens" to Portland; in 1875 married Annie McBride at Corvallis; to Marshfield 1876; successively owned and operated steamers "Bertha" and "Coos River"; later sold to Roger Brothers; conducted a tobacco store in Marshfield; afterwards in real estate business with John F. Hall. Children: Herman, Romuld Jr., Eulalia (Mrs. Robert Marsden Jr.), Josephine. Mrs. Cordes died 1925; Mr. Cordes 1935.

Cornell, Thos., b. Ohio 1843; to Curry 1858; followed gold mining; later engaged in stock raising with A. B. Greene near Salmon Mountain. Bought and sold several places in Curry; finally settled on Crystal Creek near Langlois.

Cornwall, Thos., b. Ohio 1844; to Curry 1857; settled near Cape Blanco; to Coos 1863; then back to Curry, near Port Orford. Married Ida F. Post. Three children. Engaged in farming.

Cotton, James A., b. Missouri 1863; to Coos 1877; settled near Fairview; married Clemantine Hatcher 1892; children: James R., Jesse R., Andrew C.

Cowan, James, b. Canada 1856; settled on Coos River 1890; carried on logging operations. Married Mary E. Murphy 1886. Children: James E., Marjory, Myrtle.

Cox, George Wm., b. Missouri 1870. To Coos about 1896. Married Margaret Belle Davison 1895. Children Walter E., John H., Lester C., Gussie, Beulah. Followed sawmilling and logging principally; in later years operated a dairy farm near Bandon. Died 1941; Mrs. Cox 1925.

Cox, Glen B., b. Polk County; to Coos 1857. Married Emma Etta Vowel 1885. Children: Leo L., Milton E., Nellie E., Dewey Earl. Logger, livery stable operator; mail carrier; was affectionately known by his many friends as "Uncle Glen".

Cox, H. A., b. Illinois 1840; veteran of the Civil War; to Coos 1900; stock and dairy farm; opened grocery store in Bandon 1902 and later in Curry County. Retired at Langlois, where he owned an interest in the Langlois Hotel. Married Mary J. Cramer 1861. Children: Thomas, Edward, Frank, Elizabeth, Bertha.

Cox, Isham, b. Missouri 1813. Married Mary Ann Johnston. Children: Martha, William, Joseph, Margaline, James, Frank, Sarah, Isham, Glen. Came from Illinois to Curry County where they setted and raised their family. Expert hunter and woodsman.

Cox, James H., b. 1854, son of John F. and Elizabeth Jane Cox. To Coos 1883. Married Jane Reed Hunter. Children: Euphemia Mae, Elizabeth Jane, Alice Letitia, Myrl Irene. Worked at the Libby coal mines. Died 1932; Mrs. Cox 1927.

Cox, John R., b. Lane County 1860. In Coos engaged in general farming and stock raising on Bear Creek. Married Sarah J. Haga 1887. Children: Malinda E., John F., Effie J., Wm. H., James R., George F., Jerisey A., Lilly May, Pearl Leona,

Cox, Joseph A., b. Polk County 1847; to Curry 1865; settled near Langlois. Married Susan Wooden. Children: Sarah, Wm. A., James G., Robert E. L., Mary M., Isham A. Justice of the peace many years.

Cox, Wm. B., b. Marion County 1851. Followed team work and hop drying. Married Alice Buxton 1876. Children: Carl, Hubert, Lelia, Ethel, Ray, Anna. To Coos 1900. General horse team contracting; constable. Died 1932; Mrs. Cox 1936.

Cox, William, b. Illinois 1838, son of Isham and Mary Ann Cox. To Curry 1865; settled on Sixes River; worked with George Fitzhugh, Ed Good and other neighbors in building a road leading toward Port Orford. Married three times. Children: Eugene, Effie, Adaline, Kitty, Ralph, Clove, Leonard, Della.

Crook, Thereon W., b. New York 1816. To Curry 1865; resided on Pistol River and at Port Orford. Married Nancy Hamilton. Parents of eight children.

Crosby, Charles, b. New York 1837. To Coos 1884, bringing with him considerable wealth from the gold fields of California; followed farming. Wife's name was Jennie Florence. Children: Charles, Martha, Arthur, Walter, Jeff Lee, Arthur M., Mertie, Clifford, Zelma, Iva. Died 1903.

Crouch, Shipman H., b. Alabama; early boyhood in Arkansas; crossed plains 1852; settled on Flores Creek farm in Curry, later owned by Alexander Thrift; volunteer in Rogue River Indian wars 1855-56; carried mail four years from Port Orford to Gardiner; did some black sand gold mining at Randolph on Sixes River. Later moved to Coos and settled on Haynes Inlet; did general farming. Married twice. Children by first marriage: Albert, Charles, Alice, Wallace; by second marriage, Lafe, Perry, Olive, Mary, Beecher, Lucy.

Crowley, John M., b. Missouri 1847; settled on Sixes River 1886. Married Samantha A. Cox. Children: Elizabeth, Charles, Pearly, Rebecca G., David, Sarah C.

Crunk, Geo. W., b. Montana 1869. To Coos with parents; worked on father's place on Rock Creek near Bridge till aged 25. Acquired own ranch in the same vicinity; raised, bought and sold cattle. Has well equipped and modern ranch. Married Fannie Wagner; parents of five children.

Culin, Dr. Walter, b. Philadelphia 1866; to Coos 1893; practiced medicine. Married Edith J. Taylor. One of the first in Coos County to own an automobile, which was quite a curiousity at the time. Children: Emma and Alice.

Culver, Elvarus, b. New York 1829; to Coos 1899; bought 820 acres on Rock Creek near Bridge; farmed and also operated a sawmill on his property. Married twice; first to Rubie Blaesdell; children: Charles, Mehitable, Nellie B., Mable; two sons deceased. Second marriage to Lucy E. Monzingo; children: James E., Clarence, Dwight E.

Curry, James W., b. Ohio 1832. To Curry 1875; settled on Rogue River. Married Fannie A. Coleman 1858. Children: Stephen L. Margaret, Malinda T., George W., James W. Jr.

Cutlip, Mark D., b. in Oregon 1857; settled on Coos River 1860; engaged in logging, farming, dairying. Married Mattie Haskin. Children: Minnie, Iva, Ernest Lloyd, May. Mrs. Cutlip died 1897. Mr. Cutlip married Thena Wilkins 1900.

Cutlip, S. B., b. Coos County 1870; farmed on Daniels Creek, on place settled by his father. Married Anna Laura Smith. Children: Nathan S., Guy A., Lorenzo A., Blanch E., Louis J., Mary M., Robert S.

Curtis, Wm. B., b. Maine 1853; sailed four years; to Coos 1878; farmed; clerk in Blanco Hotel 18 years, 1879-1897; Marshfield postmaster 17 years, 1898-1915; member town board. In 1886 married Rosetta Hirst. Children: Edward W., Wm. B. Jr., Alice E., Frank. Died 1925; Mrs. Curtis 1926.

D

Samuel Maxwell Dement, Coos pioneer of 1853, secured four young elk in an early day. After taming them so he thought he could handle them, he led them to Roseburg where he expected to sell them for a good price. He went a little too far in his demonstration of their domesticity; he hitched them up to a wagon; they looked a little like half of Santa Claus' team. But "the brutes" let him down terribly. They went unmanageable on him, and soon destroyed the harness and the vehicle.

Davis, Alonza, b. Illinois 1852. Married Louisa Foster 1874; nine children. In sawmill business at Smith River, California; to Curry 1884; homestead near New Lake. Mrs. Davis died 1922; Mr. Davis a number of years ago.

Davis, George S., b. Wisconsin 1863. Married Lucy Trigg 1892. Children: Harold W., Otto L. To Coos 1900; rented farm from R. C. Dement; operated Norway Creamery till 1905; sold creamery; bought a 200-acre dairy between Norway and Coquille; later years spent in Coquille.

Dement, Russell C., b. Ohio 1847, son of S. M. and Caroline. Grew up on his father's cattle ranch; bought and sold cattle; partner in a Coos Bay meat market; interested in steamboating. At Myrtle Point joined with others to organize the Security Bank; was president for many years. Married 1874 Lucy Norris (a descendant of Daniel Boone). Children: Nellie, Eunice (Braden), Ray B., Winifred (White); Lester T. and Ellis S., twins; Clara, Harry, Lorain.

Dement, Samuel Maxwell, b. Ohio 1823. Married Caroline Spencer; three children, including Russell C. Married second Luisa Lovett 1866. Children: W. Taylor, George, Clay, Caroline, Max. To Coos 1853. A blacksmith. First settled at Empire; then on donation claim on upper South Coquille; became a leading Coos cattleman. His original ranch in the Eckley area, now enlarged to about 4,000 acres of range, is still in the family.

Dement, Wallace B., b. Myrtle Point 1900, son of Lester T. (Taylor) and Nellie (Figg) Dement. Law graduate University of Southern California; attorney in Myrtle Point since 1923. City attorney; director of Security Bank; president Coos County Fair Association. In recent years devotes considerable time to livestock farm. Resides with widowed mother in Myrtle Point.

Denning, Levi Franklin, b. Douglas County 1874; married Stella Elrod, daughter of Wm. F. and Mary M. Elrod. Engaged in railroading on Marshfield-Myrtle Point run. Died 1948.

Denning, William S., b. Douglas County 1871. Married Maggie Richert 1893; one daughter, Alice, teacher in East Sacramento, California, school, struck on head by basketball in gymnasium, died from injuries a year later. Mr. Denning railroaded on Marshfield-Myrtle Point line; did construction work; in U. S. lighthouse service 1903-1936, at Cape Arago and Heceta Head; postmaster at Sunset (Cape Arago) 1910. Retired, living in Empire in home overlooking the bay.

Detlefsen, Edward I., b. Germany 1886; to U. S. 1901; to Coos 1910; rented and purchased land in Coquille Valley; carried on dairying. Married Margaret Reitz 1908. Children: Paul, Ray, Howard, Ernest. Mrs. Detlefsen died. He married Grace (Summerlin) Rackleff, widow of Lawrence Rackleff. Member of Bandon Port Commission; a successful dairyman.

Devereux, Thomas, b. Ireland 1851; married Mary Larkin 1886; to Coos same year; purchased land near Coquille and on Bear Creek; dairying, stock raising and general farming. Children: Mary Ella, John, Thomas, Margaret, Henry, James, Teresa, Lena, Phillip, David, Loretta.

Dickson, Thomas E., b. Indiana; to Coos 1889; followed contracting and building. Married Leona Johnson 1893, daughter of Z. Y. Johnson. Children: Cleo A. and John E.

Dietz, Charles E. G., b. Germany 1829. To America when very young;

settled in Baltimore. To Coos and Curry 1865; worked in mines. Married Mary Ellen Wilbur in California 1868. Homesteaded at mouth of Beaver Slough; later at Myrtle Point opened a cabinet shop with Charles E. Schroeder. Died 1904; wife 1913. Children: Joseph E., Lizzie E., William E., Grace E., Samuel E., Josie E., Gustave E.

Dimmick, Thomas M., b. Illinois 1849. Crossed plains with parents to Oregon 1853. To Coos 1880. Established a tannery near Marshfield. Joint senator from Coos and Curry 1901-1903; treasurer of Coos County. Married Fannie Lyons, daughter of Dan Lyons noted pioneer Scottsburg editor, hotel keeper and musician. Children: Daniel L., Harold H., Laura May, August E., Albert A., Victor.

Divilbiss, Daniel, b. Pennsylvania 1833. To Curry 1878; settled on lower Rogue River; followed farming. Married Mary Ann Sowers 1857. Children: George G., Emma R., Caleb N., Mary E., Ernest H., Edward H. An early miner.

Dix, Dr. George E., b. Ohio 1876, son of Peter and Ella (Chester) Dix. George was always interested in cattle, horses and other farm animals, spending much time on the farm with his grandparents; moved to Minnesota, where he spent his summer vacations on farms. Spanish-American War veteran as a private, out as a sergeant. Graduated from the University of Minnesota Medical School. Assistant Chief Surgeon with the Northern Pacific Railroad Hospital in Montana. To Coos 1907 as company doctor for the C. A. Smith Lumber Company, continuing 30 years; office in Marshfield past 45 years. In 1918 he bought the old Mark Davis farm at the forks of Coos River. In the past 30-odd years he has given constant study and effort to rehabilitating the exhausted and neglected soil so that today it is producing approximately six pounds of butterfat where one pound was previously produced. His scientific study of grass and the soil from which it springs is an important contribution to Coos agriculture.

Dodge, Edgar Allen, b. Oregon 1873, son of Orvil and Louisa (Schroeder) Dodge. Married Ethel E. Graham 1895. Commissioner for the General Land Office 1905; city recorder Myrtle Point 28 years; justice of the peace several years; built first theatre in Myrtle Point 1912. Died 1950; survived by widow and son, Austin D. Dodge.

Dodge, Orvil. (See chapters on literature and newspapers).

Donaca, Charles H., b. Illinois 1840; settled on the Rogue 1871; later moved to ranch near Ophir; engaged in stock raising and general farming. Married Nancy C. Cox 1864. Eight children.

Donaldson, Adam, b. Ireland 1867; began sailing on training ship Conway, England. Received captain's papers at age 21; followed the sea until 1933, when retired to his farm on Catching Inlet. Married Emma Maxwell 1904. Children: Martha M., Bernard M., Adam D., William H., Eva May. The family moved to their farm home 1918, which has been operated by the son, Adam, for many years. Captain Donaldson died 1944.

Donaldson, John, b. Canada 1830. Married Ann Finnegan. Children: Joseph D., Mary, Nellie. Married Mary E. Morse. To Coos 1875; homesteaded on Coquille River; later worked many years in the store of the Prosper Mill Company. Mrs. Donaldson died 1897; he 1924.

Donaldson, Joseph D., b. Canada; to Coos 1890; married Minnie Perkins. daughter of James M. and Mary (Covey) Perkins. Died 1946.

Douglas, Duncan E., b. Marshfield 1893, son of W. U. and Ida M. (Greenman) Douglas. In 1920, married Ann Flanagan, daughter of E. G. and Annie B. (Short) Flanagan. One daughter, Mary Alice. Graduated from the University of Oregon law school 1917; practiced law in Marshfield between various other jobs; served in World War I; later was captain in the Coast Artillery and served with the same rank in U. S. Army, World War II. Marshfield postmaster 1923 to 1936; served on different boards; with U. S. Veterans Administration, Portland, since 1944, Legal Specialist. Member Coos County Bar Association and Multnomah Bar Association.

Douglas, Wallace Ulysses, b. Michigan 1869. To Marshfield 1890. Practiced law many years. In 1892 married Ida M. Greenman, a teacher, born at Eastport. Children: Duncan E., Elizabeth R., Emmy Lou, Mary Lucile, Alice G., Wallace U. Jr. Died 1936.

Doyle, Cassius M., b. Coos 1870; followed stockraising on his large range near the head of Two Mile Creek. Never married.

Doyle, David R., b. Missouri 1833; to Coos 1865; farmer. Married Minerva E. Sneed 1850. Children: David W., Melisa H., Cassius M., Robert L., Elizabeth J., Dury R., Elmer E., Bert W. Died 1882.

Drane, Phillip E., b. Kentucky 1854. To Coos 1873; homesteaded near Arago; general farming. In 1877 married Mrs. Belle Pike, who had a son, George by first marriage. Drane children: Mary and Julia. Moved to Coquille about 1880; successively followed hotel keeping, meat marketing, grocery business. Retired 1916.

Drane, Thomas W., married Emma Hamblock 1885. One son, Frederick Elmore. Engaged in general farming and sheep raising. Mr. Drane died 1917; she 1945.

Drew, David M., b. New Jersey 1846; to Coos 1870; settled on Coquille River; machinist and blacksmith. Married Mary Z. Willard. Children: Thomas A., Guy, Rufus R., Zachary C., Maud M., Lou W., George J.

Dully, John B., b. Pennsylvania 1834. Setled at forks of the Coquille 1854; later moved to head of Catching Inlet on Coos Bay Wagon Road; laid out town of Sumner, where he served as postmaster. Married Henrietta Higley; nine children. Representative in Oregon Legislature 1874; county treasurer 1900-1908. Died 1908; Mrs. Dully 1905.

Dunham, H. W. (Hark), b. Pennsylvania 1849. Married Mary F. Turner 1874. Children: Hattie B., Rilla B., Harvey J., Roy W., Mils R. Licensed marine engineer and captain; engineer on first locomotive, the "Betsy" on the run from Kings Landing to J. F. Dunham's coal mine on Beaver Slough; served six years as city marshal of Marshfield and several years as marshal of Coquille, and as county juvenile officer.

Dyer, Elbert, b. Curry County 1864; with parents to Coos 1865. Married Euphemia Averill 1886. One daughter, Ethel. Owned and operated broom handle mill and small sawmills in Bandon at different times; manager of the Bandon Water Company, owned by his mother, sold later to city of Bandon. Mrs. Dyer died 1932; he 1942.

Dyer, George M., b. Ohio 1834; arrived in Curry County 1854; mined gold; served in Indian wars. Married Fannie E. Grant in Indiana 1859; back to Curry. Children: Florence E., Alice C., Henrietta; and an adopted daughter, Hattie. Continued gold mining; Curry County assessor 1862-1863; to Coos 1865; county commissioner and judge; formed partnership with W. H. Averill in laying out town of Bandon 1886; established first general merchandise store; became first chairman of town council when Bandon was incorporated 1891. Died 1896.

Charles Eckhoff, father of 11 children, was a logger, raftsman, fisherman—and an awfully good picker of land, He acquired a place at the mouth of Kentuck Inlet; coal was found and Hardy bought it at a good price. He paid Charles Merchant $400 for a part of present North Bend; the promoter of the town of Yarrow some years later gave him $16,000 for it. On the west side of Pony Slough, near the present North Bend airport, he picked up an acreage and afterwards somebody else wanted it at a good profit to Eckhoff. He sometimes boasted that he was a smart Dutchman; his neighbors answered he was just a lucky Dutchman.

Easley, Carl Patrick, b. Texas 1883; to Oregon 1912. Married Electa Brady 1922; did railroad station work 1901 to 1948, serving 35 years with S. P.;

retired 1948 with R. R. annuity; now owns and operates a stock farm near Powers; city recorder of Powers.

Easton, Teodore S., b. 1893, son of Robert A. and Emma E. Easton; to Coos with parents 1896. After spending boyhood on the family homestead on the East Fork below Sitkum, he was graduated from Albany College, the Southern Oregon Normal School and the University of Oregon; in air service in World War I; taught in high schools; wrote "The Secret of Wallowa Cave". Married in 1924. Children: Forest, Canyon, Maypril. In recent years, besides farming, has followed surveying, logging, road construction. Present residence, his boyhood home, which he has named Junglebank—"Where the leafy gorges echo, To the torrent's boisterous peal, And the rippling waters sparkle, In the crystal clear Coquille".

Edwards, Charles E., b. Indiana 1853. To Coos 1875; steamboating as engineer and captain on Coquille River, Coos Bay and Coos River. Married Mary C. Roberts. Children: Daisy B., Mignonette, Elmer Herman, Florence A. County commissioner 1884-1888. Later in life Capt. and Mrs. Edwards located near Allegany, where his widow, and daughter, Mrs. Ott, still reside. Some of the pictures in this volume were loaned by them.

Eickworth, Ernest A., b. Germany 1849; married Guzisena Windler. Children: William H., Ernest A., Susan M. (Mrs. R. F. Gebhardt), Jennie (Mrs. R. E. Pinegor). Carpenter and cabinetmaker; worked in Fred Mark's cobinet shop in Marshfield; later took over and operated the shop. German Lutheran. Died 1926; Mrs. Eickworth 1921.

Eickworth, William H., b. Germany 1857, son of Ernest A.; to Coos with parents 1881. Married Elfreda H. Wirth 1902. Children: Blanche E., Lawrence W., Merle A., John R., Alice R., Mary E., Charlotte. Carpenter. Spanish War veteran. Died 1945. His widow resides near Cape Arago Lighthouse.

Ellingseen, Arthur R., b. San Francisco 1871; to Coos with parents 1872; carpenter, boat and ship builder; built and owned several business blocks in the Coquille Valley; during later years engaged in undertaking business. Married Hulda O. Roy. Children: Denton, Dena (Mrs. Pierce).

Ellingsen, Edwin P., b. Lampa Creek 1882, son of Capt. O. P. Ellingsen. Married Pearl Sweet, daughter of John B. Sweet. Children: Herman, Pauline, Grace, John Theodore. Ship carpenter and building contractor; sheriff of Coos County; died from injuries in auto accident 1925.

Ellingsen, Ole Peter, b. Norway, Europe, 1845; sailed as cabin boy at age 16; advanced to captain before coming to U. S. 1871; to Coos 1872; settled on farm on Lampa Creek; continued as sea captain till 1896. Married Amelie Caroline Hansen 1870. Children: Arthur, Amelia, Jennie, Edwin, Ellen, Rose Lilly, Belle, Chester, Maude, Ruby. Both Captain and Mrs. Ellingsen died 1922.

Elliott, Fred, b. Jackson County 1865, son of Hiram; to Coos with parents 1865; settled on South Slough. Married Sarah May Wiley 1887. Children: Lenore Maude (Mrs. Erwin Broillier), Hiram Claude, Walter Clyde. A violinist; had his own family orchestra and at one time operated "The Oakes" in Powers.

Elliott, Hiram, b. Ohio 1812. Married Abigail Rosalie; one daughter, Mary R. died while crossing the plains in a covered wagon. Children born after arrival in Oregon 1849: Alice M., George H., William, Milton, Sarah, John F., Fred, Minnie M., Leland E. To Coos 1865; farmed and logged on South Slough, rafting logs to Empire. Died 1888; Mrs. Elliott 1911.

Elliott, Milton, b. Benton County son of Hiram; to Coos 1865; farmed and logged on South Slough. Married Frances E. Talbot. Children: Warren, Elizabeth, Abigail, Clara, Ada M., James R., Pearl. Died 1934.

Elrod, Mary (Madden), b. Nova Scotia 1861. To Coos 1877, to live with her sister Mrs. William Weir. In 1878 married William Elrod, a butcher for the H. P. Whitney meat market. Children: Mary Etta (Sacchi) and Francis S. (McLeod) 1880, first twins born in Coos County; Stella G. (Denning), Iris A., Mary Elrod. Died 1943.

Erdman, George, b. Germany 1874.

To Bandon 1908; operated meat market from 1909 until his death 1939. Married Annie Waldvogel 1911. Two children.

Evernden, T. S., b. New York 1851. To Coos 1873; homesteaded on Rock Creek. Built up a stock ranch. Noted as an expert judge of cattle and horses. Married Susan J. Applegate 1873. Children: James T., Ernie E., Fred, Alice Zoe, Lessie L., Jesse, Susie D., Joseph L., Charles.

Antonio Flores, old Spanish pilot of Aguilar's ship, at Cape Blanco January 19, 1603, created a great mystery that is still a mystery—they found a good-sized river. Now the geographical question is—was Flores Creek and Flores Lake named for him so that it should be spelled that way? Or was it named for Fred Floras who in 1852 was employed to cut a trail from Fort Orford to Rogue River? This book says Flores Lake and Flores Creek.

Fahy, Edward, b. Ireland 1826; to Port Orford 1854; followed sawmill work. Later moved to Coquille River and operated ferry near the bar in partnership with Chris Long, 1957-1858. Purchased water-power sawmill from Fundy, Stacey & Wasson 1858, which he operated for many years, rebuilding and enlarging it two or three times. Married Sarah Spoonheimer 1860. Children: Edward W., Florinda, Henrietta, Isidore P., S. W. Mary E., Francis J., Charles G., Sarah. Homesteaded near Bullards; followed sawmilling, cattle and sheep raising. Died 1906; Mrs. Fahy 1915. Members of the family still reside on the old home place.

Fahy, Florinda, b. Coos County 1862, dauhter of Edward and Sarah; worked at dressmaking trade in Coos many years, besides ten years in Portland at same trade. Still resides in the old Fahy home near Bullards; treasures a large collection of agates and Indian gems in the form of arrow heads, baskets and other works of native handicraft.

Fahy, Francis J. b. 1872, son of Edward and Sarah. In early life worked in sawmill; graduate of Healds Business College, San Francisco; bookkeeper and store manager Coquille Mill and Tug Company at Parkersburg. To Bandon 1904; with others, organized the Bank of Bandon, of which he was cashier for years and still is a director. Now residing with members of the family on the old Fahy homestead near Bullards.

Farr, Chester C., b. Washington 1890; graduate of Washington State College. Married Iva D. Haines 1913. Children: Donald H., Edythe (Thompson), Dorothy, Leonard C. County agricultural agent 1919-1921. Resigned; bought out Elwood-Collier Transfer—warehouse, storage, hauling feed and seed. In 1924, Elwood rejoined, incorporated as Farr & Elwood (now Farr's). In 1926 added store and warehouse in Marshfield. Elwood died 1941. The Farr family bought out the Elwood interests. Ownership then apportioned, one sixth each to the father, the two sons Donald H and Leonard C. and to the wife of each.

Farrier, George b. Arkansas 1842; to Curry 1886; dairying. Married Nancy Counts 1866. Children: Lucus, Charles, Andrew, Walter, Daisy. Second marriage to Mary J. Woodruff; her children by a previous marriage: Calvin, Chancey, Carrie, Carnie.

Felsher, John, b. Germany 1869; to Coos 1896; settled on dairy farm near Myrtle Point. Married Blanche Pohl. Children: Walter, Blanche Florence, Albert, Stanley (died in the "Death March" in the Phillipines in Second World War). Mr. Felsher was a chief gunner on the Battlesship Oregon during the Spanish-American War and was in the thick of battle in the sinking of Cervera's fleet. Later the Oregon went to the Phillipines; Mr. Felsher served there and was present at the surrender of the Islands.

Felter, J. W., b. Iowa 1848; served in Civil War; to Oregon 1884; resided at Bandon; married Mary A. Petitte 1875; parents of four children.

Ferguson, Duncan Sr., b. Scotland 1870; to U. S. with parents 1880; married Isabella McLean 1893. Children: John, Coos Bay public accountant and tax consultant; Duncan Jr.; Isabel; Clara; Robert, president of Ferguson Transfer Company; Dorothy; Lawrence; Wallace. The family came to Marshfield 1906. Mr. Ferguson first employed in a lumber yard; next in real estate business; organized the Ferguson Transfer Company 1908. Served on Marshfield city council; mayor 1918-1927. Mrs. Ferguson died 1922; he 1935.

Ferrey, Geo. W., b. Marshfield about 1879, son of James L. Ferrey. Married Bertha A. DeWeese; one daughter Gladys Yale. Worked with his father in the Blanco Hotel; took over the management when his father retired 1903. Later worked on various construction jobs in Coos County. Mrs. Ferrey died 1937; he 1942.

Ferrey, James L., b. Pennsylvania 1841. In Civil War three years; was transferred to construction corps, Western Army; at one time in charge of roads and bridges; followed carpenter work till 1869. To Coos 1871. In partnership with S. S. Bailey 1873 bought the Blanco Hotel which he continued to operate 30 years. Homesteaded on Isthmus Inlet 1871; owned acreage at various localities throughout Coos County. Married Henrietta W. Trott 1878. Children: George W., Eva Elizabeth, James L. Jr., Frederick A., Annie Henrietta. Member Marshfield city council, GAR. Died 1913; Mrs. Ferrey 1919.

Ferrey, James L. Jr., b. Marshfield 1883. Married Flora M. Belknap 1914. Farmed 25 years on his father's homestead on Isthmus Inlet, present site of Green Acres; two years on construction work for the Coos Bay Lumber Company; Marshfield city police force six years. Now resdies in Coos Bay.

Fetter L. B., b. Pennsylvania 1829; to Coos in late 1860's. Married Julia Day; had eight children. Operated stage station at Remote on the Roseburg-Myrtle Point highway. Their old farm home at Remote has been owned and operated by their grandson, Lawernce B. Jennings, and family during the past many years.

Figg, Ben, b. England; to Coos 1856; settled at forks of the Coquille; sold to Captain Rackleff 1859 and moved to a mile below Fishtrap. Was a cotton weaver by trade but engaged in stockraising and general farming after coming to Coos. Married Catherine Doyle of Ireland. Children: Nellie J. (Mrs. Taylor Dement, Myrtle Point), Julia A., Bertie.

Fish, Albert H., b. Connecticut 1824. Married Hannah Ann Gribble 1847. Children: John G., Samuel, William A., Anna. To Coos 1873; bought homestead right of Belieu on Myrtle Creek near present site of Bridge. Built house of five rooms out of split white cedar. Was cabinetmaker and had tools to finish the job; made brick in own kiln for fireplace and chimneys. Built gristmill complete, 12-foot overshot water wheel, all of wood, including bearings and cogs; stone burrs packed in from Roseburg. Ground wheat and corn, charging toll of one seventh. His services were in demand for building several gristmills in Coos County.

Fish, John J., b. Clackamas County 1861, son of Albert H. and Hannah Fish. Settled on Myrtle Creek 1873. Married Lillie D. Endicott. Children: Albert S., John Clarence; Frank J., Joseph R., Earl L., Ella, Arthur M., Joyce C., Donald C. Built water power sawmill on Myrtle Creek to make lumber for own and neighbor's use.

Fisher, Ben S., b. Indiana 1890; to Marshfield 1914; entered law office of John F. Hall, with whom he was associated till Judge Hall's death 1923, when Fisher took over the practice. Captain in World War I. District attorney Coos County; president Coos County Bar Association. Married Kate Cathburn 1920. Children: Ben C. and Nancy. Assistant general Council Federal Radio Commission 1930-1934; private practice in Washington, D. C.

Fitzhugh, Emily W., b. Ohio 1843. Married J. W. Canfield 1859. Children: Rolla, Lucy Nina, Stella; to Curry 1868; pre-empted a claim near Ellensburg (Gold Beach); home was ruined by flood of 1890. Mr. Canfield died 1882. She taught school in Curry County, having been educated in

Carthage, Illinois, before her marriage; county school superintendent 1892-94; postmaster Port Orford 1897.

Fitzhugh, George, b. Missouri 1844; settled on Flores Creek, Curry County 1872; moved to Sixes River 1888; farmer; married Sarah Cox; parents of nine children.

Fitzhugh, Solomon B., b. Kentucky 1804; married Polly M. Dicky; to Oregon 1851; to Curry later. Was one of the committee that drew the constitution for the State of Oregon. Children: Phoebe, Martha, Nancy, Mary, Jane, John, George.

Flam, Frank, b. Minnesota 1864; settled on Bear Creek, Coos County, 1872; in time acquired large holdings, including business and residence properties in Bandon; engaged in stock raising; school director, school clerk, road supervisor; director in Bank of Bandon. Married Docia H. Haga 1898. Children: Blanche, Rosella.

Flam, Joseph, b. Minnesota 1861; with parents to Coos 1872; settled on Bear Creek. Followed logging; later engaged in dairying and general farming on one of the best farms in the Bear Creek valley. Married Mary F. Perkins.

Flanagan, Edward George, b. Newport (Libby) 1862, son of Patrick and Ellen Flanagan. Married Annie Bell Short 1890. Children: Patrick, Evelyn, George, Florence, Elizabeth, Alice, Helen. Mrs. Flanagan died 1919. Mr. Flanagan married Mrs. Blanche Bates Colugh about 1923. A cattle dealer; hotel operator; part owner of the steamers "Comet," "Julia Ray" and the "Satellite." Operated the Pioneer Market in Marshfield, handling meat and groceries; had a slaughter house on the waterfront midway between Marshfield and North Bend, at a place named "Centerville." Owner of Coos Bay Match Factory.

Flanagan, James H., b. Newport (libby) 1869, son of Patrick and Ellen J. Flanagan. Married Alice Proctor 1901. Children: John P., Eleanor J., James H. Jr. Educated in local schools and by private tutors and in business college in San Francisco; a banker 27 years; president Flanagan and Bennett Bank 20 years; established the Marshfield Water Company 1897; later engaged in coal mining and logging operations.

Flanagan, John W., b. Libby 1879, son of Patrick; graduate of University of California. Real estate business in Coos Bay area many years; acting Marshfield postmaster 1937-1941. Married Letitia Howard 1903. Children: Elizabeth; Thomas H.; Mary J.; John D. and Roger M., who are both practicing medical doctors in their home town of Marshfield (Coos Bay).

Flanagan, Patrick, b. Ireland 1824; to America about 1843; gold fields of California 1849; about 1850 began making trips up the coast; spent some time on the Umpqua, with occasional visits to the Coos Bay country. Became interested in coal; with Rogers, made first successful shipment of coal from Coos County to San Francisco 1855. Formed partnership of Flanagan and Rogers, changed shortly afterwards to Flanagan and Mann, first successful coal mining operations in the Coos Bay area, their partnership lasting 30 years; the mine continued to operate much longer. In 1889 Mr. Flanagan, with J. W. Bennett, organized the Flanagan and Bennett Bank, first bank in Coos County, which operated about 30 years and was sold to the Bank of Southwestern Oregon. Married Ellen Winchester 1861. Children: Edward George, James H., John W. Florence, Ella, May, Annie.

Forty, Charles, b. England 1866; to Curry 1878; engaged in dairying; had extensive holdings in Port Orford. Married Olive Freund 1898. Children: Frederick, Anna, Cecelia.

Forty, George, b. England 1822; to Curry 1877; settled on Elk River. Married Caroline Bosley. Parents of five children.

Fox, Charles E., b. Coos County 1878, son of John B. Fox. Married Anna Clinton 1902. She died 1906. Served in the U. S. Life Saving Service at Bandon 1907-1910; followed steamboating; moved to Curry; bought a farm near Langlois; engaged in dairying and general framing. Second marriage 1938 to Mrs. Louise Baxter.

Fox, John B., b. New York 1823; married Violet Jane Meeker. Children: Margaret, Ida, Myrtle, Charles, Claude, Dell, Roy, Laura, David. To Coos 1869; built numerous early bridges in Coos County; put in the first water systems in Marshfield and in Coquille. (See references to him in chapters on transportation and inventions and science). He died 1914; Mrs. Fox 1932.

Fredenburg, Henry K., b. 1868 Brownsville, Oregon. Homesteaded on Halls Creek near Arago. Followed farming and logging. Married Marie Aasen, daughter of Sivert and Marie Aasen. Children: Augusta Edward E., Rosa (Johnston), H. Floyd, Hilda (Davenport), Alvin H. Mr. Fredenburg died 1937; Mrs. Fredenburg 1923.

Fredenburg, H. Floyd, b. Coos County 1911. Followed sawmill work and logging. Married Esther (Davidson) Fredenburg who had previously been married to Alvin H. Fredenburg, who shortly afterwards died in an auto accident. Children: Marie, Edward, Joanne, Christina.

Frey, James, b. Ohio 1832; settled near junction of Rogue and Illinois rivers in Curry County 1867. Children: Jacob, Ida, Eunice, Euley, Rachel, Ellen Frank, Daisy.

Fromm, John, b. Denmark, Europe, 1855. Married Christina Nielson 1877; to Curry County same year, settled near Humbug Mountain. Parents of five children. Engaged in sheep raising and general farming.

Fuhrman, Cyrus J. b. Wisconsin 1881; to Coos 1906. In 1911 married Josie O. Lyons, daughter of James A. and Maria Lyons. Two sons: Frederick A. and Ralph B. Had two years in the U. S. Indian Service; balance of active life spent as pharmacist and druggist; worked in Coquille for R. S. Knowlton; later operated Fuhrman's Pharmacy many years; set up Fuhrman and Schindler Pharmacy in Bandon with O. C. Schindler as partner and manager. Sold his Coquille business to Lucky Bonny and his Bandon interest to Schindler; retired to his ranch home near Langlois.

G

Vern C. Gorst was the first motor bus operator along the Beach Route. One of his big cars got stalled in the quicksand of Ten Mile Creek. J. E. Norton was passing along on his way to the Umpqua and saw it. In the efforts to get it out, it turned over, and was finally bottom up. Mr. Norton, returning 24 hours later, saw only a little of the wheels. It is down there to this day—preeminent sand hath Coos, dune, black, quick.

Gage, Wm. W., b. Dallas, Oregon. To Coos 1888. Purchased ranch on north fork of Coos River. Resided at Coquille. Married Lorena A. Kent. Children: Clyde A., Clara A., Nannie, William A., Virginia, Vivian A., Lee A., Gladys, Bonnie A. Served as sheriff of Coos County for a number of terms. Died 1929.

Gagnon, Andre, b. Canada. When forty years old, came to Minnesota to work as millright. Became inventor, builder and constructor. To Marshfield, with C. A. Smith Lumber Company to take charge of installation of mill. Was still active at age of 86. Died in the 1930's.

Gallier, Edmund M., b. Illinois 1861. To Coos 1873. Operated sheep ranch with brother Stephen. Learned blacksmith's trade in Coquille, conducting shop for five years. With brother Steve, bought Tupper Hotel, later known as the Gallier Hotel in Bandon. Married first 1885 to Emma L. Clemens. No children. Married in 1888 to Alice C. Tutle. Children: Edmund W., Reed A., Alice K.

Gallier, Stephen, b. Illinois 1857. To Coos with parents 1873. When 17 years old operated pack train for miners on Sixes River. Married Mary A. Langlois 1887. Children: Lentner Irvin, Edna Ellen, Gladys. Coos County sheriff 1902-1906. In partnership with brother Ed. M., operated Gallier Hotel in Bandon.

Gallier, William, b. England 1827. Married Matilda Heustis. To Coos 1873. Homesteaded in Curry; farmer, blacksmith, merchant in Coos and Curry—Coquille and Bandon. Mrs. Gallier died 1907; he in 1817.

Gant, Ben, b. Illinois 1850; to Coos 1868. Married Julia Hayes. Children: Mack, Benjamin, Clara, Levi, Rachel, Marion. Located near present site of Powers; continued general farming balance of life. Died 1936; Mrs. Gant died some years earlier. Farm at present being operated by sons, Levi and Marion.

Gant, Calvin, b. Kansas 1859; to Coos 1882; homesteaded near present site of Powers. Married Laura Hayes 1890. Children: Harvey J., Henry, Homer C., Orvin T., Elmer A., Ellis G., Olive, Eva. Retired to Myrtle Point 1914, their present home.

Garfield, Albert, b. Marshfield 1881; To Bandon 1900; operated a machine shop and iron works; added auto repair shop later; machinist for Moore Mill & Lumber Company. Married Camilla Lorentzen 1903; children: Carol and Raymond. Retired in Bandon.

Garoutte, Clay D., b. Iowa 1880; to Bandon 1892; livery and feed business, starting with his uncle, A. G. Hoyt, later buying his interest. Formed partnership with a brother under name of Garoutte Bros. stage and mail line to Langlois; added auto sale agency; brought first Oakland auto to Bandon 1912; added other makes to their agency; added auto repair garage. Director in Bank of Bandon. Mr. and Mrs. Garoutte have one daughter, Alice.

Garrett, Roy F., b. California 1875. Settled near Myrtle Point 1899. Married Rose Chandler, daughter of William Chandler, 1913. Children: Margaret Rose. Farmer and stockman. Later entered logging operations which became known as Laird and Garrett Company. Died 1936.

Garrett, Rose Chandler, is the widow of Roy F. Garrett. Her father was the late William Chandler, who had come from Missouri and settled near Myrtle Point in 1874, where he followed farming, logging and preaching.

Gasner, Casper, b. Switzerland 1876. Married Elizabeth Shmid 1898. Children: George, Bartlet, Henry, Martin, Mary. Followed dairy farming until his retirement.

Gauntlett, Alfred, b. Curry County 1861. Married Mary G. Winsor 1887. Two children. Resided at Gold Beach.

Gauntlett, John, b. England 1823. Captain's clerk in the British navy. Served in the Crimean War. Was in business at Bailarat, Australia. To California during gold excitement. To Curry about 1859 and engaged in mining. Operated the Gauntlett Hotel at Ellensburg. Father of five children. Was county clerk. Musically inclined. Died 1906.

Gauntlett, William, b. Scotland 1850. Settled in Curry County 1859. Married Annie Winsor 1880. Five children. Sheriff of Curry County two terms and county clerk five terms. Engaged in mercantile business with W. S. Winsor; later followed farming and stock raising.

Gearhart, John Neal, b. Astoria 1880. Educated in Astoria schools and in Oregon State College. To Coos 1907. Married Dora E. Bigelow 1909. Children: Hazel, Agnes, John, William, High. The family home is on a farm near Dora. Mr. Gearhart is the present county surveyor, having served in 1932 and 1933 as deputy for E. L. Vinton. Was elected, 1936. His present term, being his fourth, ends 1952.

Geisel, John, b. Germany. To Port Orford 1854. Settled a short distance north of Ellensburg. In 1843 married Miss Bruck, native of Germany. John Geisel and four sons were killed in the Rogue River Indian War of 1855-56. Mrs. Geisel and two daughters were taken into captivity by the Indians but were released later. A monument known as the "Geisel Monument" stands at the place where the massacre occurred, close to present highwav U. S. 101, near Gold Beach.

Getty, Fritz, b. Empire 1879, son of R. W. Getty, a member of the Baltimore Colony. Fritz Getty married Mabel Cottey 1903. Children: Wilmot G., Henrietta C., Anna, Mary.

Gibson, M. B., b. Kentucky 1832. To Curry 1860. Settled at Gold Beach. Shoe making business for twenty years. Married Johanna Bailey 1870; four children. Curry County treasurer 16 years. Purchased and lived on 200 acres. Moved to Langlois 1901 and retired from business.

Giles, Daniel, b. Pennsylvania 1836. To Coos 1853. Gold mining near Whiskey Run. Entered partnership in a whip saw mill. Mined on the head waters of the Coquille River. Enlisted in Rogue River Indian War 1855. Ranch near Myrtle Point. Operated brick and tile business. Married America Agnes Bruden. Children: John Henry, Samuel, Effie, Suanna, Julia Ann, Daisy Bell. In 1881 married Nannie H. Ranson. Children: Daniel, Earl, Claude, Clark. Church—Latter Day Saints.

Going, Clinton C., b. Portland 1884. Married Edna Jane Woodman 1905; to Marshfield 1906; furniture business 23 years; built Going Hotel and ran it till 1937, when Mr. Going died. Mrs. Going continued operation of the hotel 10 years. He was a member of the State Fish and Game Commission. Children: Ruth, Norman H., Catherine.

Golden, Franklin A., b. Massachusetts 1848; educated in West Virginia; taught in schools of higher learning. Married Jeannette Rae, killed in a buggy with a runaway horse. Children: Robert E. and Chas. Ray. Married Edith May Garrigus. Children: Frances Edith and Ruth Anette. In partnership with his father, Dr. Charles B. Golden, he operated a drug and notions store in Marshfield in the 1890's; superintendent of the Marshfield schools 20 years; later was rural school supervisor; then taught science in the new Marshfield High School. "Golden Field," football court, is named for him. Died 1926.

Goodman, John, b. Illinois 1837. Civil War veteran. To Coquille 1880. Married Mary Ellen Ross. Children: Carl R., Cash C., M. M., L. L., Carrie, Florence, George P. County commissioner.

Gorham, K. D., b. Kentucky 1834. To Coos 1866. Settled near Iowa Slough; later farmed near Parkersburg. Married Sally E. Harbeson. One child, July A. F.

Gould, Albert N. (Bert), b. California 1877, son of George A. and Harriett E. Gould. Settled with parents on upper west fork of the Millicoma River on the Elkhorn Ranch. (See chapter Some Pioneer Families). Hunter, trapper, logger, farmer. Studied civil engineering in correspondence courses; surveyor; awarded contract by U. S. Surveyor General to subdivide township in which Elkhorn was situated—previously unsurveyed. County surveyor 1906-1914. Furniture dealer Coquille 1919-1939. Married 1904 Bell Rich, who died in an auto accident 1940. Children: Harriet Helen (Osika), Harold H. Married 1943 Georgia Burkett, who died 1944. Married 1946 Mrs. Ethle Low. Still follows engineering; continues to enjoy hunting; residence near Coquille.

Graham, Albert, b. Missouri 1842. To Coos 1874. Settled on north fork of the Coquille; moved to Myrtle Point 1890. Married Priscilla J. May 1865. Served in Company F, 13th Kansas Infantry three years. Mail contractor and engaged in farming. Children: Arrilda B., William J., Mary D., Lillie M., Ethel E., Ruby C.

Greene, Thomas H., b. Ireland 1833. To Coos 1872. Settled where Coaledo now stands. Married Beatrice Sanley 1851. Eight children. Served in Rogue River Indian War 1855-56. A farmer.

Gross, John B., b. Ohio 1832. To Bandon 1888. Married Jennie Garoutte 1865. Children: Ettie G., Harvey A., Kittie M., John W., Daniel A., Frederick H. Served in the Civil War. Engaged in business at Bandon for a number of years.

Guerin, Addison H., b. Pennsylvania 1869. To Curry 1876; settled at Eckley. Married Ella R. Biglow 1895. One daughter, Emma. Followed farming and stock raising.

Guerin, George H., b. Alabama 1842. To Curry; settled at Eckley 1876. Married Priscilla Dobinson 1866. Children: William, Harry A., Thomas D., George H. Jr., James T., Waterman C., Charles V., Anna R., Eckley C., John.

Guerin, William S., b. New Jersey 1847. To Oregon 1877; settled at Eckley. Married Maggie W. Miller 1872. Children: A. H., William S. Jr., Charles H., Mary Charlotte, Courtland, George H., Caroline, Julia, Fredric. Later homesteaded on Flores Creek. Active in Curry County school work. County school superintendent five terms. Died 1914; Mrs. Guerin 1922.

Gulovsen, Medilius P., b. Norway, Europe, 1855. Married Ida Hansen. Children: Mamie, George, Oscar, Madoc, Arthur, Helen. To Marshfield 1882. Opened furniture store 1900, first business established on Central Avenue. Their home, the third house in South Marshfield, is still the family residence. Mrs. Gulovsen died 1907; Mr. Gulovsen 1921.

Binger Hermann's remarkable memory as exhibited at the Port Orford Agate Carnival in 1915: *In the Knapp Hotel a grinning fellow came up and put out a tanned, leathery hand to be shaken by Hermann's white one. "Do you recollect me, Mr. Hermann?" . . . "Just a moment, my good man, just a moment. It was* 20 *years ago on a steamboat up the river" . . . "Yes, yes" . . . "You and your wife and three children were on the way to a place far back in the woods" . . . "Yes, yes" . . ."I thought how brave you were—your name is—just a moment, my good man—your name is—it is Walter Bradford" . . . "That's what it is, Mr. Hermann, and you never saw me but that once* 20 *years ago."*

Hacker, Isaiah, b. Maine 1863. Injury in childhood prevented outdoor activity; was apprenticed as shoemaker. To Coos 1862; married Adrienne B. Stoddard 1886. One daughter, Mabel (Mrs. L. H. Hazard). Worked in North Bend sawmill; shoe shop and store in Empire and later in Marshfield; taught school; sheriff of Coos County; member of state legislature; county school superintendent; principal of Marshfield school; recorder and justice of the peace; collector of customs. Joined Webster and Andrew Lockhart in publishing "The Coast Mail"; established an abstract office in Empire 1888; moved with the county-seat to Coquille 1897. Director and assistant cashier, First National Bank.

Haga, Joseph F., b. Virginia 1849; to Coos in late 1880's; took preemption claim and bought additional land near Bear Creek. Worked diligently to become owner of extensive dairy and stock raising business and to rear his family of eleven children, beginning at age 16, when he married Malinda Dickson in 1865. Children: Sarah I., George, Columbus, Wesley J., Docia, Frances, John W., Polly, Gussie, Elizabeth, Joseph M.

Haga, Wesley, b. Virginia 1872; to Coos 1888; carried on general farming and dairying near Coquille. Married twice, first to Anna M. Taylor; children: Bessie, Clara, Lester, Arthur; second to Irene Evans 1910; one son, Kenneth.

Haines, J. E., b. Illinois 1828; married Eleanor Chaffee 1853; to Curry 1859; acquired land in the Eckley district, adding to it until his holdings reached more than 900 acres. Mr. and Mrs. Haines raised and educated a family of 14 children: Josephine, Cimeon Alfred, Joseph E., Charles Wm., Liberty L., Jamison L., Rupert L., Iva May, Oscar O., Ruby, Mary M., Marion Miles, Harriette, Chaffee Delong. The family moved to Douglas County to enable the children to attend the Wilbur Academy; then moved back to their mountain home. Postmaster at Eckley 1897; sold his holdings later to the C. A. Smith Lumber Company. (See story of Eckley)

Hall, Andrew J., b. 1862 Polk County; son of William and Martha J. Hall. To Coos with parents 1869. Settled on Isthmus Inlet. Began steamboating at early age on Coos Bay and Coquille River. Married Edith M. Haskins 1897. One daughter, Norma Agnes. Died 1911.

Hall, Ephriam O., b. Maine, 1835. Married Mary E. Dayton 1863. Children: Clara, Oliver J., William E., George H., Newton B., Sadie May, Ida Bell, Charles H., Ramson. For many years Mr. Hall was superintendent of the Stave Mill, located between North

Bend and Marshfield. Later engaged in the real estate business with E. A. Anderson. In 1906 operated a general store at Sumner and was postmaster. Died 1914; Mrs. Hall 1906.

Hall, James T., b. Oregon 1859. To Coos at an early age. Served as steamboat captain. Studied law; entered partnership with his brother, Judge John F. Hall, in Marshfield. Married Alice J. Stauff 1893. One chlid, Mary Elsie.

Hall, Judge John F., b. Polk County 1856, son of William and Martha J. (Cox) Hall. Received early education from his father who taught the family evenings. To Coos 1869. Various occupations: county surveyor, studied law with T. G. Owen and with Judge John Kelsay at Corvallis. Admitted to the Oregon Bar 1887. Law office in Marshfield; county judge; district attorney. Married Mary Strickling 1892. One daughter, Roxie M., who has been librarian of Calaveras County, California, since 1939. Clerk of Marshfield school board 34 years. Died 1923; Mrs. Hall 1928.

Hall, William, b. Tennessee 1821. To Coos 1869, locating on Rock Creek near Bridge. Engaged in stock raising. Later took homestead and pre-emption on land now known as Millington. County surveyor. Married Martha J. Cox. Children: Isham A., William, John F., James T., Andrew J., Ida P., Sarah A. Mary M,., and an adopted daughter, Nellie. Died in 1890's; Mrs. Hall 1908.

Hamblock, Eugene H., b. Coos, 1870, son of John F. Worked on farm, in logging camps and sawmills. After his father's death, purchased estate from heirs and carried on stock raising and general farming. Married Annie Carman 1901. Five children.

Hamblock, John, b. Prussia 1827; arrived Port Orford 1854. One of the first settlers on Coquille River, taking preemption claim 1857 near Bullards. Believed to have sawed first white cedar lumber. Opened first store at his home 1858. Married Jane Ann Long 1856. Parents of four children. Postmaster at Randolph 1863.

Hamblock, John Fredrick, b. Germany; to Coos 1869. General farming on homestead near Parkersburg. Married Mary Campbell 1869. Children: Emma, Mary F., Margaret, John W., and Eugene H. Mrs. Hamblock died 1906; he 1909.

Hamlin, Andrew J., b. in Oregon 1867. To Curry, near Langlois, 1901. Bought 250 acres which he cleared for farming. Married Alva Fitzwalter 1888. Children: James E., Delbert, Erwin V.

Hammerburg, J. W., b. Sweden 1838. To Coos 1865; settled on Coos Bay. Later moved to Prosper where he was foreman in Adam Pershbaker's sawmill. Married Alice I. Lowe, daughter of Judge David J. Lowe.

Hanly, Thomas P., b. San Francisco 1860. To Coos 1870. Married Dora L. Schroeder 1881. Children: Theresa, Thomas, Margaret. Lumber sawyer; operated and owned large dairy; stockholder and director of Bank of Bandon from its beginning until his death; commissioner Port of Bandon. Died 1936; Mrs. Hanly 1946.

Hansen, Andrew F. (My-Good-Boy-Hansen), b. Denmark, Europe, 1860. Married Madsen Christine Jensen 1886. Children: Ferdinand, Mary, Harriett, Jens, Eva, George, and a little son who disappeared at the age of three years while playing and was never seen nor heard from again, but was thought to have been carried off by some wild animal. Owned and operated a transit business in Marshfield and for 35 years carried the mail between all boats, trains and the post office. His buoyant nature and cheery "My good boy" or "My good girl" to all he met, won for him the endearing title of "Good-Boy-Hansen." Mrs. Hansen died 1938; he 1942.

Hansen, Hans H., b. Denmark, Europe, 1881; to Curry in his early twenties; dairied in Denmark before coming to America; leased Star Ranch in Curry 1915, milking 150 to 175 cows; later built cheese factory near Langlois; began experimenting in making blue vein cheese 1931; made it a commercial product two years later; in ten years built annual output up to half a million pounds per year; in 1950 shipped 35,000 pounds by parcel post direct to individual customers in all parts of the United States and to several foreign countries. His product is known as Langlois Blue Cheese.

Hansen, Kennedy H., b. Iowa 1858.

To Gravelford 1886. Married Ida Jackson. Children: Metta E., Florence M., Leonard, Carra. Taught school many years. County assessor. Owned small farm near Gravelford; moved to Myrtle Point and operated a grocery. Both Mr. and Mrs. Hansen died 1943.

Hanson, Charles E., b. Sweden 1861; to Coos 1880; worked in sawmills and logging camps; settled on Haynes Inlet farm in early 1880's; livestock, dairy, potatoes, apples; road supervisor; school board member; on same place continuously 70 years; still enjoys a game of cribbage in his 90's. Married Annie E. Nelson 1883; children: Florence E., Algie. Mrs. Hanson died about 1900.

Harlocker, Judge Lintner, b. Ohio 1848. Located near Coquille 1871. Assessor; sheriff. Married Fannie J. Coke 1889. Children: Charles S., Frank J., Edna C., Hugh, Fred L., Mary E. The family moved to Coquille 1890; postmaster; railroad station agent; county judge. Owned considerable property; active in civic affairs.

Harmon, Leason L., b. North Carolina 1849. Arrived Coos 1873, settled near Lee. Married Hester H. Mast 1886. Taught school for several years at Fairview, Norway, Gravelford, Lee, and Catching Creek. After retiring, he spent his last years working on his farm. Children: Cora M., Sadie E., William H., Charles W., Wade H., Ruby C. Died 1891; Mrs. Harmon 1934.

Harris, Capt. W. H., b. Missouri 1823. First Lieutenant in Mexican War. Was made a Mason on battlefield at Beuna Vista, under special dispensation and later became charter member of three lodges in Coos County. To Coos with the Marple Company 1853. Married Margaret Romanes 1858 at Empire City. Moved to homestead on South Fork of the Coquille. Children: Mary G., Elizabeth, Christina. Captain Harris located the first land claim in Coos County and built the first house, this being at Empire City, where he plotted the first eight blocks of the new town. Captain of Volunteers during the Indian Wars 1856.

Harrison, James W., b. Texas 1915, son of Wm. Harrison. To Oregon 1917. Attended school in Cottage Grove and Marshfield. Taught school; farmed. Married Vurl V. Mallory 1939. Children: Ronald, Norrene. County judge, beginning Jan. 1951. Residence, Sumner.

Harry, John Alva. (See chapter Some Pioneer Families).

Hartley, Irvin N., b. Minnesota 1893; to North Bend 1922, where his parents, Mr. and Mrs. I. E. Hartley, had preceded him. Worked in the Bank of Oregon several years; city treasurer 1933-1947; elected mayor 1950, still serving. In 1933, while he was city treasurer and Edgar McDaniel was mayor, they put out two issues of "Wooden Money" made of the famous myrtle wood, with which North Bend paid its city employes, water and light bills and other operating expenses. The merchants accepted the wooden dollars in payment for their merchandise. When the banks reopened a few months later, North Bend was prepared to redeem the "Chips" and issued a call accordingly. A considerable portion of the money has not been turned in to this date in 1952, being kept in many cases as souvenirs.

Hartman, J. S., b. Germany 1856; located in Bandon; lighthouse keeper 20 years; general merchandise business; motion pictures in Bandon 1909. Married Elizabeth N. Wilkerson 1887; two children.

Hatcher, Hiram, b. Missouri 1874; Civil War veteran; Texas Ranger; to Oregon about 1873; grocery business at Bridge; joined Colonel Jewel Post of the GAR at Myrtle Point, of which he was the last survivor. A familiar figure at the Coos-Curry Fair race track nearly 20 years; owned the horse "Veloskey," half-mile state champion. Married Hattie Bronson; one daughter, Hattie M. His widow, age 81, resides in Myrtle Point.

Hatcher, James A., b. Iowa 1862; son of John R. To Coos with parents 1877; settled at Fairview; farm hand, logger, stage driver. In 1888 took over an unimproved portion of his father's homestead; cleared and improved it, turning it into a fine farm, including 800 Gravenstein apple trees. Married

Alice Darnielle. Children: Everett, Violet, Vivian, James A. Jr., Carl A., Laura May, Clara Dell, Ada Pearl, Millie L., Zelma A., Lena L.

Hatcher, John R.; came from Iowa 1877; homesteaded at Fairview. Married Emily Smith. Children: Wm. A., Delaney, Simon K., James A., Robert O., Perry C., Myhulda C., Rebecca L.

Hatcher, Simon K., b. Iowa 1860; to Coos with parents 1877; farmed at Fairview. Married Ida J. Stillwell 1884. Children: Archie, Clarence, Ernest O., Bertha J., Lucinda, Sylvia M.

Hawkins, J. E., b. Missouri 1835. Married Altha Ann Wallace 1860. Children: Harvey A., James W., Sarah P., Marvin O., Lerisa E., Ellen E. To Curry 1884; settled on Flores Creek; entered dairy business. School director, county commissioner.

Hawkins, Marvin O., b. California 1871. To Curry 1884 with parents. At age 19 began teaching school in Curry County. Graduated from Monmouth State Normal school 1894. To Coos as principal of Coquille Collegiate Institute. Married Zettie Messer 1899, daughter of John P. and Nancy Messer. Children: Mamie, Marvin Jane, Ann. Deputy assessor. Director and president Farmers and Merchants Bank of Coquille. Coquille mayor; postmaster 1935-1950.

Hayes, James D., b. Tennessee 1856. To Oregon with parents by covered wagon and settled on upper Coquille River 1872. Married Jessie Adeline Self 1872. Children: Josephine, Everet, Neta, Irene, Francis Clayton, Kermit. Homesteaded at Etelka, Coos County. Farmed and raised stock until he retired and moved to Myrtle Point 1923. Youngest son, Kermit, now operates the farm and has developed it into one of the finest in the valley. Died 1928.

Hayes, John, b. North Carolina 1825. Married Susan Wagner 1854. To Coos 1872; settled on South Fork of Coquille River. Took up 160 acres as squatter's right. Martha, Dolly, Julia, Lura, Mary, Eva, Margaret. General farming. Died 1905.

Hayes, Joseph McD., b. North Carolina 1868. Came as a child to Coos. Farmer, mail carrier, road supervisor. Married Sarah Hartley 1892. Children: Adolphus, Harrison, Jesse. Mrs. Hayes died 1902.

Hayes, William, W., b. Indiana 1826. Married Martha Huntington 1847. Children: Amanda J., Maria L., Sarah, Cynthia Ann, James S., Everett E., Mary W. To Coos 1874. Entered the mercantile business. County treasurer three terms. Mrs. Hayes died 1906; he 1909.

Hayter, Melvin, b. Oregon 1863; to Coos 1865. At age 14 started work in logging camps; continued 28 years, then took up farming near Riverton. Married Nettie Pearl Steward 1895. Children: Lusta H. and Alvin.

Hazard, Louis H., b. Iowa 1867. To Empire City 1885, joining his father who had preceded him in 1873. Deputy postmaster at Marshfield, under J. M. Arrington. Store clerk with Southern Oregon Company in Empire; four years later became storekeeper for the U. S. Commissary Department. Deputy county clerk 1896; county clerk 1899. One of the organizers, cashier, then manager of Bank of Coquille until sale to the First National Bank of Portland. Married Mabel E. Hacker 1896. Children: Austin, Alice, Adrienne.

Hazard, Silas H., b. Louisiana 1838. Educated as an attorney before coming to Coos 1873; law office at Empire. Several years as district attorney; possessed large law library. Married three times; first to Maragaret Shircliff; son, Louis H.; second to Emma Watson; third to Frances Adele McKnight.

Herman, Carl F., b. Coos County 1897. Married Myrtle Philpot 1913. Three children. Followed salmon fishing, farming, boatbuilding, dairying. He and brother built a number of steamers and motor boats that operated on the Coquille River.

Herman, Frank, b. Germany 1873. Began "while a kid sailing before the mast on windjammers." To San Francisco 1888; later to Marshfield. Specialized in house and auto painting. Married Josie Peterson 1907. Residence Eastside. Died 1951.

Hermann, Henry G., b. Broadbent 1881; son of Manuel T. Hermann. Married Sarah Miller 1907. Started general blacksmithing 1907, in Myrtle Point. Later added machine works and heavy welding. At age 70 is still operating his blacksmith shop after 44 years in business.

Hervey, James C., b. Tennessee 1847. To Coos 1872; homesteaded near Bridge. Married Martha Hayes 1876. Children: LaFayette, William H., James H. Moved to Coquille 1886; a year later to a farm in Lee Velley, where the family developed a fine dairy farm. Mrs. Hervey died 1911; he some time later. Their descendants still operate the home place.

Heuckendorff, Emil H., b. Denmark, Europe. To Coos 1880. Married Mary Nielson. Shipbuilder in North Bend and Marshfield. Started a shipbuilding yard at Prosper 1905. Died 1908.

Hillstrom, Jake R., b. Marshfield 1891, son of John and Sophia (Hongell) Hillstrom. In 1911 entered into partnership with brother, J. W. Hillstrom, contracting in building of roads, bridges, ships of various types, dredging, piledriving. President Hillstrom Shipbuilding Company during World War II. President Hillstrom Rock Quarry; plant on Kentuck Inlet. Marshfield city councilman; Elks Club trustee. Married Rose Myren 1919; one son, Robert. (See chapter Assortment of Enterprises).

Hillstrom, John Wm. (Bill), b. Marshfield 1887; began work in shipyard at age 15; in partnership with brother, Jake R., since 1911; contracting of all kinds; besides his interest in the Hillstrom Rock Quarry and general contracting, he operates a general marine repair shop and ways on the Coos Bay waterfront. Married Greda Pederson 1919. Two sons: John W. Jr., George G.

Hillstrom, Rudolph J., b. Finland 1899, son of Charles J. To Marshfield 1900. Graduated in mechanical engineering from Oregon State College 1922; post graduate study in low-temperature carbonization of coal. After experimenting ten years, 1922-1932, secured patent on process. Its development will require financing running into millions. Has followed building contracting. Turned attention to harvesting of cranberries, organizing a company known as Western Harvester Inc. In 1946 patented a picking machine now used in all cranberry producing areas in the United States and in Nova Scotia; and being built in Washington, Wisconsin and Massachusetts. Married Agnes Maginnis 1925, daughter of Major T. F. Maginnis. Children: Thomas R., Joaquina A., Charles John. (See chapter on invention and science).

Hoffman, E. M., b. Oregon 1858; farming and stock raising near Myrtle Point. Married Henrietta Williams 1883. Children: Mary, Edward, Walter, Milton E., George W., Charles H., Nellie M.

Holden, David W., b. Maine 1865. To Coos 1896. Married Mary Elliott 1894. Drove stage on ocean beach, Coos Bay to Umpqua River. Operated boat "Gasgo" between Marshfield, Jarvis Landing and Empire; deckhand on ferry "Roosevelt". Died 1932; Mrs. Holden 1936. Children: Marle D., David A., Dale W., Ermin Jane.

Holland, David H., b. Scotland 1828. David, twelfth of family of 16 children, came to United States 1850. To Coos 1859, locating on the Coquille. Married Sarah Skidmore 1850. Lost all their possessions in the big flood of 1861-1862. Superintendent of Eastport coal mines. Purchased 160 acres at Rose Point 1872. Later engaged in butcher business in Marshfield. Mrs. Holland purchased an interest in the Blanco Hotel with James L. Ferry; operated by the Hollands from 1886 to 1896. Children: Anna, Nellie, Thomas D., Wm., Parker B. Mrs. Holland died 1902.

Holland, Enoch, b. Ireland 1866. Orphaned early, he lived with the family of his uncle, Dave H. Holland, at Rose Point, on east side of Coos Bay. As Enoch grew up, he worked in the Newport coal mines. Married Mary C. Kerrigan. Children: Nell, Enoch Jr., Edward, Isabel, Ann, Mary, Kathleen, Theresa, Florence.

Hollenbeck, Rev. S. B., b. Iowa 1846. To Coos 1878; farmed at Burton Prairie (Fairview) and preached. Married Amanda D. Benham. Children: Suzan M., Effie L., Ilda C., Orlando B., Mary J., Tullie B., George M., James S., Nancy P., Bessie V., Grace M.

Holverstott, Henry W., b. 1833. To Coos 1873. Settled on Burton Prairie. Married Teressa Hawley 1873. Children: John J., Homer V., Robert, Charles

A., Elmer, Harry, Dairying and general farming. Died 1917; Mrs. Holverstott 1926.

Homme, William E., b. Wisconsin 1871. To Coos 1907; started town of Cooston. Built several houses there and served as postmaster. Married Laura Nass 1903. Children: Frances, Chester, Cooston; Franklin.

Hongell, Herman, b. Finland 1872. To Coos 1888. Worked in logging camps and shipyards. Married Olga Pederson. One son, Nels Andrew.

Hooton, A. O., b. Indiana 1867; to Bridge, Coos County about 1890; farmer. Married Zua Hill 1895. Four daughters: Lou, Maude, Dorothy, Edna.

Hooton, M. A., b. 1864; to Coos 1890. Married Callie Belle Easter 1891. Children: Arthur, Ann. Taught school in Coos and Douglas counties; settled late in Coquille. Died 1935.

Horsfall, Lyda A., b. Coos River, daughter of Jasper A. and Marian A. (Rogers) Yoakam. Graduated from University of Oregon; taught school in Marshfield; married Dr. William Horsfall 1896. Children: William Jr. (deceased), George, a colonel in U. S. Army Medical Corps; Marian, a California teacher and president of California State Teachers Association two terms. Mrs. Horsfall gave private lessons in vocal and instrumental music in Marshfield many years; organized and directed the Chamande Club, a musical group of local women. Long and actively associated with the D. A. R., at different times holding national offices in that organization.

Horsfall, Dr. William. (See chapter on Early Doctors).

Houser, Evander, b. South Carolina. To Coos 1879; settled near present site of Bridge. Married Sarah Potter. Children: Mary, J. G., Maggie, Florence, Laura, Finas, Inez, Edna, Josie.

Houser, J. G., b. North Carolina 1871. To Coos 1879 with parents. Remained at home until 1895, when he married Josie Pierce. Children: Harry, Edith, Archie, Olis, Virgie, Clara. Followed logging and later farming on his own place near Bridge.

Hudson, Shadrach, b. Michigan 1830. Served in Rouge River Indian War 1855-1856. Married Ann Williams 1868. One child, Mary C. To Curry 1877; followed mining until he had misfortune to lose arm and then retired from active work.

Hughes, James, b. Curry County 1863. Married Laura McMullen 1889. Followed farming in early life and later was keeper of Cape Blanco lighthouse. Had considerable property in Curry County.

Hughes, Patrick, b. Ireland 1831; to U. S. 1831; crossed plains with ox teams; mined gold in Curry nine years; developed and operated one of Curry County's finest livestock and dairy farms. Married Jane O'Neil. Children: Edward, Thomas, Francis, James, Rev. John C., Alice. Catholics. He and others built a small church near his home on Cape Blanco; church still standing 1952 but delapidated and neglected. Staunch Republican; commissioner of Curry County several terms. Died 1901.

Huling, D. A., b. Ohio 1841. To Coos 1890. Settled at Myrtle Point. In hardware business with R. W. Lundy. Married Mary A. McAffee. Children: Mattie and C. E.

Hull, Felix, b. Indiana 1854. To Coos 1888. Married Mary Bellman 1879. She died 1918. Married Cora V. Richardson 1921. General farming and dairying. Retired and moved to Bandon 1930. Died 1950. Well known up and down Coquille River valley for his fair dealings| Did many days of hard work hewing his farm out of wilderness.

Hull, Wm. H., b. Indiana 1840; Civil War veteran. To Coos 1890; farmed and operated dairy in Coquille Valley; helped to organize and was president of the Coquille Valley Cooperative Creamery 1911. Married Kate Alexander 1872. Children: Ina, Clark, Thomas, William Jr.

Huntley, Jeremiah, b. Ohio 1845; to Gold Beach 1870; mined black sands; county school superintendent; studied law; admitted to Oregon bar; office in Gold Beach. Married Hattie Caffin 1868. Children: Jennie, Edna, Alma, Harry G., Floyd. Mason.

I

Indians — six little boys. At Port Orford small Jim appeared at Mrs. William Tichenor's door. He said he had a hiyu ache in his stomach. She mixed him a spoonful of camphor and sugar. Next day Jim and another little Indian presented themselves. With faces contorted and backs bent, they declared they had a hiyu pain. Mrs. Tichenor administered camphor and sugar. Next day came Jim with five little Indian boys with five hiyu aches in their stomachs. She dosed them and Jim with six spoonfuls of camphor and sugar. Then she sternly said this was the last time they could expect to receive the cure.

Idles, John. One of the persons killed in 1856 by the Rogue River Indians in the Whalehead Massacre, about 18 miles south of Gold Beach. For him and the others in that early conflict history has done little more than put them in a list, except Agent Ben Wright and John Geisel and his sons.

Imhoff, Anthony H, a well-known carpenter in North Bend soon after the new town was started. Children: Howard, Clifford, Garfield, Marian, Fahy. The Imhoff home on north Union Avenue, built by him, is still occupied by his son Garfield. "Imhoff's," run by two of his sons, was a popular eating house in the early days of the town, being particularly known for its pies made by "Mother Lucy" Williams.

Indian Neighbors. Chief Jackson lived until about 1920 in North Bend, with his daughter Lottie (Mrs. Alex Egenoff). He was gregarious and well liked; he was always to be seen at a parade or any kind of celebration . . . Indian Tom and his wife Kate lived on the north side of Coos Bay at Jordan's Cove, with the sand dunes as a far-stretching back yard. He was a poultryman of sorts—he had a flock of domestic chickens and sold wild ducks at a dollar a dozen to the hotel at Empire. Once J. W. Bennett's hunting dogs killed one of Tom's chickens; Bennett explained to Tom that he had no money in his pocket but would leave pay for the hen at the Simpson store in North Bend. Bennett duly left the damage amount, 75 cents, but when Tom came in for it a clerk had lost his memorandum and telephoned Bennett if it was all right. When Tom was given the money, he expressed surprise that it had come so quick; he thought it had been sent over the telephone... Gek-ka, George Wasson's grandmother, lived in a cabin on South Slough. About twice a week it was the enjoyable duty of all the grandchildren to gather at her place to hear her tell about the old Indian ways and old Indian times. George Wasson remembered her gesturing broadly and saying, 'Your hyas papas belong all this land. Someday, George, you get it back."

Ingle, Chester R. He founded in 1903 the first newspaper in North Bend, the weekly *Citizen.* With the help of his brother Roy he conducted it for only three years, suspending it in 1906.

Ingram, Rex. In 1936, with William Haglund, he bought the Pioneer Hardware Store in Marshfield, dating back to the early 80's. In 1946 he acquired the Haglund interest, and later had associated with him Leonard B. Mayfield, former superintendent of the Marshfield public schools. He died in 1951.

Isaacson, August, b. Sweden 1868. To Coos 1907. Married Mathilda Olson. Children: Leslie A., Chester L., Myrtle G. Saw filer; life member of Knights Templar, and of Elks. Mrs. Isaacson died 1946.

Ismert, Henry, b. Colorado 1873; settled on Pistol River; farmer and livestock raiser. Married Vera L. Clark 1897.

Ismert, John P., b. France 1820. To Curry County 1887; settled on Pistol River; followed farming and stockraising. Married 1863 Catherine Hafner, b. Prussia 1843. They had seven children.

Isaacs, Henry J., real estate and insurance dealer in the days before streets were paved in North Bend, selling mostly city property.

J

Andrew Johnson, who came to Empire City in 1854, mined at Whiskey Run, where he built a house. He served in Captain W. H. Harris' company during the Rogue River wars 1855-1856. When he was mustered out and returned to his place at Randolph No. 1 at Whiskey Run, "a large whale had come ashore in front of his house a few days before. He found 100 or more Indians all busy carrying away the blubber."..

Jackson, J. J., b. Boston 1815. Settled at Empire City 1856. Married Mrs. Margaret A. Noble. Children: Martha E., Andrew J., Charles H., George W. Built and for many years operated the Pioneer Hotel in Empire. Mrs. Jackson's daughter by first marriage was Emily Oregon Noble, the first white child born in Coos County. In this family was the first birth, the first marriage and the first death of white people in Coos County.

James, James H., b. Illinois 1844. Married Elizabeth McCluer 1868. Children: Laura Ann, Charles, Harvey, Alice, Walter A., Elta L. Arrived Coos 1883; located at Parkersburg. Worked as carpenter, building a mill for Captain Judah Parker after fire had destroyed first mill. County assessor 1892, serving two years.

Jenkins, James T., b. Kansas 1877. To Coos 1900. Married Myrtle M. Fox 1901. Had four sons. General farming and dairying. County commissioner five years. During late years buys and sells cattle for the California market; said to have sold over ten thousand head of cattle.

Jeub, Roy A., b. Minnesota 1885. To Coos 1912. Office work with Coos Bay Lumber Company; county clerk's office; sheriff's office; treasurer's office; second lieutenant in World War I. Returned to work in sheriff's office. Associated with A. O. Walker and N. Neimen in service station. In 1929 associated with Smith Wood Products, looking after timber and logs; mill foreman and assistant manager until the company sold out. City councilman and mayor of Coquille; president Coquille Motor Sales Company. Married Bessie Robertson 1915, killed in auto accident 1929. Married 1930 Maxine Gentry, a Coquille high school teacher. One son, Gerald.

Johnson, Charles C., b. Finland 1862. To North Bend 1882. Worked in shipyards; purchased and operated dairy farm near Cooston. Married Hilda Smith 1889. Children: Cal, George, Harry, August, Lillian, John.

Johnson, Douglas (Doug), b. 1886, son of Rev. Levi Johnson assigned to Gold Beach 1898-1899. At age 12, when not in school, worked in the Hume cannery 11 hours a day at $3.50 per week. Became enamored with Curry County. When his father was transferred, he had to leave but longed to return. Became an accountant. Married Milla Mitchell. Two daughters: Dorothy, Patricia. To Port Orford in late 1930's; mayor; away during war period; returned; again mayor. Accountant for lumber company; Hobby—Making furniture, fixtures and finishings from great variety of driftwood, for home on bluff facing Battle Rock and the ocean.

Johnson, Everett E., b. Michigan 1876, son of Alfred. To Coquille 1897. Mr. Johnson's father purchased the Morras Brothers mill, three miles above Coquille. Everett Johnson was associated with this enterprise until 1899, when he became owner and editor of the Coquille Bulletin. Purchased the Lyons Mill in Coquille 1901. Conducted it 26 years, when he went to Portland, as representative of the Robert Dollar Company, owner of mill property and large timber stands. Returned to Coquille nine years later; secured an interest in the Coquille Log and Lumber Company; became its directing head. Mayor of Coquille several terms; Bandon Port Commission. Married Julia Drane 1900. Children: Phillip E., Mary Esther. Died 1943.

Jones, Edward K., b. San Francisco 1873. Located at Marshfield 1902 as manager of the Pioneer Hardware Company. Later became agent for several manufacturers and jobbers. Married Mabel O'Connell. One son, Eugene.

Jones, J. S., b. Virginia 1848. To Coos 1875; settled at Empire City. Married Mattie J. Smith 1867. Children: Robert W., Nena M., Jennie, Charles W. Purchased William Hall place on Isthmus Slough and sub-divided it as Flagstaff and Millington.

Louis Knapp Sr. in the 60's built at Port Orford the Knapp Hotel, one of the most celebrated inns on the coast between San Francisco and the Columbia River, which was in oprea-tion for three-quarters of a century. In the early days its advertisements, in listing the accommodations for the comfort of guests, featured the fact that there was a bootjack in every room.

Kaiser, Charles B., b. Ohio 1870. To North Bend 1900. A good musician; built up and led the North Bend Band for many years. Married Wilhelmina Gehbart 1902. One child, Theodora. Trade, masonry—all kinds of brick and concrete work. Built many fireplaces, water tanks and high mill smokestacks.

Kardell, Eric W., b. Minnesota 1874. To Coos with parents 1888; settled on Isthmus Inlet 1902. Married Lulu L. Boone, a direct descendant of Daniel Boone. Children: Alton, Florence (Mrs. Chas. H. Hall), Marian L. (Mrs. Wm. E. Walsh). Followed railroading. Retired after more than 35 years of service. Member of Draft Board of Coos County during World War II. Died 1943; Mrs. Kardell 1944.

Keating, Daniel B., b. Empire City 1882; Marshfield merchant. Married Laura Sturdivant 1907. Fire chief 1913 to 1916 Marshfield Volunteer Fire Department.

Keating, Walter H., b. Massachusetts 1846. Son of Daniel B. Keating Sr. Arrived Empire City 1870. Married Alma U. Bushnell 1871. Children: Jesse W., Edith L., Frank C., George E., Daniel B., Louis H. Mr. Keating was engineer on tug "Fearless" and was drowned when wrecked 1889.

Keizer, May Rees, Mrs. b. Oregon, daughter of Chester and Sylvia Ann Rees. Taught school. Married 1907 Dr. Russell C. Keizer. Children: Ennis, Mabel (Hansen), John. To North Bend 1919 where Dr. Keizer became associated with his brother, Dr. Phil J. Keizer; established Keizer Hospital 1923. Dr. Phil died 1929; Dr. Russell C. 1939. Mrs. Keizer became superintendent of the hospital continued by her two sons Dr. Ennis and Dr. John Keizer.

Kendall, John C., b. Minnesota 1886. To Marshfield 1910; entered law practice with John D. Goss. Circuit Judge 1923 to 1927. Married Gertrude C. Walrath 1910. One son, John. Mrs. Kendall died 1933; Judge Kendall at his Crooked Riffle Lodge on Rogue River 1951.

Kennedy, Michael W., b. Canada 1841; to Pacific Coast 1862. Married Margaret Golden at Libby 1878. Children: Mary M., John E., Martin A., Thomas D., Michael R., Margaret P., Rosery C. Followed carpentry and farm work. Died 1893.

Kennedy, Willis H., b. Michigan 1878. To Coos 1906. Married Boletta Larson 1910, daughter of Julius. One daughter, Evelyn C. In the dredging business with the Larson Dredge Company. Raised beef cattle on his farm on Isthmus Inlet. Member of Marshfield City council. He is Catholic and she a Presbyterian; both Democrats. Charter member and past exalted ruler, Marshfield Elks and one of the last two living of the original twenty-five charter members, the other one being E. D. McArthur.

Kern, Henry G., b. Coos County 1875. Married Winnifred L. Chapman

1902. Children: Harry G. and Lucille (Mrs. Don McInery). Worked as cooper with his father making barrels for packing salmon; fished for salmon; blacksmith; worked in railroad shops; mined in Alaska; co-partner with L. J. Simpson in North Bend Iron Works; owner since 1903; school board; city council and mayor; president First National Bank of North Bend until sold; president West Coast Savings and Loan Association; veteran Spanish-American War; county commissioner. Resides in North Bend.

Kerrigan, Michael, b. Ireland 1834. To Coos 1857. Worked on tug for Simpson Lumber Company; later in coal mines at Libby. Married Ann Williams 1868. One child, Mary C. The Kerrigans bought the old Western Hotel in Marshfield 1871 from J. Tiegle and operated it for 13 years, rented it to John Snyder for four years, then sold it to Paul Bartholemy.

Kime, Albert W., b. Iowa 1858. Crossed plains with parents to California 1865. To Bandon 1892; opened a drug store, his father practicing medicine. Albert W. Kime graduated from the University of Oregon Medical School 1897; returned to Bandon to practice medicine. Married Kittie Rohner; two children. Served on Bandon city council.

King, William A., b. Virginia 1846. Son of Richard and Rebecca King. To Oregon by ox team with parents 1850. Civil War veteran. Attended Wilbur Academy, Douglas County; followed teaching at different places, including Denmark in Curry County. Carried mail between Roseburg and Coos Bay. Farmed until 1894. Worked for Huling-Lundy Hardware Store, Coquille. Married Elizabeth E. Ward 1884. Children: Leslie M., Allen I., Edward B., Dal. M., George I., William D., Elbert A., Effie M., Ella M., Eva M. Died 1927.

Kinnicut, Frank C. To Curry 1868; settled on Sixes River; later moved to Coquille. Married Hannah Beckworth 1892. Seven children. A leading school teacher in Coos County.

Knapp, Louis Sr., b. Maryland 1843; to Myrtle Point 1859 with his mother, where they filed on and proved up on a timber claim. Later took up land near Port Orford. Built up a great sheep and cattle ranch of two thousand acres, owned a dairy, built and operated a widely-known hotel at Port Orford. In 1893 married Ella Stagg. Children: Louis, Orris, Lloyd.

Knapp, Louis L., b. Curry County, son of Louis and Ella (Stagg) Knapp; closely followed in the footsteps of his father as an active leader in community and civic development; Port of Port Orford commissioner; joint representative of Coos-Curry in state legislature 1928-32; one of organizers and president of Curry County banks. Taking over the home ranch after his father's death, he continued to operate, improve and build up the land to make it one of the leading dairy and livestock farms of Curry County. Recently bought the former large Thrift ranch near Langlois; built new home for himself and mother; turned original Knapp place over to younger brother, Orris.

Knight, Joseph L., b. Illinois 1867. To Coos 1874. Married Mrs. Rose Elliott 1888. Children: Sue, Loren, Cina, Joe, Flossie, Elmer, Thelma. Bought land on Catching Creek; logged the timber, floating the logs down the creek to main river and to mill. Bought and sold stock, raised cattle and sheep and race horses. Operated a butcher shop at Myrtle Point. One of the prime movers in starting the Coos County Fair; had some fine race horses. Died 1941. Mrs. Knight still operates the old place.

Knowlton, Rudophus S., b. Tennessee 1855. To Empire 1888. Worked as drug clerk for Henry Sengstacken. In 1890 purchased Coquille drug store of J. H. Nosler. In 1892 married Annie Hayter, daughter of W. L. and Sarah Crowley Hayter, who had settled in Fish Trap Valley 1865. Children: Owen H., R. Clay, Naomi. First president of Farmers and Merchants Bank of Coquille.

Koch, J. A. H., b. Prussia 1824; followed the sea. Arrived California 1851; served in the U. S. Army during the war with Mexico; to Curry 1871. Proved up on a homestead; later retired; obtained U. S. pension 1890. Sold homestead; moved to Port Orford.

Kranick, Leslie M., b. Marion County 1892. To Coos 1892. U. S. Coast Guard at Bandon. Married Ethel M. Metzler 1918. Engaged in cranberry culture in 1926 south of Bandon. Now in partnership with son, Marlin E. Kranick; among largest cranberry producers in the Coos-Curry area.

Kronenberg, John, b. Germany 1826; to U. S. 1837; apprenticed to a shoemaker; to California 1849; gold mining. In 1856 married Catherine Buechler. Children: Emma (Blakely), John Lewis, Fred, Rachel (Marsh), Ida (Owen). To Coos 1858; homesteaded on Halls Creek near Arago; 30 years later sold out, moved to Coquille and bought out a hardware business; burnt out, losing entire stock, no insurance; rebuilt and continued business. Mr. and Mrs. Kronenberg spent their retirement days in Coquille.

Kronenberg, John Lewis, b. 1861 on homestead near Arago, son of John and Catherine (Buechler) Kronenberg. Helped parents develop the farm homestead. In 1887 married Otillia Parker, daughter of Captain Judah Parker. Children: Harry, John F., George F. Began working in logging camps and sawmills; became sawmill foreman. In 1909 headed a group to take over the properties of the then deceased Captain Parker; incorporated as the Coquille Mill and Tug Company. Carried on sawmill operations; built and operated ocean-going lumber carriers; associated with others in organizing Bank of Bandon as well as other local commercial and community activities.

Kronenberg, John F. (Jack) b. at Parkersburg 1899, son of John Lewis and Otillia (Parker) Kronenberg. In 1933 married Agnes Hansen of Alaska. Children: John and Jean. At age 19 became manager of his father's electric power system, then serving the Bandon area. Maternal grandfather was Captain Judah Parker, founder of Parkersburg; paternal grandfather was the late John Kronenberg, noted above. In the third generation of active lumbering and shipping pioneers, he is maintaining the tradition; seldom found asleep after five in the morning, not uncommon to see him (if you chance to be awake) departing from his Bandon home hours before smoke begins to rise from chimneys of other city homes. With his pickup he is heading for the tall timber of Coos or Curry, viewing his holdings or some prospective purchase. Perhaps no other living person today has a more comprehensive knowledge of Coos-Curry timber belt. Bandon city councilman; president chamber of commerce.

Kronenberg, George F., b. at Parkersburg 1904, son of John L. and Otillia (Parker) Kronenberg. Married Marie E. Wooley 1944. Connected with Bank of Bandon 1923-1942; with Portland Branch Internal Revenue 1943-1944; Bandon city councilman; president chamber of commerce; chairman, Coos County Democratic Central Committee. Engaged in real estate and insurance.

Judge D. M. Lowe in November of 1856 arrived with three companions at Port Orford, which "looked quite gloomy to us. There was in the place what they called a hotel, kept by one Billy Craze." The establishment offered little to eat except potatoes. Then a southwest gale blew for several days. This tore the kelp off Port Orford reef, and the kelp formed a kind of seine. When it was tossed back upon the beach it held all manner of fish in enormous quantities. Then there was plenty to eat. "With the fine potatoes and that fish bank, and Billy Craze to chowder it up, we lived fine."

Lafferty, S. L., b. Coos County 1873; owned and operated dairy farm near West Norway. Married Amelia Ellingsen, daughter of O. P. Ellingsen. Children: Everett, Lester, Fred, Crystal. After his death, his son Fred operated the farm several years, until he bought a place of his own. Mrs. Lafferty still resides on the farm home, leasing the land to a tenant.

Laird, Binger H., b. Sitkum 1882, pack horse mail carrier; telegraph line rider; railroad worker; Roseburg-Myrtle Point auto stage operator; Standard Oil Company employee 30 years; retired 1948. Married Anna Weekly 1907. Children: Gertrude D., Alto M., Burton H.

Laird, James, b. New York 1832. To Coos 1874, homesteaded in Brewster Valley; stage operator; Sitkum hotel keeper and postmaster. First marriage Katie Smith. Children: Eunice, Anice, Isco, Emma, Fannie, James D. Second marriage to widow, Chloe Harry. Children: Walter, Joseph L., John Hailey.

Laird, Nancy Belle (Mrs. James D.), b. Coos 1865, daughter of John Alva and Chloe (Cook) Harry. Lived on farm near Myrtle Point. Married 1881 James D. Laird. Children: Binger Hermann; Ethel (Abernethy), postmaster at Sitkum since 1917—35 years, longest record in Coos or Curry; Eva, Mildred, Ivan, Clifford, Otto Kenneth, Carl E., Jesse. Mrs. Laird was telegraph operator at Sitkum during the life of that line 1875 to about 1917 – more than 40 years. She still resides at the old Laird home, more than 70 years of continuous residence.

Laird, Ivan C., b. Sitkum 1894. Dairy and stock raising Brewster Valley; logging and sawmill operator; Marine Corps World War I; active in civic affairs; local school board 18 years; Coos Rural School Board; President Coos-Curry Electric Co-Op since it was organized; Coos representative Oregon legislature. Married Daisy Wilson 1920. Children: Murl, now in U. S. Navy; Lila (Mrs. Ray Clarno).

Laird John C., b. New York. Arrived California 1851. Worked at farming and teaming. Married Janey Norris 1872. To Coos 1879; followed farming and dairying near Coquille. Owned one of the finest farms in the valley. Children: Eunice L., Anna A., James W., Pinkston Wade, Charles Warren, George Preston. Died 1904.

Laird, Joseph L., b. Sitkum 1878. Married Ora E. Weekly 1905. Children: Wilferd, Eugene, Cal, Shirley, Hooker, Averil. In the transportation business in the stage coach days; contractor, carrying U. S. mail; postmaster at McKinley; school clerk at Sitkum; farmer; logger; stockman.

Laird, J. W., b. California 1873; to Oregon with parents in boyhood days; engineer in Johnson Lumber Company sawmill near Coquille 10 years; purchased and operated dairy farm. Married Mabel Baxter 1896.

Laird, Pinkston, b. 1877, son of John. To Coos 1879. Attended public schools and Coquille Academy. Married Flora M. McCloskey 1903. Dairy and general farming. To Myrtle Point 1914. Assistant cashier Bank of Myrtle Point. Partner with Roy F. Garrett in timber and logging business. Interested in improved livestock and model farm management. Owned dairy farms. Children: Marguerite J., Vernita, Elda. Died 1943.

Lamb, James A., b. near Coquille 1873. Son of J. J. and Mary Ann. Educated in public schools and Bowen's Academy, Berkeley, California. Married Virginia Woodford 1903. One son, Irving. First business venture was in the newspaper field as partner with B. F. Lawrence, in "Coquille Bulletin", 1895. After one year, took employment in the hardware store owned by his father and A. L. Nosler. In 1899 he took over the hardware business with Denholm and Kribs, eventually becoming sole owner and continuing till 1945, when he sold to M. F. Pettit, retiring after 46 years in the hardware business in Coquille.

Lamb, John J., b. Alabama 1843. In Confederate army during Civil War. Married Mary Ann Lindley 1866. Children: Ada E., Leona A., James A., May M., Florence I. To Coos 1873. Purchased and operated farm on Rink Creek. Later moved to Fish Trap; cleared land with ax, shovel, and hoe. County clerk eight years. Operated hardware store; helped organize the Coquille creamery and other enterprises. County assessor two terms. Died 1916; Mrs. Lamb 1913.

Lamb, J. J., b. Alabama 1839; Confederate army 1861-1865; to Oregon 1874. Settled in Coquille Valley and followed general farming. Married Ann M. Drummond 1866. Children: Phoebe H., John B., and Mary N.

Landrith C. S., b. Lane County 1857. Married Jennie Richmond at Coos

River 1883. Children: James, Roy, Helen, Blanche, Phillip. Followed farming. Died 1893.

Landrith, Cyrus, b. Virginia 1817. Crossed plains by covered wagon to Oregon 1853. To Coos 1860; settled on Coos River. Married Martha Coulson. Children: George, Benjamin, Delia, Joseph, Oliver, Nancy, Martha, Dora, C. S., Isaac. Mrs. Landrith died 1879. He married Mrs. Condron 1884. Died 1891.

Landrith, George, b. Coos River 1911; son of James. Married Lynette Hagquist 1942. Children: Judith Helen, James William. Followed the dairy business, operating the home place on South Coos River for his mother, and another farm at Sunset Bay, purchased 1949.

Landrith, James, b. Coos County 1884. Coos River dairy farmer throughout his adult life. Married Jessie Myers. Children: George James, Helen Jean. Died 1932.

Langlois, Frank M., b. Oregon 1850. Although he had but 18 months of schooling, he built up a fine dairy farm, became a merchant and postmaster of the town named for him; carried on extensive sheep raising from blooded English stock, and developed a large real estate business in Langlois. In 1886 married Georgia E. Hormen. One daughter, Ivy.

Langlois, James, b. Silverton, Oregon, 1848, son of William V. and Mary A. To Curry with parents 1854; settled on Flores Creek. Married Elizabeth A. Rudolph 1873. Children: Murton, Oscar R., Mary G., Idella, Audrey E. Assistant keeper of Cape Blanco light 1875, under Captain Pierce. Later became keeper, continuing for 42 years, perhaps the longest continuous service on the Pacific Coast. Retired, moved to Bandon.

Langlois, Oscar, b. Cape Blanco 1880 where his father was light keeper. Oscar attended school there and in 1905 became assistant light keeper at Cape Arago under Captain Frederick Amundsen, continuing under Captain William Denning. Later went to Coquille light as assistant to Captain Wiren and followed Wiren as keeper until 1939, when he retired. Married Marie Amundsen 1907. Children: Elmer and Walter. Mr. and Mrs. Langloís now live in Coquille.

Langlois, William, b. On Isle of Guernsey, England. Followed sea in early life; to California during the gold rush. Settled in Curry County 1854. Married Mary A. King. Children: James, Frank M., John, Thomas, Charles, Ella, Mary. Engaged in farming and merchantile business. Died 1880; Mrs. Langlois 1898.

Larson, Carl Julius, b. Empire City 1892, son of Ludwig and Hedwig Larson. Married Carrie E. Ross 1920. Children: Carl D., Audrey B. Worked for The Hub at Powers and at Henry Lorenz' store in Coquille. Served in World War I in France. On his return, worked in Oregon Woolen Mills store, and then went into partnership in the furniture business with Colby Perry; bought latter's interest 1931. Served with local unit National Guard, finally as captain for several years. Charter member of American Legion. Died 1933.

Larson, Julius, b. Norway, Europe, 1842. At age of five he lost his father; at 13 started out to make his own living. To sea and able seaman at 18. To Coos Bay in the winter of 1861-1863, on the brig "Energy"; wrecked at Coos entrance; worked at Simpson Lumber Company sawmill, North Bend. Married Marie Olsen in Bergen, Norway, 1866. Took pre-emption claim on Larson Inlet 1867. Children: Jennie, Hermann, Elizabeth, Julia, Phoebe, Fred, Lena, Lettie, Mary Ann, Edward, Reuben. Besides being a successful farmer, he started the Larson Dredging Company; built and operated three dredges with his sons Herman and Fred as partners. At time of his death was most elderly member of Elks Lodge in Oregon. Died 1923; Mrs. Larson 1928.

Larson, Ludwig J., b. Sweden 1858. To sea with his father, a sea captain. To Empire in early 1880's. Sawmill and other work. Invested in income property. Married Hedwig L. Carlson 1888. Children: Edla L., Carl J., both born in Empire. Died 1944; Mrs. Larson died 1951. Their daughter, Edla L., is music teacher in Portland.

Lawhorn, L. A., b. Virginia 1852. Sawmill work. Arrived Coos 1871 in company with John S. Coke Sr.; settled on Coos Bay Wagon Road. In 1877 took up a homestead claim and engaged in stockraising and general farming. Married Louisa Norris. Children: Walter, Mabel, Chester, Hugh, Ratcliff.

Leach, George C., b. Missouri 1868. To Coquille 1888. Married Callie E. Wickam 1891. Two sons, Tracy A. and Jackson A. Several years in Coos County tax department, retiring as chief deputy in the middle 1930's. With exceptional musical and dramatic talent, he led the Coquille Trombone Band and Star Comedy Company and later organizations. Died 1936.

Lee, Alva, b. Douglas County 1859. Followed logging; ranching; steamboating on the Coquille River. Married Lillie May Hoyt 1896; five children. Upon death of his father, Mr. Lee returned to the old homestead on the North Fork of the Coquille and carried on dairying and general farming.

Lee, J. D. B., b. Iowa 1830. To Coos near Myrtle Point 1874. Married Marilla Huntley 1856. Children: Sylvia C., Alva, Milton R. Operated a harness shop in Myrtle Point, but devoted most of his life to farming. Died 1902.

Lee, M. R., b. Oregon 1863. Married Martha Roberts 1887. Children: Chester, Ernest, Eva Ruth. Mrs. Lee died 1893. Married Louisa Sowash 1894. Children: Sylvia, Hazel, George, Blanche. Followed steamboating on Coquille River; la'er a merchant in Bandon, Powers, and Myrtle Point. Member of Masonic Lodge 63 years. Died 1948.

Leep, Kersey A., b. Kentucky 1855. To Oregon 1879. Practiced medicine in Myrtle Point. Married Catherine Reed 1886. One son, Roland V. Mrs. Leep died 1887. He married Ella Endicott 1891. Children: Homer, Hallie, Freda, Kersey A. Jr. Served city council of Myrtle Point seven years.

Leep, Roland V., b. Oregon 1887. To Myrtle Point with parents 1891. Graduated from the University of Oregon 1911. Practiced medicine in Bandon until accidental death. Founded Leep Hospital, Bandon. Well known as surgeon and medical doctor.

Lemanowsky, Benjamin C. (Charlie), b. Indiana 1859, son of J. J. Lemanowsky, a Polish follower of Napolean. Operated general merchandise store in Myrtle Point 1893. Married Anna Rackleff. Children: William E., Leslie L., Lenore, Clare S. Died 1920.

Lehmanowsky, Clare S., b. 1903 California. Married Illma Langworthy 1928. One daughter, Andrea. Registered professional engineer 1936. Civil engineer for Coos Bay Lumber Company.

Leneve, George W., b. Illinois 1850; to Coos with parents 1860. Captain on Coquille River steamers "Dispatch," "Alert," "Relief," "Fawn," "Antelope,' "Favorite,' and others. Married Susan F. Wagner 1877; parents of four children. Died 1944; Mrs. Leneve 1938.

Leneve, John W., b. Coos County 1867, son of Dr. Samuel L .and Elizabeth. Coquille merchant (See chapter on pioneer merchants); Coquille Ice and Cold Storage; deputy county clerk; postmaster. Married Kittie Cox. One son, Lans.

Leneve, Dr. Samuel L., b. Illinois. Married Elizabeth Wiley 1851. Ten children—five sons and five daughters. To Coos 1861; located on lower Coquille near Bear Creek; kept a stock of drugs; practiced medicine. Later operated drug store and practiced medicine in Coquille. Died 1901. (See chapter on early doctors).

Lett, Joseph C., b. Oregon 1877. Marrined Elva Elizabeth Wagner. Children: Leslie H., Dorma A. Bought a large dairy farm near Norway which he operated successfully for many years. Died 1932.

Lewellen, J. L., b. Indiana 1851. To Coos 1874. Opened furniture store in Myrtle Point 1888. Married Ella J. Partillo 1872. Children: Wm. Edgar, Hattie M., Arthur H., Elsie A., Laura B., Harry B., Ernest W.

Lewis, Daniel R., b. Tennessee 1862. To Coos 1885; settled at Gravelford; farming and dairying. United Brethren Church. Married Carrie C. Sumerlin 1883. Children: Bessie, Butler, Ola C. Married Nora B. Fletcher 1910. Child: Oveda.

Lightner, James R., b. Pennsylvania 1839. To Coos 1875; settled at Coaledo, later moving to Marshfield. Married Mary C. Dunham. Children: Clyde C., Lottie D. Captain Lightner was owner, master and pilot of several steam vessels on Coos Bay.

Lindberg, P. J., b. Sweden 1851. Followed the sea and saw many parts of the world. Learned carpentering, bridge-building, plumbing trades. To Port Orford 1882. Followed contracting and building. Operated undertaking business. Married Mrs. Frances Lane 1881. Two children. County commissioner; road supervisor; constable at Port Orford.

Lindros, Adolph, b. Finland 1876. To Marshfield 1897. Helped construct jetty at mouth of Coos Bay. Homesteaded and developed dairy farm near Lakeside on Ten Mile Lake. Married Annie Nieminen 1905. Children: Suma W., John E., Lizzie M., Carl William, Leo.

Lindstrom, William, b. Finland 1861; to North Bend 1890; worked in shipyards 11 years. Owned and operated dairy farm at Cooston. Married Sophie Jacobson 1889. Children: Annie, Victor, Carl, Hilda, Francis, William.

Lockhart, Freeman G., b. New York 1822; married Esther M. Selover 1848; crossed plains with family 1851. To Coos 1853; gold mine prospector; county school superintendent; county clerk; represented Coos County in state legislature. Made first settlement at North Bend. Children: Ella, Eva, Agnes, Herbert, Andrew.

Logan, John C., b. Ohio 1845. Followed farm work. Taught school in Ohio, Florida and Colorado. Married Ella M. Moore 1884. To Oregon 1893; taught school in Coos County. Spent later years on his Bear Creek ranch.

Loggie, Peter, b. Canada 1847. Married Elizabeth T. Williston. Five children. To Coos 1891; contracting and building work; operated a building material business in North Bend. Active in Coos Bay harbor improvements. Prominent in local affairs.

Long, Christopher, b. Canada 1837. To Curry County 1854. In dairy business 30 years; in 1894 purchased land on Bear Creek. Married Alice Cheney 1872. Children: May, Rose J., Amedia, Georgia, John M., Charles A.

Lorenz, Henry N., b. California 1870. To Coquille 1887. Employed in his father's general merchandise store. Married Eugenia Harper 1899. Children: Frederick N., Camilla. When father retired, he took over the business, which he operated until 1941, when he retired, son Fred succeeding him. Died 1946.

Lowe, Clarence Y., b. Oregon 1869. Educated as druggist. Started drug store in Bandon 1890; closed business 1922. Worked as druggist clerk for Fuhrman and Shindler. With Ed Capps in a large service station and garage building which was destroyed by Bandon fire 1936, in which he lost heavily. Married Hattie Dyer 1892; one daughter. Died 1945.

Lowe, David J., b. Maryland 1823. To California 1849; 1856 located on Coquille River. Married Eurilla Slayback 1857. Children: Annie, Alice A., Mary Lee, Maggie, Frank L., David John. Parkersburg school board; justice of the peace; county commissioner; county judge. The Lowes were well known for their early-day hospitality to all new settlers. Died 1911.

Lowe, Frank L., b. Near Parkersburg, 1868. Followed shipbuilding and boat business in Coos County many years. Only surviving member of the Judge David J. Lowe family; retired in Coos Bay.

Lowe, Yelverton M., b. Maryland 1826. Married Mary A. Slayback 1857. To Port Orford same year, then to Coquille, settling on farm near Myrtle Point. Moved to the mouth of Beaver Slough late 1860's, taking up a preemption. Built a home, operated a farm and guest house, providing rest and food for many early travelers. In 1878 a post office was established at the Lowe home and given the name of Freedom; Mr. Lowe its first postmaster. Children: Viola R. Rosa, Thomas C., Clarence Y., Florence.

Lyons—five generations in Coos; among oldest logging and sawmill families in Coos-Curry area.

Lyons, Wm. B., b. Canada 1820; to Coos 1884; sawmill and store on river above Coquille City. Died 1886.

Lyons, James A., b. Michigan 1844, son of Wm. B. Worked with his father in mercantile and sawmill enterprises; to Coos 1884; lumber salesman; took charge of the Lyons mill following death of his father 1886. Married Emma M. Bowlby. Children: Lottie, Aggie,

Lillie (Mrs. Frederick Kronenberg), Wm. H., Fred E., Stewart, Josie.

Lyons, Stewart, b. Canada 1878; to Coos 1893. Lumber mill and logging; machinist. Owned and operated machine shop in Marshfield, specializing in building the "Koos King," an oil-operated donkey. (See Inventions and Science). Married Fannie B. Endicott 1896. Children: Thelma, Frances, Audrey, James A. Died 1951.

Lyons, James A. (Jimmy), b. Coquille in the 1890's. In sawmill, logging and general lumbering business since early life. Member, Irwin-Lyons Lumber Company, North Bend; this company among the ten highest taxpayers in Coos County 1950-51. Married Jane Marr Sullivan. Children: James Stewart, Susan Jane. Residence, North Bend.

Lund, Ole O., b. Norway, Europe, 1862; to Marshfield 1907. Entered business making harness, shoes, and operating a retail shoe store. Married Anna Oleson 1890. Children: Lulu, Pearlie Oliver, Myrtle, Margaret.

Lundy, R. W., b. Ohio 1844. To Myrtle Point 1890. In hardware business with D. A. Huling. Married Mary J. Emerson. Children: Eva E., Mabel E., William E.

Lundy, Vern, b. Kansas 1890. To Oregon 1910. Married Mary E. Cooper 1910. Children: Dorothy J., Robert C. Mr. Lundy has continued to carry on dairying on the old home place south of Myrtle Point for the past 40 years.

John Mule—was there an early prospector of this name? Some accounts claim there was and that Mule Creek, a tributary of the Rogue and locale of the Pot of Gold folk story in this volume, was named for him. Another account, and perhaps the truer one, is that a mule named John was turned loose to graze on the stream in 1852; he was the mount of a lieutenant there with some troops. The mule wandered off and couldn't be found. Whereupon the soldiers called the mountain watercourse John Mule Creek, later shortened by sober geographers to Mule Creek. John Mule himself wasn't eaten by bears or cougars after all. A few years later he was seen at the Siletz Reservation. An Indian had salvaged him from the wilderness and, when deported with the other Rogues after the war, had taken him along.

Machado, Alfred, b. Portugal 1844. Followed the sea in early life and became captain. To Coquille River 1876 in a small vessel "Mary"; on a later return trip was wrecked on Coquille River bar. He and his companion, R. Beatty, swam ashore. Married Mrs. Jennie Stone, who died in Coos County 1912. No children. Captain Machado was pioneer salmon fisherman. Died 1915.

Machado, Jason, b. Portugal 1846, brother of Alfred Machado. To Prosper, Coos County, 1878. Opened a butcher shop and grocery store. Operated a hotel in Coquille one year; later operated a meat market and merchandise store in Myrtle Point until 1912. Married Bessie Deary who died 1906; four children. Married Mary Morris 1910. Owned considerable property.

Macnamara, John S., b. Ireland 1823; to U. S. 1848; to Coos 1855. Hotel keeper; gold miner, school teacher at Empire, sheriff, carpenter. Married Mary A. Rose 1851. Children: Mary (Mrs. Randleman), John F., Daniel W., Robert M. Wm. Dennis, Violet M. He ran the first hotel in Marshfield about 1867—the Macnamara House, located on what is now North First Sstreet. There were eight bedrooms, with spool bedsteads and with mattresses filled with the fluff from a local marsh plant; when fresh it was somewhat like wool but had a tendency to "ball up" and make a lumpy bed.

Madden, Cyrus, b. Ohio 1832. To Curry 1865; followed mining over 40 years. Married Lucretia V. Kent 1872, who died 1893. Operated the rich Lane Mine on Cut Creek north of Coquille River.

Magee, James B., b. Ireland 1841. To Coos Bay 1867 to assist in building a sawmill and three vessels, including tugboat "Escort." Captain Magee was rated as one of the most capable bar and ocean pilots on the Pacific Coast from San Francisco to Seattle, usually in the employ of the Simpson Lumber Company. Married Sarah Gigar 1873. Children: Edna, Charles, James, William, May.

Magee, Joseph D., b. Pennsylvania 1863. To Coos 1897. Married Ida V. Morgan 1897. Children: Leon, Buell, Mabel, Elsie, Helen, Florence. Wood business, hotel operator, postmaster at Lakeside.

Mann, Stillman S., b. Massachusetts 1819. Joined a company to provision and man the ship "Lenore" and sailed for the gold fields of California 1849. With others he chartered the bark "Katie Heath" 1850 and sailed to the Umpqua River. To Empire City 1854. In partnership with Patrick Flanagan, owned and operated the Flanagan and Mann coal mines at Libby. Became Coos County's first county judge. Married Elephol Tower 1863. Two sons: Charles and Fred A. Re-elected county judge 1866. Served as U. S. marshal; collector of customs. Disposed of mining interest and moved to San Francisco 1883. Died 1885.

Marcy, K. E. (Ed), b. Ohio 1873. To Coos 1894. Sailor between Coos Bay and San Francisco; served in Cape Arago Life Saving Service. Married Lois A. Haynes, daughter of Jerry K. Haynes. Children: Majory B., Dale A., and Lyle E. Operated farm at Dora. Mrs. Marcy died 1949. He is retired, living at Coos Bay.

Mark, Fredrick, b. Denmark 1830. Learned cabinet and piano manufacturer's trade. To Marshfield 1873. Built and operated furniture factory on North Front Street. Building still stands 1952. Married Mary Eickworth. One daughter, Jennie (Mrs. G. A. Bennett).

Mars, James T., b. Boston 1872. To Oregon in 1880's; worked in saw mills on Coquille River. Married Mary Gauntlett 1893. Two daughters: Reta, Alba. Operated first moving picture show business in Bandon. Prominent in baseball playing in early days. Both Mr. and Mrs. Mars died 1936.

Marsden, Robert Sr., b. England 1847. Married Rachael Barnes. To Coos 1897. Coal mining at Riverton. Moved to Marshfield but continued to manage Riverton Coal Company at Klondike near Beaver Hill. When he retired 1911 he was one of Marshfield's largest holders of real estate. Mrs. Marsden died 1910; he 1924. Children: Richard, Peter, James, John, Rachael, Alice, Robert Jr., Samuel.

Marsden, Robert Jr., b. England 1882; to Coos 1898; to school in Marshfield; delivered newspapers; Oregonian agency; confectionery store; early telephone operator; moving picture business since its beginnings in Marshfield and North Bend until he sold out in the mid-1940's. Married Eulelia F. Cordes 1906. Serving second term as mayor of Coos Bay. One son.

Marsh, Alfred J., b. New York 1861; to Curry 1883; married Rachel Kronenberg 1885. Children: Mary, John, Louis, Donald, Dorothy, Fred, Nicholas, Beatrice, Kate. Acquired considerable land on Elk River which was improved and developed into a large dairy farm. Active in political and community affairs and served as county assessor, road supervisor, and other county offices.

Marsh, Nicholas B., b. Near Port Orford 1901. Married Catherine Wehsly 1926. Children: Delores Ann, Nicholas, Judy Lynn. Successfully engaged in logging and trucking business; recently engaged in farming. County commissioner; on city council of Port Orford.

Marsters, Rev. Ora E., b. California 1873; to Coos with parents 1881; settled on Catching Creek, where he still lives. Married Florence Carman 1897. Children: Carmel, Kathleen, Kent, Kenneth, Cales. Farming and cattle raising. In 1917 became minister of the United Brethern Church. Built and for years maintained a small church on his farm. Mrs. Marsters died 1947. He still resides on the old place.

Martin, Clifford W., b. California 1879. To Oregon with parents 1887. Married Mabel Sanford. No children. Worked in logging camps and sawmills. In 1908 purchased half interest in Riverton store and post office from Wesley A. Bean. Was postmaster five years and postal clerk about 35 years.

Mr. and Mrs. Martin still reside at Riverton.

Martin, Dr. June (Miss Amelia J. McCall), b. Missouri 1879. Graduated in osteopathy 1904. Practiced in Marshfield. Married Dr. George A. Martin 1916. Ill health caused him to give up his practice; opened candy factory and soft drink bottling works. She resumed osteopathy practice. D.A.R.; active in lodges and clubs. Died 1952.

Mast, Eli (Lark), b. North Carolina 1848. Married Emeline Woodring 1866. Settled on Middle Creek, Coos County; built home in wilderness. Children: William Lee, Sarah Caroline, Fred, Jack.

Mast, Hardee, b. Douglas County 1873. To Coos with parents 1873; settled in Lee Valley. Grew up on the home place. Married Maude Dora Brown 1897. Children: William, Lloyd C., Hardee Jr., Myrtle H. Hardee's father, Wm. P. Mast, died in 1889; Hardee, the youngest of five sons, remained with mother, where he continued to make his home. Mother died 1920; his wife 1937. He and his brother Webb gave to the Masonic bodies of Coos County a beautiful Myrtle Grove on the banks of North Fork of the Coquille, in Lee Valley, known as the Shrine Grove.

Mast, James W., b. North Carolina 1865. To Oregon with parents; settled in Lee Valley 1873. Taught school; worked in assessor's affice; bookkeeper for Prosper Mill Company; associated with the R. H. Rosa Company as secretary-manager. In grocery business in Bandon; city councilman and mayor. Died 1925.

Mast, Joseph, b. Rowland Prairie. Coos County 1879. Mother died when he was only two. With his father he spent early life in east. Married Sarah Isaacs 1897. Children: Ray J., Mollie O., Nellie G., Daniel G., Zaida N., Dena D., Alden A., Milton J., Gilnard D., Danford H., Oliver C., Newton. To Coos 1905. Dairy farm operator; Standard Oil Company employee since 1911. City councilman in Myrtle Point.

Mast, Lee, b. North Carolina 1868. To Coos 1873; settled on Middle Creek. Married Josie Chandler. Children: Wilford, Mildred and Ray. Died 1948.

Mast, Reuben H., b. North Carolina 1854. To Coos 1873; settled on North Fork of Coquille. Married Lola M. Leabo. Children: Leta Ray, Reuben, James. Farmed; taught school; bookkeeper. One of the organizers of Farmers and Merchants Bank; served as cashier; county judge; county juvenile officer. Died 1949.

Mast, Webb, b. North Carolina 1868. To Coos 1873 with parents. Settled in Lee Valley, where he grew up and spent his entire adult life. Married Bessie Durnberger. Children: Webb Jr., Helen, and Hollis. Died 1951.

Mast, William L., b. North Carolina 1863. To Coos 1873. Settled North Fork of Coquille River. Took employment with U. S. Government on harbor improvements and worked much of his life as deep sea diver. Died 1926.

Mast, Lieutenant Wm. P., b. North Carolina 1834. To Coos 1873. Married Charlotte Helen Mast 1857. Children: Reuben H., William L., James W., Webb, Hardee. With help of sons extended property by purchase of more land and developed an extensive dairy. Established post office at Lee. Coos County Commissioner 1884. Died 1889. (See chapter on pioneer families.)

Matson, Alexander, b. Finland 1845. To Coos 1870's. Carpenter work until 1909. Married Fredrika Rontgeroe 1878. Children: Albert, A. August, John F., Elmer, Esther J., Selma, Ernest, Otto, Carl, Ira, Lena F. Owned and operated a large farm on Catching Inlet.

Matson, J. Albert, b. Marshfield 1875; son of Alfred and Amelia. Prominent merchant and life insurance salesman, oldest locally-born living resident of Marshfield (Coos Bay); continuous resident nearly 77 years. Married Virginia Alice Kruse 1902. Children: Julius A., Virginia A. (See chapter on pioneer merchants.)

Mattson, John, b. Finland 1855. To Coos 1877. Home on Catching Inlet; engaged in dairying. Married Sophia Stora 1880. Children: Selma, Arthur, Carl, Edna, Reuben, Walter.

Mayse, Andrew J., b. Missouri 1864. To Coos 1884. Settled near Dora. Married Laura Belle Krantz 1891. Children: Lester L., Emmett M., Macie, Eula. Logging and farming. Died 1949. Mrs. Mayse lives with daughter at Arago.

McAdams, James C., b. California 1871; to Coos 1877; later farmed near Langlois; cattle, sheep and general farming. Married Maude C. Cox. Children: Harry L., Claude H., Austin A. Died 1951. Mrs. McAdams resides in North Bend.

McArthur, Edwin D., b. Iowa 1869. Married Louise Harrison. Children: Mary, William. To Marshfield 1906; pharmacist. One of the two surviving charter members of Marshfield Elks.

McCloskey, James H., (Berdie), b. Gravelford 1877; son of Sol J. Steamboating on the Coquille. Married Sarah Wagner 1905; purchased Norway creamery from George Davis; operated it 23 years. In 1918 purchased Coquille creamery; sold to Swift & Company 1928. Member state legislature 1933-1939; elected 1940 but resigned due to severe injury when struck by auto. Mr. and Mrs. McCloskey live on their old home place at Norway, where they own two dairy farms.

McCloskey, Thomas Wm., b. Kansas 1866; son of Sol J. To Oregon with parents by ox team 1876, located at Gravelford. To Norway 1882. Married Ida J. Self; moved to Myrtle Point. Children: Reta Myrl, Earl, Roy Elsworth, Jasper J. Owned and operated steamboat line between Myrtle Point and Coquille, carrying mail, passengers and freight; boats included the Myrl, Echo. Did thriving business on upper Coquille many years. Died 1921.

McCloskey, Sol. J., b. Pennsylvania 1836. Married Mary Ann Stewart 1859. Civil War veteran. To Coos 1876; homesteaded at Gravelford; its first postmaster 1878. Moved to small farm near Norway 1882. Bought Norway store from Oden Nelson 1886 and became postmaster. Two terms as county commissioner; justice of peace for many years. Children: Agnes J., Anna Statia, Lucinda Ann, Thomas William, Clara E., Mary Eliabeth, Margaret Florida, James Hildebert, Roy Edmond. Died 1908. (See chapter on pioneer families.)

McCormac, Dr. James T., b. Oregon City 1857. Married Hattie E. Bay 1878. Children: Grace (Mrs. Alfred J. French), Alice B. (Mrs. M. C. Maloney), Fred B. Served as Marine Hospital Surgeon of Coos Bay 35 years. On Marshfield school board; county school superintendent. Owned log booms on Coos Bay and on the Coquille. Died 1925.

McCue, James, b. Ireland 1820. To Coos 1859. Settled near Parkersburg. Farmer and salmon fisherman. Married Clementine Thrush. Children: John, Antony M., Armenia, Agnes E., James E., Chas. H., Cornelia C. Died 1888.

McDaniel, Edgar, b. Missouri 1875; married Annie Peppmuller 1901. Children: Hobart, Harold, Gordon. To North Bend; bought and published the "Coos Bay Harbor" 1907-1945. (See chapter on newspapers.) Strongly pro-North Bend; kept and bound most complete newspaper file in Coos-Curry area. Took and finished many photos; was free, generous and liberal with them. "Your Friend and Mine" was his motto. Died 1949.

McIntosh, Donald, b. Nova Scotia, 1847. To Marshfield 1868. Fisherman, sailor, ship builder. Married Nancy Davis 1870. Children: Eleanor, Josephine (Mrs. H. E. Bessey), John A., May Belle (Mrs. Christensen), George Kenneth. Purchased farm on Coos River, where the family made their home. A leader in building Coos Bay Mutual creamery 1892; its manager many years; county commissioner. Died 1903.

McKenzie, Robert, b. Scotland 1835. To Curry 1875. Purchased land at mouth of Elk River. Owned and operated a 1000-acre stock ranch, having cattle, sheep and hogs. Married Georgina Tulloch 1863. Children: John, Annie Schuyler, Isabelle Ashman, Ena, David, Eliza, Margaret, Flora, Robert.

McKeown, Arthur, b. California 1880; graduate of University of California. To Coos as baseball player 1904. Married Elsie Kate Bennett 1906. Children: Joseph Arthur, Grace Elsie, Scott Arthur. Associated with Bennett and Swanton law firm in Marshfield. Died 1922.

McKnight, Charles F., b. Marshfield 1876. Graduate of Oregon State College 1898. Studied law with S. H. Hazard of Marshfield and became his partner. Continued the practice after Mr. Hazard's death. Married Lulu Maud Spangler 1911. Two daughters; Jennie Lind, Mary Lu. Died 1928.

McLain, Hugh, b. Indiana 1857. To

Coos as a young engineer, when Beaver Hill coal mines first opened. His wife and two babies, Leo and Alice, joined him later. Children born in Marshfield: Regina, Wilfred, Jane, Lucille, Agnes. Postmaster at Marshfield; city councilman; Eagle, Knight of Colubus; Catholic. Died 1940; Mrs. McLain 1945.

McLeod, Mrs. Frances S. (Elrod), b. North Bend 1880. Married Malcolm A. McLeod 1902. One daughter, Leona. Mrs. McLeod is the oldest credit woman in Oregon, having been in the business since 1916 and operated her own credit organization 30 years.

McLeod, John, b. Scotland about 1823; married Flora Martin about 1858. Children: James, Charles, Mary (Mrs. Joe E. Schilling), Flora A. (Mrs. Joseph J. Murphy), Malcum A., Dan. To Marshfield 1875; ship carpenter. Died 1909; Mrs. McLeod 1888.

McLeod, John K., b. Canada 1855; to Coos 1890; settled in Coquille Valley. Married Mary K. Rhue 1886. Children: Alex, Etta Belle, Wm. R., John K., Flora May. Piledriving and contracting. Died 1912; Mrs. McLeod 1937.

McLeod, Wm., b. Coquille 1891, son of John and Mary. Contractor; secretary-treasurer Coos Bay Dredging Company since 1924; active in highway construction and general harbor work. Married Alice Curtis 1933. Son, Curtis. Home, Coos Bay.

McMullen, Frank T., b. Connecticut 1871; to Curry 1885; owned and operated large farm devoted mainly to dairying. Married Mary Hughes 1898. Children: Marguerite, May, Theresa, John, Rosalie, Edith.

McNair, Archibald, b. Canada 1854. Married Martha Archibald 1877. Nine children. To Coos 1883. Farming until 1899. Served on local school board and Port of Bandon Commission. Died 1917. Mrs. McNair lives at Bandon.

McNair, David, b. Canada 1844; married Elsie Ann Chase 1872. Purchased ranch near Myrtle Point; operated it as dairy. Retired and moved to Myrtle Point 1908. Children: William A., Howard F., David N., Lulu I. Died 1922.

McNair, George Ray, b. Myrtle Point 1889. To Bandon with parents 1899. Clerk in his father's hardware store. Learned plumbing and sheet metal work; stockholder, director and manager McNair Hardware Company 1913. Married Alfa Weddle 1913. A son, Raymond, practices dentistry at Klamath Falls.

Mecum, Isaac, b. Massachusetts 1822. To Coos 1869 with his wife; settled at Four Mile. Built small schoolhouse; taught school 1871-1873 without compensation; justice of the peace. Six children. Died 1889; Mrs. Mecum 1920.

Mehl, Fred A., b. Roseburg 1868. To Coquille with parents 1874; to Bandon 1900. Member of U. S. Life Saving crew. Carpenter and boat builder. Operated planing mill, making sash and doors, box shooks, all kinds of finishing lumber. Sold out, retired 1936. Married Mertie Graves 1900. Both Mr. and Mrs. Mehl died 1946.

Mehl, Gottlieb, b. Germany 1823. To Coos 1874, settled at Coquille. Operated first brewery in Coos County. Married Mary A. Hervey 1867. Children: Fred, Mary, William G., George, Thomas. Died 1893.

Merchant, Charles, b. New York 1838. To North Bend 1860 as manager for A. M. Simpson's lumber yard, sawmill and store. Married Mary Gunn 1862. Children: Ella, Fanny, Stella, Ruby E., William T., Robert S., Benjamin T., Francis E., John C. G., Charles W., Albert F. S., James, Mary, Lydia, March Lily. Died 1906. (See chapter on pioneer merchants.)

Merchant, W. T., b. Oregon 1870, son of C. H. Large general merchandise establishment in Marshfield. Married Elizabeth Preuss. Children: C. H., John W., Helen.

Messer, John P., b. Tennessee 1837; married Nancy J. Hatcher 1860; to Coos 1870 over pack trail from Roseburg; farmed on Cunningham Creek; later operated The Antlers, first hotel in Coquille, 1873; next operated the Robinson House and then the Stewart Hotel. Later established the Pioneer Barn, a livery and feed stable. The Messers had eight children in all; one died early; diphtheria epidemic in Coquille 1880 took the six remaining children. In 1881 was born another daughter, Zettie (the present Mrs. M. O. Hawkins of Coquille). He died 1929; Mrs. Messer 1930.

Metlin, Charles A., b. Ohio 1858; to Coos about 1885; took homestead and timber claims; livery stable, express business; mail carrier; coal mining; interested in water works; hotel business; operated in and around Marshfield and Empire. Married Margaret McKnight 1891. Children: Elton C., Mary M.

Miller, Alfred S., b. Oregon 1862; married Eliza Cunniff, a native of Gold Beach. Children: Pearl, Sylvia, Ethel, Georgia, Carl, Gladys, Howard, Robert. Owned and operated large dairy and livestock ranch near Gold Beach.

Miller, Francis M., b. Missouri 1844; to Coos 1877; married Cerilda Miller 1876. Children: Minnie, Maude, W. F., Sadie, Ettie, Robert, Jessie, Grace. Farmed on Fish Trap Creek.

Miller, George P., b. Missouri 1861; to Coos 1873; settled near Dora. Married Martha J. Johnson 1883. Children: Charles W., Ida Mae, Mintie R., Della Ruth.

Miller, John H., b. Missouri 1854; to Coos 1873; settled on Big Creek. Married Mattie Hunt. Children: Hattie M., James M., Emma C., Fannie D., Esther M. Later moved to Elk Creek, Curry County.

Miller, John R., b. Oregon 1864; to Curry with parents 1869; settled at present site of Gold Beach; took charge of his father's ranch 1892. Married Addie L. Burrow 1893; she died 1898. Operated a general merchandise store in Port Orford. To Alaska 1900; sold supplies to miners; back to Port Orford 1904, again in general merchandise business. Married Belle I. Norberg 1902.

Miller, Marion C., b. Virginia 1869; to Coos 1892; settled on farm near Dora. Did general farming; road supervisor; active in church, grange and community movements. Married Pearl D. Abernathy 1898. Children: Connor, William L., Felix G., Virginia, Lincoln L., Theodore R., Priscilla. An interesting and unique custom in this family has been practiced since 1899. At Christmas time following the birth of each child, a Douglas Fir tree has been dug up, set in a box and decorated for the Christmas occasion; later the tree would be planted in the front yard. There are now seven Christmas trees growing in the Miller front yard.

Miller, M. W., b. Indiana 1823; to Coos 1873; built and operated first hotel in Coquille, later operated by the Messers, same location as the present Coquille Hotel, entrance on Front Street. Married Charlotte Barbee 1843. Children: Mary C., Wm. L., Fedelia M., Amanda A., Francis A., George W., Henry W., Florence A., Emma W.

Miller, Wm. A., b. Wisconsin 1859. Farmer, carpenter, steam engineer. To Curry 1893; carried mail six years. Married Mary J. Miller 1894; 12 children; operated hotel in Gold Beach. Sheriff; road supervisor; constable.

Miller, Wm. T., b. Missouri 1839; Civil War veteran. General farm work; carpenter, contractor. In 1873 homesteaded on Fish Trap Creek; general farming. Married Orvilla Robinson 1871. Children: Wirt, Mary, George, Orvis, Martha.

Minard, Harvey J., b. Douglas County 1856; to Coos 1875; settled near Dora. Married Roxana Krantz. Children: Leland S., Stephen L., Michael M., Florence F., Ruth Z., Manta A., John H. In 1882 purchased sawmill from Joseph Wright; added flouring mill. Died 1896.

Mirrasoul, John Sr., b. France 1874; to Coos 1889; worked in coal mines at Libby, Beaver Hill and Southport. Married Louise A. Girard 1899. Children: Loretta, Marie, John Jr. With his brother, owned and operated National Bottling Works, Marshfield.

Moomaw, Capt. John C., b. Kansas 1870; to Coos 1887; located at Norway; farming and logging. Married Carrie Dement 1894. Children: Claude, Gladys, Harold, Elda. In 1897 became interested in steamboating on the Coquille River; owned and operated the "Favorite," "Dispatch," "Liberty," "Antelope," "Coquille."

Moore, Ralph T., b. Michigan 1892. To Bandon with parents about 1900, when his father was head of the Moore Mill and Lumber Company. Principal owner of the Moore Mill at Bandon and the Cape Arago Lumber Company at Empire until he disposed of his interests in 1951 to move to Grants Pass to be associated with his son in the Timber Products Company. Coos representative in state legislature 1943-1949; writer of weekly column in the "Western World" and other newspapers. School board member, city councilman, library board, chamber of commerce president. In 1917 married Hattie Boak. One son, Ralph T. Jr.

Moore, Silas A., b. Missouri 1844. To Curry 1859; settled among the Indians. His father broke the first land in Chetco Valley. County judge. Married Margaret Jordan 1869. Purchased 400 acres adjoining father's homestead in Curry. Did general farming. Operated sawmill in partnership with brother.

Morgan, John, b. Massachusetts 1856. To Empire 1876. Operated Arago Hotel nearly 40 years. Married Jane Roberts. Children: Nellie, Lottie, John, Arthur, Chester P., and David. Died 1916; Mrs. Morgan 1949.

Morras, William, b. England 1828. To Coos 1873; located in Beaver Slough. Later moved to Coquille. Married Elizabeth Jaques. Children: E. Jane, Judith, George, Mark, Alfred, Edith. Died 1887. Had started to build sawmill near Coquille; completed by his sons; operated by them until sold to Alfred Johnson 1897.

Morrison, Arthur T., b. Alabama 1866. Married Anna Nosler 1888. One daughter, Lois Genevieve. In 1906 engaged in laundry business with brother-in-law, S. M. Nosler. Later carried on business alone. Purchased land near Bandon 1927; built home and developed one of the finest cranberry bogs in the county. Coquille city councilman; mayor; member of school board; county truant officer. Active in organizing Coos County's first Good Roads Association 1912; two years as president. Died 1950.

Morrison, James A., b. Indiana 1867. To Coos with parents 1868; settled at Whiskey Run Creek. In early life followed beach mining and salmon fishing, later house building and ship carpenter work.

Morrison (father of James A.), b. Scotland 1816. Settled at Whiskey Run Creek 1868. Married Ellen Potts. One child, James A. Mrs. Morrison died 1891; he 1898.

Morse, David Jr., b. Maine 1840; to Empire City 1860. Married Mrs. Ella Elliott 1882. One daughter, Josephine Anette. County clerk; county treasurer; postmaster at Empire 12 years; president of first city board of Empire; operated logging camp on South Slough for match wood. Established and operated Morse's Store in Empire. Died 1926.

Morse, Frank, b. California 1865. Store clerk; engineer in mines and in steam electric power plants. To Coos about 1900; pioneered electric power and lighting in Coquille Valley. His first plant in Coquille burned in 1910; built new plant to serve Coquille, Norway, and Myrtle Point. Married Margaret M. Smith 1897. Children: Phillip and Ruth.

Morse, Mrs. Maryetta, b. Josephine County 1866, daughter of Thos. J. Perkins. To Coos with parents 1872. Married A. D. Morse, Civil War veteran, 1893. Two children, Mildred and Harold. Justice of peace; notary public; real estate business at Bandon. Died 1912. Mrs. Morse still resides at Bandon.

Moser, Fred, b. Switzerland. To Coos 1895. Established creamery at Myrtle Point; moved to Gravelford 1896; established and operated creamery, store and farm; Gravelford postmaster 1906-1918. Married Ida Segessenman 1895. Children: Clara, Frank, Annie, Ernest.

Moulton, John T., b. Maine 1826. Miner in California. To Coos 1865. Homesteaded on North Bank of Coquille. Installed hydraulic equipment in Lane Mine near Randolph 1868. To present site of Coquille 1871; bought small store from T. W. Vowell, which he enlarged and operated for number of years. Married Mary J. Brenn. Children: George T., William, Lula.

Mulkey, Charles E., b. Lane County 1881, son of Isaac N. and Sarah F. Mulkey. Taught school in Polk, Lane, Klamath and Coos counties. Married Martha E. Foster 1917. Children: Emma Frances (Farr) and Charles E. Jr. Rural school supervisor for Coos County 1917-18; county school superintendent 1918-1925; was accidentally killed by a falling tree in 1925. Said Charles A. Howard, then superintendent of the Marshfield schools; "For eight years without bluster or flurry, but in the quiet performance of his duty, Charles Mulkey had gone up and down this county touching the lives of our people. Wherever he put forth his hand it was a hand of helpfulness; never a grasping hand, eager to possess, or to draw himself into a more advantageous position. Once, on the advice of Mr. Mulkey, the district boundary board had changed a line so a family of children might have access to a school. Shortly afterwards, a man whose property had been involved, phoned to Mr. Mulkey, berating him severely, saying, "You did it for a dirty bootlegger!" "No," said Charles Mulkey, 'I did it for the bootlegger's children."

(Mulkey) Purdy, Martha E., b. California 1892, daughter of Adam S. and Mary Emma Foster. Teacher in Klamath and Coos counties; married Charles E. Mulkey 1917. When Mr. Mulkey was accidentally killed in 1925, the county court appointed his widow to the office of county school superintendent, a position efficiently filled during the past 27 years, the longest continuous service of any Coos County official. The two Mulkeys, in a combined service covering more than a third of a century, have contributed more than any other individuals to the development of Coos County schools. In 1945 she married Bruce R. Purdy; their residence is in Coquille.

Mullen, John G., b. Michigan 1885, son of Francis and Julia (Maher) Mullen. Graduate of Detroit College of Law; office in North Bend since 1908—corporation, banking and shipbuilding counsel; represented Coos Indians in their long-delayed claims for lands taken in the 50's. City attorney; city recorder; selective service board for Coos County. Married 1914 Dorothea H. Kruse, daughter of K. V. Kruse, shipbuilder. Children: John F., Helen (Davis).

Mumford, John F., b. Kentucky 1884. Civil War veteran. To Coos 1871; settled on North Fork of Coquille; later took homestead on Hall's Creek. Married Juliet Benham 1878. Four children.

Murphy, Charles, b. Missouri 1874; to Portland 1910; later to Coos. Married Ida May Hornung. One daughter, Helen. Worked on Portland Oregonian and Coos Bay Times as linotype operator. Moved to Bridge 1913; operated store and post office until his death 1939.

Myers, Elijah D., b. Tennessee 1854; to Coos 1870; logger and farmer. Married Mary L. Grindstaff 1876. Children: William H., Phoebe E., Minnie, Joseph B., Grover C., Walter.

Curtis Noble and Mrs. Noble came to Empire City in October of 1853. They found a long log hut about seven feet high and with only a dirt floor. In this they opened the Pioneer Hotel, the one whose sign was quoted in Harper's Magazine *in 1856—"Pioneer Hotel. Donuts. Wom Meels." The first three sacks of Umpqua spuds which the Nobles bought, cost $30. "Mrs. Noble was fortunate enough to own a real cow bell with which she called her boarders together."*

Nasburg, Claude, b. Marshfield 1882. Married Alice Herron 1929. Children: Barbara Alice, Charles David, Claude Andrew. Insurance agency in Marshfield 1906-1947. An original director of the Coos Bay Country Club; active in Marshfield chamber of commerce; served on Port Commission. Died 1947.

Nasburg, Harry, b. Marshfield 1880. Married Hazel McGraw 1911. Daughters: Hazel Ann, Ellen Edna. Employed in Lockhart Grocery store of Marshfield; entered partnership of Ollivant and Nasburg grocery store. Bought Coos Bay Stationery from I. S. Smith 1921; sold out to J. C. Hanen 1949.

Nay, Joseph L., b. New Hampshire. To Curry in 1860's; took over the remains of the A. M. Simpson saw mill property on Elk River after the destructive fire in October 1868. Built a mill and operated it for many years. The old mill building still stands, used as a hay barn on the Sweet Dairy farm.

Said to have owned 1000 acres in Coos and Curry. Joe Nay Slough near Charleston was named for him.

Neely, Willis E., b. Josephine county 1870. To Fairview with parents 1874. Attended public schools and Coquille Academy. Homesteaded in 1891; taught school; worked in logging camps. Married Lenora Bennell 1892. Children: Alva, Sylvia, Myrtle, Elmer, Mildred. Followed farming in later life.

Nelson, Frederick E., b. Kansas 1869. Married Mary E. Smith 1900. Children: Herschel F., Max L., Rose B. Owned and operated machine shop; founder of the Nelson Iron Works in Marshfield 1902; sold to Stewart Lyons 1922. Moved to Bandon and took over the Bandon Iron Works. Died 1935.

Nelson, Oden, b. Norway, Europe. In 1873 he and Olaf Reed erected a building on south side of Coquille River, put in a stock of goods, and named the place Norway. In early 1880's purchased Reed's interest and moved to the north side of the river, where he bought out W. T. Perry in 1881; became Norway postmaster 1882. Children of Oden and Anna Nelson: Emma, Donald, Ervin.

Nicholson, William S., b. Iowa. To Coos 1911. Married Kathrun A. Baker. Children: William R., Kathrun. Mr. Nicholson owned and operated the Nicholson Drug Store in Marshfield. Died 1945. His son now runs the store.

Nielson, John, b. Arago 1882. Graduate of Heald's Business College. In early life followed salmon fishing and carpenter work. Operated the first two air compressors brought into Coos County in shipbuilding. Managed salmon cannery on Coquille River 1909-1914. Bandon city councilman and city marshal. Accounting work and insurance over 40 years. School director and clerk; assistant secretary of Port of Bandon 27 years. Married Martha E. Blundell 1912. Children: Vernon B., Roderick J. Home on cranberry meadow near Bandon.

Nielson, Neils J., b. Denmark, Europe, 1841. Ship carpenter. To Coos Bay 1870's; worked in shipyards; purchased small farm near Arago. Married Mary Pederson 1881. Sons: John, Niels P., Thomas M., Andrew F. Died 1891; his widow 1936.

Noble, William H., b. Arkansas 1844, son of Curtis and Mrs. Noble, among first pioneers to Coos, 1853. His father died in 1856 and his mother married J. J. Jackson, first postmaster in Empire City. Young Noble grew up in Empire, where his mother and stepfather continued to operate the Pioneer Hotel many years. William (Bill) Noble and his brother Lyman became loggers and were long known as leaders in bull-team logging operations. Bill was a pensioner of the Indian wars. Accumulated considerable property. Married Mary E. Rhodes. Children: Harry C., Richard, Charles A., Mrs. Frank Bowron, William F., Calude C., J. G. At the time of his death he owned a large dairy farm on Hopkins Creek east of Lakeside. Died 1910; Mrs. Noble 1930.

Norris, George Wm., b. Oregon City 1847. Came to Coos over Brewster Trail 1868; settled at Burton Prairie (Fairview). Married Mrs. Mary J. Dyer 1884. Mrs. Dyer was the mother of two children: Carrie, Delma. Norris children: Mary L., Walter Boone, George Ray, Myrtle A., Olive Irene.

Norris, Thomas, b. Maryland. Crossed plains to Oregon 1845. Married Mary E. Boone, descendent of Daniel Boone. Built the first foundry in Oregon City and the first plow factory in the state. To Coos over pack trail 1868; settled at Burton Prairie (Fairview). Children: George Wm., Mary (Mrs. J. L. Barker). Lucy Ann (Mrs. R. C. Dement), Louise S. (Mrs. L. A. Lawhorn), C. L., Thomas C., Albert.

Norton, Jesse Eugene (Gene), b. Nebraska 1874, son of George W. and Frances F. (Johnson) Norton. After age 12 obtained education principally in newspaper offices. To Coos with parents 1886. Worked for Coquille "Herald;" in logging camps; retail and wholesale grocery business in field from Port Orford to Scottsburg. Baseball his hobby—organizer and captain of Coquille team before Coos League was established; member of Corn-Fed Canaries. President of first Coos County good roads association; represented Coos County before the State Highway Commission when roads in Coos were being located and built; instrumental in securing the Rogue River bridge. President of Port of Bandon Commission; representative in state legislature; county judge. Furnished vision, leadership, persistence for "A Century of Coos and Curry," perhaps the most substantial county history enterprise ever carried out in the state. Developed one of Coos County's fine dairy farms. Married first Grace McEwin 1894. Children: Althea G. (Kraft), Harry Stewart, Mildred M. (Hudson), Marian L. (Thomas). Married second Bertha M. (Stark) Kalbus 1929. Home on the river six miles below Coquille.

Norton, F. P., b. Maine 1853. To Coos 1884; settled in Marshfield. Married 1888 Alice M. Snyder. In a stationery business in Marshfield in a firm known as Norton & Hansen.

Nosler, Amos L., b. Iowa 1852; to Coos 1870. Settled on Iowa Slough; later moved to Coquille. Married Annie R. Hatcher. Children: Claude H., Fred N., John H., Maude M. Active in early business life of Coquille; owned farm north of town; platted Nosler's addition. Engaged in various lines of business, selling out to N. Lorenz. Moved to Bridge; conducted a store and post office. Returned to Coquille; constable and court bailiff.

Nosler, James T., b. Iowa 1854. To Oregon by ox team 1870. Married Florence A. Miller 1876, the first couple married in Coquille. Logged with ox team on Cunningham Creek and at Bullards. Operated livery and feed stable in partnership with his brother Wes. Coquille school clerk; janitor at court house; circuit court bailiff. One son, Ralph E., who operated barber shop in Coquille 1899-1947, 48 years, the oldest business man in Coquille in point of continous service.

Nosler, Judge J. H., b. Indiana 1831. Married Matilda E. Farmer. Children: Amos, James, William, Wesley, Bird E., Emma. To Coos 1870; located on Iowa Slough. Here misfortune overtook them. While clearing land on a hillside, two children were caught between two logs; son killed; daughter Emma permanently injured. Later their home burned and they lost all their possessions. Sold out in 1875 and purchased 45 acres adjoining Coquille. County judge of Coos County; drug business in Coquille 1883, selling to R. S. Knowlton in 1888. Postmaster; school director; justice of the peace; road supervisor; G. A. R.

Nosler, R. Wyatt, b. Indiana 1822. Married Martha J. Gentry. Children: Alkana, Mary Ann, Quincy, Laura, Florence E., Abe L., Frank S., Julia V., Ada M., Charles. To Coquille 1863 by ox team from Iowa. First of the Nosler family to arrive in Coos, he was followed from Iowa by three brothers and two sisters and their families, all settling along a slough, soon to be known as the Iowa Settlement, then Iowa Slough.

Nosler, Samuel M., b. present site of Riverton 1872; son of Wm. and Esther. To Coquille 1873. With the arrival of the Nosler family of six, added to the John T. Moulton family of four, the population of Coquille increased 150 percent, to ten. In 1895, Sam married Lulu M. Moulton, born in Coquille 1876, daughter of Jorn T. and Mrs. Moulton. In 1951 Mrs. Nosler had resided 75 years within a few rods of her birthplace. Sam started work in the O. K. Creamery 1897; established the Coquille City Creamery 1901; sold out and started Coquille Laundy 1904; later sold his interest to A. T. Morrison; entered grocery business 1911; retired 1941. City councilman and mayor.

Nosler, Wm. H., b. 1840. Married Esther Rittgers 1864. Children: Alva A., Oscar L., Anna S., Samuel M., Mary C., Israel, Alberta, Minnie E., Eugene E. To Coos 1871. Carpenter work; built the first frame buildings in Coquille, including hotel for M. W. Miller, also the first school building in town, on present site of First National Bank. He taught the first school there. Civil War veteran.

Noyes, Joseph E., b. Ohio 1847. To Coos 1873. Settled on the North Fork of the Coquille. Moved to Myrtle Point 1892. A pioneer nurseryman of the Coquille Valley. Civil War veteran, enlisting at the age of 16 already as a good deal of a trained soldier from being in the Ohio militia since he was 14.

Eugene O'Connel, when he went into partnership with H. P. Whitney about 1870, would take meat from the slaughter house at Centerville, by rowboat, through the head of Coalbank Slough to within a mile of Libby, one of their big customers.

Oakes, Edward E., b. Wisconsin; Coos 1893. Interests ranged through trapping, the operation of a broom factory at Parkersburg, work in a lumber plant before establishing his real estate and insurance business in Bandon 1907. Owned and platted Oakes addition to Bandon. One of the founders and assistant cashier of First National Bank. Married Ethel Perkins 1900. Children: Wallace, Gladys, Maxine.

O'Connell, Eugene, b. Ireland 1844. To Coos 1869. Settled in Empire City; meat and butcher business in partnership with H. P. Whitney. Moved to Marshfield and built first meat market 1872. Operated first hardware store in Coos County, still operating as the Pioneer Hardware Company. Built the first modern apartment house in Marshfield. Married Rose Hague 1876. Children: Edna, Mabel, Letta Elizabeth.

Oerding, George E., b. North Dakota 1893; to Coos 1907 with parents, six brothers and three sisters; followed myrtle wood and other wood manufacturing business; sold out and followed real estate and insurance in Coquille. In 1936 married Vera P. Nodine, daughter of John H. Nodine.

Ollivant, Ray A., b. Lookingglass 1882. To Coos 1905. Grocery business 1905-1932, first in partnership with Fred Weaver (Ollivant and Weaver) and next with Harry Nasburg (Ollivant and Nasburg); later in business for himself 1932-1946. Married Vivian Whitmore 1913.

Olsen, Reynold H., b. Norway, Europe, 1867. To Coos at age 16 years by boat in company with Mr. and Mrs. Edward Erickson. Married May Wiliams 1906. Children: Reynold, Elizabeth. First worked for Fred Marks as cabinet maker. Later studied architectural engineering in San Francisco. Worked at Kruse & Banks shipyards 25 years. President Scandinavian-American Bank 1919. Empire City conucilman and first mayor under charter. Died 1944.

Olsen, Samuel M., b. Norway, Europe, 1868. To Coos 1889. Worked in sawmills for five years. Homesteaded near Myrtle Point. Bought and operated dairy farm near Coquille. Married Mary Shields 1898. Children: Elmer, Edna, Lavinia, Myrtle, Basil.

Captain Judah Parker, founder of Parkersburg in 1876, had previously been a searcher for treasure sunk in the sea. In 1862 he and his crew raised $640,000 of the $2,000,000 that went down with the City of San Francisco; *a second time in the winter of 1863-1864 he recovered $60,000 more; a third time in 1870 he found the wreck buried in 20 feet of sand. A short time later he went to South America to raise the immense amount of money in the* Leo Candia *which had foundered in 1802. Captain Parker secured about 5,000 Spanish dollars, "but on account of the long period they had lain in the salt water, they were utterly worthless."*

Panter, Thomas W., b. Coos County 1881. Farming, steamboating, salmon fishing on the Coquille; hotel operator and general merchandise business in

Bandon. Back to steamboating 1908-1925. Captain on eight different river boats. When all-season highways displaced river transportation, Captain Panter turned to the business of handling motor oil products, with service station and garage in Bandon. City councilman. Married Clara Herman 1901. Children: Ernest R., May E., Fred A. Resides on small farm which has cranberry bog.

Panter, William, b. England 1835; to Coos 1860; settled on North Fork of Coquille. Later engaged in general farming on Alder Creek near Riverton; farm has been held by members of the Panter family ever since. Married Fannie Weitten; one son, William R.

Panter, William R., b. 1858 in a covered wagon in Nebraska, son of Wm. and Fannie. To Coos 1860; on Panter ranch near Lampa Creek 1863. Steamboating experiences began in 1870's; worked as deck-hand on stern-wheel steamer *Annie,* under Captain Rackleff. Married Ella E. Hutchinson 1880. Children: J. Walter, William A., Mary E., Allen R., Ruby, Stacy O., Dora, Albert E., Archie E. Mining, logging, farming and steamboating. His sons took an active part in such operations. During his residence in Coquille valley he saw many changes in its growth over a period of 86 years. Died 1946; Mrs. Panter 1948.

Parker, Captain Judah, b. New Jersey 1829; in earlier life followed sea as sailor and ship carpenter; mining; followed treasure hunting on coast of Mexico and South America. To Coos 1875; erected sawmill at Parkersburg; instrumental in having first jetty work done on Coquille River bar. Built first tug "Katie Cook" at Parkersburg, to operate on Coquille River and bar; owned timber land. Married Mrs. Ottilie Frederick 1863. Children: Tom Lewis, son of Mrs. Parker by a former marriage; Ottilie K. (Mrs. John S. Kronenberg); Georgia; Warren C. Died 1899; Mrs. Parker 1900.

Pederson, Neils A., b. Norway, Europe, 1851; followed the sea until he became captain. Married Gerda Olson. Arrived in Oregon 1880 with wife and sister. Followed carpenter work, ship caulking, salmon fishing. Became interested, with others, in salmon canning business at Prosper until Coquille River was closed to commercial fishing. Early day pioneer in salting and packing of salmon in wooden barrels for shipment to San Francisco. Children: John P., Amelia C., Olga J., Arnold, Norman G., Gerda, Percy, Norma M., and Arthur S. Died 1907; Mrs. Pederson 1938.

Pemberton, Dr. W. L., b. Iowa 1882. To west coast 1895. Married Ivy N. Langlois, daughter of F. M. Langlois, 1913. One son, Wilfred Rex. Dr. Pemberton, physician and surgeon, started practicing at Langlois 1912; to Myrtle Point 1916-1924. Retired 1945, residing at San Jose, California.

Perkins, Flentge A., b. Myrtle Point 1898. Married Mollie V. Johnson 1922. One son, Thomas. Studied pharmacy and graduated from the University of California 1919; bought drug store from N. G. W. Perkins, his father, 1936, and is still operating it.

Perkins, Frederick N., b. Kansas 1856. To Coos 1891; settled on Two Mile Creek, south of Bandon. Married Ida May Healey 1880. Children: Ruth, Kenneth, Edna. General farming. Died in Idaho some years ago; Mrs. Perkins 1943.

Perkins, N. G. W., b. Mississippi 1860. To Myrtle Point 1888. Married Emelia Josephine Flentge 1889. Children: Opal, Lois A., Nicolas W., Ala E., Flentge A. First wife died 1933; he married Daisy Giles Short 1934. She died 1942. Mr. Perkins was a druggist all his life. Died 1947.

Perkins, Thomas J., b. Tennessee 1831. To Oregon 1852. Married Eliza Huffmaster 1852. Children: William J., Delcina, Lydia, Andrew, Maryette. To Coos 1872; settled on farm on North Bank of Coquille. Started nursery and planted fruit trees in many places. Died 1912; Mrs. Perkins 1930.

Perry, Wm. T., b. Connecticut 1809. Worked on railroad; carpenter; school teacher. Married Ann Abell 1839. Children: Mary, Vale N., Emily, Dora C., Louisa K.; the three older girls married three sons of Henry Schroeder. To Oregon City 1842; built first flour mill in Oregon. Built Roseburg flour mills 1851. To Coos 1858; settled at present site of Norway. Planted first orchard in Coos, still bearing, owned by J. H. McCloskey. Died 1882; Mrs. Perry 1879.

Pershbaker, Adam, b. Missouri 1838. To Coos early 1870's; married Ella Dame 1875; two daughters: Ruby E., Amice. Took over merchandise store at Randolph founded by his brother, who had died. Various enterprises: logging camps; sawmill at Prosper; Randolph store moved to Prosper.

Peterson, Chas. A., b. Scotland 1832. To Coos 1873; settled near Riverton, where he eventually accumulated 400 acres; engaged in general farming. Married Mary L. Gamble 1872. Children: Harrison J., Susan, Elson, Charles A. Died 1910.

Peterson, David and Percy, brothers born in Coos County. Dairying, livestock, general agriculture carried on successfully for many years on farm near Arago. Never married. Now semi-retired, still reside on the same place.

Peterson, N. P., b. Denmark, Europe, 1847. Married Sarah Nisson 1874. Three daughters: Emma, Agness, Laura. Merchant in Myrtle Point 20 years.

Peterson, Peter, b. Sweden 1844; sailed the "Seven Seas" as cabin-boy and ship-carpenter. To Coos 1865. Married Hilda Erickson 1874. Children: M. Annia, John E., Florence H., Elizabeth C., Emil R., Charles V., Pere A., May J. Construction work—coal bunkers, trestles, bridges, houses, boats; very fond of sailing; among the early builders of gasoline launches, including the Mayflower, Vega, Fram, Elida. Moved to farm on Haynes Inlet 1886; reclaimed large acreage of tide land; was a builder rather than a farmer; Mrs. Peterson was the farmer and home builder. A post office in the home, named "May" after the youngest of the children. Mr. Peterson died 1925; Mrs. Peterson 1931.

Peterson, P. August (Gus), b. Sweden; farmer on Larson Inlet, dairy and general farming. Married Mrs. Mary A. (Krantz) Rustic. Children of Mrs. Rustic's first marriage: Emma, Pauline, Josephine. Children of Peterson marriage: Augusta, Frank E., Millie, Edward. Both Mr. and Mrs. Peterson died in the early 1920's.

Peterson, Swanie, b. Sweden 1864. To Marshfield 1882. Commercial fisherman, lath mill operator, farmer. Owned and developed 30-cow dairy farm on Haynes Inlet. Married Annie Olson 1896. Children: Shirley A., Russell A., Ervin L. Died in the late 1930's; Mrs. Peterson in the late 1940's.

Phillip, Archie, b. Scotland 1868. To Coos 1903. Timber cruiser; logging operator; owned and operated farm on Larson Inlet; county commissioner. Married Nellie Kenyon 1893. Children: Percy F., Archie, Olive, Carol.

Pierce, S. P., b. Washington. To Curry 1875. Settled at Cape Blanco. Married Jennie E. Huntley. County clerk; Coos-Curry joint representative in legislature several terms.

Pierson, Milo M., b. Missouri 1883. To Oregon as small boy. General merchandise store in Lakeside; logging and lumbering. Married Flora Krick 1905. Children: Mary Ethel, William, Irvin, Hazel.

Pike, George E., b. California 1869. To Coos 1877. Followed logging and was one of the top teamsters in the 80's and 90's. Operated logging camps many years. In 1907, logged the Fat Elk section near Coquille where he used seven yoke of oxen, the largest team in Coos County. In all his experience the highest price he ever received for logs was $6.50 per thousand. Married Maggie Stone 1896. Children: Howard E. and Mary (wife of Dr. Lucas of Bandon). Lives in Portland.

Platts, E. S., b. Iowa 1861. To Curry 1895; settled on Sixes River; farmer; miner. Coos-Curry joint representative in legislature 1890. Married Mary E. Mather. Children: Jesse and Benjamin H.

Pomeroy, Richard, b. Maine 1840. Early life spent as sailor. To Oregon 1883. Operated the New Lake dairy in Curry County. Married Emma A. Thoits 1864. Died 1923; Mrs. Pomeroy 1895.

Pomeroy, Wallace P., b. Maine 1869. To Oregon 1883. Married Marie Guerin 1900. Parents of one child. Owned and operated dairy farm near New Lake, Curry County. Moved to Bandon 1944 where he had property. Died 1950; Mrs. Pomeroy 1920.

Powell, John L., b. Ohio, 1816. Married Clarinda Campbell 1837. Children: F. M. Powell, Mrs. E. E. Topping, F. A. Powell, Mrs. James Turvey.

To Coos 1856; homesteaded on Williams Creek; constructed farm buildings and fences of logs and poles. Left his homestead one season on visit to Willamette Valley; in his absence all property and buildings were burned. He simply set to work rebuilding. Died at Bandon 1900.

Powers, Albert, b. Canada 1862. Married Johannah Hogan 1887. Children: Frederick Wm., Ethel, Hazel E., Lucy M., Florence M., Albert Jr., Margaret E. Began work in Michigan logging camps at 16. To Marshfield 1907 as vice-president and general manager of the Smith-Powers Logging Company; president Powers-Davis Logging Co. 1928-1930. Civic minded; interested in schools and sports. Marshfield city councilman and school director; Port Commission; State Fish Commission. Died 1930. (See his portrait in the page of pictures of City of Powers.)

Powers, Charles E., b. Wisconsin 1876. Managed creamery in North Dakota before coming to Oregon 1903. Married Sara Ethel Cox 1908. The Powers entered grocery business in Marshfield 1910; still in same business 1952. County commissioner 1940.

Pratt, Vince O., b. Michigan 1868. Walked with his father, Calvin O. Pratt, from Roseburg to Marshfield 1890. Vaudeville entertainer, singer, banjo player. (See chapter on music and drama.) Clerked in grocery stores and operated a transfer business in later years until his retirement. Member of Marshfield fire department from 1897. Still held office of president at age of 82, and never missed a meeting. Married Edith Keating 1892. Children: Della E., George E., and Alma. Died 1952.

Prewett, Esau, b. Indiana 1836. Settled near Parkersburg 1875. Married Sarah E. Archer. Children: Cornelia, Nancy, Mary, Martha, Thomas, Amanda, May E. D., Lillie G., Rosilla E. B.

Prewett, Jacob F., b. Indiana 1834. To Coos 1869. Settled on Bear Creek 1870. Married Mary J. Follis. Children: David H., Mary C., William A., Sarah J., Jacob F., Samuel T.

R

One Rohrer, a timid fellow was a hired man of the Lockharts near Empire in the 50's. While he and two others were cutting wood, a bunch of naked Indians appeared and began to utter threats in Chinook Jargon. Rohrer turned white with fear, which the Indians soon perceived. A buck stepped up to him, opened his shirt, and placed a hand upon the white man's heart to feel its tumultuous beating. Said the buck scornfully, "Nica tumtum hiyu wawa—Your heart talks very much." Giving each of the three palefaces an Indian name, the savages went away, with a final order for them to be ready when they were called for that night.

Rackleff, Edward, b. Douglas County 1866. To Coos with parents 1870; settled at Myrtle Point. Married Mary J. Roberts 1888. Children: Lawrence, Arthur R., Sylvia L., Leland R., David, Melvin, Donald, Lowell, Beulah, Allison, and Spencer. County clerk 1896-1899. Engaged in mercantile business and farming.

Rackleff, Wm. E., b. Maine 1834, son of Wm. and Mary. To Myrtle Point with father 1870; built a small river steamer, the "Mary," which was used for towing. Built and operated a grist mill and later a sawmill at The Forks. Married Cordelia Ransom. Children: Edward, Mary, Annie, William, Charles, Ralph R., George, Lyman, Nelson, Ellen, Owen. Died 1908.

Radabaugh, Andy, b. Ohio 1860. To Coos Bay 1875. Farmed near Norway; was first road supervisor to build rock base road between Myrtle Point and Coquille. Bought an interest in Myrtle Point bank; director and president several years. Died 1943.

Radabaugh, Henry J., b. Ohio 1866. To Myrtle Point 1875. Married Mary

Pope 1893. Children: Albina and Esther. Farmed near Norway; sold farm in later years and moved to Myrtle Point, where his widow still lives.

Radabaugh, John, b. Ohio 1829. To Coos 1875; settled on homestead near Norway. Married Nancy Mack. Children: Joseph H., Andrew J., Albert S., Sarah M., Henry J., Mary L. Died 1898.

Radabaugh, Joseph, b. Ohio 1859. To Coos with parents 1875. Farm owner and operator in Coquille Valley. Married Mattie Weimer 1891. Children: Mable, Hazel, Flossie, Herman, Reuben.

Radley, Florence E., b. Curry County 1860, daughter of Mr. and Mrs. Geo. W. Dyer, early pioneer settlers. Married John Garfield 1878. Children: Albert, Grace and Maud. Mr. Garfield died. Mrs. Garfield married L. J. Radley 1908. Still living in her 90's.

Randleman, Evander, b. California 1870. To Coos Bay with parents 1872. Worked as a carpenter, earning sufficient to purchase his father's farm on Bear Creek, which he has continued to farm. Married Polly C. Haga 1895. Children: Aloma, Alta, Thelma, Orrin, Elfleda.

Randleman, Henry, b. Missouri. To Coos 1872; settled on homestead lower Coquille River. Married Rachel Steel. Children: Dewitt C., Martin L., Mary H., Jason L., Madora A., Louise F., Evander Melvin, Lafayette.

Randleman, Jason L., b. California 1860. To Coos with father 1872; settled on Bear Creek. Married Mary E. Prewett 1881. Wife died soon after. Moved to Norway, Coos County. Logger and farmer. Married Sarah Barklow 1886. Children: Birdie I., Claud A., Ruby E., Lester.

Ray, Wade Lee, b. Nebraska 1866. Farmer and machinist. Married Nellie King 1890. To Coos 1901; purchased farm near Myrtle Point. Children: Maurice, John S., Floyd, Nona May, Calvin, Oro, Lois Grace.

Raymond, Edgar C., b. Massachusetts 1857. To Coos 1890. Helped build and later served as the first conductor on the Coos Bay, Roseburg and Eastern Railroad. Worked at lumbering. Bought 240-acre farm; conducted dairy; raised purebred stock. Married Lillie Dunham 1895. Children: Blanche L., Jack L.M.

Raymond, Jack L., b. Coos County 1897, son of Edgar C. and Lillie (Dunham) Raymond. Owns and operates dairy farm in Ten Mile area near Lakeside. Married Esther Wisti 1920. Children: Mary I., Lillas.

Reed, Captain Hans R., b. Norway, Europe 1840; to Coos Bay 1869. Married Jennie Eliason 1873. Children: Ralph R., Eleanor A., Maude, Henry. A leading shipbuilder in Coos County many years. (See chapter on shipbuilding.) Settled in Marshfield 1874; later moved to Bandon. Died 1916; Mrs. Reed, 1922.

Reed, Olaf, b. Norway 1824; (brother of Captain Hans Reed.) To Coos Bay in the early 1870's. Town of Norway in Coos County was named by him. Had extensive holdings in this vicinity and ran a store. For many years operated steamers Ceres and Antelope on the Coquille River, one of the early pioneers in this business. Died 1906.

Reed, Stephen S., b. Gaylord, Coos County, 1869, son of Oscar and Mary Catherine (Lehnherr) Reed. At age ten began helping his father operate grist mill on Middle Fork near Sugar Loaf Mountain; later worked for Daniel Giles, carrying mail from Myrtle Point to Eckley and other points. In 1891 married Anna C. McCracken, daughter of Mr. and Mrs. J. F. McCracken. One daughter. Followed dairying and general farming; developed one of the fine dairies near Broadbent, which they sold and retired to Myrtle Point. Mrs. Reed died 1951.

Reiher, Matt Herman, b. Finland 1867. To Coos Bay about 1890. Engaged in rafting and shipyard work. Bought the former Charles Westman place on Haynes Inlet, where he carried on dairying and general farming. In 1896 married Ida Kotka. Children: Ida, Hugo, Esther, Rudolph, Ina, Albert, Gunard, Ellen, Leonard. Hugo, the oldest son, has operated the farm during the past several years since the death of his parents. His sister Ida and the youngest brother, Gunard, reside on the place with him.

Rice, Al, b. Washington 1877. Married Stells Crunk. Children: George, Orvil, Erma (Briggs). City marshal in

Myrtle Point; had a livery barn. In 1908 he bought a stock farm near Bancroft, operating it till 1949. Now resides with son George in Douglas County.

Richard, Joseph, b. England 1835, son of Mark and Mary. Married Agnes Bowden 1860. Children: Mary A., Joseph H., Phillippa J., Annis, George, Ella, Bessie, William, John. A miner by trade; came to Newport (Libby) coal mines 1867. Later homesteaded on Shingle House Slough, where he spent the remainder of his days farming. Died 1914; Mrs. Richard 1925.

Richmond, Mrs. Georgia, b. Elkton, Oregon, 1884. To Coos with parents 1887; settled at Elkhorn Ranch; one of four sisters who became nurses; followed nursing many years; was superintendent of Southwest Oregon General Hospital, owned and run by doctors Culin and Richmond. In 1908 married Dr. James Richmond. Children: Barbara Arenz and James Gould Richmond.

Riggs, James, b. West Virginia 1842. To Coos 1889, opening a photographic studio in Marshfield which he continued to operate for many years. Married Josie Margaret Bonebrake. Children: Elfie E., Hershel B., Pearl.

Roberts, Daniel, b. Ohio 1818. To Coos 1874; settled near the forks of the Coquille River. Married Keisiah Beatty. Children: John H., William, George, Manley, Mary (Mrs. C. E. Edwards), Lizzie (Mrs. W. H. Bunch).

Roberts, Edwin C., b. Myrtle Point 1880. Associated with his brother, J. C. Roberts, in publishing the Myrtle Point Enterprise. Later entered law office of his brother, L. A. Roberts; admitted to the bar 1913. City recorder four years. Now devotes his time to real estate and insurance. In 1914 married Ivy Miller, daughter of Al and Emily Miller. One daughter, Bessie.

Roberts, John H., b. Ohio 1841. Married Louisa De Vaul 1864. Children: Louis A., Martha A., Emma K., Mary J., Lydia E., David A., Priscilla R., John C., Levi J., Edwin C.; Bessie K. and Gracie, twins; Jennie, Sarah L., Annie K., William Allison. Family settled at Ott, now Myrtle Point, 1873. The father was a carpenter; in 1886 entered the mercantile business; represented Coos County in state legislature three terms. Reported to have constructed first brick building in Myrtle Point 1890. At one time owner of the "West Oregonian," Myrtle Point's first newspaper.

Robinson, Eugene, b. Wisconsin 1861. To Bandon 1887. Operated a butcher shop. Married Lora Cope 1890. Children: Geneva (Mrs. O. C. Schindler) and Constantia. Followed the salmon fishing business on the Coquille River for many years. Died 1944. Mrs. Robinson still living.

Robinson, George F., b. Missouri 1874, son of George T. and Priscilla (Medlock) Robinson. Married 1907, Mary W. Lamb, daughter of J. H. Lamb. Children: Ruby A., Opal, Houston T., Iola, George Woodrow, Marguerite, and Lois. Mr. Robinson followed farming and dairying. Died 1950.

Robison, Price, b. Missouri 1858; settled at Fish Trap, Coos County, 1873; married Laura B. Hoover 1886. Children: Caleb C., Beulah, Walter C., Della L., Franklin R., C. Lucinan; twins, Bunice and Benice; Florence, Glenn. Dairy and general farming; long an active leader in Grange work.

Robison, Samuel L., b. Pennsylvania 1805. Married Louisa Lamon. Seven children: Arvila, George T., Frank B., Rock C., Tennesee K., Price S., Martha J. To Coos 1871; homesteaded at Fish Trap 1882; farmed balance of life. Died 1892.

Robison, Rocky C., b. Missouri 1852. To Coos County 1871, settling on Fishtrap. Married Cathleen T. Johnson. Children: Edward P., M. Rubie, B. Rock. Mr. Robison followed farming.

Rogers, Anson, b. Vermont 1829. son of Joseph and Lydia Rogers. To Coos 1859; purchased 319 acres of farm land on South Coos River. Married 1869 Elizabeth Dillingham. Children: Dillingham, Lydia E., Alice (Mrs. Arthur S. Eldridge), Anson Otis, present owner and operator of the family farm. County school superintendent 1866-1868. Died 1913; Mrs. Rogers 1923.

Rogers, Anson Otis, b. Coos River 1880, son of Anson and Elizabeth Rogers. Married 1908 Lena B. Larson, daughter of Julius and Mary. Children: Marie (Mrs. Reynold B. Olsen); Otis Dillingham. A successful dairyman, having lived continuously on farm which was first his father's. Treasurer, Port of Coos Bay 1912-1930; president Coos Bay Creamery 1928-1940.

Rogers, Stephens C., b. Vermont 1834, son of Joseph and Lydia (Carpenter) Rogers. About 1859 married Delia M. Parker. Children: Herbert H., Cynthia (Mrs. A. J. Sherwood), Frank E., Emma (Craddock), Nellie. To Coos 1870; secured land on South Coos River; built up and developed one of the best dairy farms in the area. Operated several gasoline and steamboats, carrying passengers, freight and mail to and from Marshfield and the farms along the river, thus being known as Captain Rogers. Served as justice of the peace.

Rookard, James H., b. Oregon 1876. To Coos 1903, operating his father's farm at Bridge until 1909, when he bought a place of his own. Married Lottie Belieu 1904. Children: Freddie, James, Velma, Ardest, Vera.

Rookard, Thomas, b. Indiana. Married Catherine Howell. Settled near the present site of Bridge 1876. Children: Emma, Marjory, Elizabeth, Eva E., James H., Lena, Louisa, Ida, Thomas. Died 1902.

Rooke, James W., b. Ireland. To Coos 1854. Served in Captain W. H. Harris' Company in the Rogue River Indian War 1855. Worked for A. M. Simpson in mill and as engineer and on tug "Fearless." Moved to farm on Coos River and married Helen Gurney 1863. Children: Thomas R., Elizabeth Ellen, James W., Florence E., Rose. In 1900 sold his farm to his son-in-law, Ivy Condron, and moved to Marshfield. Died 1903.

Root, John, b. Ohio 1826. Married Susanna Noffsinger 1849. To Coos 1874; settled on a farm at Fish Trap. Children: Andrew, Eli, Uriah, Daniel, Jacob, John, Mary, Joel, Hezekiah, Sarah, Abraham. Died 1887. Mrs. Root married 1892 David Brower, a minister of the Baptist Brethren Church, of which the Root family were members.

Rosa, Archie A., b. Bandon 1892, son of Ralph H. and Viola (Lowe) Rosa. Married Esther J. Solve 1915; one daughter, Betty. Employed in Bandon post office 1915-1918; bookkeeper and cashier Bank of Bandon 1918-1933; appraiser Federal Land Bank 1933-1934; worked for W. J. Sweet and C. E. Dick Logging Company 1934-1939. Cashier since 1939.

Rosa, R. H., b. New York. Civil War veteran; lieutenant-colonel in National Guard; to Coos 1870; worked in merchandise stores a number of years. Built and ran a sawmill two miles south of Bandon on the old county road, in the 80's, which he continued in operation till 1911, when he retired from active business. Interested in a number of projects. Married Viola Lowe, daughter of Y. M. Lowe. Children: Florence A., Lloyd L., Kate, Archie H. Served in Oregon legislature; commissioner of Port of Bandon; an energetic booster in the upbuilding of Bandon and community. Died 1921. Mrs. Rosa still resides in Bandon, past 90.

Ross, Benjamin F., b. Indiana 1827; brick mason by trade; to Coos 1853; built first hotel in Empire; later in butcher business in Marshfield; homesteaded in 1857 on a branch of Catching Inlet, which took his name as Ross Inlet. Served in Rogue River Indian Wars 1856. Married Rhoda E. Bonebraken 1864; one son, George F. Ross. Died 1912.

Ross, George F., b. on Ross Inlet 1865; farmed his father's homestead. Director and secretary of old Coos Bay Creamery for many years; first to market bottled milk in the Coos Bay area, at North Bend. Married Lucy Black, daughter of Mr. and Mrs. Henry Black. Children: George F. Jr., Mary Elizabeth, Robert E. Active in many community projects. Both Mr. and Mrs. Ross died during the 1940's. George F. Jr. continues to run their dairy farm.

Roy, Captain Jesse L., b. Tennessee 1830. At 18, enlisted in U.S. Army and served ten months in Mexican War. Captain in Confederate Army from Arkansas. To Coos 1875. Settled on river near Coquille. Married Emily Courtney 1849. Mrs. Roy died 1874. Married Delia A. Brown 1875. Two daughters, Mary E. and Hulda O.

Rozell, Samuel, b. Pennsylvania 1813. Married Annah Marriah Wilson 1867. Children: Merton Clark, Eletta Maude

(Mrs. Jerry Gilbert Haynes), Glenn Garfield, Roy Henry, Sarah May (Mrs. John Angus Prentice). The Rozells came to Coos County in a covered wagon 1872. Bought homestead rights near South Inlet. Raised cattle. He died 1898; his wife 1936.

Rudnas, Mrs. Bertha, b. Finland 1870. To Marshfield to visit brother Victor Anderson 1889. Married Otto Nystrom; to Coos Bay 1880. He was drowned while duck hunting in 1893. One daughter, Ellen. Mrs. Nystrom remarried 1895 to Victor Rudnas. Mrs. Rudnas died 1938; Mr. Rudnas 1944. The daughter, Ellen, has been known by the name Rudnas since her mother's second marriage.

Rudnas, Ellen, b. Marshfield; assistant librarian under Miss Mary Jamison; secretary respectively to Judge John F. Hall, Ben S. Fisher and William E. Coleman; school district clerk; secretary Coos Bay community chest; secretary Coos Country Club; secretary and director Odd Fellows Cemetery Corporation; secretary Associated Employers of Coos Bay; director Oregon Interment Association.

Rumley, Uncle Bill, b. about 1846, pioneer negro homesteader of Curry County. He was married to an Indian woman, who was drowned in a stream which took the name of Squaw Creek. He had been a slave, and escaped from his master. All who knew him were reminiscent of his good deeds. Often, with a lantern to light him on a dark and rainy night, he walked miles along mountain trails to care for a sick neighbor. Though he had spent much of his life with horses, he enrolled at the age of 70 in a Boston correspondence school to learn how to break horses. He retained frequent use of the southern by-word "By gonnies."

Russell, Elmer F., b. Florida 1874, son of J. W. and Helen Russell. To North Bend 1903; engaged in grocery business with brothers Willard and Walter; postmaster 1907-1916; mayor of North Bend 1917-1919. To Myrtle Point 1923; bakery. Returned to North Bend 1936; real estate and insurance. Justice of the peace since 1945. Married 1906 Picciola Kern. Children: Helen D., Mildred A., Elma K.

Russell, Horace N., b. Douglas County 1870. Moved with parents to Seven Mile Ranch 1875 on which he and family have since lived. Engaged in logging and general farming. Married Mary Shinn. Children: Gareld, Nelson, Monte, Dairy, Vance.

Henry Schroeder Sr. was a host to Joaquin Miller when the latter came across the mountains from Eugene to quickly woo Minnie Myrtle Dyer at the mouth of Elk River. The Schroeders had him for dinner, and they thought he was a decidedly queer duck. His saddle, of Mexican fashion, was covered at all the fastenings with silver half-dollars and quarters.

Sabin, William Upton, b. Denmark, Oregon, 1886. Married 1909 Leah Emma White, daughter of Mr. and Mrs. Joseph W. White, who came to Curry County in 1894 and settled on a homestead on Flores Creek, later moving to Langlois, where they operated a hotel. Children: William Hill, Laura Etheleene, Loren L. Mrs. Sabin died 1947. He married 1948 Velma Sabin, his brother's widow.

Sacchi, Frank A., b. Switzerland 1867. T. Coos 1898. Married 1900 Mary Etta Elrod, daughter of William Francis and Mary M. Elrod. Children: Francis, Jack L., Joseph F. Grocery merchant and retail dairy and creamery operator. Councilman of Marshfield two terms. Promoter and leader of Marshfield band and of music in churches. Now retired.

Sanderlin, F. M., b. Ohio 1846. Another Ohio immigrant to Coos who went into the Civil War very young, at 15. Married Amanda J. Burwell, who died 1885, leaving seven children. Mr. Sanderlin to Coos 1891. A few months in Marshfield, then settled at Bandon.

A Methodist minister; he organized several churches in Coos and Curry.

Sanford, Richard D., b. Illinois 1851. Married Mary C. Orchard 1875. Children: Oliver C., Curtis J. To Coquille 1887. Purchased a farm and established a dairy, part of which is now Burns Acres, Coquille. Formed partnership with A. J. Sherwood in real estate business. Platted Sanford Heights. Retired, and he and Mrs. Sanford passed their last years in Ashland.

Sanford, Oliver Carl, b. Turner, Oregon, 1879, son of Richard D. and Mary. To Coquille 1888. Married 1910 Florence E. Walstrom, daughter of John L. and Elizabeth M. Succeeded his father in the real estate business and followed banking from 1906 to 1937; then practiced law until his death 1950.

Saunders, William, b. Pennsylvania 1844. Married 1873 Emily Oregon Noble, the first white child born in Coos County (at Empire April 24, 1854), daughter of Curtis and Margaret Ann (Harrison) Noble. Mr. Saunders died 1914; Mrs. Saunders 1929. Sons: William Francis, Charles Alfred, Jack Curtis.

Savage, Byron F., b. Michigan 1860. Married Harriet Irene Howard. Children: Mabel, David Howard. To Coos 1892. Taught at Old Town, Allegany, Libby and in other Coos County schools. Farmed on North Inlet. After first wife's death, he married Jennie Robertson, who died a few months later. Married Emma Stephens. One son, Harold G. Died 1911. Mrs. Savage resides in North Bend.

Savage, David Howard, b. Kansas 1882, son of Byron F. and Harriet Irene. To Coos Bay with parents 1892. He was a master plumber. Married Bessie Brown 1904. Children: Josephine Irene, Howard Lee, Grace Elizabeth. Mrs. Savage died 1946. He married Dorothy Hoskins 1947. Died 1951.

Schilling, Joseph E., b. Ohio 1863; to Marshfield 1886. Married Mary McLeod. Children: Eugenia (Kilgore), Joe McLeod. Steam engineer on river boats, construction jobs, logging trains. Operated a bakery in Marshfield; ran a hotel in Gardiner which burned down; then operated a hotel in Myrtle Point. Died 1937. Mrs. Schilling still resides with her family in Myrtle Point.

Schetter, Frederick, b. Maryland 1831. Married Emma G. Chase 1856. Children: Lottie Julia (Mrs. Wilmot Getty), Fred, Eugene, Grace, William, Emma Florence (Mrs. Ralph F. Williams), Otto Herman. Died 1902; Mrs. Schetter 1894. (See chapter on communication.)

Schetter, Otto, b. Eastport (now Englewood) 1874, son of Frederick and Emily Schetter. Married 1905 Alice Olive Aiken, daughter of Andrew Glenn and Augusta Aiken. Children: Frederick Glenn, Gardner Chase, Alice Augusta, Wilmer Culver Alter. Manager of Western Union Telegraph Company in Marshfield from 1892 until his death 1936. (See chapter on communication.)

Schindler, Otto C., b. Wisconsin 1894. To Marshfield 1914; druggist in Winkler's Store; veteran of World War I. To Coquille, clerk in Fuhrman's Drug Store; became partner in the business. In 1922 moved to Bandon and opened the Fuhrman-Shindler Drug Store. Burned out by Bandon fire 1936; rebuilt and bought out Fuhrman. Married Geneva Robinson 1922. One son, Franz.

Schliemann, Dr. Frederick J. b. Illinois 1852. To Gold Beach 1903. Left the practice of medicine for a few years while he operated 200-acre ranch. Later established a mercantile business at Gold Beach and continued medical practice. In 1875 married Charlotte L. King. Children: Frederika Miller, John.

Schmidt, Martin M., b. Germany 1889. To Coos 1909; followed dairy farming. Married 1913 Marie Anna Reitz Dean, daughter of Mrs. John Gasner. Children: Fred, Elton, Donald. Mrs. Schmidt died 1938. Married Frances Smith (1941). Owns a large dairy farm near Norway which he operated until he retired in 1946 and his youngest son, Donald, took over. He still lives on the same farm, which is named "The Linden Dairy."

Schroeder, Charles, b. near Coquille 1871, son of J. Fred and Mary Perry. Married 1893 Rachel Simons, daughter of Thomas Simons. Children: Eugene, Mabel, Marion, Rosanna, Ruth. For many years has operated the Schroeder farm where he has a large herd of dairy cows.

Schroeder, Elton A., b. near Coquille 1906, son of Henry A. and Laura E. Married 1934 Averil Irene Laird, daughter of Mr. and Mrs. J. L. Laird. Children: Mary-Jo, Keith Henry, Jane Ashton. Postmaster of Myrtle Point 10 years. Partner in Schroeder Brothers Mortuaries in Coquille and Bandon, and for past 10 years manager of the Henry A. Schroeder & Sons furniture business at Myrtle Point, Powers, Gold Beach.

Schroeder, Gustave, b. Arago 1883. Jewelry business for two years at Myrtle Point, then took up farming on rented land near Arago. Married 1907 Susie Smith. Children: Vivian G., Irene E.

Schroeder, Henry A., b. Norway, Coos County, son of August H. and Dora C. On farm with parents till age 18. Married Laura B. Berry 1905. Children: Elton A., Elbert L. Worked at Johnson mill near Myrtle Point; with A. H. Bender 1912; showed first motion pictures in Myrtle Point; later operated a movie in Powers; sales agency for Ford Motor Company. Furniture business and funeral service since 1917. Myrtle Point school budget chairman; third term as commissioner of Port of Coquille.

Schroeder, J. Frederick, b. Maryland 1844. To Coos 1859 with Baltimore Colony; settled near Myrtle Point. Married Mary Perry 1866. Children: Clara C., Abbert, Frank E., John Finley, Eva. Engaged in farming.

Schroeder, William H., b. Norway, Oregon, 1866, son of John Henry and Emily (Perry) Schroeder. Early life at home; later set type in Coquille Herald office. General merchandise store in Arago 1886-1904. Married 1892 Mary Clinton, daughter of Mr. and Mrs. John Clinton. Children: Leslie A., Earl L., Lorin C. About 1905 he started a jewelry and watch repair shop in Coquille, which is still being operated by his two sons, Earl and Leslie.

Scott, Alexander, b. Indiana 1848. To Curry 1859; settled on Flores Creek. Married Sarah E. Elliot 1874; she died 1889. Children: Mary Scott Woodruff, Harold, Marn, Lilian, Francis. He married Jennie Yoakam 1897. Moved to Coos County 1880. In life saving service at Cape Arago; keeper of Coquille River station a number of years.

Seelig, Albert, b. Germany 1882. To Marshfield 1902. Worked in Geo. Farrin's "Broiler"; wholesale liquor house; gold mining; creamery manager; life insurance salesman. Married Ellen Johnson. One daughter, Sylvia. Mrs. Seelig died. Second marriage to Susie M. Wirth; children: Albert Jr., Marquitta Leona.

Shelton, J. R. B., b. Virginia 1850. To Coos 1882. Married Eliza C. Williams, b. Missouri 1860. Children: Lara N., Elmer, George H., Fred R., Alva B. He followed farming.

Sheridan, Thomas R. Married at Newport (now Libby) 1879 Catherine Florence Flanagan, daughter of Patrick and Ellen Janes Flanagan, b. Empire City 1860. Children: Minnie and Grace (now living in San Francisco); George. Sheridan Avenue in North Bend is named for this family.

Sherrard, William H., b. Ohio 1829. To Coos 1873; settled on Catching Inlet near Sumner. Married Sarah J. Demming. Children: Mary F., Hattie A., Addie K., Elizabeth L., David W., Shephen H., Martin H., Lincoln. He followed logging and farming.

Sherrard, Martin D., b. Marshfield 1876. Married Anna Carey 1902. Married second time 1931 Mrs. Ida Tyler Bohrer. Veteran of the Spanish American War; a machinist by trade; operated an early garage in Bandon; served as head machinist for Kruse and Banks during two world wars. Died 1951.

Sherwood, Andrew Jackson, b. Iowa 1858. To Coos 1883. Married 1885 Cynthia Rogers, daughter of Mr. and Mrs. Stephen Rogers of Coos River. Five daughters: Claire, Emma, Gretchen, Helen, Delia. A graduate of the University of Iowa, he taught school after his arrival in Coos County; county school superintendent 1886-1888. Operated a law office in Coquille. One of the organizers of the First National Bank of Coquille in 1903, later serving as president until his death 1929. Mrs. Sherwood died 1950.

Shriver, Ernest M., b. Illinois 1879. To North Bend 1907. Married 1902

Mabel Matson. Children: Irwin, Vivian, Frank, Gale, Phillip. Engaged in real estate and insurance business; justice of the peace. Died 1949.

Shull, Ben C., b. North Carolina 1845. To Coos 1872. Married 1886 Olive Berry, daughter of John Berry. Nine children: LeRoy, Ada, Jane S., John R., Ellis, Boby, Elizabeth, Ray, Lloyd. Farmer, logger; had an interest in a sawmill. County commissioner. Died 1926.

Siglin, J. M., b. Pennsylvania, son of Jacob Siglin. Lieutenant in Civil War. Married Ellen Sherman, a relative of General William Tecumseh Sherman. To Empire City 1872. Editor of the Coos Bay News. A practicing attorney on the Bay for many years and much in demand as a public speaker.

Simpson, William R., b. Maine 1843. Civil War veteran. To North Bend 1865. Married 1873 Annie Elizabeth Holland, daughter of David and Sarah Holland. Children: Ethel (Mrs. Charles H. Worrel), William, Edna (Mrs. Edward W. Fahy), Garfield, Robert, Harold. Worked in Simpson mill and store; many years as a lumber inspector. He died 1933; Mrs. Simpson 1937.

Skeels, C. M., b. Ohio 1848. Married Nellie J. Henry 1873. Children: Charles T., Mary, Oreta, Grace; Portus and Nellie, twins; Dolly May, Paul. To Coos 1889. At Bandon established a general merchandise store; a year later moved to Coquille and operated a general store until his death 1911.

Skeels, Charles T., b. Indiana 1875, son of Clay M. and Nellie. With parents to Coos 1889. For a time at Marshfield and Bandon before coming to Coquille. Drove stage, carried mail between Bandon and Langlois. Head sawyer in Johnson mill. Entered mercantile business with father in Coquille. Associated with J. E. Norton in Coquille Valley Mercantile Association till his death 1930. Married 1900 Alberta Nosler, daughter of W. H. and Esther Nosler. Children: Marvel, Charles. On Coquille city council; one year as mayor.

Skogg, Captain Edward, b. Florence, Oregon, 1888. To Empire 1897. Followed the sea. In 1915 was the youngest captain to take a ship through the Panama Canal. Coos Bay bar pilot 1925-1948. Married Leah V. Elliott 1928.

Smith, Benjamin F., b. Arkansas 1861. Married Nina DeCasher; one son, Walker. Mrs. Smith died 1881. In 1890 married Elizabeth McCue; children: Alma, I. Bonnie, Ezra, Warren B., Lyle C. Worked in sawmills; later engaged in farming on homestead near Riverton. Died 1915; Mrs. Smith 1942.

Smith, Edward A., b. Arkansas 1876; to Coos 1888. Married Minnie McCue 1894. Children: Howard, Dora, Daniel, Ralph, Lucy, Eugene. Following sawmilling, logging, farming. Later built and ran service station at Riverton. Was musically inclined; played for many a dance up and down the river. Died 1940.

Smith, Frank W., b. Douglas County 1879, son of Levi and Dolly Smith. Married Eva Catching 1921, daughter of Watson E. and Florence Catching. Fish culturist, working for the Oregon Fish Commission since 1900; in charge of Coos River Hatchery.

Smith, George W., b. West Virginia 1865; to Curry 1891; taught school at Langlois a number of years; engaged later in mercantile business; elected county clerk in 1902; elected county school superintendent in 1912. In 1899 married Marion B. Russell. Children: Marshall, Homer, Harold, Nancy.

Smith, Ira S., b. Polk County, 1859. Married 1888 Sarah Agness McNary. Children: Ruth McNary (Clark), Hugh I., Kathryn M. (Ball). Came Coos 1905; located in Marshfield; grocery, stationery and real estate business more than 45 years. Represented Coos-Curry in state senate; author of several important bills, including Workman's Compensation, Widow's Pension and highway legislation. Died 1950 at age 91; Mrs. Smith died 1939.

Smith, J. L. (Jay) B., Kansas 1881. Married Blanche Robertson 1910. Both graduated from Kansas State Agricultural College. Children: David R., Donald R., Margaret. To Coos 1913. Coos County's first agricultural agent, serving six years. Main projects featured crop demonstartion and improvement of dairy herds. Fathered the Corn Show in Coquille. (See chapter on music and drama). After resigning as county agent, he acted for a time as farm representative for a group of Coos County banks. He then entered business for himself, dealing in live stock and grass seeds. A director of the Coos County Fair Board 20 years. Resides in Coquille.

Smith, Levi, b. Marion County 1853; to Coos 1865; settled on Coos River. Married Dolly J. Flook 1876. Children: Ernest W., Frank W., Odessie E., Edwin E. Farmer and logger. Mrs. Smith died 1915. He married Della Able 1918. Mr. Smith died 1938; the second Mrs. Smith 1945.

Smith, William D. L. F., b. Connecticut 1828; mined gold in California and at Randolph in Coos County. To Curry from California 1855; served with Mounted Oregon Volunteers, in Rogue River Indian War. Mustered out in 1856; worked in Tichenor's sawmill at Port Orford. To North Bend in 1857, worked in Simpson mill. To Empire in 1859; associated with H. H. Luse in his sawmill; married Mary R. Luse, daughter of H. H. Luse. Purchased a farm on Coos River; lived there 1864-1896; then moved to Marshfield. Children: Ada, William, Florence, Augusta, George. Justice of the peace, school director, school clerk.

Snead, Albert, b. Ohio 1855. To Coos 1862; settled on Bear Creek 1876. Married Medora A. Randleman 1882. Children: Marion H., Annie R., Martha V., Melvin A., Clara B. Engaged in logging and in later years operated a dairy and did general farming.

Sneddon, Charles, b. Scotland 1841. To Coos Bay 1861. Married Ellen Blakely. Children: Charles Hugh, Walter, Robert, Hannah, John B., Ellen, Jeannette.

Snyder, Alexander H., b. Pennsylvania 1830. Settled at Myrtle Point when there were only two houses. Later settled in Pleasant Valley. Married Sophia S. Hansel. Children: Amanda, Elizabeth, Nancy, John H., Levi, Edward A., Annie C., Samuel S., Alexander M. Farmer.

Snyder, George H., b. Marshfield 1885, son of John and Amanda. Children: Naoma, George F., Bernice E., Doris E., Donald. Logging railroad engineer.

Snyder, John, b. Germany 1838. To Coos 1869; ran hotel in Coquille; also photograph gallery, taking tintype pictures. Married Amanda Hayes 1865. Children: Alice, Addie, William, Herbert, Matha, John Jr., George.

Snyder, Levi, b. Pennsylvania 1859; to Coos 1873. For many years served as captain on Coquille River bar. Well known by long residence in Coquille Valley. Died 1950 at age 91. Survived by two daugthers, Ruby and Pearl, twins; and a son, Walter.

Spires, Lloyd, b. California 1857. Married Emma Landey 1881. Children: Oliver R., Fred, Winifred A., Roy, Elton C. To Coos 1884. Engaged in stock raising; lived in Myrtle Point for some time. Owned interest in Spires Drug Company; city councilman; county commissioner; school director.

Stadden, John H., b. Pennsylvania 1873; learned trade of wood carving, engraving and furniture making. Came west for health; worked on farms and in hop yards to be out of doors. Picture taking became a hobby. To Marshfield 1907, opened a photograph gallery, continuing to present. (See page of dune pictures). Married Emma B. Pease 1910; one daughter, Emma Bell Stadden, now dean of women in a Seattle school.

Stadden, Mrs. John H. (Emma B. Pease), b. South Dakota 1884. Taught school in State of Washington. Married John H. Stadden 1910. In 1918 called into Marshfield schools as a temporary substitute; not relieved until she had rendered 31 years of continuous service. Retired 1949. Hobby, library work and research. Member D. A. R.

Stanley, J. J., b. Iowa 1864; to Oregon 1888; taught school in Coquille, at Cape Arago and Randolph; county clerk; deputy sheriff. Married 1892 Carrie B. Goodman, daughter of Mr. and Mrs. J. P. Goodman. Children: Mary A., Carrie A., John F., Ruth Ann. Published the "Coquille Bulletin" 1899-1902. Studied law; had law office in Coquille; city councilman; road supervisor; justice of the peace.

Stannard, John R., b. New York 1890. To Curry 1908; taught school; principal at Gold Beach; county clerk; studied law. Married Mary E. Anderson. Children: Clarence, Ralph K., George, Lawrence. Elected 1918 to the state legislature to represent Coos and

Curry. Family taken down with the flue; Stannard, feeling sufficiently recovered early in January, started in an open car for Salem; reached Bandon, where he died. Back in Gold Beach, Mrs. Stannard died about the same time. Four boys recovered; adopted into different families; now successful men in their thirties and early forties, with families.

Stauff, Alexander, b. Germany 1839. Took up homestead near Arago. Married Mary Isaacs 1875. Children: Alice J., Ernest A., Charles F., Edward C., William H., James A., Mary R. Assessor; county clerk; deputy sheriff; deputy collector of customs for Southern Oregon. Operated dairy farm many years.

Stauff, Charles F., b. Arago, Coos County, 1876, son of Alexander and Mary E. Moved to Empire with parents when his father was a county employe. (See chapter on cities). Clerked in merchandise and grocery stores at Empire, North Bend and Marshfield. Owned and operated grocery business in Marshfield. Married 1904 Clara A. Johnson, daughter of Peter and Johanna. Children: Margaret L. (Turkel) and Alice Marian. Appointed Coos County treasurer 1930; nominated by both major parties in each successive election; served till time of death 1948. Played in bands and orchestras; sang in church choirs and home talent musicals.

Stauff, Clara A., b. Marshfield 1884, daughter of Peter and Johannah Johnson. Active in music; member of Chamandade Club, Johnson Sisters' Quartet, church choirs, many home talent musical productions. Treasurer Emanuel Episcopal Church 10 years; secretary Marshfield Women's Civic Club 10 years. Married Charles F. Stauff 1904. Children: Margaret Leona (Turkel), Alice Marian. To Coquille 1936, when Mr. Stauff became county treasurer; assisted him in office; appointed county treasurer 1948, when Mr. Stauff died.

Stauff, Victor, b. Finland 1866. To Coos 1884; worked in shipyards 15 years. Purchased, developed and ran dairy farm near Cooston. Married Vendla Smith 1888. Children: Oscar, Hugo, Violet, Gladys, Ivy.

Stephens, William, married Emily Steva in Germany 1866; to Coos 1867; settled on farm on Kentuck Inlet. Home destroyed by fire, taking the lives of their three children, ages five, four and two years. Children born later: Minnie, Emma (Savage), Frank, Willie, Lillie (Klockars), Wanda (Swanton), Effie, Herbert, Leo. Mr. Stephens died 1891. Mrs. Stephens ramained on the farm till 1907, when she moved into town. She died 1938.

Stevens, Francis W., b. Michigan 1857. Learned and followed printer's trade. Married Caroline McClatchie 1882. Childdren: Bertha Jane (Pretzel), James L., Carrie M. (Clinkenbeard). With family to North Bend 1907; printer with "Coos Bay Harbor." Established F. W. Printing Company 1908. Daughter Carrie learned the trade. After graduation from the University of Oregon, she continued to work with him. He died in 1932. Carrie (now Mrs. George Clinkenbeard) took over, continued the business as usual under the same name. In 1951 she moved the plant and business of the F. W. Stevens Printing Company into her own new concrete building on McPherson Avenue, thus continuing one of the few enterprises steadfastly maintained by a single family through all the ups and downs of nearly half a century of North Bend history.

Steward, George A., b. Coos County 1872, son of Steven E. and Mary F., who had settled at Lampa Creek 1864. Worked on the farm; later as steam engineer. Married Lillie M. Thomas. Three sons: M. Earl, William H., Henry. Farmed near Riverton before retiring to Coquille, where they now reside.

Steward, Henry B., b. Maine; to Coos 1894. Followed carpentering and contracting; constable seven years; postmaster at Myrtle Point. Married 1898 Estella Volkmar. Children: Harry B., Melba H., Darrell C.

Steward, Steven E., b. Maine 1835; to Coos 1884; homesteaded near Lampa. Married Mary F. Hamlin. Children: Frank E., Charles W., George A., Robert S., Nellie M., Nettie P., William E., Richard F., Walter, Steve. Farming and logging; later engaged in butcher business in Coquille. Died 1887.

Stillwell, Elias N., b. Ohio 1822. To

Coos 1864; settled on the south fork of the Coquille; to present site of Coquille in 1866, taking a place on Cunningham Creek; to Bandon 1888. Married Isabella Smith. Children: Mary R., Eliza A. E., Suzan J., Eva O., Frank, Peter A., Amey I., William A., Lilious C., John R., Edwin E.

Strang, Charles E., b. Oregon 1866. To Coos as a small child. Farmer and locomotive engineer. First married Mary Cecil. One child, Cora Ziem. Second marriage to Mrs. Rachel Rutledge. Her child by first marriage, Della.

Strang, D. P. Sr., b. Massachusetts. Homesteaded in Minnesota. Served through Civil War; also aided in Sioux Indian wars in Minnesota. To Oregon 1871. Took up claim of 160 acres near Coquille. Married Emily M. Warren. Three sons: David P., Zenie C., Frank E.

Strang, Robert M., b. Prince Edward Island 1836; to Coos 1868; settled below Cedar Point on the Coquille. Followed farming. Married Evaline Collier. Children: Charles E., Ida J., Hulda A., David H., Frederick, Franklin, Sarah A., George L.

Strang, Zenie C., b. Minnesota 1866, son of David P. and Emily M. Married Ella Wagner, daughter of Zelma C. An expert farmer; owned and operated several fine farms in the Coquille Valley. Interested in mercantile business in Coquille. Died 1945.

Strong, Henry B., b. Jackson County 1870; to Coos with family; settled on south fork of the Coquille. Helped run a small sawmill on his father's place. Married Marie Berry 1894. Children: Clarence, Bertha E., Griffeth, Audrey B., Stark, Deloss A., Ardyce M., Penn. After marriage, bought a farm below Mrtlye Point; developed and ran a fine dairy till time of his death 1936. School director; road supervisor.

Strong, Jacob, b. Yamhill County, 1886; to Coos 1889. Married Margaret W. Brown, who died shortly after. No children. In 1919 married Bertha Fox. Children: Genevieve, Aileen, Lucele, Kenneth. A successful farmer and dairyman many years. Mrs. Strong died 1927; he 1945.

Sweet, Alfred J., b. Canada, son of John B. and Susan. Langlois merchant many years. Married Lenora Hofsess. One son, James.

Sweet, Arthur P., b. California, son of John B. and Susan. To Coos with parents. Curry County farmer. Married Docia Smith. Children: Neonta, Effie, Ernest S., Ralph.

Sweet, John B., b. Canada 1848; married Susan Gromley 1877. Children: Sadie, Maggie B., Alfred J., William J., Arthur P., Pearl A., Maude G., Jessie M., Hattie. To California, dairying on Eel River; flood ruined farm; moved to Coos; dairy and general farming on Coquille River. Died 1926.

Sweet, Wm. J., b. Canada 1882, son of John B. and Susan; with parents to California; later to Coos and Curry. Prominent as dairyman, merchant and postmaster; banker, lumberman. Author of "Dairy Ranch Rhymes and Sweet Family Yarns." Bandon postmaster; city treasurer; Married Teresa Hanley 1908. Children: Helen, Piercy, Alfred W., Donald H., Susan Anne. Mrs. Sweet died 1948. Mr. Sweet married Clara (Haga) Perkins 1950. Residence in Bandon.

Sumerlin, John N., b. North Carolina. Married Martha Rickie. Two children: Alvin and Elizabeth. The mother died. Married 1857 Eliza Lippa. Children: Carrie, Reuben G., Michael P., Thomas G., Cordia Belle, Cordia Elizabeth, Frona, John Cleveland, Lester, Henry Grady. To Coos 1884. Settled on North Fork of Coquille. Followed farming. To Myrtle Point 1908. Died 1911.

Sumerlin, Thomas G., b. Tennessee 1874; to Coos with parents 1884; settled on North Fork. Married Florence Carter 1906. Children: Verla, Lucile (Barklow) Katharine (Griffin). Farmer and meat market operator. Mrs. Sumerlin is city librarian in Myrtle Point.

Swan, Grove G., b. 1850; to Coos 1870; settled on East Fork. Married Mary I. Dysert 1882. Children: William, Annie, LeRoy J., Edith, Itty True. Improved and operated farm; director and clerk of school board: justice of the Peace.

Sypher, Edward, b. Wedderburn, 1865. Married Annie E. Russell. Farmer, builder, road contractor; carried mail in early days; Curry County commissioner 24 years. Died 1950. Survivors: J. B., Harold, Wilbur, Florence (Sydnam), Elsie (Strain), Helma (Anderson), Ethel (Robinson), Edna Nettie (Anthony).

T

George W. Thomas was his real name but everybody called him Kentuck. Then having called him that they named Kentuck Slough and Kentuck Creek after the nickname. He lived on the slough with his Indian wife; about 1860 *he had a contract to furnish elk meat for crews of windjammers coming to load lumber at the North Bend mill.*

Tedson, Herman F., b. Germany 1892. To Coos 1920; located near Myrtle Point; operated a dairy farm for eight years. Purchased Norway store and service station 1928. Norway postmaster 1934 to present. Married Agnes Elzner. Daughter, Anita (Mrs. Pat McKeown).

Teeters, Burr Benjamin, b. Ohio 1846. To Coos over Coos Bay Wagon Road; settled at Fairview 1875. Married 1875 Malinda Ellen Benham, daughter of Mr. and Mrs. Peter Benham. Children: Mary Jane, Lawrence Edmond, Amanda Susan, Nancy, John William, Peter Francis.

Terry, George Henry, b. Eastport (now Englewood) 1876, son of John William and Artlissa. Grew up on Kentuck Inlet; entered logging industry. Became one of outstanding steam donkey punchers and shay geared locomotive drivers in Southern Oregon. Long associated with McDonald & Vaughan Logging Company on Blue Ridge. Later, with brother, operated Port Orford cedar sawmill. Married 1903 Frances Augusta Gould, daughter of George A. and Harriet E. Gould. Children: Vella, Jack, Allen, Mrs. Terry died 1935. He married 1942 Mrs. Della Ralston; their home is on Coos Bay, on the Empire Road.

Thom, Charles Albert, b. England 1868. To Oregon 1897; to North Bend 1907. A timber cruiser; owned and operated Coos Bay Brewing and Bottling Company; in 1920 had built for his coast trade gasoline schooner "Wilhelmina." He and his wife, Elizabeth Louise, had four daughters: Eva Pearl (Mrs. Henry Johnson), Sadie Grace (Mrs. Edwin E. Smith), Dora May (Mrs. Adolph Schultpelz), Wilhelmina Elizabeth (Mrs. Gerald W. Carlson). Died 1927; Mrs. Thom 1923.

Thornhaven, E. A., b. Denmark 1841. Settled in Curry County 1883. Married Anna Juhl. Children: Anna L., Daisy E., Andrew A., John A. and Clara G.

Thrift, A. H., b. Ohio 1837. To Coos 1853, with Perry B. Marple, who piloted the first settlers to Empire, the Coos Bay Company. One of the locators of the mine at Whiskey Run later known as the Lane Mine. Fortunate in the mines; invested his savings in land on Flores Creek. He laid out the town of Dairyville, now Langlois. Married Mary Jane Goodman. Parents of eleven children.

Thrift, Thomas Jefferson, b. Josephine County 1861. To Curry 1863; settled at Port Orford. Married 1891 Sarah P. Hawkins, daughter of J. E. and Altha Ann (Wallace) Hawkins. Children: Theresa, Frank, James. Moved to Bandon after his marriage and worked as carpenter and contractor. Deputy county assessor 1899; elected to that office 1902.

Thrush, Nathaniel, b. Iowa 1841. With the First Oregon Cavalry two years. To Coos 1865. Settled on homestead where Riverton now stands. His father and niece were killed in a landslide at Randolph in 1890. Married Saphonia Hunt 1873. Children: Frank, Norris, Richard, Susan, John. Engaged in farming.

Topping, George P. b. Josephine County 1871. To Coos 1895. Started practice of law in Bandon 1896. Married Amy Wilkins, daughter of Mr.

and Mrs. Charles Wilkins 1898. Children: Ethel, Paul, Rex, Katherine. Elected to state legislature 1898. Continued law practice until his death 1943.

Tower, Isaac Russ, b. Marshfield 1885, son of Dr. C. W. and Minnie (Burrell) Tower. Graduate of Stanford University. Married Isabelle Stearns 1918. Auto sales and service in Marshfield since 1909; today known as Tower Motor Company and Tower-Day Motors. A founder of Coos County Club. (See chapter on transportation).

Tower, Morton L., b. Boston, son of Morton and Annie M. (Louden) Tower. With parents to Empire City 1873. Married Cornelia M. Smith 1894. Children: Gladys F., Ella Gwenedde A. (Mrs. Jas. G. Maple), Cornelia M. H. Taught school; on U. S. engineering work from late 1880's; with U. S. Engineers from 1891; junior engineer in charge of local government works on river surveys, dredging, construction of jettties. As senior engineer he designed and constructed a combined dredge and snagboat and operated it on the Coquille, Tillamook and Coos bays; Columbia, Umpqua, and Siuslaw rivers; jetty and fortifications at various Oregon and California coast points.

Tower, Charles, M. D., b. Massachusetts 1842. Married Minnie Burrell 1874. Children: Edward, Jay B., Isaac R., Nellie B. (Mrs. L. L. Day). To Empire City 1868. Practiced his profession; drug store 1872-1880. Mrs. Tower talented in music, dramatics, and art. Dr. Tower died 1920; Mrs. Tower 1934. (See chapter on early doctors).

Tower, Jay B., b. Marshfield 1883, son of Dr. C. W. and Minnie. Married Ruth Hill 1913. Two sons: Jay B. Jr., Jack Walter. Very talented musically; member Golden West Quartette; provided music in early picture show house and composed wordes and music for several popular songs. Partner in in the Gunnery, the first sporting goods store in Marshfield; later an automobile salesman for the Ford Auto agency. Died 1928.

True, Fred C., b. Iowa 1882. To Coos 1906; employed in First National Bank of Coos Bay; with F. S. Dow wholesale grocery and feed business; to Coquille as manager of Coquille warehouse. Retail grocery business in Coquille, later in Broadbent. County commissioner since death of Commissioner Pete Cullver. Married Lulu Lund 1908, daughter of Mr. and Mrs. O. O. Lund. Children: Frank O., Frances Littrell.

Turpen, William, b. Missouri 1847. To Coos 1861. Married Alice A. Stokes 1871. Children: Laura (Mrs. Chauncey M. Byler), Edward, Alice, William S. Worked in logging camps; then purchased an interest in one which he kept until his retirement. Justice of the peace and city recorder in Empire. Died 1934; Mrs. Turpin 1893.

Tupper, J. P., b. Nova Scotia 1833; to Marshfield in the 1870's. Ship carpenter; government jetty work. Purchased land near Tupper Rock and built hotel called "Ocean House." Later he successively owned and operated the "Lewis" (later known as the "Tupper" and then the "Gallier"); the "Curren Hotel" in Coquille, which he sold to Baxter Brothers. Married in 1862 to Martha A. Lynch. Son, Benjamin Frasier. (See also sketch on transportation chapter).

Fred Unican lived with his family three miles north of Port Orford during the great forest fire of 1868. *He dug pits in the ground in which they found refuge, being in addition wrapped up in wet blankets. They lost everything but one chicken and a few head of cattle.*

Ulett, George A., b. Massachusetts 1889. Active imaginative in wood products in New England. To Coquille 1928; became vice-president and general manager of Smith Wood Products Company, Inc., in association with Ralph Smith. Built a Port Orford Cedar mill; a factory for the manufacture of separators and Venetian blind stock; in 1936 built plywood plant to use second growth fir; first plant in Southwest Oregon; operated it for 17 years; sold to Coos Bay Lumber Company. Now heads a new company building a big plywood plant at Cedar Point, a mile below Coquille. (See chapter on lumbering).

Urquhart, Alexander, b. Nova Scotia 1843. To Coos 1867; settled successively at Marshfield, Empire, Coquille. A millwright by trade. Married Frances C. Burton. Son, Irwin W.

Urquhart, Dunken, b. Nova Scotia 1836. To Coos 1869. First settled on Coos Bay, later in Coquille. A ship carpenter. Married Florence Nosler. Daughter, Flora J.

Upton, J. H., b. Ohio 1832. Civil War veteran. To Oregon 1863. Came in 1881 to Curry County where he established the "Port Orford Post." He proved up on 160 acres of land, bought 40 more, and established himself as a general farmer, continuing for 29 years, then resided at Langlois. He contributed the chapter "Two Decades in Curry" to Dodge's history. He married Cloey Mitchell 1856. Children: James M., Arthur W., and an adopted son and daughter. In politics he called himself "an ardent socialist." (See the newspaper chapter).

Utter, "Bill." Coal mine operator; owner of the spectacular Isthmus Railroad; Utter City was named for him. (See chapters on coal, transportation, ghost towns).

Til Vowel was only 19 years old when he urged Uncle Tite Willard to plat a town on his claim that is the present site of Coquille. "Uncle Tite held him at arm's length, declaring that he did not want a town on his land." Vowel, however, was allowed to open a store in 1871. In discouragement he sold out. Then in 1872 Uncle Tite laid off five blocks of a town. Vowel's persuasion was working but too late for himself.

Vanderburg, John K. To Marshfield 1864; became a prominent early pioneer. Removed to Western Lane County 1880. Wife's maiden name Emily Culver. They had 10 children; one daughter became Mrs. J. J. Clinkenbeard. Mr. Vanderburg died 1888; she 1906.

Van Leauven, John F., b. Coos County 1881, son of W. H. and Rosella (Flam). Engaged in dairying and general farming on the old home place, about 5½ miles from Bandon on the Bear Creek Road. Married Elizabeth Haga 1903. Children: Rose Elizabeth, Willis.

Van Leuven, W. H., b. New York. To Oregon 1870. Settled on Bear Creek. Married Rosella Flam; Children: Laura, Mary Alice, John F., Horace J., Rosella. Died 1883. Mrs. Van Leuven later married W. L. Beach.

Van Pelt, Thomas, b. Illinois. Played an adventurous part in the Rogue River Indian War. Postmaster at Chetco 1871-1873. He married Amelia, a Rogue River Indian woman. His son, John Van Pelt, continued during a long life to reside at Harbor, was one of those strongly urging the Indian claims for loss of their lands in the 50's.

Van Zile, Abraham, b. 1854, New York State. To North Bend 1903. Organized Coos Bay Tideland Company, also Oregon Trust Company and helped organize the First National Bank of North Bend, of which he later became president. Engaged in real estate and insurance. First married Arika Parsons. One child, Harriet DeRoe. Second marriage to Caroline Parsons, cousin of deceased first wife, Their children: Ethel and Eva.

VanZile, Charles J., b. New York 1857. Many years in Coos and Douglas counties as a cruiser and timber claim locator. To North Bend 1905. Associated with brother Abraham in First National Bank of North Bend, and in the Oregon Trust Company. Married Minnie LaSalle. Childen: Edith M., Mary J., Harriett W., Charles J. Jr., Jeanette, Ruth, Forrest, Hazel, Dorothy.

Vaughan, "Bill." Resourceful and inventive pioneer in the logging industry. (See the chapters on lumbering, inventions and science).

Vincamp, William J., b. Coos County 1875. Engaged in farming on Coos River. He married 1897 Alma S. Morgan, b. Coos County 1882.

Vinson, William R. A resident of Douglas County; his principal relationship to Coos County was as a stage driver for three years in the late 70's and early 80's over the old Coos Bay Wagon Road from Roseburg to Coos City.

Volkmar, Albert L. Born Coos County 1866. Son of William C. Volkmar, of the Baltimore Colony. His father was a tinsmith and started a hardware store in Myrtle Point. Albert worked with his father, learning tin work and plumbing trade. Sold his interest to his brother Henry, after his father's death. He bought a small farm west of Myrtle Point, where he now resides. Married, in 1909, to Amelia Shunke. Children: Audrey L. Bradburn; Beneva Keltner; Alberta Steward; and Reola Huckins.

Volkmar, Wm. C., b. Germany 1816. Married Wilhelmina C. Diffenbach. Children: Johanna C., Carl H., James M., William F., Clotilda W., Albert L., Estella M., Henry G. With Dr. Hermann's Baltimore Colony to San Francisco 1859; sailing vessel to Port Orford. Up ocean beach with ox team to Coquille River. In scows and canoes up the Coquille and located on the south fork. Operated sawmill, grist mill and carried on general farming. Moved to Myrtle Point in 1884 and opened tin shop and hardware store.

Vowell, Bird. Born Missouri July 10, 1826. Married Mary Ann Nosler. Children: Siotha, William, Tilman, Molly, Julia, Etta, James. The Vowels came to Coos County in 1870, settled in the Nosler Colony on Iowa Slough. In the years that followed, resided at different places along the Coquille from Bandon to Coquille City. Mr. Vowel was a farmer and a nurseryman.

George L. Weeks lived on the river between Coquille and Myrtle Point in a small cabin surrounded by timber and brush. "At an early day he drove in a few swine from the Umpqua Valley and turned them loose in the densely-wooded bottoms around his place. It is said that the old bachelor blazed trails through the timber so that the pigs could find their way home at night after looking for myrtle nuts during the day."

Wagner, David, b. about 1810; from Tennessee to Coos 1873 with Wagner-Hayes group. Two sons, John L. and William D. Donation claim at present site of city of Powers. With others established post office of Rural; built grist mill; general farming.

Wagner, James M., b. Coos 1874, son of Wililiam Daniel and Mary E. Married Nellie Hermann 1902, daughter of Mr. and Mrs. T. M. Hermann. Children: Irma E., Audra M., Leland H., Truman B., Leo J. Operated large dairy farm near Broadbent many years. Now lives near Eugene.

Wagner, John L., b. Tennessee 1848, son of David Wagner. Married Mary E. Horton 1872. To Coos 1873. Located near his parents' place. Later purchased his father's donation claim, now the the city of Powers. Children: Lee, Fannie (Crunk), Charles, Dollie (Barr), John, Alice (Evernden), Nellie (McClees), Glen, Wilbur, Sterling, Died 1917.

Wagner, Robert Lee, b. North Carolina 1871, son of Wm. Daniel and Mary E. To Coos with parents 1873; settled on South Fork of Coquille, present site of Powers. Married Oma L. Mc-

Cracken 1897. Children: Gertrude (Zumwalt), Clyde, Paul, Vera (Sutton), Clarence. Farmer; bought and sold cattle. About 1917 bought farm near Port Orford on Elk River. County commissioner for Curry County; commissioner of Port of Port Orford; president of Curry County Fair Board. Died 1938.

Wagner, William Daniel, b. Tennessee 1834, son of David. Married Mary E. Miller. Children: Susan, Emma, Robert L., James M., Ella, Lilly, Elva, Sarah Ann. To South Coquille River 1873; settled near his parents. Built a grist mill on what later became known as Mill Creek, now a log pond of the Coos Bay Lumber Company at Powers. Later bought a farm at mouth of Catching Creek. Died 1884; Mrs. Wagner 1890.

Waldvogel, Jacob, b. Switzerland 1853. Married Clara Robitch 1883. Children: Annie, Oliver C., Clark W., and Helen I. To Bandon 1903; opened City Meat Market, sold to George Erdman 1909. Owned a small homestead ranch near Bandon, where he lived until his death in 1929. Mrs. Waldvogel died in 1913.

Walker, James J., b. Canada 1845; to Curry 1871; settled near Gold Beach. Married A. Zahner 1877. Parents of six children. Engaged in livestock raising.

Walker, Robert, b. Canada 1844. Served three years as a sergeant in the Union Army during Civil War. To Coos; then to Curry; sheriff 1874-1878. Returned to Coos. Postmaster at Bandon 1901-1909. Married Mary E. Frame 1875. Children: Mary L., Robert F., Pearl R., Harry J., Claire I. Member of Republican state central committee, State Board of Equalization, Bandon City Council, school board. Died 1909.

Walstrom, J. E., b. Marshfield 1875. Married Ella Buck 1903. Children: Lowell and Margaret. Freight and warehouse business at Bandon 1907; freight agent for steamer "Elizabeth." After construction of all-year highways, he began truck-freight and warehouse business. Sold 1949. Present manager of Port of Bandon; member of city council.

Walstrom, John, b. Sweden 1842. Married Margaret E. Swensen 1873; arrieved Marshfield same year; to Coquille River 1882; lumber mill sawyer and carpenter. Children: James E., Florence E., Almer and Ella. Mrs. Walstrom died 1915; he 1923.

Warner, Calvin M., b. Indiana 1833. To Coos 1860; settled on South Fork of Coquille. Married Fannie Getty. Children: Maggie E., Seldon W., G. E. Vernon, William T., John C., Mollie, Robert E., Charles S., Henry D., Jessie J., Harris N. Farming and stock raising. A well known dance fiddler and hunter. Died 1881.

Warner, Charles S., b. Coos 1875. Stock raiser and dairyman on 200-acre farm on Myrtle Creek near Bridge. Married Florence Houser. Children: Hulda, H. E., Ada F., Delma A.

Warner, Seldon, b. 1863 at the old Warner homestead where he still lives near Broadbent. Married 1892 Viola Strong, daughter of Mr. and Mrs. Lewis Strong. Children: Constance, Roland, Ellis, Katherine, Frances. Has spent his entire life on the old place, developing a fine dairy. Like his father, he likes to play the fiddle. Mrs. Warner died 1947.

Wasson, George R., b. New Brunswick 1823. Mined gold in California; next at Jacksonville, Oregon; at Randolph in Coos County is said to have cleaned up $30,000. Built a log house at present site of Empire 1852, a year before the coming of the "Coose" Bay Company, said to be the first house at Empire; first postmaster at Randolph, 1859; Justice of the peace; with Stacy and Fundy, built first power sawmill in Coos County, with undershot water wheel. Settled on South Slough; operated a logging camp many years by ox team and horses; built first logging railroad in Coos County, using poles for rails, concave wheels; built a water-power sawmill on his place. Married 1866 the widow of Charles Hodgkiss. Adulsa (daughter of Chief Kit-zun-gin-um of the Miluk band and Princess Nes-til-cut of the Coquille band). After marriage to Mr. Wasson, she took the name of Susan Wasson. By her first marriage, she had a daughter, Laura, the present Mrs. Ira Metcalf. Wasson children: James, Annie, Fred, Johnson, Nellie, Thomas, Daisy, George B., Mary. Mr. Wasson died 1910; Mrs. Wasson 1917.

Waterman, Clarence F., b. Kansas 1875; to Coos 1888. Taught school; had ranch of 322 acres with large dairy facilities. Married Etta Hardman 1898. Children: Clyde, Elvin, Perry, Echo, Irene, Grace, Andrew.

Watson, David L., b. Iowa 1842. Married Laura Lavina Owen 1870. Children: James, Mary E., David L., Jotty (Folsom), Robert R., Edward E., Neil O., Dorothy (Tuttle), Laura Lavina (Kramer). To Coos 1867; in partnership with Orvil Dodge, opened Coos County's first drug store in Empire City. Practiced law. County judge 1886-1894. Died 1917.

Watson, Edward, M. D., b. New York City 1857. Graduate of Medical School of Drake University, Iowa. Practiced medicine in Iowa and Washington before coming to Coos. Opened the North Bend drug store, later bought by M. E. Everett and now owned by Theron F. Northrop. Married Helene Flieschman 1913. Children: Emma Lore, Edward, Helen.

Watson, James, b. Empire City 1871, son of D. L. and Laura Watson. Married 1920 Eva Laura Schroeder, daughter of Mr. and Mrs. J. Fred Schroeder. Children: James Frederick (lost in World War II) and Clarabel. Clerk of Coos County 1904-1915; then became county judge serving till 1919, when he opened a law office in Coquille. Now living in Seattle.

Watson, Robert R. (Pete), b. Coos City 1878, son of David L. and Laura. Married 1906 Kate Steckle. Children: Mary K., James L., Robert J., Jotty V. County clerk 1915-1932. Retired to farm in North Coquille. Died 1936.

Way, W. M., b. Pennsylvania 1854. To Coos 1875. Married Malinda Leneve, daughter of Dr. and Mrs. S. L. Leneve. One daughter, Lily Sterling. First telegraph operator in the Coquille Valley over a local line from Marshfield to the James A. Lyons Mill Company in Coquille.

Weekly, Edmund E., b. Douglas County 1859; to Coos 1871. Settled on east fork of the Coquille. Sold; moved to Douglas County; returned and bought a farm near Bridge. Married Mary J. Watterman. Children: Ora, William W., Opal L., Irene J., Smith A., Edwin, Edith.

Weekly, Isaac Taylor, b. Missouri 1859; to Coos 1878. Took up a claim near Gravel Ford. Packed supplies in by horse. Helped build wagon road between Roseburg and Marshfield. Married 1874 Queen Victoria Krantz. Children: Mattie, Onie, Vance, Josie, Maude.

Weekly, J. D., b. Douglas County 1861. To Coos 1871; settled on east fork of Coquille River on a farm where he lived until his death in 1889. Married Agnes McCloskey. Children: Viola, Mable, Anna, Verna.

Weekly, Robert L., b. Douglas County 1864. To Coos 1873; settled on the east fork of the Coquille. Married Mary P. Bright 1885. Children: Estella, Winnie, Thomas, Robert S., Effie, Gerry Elza. Followed farming and stock raising.

Weekly, William E., b. Kentucky 1812. To Oregon, 1853. Settled in Douglas County; helped locate the old Coos Bay Trail from his place to the south fork of Coos River. One of the stockholders and contractors of the Coos Bay Wagon Road. Married Jane Skaggs 1849. Children: John Samuel, Nancy Jane, Isaac Taylor, Ursula, Stephen, Mary, Francis, Edmund E., Jefferson D., Robert L., William Elza. Moved 1874 to a farm at Gravel Ford. Died 1889; his wife soon after.

White, James, b. Ireland 1841. To Oregon 1865; settled in Curry County near the mouth of Winchuck River. Engaged in farming. Married Margaret Cuniff, born in Curry County. Children: Ellen, Maggie, Annie, and James.

White, Willis T., b. Maine 1847. To Curry in 1870's; worked at tanning trade, lumbering, farming, stock raising, various other occupations. Bought and sold considerable real property; moved to Port Orford 1912. Married Margaret Curry 1882. Children: Eugene, Willis, Violet, James Carl, Leland L., Magnolia. Two terms as Curry assessor; deputy sheriff and enumerator 12 years; port commissioner Port Orford; died a number of years ago.

White, Thomas D., b. Iowa 1866. Married Margaret Ohman 1898. Children: Thomas C., Margaret, Hugh B. To Coos 1888; worked on side-wheeler steamer "Coos;" with H. W. Dunham, ran a livery stable in Coquille; operated stage line between Coquille and Utter City. With Coquille River Transportation Company; captain of steamer "Dispatch" between Bandon and Coquille 1903-1925. Captain on ferry across Coos Bay at North Bend for State Highway Department 1926-1936. Retired; home in Coos Bay.

Wilkins, Charles, b. 1841. To Coos from Washington 1870; settled near Myrtle Point. Married Elizabeth McAboy 1865. Children: Minnie, Iona (Smith), Martha (Baker), George, Marthena (Cutlip), Amy L. (Topping), Bertha, Earnest. Photographer; built and operated a gallery in Coquille in the 1890's. Justice of the peace. Died 1894; his wife 1903.

Willard, Oscar R. Jr., b. Wyoming Territory 1868. With parents to Coos 1872. Settled on Coquille River. Married Dora Belle Dodge 1870. Children: Elmer E., Louisa B., Charles O., Beulah P., Vanney K. Followed farming and steamboating.

Willard, Orson R. Sr., b. Michigan 1841. To Coos 1871; settled on farm on Coquille River. Married Matilda Shaw. Children: Orson R., R. Alvin, Charles B., Frank E., Fred A., Annie M., Lottie P. Civil War veteran; serving in both army and navy.

Willard, Thomas R., b. New York 1825. To Oregon 1868; settled at Coquille. Married Rachel Shaw. Children: Mary, Rufus, Titus, Bell, Eliza, Bates. Followed carpentering and cabinet making. He was a brother of Titus B. Willard who founded the city of Coquille. Died in the 1890's.

Williams, George Fuller, b. Ireland 1851. To Empire City 1873; worked for George Bennett at Bandon two years, for Judge Dyer in general mercantile store, for Henry Sengstacken in Empire, and for J. D. Denholm. Homesteaded on Bear Creek. Married Kathleen Abbott 1892. Children: Francis Bennett, and George William. Mr. and Mrs. Williams lived their entire life in Bandon, on the bluff overlooking the bar, until the fire on September 26, 1936, when both were burned to death.

Williams, Ralph F., b. Ireland 1861; to Coos 1881. Worked on dairy farms on lower Coquille River; mill hand at Parkersburg; later worked for H. P. Whitney in grocery and meat markets at Marshfield and Empire. With establishment of Flanagan & Bennett Bank at Marshfield, first in Coos County, he became its cashier, continuing in banking business until retirement. Member city council; school board member; city treasurer. Hobbies: his home vegetable garden (Mrs. Williams won't let him work in her flower garden); and historical collection pertaining to Coos County. They reside in Coos Bay (but prefer to remember it as Marshfield).

Wilson, James H. C., married Sarah Clark. Children: Annah M. (Rozell) Hulda (Getty), George H. To Coos about 1872; bought 160 acres near present Barview south of Empire. The family lived in Empire many years. A building contractor. Died 1882; Mrs. Wilson 1908.

Wilson, James W., b. Arkansas 1832. Married Susan Netherby 1865. Children: Jefferson.; twins — S. J. (Jack) and Clarinda L. (Crew); Mary (Cooley); Wade H.; and a stepson, Will Netherby. To Coos by pack and saddle horses from California 1868; settled on upper south Coquille River near present site of Powers; later to permanent home known as Calf Ranch 1870; acquired and built up range of 800 acres and large herd of cattle; leading cattle man in that area during his time. Sold Calf Ranch to Russell Dement 1891; sold all 1894; retired and moved to Port Orford. Died 1897; Mrs. Wilson 1917.

Wilson, Jeff D., b. California 1867, son of James W. and Susan. To Coos with parents 1868. Married Phoebe Frances Anderson 1892, a trained nurse. Children: Minnie, Dillard, Edgar, Agnes, Lloyd, John, Lenore, Harry. Family home at headwaters of the Sixes was known as Summit Ranch, one of the early livestock ranches of Curry. To Myrtle Point 1905 and to Coquille 1906, where they owned and operated the City General Hospital, the Grayce Hospital and the Coquille Maternity Home.

Mr. Wilson died 1918; Mrs. Wilson 1938.

Winsor, Charles S., b. Pennsylvania 1865, son of William and Charlotte (Wythe) Winsor. To Curry 1871. At age 16 became employe of R. D. Hume in salmon canning and mercantile enterprise; at 18 was managfer of Hume's Rogue River operations; later general manager of all Hume establishments; continued with Mr. Hume 23 years. In 1904, became first cashier of Bank of Oregon in North Bend; later was president and board member. Afterwards manager of the Oregon properties of the (A. M.) Simpson Estate Company. Married 1892 Kate Anthony, daughter of Joseph and Emma (Bailey) Anthony. Children: Charles Joseph (Joe) and Helen C. (Johnson). He died 1931. Mrs. Winsor, still residing in North Bend, has been a member of the school board; in Red Cross work; a founder of the city library.

Winsor, William, b. New York 1832; to Port Orford 1854. In Company K, Oregon Mounted Volunteers, under Captain Bledsoe and General Lamrick. Rented a sawmill in Port Orford; sawed and shipped the first white cedar to be put on the market under the name of Port Orford cedar and is credited with originating that now famous name. Married Charlotte Wythe 1858. In Curry during most of their married life of 40 years. Children: Anna (Gauntlett), Mary (Gauntlett), Charles, Harvey, Nettie, Ruby. Treasurer of Curry one year. General merchandise, hotel and sawmill business; general contracting and building; is credited with supervising the construction of the "big" mill at Empire for the Southern Oregon Improvement Company in the eighties. The building is still in use, much of the original Port Orford cedar in its under structure being "sound as a dollar."

Wirth, Antone, b. Austria about 1847; to Coos 1878. Married Eliza Schultz 1871. Children: Oswald A., Elfreda H. (Eickworth), Wilfred L. Settled on Coos River; nurseryman and truck gardener; had one of the first fruit nurseries in Coos County; trees from his nursery are still bearing in many of the older orchards. Mrs. Wirth died 1905. Mr. Wirth 1906.

Wirth, Wilfred L., b. Missouri 1878, son of Antone and Eliza. To Coos with parents same year. Married Iva B. Cutlip 1903, daughter of Mark D. and Mattie. Children: Susie May, Wilfred M., Evelyn L. (Green). Farmer and towboat man. Mrs. Wirth died 1950.

Woodruff, Calvin A., b. Curry County 1861; engaged in farming and fishing in Rogue River area. Married Harriett L. Gilespie. Children: Jane K., Cornelius S., William S.

Worrel, Charles, b. Ohio 1881. To North Bend 1904 as bookkeeper for Simpson Lumber Company. Has since worked continuously as a bookkeeper and timekeeper with different lumber companies. Married 1905 Ethel (Simpson) Turpin, daughter of Wm. R. and Annie E. (Holland) Simpson. Mrs. Worrel, a graduate of the University of Oregon in music, has taught in public schools and has given private music lessons during many years. Member of the D. A. R., Daughters of Union Veterans, and University of Oregon Half Century Club. Residence, North Bend.

John Yoakam was one of the two men of Southwest Oregon accorded the rulership of important streams, different from just having one named for him. ..He was referred to as "The Governor of Coos River," while R. D. Hume was called "The Lord of Rogue River."

Yager, J. W., b. Michigan 1844. To Coos Bay 1874; settled near Halls Prairie; later in hardware business in Bandon. Clerked in W. E. Rackleff's store at The Forks; helped Rackleff install machinery in the "Little Annie."

Followed steamboating on the Coquille, as engineer and master, till 1888; then had hardware store in Coquille with George McEwen; sold out to John Kronenberg. In 1881 married Nancy E. Legg. Children: Mary Emily, Nancy E.

Yoakam, John A., b. Ohio 1820. Married Eliza Davis 1843. Children: Druscilla, Susan, Henry C., Jasper A., George W., Harriet R., Nancy E., Martha, John, Joseph H., Mary E., Asa S., and an adopted girl, Caroline Holderman. (Six of the children were born after coming to Coos County). To Coos Bay 1854; homesteaded near Empire; a falling tree destroyed the house and killed the five girls including Caroline, the adopted child. The two boys, Jasper A. and George W., were in the house but were not injured. Leaving the place, the Yoakams operated a boarding house in Empire for about a year; moved to farm on South Fork of Coquille; moved 1867 to farm purchased by the son, Jasper A., at Forks of Coos River; built a house, said to be still in use, since known as the Landrith place. John A. Yoakam died 1876.

Yoakam, Jasper A., b. Illinois 1848, son of John A. and Eliza. With parents to Coos 1854. (Escaped unharmed in tragedy of falling tree reported above). Life devoted to farming, sawmilling, logging. Began at age of 15 in Simpson's North Bend mill; strictly opposed to use of liquor by self or men in mill, in camp or on the farm, he early became a foreman and commanded the respect of his men. Married 1876 Marian A. Rogers (sister of Anson and Stephen Rogers). Children: Edwin R., George H., Lydia E. (Mrs. Wm. Horsfall), Stephen J., Jasper A. Jr. Mrs. Yoakam died 1920; Mr. Yoakam 1930.

Yoakam, John, b. Coos County 1859, son of John A. and Eliza. An early logger, later turning to farming and stock raising. Married three times. Children: Edwin D., Jasper, Clinton, Madge, John. County commissioner; commissioner of Port of Bandon; active in public affairs.

Yoakam, Joseph H., b. Coos County 1862, son of John A. and Eliza. Married Harriet A. Jones. Children: Eliza D., Laura C., Stacy J., Lillie K., Eulalie.

Young, W. H., b. 1848; died 1927; publisher of "Coquille Valley Sentinel." (See chapter on newspapers).

Younker, Joseph A., member of crew of the U. S. Living Saving Station, beginning at Cape Arago in 1891. Participating in life-boat rescue to steamer "Arago" on South Spit 1891, and again five years later when the same ship was wrecked on the submerged jetty; to the steamer "Emily" on the North Spit and again when the "Emily" was wrecked on the South Spit in 1893; numerous other cases of assistance to vessels in distress.

Zahniser, Porter, b. Portland 1868; to Curry 1884; farmer and fisherman near Ellensburg. Married Cora Merrill. Children: Irene M., Albert D., Charles L.

Zeek, Horace L., b. Michigan 1860; to Oregon 1871; to Curry 1890. Stock raising and general farming near Gold Beach. Opened a hotel at Wedderburn 1898. Married Mary Dillman. One son, Frank F.

Zumwalt, Charles W., b. Missouri 1847; to Curry 1869; married Sarah B. Clymer 1868. Married again 1887 to Agnes E. Blacklock. Six sons: John Henry, Marion R., Clarence Wm., Charles P., Raymond B., Harold W. County commissioner and assessor; justice of the peace; deputy collector of customs at Port Orford; owned and operated one of the best dairy and stock farms in Curry, on Sixes River.

Zumwalt, Henry J., b. Missouri 1819; to Curry 1869; settled on Sixes River. Married Elizabeth E. Rupard. Engaged in farming. Children: Charles W., Francis E., Mary A. P.

INDEX

INDEX

Not included are proper names in lists; references to Coos and Curry as geographical areas; incidental mention of persons, events and places; the biographies.

C

G

H

I

J

N

O

P

Q

R

S

T

U

V

W

Y

Z

PORT ORI